ARTISTS, SIBLINGS, VISIONARIES

Also by Judith Mackrell

Going with the Boys: Six Extraordinary
Women Writing from the Front Line

Bloomsbury Ballerina

Flappers: Six Women of a Dangerous Generation

The Unfinished Palazzo: Life, Love and Art in Venice

ARTISTS, SIBLINGS, VISIONARIES

The lives and loves of Augustus and Gwen John

JUDITH MACKRELL

PICADOR

First published 2025 by Picador
an imprint of Pan Macmillan
The Smithson, 6 Briset Street, London EC1M 5NR
EU representative: Macmillan Publishers Ireland Ltd, 1st Floor,
The Liffey Trust Centre, 117–126 Sheriff Street Upper,
Dublin 1 D01 YC43
Associated companies throughout the world

ISBN 978-1-5290-9584-5

Copyright © Judith Mackrell 2025

The right of Judith Mackrell to be identified as the
author of this work has been asserted in accordance with
the Copyright, Designs and Patents Act 1988.

The list of illustrations on pp. ix–x constitutes an extension of this copyright page.

All rights reserved. No part of this publication may be reproduced,
stored in a retrieval system, or transmitted, in any form, or by any means
(including, without limitation, electronic, mechanical, photocopying, recording
or otherwise) without the prior written permission of the publisher.

Pan Macmillan does not have any control over, or any responsibility for,
any author or third-party websites (including, without limitation, URLs,
emails and QR codes) referred to in or on this book.

1 3 5 7 9 8 6 4 2

A CIP catalogue record for this book is available from the British Library.

Typeset in Baskerville by Jouve (UK), Milton Keynes
Printed and bound by CPI Group (UK) Ltd, Croydon CR0 4YY

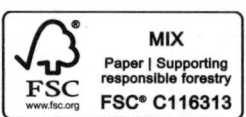

This book is sold subject to the condition that it shall not, by way of
trade or otherwise, be lent, hired out, or otherwise circulated without
the publisher's prior consent in any form of binding or cover other than
that in which it is published and without a similar condition including this
condition being imposed on the subsequent purchaser. The publisher does not
authorize the use or reproduction of any part of this book in any manner
for the purpose of training artificial intelligence technologies or systems.
The publisher expressly reserves this book from the Text and Data Mining
exception in accordance with Article 4(3) of the European Union
Digital Single Market Directive 2019/790.

Visit **www.picador.com** to read more about all our books
and to buy them.

In memory of Anna Perring and June Mendoza

CONTENTS

List of Illustrations ix
Author's Note and Acknowledgements xi
Introduction 1

1. TENBY 7
2. THE SLADE 22
3. LONDON AND PARIS 44
4. TWO SELF-PORTRAITS 66
5. DORELIA 79
6. RODIN 102
7. IDA 120
8. CROSS-CHANNEL AFFAIRS 135
9. GRIEFS AND DUTIES 157
10. MONEY 178
11. SEARCHING FOR ARCADIA 193
12. SEARCHING FOR RELIGION 215
13. THE GREAT WAR 234
14. THE PEACE 260
15. GOOD INTENTIONS 282
16. ALTERED MOVES 301

17. THE BLOODY DECADE 319
18. MORTALITY 341
19. A NATIONAL TREASURE 361

Notes 387
Bibliography 415
Index 417

LIST OF ILLUSTRATIONS

Photographic credits are shown in italics

1. Gwen and Augustus John's father, Edwin John. *Photo: Private Collection, London.*
2. The four John children (left to right: Augustus, Thornton, Winifred and Gwen) with their nurse, c. 1880. *Photo: courtesy of the author.*
3. Tenby beach, c. 1890. *Photo: KGPA Ltd / Alamy Stock Photo.*
4. 'The talented and ornamental Slade girls' – Ida, Ursula and Gwen by Augustus John, 1898. *Photo: © Estate of Augustus John. All rights reserved 2025 / Bridgeman Images.*
5. Drawings of Gwen by Augustus John, c. 1900. *Photo: © Tom Graves Archive / © Estate of Augustus John. All rights reserved 2025 / Bridgeman Images.*
6. *Mrs. Atkinson*, Gwen John, 1898. *Photo: ARTGEN / Alamy Stock Photo.*
7. *Self Portrait*, Gwen John, 1899–1900. *Photo: incamerastock / Alamy Stock Photo.*
8. *Merikli*, Augustus John, 1902. *Photo: © Manchester Art Gallery / © Estate of Augustus John. All rights reserved 2025 / Bridgeman Images.*
9. Augustus, Ida, Gwen and David John, Liverpool, 1902. *Photo: Private Collection, London.*
10. *The Student*, Gwen John, 1903–4. *Photo: ARTGEN / Alamy Stock Photo.*
11. Sketch at Matching Green with Elm House in the background, Augustus John, c. 1904–5. *Photo: courtesy of the author.*
12. *Woman Smiling*, Augustus John, 1908–9. *Photo: © Estate of Augustus John. All rights reserved 2023 / Bridgeman Images.*
13. Sketch of Ida and Robin, 1905. *Photo: courtesy of the author.*
14. 'A dream of the nomadic life'; Augustus and his family, 1909. *Photo: Private Collection, London.*

15. Augustus John, Jacob Hilsdorf, 1909. *Photo: Wikimedia Commons.*
16. *The Blue Pool*, Augustus John, 1911. *Photo: © Estate of Augustus John. All rights reserved 2023 / Bridgeman Images.*
17. *A Corner of the Artist's Room in Paris*, Gwen John, 1907–9. *Photo: The Picture Art Collection / Alamy Stock Photo.*
18. *Nude Girl*, Gwen John, 1909–10. *Photo: © Estate of Augustus John. All rights reserved 2025 / Bridgeman Images.*
19. Gwen posing nude, possibly for Ruth Manson, c. 1911. *Photo: The National Library of Wales.*
20. *Self-portrait*, sketching, Gwen John, c. 1909. *Photo: Patrick Bourne & Co., London.*
21. Auguste Rodin. *Photo: GL Archive / Alamy Stock Photo.*
22. *Whistler's Muse*, Auguste Rodin, c. 1908. *Photo: Wikimedia Commons.*
23. Chloe Boughton-Leigh, Gwen John, 1910. *Photo: ARTGEN / Alamy Stock Photo.*
24. *Interior*, Gwen John, 1915–16. *Photo: incamerastock / Alamy Stock Photo.*
25. Mère Poussepin, Gwen John, c. 1913–20. *Photo: incamerastock / Alamy Stock Photo.*
26. *Young Woman Holding a Black Cat*, Gwen John, c. 1919–early 1920s. *Photo: ARTGEN / Alamy Stock Photo.*
27. *The Convalescent*, Gwen John, c. 1923–4. *Photo: VTR / Alamy Stock Photo.*
28. Jeanne Robert Foster. *Photo: The National Library of Wales.*
29. *Girl with a Blue Scarf*, Gwen John, 1923–4. *Photo: ARTGEN / Alamy Stock Photo.*
30. *Three Children Bathing*, Augustus John, c. 1910. *Photo: © Estate of Augustus John, image courtesy Piano Nobile, London.*
31. *Madame Suggia*, Augustus John, 1920–3. *Photo: The Print Collector / Alamy Stock Photo.*
32. *Portrait of James Joyce*, Augustus John, 1930. *Photo: Stan Pritchard / Alamy Stock Photo.*
33. *A Jamaican Girl*, Augustus John, 1937. *Photo: © Estate of Augustus John. All rights reserved 2025 / Bridgeman Images.*
34. *Portrait of Tristan de Vere Cole*, Augustus John, 1951. *Photo: © Estate of Augustus John. All rights reserved 2025 / Bridgeman Images.*
35. Augustus John at Fryern Court, 1959. *Photo: Pictorial Press Ltd / Alamy Stock Photo.*

AUTHOR'S NOTE AND ACKNOWLEDGEMENTS

In writing this double biography of Gwen and Augustus John I have chosen to focus not only on their art, and on their individually remarkable stories, but also on the complexities of their sibling relationship – a relationship that ranged from profound intimacy through periods of mutual exasperation to moments of outright antagonism. They were a brother and sister between whom the ordinary tensions of family were made particularly fascinating by a combination of circumstance, talent and reputation.

To maintain that focus I have taken the decision to refer to Augustus, throughout most of the book, as Gus. As an adult he preferred to be known as Augustus, or simply John. Gwen, however, was one of the very few who continued to use his childhood diminutive, and I have adopted this particular marker of their sibling bond as a way of keeping it at the forefront of my narrative.

My work on *Artists, Siblings, Visionaries* has been assisted and inspired by other biographers and scholars. All are listed in the bibliography, but I would especially like to acknowledge Michael Holroyd, Mary Taubman, Cecily Langdale, Sue Roe, Alicia Foster and David Boyd Haycock for their stellar, groundbreaking research. I would also like to honour Ceridwen Lloyd-Morgan for her edited collection of Gwen John's letters and notebooks, and Rebecca John and Michael Holroyd for their edited collection of Ida John's letters.

During the course of my writing, I have been given generous support and assistance by several people. Cecily Landgale was very kind in offering me her thoughts on Gwen John; Anthony d'Offay and Caroline Cuthbert were very generous in relating their experience of handling Gwen's estate, and I owe a special debt to Marie-Louise Laband for facilitating our conversations. Thanks also to Ariane Bankes for introducing me to the John family, who have kindly given permission for me to quote from the correspondence of Augustus, Gwen and Ida John; and to Matthew Meadows, David Weller and Debra Craine for reading and commenting on the manuscript in its early draft.

I received particular help from the superb archivists at the National Library of Wales, and am grateful for their additional permission in quoting from the Johns' archives.

Huge thanks finally to the mighty Georgina Morley and her marvellous editing team at Picador, Rosie Shackles, Laura Carr and John Sugar; to Penelope Price for her patient and eagle-eyed copy-editing; to Nicole Foster and Kate Berens for their equally meticulous proofreading; to Sarah Ereira for the comprehensive index; and to Tiana-Jane Dunlop for designing such a clever and compelling cover. Gratitude as always to my brilliant agent Clare Alexander for seeing the possibilities in this book.

And, to my family and friends – huge love.

INTRODUCTION

In November 1985, two exhibitions opened in Manchester which had the symbolic effect of a family reunion. Gwen and Augustus John had been brother and sister, they had studied at the same art school and had shared overlapping circles of friends. Yet they had gone on to live and work in quite separate worlds. And it was only in Manchester – forty-six years after Gwen's death, twenty-four years after Augustus's – that so much of their art would be seen in such close proximity.

'Augustus John and Friends' was hung in the grandly neoclassical space of the Manchester City Gallery, and with its parade of portraits – of poets, painters, actors and expensive women – it played to all the swagger of Augustus's public image. 'Gwen John: An Interior Life' was, by contrast, everything its title intimated. Housed within the cool grey space of the Athenaeum, the paintings and drawings were not only smaller, but their palette was more muted, their forms and atmosphere more quietly strange.

As critics observed, the pairing of these shows was a unique opportunity to analyse the contrasting registers of the siblings' work – the 'variable, strident chords' of his, the 'sustained minor key' of hers – an opportunity, also, to speculate on the contrasting registers of their lives.[1]

Augustus had been the younger of the two by eighteen months, yet his career had rapidly outstripped his sister's. His draughtsmanship had been compared to Raphael, to Rembrandt; his painting had crossed genre from portraiture, to modernist landscape, to epic, lyric fantasy. By the time he was thirty-five, he was recognized as one of the most imposing personages on the London art scene, and the writer Virginia Woolf was only being half ironic when she described the early years of the twentieth century as 'The Age of Augustus John'.

But the trajectory of Augustus's success was driven not only by his art but by his personal notoriety. He was charismatically handsome, he dressed like a bohemian, he lived, drank and travelled like one too. And the women in his life became the stuff of legend – not only his wife Ida and lover Dorelia, with whom he tried to create a radically open marriage – but the many, many others with whom he had affairs. This, at the time, was fabulously wicked behaviour, and the prices Augustus was able to command for his work were driven in part by the thrilling adumbrations of his image.

Living and working in the shadow of her prodigious brother, Gwen's story inevitably appeared smaller. Talented though she was, she lacked Augustus's boldness and, when she settled in Paris in 1904, she had no interest in emulating his world. She had a decade-long relationship with Auguste Rodin, yet she never chose to advertise her intimacy with the sculptor, and never sought to become part of his milieu. Her own work, as it evolved from meticulous self-portraits to rapt explorations of colour, texture and form, became, in part, a study of her inner life. By the time Gwen converted to Catholicism in 1913, she was already regarded as something of a recluse – a pale anchoress who was dedicated to God and her art. She died in 1939, and it would be several decades before her talent received the same critical and biographical scrutiny as her brother's.

Much of that scrutiny would centre on the differences between them. Yet, although the two Johns were powerfully complex as individuals, the starting point of this book is what connected them as siblings – the forces that shaped their lives, the friends they shared, the books and the art they had in common, and, above all, the tangle of love, antagonism, exasperation and sympathy they felt towards each other.

As Augustus himself acknowledged, the closeness between them had been forged in the darkness of their childhood. Growing up in the Welsh seaside town of Tenby, they and their two siblings had suffered the bewildering early death of their mother, and the painfully inadequate parenting of their father. Edwin John had tried to do his best by his children, but, an anxious inhibited man, he'd turned into a petty disciplinarian. The four little Johns had feared him at first, then they had learned to mock him.

However, if this sad, semi-orphaned childhood had blighted the Johns, it had also steeled in them a determination to escape. For Gwen and Augustus, who'd been drawing since they were small, their route out of Tenby was art. In 1894, when sixteen-year-old Augustus was allowed to enrol at the Slade, it was imperative to Gwen that she would follow, and when they were students in London, shedding their awkwardly provincial teenage selves, they shared a rackety lodging house in Fitzrovia, went to parties and anarchist meetings, fell in and out of love – and recorded much of it on paper and canvas.

Years later, when Augustus wrote about Gwen, he would argue that, however widely their lives had diverged, they had always been cut from the same temperamental cloth: 'We were not opposites but much the same really . . . we took a different attitude.'[2] Beneath the surface of his own public flamboyance and Gwen's reclusiveness, they had other qualities in common – a scorn for banality, a yearning for beauty and love. They were also, equally, victim to tendencies which Augustus believed were genetic – a susceptibility to depression (which in his case could be crippling) and an awkwardness with strangers (which he was much more successful at concealing). They recognized themselves in each other and, when Ida died in 1907, and when Rodin died in 1917, they came instinctively to each other's support.

Gwen would be almost the only person to continue calling her brother by his childhood diminutive 'Gus'. Yet their relationship was not easy. If there was love and sympathy between them, there was also conflict – a conflict which, for Gwen in particular, was bound up with an old and unexamined sibling rage. Growing up as the two middle children of the family, and very close in age, they had naturally been competitive with each other. But Augustus, infuriated by his sister's eighteen-month advantage, had gone through a period when his competitiveness had hardened into bullying. Gwen had battled against him then, and, long after she'd gone to Paris, she still had occasional nightmares about their fights. When Augustus, generously flush with money and contacts, had wanted to help Gwen, she had sometimes felt only that he was trying to control her.

Augustus had been a foot taller than Gwen, larger in every way, and he'd been able to dominate her with all the advantages of his sex. As a boy, he'd been given a far more solid academic education than her, and even at the Slade, famously progressive in its acceptance of women students, there had been a subtle enforcing of that same inequality. With an all-male teaching staff and a curriculum focused around old masters, it was tacitly acknowledged that, once the students graduated, only the men were likely to have successful careers.

In 1898, when Gwen and Augustus left the Slade, the art world was a harsh place for women to thrive. Very few of them ran their own studios or schools, very few of them sat on the juries which selected work for exhibition, and – unless they had money, exceptional luck or nerve – most of them would be forced to put aside their painting ambitions and accept the security of marriage.

Gwen was too proud, or too stubborn, to cast herself as a victim of the patriarchy or of any other system. Yet the difference in how she and her brother survived the first years of their careers was striking. Augustus may have been the more naturally assertive, yet the success he enjoyed was boosted by a network of men – friends, artists, buyers and patrons – who provided him with material and public support. He might often have been broke, and badly in debt, but he could always count on sufficient commissions and sales to pay for his studios, his art materials and models.

Gwen had no such network, and for a long time she could only support herself and her art by hiring herself out as a model. Living alone, often in small, squalid rooms, she might have looked wistfully at the comfort of her married friends. But she had made her own choice: 'I think if we are to do beautiful pictures, we ought to be free from family conventions and ties', she wrote, and although she would fall in love several times – with men, with other women and, above all, with Rodin – it was never domestic happiness Gwen sought, but passion and grandeur.

Freedom worked both ways, though. While Augustus appeared to roam in a more privileged world, the life he chose also cost him part of his liberty. In 1904, when he first set up house with Ida and Dorelia, he thought he'd embarked on a glorious experiment. Over the years, however, that experiment spawned nine children, plus the expense of several households and studios, and the financial burdens that seemed to gather around Augustus were one reason why he drifted into painting the rapid portraits that came so easily and profitably to him. He never quite sank to being an artist for hire, but neither did he ever fulfil his youthful ambition of finding his own way to put the world down in paint.

If debts and responsibilities became an impediment for Augustus, so too did the exhausting puzzle of his own personality. When he was young, the 'heaven and hell' of his moods, the mania of his excitements, the blackness of his despairs had all been fuel for his art, but by early middle age they were sapping his powers and driving him to greater excesses. There were times when Augustus deeply envied his sister's ability to recuse herself from the world and focus on her painting, many times when he wished they'd been able to live and work more closely together. But Gwen became increasingly protective of her solitude and, in her final decade, she not only stopped visiting Augustus, she all but stopped writing to him.

When she died in 1939, Augustus grieved for the distance between them, and when he came to sort through the mass of paintings, drawings and writings she'd left behind, he was haunted by their delicate rigour. 'I feel ashamed of wasting my time, thinking that life could last almost for ever,' he wrote. But although he still had over two decades to live and would become celebrated as one of the grand old men of British painting, Augustus never did recover the joyous brilliance of his youth. However hard he worked, he could never achieve the one final vision that would absolve him of his wasted years.

History, in fact, would turn against him. After his death in 1961, the market was flooded with too many of his late, inferior works, and, two decades later, when the world began to take notice of Gwen, a critical consensus began to form that not only had her talent been greater than his, but so too had her character, her integrity as an artist. Just as there was a move to disparage Gus as a philanderer and a charlatan, a painter who'd used the cheap magic of his personality to convince the world he was a genius, so too was there a move to cast a halo around Gwen, to sanctify the discipline that she'd brought to her life and work, and the indifference she'd cultivated towards money and artistic fashion.

But the truth of a life is hard to excavate and even harder to judge – even those who knew the Johns well could struggle to decide whether they were admirable or awful. Augustus, with his reckless volatile passions, could be a danger to himself and to others, but to those who loved him he could also be a hero, a kind of visionary who saw his life in brighter, more exciting colours. Gwen, in her refusal to compromise her independence and her work, could equally be revered as a saint, yet to her family and friends she could also appear cranky, ruthless and even coldly ungenerous.

The one unarguable fact about the Johns, however, is the extraordinary journey they made: two shy and angry young teenagers who, without money or influence, made the world of art their own, and found distinction and acclaim. Critical fashions may fluctuate, the verdict on their work may change, but as a story of two siblings, of two unexpected and idiosyncratic talents, the lives of Gwen and Augustus John must always be remarkable.

Chapter One

TENBY

'Even at that early age we were vaguely
aware of Art and Beauty'
AUGUSTUS JOHN[1]

For a few weeks in summer, when the waters of Carmarthen Bay glittered blue under a sharp sea breeze, the Welsh town of Tenby was transformed into a busy seaside resort. Music from the local brass band competed with a visiting troupe of black-faced minstrels; elegant couples strolled along the curving esplanade; bathing machines lined up at the water's edge, cumbersome wagons on high spindly wheels. And there were children everywhere, flying kites in the sharp summer winds, paddling in the shallow surf and begging for rides on the donkeys that padded patiently up and down the sand.

For many of those children, the beach was their annual treat, but for the four John siblings it was their familiar playground. The rock pools where they paddled and fished for shrimps, the dark caves, the secluded swimming spots – all these had been known to them since they were small. And, for Gwen and Gus, who kept pencils and scraps of paper in their pockets wherever they went, the beach was also their studio. It rarely failed to throw up new subjects to sketch – the beaky outline of a seagull, a bleached sculpture of driftwood, the faces of new children. And, when they were lucky, there were visiting artists to spy on, too – amateur painters, who set up their easels to capture views of the sea, the cliffs and the old town walls.

'Gwen and I, full of curiosity, would approach as near as we dared, to watch the mystery of painting', Gus recalled, and years later, when Gwen was a student, she would paint her own landscape of Tenby. It was a panoramic view of the beach, with the harbour wall curving steeply round a crescent of golden sand; and it captured the moment between daylight and dusk, when families were taking their last seaside stroll. In the foreground, a young woman in a fashionably trimmed hat was walking with a small girl, their closeness evident in the child's bright uptilted face. A little way behind was a slightly older mother, talking attentively to her own small daughter. The only other figure in the painting – a youth in a hat – walked alone.

As a painting, *Landscape at Tenby with Figures* was the work of a novice, its detail undercut by awkward hitches in perspective. But as a biographical image, it was tantalizing. There were no fathers in either family group, and something about Gwen's placing of her figures on the otherwise deserted beach, her exaggerated contrast of light and shadow, had given the scene a quality of dream or memory. The woman in the foreground (who'd been modelled on Gwen's sister Winnie) may have been a dim recollection of her own dead mother, Augusta; the child may have been Gwen herself; and this painting may have drawn on the last happy moments Gwen could recall before Augusta John had fallen seriously ill and Edwin John had shuttered himself away in grief.

Gwen had been eight, Gus just six and a half, when tragedy struck. 'I used to cry all the time,' Gwen claimed, 'I never expected any happiness in my life'. To Gus it seemed that the death of their mother had robbed them not only of joy, but confidence too, causing all four children to retreat behind a wall of 'invincible shyness'.[2] They had no help from their father, who was unable to articulate his own loss, let alone comfort theirs, and Augusta's death remained a bewildering mystery to the little Johns, an inexplicable rupturing of their childhood.

There had been a time before that rupture when the family was happy. They lived in Haverfordwest, a market town twenty miles northwest of Tenby, where their slightly cramped, narrow home was graced by dramatic views of the old ruined castle and the surrounding hills. It was graced too by the lightness of touch which Augusta brought to 7 Victoria Place when she came to live there as Edwin's wife in 1873, and by the gentle transformation she worked on her husband, turning him from a painfully shy and undistinguished young solicitor, to a contented family man.

As a small child, growing up in Haverfordwest, Edwin had been a bright and inquisitive boy, musical and fond of books, but as a teenager he'd developed a disabling social anxiety, which had been provoked in part by his father's determination to turn all of his three sons into gentlemen. William John had been a dynamic adventurous man, working and studying his way out of poverty and eventually buying a lucrative solicitor's practice. His decision to send Edwin away to school, however, to board among richer, more entitled boys, had wrecked the child's confidence. Edwin had returned home a timid misfit, ashamed of his Welsh accent and origins, yet ignorant of how to rise above them. While his older brother Alfred had run away to study art and play the flute, Edwin had seen no option but to join his father's practice. Half-hearted about the job, and having no local friends, the future seemed to spread drearily ahead of him.

Then, at the age of twenty-seven, he went to Brighton to visit relatives and met Augusta Smith, a delicately pretty young woman with an expressive light in her eyes and a tumble of dark curls. She was artistic too. Her father, Thomas, a master plumber and glazier, had sent her to a modest finishing school in south London, where she was encouraged to study music, painting and drawing. Her work, though girlishly sentimental, showed a gift for colour (years later, a landscape signed *A. John* was hung in an American gallery, having been mistakenly attributed to her son), and when the Slade School of Art opened its doors to both men and women in 1871, it's possible that Augusta dreamed of continuing her studies there.*

However, 'Mrs Leleux's Establishment' was all the education Thomas Smith would permit. A widower of vehemently religious and patriarchal opinions, he expected his oldest daughter to return home and take over the running of the house. The two younger daughters, Rosina and Leah, were excused because they'd joined the Salvation Army and were doing God's work. For Augusta, alone in the house, there had seemed no chance of escape from the making of lists and the managing of servants, but, in February 1873, Thomas Smith suffered a fatal stroke. When

---

* The painting was titled *Landscape with Cows* and had been part of the Dalton Collection, Charlotte, North Carolina.

Edwin appeared in Brighton three and a half months later, timid but rather handsome, with an upright posture and a ginger moustache, Augusta was ready to accept him as a suitor.

The early years of their marriage were sunny; the young couple played music together, read books and had four healthy babies: Thornton in 1875; Gwendoline Mary, a year later, on 22 June 1876; Augustus Edwin on 4 January 1878; and Winifred in late 1879. Although Augusta may have felt the effects of delivering four babies in almost as many years, she had a small staff to cook and clean, and a nursemaid, Mimi, to help with the babies. She played the piano, she painted and she took pleasure in her children, teaching them their letters and numbers, encouraging them to draw and colour as soon as they could hold a pencil, and taking them with her on her errands around town.

Edwin thrived in his marriage: his shyness eased and he blossomed, a little stiffly, into fatherhood. Every Sunday after church, he led the children on a walk, marching them along the banks of the river Cleddau, or through the country lanes above the town. He took them to the circus once, leaving Gus with the indelible memory of a 'superb woman in spangled tights'.[3] And, anxious for his children to benefit from the nearby coast, he had a small holiday house built in the seaside village of Broad Haven, a magical place the children remembered, where they learned to swim and where they fell asleep to the gentle wash of the waves.

One summer at Broad Haven, the children witnessed a crowd of skimpily dressed young women immersed in the sea for a collective baptism. Such scenes were an indelible part of the colour of their lives. Haverfordwest, on market days, was loud with pig farmers and cattle drovers, with oyster women in tall Welsh hats, with gypsies who appeared from the countryside. These ragged, dark-featured strangers, said by Edwin to kidnap unwary children, became figures of romance to the little Johns, as did the miller who used to emerge from his work with a coating of flour, the little workhouse girls in their ill-fitting pinafores, and the woman in her ramshackle cottage who they believed was a witch.

'Had our mother lived it would all have been different', wrote Thornton, years later.[4] But early in 1880, shortly after Winnie was born, Augusta fell ill. Her doctor believed it was rheumatism and advised her to spend the winter away from the Pembrokeshire damp. Yet, on her return, she was no better and, as she was sent away for a succession of rest cures, life in Victoria Place underwent a miserable transformation.

Edwin, unable to manage the children on his own, had been obliged to accept the help of his sisters-in-law, Rosina and Leah Smith. They were not unkind women, but they blazed with the terrible piety of their vocation and, once in the house, they imposed a strict routine of prayers, replacing the children's library of fairy tales with drearily titled pamphlets like *Jessica's First Prayer*. Even out in the town there was no escaping their zealotry; every day, the sisters would ride through the streets in their pony and trap – their 'Hallelujah Chariot' – preaching sermons and handing out tracts, blithely indifferent to the embarrassment they inflicted on their family.

Edwin lacked the courage to intervene, while Augusta was too weak and too often absent. When the children were photographed in 1881, they already appeared to be feeling the strain, even accounting for the effort of holding themselves still for the camera. Thornton, always a slow, quiet boy, stared impassively in front of him; Gus was planted, wide eyed, in his infant chair, looking as though he expected a rebuke; and Gwen, standing very straight in her neat black dress, her hands clasped in front of her, wore an expression of precocious wariness.

The most comfortable of the four was little Winnie, sitting on the ample lap of their nurse. Mimi at least had remained a constant. But just a short time after that photograph was taken, Leah and Rosina decided her services were no longer required. They sent Mimi away and, in the summer of 1884, when Augusta died, the children had no nurse to cuddle away their tears, no refuge of cosy familiarity.

Augusta had been in Derbyshire, consulting a new doctor or taking the Buxton waters, and Edwin had apparently been given no warning of her sudden decline. Shocked as he was, he did not think about how to prepare his children, and simply informed them of their mother's death along with the servants and the aunts. It was all too much and, overwhelmed by the magnitude of the news, the four little Johns raced hysterically around the house, chanting 'Mama's dead! Mama's dead!' – hectic with emotions they could neither name nor control.

Rheumatic gout and exhaustion were given as the official cause, although no doctor could account for why those conditions should be fatal in a young woman of thirty-five. It's possible Augusta had inherited a genetic condition like lupus or Crohn's, some fundamental and critical disorder of her immune system. The fact that Augusta's sister Rosina suffered from chronic gut and joint pain, and that Gwen and Thornton went on to develop similar symptoms, would raise a flag with any twenty-first-century diagnostician. But the Victorians knew little of such things, and the mysteriousness of Augusta's death would provoke beady gossip in Haverfordwest, especially when it was revealed that Edwin was the major beneficiary of her will.

Gus later recalled that his father had seemed 'full of secrets'. Perhaps he was ashamed that Augusta had been alone when she died; perhaps he worried he could have done more to find a cure. But there was no one with whom Edwin could share his distress. He had quarrelled with his sister Clara over their father's will, and his two brothers were all but lost to him – Alfred having turned to drink and semi-vagrancy, Frederick in prison for some unnamed offence. Bereft, and flinching from the threat of scandal, Edwin decided to leave Victoria Place and make a new start in Tenby. The town had happy associations – Augusta had always liked it, the children had always enjoyed playing on its beach – and, for Edwin, it would put a good twenty miles between him and the tittle-tattle of Haverfordwest.

The tragedy of Augusta's death could not be shaken off, however, and it settled in every corner of their new Tenby home, 32 Victoria Street. The house was grim and unwelcoming, dark and meanly proportioned, set in the middle of a nondescript terrace, and it was made even more uncomfortable by Edwin's hapless attempt at furnishing. Gus remembered it becoming 'a kind of mortuary', a 'museum of rubbish' – every room crammed with the stuffed birds and cheap mahogany furniture Edwin had inherited from William John, every wall hung with his mediocre collection of paintings.[5]

Far more oppressive, though, was Edwin's own presence. He'd become a man of modestly independent means with the deaths of his wife and father, and had decided to throw away his professional brass plaque and retire. He was almost constantly around the house, reading and playing the piano, and now that he had no work to occupy him, he became fixated on his duties as a single father. The family may have been free of the hallelujah aunts, who were harrying souls elsewhere, but Edwin set strict rules for the children and for the running of the household, and, obsessive about economies, he rationed both fuel and food. There were to be no more fires in the attic bedrooms where the children slept – they had to pile rugs and overcoats onto themselves to keep warm – and no pandering to the children's taste at meals – Gwen, always picky about food, developed a loathing for the rice puddings which Edwin routinely demanded from the kitchen.

It was at mealtimes, too, that the children felt the worst of their father's temper. Without Augusta, he lost much of his ability to enjoy family life. He criticized the children's table manners, was irritated by their chatter; he alternated between irascible demands for silence and impatience because they had nothing useful to say. Winnie recalled that, if ever she ventured some whispered comment at dinner, Edwin would pounce on her sarcastically: 'Oh you've found it have you . . . your tongue?' When she and Gwen invented a mute rebellious language of eye rolling and grimaces, they were ordered to leave the table.

As the children grew older and learned to make comparisons, they could see their father was odd. His extreme social anxiety had returned and he was so easily agitated by chance encounters that, when he was out on the street and saw an acquaintance approach, he would quicken his step and pretend he had an appointment to keep. Even his attempts at discipline were embarrassing. Edwin, to his credit, detested physical punishment and tried hard to avoid it. Yet the children saw no virtue in his mildness. When Gus came home from school with a report for delinquent behaviour, he simply laughed at Edwin's feeble attempt at a caning. Later, he wrote that, the more ridiculous he found his father, the more determined he was to become his opposite: 'taking [him] as a model I watched him carefully, imitating his tricks as closely as I could, but in reverse'.[6]

But Edwin did love his children and, within the narrow limits of his ability, he tried his best. Years later, Winifred would acknowledge how hard it must have been to raise these 'strange, silent and sometime mutinous' siblings; Gus too could look back and remember exceptional moments when their father had managed to be 'playful and humane'.[7]

Edwin did what he could to maintain some of Augusta's traditions: he allowed the servants to organize birthday teas and balloons, he read stories to the children after supper and played the piano for them. He also bought pets for the girls – a spaniel for Winnie and a cat for Gwen – and, although he couldn't abide the latter, a vicious bruiser of a tom called Mudge, when Floss the spaniel went missing, he asked the town crier to advertise a search.

Most crucially, as Gus recalled, he allowed his daughters as well as his sons 'to run happily wild'. Led by Thornton, who planned to become an explorer, a prospector for gold, they were permitted to tramp off alone to deserted beaches, to walk all the way to the common at Begelly, where the gypsies camped. Here, they would stare shyly at the hordes of enviably ragged children and wonder why their father was so worried about kidnapping when the gypsies had so many offspring of their own.

Gus in particular could imagine nothing more glamorous than being stolen by gypsies – apart from being born a Red Indian, perhaps. For a time, the only book he read was a collection of stories by Gustave Aimard which featured thrillingly bloody accounts of the American Wild West. The more alienated he became from his father and from the mausoleum of Victoria Street, the more gripped he was by the belief that he was the son of an Indian brave and had been mysteriously transported to Wales. He schooled himself to live by what he called 'the Red Man's code'; he attempted to gallop bareback on a wild horse and, with a gang of local boys, he devised other ritual tests of courage – daring them all to hang perilously over the edge of a disused coal pit, to dive off the highest rocks and to swim through the roughest seas.

Gwen also occupied a world of fantasy, but much of it was confined to her bedroom, where she read and drew, arranged wild flowers, cuddled her cat Mudge and dreamed of escape. In a photograph, taken around the time she turned eleven, her expression was pensive, and years later she claimed that adults always used to tell her off for crying so much, warning her that 'when you're a grown up you'll have something to cry about'.[8] Yet Gwen's memory was patchy. Her siblings would remember her excitement at birthdays, her yelps of delight when she stripped off her clothes and ran into the sea. When Edwin bought bicycles for her and Winnie, the two of them would go pedalling around

Tenby at hysterical speeds, skirts whipping around their legs, hair streaming loose in the wind.

A local family with whom they occasionally went to stay remembered all four children as the 'turbulent Johns', a farouche, untamed and close-knit tribe. But this was during the holidays; when the children were in school their lives not only became more physically muted, but a divide opened up between them as the two boys and two girls were educated in very different institutions.

Gwen and Winnie were happy at first at the dame school they attended until the age of ten. It was small and cheerfully run by an intelligent, liberal-minded woman named Mrs Mackenzie, who became something of surrogate mother to the Johns (it was she who invited them to stay in the holidays) and whose daughter, Irene, became Winnie's special friend.

The girls' enjoyment came to an abrupt end, however, when they were moved on to 'Miss Wilson's Private Academy', and made to suffer through five years of schooling that was as overbearingly strict as it was intellectually inadequate. Although Miss Wilson provided a veneer of academic learning for her pupils – the acceptable parts of English history and geography, a smattering of French, some simple arithmetic – her principal concern was equipping them with an armoury of social accomplishments. Some of her lessons would stick with Gwen for the rest of her life: she was always prompt in writing her thank-you letters and she rarely left home without a hat. But Gwen was bored and humiliated by the shallowness of her education and fiercely resentful that, when she was finally released from the academy, around the age of fifteen, her spelling and her grammar were poor and there were shaming gaps in her knowledge.

She blamed her father, although at that time there were few good options for girls* and Edwin did make an effort to supplement his daughters' education. He paid for Winifred's violin lessons, provided drawing materials for Gwen, and the books he read to them, including *Jane Eyre*, were unusually sophisticated for the time. He also hired a governess to

---

* Most were boarding schools, like Cheltenham Ladies or Roedean, which had been founded in the mid-nineteenth century.

teach them French – but the lessons came to an abrupt halt when the governess, impressed by the girls' progress, enquired if there was any French blood in the family, which Edwin took as an obscure and worrying insult.

For the boys, there were better options in Tenby. Greenhill, which Gus and Thornton attended, gave its pupils a rough but solid academic grounding and even though both John boys were chronically innumerate, Gus did reasonably well in his other subjects, well enough, at least, for him to start boasting of his superior learning to Gwen and start using it as a weapon in their battle for dominance.

Gus wasn't a naturally cruel child: he could weep for little Kay and Gerda in Andersen's *The Snow Queen*; he could shed tears for the boys who were hurt in playground fights – even though he was often at the centre of the brawl. Some part of his need to tease Gwen was to cover up the fact that he too was often unhappy at school; he was routinely punished for dreaming in class, or for doodling cartoons of teachers, and sometimes, he felt, he was unreasonably picked on. One day, when his fidgeting provoked a master to give him a vicious clip around the ear, he was so outraged by the injustice, he instinctively hit back.

This was the offence that drove Edwin to bring out his cane, but it also convinced him that the discipline at Greenhill was inadequate. Forgetting his own wretched experiences at boarding school, he found an expensive institution near Bristol which had a reputation for grooming middle-class boys into gentlemen. But Clifton School only exacerbated his sons' problems. Thornton, so quiet and so slow, withdrew further into himself, while Gus, chafing in his tight Eton jacket, became even more inattentive. Loafing on the sidelines of the cricket pitch one day, a ball smacked him so hard on the side of his head, his hearing was permanently damaged.

'Gloom, boredom and sometimes anguish of mind were my abiding states', he recalled, and he was driven to offload even more of his misery onto Gwen.[9] Later, he would admit that his need to bully her was complicated by 'fraternal jealousy', but Gwen saw only his power to hurt. Almost two decades later, she could still recall how she dreaded Gus's return from school: 'I revolted against him at the beginning of each holiday, but he won by telling me horrible things and when I threw myself on him to fight and pull his hair . . . he always won for of course he was the stronger. He used to discourage me so much because he would say [that] I [forgot] everything I learnt and it was always a long time before I had enough confidence to start again.'[10]

It was a relief, not only to Gwen but also the rest of the family, when a new school opened in Tenby and Gus was allowed to attend. There were only seven pupils at St Catherine's, but the headmaster, Allen Evans, was a perceptive man who was committed to getting the best from each one. He had the wit to turn sports lessons into games – four-a-side football, roller-skating hockey, golf among the dunes – and his lessons were no less flexible, designed to encourage the boys at what they did best and not to punish their failings.

For Gus, Evans's methods were a revelation – his essays and stories were read out in class, he won a certificate for drawing – and his confidence showed in the school photograph that was taken at the end of his first year. While all the other boys were sitting cross-legged on the sand, Gus, at thirteen and a half, had perched himself a little way up the cliff. Even though his image was slightly blurred, his grin of triumph was unmistakeable.

In Evans, Gus had found all the appreciative sympathy his own father had withheld. During the next two years, he thrived both intellectually and emotionally, discovering the plays of Shakespeare, the poetry of Walt Whitman. But then an incident occurred which provoked an abrupt and, to Gus, inexplicable withdrawal of Evans's warmth. The boys had been taking their daily walk along the sands, and Gus, following behind his headmaster, had been seized with a rush of sudden happiness. His whole body had seemed to fizz and thrum, and, barely conscious of what he was doing, he stripped off half his uniform and began to dance, improvising a wildly capering, somersaulting jig.

Years later, he remembered that moment as astonishing, a kind of 'Dionysian Fury when the sun [had] shone approvingly, the sea turned a deeper blue' and he had felt himself uniquely invincible.[11] The other boys had stared at Gus with trepidation, expecting him to be punished. Yet Evans had remained strangely silent, and only when Gus recalled that incident as an adult did he suspect that Evans, shocked by the beauty of his pupil's bare adolescent limbs, had been fighting down a shameful impulse of desire. Gus, at fifteen, could make no sense of this.

He'd never heard of a homosexual; he'd never thought to question why the priest who also taught at St Catherine's was so quick to encourage him in the drawing of classical male nudes. And he had no way of understanding why, after that incident on the beach, Evans had felt compelled to keep his distance. All Gus could see was a hurtful withdrawing of his headmaster's regard, a new tendency to punish him, and it made him bitter. Even as an adult, when he learned that Evans had committed suicide, Gus could not find it in himself to forgive.

Edwin, inevitably, had told his children nothing about sex, and when Gus was crudely enlightened by one of his friends, he was traumatized. The idea that his own parents had ever engaged in so filthy an act overwhelmed him with 'terror and bewilderment' and he went immediately in search of Gwen, needing to share this horrible knowledge, but also inflict on her the same distress.[12] Puberty apparently came late to Gus – and so did girls. He was puzzled at first when members of his gang began abandoning the Red Man's code in favour of Sunday afternoons spent flirting with local girls. When Gus was persuaded to join them, he still felt wretchedly ill at ease. He knew that the girl who'd been assigned him had a crush on another boy and, in any case, he could see no connection between the gauche embraces of his Tenby friends and the images of love he had formed from the poets and painters. It was, he recalled, a long time before he even dared to hold a girl's hand.

Gwen left little record of her own teenage years, but they must have been difficult. She had no mother to soften the ordeal of her first period or to explain what was happening to her body as she developed breasts.* Although she was very close to Winnie, very reliant on her sweet good sense, Winnie was three years younger than her and had yet to experience such things. Gwen also had no friends, as Gus did, to initiate her into the alarming world of adolescent flirtation. At the age of fourteen or fifteen, she may even have begun to sense her own sexual ambivalence, to wonder if she might find girls more interesting and attractive than boys.

Isolated and ignorant as she was, Gwen flinched from almost anything

---

* Presumably Edwin left this task to one of the servants, who would have to deal with Gwen's bloodied sheets and menstrual rags.

that hinted at sex. Once, when she was out cycling and had to pass a company of foot soldiers, she felt the agony of her own conspicuousness. It felt even more of an assault when her father, emerging from his long bereavement, began a shy courtship of two local women. The mere idea of Edwin having any physical desire, of him wanting a replacement for their mother, was morally and physically repugnant. 'Gwen had an implacable nature when roused,' Gus wrote, and when she rounded on Edwin, abusing his disgusting behaviour and commandeering Winnie to join in her attack, Gus felt so badly for Edwin, he was obliged to come to his father's defence.[13]

Although these adolescent years were often lonely and angry for both Gwen and Gus, the one fixed point between them remained their art. They never lost their childhood habit of carrying sketchbooks and pencils in their pockets; as Edwin later recorded, they drew everywhere: 'on walks along the beach, on excursions into the country'. Even when he took them to London for their first taste of the theatre, the two of them would compete 'feverishly to draw some person [in the audience] who had interested them.'[14] Edwin was proud of their talent and of his own efforts to let it develop freely and naturally; he resigned himself to the clutter of pencils, charcoals and paper in the house, and even to the stray children whom Gwen brought home to pose – although it caused great alarm to him when the mother of one of them, a boy in a green velvet suit, who belonged to a troupe of street entertainers, also turned up at Victoria House and Edwin was convinced that the gossip would spread all over Tenby.

It hadn't occurred to him, at first, that the children's drawing could lead anywhere. But, when Gus was leaving St Catherine's, Edwin was urged by one of the masters to find his son a professional art tutor and was recommended a local painter, Edward Head.* Edwin was gratified by this acknowledgement of Gus's talent, and snobbishly impressed that Head was a member of the Royal Academy. When Head, on seeing the

---

* The only tuition Gus had received in school was the drawing of simple objects and the mastery of 'stumping' – a technique in which a cylinder of paper, shaped to a soft point, was used for smudging and shading lines.

quality of Gus's drawing, suggested he might do well at the Slade, Edwin was too flattered to dismiss an idea which, normally, he would have considered impossible.

The question of what his sons might do for a living had actually been bothering Edwin for some time. His brief expectation that one of them might follow him into law had long since passed. Thornton, now aged nineteen, had remained stubbornly faithful to his dream of the pioneering life and was already planning to leave for Canada. But Gus's own unruly imagination made him equally unfitted for a solicitor's desk, and his own ideas about his future had recently wandered towards the army. However badly he'd dealt with regulations and uniforms at school, he imagined that soldiering might be his route to adventure and even got as far as questioning whether Sandhurst or Woolwich would be the better place to train.

Then Head suggested the Slade and there was no more talk of the army. Edwin was thrown into a predictable flurry of indecision at first: he was worried about letting Gus loose in London, and worried about the expense. But Head dismissed the first of his anxieties, assuring him that the Slade was a highly reputable school, part of the University of London. And when Edwin realized that Gus could lodge with one of the hallelujah aunts, who now lived in Acton, and when he calculated that his son's share of income from the family trust could cover the bulk of the school's twenty-pound fees, the financial implications became less alarming. Perhaps what really moved him to say yes to the Slade was the enthusiasm he saw burning in Gus. He'd never known his son to be so focused or fierce, and eventually, with a grudging warning that he could go off and 'be a Michelangelo' if he liked, but must 'first make his living', Edwin finally gave his permission.[15]

Ungraciously, Gus chose to believe his father had only agreed to the Slade because he wanted to restore peace to the house. But, as soon as Edwin gave way to Gus, he had a second battle brewing with Gwen. She and Gus had always fantasized about becoming artists, even though, for Gwen, that fantasy had been hard to visualize, given the absence of women from most of the art books and magazines she read. She may even have begun to wonder if the only way a woman could paint or draw was to be like her mother and do it under cover of marriage. But then the possibility of the Slade had arisen, and as soon as Gus had been given permission to attend, as soon as Gwen realized that girls could enrol there, too, she was ready to use the full force of her will to fight for the same opportunity. Later, Gus would write, with wry admiration, '*She* wasn't going to be left out of it.'[16]

Chapter Two

THE SLADE

'We continue to produce geniuses,
we turn them out every year'
HENRY TONKS[1]

When Gus went down to London in the autumn of 1894, he was only sixteen, and very much a boy from the provinces. The scale of the city, its sulphurous, smoky air and rattling horse-drawn traffic were daunting to him, and his aunt's Acton house seemed miles away from the Slade, which was in Gower Street, close to Euston Station. On the first morning of term, as Gus dressed himself in the stiff black suit that had been approved by his father, as he packed his bag with provisions for lunch, with a box of charcoal and sheets of *papiers Ingres*, he must surely have been anxious about navigating the long, unfamiliar journey in time for the start of classes at ten.

Everything was overwhelming that day: the size of the Slade behind huge iron gates, the uniformed beadle who was instructing new arrivals to sign the register. The Antiquities Room to which Gus was first directed was also like no classroom he had ever seen. Along the length of one wall were full-sized plaster casts – copies of classical and Renaissance sculptures – while heaped together dustily on shelves were small sculptural fragments – headless torsos, broken-off limbs. In the middle of the space was a semicircle of 'donkeys' – stubby wooden benches with easels attached – where the students would work that term. And more fabulous still to Gus's apprehensive gaze were the students themselves who crowded into the room alongside him.

There were women among them – women who seemed infinitely more sophisticated than any girl he'd known in Tenby – and, among the men, there was one noisy group which appeared frighteningly experienced. They had apparently just spent the summer at a variety of Paris art academies and, comparing notes about the freedoms they'd enjoyed, were now protesting the rule at the Slade which required all pupils to spend a probationary period drawing in the Antiquities Room before being allowed to work with live models. As Gus listened, awed, to the hubbub, as he quietly seated himself astride the donkey he'd been assigned, his nervousness was very apparent to the young woman next to him. Ethel Hatch wrote later that Augustus John had looked unusually young, neat and conscientious that first morning, carefully unpacking his charcoal, pinning a sheet of paper to his easel and printing *John* in very large letters at the bottom.

All eyes had then turned to their drawing master, Henry Tonks, a tall, gaunt man, who'd appeared suddenly in the classroom and, with practised sarcasm, had quelled the entitled young men into silence. Tonks was famously strict, and famously fastidious in his methods. He'd formerly practised as a surgeon and told his students that, before they could consider themselves artists, they needed to acquire a fundamental knowledge of human anatomy – the bones, tendons and muscles beneath the skin. They could learn this from textbooks, but also, he pointed out, from the sculptures in the Antiquities Room. All were masterpieces of observation and execution, object lessons in proportion and form, and Tonks made it plain that when he tasked his students with copying these sculptures, he expected 'clear straightforward drawings with beautiful lines' – specifying further that he would have no patience with tricks of technique, that he particularly frowned on excessive use of smudging, cross-hatching and rubbing-out.[2]

The first task he set the class was to draw the *Discobolus*, the statue of a naked Greek discus thrower, his body torqued low in a graceful twist. A collective concentration descended, the silence broken only by the scratchings of charcoal and pencil, the occasional apologetic squeak of an India rubber – and by murmured comments from Tonks. These comments, the class soon learned, could be brutal, for there were no formal entry requirements at the Slade and Tonks considered it his duty to weed out the lazier, least gifted of his students. 'Is that an insect?' he lethally enquired of one hapless drawing; and he would give no quarter to any student who came to class with a blunt pencil or failed to realize they were 'sitting in their own light.'[3]

Gus escaped the most scathing of Tonks' abuse. His own drawing of the *Discobolus*, which he'd finished eagerly in under ten minutes, was judged 'summary' but accurate, and Tonks evidently saw in him a willing pupil.[4] So unquestioningly did Gus follow Tonks' instructions, so eager was he to unpick every bad 'stumping' habit, every precocious mannerism he'd brought with him from Tenby, that he was among the first batch of students deemed ready to graduate from plaster-cast antiquities to drawing from life.

The Life Room was almost a sacrosanct space at the Slade. It was lofty, filled with light from five high windows, and its semi-circles of donkeys were arranged around a central dais, on which the model of the day was posed. Junior students were only permitted one session per day, and when Gus first set foot in the room, he wondered if he would survive even that. Their model was a young Italian, and she was probably the first adult woman that Gus had seen naked. When he realized that he was permitted to study every detail of her breasts, her pubic hair, her thighs, the flush of her skin from the warmth of the stove, he became weak at the knees and his hands trembled so badly he could barely draw. Glancing around at his fellow students, he couldn't understand how they appeared so calm.

As the school year advanced, the curriculum expanded to include formal lectures in perspective, anatomy and the history of art. Knowledge of the old masters was considered critical and the students were encouraged to spend an hour each day visiting one of London's major art collections – the National Gallery, the Prints and Drawings Room at the British Museum or the eclectic treasures of the Soane. During that hour, they were told to focus on one picture, to copy it in pencil or paint, to absorb all they could from its composition, style and technique. According to the Slade's professor, Fred Brown, any student who was having 'difficulties' with their work would be able to find the answer to their problem in the masters of the past.

Gus spent obedient hours in the galleries, but the abundance of art on the walls, the wealth of genius, was impossible to assimilate. He thought he should concentrate on one specific artist or school, but, lost between the luminous colours of Titian, the earthy physicality of Rembrandt, the quick-limbed grace of Watteau's figures and the 'voluptuous ghosts' of his favourite Pre-Raphaelite painters, he didn't know how to choose. Later, he would describe how he'd all but paralysed himself, 'loading my mind with a confusion of ideas which a lifetime hardly provides time to sort out.'[5]

And painting, as a discipline, was to come much harder to Gus than drawing. It wasn't only the question of how to paint, but what, and his tutor, Philip Wilson Steer, offered far fewer pointers than Tonks. A large, quiet man, who'd been influenced in his youth by the French impressionists, Steer was either too indecisive or too reticent to direct his students' work. Rather than offering corrections, he preferred to silently rework parts of their canvas he considered weak. Gus admired Steer as a painter, he was fascinated by the 'flickering and voluptuous touch', the handling of light which he'd learned from the French, but he had no idea yet how to learn from him.

At first, there was no one to whom Gus could confide the thoughts and worries that churned in his head. He lacked the money and the courage to join the students who lunched together in cafes and drank in bars after school. A classmate of Gus's, John Everett, remembered him then as 'a very quiet boy, a great reader, a studious youth who avoided all the organised rags [and] was thought by some to be a "nonentity".'[6] Alone as he was, Gus spent much of his free time walking around London, the city and its people becoming his company and his entertainment.

He felt uneasy, at first, when he ventured too deep into the manicured streets of Belgravia but, wandering through the East End docks and the slums of Soho, he delighted in the variety of food vendors on the streets, in the beggars and prostitutes, the musicians on the corners, the foreigners who shouted in strange accents. His favourite activity on a Sunday was to join the crowd at Speakers' Corner in Hyde Park, where he could stand for hours, listening to the polemics of preachers and radicals, joining in with the jeers and applause. Very occasionally, if he skimped on food, Gus could afford an evening at the music hall – the Alhambra with its extravagant Moorish décor, the plush and gilt splendour of Sadler's Wells, or the cockney cosiness of Wilton's. And, for his first few months at the Slade, it was only in the bawdy intimacy of the music hall, the friendly dazzle of performers like Marie Lloyd, Harry Tate or Arthur Roberts and the raucous energy of the audience, that he could forget his abiding loneliness.

Then, sometime in his second or third term, Gus found a friend. Ambrose McEvoy was a long, skinny, short-sighted boy with a limp fringe of hair and an ardent enthusiasm for the art, aestheticism and dandified style of the American painter James McNeill Whistler. Gus admired McEvoy's courage when he began sporting a replica of Whistler's monocle and his own cheap version of Whistler's dressy black suits; but he was even more drawn to the streak of poetic melancholy in McEvoy's character, a sensitivity which made him far more sympathetic than the bluster of some of their peers.

Once Gus had gained his confidence with McEvoy, he made two other friends – Benjamin Evans, who turned out to have suffered his own 'frightful' years at Clifton boarding school, and Michel Salaman, a small, handsome, red-headed young man who came from a huge, wealthy family and was generous with the allowance he received. They formed a little group, these boys. At weekends, they trekked together across London, going to distant art galleries in Dulwich or Hampton Court, pausing for mugs of tea and bread at the cabbies' stands. In the evenings, they explored the sprawl of cheap restaurants around Euston, where, for the price of a beer, they could loiter for hours. They sketched the other drinkers, stared at the occasional group of frock-coated Russian anarchists, argued over the merits of painters and studied every page of the latest edition of *The Yellow Book*.

This new quarterly journal was a platform for dangerous ideas, for the continental aestheticism that promoted art for art's sake. Its sinuous, often fantastically erotic cover designs, by the young Aubrey Beardsley, had been condemned by *The Times* as 'repulsiveness and insolence', and this, to Gus and his friends, made everything about *The Yellow Book* feel even more intoxicatingly adult.[7]

Under the magazine's influence, they learned about paganism, bohemianism, vegetarianism, and were able to parrot the more outrageous witticisms of Oscar Wilde. Under its influence, too, Gus became less the earnest schoolboy, and by the end of the year he was making plans to leave his aunt in Acton and move to a lodging house in Montague Place, close to the school.

When Gus returned home for the holidays, his stories about London and the Slade were both enraging and inspiring to Gwen. She became quite brutal with Edwin when she tried to argue for her own right to attend, giving him no rest as she repeated over and over again all that Gus had reported about the school's proper care of its female students and about the respectability of the girls in his class, some so elegantly proper they were driven to and from the Slade by carriage and were attended by servants.

Despite all of Gwen's arguments and Gus's reassurances, the idea of sending a daughter off to art school still seemed a fearsome proposition to Edwin; until now, he'd only ever worried about how he was going to get Gwen married. Yet, if he refused his permission, he quailed at the rows which would follow, and, as with Gus the previous year, his longing for peace overcame his apprehensions. He told Gwen she could go to the Slade on the strict condition that she lodged in a place where her movements could be properly monitored. Since the aunt's house in Acton was apparently unavailable, they found an alternative in 'Miss Philpot's Education Establishment', an institution in Bayswater which was something between a finishing school and a boarding house. It was, for them both, an ideal compromise; for while Edwin could comfort himself with the belief that he'd acted responsibly, Gwen knew perfectly well that, once she'd made her escape to London, she could do as she pleased.

Even so, as Gwen prepared for her first term at the Slade, she was very apprehensive. She'd never lived away from home, never attended a proper school, never even had a formal drawing lesson. And, relieved though she might have been that Gus had helped pave her way, she minded that he'd had a full year to establish himself at the Slade, that he'd already commandeered the family name for his artist's signature and that she would struggle to make herself known as anything more than his smaller, quieter sister, as anything more than the 'other' John.

According to the observant Ethel Hatch, who'd been quick to notice Gus at the start of the previous year, Gwen had seemed almost invisible when she first arrived – 'very fragile-looking and very quiet in her manners'.[8] Even now that she was fully grown, Gwen was barely five foot tall, she had tiny hands and feet, delicate features, and her slightly accented voice was so soft as to be sometimes inaudible. When she walked through the corridors or sat in class, she was careful not to draw attention to herself, finding it even more impossible than Gus had to imagine she could be on sufficiently intimate terms with her fellow pupils to consider some of them her friends.

Yet solitude had never frightened Gwen and, because her days were so rich in discoveries – about anatomy, composition, line, colour and light – she didn't mind being alone. She was assiduous in filling her neatly ruled exercise books with notes from lectures, with lists of important painters; she made a meticulous study of her anatomy book, noting down all the recommended proportions of limbs to body; and, even though she lacked her brother's precocious facility, an early copy she made of a Raphael nude was very beautiful in its clear delineation of muscle and physical heft.

For Gwen, the Slade was a cathedral of learning and it didn't occur to her, at first, to question her place in it. When she was allowed to graduate from the Antiquities Room into life drawing class, she didn't challenge the fact that she and her female peers were taught in a separate, rather inferior room from the men and were also barred from drawing fully naked bodies – their models discreetly draped with cloth below the waist.

Many of the teachers believed that this was the only form of segregation enforced at the school and that no other distinctions were made. Tonks always insisted that his battery of sarcasm as well as his grudging crumbs of praise were distributed equally between the sexes. Yet it was not the case, for Tonks also conceded that his expectations of women were lower. 'They improve rapidly from sixteen to twenty-one', he claimed, 'but then the genius that you have discovered goes off and they begin to take marriage seriously'.[9] Apparently, it didn't occur to him that this disappointing failure of ambition on the part of his female students might stem from the meagre opportunities they saw available to them. The professional art world was still a very male preserve, so male that when Tonks chose to compliment the work of one newly arrived pupil, by observing that she had the makings of 'a second Burne-Jones', he was completely unconscious of the implications of his remark. So unexpected was the spirit with which this fourteen-year-old girl then replied that she would 'rather be known as the first Edna Waugh', her comment became enshrined in the folklore of the school. Certainly, Edna's ambition for herself ran counter to the more orthodox views at the Slade, which were espoused by one of its teaching assistants, Miss Elder. To the girls in her care, Miss Elder was always keen to encourage a proper modesty of expectation, warning them that, while they might excel in the 'feminine grace and beauty [of] drawing', they could never aspire to the 'greater creative more imaginative force' of men.[10]

There was a difference between the sexes, Miss Elder said, which explained why there had 'never been any very great woman painter', and to the female students at the Slade there seemed little evidence to contradict her, either in the books they read or the art they studied in galleries. Sometimes they found themselves being hustled by officious attendants, who claimed that unaccompanied females were not welcome. If they wanted to sketch people or street scenes in London, they had none of the unquestioning freedom which Gus and his friends enjoyed. A young woman walking on her own would always face the risk of physical attack or the shame of being mistaken for a prostitute.

One of the angrier women in Gwen's class boldly swore that being a girl was 'an awful curse', yet there was little they could do but band together, eating their lunch in the safety of a nearby department store, gathering at each other's rooms.[11] Gwen saw groups of these women around the school – arm in arm, chattering intimately with each other – and at first they seemed completely inaccessible. But, sometime in the middle of her first year, she mustered the courage to move out of Miss Philpot's to a cheap boarding house just minutes away from the Slade. And now that she was able to spend more time around the school, she was also becoming more noticeable.

Years later, Edna remembered her first impressions of Gwen as a rather 'odd' person 'wandering about'. Her curiosity, she recalled, had been so piqued that she'd approached Gwen to suggest they might lunch together in a cafe, and when Gwen bluntly replied she had very little money, so 'had better go without', Edna insisted on paying for them both. The matter-of-factness with which Gwen agreed to this treat, and the naive delight she took in it, were both very touching to Edna. '[Gwen] thought it marvellous to sit down and have food brought to her, a luxury to have an egg and coffee served.'[12]

Yet for Gwen herself the true marvel was finding herself no longer alone. Edna, as sympathetic as she was talented, was undeterred by Gwen's shyness and over lunch she patiently coaxed her into conversation and gave her the confidence to share some of her most private and passionately held thoughts. Edna was generous too, and during the weeks that followed she gradually introduced Gwen into her own circle of friends, so that tentatively, even a little painfully, Gwen was drawn into a more sociable world.

They were a gifted, ambitious group, her new companions at the Slade. Ursula Tyrwhitt was a small, sharp woman, a little older than the others, with a wry humour and a flair for style; Gwen Salmond was very sure of herself in calling out the injustices of the art world; and at the heart of the circle was Ida Nettleship, who seemed quite fabulously fortunate to Gwen in having grown up in a family where artists, writers, even actors were counted as friends.

Ida's father, Jack, was a painter who had been close to the Pre-Raphaelites; her mother, Ada, ran a dressmaking business, counting the wife of Oscar Wilde and the actress Ellen Terry among her clientele. Ida, despite the beautiful dresses her mother sewed, was also a tomboy romantic, a 'wild spirit' according to her friends. When Ida went with two of them on a painting holiday to Aldeburgh it was she who insisted they all bathe naked in the sea, that they walk through the night in high winds, returning to their lodgings with soaking skirts just before dawn. It was she, too, who gave the most fervent expression to their collective determination to become as free and focused in their art as any man. 'Above all things I desire a studio and an ability to paint for myself', Ida wrote to Edna one Christmas holiday. 'I want to paint people – portraits. Oh I want real things – I know I can get them and I will.'[13]

Gwen had never imagined such friends as these. They shared her craving for swooping, remarkable experiences, they were passionate about their work and, even when classes were over, they would meet for informal drawing sessions, taking it in turns to model for each other. One surviving sketch of Edna's, showing Gwen deep in thought, was a celebration of their seriousness, yet these sketching sessions were also sweetly sociable occasions, when the women trimmed hats, talked about clothes, gossiped about boys and marriage.

They taught Gwen to love her new friends for their frivolities as well as their earnestness, although even now, there were moments when she floundered in the effort to express herself. The temporizing 'oh dear' with which her sentences tailed away became a fond joke among the other women. Gwen was physically shy, too, about giving and receiving the casual caresses and tokens of affection that were habitual to the group. When Gus made a drawing of her together with Ida and Ursula, he placed her on the very edge of the paper, her hat clasped in her hand as if she were not quite a part of the others' intimacy.

But that drawing was still a little way in the future, for Gus was still overawed by 'the talented ornamental' girls at the Slade. With the men, however, he was gaining tremendously in confidence, developing the kind of friendships he'd known with his old Tenby gang. He was joining in the student pranks and ragging; when he went to a night at the music hall, he shared a 'shilling box' with friends, from which he would raucously bellow out the words of the performers' songs. His work, too, was becoming assured. Already skilled at catching a likeness, Gus was starting to get at something quick, alive and true in his subjects. His sketchbooks were filling with lyrical studies of people, guitars, animals, hands and feet, any small detail that caught his eye. A male nude that has survived from around this time appears to have been drawn in one fluid, vigorous line, and Gus's progress was marked not only with two second-year certificates, in drawing and advanced antique drawing, but with a scholarship that added a princely thirty-five pounds to his annual income, the equivalent of about £35,000 today.

With his painting, though, Gus had yet to find his way. He'd learned to imitate with panache (in 1897, his homage to Watteau would be awarded 'Best Copy of an Old Master'), but he had little faith in his own ideas and was uncertain where to look for inspiration. Unlike McEvoy and Evans, with their committed allegiances, he was still swerving between Titian, Reynolds, Gainsborough and Goya, and was even more unsure about his taste in more contemporary art. He'd seen reproductions of the leading French impressionists and had puzzled over their radical techniques for capturing texture and light, their representation of the fleeting moment of the artist's perception. Yet Tonks, whom Gus revered, was inclined to warn against their influence, believing his students should master his own strict principles of accuracy before deviating into a more subjective way of seeing and painting.

Tonks was especially cautious about Whistler, one of the most radical of the impressionists' followers, who had divided the British art establishment with his claim that painting should reach beyond representation to a state of pure emotion. There 'are no short cuts to poetry,' Tonks warned, yet his reservations only added to the thrill of Whistler's notoriety. When the painter paid a visit to the Slade, wickedly dapper, genially grand, Gus remembered that 'an electric shock seemed to galvanise the class'.[14]

None of this helped Gus to settle on the school of art he should follow. Gwen, however, had already chosen the seventeenth-century Dutch masters as her principal models. She liked their quiet domestic interiors, their images of women, and when she painted a copy of Gabriel Metsu's 1650 painting, *A Woman Seated at a Table and a Man Tuning a Violin*, she made very specific changes to the original, transforming the man into a shadowy anonymous presence, focusing both the light and the emotional drama on the woman.

Gwen, in her second year, was gaining a steady authority in her painting. A sketch, drawn by her fellow student Elinor Monsell, showed her standing erect at her easel, her hair escaping from its habitual bun, her palette crooked over her arm, her expression intently absorbed. Another student's sketch showed her in the same position, with the Slade professor Fred Brown apparently observing and correcting her work. From the lift of her chin and the narrowing of her gaze, it was apparent that, while Gwen might have been interested in Brown's comments, she was not inclined to be cowed by them.

By the time Gwen reached her third and final year, she was sure enough of her own direction to progress beyond her Dutch masters, and the portrait she painted of the elderly woman who cleaned her lodgings was quite different from anything she'd previously attempted. Gwen had grown fond of Mrs Atkinson – so much so that she used to kiss her in greeting, a breach of social class that was still unusual for the time – and she painted her affection for the charlady into the detail of her portrait: the stubbiness of Mrs Atkinson's work-worn hands; the thin, wry set of her mouth; the modest vanity of her fur-trimmed tippet and hat; and the rheumy tiredness of her eyes.

Yet Gwen had also attempted something more remarkable than a straightforward likeness. She'd positioned Mrs Atkinson at the very forefront of the painting and had heightened the garish orange wallpaper behind her so that the figure of the charlady, dressed in deepest black, seemed almost superimposed against the background brightness. The strangeness of the composition was boldly discordant, almost precociously modern, and, three decades later, the critic Mary Chamot would compare it to the work of Édouard Vuillard, the radical French *interioriste*, claiming no one else could have painted the same image 'so sensitively, getting beauty out of its very drabness, and breadth combined with minuteness.'[15]

The room where Gwen painted that portrait was at 21 Fitzroy Street, the boarding house just south of Euston in which she lived for her final year. Gus had moved there too and, for both of them, it was the richest of all their time at the Slade. The house itself had formerly been a brothel, and, in every way, it was as far from Victoria Street as the Johns could have hoped. Rents were low in the neighbourhood and it was popular with artists, students and foreigners; the pubs and restaurants were cheap; the streets were busy with organ grinders and food vendors; and, above all, the two Johns had the luck of an extravagantly eccentric landlady.

Mrs Aurelia Everett was the mother of Gus's classmate, John Everett. Stoutly booted and never without her Salvation Army hymn book, she had enrolled herself as a mature student at the Slade, where she'd become something of a legend. Tonks, infuriated by her habit of singing hymns in his class, and even more so by the quality of her work – which he said looked like 'a gorilla drawn by a savage' – had relegated her to the basement.[16] But the students adored her, and Gwen and Gus were part of the group who'd been lured to her Sunday afternoon prayer meetings with the promise of free bread and jam. They had also been offered cheap rooms in her boarding house, where, despite her religious convictions, Mrs Everett proved to be astonishingly tolerant of them receiving visits from both male and female friends.

This was exceptional in their experience. Even at the Slade, men and women were discouraged from talking to each other – if Fred Brown, patrolling the corridors, saw any couple whispering together, he would bark that he was not in the business of running a matrimonial agency. So habitual had this distancing become to the Johns that, the previous summer, when Gus had invited Michel Salaman to Tenby for a week, the two men had played cards alone, while Gwen retreated into awkward giggles with Winnie.

At Mrs Everett's, everything was different, and, that year, 21 Fitzroy Street was the place to be. William Orpen, newly arrived from Dublin, was willing to lodge in its basement – dankly cold, with a crude earth floor – simply to be part of it. As the young people mixed together, they grew easy in each other's company; they talked and drew, they smoked cigarettes. Romantic theories of life were entertained; there was a brief fad for vegetarianism; a fancy-dress party was held at which Gwen wore a Spanish costume and the diamonds she'd inherited from her mother. Led by Gus, they went to meetings of the local anarchist group, where they heard the celebrated 'Red Virgin', now very old, reminiscing of her days behind the barricades of the Paris Commune.

Gus was the instigator of most things. In May 1898, when Mrs Everett organized a picnic for the students, Ethel Hatch observed that he was now the centre of everyone's attention, whether he was chasing 'a red-haired girl through the trees' or performing a comic double act with William Orpen on the train home – the two of them 'standing up in the carriage, singing all the latest songs from Paris, with a great deal of action'.[17] In a photograph taken of the picnickers on their drive back to the station, Gus also stood out. While the other men were wearing boaters and blazers, he was sporting a shabby workman's jacket, with a new, thickly curling beard. And while the rest of the party were jammed into a farmer's cart, he was sitting jauntily astride one of the horses that pulled it, sharing his ride with Orpen, who was seated at his back, and Gwen, who was squeezed in at his front.

There were times when Gus worried that his sister was still too solitary, too dedicated to her studies, and in the drawings he made of her,

her expression was always grave. Yet those drawings also captured her newly confident appearance, the delicate receding curves of her profile contrasting with the thick weight of her swept-back hair and with the girlish vanity of her favourite, elaborately ruffled blouse.

Quiet though Gwen often was, she'd also become unrecognizable from the eighteen-year-old girl who'd slipped so invisibly through her first months at the Slade – so much quicker to laugh, to show herself off in her mother's diamonds or in an elegantly trimmed hat. Living with Gus at Fitzroy Street, she was also much less touchy about being his sister. There was a cachet, they both discovered, in their being siblings, in their sharing of the same mysterious, motherless Welsh background, in their being artists from the same family. The two of them had never been so close, and it made them additionally lovable to their friends. When it was time for their group to graduate, in the summer of 1898, Ida Nettleship confessed to Edna Waugh how much she would miss them. 'These Johns you know have a hold that never ceases – and the ache is always there in place of them when absent.'[18]

Despite their closeness, despite the drawings Gus made of Gwen, the only surviving image that Gwen did of her brother was in *Portrait Group*, a watercolour, which she painted that year. Gus was one of the four young people crowded together in a room at Fitzroy Street: a group which featured Edna's sister Rosa, showing a few inches of striped stocking beneath her roguishly lifted skirt; a second young woman who was seated at a desk; and Michel Salaman just behind. Gus himself was perched against the mantelpiece, as though surveying the scene, while glimpsed through the window were two other figures – possibly Gwen herself and Ambrose McEvoy – talking on the pavement outside.

As a painting, *Portrait Group* was awkwardly composed, the figures too large for the space; yet it concentrated all the energetic student life in that room. It was the opposite of the haunted emptiness in Gwen's earlier group painting *Tenby with Figures*, and it was significant, too, because the second young woman in the painting was Winnie, who'd just taken a room in the house.

Winnie had been just as determined as the others to leave home and had worked on Edwin until he'd agreed to her continuing her music studies in London. He may have made his permission conditional on

Winnie staying with her two older siblings, knowing little, of course, about the kind of life they led. In a sketch Gus drew of Winnie, shortly after her arrival, she lay sprawled on a daybed – her hair piled high, her dress an almost wanton tumble of ruffles and flounces.

Gwen drew her sister, too – studies for an oil portrait in which Winnie was dressed for the street in a jauntily angled hat and cherry-pink scarf, an open book on the table in front of her. She appeared a little flushed, but her gaze was quizzical, alert, and she was very much the sweet, practical sister who'd been both friend and support to Gwen in Tenby. And, when life at Fitzroy Street became too exciting, too intense for them all, Gwen was sometimes very glad of Winnie's presence.

Meeting as they did without parents or chaperones, the friends who gathered around Fitzroy Street inevitably became dizzied and disturbed by love. Gus was among the first, jolted from his schoolboy terror of women by the beauty of Ursula Tyrwhitt's appearance when she arrived at the Slade's summer party in June 1897. That had been just prior to his move into Fitzroy Street, and, throughout the long school holidays, Gus had courted Ursula by letter, writing mistily poetic screeds in which he'd compared her loveliness to 'the dawn which [makes] the stars turn pale and flee', and sending effusive thanks for her replies, which 'smelled of violets' and made his heart 'beat faster'.[19] He begged permission to walk his 'angel' home when they met the following term. However, once Gus began meeting Ursula in the rackety freedom of Fitzroy Street, he was emboldened to hope for more. So rapidly had their intimacy advanced that Ursula's father – a vicar, who'd always been suspicious of the Slade and had allowed his daughter only one year of formal tuition – thought it wise to send her away to Paris.

There had been no sex. If Gus, at the age of nineteen, could fantasize torridly about making love to Ursula, he was almost certainly still a virgin, and too poor to follow the example of the few experienced men he knew who used prostitutes or made liaisons with female models.* He also knew that Ursula herself would hardly allow him access to her body unless they were married. Love outside of marriage was dangerous; and

---

* In his memoir, Gus would recall a couple of compliant 'Tenby maidens' with whom he'd some experience, but he was extremely vague about what that experience was.

even Ida Nettleship, with her fierce desire for liberty, had yielded to convention when, drifting into a romance with Clement Salaman (the brother of Michel and of her close friend Louise), she'd accepted Clement's proposal. When she'd subsequently realized that the engagement was all wrong for her, it had taken all of Ida's courage to extricate herself.

Edna Waugh had been unable to muster such clarity when she accepted the proposal of her own suitor, William Clarke Hall. Willie was a close friend of her parents, a brilliant man who would eventually be knighted for his work in juvenile law, and Edna, who'd known him since she was thirteen, admired him very much. But Willie was twelve years her senior and it was partly her sense of being obligated to him and to the flattering ardour of his courtship that had made her, in the spring of 1896, agree to an informal engagement.

As soon as she'd done so, she was riven with doubt. She was afraid she might not love Willie enough and afraid that marriage to him might stand in the way of her having a career. While Willie was proud of Edna's talent and had encouraged her parents to send her to the Slade, he had conventional views on what he thought a wife should paint. He certainly would not want Edna to continue in the vein of the prize-winning watercolour *The Rape of the Sabines*, which she painted the following year.* It was an extreme, even transgressive subject for a seventeen-year-old girl, and Edna had actually used herself as a model for each of its figures, confessing to her diary how she'd stood in front of her bedroom mirror and systematically assumed 'the awful positions of being raped'.[20]

As Edna agonized over Willie, unable to commit to a wedding date, it was Ida who urged her to 'look things in the face and be a man', and to remember 'there are many things to learn, many things to think of before one thinks of marrying'.[21] Gwen apparently had no advice to offer. Her own hard-won independence was too precious for her to imagine trading it in for marriage, and, in any case, she wasn't even sure she could love a man. Women seemed so much more beautiful and complete to her. 'We are more than intellectual and animal beings. We are

---

* It received second prize in the end of year competition.

spiritual also', she later wrote; and, when she first fell in love at the Slade, it was with another female student.[22]

Years later, Gus would refer to the object of Gwen's passion as 'Elinor' (the quotation marks were his), and she was possibly the Elinor Monsell who'd drawn Gwen at her easel.* Even in the mid-twentieth century, however, Gus would be wary of defining the exact nature of the relationship – avoiding terms like 'lesbian' or the more acceptable 'sapphic' – and would only describe how entirely it had consumed Gwen. 'Her passions for both men and women were outrageous and irrational,' Gus wrote. 'She was capable of a degree of exaltation combined with ruthlessness which like a pointed pistol compelled surrender.'[23] When Gwen discovered that 'Elinor' was also seeing a married man, she was so ravaged by hurt and disgust, she threatened to kill herself. 'The atmosphere in the flat became almost unbearable with its frightful tensions, its terrifying excursions and alarms,' Gus recorded, and at one point Ambrose McEvoy rushed in to tell him that Gwen had gone mad.[24] Finally, Gus decided it was his duty to confront Elinor's admirer and demand his retreat. But there could be no reconciliation for Gwen. She was as intransigent, as idealistic in love as she was in her dedication to art, and Elinor would be the first of several – women and men – who would bewilder and break Gwen's heart when they failed to live up to her exacting expectations.

During that formative year at Fitzroy Street, Gwen had discovered much about herself, but it was Gus who'd undergone the most radical alteration, and that change had been a consequence not only of his sudden passion for Ursula, but of a near fatal accident he'd suffered just before the start of the autumn term and just before the era of Fitzroy Street had even begun.

He'd grown hideously impatient with life in Tenby. Even though he'd gone camping in Ireland with McEvoy and Evans, tagging along with a group of tinkers who'd taught them to snare rabbits and cook them over a fire, the rest of the summer had passed drearily. Gus was missing

---

* Others, on the basis of a tenderly pensive portrait that Gwen painted, have speculated that she may have been in love with a music student called Grace Westray.

Ursula, dreaming of their last encounter at the Slade, and his father's house in Victoria Street felt more claustrophobic than ever.

One afternoon, he was killing time on Tenby beach with Gwen, Winnie and Irene Mackenzie, when he decided to go diving from the rocks at Giltar Point. He'd dived there countless times before and thought he knew every inch of the water, but he failed to notice a submerged rock that was masked by seaweed. 'The universe seemed to explode' he wrote later as his head smashed against that rock and he believed it was only the coldness of the water that saved him from losing consciousness.[25] With blood pumping from his wound, a flap of lacerated skin hanging over one eye, Gus managed to swim to the shore, wrap a towel around his head and limp his way back to the girls.

With Edwin's help, they managed to get him home, where he finally passed out. Gus was lucky, preposterously lucky, writing to Ursula that the doctor who'd come to stich up his wound had said it would almost certainly have been fatal had he not had such an 'uncommonly thick skull'. Confidently, he assured Ursula, 'I am healing like a dog', but his convalescence would take another few weeks and, once Gwen had returned to London, Gus was left in the tedious company of his father with nothing to do but write letters to his friends, draw fantastical cartoons of himself and annoy Edwin by growing a beard.

He'd also taken to wearing a velvet smoking cap of Edwin's to cover his still-livid scar, and, when he was finally allowed back to the Slade, the smoking cap came with him. Combined with his beard and the drama of his accident, it gave him a dashing, disreputable air, which, Gus later wrote, felt like a far truer version of his 'own unadulterated self'.[26] And, caught up in the chameleon thrill of changing his image, he became progressively bolder, throwing out his suits and stiff white collars and replacing them with a labourer's jacket, a black silk scarf and a silver brooch. He left his shoes unpolished to a precise degree of provocation, let his hair grow long and bought himself a pair of gold gypsy earrings. And, if this new version of Gus was rather stunning to his friends, if it would make him stand out in the photograph of their picnic the following summer, it also made him shockingly visible on the streets of Victorian London. Gangs of children would now walk behind him, shouting, 'Get your 'air cut, mister!' And Gus would enjoy himself hugely by snarling back at them, 'Get your throats cut!'

Clothes can work transformations, especially for the young. Gus, who'd already shed much of his schoolboy shyness, now felt liberated to a near excess of confidence. He emerged as the natural leader of the Fitzroy Street group, his jokes, his opinions and his recklessness becoming the talk of all their friends. Edna Waugh, at the age of ninety-five, could still recall how she'd watched 'in horrified silence and suspense' as Gus, having forgotten his key to Fitzroy Street, climbed in through a top-floor window, going 'straight up the face of the house using the crevices between the flat stones as hand-hold and foot-hold'.[27]

After Gus became famous, and his life became the subject of gossip and invention, it was said that the alteration in his dress and his personality had been accompanied by a comparable change in his art – that Augustus John had 'dived into the sea and come out a genius.' According to John Everett, 'he started doing brilliant drawings, fellows used to watch him draw'; and Tonks became almost embarrassingly effusive, predicting to the class that Mr John was likely to become 'the greatest draughtsman since Michaelangelo'. The praise made Gus awkward. 'I can't agree with you', he demurred, but Steer also thought he showed the promise of 'genius' and, when the celebrated John Singer Sargent came to visit the Slade, he pronounced Gus's drawing to be 'beyond' anything that had been achieved since the Italian renaissance.[28]

Gus would always challenge the myth of his own transfiguration. There were other exceptional students in his year – Edna Waugh, William Orpen and the recently arrived Spencer Gore – and Gus, very conscious of having to fight for his place among them, was still plagued by his own 'wool-gathering' doubts.

Yet there was a difference in him that year, as though his frustrating convalescence had accelerated his drive for work, had sharpened his hunger for life and for love. After Ursula had been dispatched to Paris by her nervous father, Gus had thought he would wait faithfully for her return. Within less than a month, however, he'd recovered from his heartbreak and pledged himself, ardently, to Ida Nettleship.

Ida, with her olive skin, her dark shock of hair, her full mouth and lovely curves, had always seemed to Gus the most beautiful of the girls at the Slade. But in the spring and summer of 1897 he'd temporarily lost sight of her when she'd gone travelling to Florence in the wake of her broken engagement.

For Ida herself, that period had been intoxicating. She'd learned Italian, she'd studied the paintings in the Uffizi and Pitti galleries, she'd been admired by a succession of young men and had learned how to blow 'seven perfect smoke rings' with Italian cigarettes. Every morning, she'd woken to the view of red-tiled rooftops against a clear blue sky, to mules plodding past her *pensione* windows, and never had her world felt so alive. 'I simply gasp things in now', she wrote to her mother, 'in my effort to live as much as possible'.[29]

That autumn, when Ida returned to the Slade, she looked even more magnificent to Gus – but, while she had formerly seemed unattainable, he now had the confidence to start courting her. He invited her to join him on walks around London, on visits to galleries, he sat talking with her for hours; and for Ida this new Gus, with his gypsy flourish, his exhilarating energy, was exactly the kind of unfettered spirit, the kindred artist, she'd always dreamed of loving. She was stirred by his passions, his jokes made her weep with laughter, his ideas about life promised infinite possibilities. There was a game that she and her sisters had played since childhood, which they called, 'What do you like doing best in the world?' These days, Ida's only whispered contribution was, 'going to a picture gallery with Gus John'.[30]

Soon, they were spending all their free time together. Gus was ecstatic in the knowledge that his feelings for Ida were reciprocated, and he longed for their cautious kisses to progress towards the rapture he believed their love deserved. But Ida's body was no more available to him than Ursula's had been. As a girl she'd been profoundly religious, and she still regarded sex as something holy. However fervently she might yearn to be with Gus – as his lover, his soul mate, his fellow artist – she would only do so as his wife.

For Gus, however, marriage was a remote, even impossible idea. He had no money with which to support Ida or any children they might have, and, in any case, he'd been taught by his new anarchist friends to believe that marriage was a bourgeois institution, a conspiracy to trap the unwary. His beloved Whitman had written that a man's only truth lay in 'freedom and the open road', and Gus, who had yet to turn twenty, thought he had plenty of road still to travel.

Even if he'd been more inclined towards matrimony, it was made clear to Gus, on meeting Ida's mother, that he was far from acceptable as a future husband. Ada Nettleship was a remarkable woman, turning serious profits from the dressmaking business she ran from the family home in Wigmore Street. But she was also a traditional mother. Her own husband, Jack, had never fulfilled his early promise as an artist, had been reduced to selling his highly coloured animal paintings to magazines like *The Boy's Own Paper*. While the Nettleships were far from poor, it was Ada who'd been left to worry about maintaining the family income, and she had long ago vowed that none of her daughters should suffer the same financial insecurity. When Ida had first brought Gus to Wigmore Street, his scruffy clothes and unkempt air had been an embodiment of all that Ada least wanted for her girls. And Gus himself had done little to dispel that impression. He had been intimidated by Ada's large, scrutinizing bombazined presence, had felt tongue-tied and awkward, and had known that his new gypsy clothes looked ridiculous in the family drawing room. Ida's father had restricted his own reservations about Gus to a mild-mannered dismay at the unpolished state of his shoes – 'it's so bad for the leather.'[31] Ada, though, had been overtly hostile and her manner left Gus in no doubt that she would fight against any claim he might make for Ida.

Love, without a future, was hard to sustain. For Ida's sake, Gus continued to brave the Nettleships' drawing room; he continued to believe she was the most interesting and beautiful woman he knew. But Ada's disapproval and his own enforced chastity took their toll and the girl he was later seen chasing at Mrs Everett's summer picnic was one of several with whom he'd begun to flirt. At the end of the school year, when the Fitzroy Street household was dismantled and the students were dispersing, Gus made no plans for how he and Ida might see each other again. What mattered most to him now was setting the course of his own independent adult life.

There were times during the summer when, back with his father and the grinding predictability of Tenby, Gus could hardly believe that such a life would be possible. Early in the autumn, however, he went with Evans and McEvoy to a Rembrandt exhibition in Amsterdam and all his buoyancy was restored. Gus had never been abroad before – simply to catch the boat to Rotterdam, to find a cheap lodging house in Amsterdam, to dine off herrings and schnapps every day was an adventure. Then, the exhibition itself was a revelation. Four hundred paintings, drawings and etchings were hanging in the Stedelijk Museum, and Gus felt he had never before understood the essence of Rembrandt, never appreciated his genius for illuminating the ordinariness and the humanity of his subjects. 'The scales of aesthetic romanticism fell from my eyes,' Gus wrote, and after his anxious years of wavering between Titian, Watteau and the Pre-Raphaelites and the Mannerists, he vowed he would take 'the Dutchman' as his future model and master.[32]

Fired by the inspiration and the absolute freedom of being abroad, Gus also decided that this was his chance to get shot of his virginity. Rather than returning home with Evans and McEvoy, he made a separate detour through Belgium, where he planned to seek out a prostitute or two. The one he found in Brussels was older than he'd visualized in his fantasies, but she must have been generous; afterwards, when Gus boasted of his adventure, he admitted he had 'blushed' for his naivety in imagining that only 'the young wenches' could pleasure a man so well. His second encounter, in Antwerp, felt more transactional: the woman's 'white-haired bundle of a mother' was sleeping in an adjoining bedroom, and Gus was aware of the cheapness of the prostitute's boots and the 'tint of azure under her eyes'. He wondered how Rembrandt would have painted her. Yet, if these first experiences had fallen short of the rapture he'd imagined with Ida, he felt liberated by them, and grateful: 'You will shrug your shoulders when hearing of my aberrations,' he wrote to his friends, 'but I feel more competent for them, and that is the main thing.'[33] He'd become a man, and, now that this essential hurdle had been cleared, Gus felt more equal to the challenge of making himself an artist.

Chapter Three

LONDON AND PARIS

'We all go suddenly daft with lovely pictures we
can see or imagine, and want to do'
IDA NETTLESHIP TO MICHEL SALAMAN, AUTUMN 1898[1]

For a twenty-year-old like Gus, with little money and no social pull, his route to a professional career was not obvious. To maintain his place in London would be difficult: studio rents were twice as expensive as Paris and the market was less friendly to new talent. Yet it seemed to Gus there was no other city for him, so even before he'd left the Slade, he'd already begun talking with McEvoy, Orpen and Evans about the possibility of sharing a studio in Soho.

The money from his scholarship was all spent, however, and when he was forced back home to Tenby, to await the next meagre instalment of his allowance, he wondered tearfully if he would ever fully escape: 'I feel an exile in my native place,' he wrote; 'the town [has never appeared] so smugly insignificant nor the paternal roof so tedious and compromising a shelter.'[2]

His best chance of deliverance would come from winning the Slade's annual Summer Competition, which offered a prize of thirty pounds. Participating students were recommended a list of classical and biblical scenes, and Gus had chosen 'Moses and the Brazen Serpent', the story in which Moses delivers the Israelites from a plague of snakes. The subject had excited him as he'd worked on the painting that summer, for, even though his style was a mishmash of borrowings, from the Italian Mannerists to the 'flickering' brushwork of Steer (his conversion to Rembrandt was yet to come), he felt a new confidence in his technique. His painting of the surging crowd of Israelites came particularly easily, since he'd based the majority of the figures on existing drawings of himself and his friends. And evidently the freshness of his interpretation impressed the judges, for Gus was awarded the thirty pounds. By the end of the summer he was able to leave Tenby for good, to fund his trip to Amsterdam and to pay the first month's rent on his studio.* Even though he would struggle to support himself through the coming winter, he felt he could consider himself launched.

Earlier that summer, Gwen too had been forced into comfortless exile in Tenby. Once term had ended, her own close friends had either gone home or dispersed on holiday, and none of them had plans for renting studios. If Gwen wanted to go back to London, she would be on her own and facing a much harder battle than Gus to survive. While she too had graduated with an award, the Melville Nettleship Prize for Figure Composition, it was worth far less than her brother's and, if she was going to support herself financially, her only obvious option was to teach. She could give lessons to private pupils, perhaps, or apply to one of the small art schools that were run for young ladies. But that would be a compromise for Gwen, a violation of her own high ambitions, and, as she had mooched drearily around Tenby that summer, she was even more fearful than Gus of becoming stuck at home.

Then, late in August, she received wonderful news. Ida Nettleship and Gwen Salmond had decided to go to Paris for the autumn, to rent an apartment and enrol for a term in one of the city's private art academies. Both their families approved: Gwen Salmond had the luck of wealthy liberal parents; Ida's were possibly keen to separate her conclusively from Gus. But, just as they were finalizing their plans for Paris, it occurred to Ida that three would be a better number, and Gwen would be their ideal companion.

Of course, she wanted to go. Even though her allowance wouldn't stretch to the fees of an academy, it would be enough to pay her share of a cheap apartment, and to be living with her friends, in the centre of the art world, seemed like everything to Gwen. The only sticking point,

---

* Even though Edwin had recently moved, the new house was just as meanly proportioned and depressingly cluttered as the old.

the colossal sticking point, was getting her father's permission. Even now, at twenty-one, Gwen had no control of her own money; as an unmarried woman, she was barred from opening a bank account. There was no chance of her going to Paris unless Edwin agreed, and, exactly as she had feared, he fussed dreadfully at the idea. The city had long held terrors for him – his errant brother, Alfred, had ended up there, drunk and unemployed – and he dared not imagine the threats it might pose to his daughter. But Gwen had already fought her father over the Slade, and she was no less ruthless now. She made Edwin's life intolerable, marching noisily around the house and singing 'to Paris, to Paris' at the top of her voice; she belittled all his fears, insisting repeatedly that she would be living and working exactly as she had been in London and would be sharing a flat with two of her most respectable friends.

Her vehemence was particularly awful to Edwin because he'd started to build a contented life for himself in Tenby. Released from the anxiety of raising his children, he'd acquired a modest popularity around the town, had found new hobbies to enjoy – photography and composing music. The prospect of Gwen living permanently back home, a moody, contemptuous disruption to his peace, was almost as awful to him as it was to her and by mid-September, Ida was able to write triumphantly to her mother, 'Gwen John is coming hurrah. It makes all the difference, a complete trio.'[3]

On 25 September, Gwen went to London to catch the boat train to Paris with as much equipment as she could carry – a portable easel, some rolled-up paper and canvas, some boxes of charcoals, pencils and paints. She was travelling cheap – Ida had insisted that 'the third-class deck [was] charming . . . full of peasants and lovely people' – and the ten-hour journey was the longest she'd ever attempted.[4] Her French, however, was good enough to make herself understood, and, when her train eventually steamed into Paris, she managed to navigate her way to the 'very old lady style of pension' on boulevard Raspail, where Gwen Salmond and Ida were awaiting her.

They were impatient to begin their hunt for an apartment and had already settled on Montparnasse, a working-class district south of the Seine which was becoming popular with artists – its streets busy with bookshops, studios and pavement cafes, with restaurants where a three-course meal could be had for a couple of francs. As soon as Gwen arrived, the women began exploring the neighbourhood together, learning to avoid the streets that were most clogged with rubbish, most stinking of drains, debating whether the views from a top-storey apartment were worth the climb of five flights of stairs.

Eventually, they settled on a three-room apartment on rue Froidevaux, a wide, tree-lined street in the 14th arrondissement, which ran alongside the Montparnasse Cemetery. The plumbing was primitive, and there was only one shared tap in the corridor outside. But the rooms were large and elegantly proportioned, and they would be within walking distance of the Louvre. Once the landlady had made it clear she would allow no male visitors, she became quite obliging, agreeing to the women's request to have the walls stripped and whitewashed. And, while the rent was higher than they'd budgeted, 900 francs for the quarter, Ida calculated that the allowances which she and Gwen Salmond each received (around 1,500 francs in total*) would be enough to subsidize Gwen's more modest share and still leave plenty for 'Dej and dinner in cafes, breakfast at home, trams . . . furniture and washing'.

The move into Cold Veal Street – as they called it – was the start of the most hopeful, happy period Gwen had known. Every morning, at breakfast, the three women took it in turns to read aloud to each other: Shakespeare's history plays (which they borrowed from a nearby library); cheap editions of Schiller and Rousseau (which they bought from bookstalls along the Seine). They toured the masterpieces in the Louvre and explored the little galleries, looking at works by impressionists, symbolists, and other styles of painting they could not even name. They were diligent even in their frivolity; if Paris was the epicentre of the art world, it was also the capital of fashion, and, as the new season's styles came into the shops, they spent pleasurable hours looking at the windows of couturiers and department stores, scrutinizing the expensively dressed women who frequented them. Although such clothes were far beyond their means, all three of them could sew, and, with the occasional help of a cheap young seamstress, they updated their own small

---

* The equivalent of about £4,000 today.

wardrobes, Ida sending home sketches of the dresses she begged Ada to make.

Their reward each evening was a meal in one of the local restaurants – their favourite a cafe run by anarchists, where the customers had to fetch and carry their own plates of food. Meals and wine were cheap – they felt themselves almost rich – and Gwen, who'd commemorated the student freedoms of Fitzroy Street in *Portrait Group*, now began work on a homage to the more grown-up, feminine intimacy of rue Froidevaux.

Interior with Figures was a double portrait of Ida and Gwen Salmond, the two of them reading together from the same book, their hair loose around their shoulders and their dresses a conscious statement of style. Ida had just acquired an illustrated volume of fashion history, *Une siècle des modes feminines, 1794–1894*, and, while the simple white frock that Gwen Salmond wore was probably copied from Whistler's painting *The White Girl*, Ida had apparently modelled her own flounced, Victorian crinoline on an illustration from that history. There was something, too, of the classic fashion plate in the composition of Gwen's interior, for she posed her friends in a near empty space, leaving out all the clutter of pictures, clothes and painting things that were actually crowding their flat.

All three women were now painting at Cold Veal Street. There were easels, tubes, rags and bottles of turpentine scattered about, and the walls, protected with brown paper, were covered with their art. 'It is so untidy,' Ida reported jubilantly to Michel Salaman. 'We all go suddenly daft with lovely paintings we can see or imagine and want to do.'[5] They were taking it in turns to sit for each other. Gwen drew an exquisite study of Ida, her face modelled in precise detail, her body a near abstraction of fluid lines. Ida's own sketch of Gwen was less flattering, too heavy in the jaw and full in the face. But other, more interesting versions of Gwen were also being pinned up on the walls – images she was sketching of herself. She'd become intrigued by the idea of self-portraiture, had taken to staring at her reflection in the mirror, experimenting with poses, working out how to simultaneously observe and draw. Ida, watching her indulgently one day, reported to Michel, 'She has been at it for half an hour'.

Durer, da Vinci, Rembrandt – Gwen had studied the masters of the genre, she understood how the best of their works had been a revelation not only of the artist, but of the deeper mystery of the human face. Tonks had said repeatedly that the 'drawings of great men are like lines in Shakespeare, the beauty of which are beyond explanation'. And, here in Paris, as Gwen began studying the emphatic line of her eyebrows, the curve of her cheek, the slightly downward pout of her mouth, she was trying to peer deeper into herself.

More pragmatically, she was also preparing for the fact that, shortly, she would have no one to draw but herself, for Gwen Salmond and Ida were about to start classes at their chosen academies and she had no money to pay a professional model.

It was difficult for Gwen not to envy her friends' advantages, their luck in having liberal, enlightened parents; it was even more difficult when Gwen Salmond announced she had successfully enrolled at Académie Carmen, the private atelier where Whistler taught. Gwen herself had become interested in Whistler during her last year at the Slade; she had learned from Ambrose McEvoy to appreciate the American's famously 'symphonic' handling of tone, to admire his conjuring of emotional atmosphere. In the portrait Gwen had painted of Winnie at Fitzroy Street, she had borrowed her sister's pose from Whistler's *Miss Agnes Mary Alexander*.

When Gwen Salmond came back from her first week at Académie Carmen, boasting that Whistler 'was very beautiful & just right . . . a regular first-rate master', Gwen struggled to remain gracious.[6] But the other Gwen was generous, and when she saw how Gwen was fighting down her envy, she offered to pay for her to attend Whistler's classes as well.*

Whistler himself was in declining health, not quite the galvanizing presence who'd visited the Slade. But he was still a performer. Dressed in one of his exquisitely tailored suits, his monocle glinting, he delivered his instructions to the class in a stream of witty aperçus that were the opposite of Tonks' bluntly surgical commands. His charm worked particularly well on the women, yet it was the analytic beauty of his painting

---

* Ida had enrolled in the less expensive Studio Colarossi, where she complained her teacher was mediocre and the 'other girls somewhat feeble'.

method that captivated Gwen. After making just a few charcoal marks on his canvas, Whistler would apply his colour in very fine layers, one after another, until the image was fully formed. One of his subjects recalled that it was as though his own face had been 'hidden in the canvas', emerging slowly through each film of paint, 'like a photograph being developed in chemicals'.[7]

'I do not teach art [but] the scientific application of paint and brushes,' Whistler told his class, and he made a severe point of studying each student's palette before they started work, scrutinizing their choice of colour, enquiring what 'tone picture' they were hoping to achieve. For Gwen, it was all so interestingly different from the teaching at the Slade, and she must have written to Gus about it because, rich with the money from his prize (news of which he'd sent in a jaunty pen-and-ink sketch of himself), he came over to Paris to learn more.[8]

He was terrifically impressed by the women's apartment and by their newly Parisian style. His attempts to make himself known to Whistler, though, were disappointing. He encountered the painter one day at the Louvre and, overcoming a twinge of anxiety that Whistler might think him a 'tramp' in his scruffy clothes, he introduced himself as Gwen John's brother. Hoping to initiate a conversation about art, he asked Whistler if he didn't think Gwen showed a fine 'feeling for character'. The response was dismissively brief: 'Character?' Whistler sniffed. 'What's that? It's *tone* that matters. Your sister has a fine sense of *tone*.'[9]

If Gus felt rebuffed by Whistler's comment, Gwen knew it was a compliment to treasure. She was flourishing in his classes, and had gained confidence, too, because, here in Whistler's elegant third-floor studio, she wasn't known as the sister of the more famous Augustus – only as herself. Loving Paris, and particularly loving Ida, to whom she now believed she could trust all 'my thoughts and feelings and secrets', Gwen wished this time would never end. She had the promise of a winter ball at Whistler's atelier, so much more to discover and learn. Yet her father had only agreed to her spending four months in the city, and early in the New Year he would be expecting her home.

In a bid to change Edwin's mind, Gwen pretended that she'd been awarded a scholarship to the Académie Carmen, hoping he would be proud enough to regard this as a solid reason for her prolonging her stay.

Instead, however, he proposed coming over to visit. This was entirely out of character, Gwen thought; Edwin had rarely ventured further than London. But she decided she must make the most of her father's visit and, having cleaned and tidied the apartment, she arranged a special dinner in his honour, at which she planned to wear a new dress, with a design she'd copied from a painting by Manet.* The dress was a disaster, though, for Edwin knew nothing of fashion and could only stare, appalled, at the inches of bare neck and wrist Gwen showed. He told her she looked like a prostitute, and she was so hurt by his attack, so disgusted by his prudish provincialism, she vowed never to go home again. She said she would not even accept any more money from him beyond the interest she earned from the family trust.

That money was stretched very thin, though, and while Gwen began to earn a little cash from modelling, most likely sitting for students at Académie Carmen, she couldn't afford to accompany her friends when they went briefly back to London for Edna and Willie's long-postponed wedding. The ceremony was on 22 December, which meant Gwen was alone over the Christmas holiday; and although she'd received an invitation to dine with a woman she'd recently befriended, she chose instead to spend her Christmas day tramping through the woods around St Cloud, wearing her best coat and hat.

'I walked until dark in strange places – over a hill covered with trees – and then came home quite footsore,' she boasted to Ida. 'The people look on me as one of the sights of Paris'.[10] Gwen had the same urge to explore that she'd always had as a child – it was her way of imprinting herself on a place, of feeling herself at large. Yet, in Paris, as in London, it wasn't always easy for a woman to be out on her own, and, as Gwen admitted to Ida, when she'd crossed paths with two men on the street and wished them a 'Joyeux Noël', the men had taken her for a prostitute and insulted her with a 'freezing bow'. Without the company and protection of her friends, Gwen was beginning to feel vulnerable, and so on edge that, when they returned to the flat, late one night, she was convinced the footsteps she heard were those of thieves. 'We heard a loud

---

* The painting was possibly *A Bar at the Folies-Bergères*, and Gwen may have made it to wear at Whistler's ball.

O, and then again O,' Ida reported back to her mother. 'A queer reception for a burglar'.[11]

Afterwards, when Gwen's heart had stopped racing, the women talked late into the night, celebrating their reunion with plates of ham and glasses of warm milk. But their time together was almost over for the lease on their flat had only three weeks to run. Gwen Salmond had decided to stay on in Paris for a second term at the Académie Carmen while Ida was returning home to Wigmore Street. Gwen, though, had no plans beyond knowing that she would never go back to Tenby and must somehow find a place of her own in London.

Gus could do nothing for her. His shared studio in Charlotte Street was already so cramped that he and his friends were having to work and sleep in rotation. None of Gwen's other close friends could offer her rooms and, after a miserable search, she was forced to settle for a foetid basement in Howland Street, just off Tottenham Court Road. Gus thought it unbelievably grim, a 'kind of dungeon into which no ray of sunlight could ever penetrate'; yet even this squalid space ate deep into Gwen's allowance and, if she wanted to paint, let alone feed herself, she needed to earn money.[12]

To profit from her work at this point seemed impossible; she knew of no buyers and had very few pieces to sell. But Gwen did know how to model. Her years of sitting for friends at the Slade had taught her how to find and hold a pose, how to direct the line of her body, and had even given her a sense that modelling could be an art in itself. (A year or two later, when Orpen asked her to model Ophelia for his new *Hamlet* painting, she refused because she thought the pose he wanted was gratuitously histrionic.) Yet Gwen was not so innocent or so elevated in her ideas that she was ignorant of the risks she would run in sitting for strangers. In 1899, it was mostly prostitutes, actresses, or women who were down on their luck who worked as models, and among the artists who hired them they were routinely regarded as fair sexual game.

Later, when Gwen was in Paris and looking for work as a model, she wrote about some of the abuse she encountered. Of her experiences in London, however, she left no record. And while she must have endured some humiliation, even fear, those traumas also made no impression on the self-portrait she painted during her first months in Howland Street. On the contrary, her portrait glowed. Working in a palette of browns and golds, Gwen posed herself with an almost flamboyant air of challenge, her head held high, her hands firmly planted each side of her narrow-belted waist, giving full display to the gorgeous leg-of-mutton sleeves and extravagant bow of her blouse. This was Gwen's post-Parisian self, and everything about the resolute light in her eyes, the set of her mouth and the tensile nubby strength of her little hands declared her authority, both as painter and subject.*

She knew it was good and, early in 1900, she submitted it for exhibition at the New English Art Club. The NEAC had been launched fourteen years earlier as a deliberate provocation to the fusty elite of the Royal Academy; it held two-yearly exhibitions at the Dudley Gallery in Piccadilly and it was a rite of passage for any young British artist to be included. With Fred Brown and Henry Tonks on the selecting jury, it was also a regular showcase for Slade graduates. Gus would exhibit there for years, but women were still quite a rarity; when *Self Portrait* was accepted for the Club's summer show, Gwen was one of only sixteen among the ninety participating artists.

It was her first professional accolade, her first precious foothold in the London art world, and the lift it gave to her courage was bolstered the following year when her student portrait of Winnie was also selected and was then purchased by Louise Salaman. Even so, Gwen's life remained hard, and often solitary. Gus, Ida and Winnie were all in London, but they were busy with their own work and studies, and Gwen herself had no money for outings to cafes or bars. Some of the time, she could convince herself that anything was worth enduring for the sake of her work. But some of the time she was very low, and, six years later, when she looked back at this period, she would remember herself as a 'starved little creature,' who crept through a 'subterranean life'.[13]

Gus felt real concern for his sister, but he too was short of funds. Although he had found buyers for his work much sooner than Gwen, the money seemed to spend itself – on paints, paper and canvas, but also on

---

* Years later, the artist Allen Gwynne Jones singled out *Self Portrait* as an outstanding example of the genre: 'It has grandeur, delicacy, most beautiful colour and above all intensity'.

pubs, cafes and the music hall. At Sadler's Wells, he'd become such a regular that the punters in the stalls had given him a nickname – Algie, on account of his long hair – and had united in mocking him when he sang along with the performers. So extravagantly did Gus spend that, when the lease of the Soho studio came to an end, he had to flit from one cheap room to another, escaping his debts. Spencer Gore remembered that, whenever he changed lodgings, friends tried to gather up any sketches or fragments of sketches he left behind: 'I know people who got many wonderful drawings that way.'[14]

But Gus was too busy to mind where he slept. While Gwen starved for company, his own days were jammed. He owed many of his meetings with new friends and artists to William Rothenstein, an artist to whom he'd been introduced shortly after graduation. William – Will – was the older brother of a fellow Slade student, Albert Rothenstein, and he'd just returned from four years painting in Paris, where he'd acquired an extraordinary network of colleagues and friends, among them Whistler, Toulouse-Lautrec, Oscar Wilde and Degas. Although he was only twenty-six, Will was a great gatherer-up of people and a generous promoter of other careers – Walter Sickert would call him 'Puffing Billy' in half-mocking gratitude, but it was now onto Gus that Will was focusing his support.

A small, unathletic man himself, with horn-rimmed spectacles and a clever, unassuming face, Will admitted he'd been physically beguiled by Gus: 'a young fawn with beautiful eyes, almond shaped, broad cheekbones, thick brown hair parted in the middle.' But it was the beautiful fawn's drawings that Will had thought 'truly remarkable' – 'masterly' in their composition, 'poured out [with] the copiousness that goes with genius.'[15] And, once he'd decided to champion Gus, Will was assiduous in spreading word of his talent and in persuading others, like Sargent and the thirty-year-old impressionist Charles Conder, to purchase his drawings, at two pounds apiece.

Will also let it be known that the young Augustus John was in the market for commissioned portraits, and when Gus was introduced to his first client, an elderly widow in Eaton Square, he was emboldened to ask for a forty-pound fee (the equivalent, now, of several thousand pounds). He took care with the portrait, which was the closest his style ever came to Gwen's: a Whistlerian palette of sober tones and delicate highlights, through which he captured something stiff, proud and lonely in the widow's tightly drawn features. Yet his client had a sharp temper, she clearly disapproved of Gus, with his shabby trousers and unpolished shoes, and he in turn found the long hours spent in her over-furnished room quite unbearably oppressive. When he got into difficulties with the widow's hands, unable to capture their arthritic tension, he'd suddenly had enough: even though he'd got close to finishing the portrait, he left it as it was, walking away with only half his fee.*

Still, Gus was undeterred. Two smaller commissions came to him, from women living outside London, and both apparently entangled him in some sexual flirtation. Will had observed on first meeting Gus that, with his 'looks and his ardour', he was destined to become 'a dangerous breaker of hearts'.[16] And, once he'd returned from his liberating experiences with the two Belgian prostitutes, Gus was discovering that all kinds of women were attracted to the reinforced gleam of his confidence.

Nor was it just bored wives and impressionable young girls who responded. Late that autumn, he was invited by Tonks to give a demonstration to the first-year life-drawing class. The students already knew about Gus from two of his pictures, a nude drawing and the prize-winning *Moses and the Brazen Serpent*, which had been hung prominently on the walls of the Slade. Yet it was his physical presence to which the young men immediately thrilled. Percy Wyndham Lewis, then an impressionable sixteen-year-old, recalled that, when a tall 'figure with an enormous black Paris hat, large gold earrings [and] a carriage of utmost arrogance strode into the room, the whisper "John" went around the class.'[17]

That same arrogance held them captive, too, when Gus sat down to demonstrate his drawing. The female model that day was 'a squat little figure', and Gus, fresh from his discoveries of Rembrandt, did nothing to flatter her, using a flourish of dense, dark cross-hatching to exaggerate the ungraceful lines of her body. To the watching students, his sketch was both an electrifying demonstration of technique and an electrifying deviancy from all that Tonks had taught. It was Gus's homage to all that

---

* Titled *An Old Lady*, in 1941, it would be purchased by the Tate.

was most raw and unsentimental in Rembrandt, and afterwards, Lewis claimed, a vogue for 'Dutch squalor' spread like wildfire through the school.

Contemporary Dutch squalor didn't have a ready market, though, and several buyers whom Will tried to interest in Gus's work were put off by the style and subject matter of his most recent sketches, his perverse attraction to what one critic would describe as the 'gossip of the slums' — toothless women, squint-eyed urchins and 'shuffling old men in dingy shapeless coats and top hats'.[18] But, in March 1899, Gus had his next piece of luck when Will included some of his drawings in 'Moderns and Old Masters', an exhibition he'd organized at the newly opened Carfax Gallery, in Piccadilly. It was an eclectic show, ranging from Titian and Goya to Conder and Rothenstein, but it was enough to get Gus noticed. He received words of praise from the Scottish painter Dugald (D. S.) MacColl in *The Spectator* and he netted thirty pounds in sales.

It was enough to keep him in food, rent and paint for several more months, but the money was burning too big a hole in his pocket for him to put it sensibly aside. Impatient to get out of London and conscious of Gwen in the subterranean gloom of her basement, Gus proposed an early summer holiday for them both in Swanage. Their beloved Mrs Everett ran a seaside boarding house, Peveril Tower, in addition to her house in Fitzroy Street; for the Johns, she would lower her modest rates. Already, Gus was looking forward to sharing with Gwen a seaside reprise of their happy student past.

The holiday didn't quite turn out that way, because Gus developed conjunctivitis and had to remain confined to a darkened room. At first, Gwen was happy in her own company: she painted and read; at night, she went walking over the cliffs, following the moonlight and catching fireflies to put in her hair. Yet, her solitary months in Howland Street had left her prone to strange impulses, and one afternoon, when she went to swim in the sea, she had a sudden longing for intensity and risk. Writing afterwards to Michel Salaman, she explained that, while the rocks on her beach were 'treacherous . . . & The sea unfathomable', there had been 'no delicious danger' for her there, so she had experimented with sitting right on the 'edge of the rock to see what would happen'. It was with a certain pride that she admitted to Michel she'd almost drowned: 'A great wave came & rolled me over and over which was humiliating & *very* painful & then it washed me out to sea & that was terrifying – but I was washed up again.'[19]

Ever since childhood, Gwen had felt an instinctual, almost primitive connection to the sea, but she had a more adult motive, now, when reporting her dramatic immersion to Michel. She wanted to create an impression, to make herself more visible and interesting, because, in her last year at the Slade, she'd come to value Michel as an unusually intuitive and sympathetic friend, and had lately begun to wonder if she might love him. After exaggerating the recklessness of her escapade in her letter from Swanage, and hinting to Michel about the paintability of the landscape, Gwen concluded by suggesting he might join her and Gus for the rest of their stay.*

Carefully, she added that he must not 'take any notice' if the idea didn't suit. And apparently it didn't, for, while Michel admired Gwen, he'd witnessed the full fury of her passion for 'Elinor' at Fitzroy Street and had no desire to expose himself to anything similar. He sent no reply, and Gwen, gnawed with the horror of having made a fool of herself, felt exposed and alone. Once she was back in London, she couldn't even count on Gus for company, because he was to spend most of his summer in Normandy, having been invited there for a painting holiday organized by Will and his new wife, the actress Alice Knewstub.

William Orpen, Charles Conder and Alice's sister Grace were also among the party, and for Gus it was an enchanted time. He felt limitlessly energetic, swimming naked in the sea and half falling in love with Grace when she sat for him. He was up early each morning, to bed very late, often sharing a bottle of Calvados with Conder, who became something of a hero to him. Impressively dissolute, if slightly 'gone at the knees', Conder regaled Gus with stories of his student years in Paris, of meetings with Wilde and Beardsley, of evenings spent drinking and whoring with Toulouse-Lautrec. To Gus, Conder also seemed to possess a marvellous instinct for style, dressing in theatrically old-fashioned

---

* Gwen was still unsure of her feelings and had first invited Michel's sister, Louise, to Swanage.

clothes which he'd picked up from Parisian flea markets. Bored all at once with his own shabby wardrobe, Gus used up more of his dwindling funds to order an extravagant suit from a local tailor – pale blue corduroy, with a tight waistcoat and pegtop trousers.

Orpen thought Gus cut a 'splendid' figure in his suit, but also recorded that, the first time he wore it, he seemed overcome by a mad elation. 'Suddenly John jumped into a bucket that was wound to the top of a very deep well; he went down with a rush; it was all we could do to haul him up again.'[20] When Gus stepped out of the bucket, he was crowing with laughter, as high on his own bravado as he'd been as a half-naked schoolboy capering wildly on Tenby beach. Everyone was entertained, for, while Gwen had alarmed Michel with her own near-drowning, Gus, according to Orpen, had displayed a classic 'Byronic recklessness'. Behaviour that made Gwen appear worryingly odd only made her brother fascinatingly mad, bad and dangerous to know.

When the painting party broke up, Gus moved on to Paris with Conder and Will. He was still supercharged with energy and very excited when he was taken to the Café de la Régence and introduced to the 'distinguished reprobate', Oscar Wilde. Even though Wilde had been physically diminished by his recent incarceration – serving a two-year sentence for the crime of homosexuality – he remained a brilliant conversationalist, leaving Gus with the impression of an 'enormous sense of fun, infallible bad taste and a gleam of profundity'. Wilde also took flattering flirtatious notice of Gus himself, scolding him skittishly for having had several inches trimmed off his hair – 'you should have consulted me', he said, 'before taking this important step.'*

But, although Gus was moving in sophisticated company with Will, he was not always comfortable. He could still experience blanks of shyness, bristles of antagonism towards those he considered facile or fake. Wilde, in Paris, had surrounded himself with an entourage who seemed to Gus made up of 'snobs, lickspittles, social hangers and crawlers up', and it tainted his admiration for the man to see him tolerate such fawning mediocrity.[21] It was a relief when Conder suggested they abandon

---

* Wilde would die the following year.

the soirées at Café de la Régence and begin the tour of Parisian nightlife he'd promised. This too was a revelation for Gus, who'd never imagined brothels of such number and variety; and in his enthusiasm for sampling them all, it never occurred to him he might catch an infection. Conder had already contracted syphilis, although his symptoms were not yet apparent. Gus, however, seemed to have been gifted with some fluky immunity – not just in Paris, but for the rest of his life. 'How he escaped getting the Ladies Fever we couldn't make out,' John Everett recalled. 'Tonks used to say it must be his natural dirt.'[22]

It felt to Gus, then, that his body could do anything. After visiting brothels with Conder, he still had the energy to go walking on his own, striding up to the top of Montmartre to watch the dawn. During the day, he spent hours in the Louvre, where he became obsessed with the symbolist canvases of Pierre Puvis de Chavannes. The Arcadian simplicity of Puvis's landscapes, the lyrical choreography of his figures, had an effect on Gus as profound as Rembrandt. He didn't yet know what to do with them, but he kept them lodged in his imagination.

By October, Gus had exhausted his funds and had to go back to London. With little money left for lodgings, he had to beg one of the old Fitzroy Street rooms from Mrs Everett – which seemed rather 'comfortless quarters' now, without all his friends. But, later in the autumn, Will came to his aid yet again, offering Gus the use of his old bachelor cottage in Kensington, lying empty now that he and Alice had moved to their new house in Hampstead.

There was enough room at 1 Pembroke Cottages for Will to suggest Gwen might stay there too; he'd taken an interest in her work and he enjoyed the idea of supporting both the John siblings. He would soon, however, come to regret his generosity. Neither Gus nor Gwen had any interest in domesticity, and, when Will called round to see them, he found his cottage in a state of desolate filth. The hallway was littered with muddy boots, the sitting-room fire was 'a cold grate choked with cinders', and, as Will gazed around at the mess, he heard the sound of a window being forced open – Gus, as usual, having forgotten his key. 'There were none I loved more than Augustus and Gwen John,' Will wrote loyally, 'but they could scarcely be called "comfortable friends".'[23] Guiltily, he had to ask them to leave – and Alice was so horrified by the state in which they'd left the cottage, she had the walls whitewashed and the floorboards scrubbed.

It was early February 1900, the dead of winter, and Gwen was so short of money she had to break into an empty building on Gower Street and sleep in an unfurnished room. Gus at least had friends to offer him a couch or mattress, and, for a brief, comfortable period, he was able to share the bed of a young woman who'd fallen in love with him – although, he was ejected when she discovered that her feelings were not reciprocated. But, while Gus always had a roof over his head, this itinerant life was no longer good for his work. At Will's suggestion, he'd started to think about painting more directly from his imagination, and he was forming plans for an epic tableau of Faust being tempted by Mephistopheles – a Walpurgis-night fantasy, which he visualized as a swirl of naked bodies with 'a carrion-laden gibbet'.[24]

But, to realize his painting, he needed to be settled in a good room, with good light, and in March he went with Conder (probably at the latter's expense) to stay with Mrs Everett in Swanage, to begin work on a preliminary study. His progress on the work was slowed, however, firstly, because he was confined to bed for a week with German measles, but then, as he admitted to Orpen, because he'd become 'fatally smitten' with Mrs Everett's new parlourmaid.

Gus's heart was initially touched by the story Maria Katerina told him of how she'd been born into the Viennese aristocracy but had been forced to find work after escaping an abusive marriage. Yet, as he told Orpen, it was the seductive elegance of Maria's patent leather shoes and lacy stockings that had 'wrench[ed] away a considerable portion of my already mutilated heart'.[25] He begged to see her naked and make love to her, but Maria was far too cautious, and it was Conder, the experienced cynic, who advised Gus to buy her a ring and let her believe that it came with the promise of marriage. Even if Gus had felt a momentary pang of shame as he climbed up the drainpipe to Maria's window with the ring in his hand, it was overcome by the joy of being welcomed into her bed, where, as he wrote deliriously to Will, she 'sucked out my soul with her lips'.

Gus believed he was in love, and, on his return to London, he made Maria promise she would join him later that summer in France, where he would be on yet another painting holiday. This was to be paid for by

Michel, who had confided to Edna his concern that Gus, under Conder's influence, was drinking too much and behaving more wildly than was good for him. Only a couple of weeks after finding himself an affordable room in London, he'd been thrown out by his landlady because he'd come home with a prostitute and a crowd of paralytically drunk friends.

When Gus arrived in France, he was at least sober – and impatient to paint. Michel had found a spot, deep in the Auvergne, in the medieval village of Le Puy-en-Velay. 'Wonderful country', Gus told Ursula, 'with the most exquisite hills, little and big, Rembrandtesque, Titianesque, Giottoesque, Turneresque.'

He set up his easel at a nearby chateau, and also started work on a portrait of Michel. One evening, in the park, as the two men sat listening to 'an excellent military band', Gus felt graced by a sudden epiphany, a heightened awareness of the people around him. 'Rendered clairvoyant by the music one feels very intimate with humanity', he wrote – and, throughout his life, he would sometimes be visited by such moments of calm, when, lost in a crowd, a drink in his hand, a melody in the air, he felt peculiarly at ease with himself and the world.[26]

The work and the clairvoyance, however, were then dispelled by Will and Alice, who were on a cycling tour of France and insistent that Gus and Michel should accompany them on a strenuous fortnight of pedalling. By this time, Maria should also have arrived, but, when Gus returned to Le Puy, he received a bombshell letter, announcing that she would not, could not join him. Mrs Everett (who'd coaxed out the truth of their affair after discovering some hairpins in Gus's bed) had been very blunt with Maria, warning her that, however charming Gus might be, however winning his promises, he would inevitably tire of her.

'When you will no longer have me, what will I do then?' Maria asked plaintively – but, if she'd been hoping to elicit some guarantee from Gus with her letter, she was disappointed. He was hurt, morally enraged by her lack of trust. 'Women always suspect me of fickleness but will they never give me a chance of vindicating myself?' he demanded angrily of Alice. 'They are too modest, too cautious . . . I am not an exponent of the faithful dog business.'[27]

Alice might well have responded that it was easy for Gus to disdain the 'faithful dog business', but much harder for a woman like Maria, who was a long way from home and without financial security. Gus, however, was too blinded by self-righteousness and frustration to be reasoned with, and indifferent to his effect on Michel, he retreated to his room in a sour and selfish depression, painting and reading Balzac.

But his was not the only emotional drama to destroy the peace at Le Puy, for, days after Maria's letter, Gwen arrived at their lodgings with Ambrose McEvoy. Gus had invited his sister because he'd wanted to give her a holiday away from her miserable squat, and it was Michel, perhaps afraid of being exposed to the force of Gwen's passions, who'd invited Ambrose to join them, sending a cheque because Ambrose had no money for the fare. Neither he nor Gus apparently realized, however, that it was not their planning alone which was bringing Gwen and Ambrose to Le Puy, rather that the two 'unfortunates' had begun seeing each other in London and were on the brink of an affair.

What happened next was unclear, except that it was miserable. By the time Gwen and Ambrose arrived in Le Puy, Michel had left, driven out by the relentless bitterness that was emanating from Gus. Left to play host, Gus attempted to be sociable. 'I am conducted about by McEvoy and Gwen,' he wrote to Michel, 'and seeing some surprising spots'.[28] But he was too wrapped up in his own private calamity to sustain the effort for long. After a couple of days, he was back in his room and, as Ambrose informed Michel, he 'would not be budged from his easel'. A grim paralysis then descended on the house, for when Gus was painting as intently as this, the force of his concentration could disable those around him. Neither Ambrose nor Gwen could settle to their own work and, left to each other's company, they were wretchedly uncomfortable.

Ambrose had already admitted to Michel that he'd been going through a 'strange period of mental and physical bewilderment' in London, and it seems to have been now that he felt morally bound to tell Gwen why. There was another woman in his life – a former Slade student called Mary Spencer Edwards whom he'd met a couple of years earlier.[29] And according to Gus's version of events, even though Ambrose hadn't yet made a formal commitment to Mary, he was in sufficiently deep to feel he owed a confession to Gwen, a confession which left her 'quite inconsolable' during her remaining time in France, and drove Ambrose to drink himself guiltily into a 'wreck'.

After they all returned to London, Ambrose decided his loyalties must be to Mary. Yet, although he proposed to her, he still insisted their engagement remain a secret, and he still carried on seeing Gwen. She either knew nothing about the engagement or chose to love Ambrose regardless, and, the following summer she moved in with him, the two of them sharing a tiny flat above a tobacconist's shop on Southampton Street. It could have been a charming setting for Gwen's first adult affair, almost Parisian in its proximity to the vegetable and flower markets of Covent Garden, the department stores of Oxford Street. But domesticity seems to have put too much strain on her already complicated relationship with Ambrose. By late autumn they had separated, and, in January 1902, Ambrose and Mary were married.

The ending of this relationship was crushing for Gwen. For months, she was grieving and wrung with self-doubt. 'I don't pretend to know anybody well. People are like shadows to me and I am like a shadow,' she wrote. Love – true, mutual love – seemed impossible and she believed it was her own disabling shyness that was to blame. In a long confessional letter to Michel, Gwen described how much of a struggle it was for her to communicate her ideas and emotions to anyone, explaining that the only way she could confidently express herself was on paper: 'To me the writing of a letter is a very important event. I try to say what I mean exactly. It is the only chance I have, for in talking, shyness and timidity distort the meaning of my words in people's ears – that I think is one reason why I am such a waif.'[30]

Michel, who remained wary of Gwen, had already tried to refuse the responsibility of becoming her confidante, and his resistance had confused and upset her. 'I cannot understand what you say about yourself but it does not change what I said & I feel at ease with you & I should like you to read at will all my thoughts & feelings, I trust you as much as Ida and Winnie . . . You say this does not matter to you. I know but still don't be bored and whatever you do don't *laugh*.'[31] At times like this, it seemed to Gwen she was truly an outcast, living in a world whose rules and relationships she'd failed to master. After the unravelling of her affair with Ambrose, she had nowhere to live and was forced to accept the temporary generosity of his elderly father, who offered her a room in his Bayswater home. Talk of Ambrose and Mary must have been impossible to escape, intensifying her sense of exclusion. And Gwen could no longer turn to Gus – the principled anarchist, mocker of 'the faithful dog business' – for support in her single state. At the beginning of 1901, when she and Ambrose had still been dithering around the edges of their love affair, Gus had turned all his own beliefs upside down and got married.

Back in the autumn of 1900, Gus had come back to London convinced he'd put Maria behind him. He doubted, in fact, how much he'd ever cared for her, and even wondered whether, at the cynical age of twenty-two, he'd already lost 'the art of loving fanatically'.[32] But then he met up with Ida again, and realized that her courage, integrity, talent and wit had once aroused feelings that were both more ecstatic and more enduring than his infatuation for Maria. Even after he'd drifted away from Ida, she'd remained loyal to him: she had never abused him to their friends, she had willingly sat for him (a portrait in a red dress he never finished) and had sent him valiant notes on his travels – 'Don't forget old Ida. Come home soon.'[33]

Suddenly, it was obvious to Gus that Ida had always been his woman. He wanted to draw her again, to capture on paper the particular mix of delicacy and earthiness that was so moving to him, and above all he wanted her in his bed. Against the burning necessity of his desire, his old principled stand against marriage seemed juvenile – a folly of hot air. Just two months after he'd begun seeing Ida, Gus was writing jubilantly to Winnie: 'I have news to tell you. Ida Nettleship and I got spliced at the St Pancras Registry Office last Saturday. McEvoy and Evans and Gwen aided and abetted us. Everyone agreed it was a beautiful wedding – there was a wonderful fog which lent an air of mystery unexpectedly romantic.' Ironically aware of his own moral reversal, Gus signed off the letter with a cartoon of himself standing clownishly on his head.[34]

The modest ceremony had taken place on the morning of 12 January – and, while Gus had his sister and his friends as witnesses, none of the Nettleships were present. Afterwards, when Ida went home to Wigmore Street to confess what she'd done, her mother's reaction was as hysterical as she'd feared. Even if Ada hadn't been quite so fiercely opposed to Gus, the hugger-mugger secrecy of this wedding had been hurtful, destroying her dream of seeing her favourite daughter beautifully wed among family and friends, and wearing a gown that she herself had made.[35]

Jack Nettleship had at least been able to calm Ada in time to attend the impromptu party hosted by Will and Alice in the evening. According to Albert Rothenstein, it was a delightfully Slade affair – with 'Miss Salmond, Miss John, Messrs Steer, Tonks, McEvoy, Salaman and myself' all gathered to toast the new couple and to play games of charades.[36] Ida had looked 'radiant' in a simple white dress, but Gus, bizarrely, had arrived two hours late to his own party, wearing a loud checked suit and gold earrings. He claimed he had been getting himself ready at the public bath – but, to his friends, he already appeared half drunk.

This was aberrant behaviour even for Gus and, if it had confirmed Ada's worst fears about her new son-in-law, it may also have shaken Ida. She hadn't hesitated when Gus proposed; she believed in his genius, she knew she couldn't love anyone as she loved him. But she also knew he could be dangerous to her. The stories she'd heard of all his other women had made her more jealous than Gus knew; to her friend Dorothy Salaman (another of Michel and Clement's many sisters), she'd intimated that her own thoughts had 'become poison' to her.[37] And, even now, when Gus had made this enormous gesture of marrying her, Ida was too clear sighted to believe he could ever deny his restless hungers. She knew who he was and she knew that her future with him was always going to be uncertain.

Earlier in the day, when Ida was breaking news of her wedding to her parents, she had revealed none of her private fears. Her response to Ada's noisy lament that she 'could have married a king' was only to insist that 'Gussie *is* my king'.[38] Afterwards, when Ada was quieter, Ida had gone upstairs to her mother's workroom to share her news with Elspeth Phelps, a young trainee seamstress with whom she'd become close. The dramas of the day, however, and her own suppressed anxieties had suddenly become too much. 'I want to tell you something,' Ida had started to say, but then she had begun to weep violently. Burying her face in her hands, she had sobbed, 'I want to tell you I've married Gussie, and I think I'm a little frightened.'[39]

Chapter Four

TWO SELF-PORTRAITS

After the wedding, Gus took Ida down to Swanage, their honeymoon a gift from Mrs Everett, who now liked to think of herself as godmother to the new Mr and Mrs John. They were very happy, at first: 'We have taken the most convenient flat imaginable in Fitzroy Street,' Gus crowed to Winnie. 'It has an excellent studio. The whole most cheap.' The novelty of having Ida beside him was still wonderful to Gus. Together, they had vowed that marriage would not limit them in any way, that they would continue to make art and see friends as they'd always done, and, while Gus might sometimes joke, a little savagely, about the comedy of their wedded state, he also wrote letters to Ida so ardent that, years later, he would be embarrassed by their callow sentimentality.*[1]

Gwen's feelings about the marriage were mixed. Gus and Ida were two of the people she cared about most and there was a certain satisfying simplicity in them becoming husband and wife. Yet she was also conscious that their life as a couple excluded her and, as she fought to

---

* Around this time, he wrote a wicked limerick:

'There was a young woman named Ida
Who had a porcelain heart inside her
But she met a young card
Who hugged her so hard
He smashed up her crockery, Poor Ida!'

sustain her own affair with Ambrose, she often feared what her future might be.

Her painting, though, was still the centre of her life, the stubborn grit that made sense of everything. And the picture Gwen painted of herself during the winter after Gus and Ida were married was, among many things, a statement of her will to survive.

Technically, *Self Portrait in a Red Blouse* was the closest she'd come to matching the finesse of her master, James Whistler – the near invisibility of his brushstrokes, the elegance of tone. Against a dark, subtle background, she had painted a controlled lustre of colour, the auburn tints of her hair chiming with the glimmer of gold at her ears, with the flush of her cheeks and the crimson of her blouse. But the power of the portrait was in the force of its self-expression. Through some beautifully rendered chemistry of detail – the vestigial frown that puckered her forehead, the slight canting of her head, the pursing of her lips and, above all, the nakedness of her gaze – Gwen had made her interior life visible. She had painted a window onto her proud and troubled spirit, and it wasn't necessary to know her history to see her, in this painting, as a woman who could both suffer and endure, who could set aside the disappointments and failure of her life and state very simply – *This is me.*

It may have been pure coincidence that Gus began work on his own self-portrait that year – although he'd certainly been watching Gwen's progress with interest. Viewed side by side, as family portraits, there was an arresting sibling resemblance – the genetic similarity of their almond-shaped eyes, the length and strength of their nose more evident in paint than in any photograph. But the character of each portrait was very different. While Gwen had chosen to pose with quiet formality, in a pleated, high-necked Victorian blouse, Gus had painted himself as the bohemian artist, with the buttons of his loose white shirt half undone, and with subtle flourishes to the detail of his curling beard, to the rich carmine red of his lips. And, while Gwen's gaze was unwavering, Gus had captured some sliding, sideways hesitancy in his own. Beneath the romantic theatre of his portrait, he'd allowed himself to reveal the anxieties which had always churned within him – and which still churned, despite his new adult status and his growing success.

Gus was only twenty-three when he married Ida, and he'd been too impatient to worry much about the practical and financial consequences. Money, however, soon became an urgent issue. There were long periods when Gus was still earning very little, and even though Ida was getting an allowance from her family, it wasn't enough to buffer against lean times. As a married man, Gus could no longer flit from his lodgings when he was short on rent, he could no longer expect his friends to subsidize his painting holidays, he needed some steadier income. Shortly before the wedding he'd applied for a scholarship from the British Institute, which would have kept him afloat for a while, but, to his genuine shock, his application failed. Although Gus was exaggerating when he told Conder he was unable to get out of bed until Ida had mended his only decent set of clothes, the threat of poverty had rarely felt more close. He was conscious that, when Ida visited her family, the staff at Wigmore Street all whispered that he wasn't 'half good enough' for her.

But, in February, Albert Rothenstein came round to Fitzroy Street, delivering the late wedding present of a kitchen table and some interesting news. Liverpool Art School (a faculty of the city's university) had urgent need of a temporary teacher, its current professor having enlisted to fight in the Boer War. According to Albert, the post came with an annual salary of between £300 and £400, plus the use of a rent-free studio, and, while Gus had no teaching experience, Dugald MacColl had promised to vouch for him. Everything then happened fast: letters were exchanged and, by early March 1901, Gus and Ida had moved to Liverpool, where a student was able to report the 'heartening sight' of Augustus John arriving for his first morning's class – 'striding across the drab quad to the studios in his grey fisherman's jersey and with gold rings in his ears.'[2]

Gus wanted to make a success of the job. Even though he did little more than draw and paint alongside his students, explaining his methods as he went along, his lessons were flatteringly popular. According to Steer, it was mesmerizing to watch Gus at work, making his first, rapid series of lines, some of them apparently 'superfluous or even wrong', and then working them into a drawing that 'in the hands of any other man would have become . . . a failure.'[3] Certainly Gus believed his

Liverpool students were making progress, and for his first two terms he was very proud of them.

He was also, for that period, delighted by Liverpool. 'It is a most gorgeous place,' he told Michel, with 'wondrous' docks, an opium-scented Chinese quarter and a heaving shanty town that was home to 'rough nomadic tinkers'.[4] There was such a variety of people on the streets of this tough northern metropolis – a variety with which Rembrandt could have done much – that Gus felt he had been gifted a world of new subject matter. Within a few weeks, he was sending parcels of drawings and pastels back to Will – pictures of beggars, tramps and urchins, which Will considered quite extraordinary in their embrace of the savage, the squalid and the sublime. 'Such power combined with a marvellous subtlety,' he wrote, 'no one living has his range of sensuous lofty and grotesque imagination.'[5]

These Liverpool sketches were mostly done at speed – the impression of a moment – but Gus was also starting to explore the slower, more meticulous process of etching. He'd been astounded, in Amsterdam, to see what Rembrandt had achieved in the medium, the heightened contrasts between light and dark, between harshness and delicacy, and, in Liverpool, where the school had a strong tradition of etching, he had access to materials and tools. 'I have taken to nitric acid like a duck to water,'[6] he would tell Will. He relished the physicality of the process – the scratching of needle onto copper, the loading of ink onto roller, the alchemical action of the acid – but he embraced its discipline too, the slower pace at which it forced him to work, the extended focus on the image he was constructing.

Some of Gus's first experiments were heavy-handed, others too obviously indebted to Rembrandt. But there were etchings he made in Liverpool where the transfer from paper to copper made the grime of the city more visceral, its character more cussedly alive. Gus created beautiful prints of Ida, too, from which the strong clear planes of her face, the solidity of her body emerged with gorgeous force. He was flying so high on discovery, he believed he'd gathered what he needed from the art of the past and was getting close to creating a vision of his own. To Will, he wrote, in a euphoric mix of metaphor, 'Hitherto I have been Art's most devoted concubine but now and then the seed takes root. I *am*

O Will about to become a mother – the question of paternity must be left to the future. I suspect at least 4 old masters.'[7]

Liverpool was generous to Gus in other ways. He and Ida were offered cheap, commodious lodgings with the university's 'very absent minded and charming' professor of ancient history, and through him were introduced to Harold Chaloner Dowdall and his wife Mary. The Dowdalls were among the city's elite – he was a barrister and local politician, while she was the daughter of a lord – yet Mary, in particular, struck Gus as the 'most charming and entertaining character in Liverpool.'[8] Small, auburn-haired, sharp witted and attractive, Mary wrote cynical novellas about love and marriage, and had acquired a mild reputation for wickedness through her willingness to sit for slightly disreputable artists.

Ida was initially unnerved by Mary's careless brilliance, and felt young and naive in her presence; but, over time, she came to love her candour. She nicknamed her 'the Rani', Hindi for 'queen', and eventually came to entrust her with confidences she could share with no one else. She was far less ready, though, to trust the other new friend they made in Liverpool, John Sampson, who was the university librarian. A large Irishman, a self-taught scholar of literature and lost languages, Sampson often dressed like a tramp, in baggy trousers, a battered hat and food-spattered waistcoat. Gus, who loved him immediately, thought he resembled 'a magnificent ship on a swelling sea . . . very heavily built, rather slow of movement and speech but with the soul of a poet.'[9] And the hold he came to exert on Gus, the principal reason why Ida came to distrust him, was because of his profound, and passionate, kinship with the Roma people.

Gus had never lost his own fascination with gypsies. His urgent wish to be stolen away in one of their caravans had burrowed deep into his childhood imagination and, when he first started to wear his gold earrings and colourful silk scarves, he'd been conscious of returning to his schoolboy fantasy. Through Sampson, however, he discovered new adult depths to his fascination. In 1888, a group of British enthusiasts had founded the Gypsy Lore Society, with the aim of gathering more knowledge about Roma language and culture; and, although the Society had been temporarily suspended, Sampson and his small team of researchers were keeping its work alive. Sampson himself was now recognized as an honorary Roma and, each year, when groups of gypsies came to camp on waste ground just outside Liverpool, he was invited to stay with them as their guest and friend.

The first time Gus was invited to accompany Sampson on a visit to 'Cabbage Hall', he experienced an exhilaration so profound it was physically painful. To be sleeping in one of the gypsies' caravans, to be eating their *otchi-wichi* (hedgehog) stew was beyond his childhood dreams. He marvelled at the beauty of his hosts – their brilliantly ornamented clothes, their oiled black hair – and he committed to memory the exotic music of their names: Sinfai, Counseletta, Kenza, Tihanna. On Sampson's advice, he'd brought gifts of wine, earning himself the right to sit with the men and hear their 'tribal secrets'; also on Sampson's advice, he kept himself at a respectful distance from the women. They were attractive to him, radiating an 'oblique derisory intelligence', but Roma etiquette was strict and the one portrait Gus painted of those women, *Athaliah*, was deferentially classical in style.[10]

Those days in Cabbage Hall became the start of an obsession. Gus could hardly explain the hold the gypsies had on him, except that they looked beautiful and they lived as he'd always longed to do, following the sun and the seasons. Even if Gus couldn't go out on the road with them, he could study their ways and learn their language, and, with his quick ear, he was soon able to swap limericks and dirty jokes with Sampson, sharing the older man's excitement over the 'strange grammar and voluptuous syllables' of the multiple Romani dialects.

This new friendship became almost as exclusive and absorbing as a love affair. To Sampson, Gus seemed blessed with more beauty, talent and temperament than 'one mortal deserves', while 'Beloved Sampson' became an intellectual hero to Gus.[11] He called him 'Rai' (Romani for 'gentleman scholar') and he was greedy for everything Sampson could teach – Celtic folklore, the history of poaching, the 'wonderful' poetry of William Blake and Thomas Hardy. Through Sampson, Gus came to identify himself as an inheritor of the Romantic tradition, living by the laws of art, love and freedom; he was impressed by the ease with which Sampson justified his own frequent breaks from responsibility, leaving his young wife, Meg, and their three small children for weeks at a time while he went travelling for research, accompanied by his team of young and often attractive assistants.

Ida, Gus sensed, would not like to be left so alone. She didn't directly complain about the hours he spent with the Rai – she was working on a portrait, an elderly man who posed for her 'like a rock, occasionally wiping his old eyes when they get moist'[12] – but time hung heavy and social calls from the university faculty wives were more of an irritant than a pleasure. Gwen had promised to visit, yet she was too preoccupied with work and with Ambrose, and soon Ida began to talk wistfully of starting a family.

Gus's own thoughts about babies were ambivalent. They were to be expected, of course, and he was rather taken by the image of himself as father to a tumble of picturesque infants. Yet he felt too young still for the expense of a family, the encroachment on his liberty, and, early in the summer, when he reported to Will that Ida had started to look 'suspiciously pregnant', his pride at having proved himself a man was shadowed by a secret, shameful alarm.

Then, for a moment, it seemed there might be no baby, because Ida showed signs of miscarrying. Although the bleeding and cramping eased, the doctor insisted she must rest, so she went home to her mother in London, leaving Gus to finish the term on his own. He minded the separation from Ida, but he also relished the return of his bachelor life, his freedom to closet himself away with Sampson, to paint through the night, even to wake up one morning and decide, on a whim, to travel to Bruges and look at Dutch art.

It was late August before Gus rejoined Ida, who was now rosy and round in her sixth month of pregnancy and was visiting Edwin and Winnie in Tenby. Gwen also arrived, although Ida reported she was often in an 'unconversable state', unwilling to spend time with her father, unhappy over Ambrose and retreating to the works of Turgenev, which she was reading in a new French translation. After Tenby, though, they were planning a painting holiday in the nearby port of New Quay, where Gwen, Gus and Ida were to be joined by Gwen Salmond, and this proved to be almost as cheerful as their time together in rue Froidevaux. Every day began with a swim, after which they all went to work in a disused schoolroom, sketching the butcher and other locals whom they'd persuaded to model. Ida wrote of her quiet contentment as she sat and watched the 'very gay regatta' which marked the end of the season, and felt the baby's reassuring flutters inside her belly.

By the end of the holiday, Gus had become cheerfully reconciled to the baby and, on their return to Liverpool, his mood was given an extra fillip by news that his teaching load had been reduced to three days a week, while his salary had been raised by a 'smug £200'. With his account freshly bolstered, Gus could move Ida to more private and spacious lodgings, and, with his additional free hours, he could devote more time to work. Early that autumn, he sent a batch of drawings, pastels and etchings back to London, and Will's extravagant response made him weep with gratitude. 'Beloved Will', he wrote. 'You know nothing delights my soul more than your laudation! You have made me tickle and thrill, and gulp tears to eye and water to lip.'[13]

Yet Gus had never mastered the habit of day-to-day contentment. In mid-October, he slipped from a ladder, breaking his nose and dislocating a finger, and the few days during which he was stuck at home and unable to paint triggered something of the frustration he'd endured during his protracted convalescence back in Tenby. He was appalled by the university wives who called at their rooms to quiz Ida about her delivery date and offer oblique but ghoulish warnings of what awaited her. Ida, unnerved by their influence, began to suffer nightmares: in one of them, she dreamed she had given birth to a grotesquely oversized baby with 'thick lips, little black eyes near together . . . altogether very like a savage'; in another she dreamed the baby had come out as a tiny adult, 'the size of the 1st joint of a finger.'[14]

As the birth drew near and as their rooms began to fill with baby shawls and maternity gowns, Gus seized every chance to visit Cabbage Hall, where the gypsies had returned for the winter. He spent many hours at the camp, sitting around the fire as the men made music and related their travellers' tales, and the more time he spent with gypsies, the more disgruntled he became with his life. Liverpool now felt too small to him; with the exception of Sampson and the Dowdalls, there were few people who interested him, even fewer who took any serious interest in his work. He'd found no buyers for his pictures, the Liverpool Academy of Arts had inexplicably refused him membership and he now regarded his teaching post as a hideous mistake. 'The three days I prostitute to foul-faced commodity weigh on my soul,' he fumed with melodramatic indignation. 'I see the evil of my ways.'[15]

Gus pined for his old London life, but, when Will urged him down for a visit, he replied, martyrishly, that he was obliged to wait until 'our baby has squeezed its way through the narrow portals of life.'[16] At last, on 6 January 1902, Ida went into labour and their baby, a boy, was safely delivered. 'I *cannot* believe I am a mother,' she wrote to her sister, Ursula. Contrary to all her nightmares, her baby seemed perfect, with 'an intelligent little face . . . a wonderful mixture of Nettleship-John.'[17] Gus drew a sketch of her, lying in bed with the baby in her arms, and, in the joy of her gaze, the cradling of her touch, he portrayed his own deep sense of wonder. To Will, he marvelled diligently over the baby's growth – 'he is becoming a surprising bantling with muscles like an amorillo' – and so miraculous did Gus find each small change in his infant son, he could not decide what to name him.[18] One day, he favoured the simplicity of Lewis, Peter or Anthony; another, he felt only the exoticism of Honoré or Pharoah would be adequate. Ida simply waited for Gus's indecision to exhaust itself. 'It changes every week,' she reported placidly. 'I don't mind what it is.' Yet, even after Gus had finally agreed on David Nettleship John, he couldn't fully commit to it – and, for several years, would confuse the little boy by calling him Dafydd, the Welsh for David, or sometimes just Tony.[19]

During this first proud flush of fatherhood, Gus was determined to apply himself more steadily to life and to work: 'the arrival of Honoré gives me to see I cannot dally and temporise with fate'. But David was not an easy baby, and, over the next few weeks, the difficulties of parenthood began to weigh on them both. Ida, inevitably, bore the brunt. In March, they changed lodgings again, to rooms close to Sampson, and the upheaval of the move, combined with the broken nights, the anxiety over David's feeding, was almost more than she could manage. She feared she was a bad mother and little David was suffering. 'He *howls* . . . I have done all I can for him and I know he is not hungry. I suppose the poor soul is simply unhappy,' she admitted to Alice, feebly joking that her baby seemed almost to wish he hadn't been born.[20]

Ruthlessly honest with herself, Ida also admitted she sometimes wished the same. It was hard for her to love David when he refused to be pacified, and, as the weeks passed, she observed with dismay that she was feeling as fuzzy, as depleted in her mind as she was in her body. She couldn't seem to read, she certainly couldn't draw or paint, and she was acutely sensitive to the fact that Gus rarely asked her to sit for him. The first of her friends to have a baby, Ida had no idea of the effect that hormones could have on her, and postnatal depression was not then widely understood. It seemed to her only that she was being weak, and she was too ashamed to admit how unhappy she was. Ida also knew Gus well enough now to understand that a discussion of her feelings was one from which he would flinch. However eloquent he might be on the subject of love, or art, or gypsies, Gus had neither the language nor the talent for talking about more humdrum or unattractive emotions. Growing up in Tenby, he'd never been encouraged to share his own feelings, and the authors he now preferred, like Whitman and Baudelaire, wrote little about the cross-currents of domestic life. But, while it was simpler to brush aside Ida's depression as ordinary fatigue, Gus was frightened by it. He missed the woman with whom he'd fallen in love, and was unsettled by the monotony into which his marriage had slumped. In the middle of April, when Ida's father fell seriously ill and she and the baby went down to London, Gus admitted to Will he was glad of their absence: 'Decidedly it is inspiring to lie alone at times. I fear continued cosiness is risky.'[21]

Both he and Ida had been hoping that Gwen would visit, but she didn't appear until March. She'd had her own misery to contend with, Ambrose having married Mary in January, and she'd retreated to New Quay to spend time on her own. She was not so self-absorbed, however, that she couldn't see how difficult things were with Gus and Ida, and, during the four or five days that she spent with them, she tried to help. She took the baby out for very long walks in his pram, sitting down in doorways when she needed to rest; she talked to Gus and Ida about books and painting, the admiration she now shared with them for Puvis de Chavannes.* 'I have been very busy,' she told Michel, urging him to write more often, especially to Ida, who needed her friends.

---

* Gwen Salmond may have sparked Gwen's interest, and her vanity, by claiming that Puvis's pale wavering women bore a strong resemblance to Gwen herself.

But, concerned though she was, Gwen had no intention of entangling herself too deeply in Gus and Ida's marriage. She was uncomfortable with their cluttered domesticity, and critical of what they, especially Ida, had given up for it. In little more than a year, Ida's brave, youthful determination to achieve 'real things' in her art and her life had been eroded by marriage and motherhood. And Gwen had seen an equal diminishing in the hopes and talents of their friend Edna Waugh. Although she had no children yet, Edna had nonetheless become victim to her husband's controlling views. Willie not only disapproved of Edna's former crowd at the Slade, he disapproved of the ideas she wanted to explore in her art. Now, if she painted at all, it was in the isolation of her marital home.

Many years later, Gwen would copy out part of an article from *The Times Literary Supplement*, which argued that a married woman could never hope for equality because her 'true happiness was invested in the well-being of her dependents.' She was witnessing the truth of that even now, and, although she agreed to pose with Gus, Ida and David for a photograph in Liverpool, a small pale figure beside her brother and her friend, this would be the last time that Gwen involved herself closely with any of the John babies, and it was almost certainly the last family photograph in which she featured.

But Gwen was not happy in her solitude. It was while she was in Liverpool that she wrote her long letter to Michel, describing herself as a waif and a shadow, and on her return to London it seemed that everyone around her had work and plans. Michel himself was about to go travelling, while Gwen Salmond had secured two teaching posts, with London County Council and with Clapham School of Art. Even though Gus and Ida were about to return to London for good, he having finally lost all patience with his teaching job, they would be preoccupied.* A 'magnificent' group exhibition was due to be held in Wolverhampton, to which Gus was contributing work and Ida, left to deal with the move and the baby, was also busy with the rest of her family. Jack Nettleship had not recovered from his illness, he was now clearly dying, and Ida was far

---

* Gus had virtually forced his own dismissal from the art school by blatantly neglecting his students and refusing to stand for the King's toast at a university dinner.

too caught up with her grief, and that of her mother and sisters, to have much energy or time for Gwen.

Gus was not unaware of his sister's unhappiness. He took her up to the opening of the Wolverhampton show – 'Art and Industrial Exhibition' – which also featured works by Will; he stood by her loyally when the NEAC accepted only one of her works that autumn, *Interior with Figures*, which they then inexplicably failed to hang. But it was hard for Gwen to feel gratitude for the vigorous protest which Gus made on her behalf when his own two submissions had been prominently displayed and glowingly reviewed. Although she declared proudly to Ursula that she refused to care about the snub, the wound to her pride had cut deep.

In need of money and distraction, Gwen began to do a little private teaching. Edna and her sister Rosa came for painting tuition, and an 'exquisite' fifteen-year-old girl began sitting for her in exchange for drawing classes. But, as Christmas approached, marking the passage of yet another unhappy year, Gwen was close to despair, feeling herself further away than ever from love and a career. And she could hardly have been in a more susceptible state when, one evening, she ventured from her basement to a party at the Westminster School of Art and encountered a young woman of quite disconcerting loveliness.

It had been impossible not to notice Dorothy McNeill in the middle of that noisy posturing party. Her dress was plain, her long dark hair was drawn back in a simple bun and she spoke very little, yet, as Will would write a few months later, 'One could not take one's eyes off her.' Dorothy was beautiful in ways that went deeper than the graceful curves of her body, the large slanting eyes, the broad planes of her face, the enigmatic play of her smile – she appeared preternaturally calm, in possession of herself, and it made her loveliness almost embarrassingly hypnotic.

Gwen lost her shyness in the face of such beauty and, having introduced herself, she learned that Dorothy came from a very ordinary family – her father a clerk, her mother a farmer's daughter – that she worked as a junior typist in a solicitor's office and had enrolled herself into evening classes at the Westminster School of Art. About her own modest talent, Dorothy had few illusions, yet she admitted to Gwen that she yearned to become part of the artistic life. She rented a basement in Fitzroy Street so that she could be close to the painters and their studios;

she was a diligent visitor of galleries and exhibitions; and, between her evening classes at Westminster, she frequently sat for her teachers and fellow students.

Dorothy was willing to sit for Gwen as well, and, over the rest of the winter, the women became friends. As Gwen basked in Dorothy's quietly admiring interest – for her work, for her studies in Paris, for her future plans – she felt her own eloquence and confidence gathering force. This was a friendship over which Gwen had some power and – even if she may have hoped, in vain, that Dorothy might come to see her as more than a friend – their chaste but passionate intimacy was like a feast for her.

For a while, she apparently wanted to keep that intimacy secret, especially from Gus. He had already taken effective possession of Ida, and Gwen could easily imagine his greedy response to her beautiful new friend. But, whatever pains Gwen might have taken to keep Dorothy and her brother apart, the London art world was small. Dorothy had already noticed Gus when she'd seen him at a gallery and, magnetized by his presence, had been certain that fate would someday bring them together. Then, sometime around the spring of 1903, Gus saw Dorothy coming out of her Fitzroy Street basement. He asked her to sit for him and, after an all too predictably short time, he was lost to her beauty: 'The smell of you is in my nostrils', he wrote, 'and it will never go and I am sick for love of you.'[22]

Chapter Five

DORELIA

'I want to look long & solemnly at you. I want to hear you laugh and sigh – my breath is on your cheek . . . I kiss you on the lips . . . I possess you as you possess me and I will hear you laugh again and worship your eyes again and touch you again and again and again and again . . . write a line to your lover Gustavus'
AUGUSTUS JOHN TO DORELIA MCNEILL[1]

The letters Gus began writing to Dorothy were mostly undated and no record survives of when, precisely, they became lovers. His drawings, too, were undated, but they were as blatant in their longing as the letters – hot lyrical images in ink, pencil or red chalk, which cast Dorothy as a coquette in petticoats and stockings, an elusive Giaconda, a peasant woman or a siren. She was the essence of poetry to him, his protean muse, and because he could not bear to call her by so humdrum a name as Dorothy he rechristened her Dorelia – a name she would keep for the rest of her life.

If Gus was intoxicated by Dorelia's beauty, if he was in a frenzy to possess the mystery of her on paper and in bed, he was also reacting against the insidious dissatisfactions that had crept into his marriage. He and Ida had been happy when they'd first made their escape from Liverpool in the summer of 1902; Ida's depression had lifted and Gus had painted a portrait of her, which he called *Merikli*, Romani for 'jewel'. Ida, in that picture, was the sensualist, idealist and artist with whom he'd fallen in love. Sitting with a bowlful of flowers and cherries in her lap, a strand of brilliant coral beads around her neck, she looked magnificent, her face lambent, her dark eyes pooling with a secret intelligence, her hands delicately tactile. Although Gus had painted the portrait with a certain classical gravitas, the free loose rhythms of his brushstrokes had channelled something of Ida's old wild spirit, and when *Merikli* was submitted to the NEAC, it was voted picture of the year.

Gus remained hugely energetic throughout that autumn, working hard and plunging into London society with all the enthusiasm of a returned exile. Often, he was at the Rothensteins' Hampstead home, mixing with their clever and cosmopolitan guests. There were times when Gus could feel a provincial still, too easily thrown off balance by the urbane wit of the cartoonist Max Beerbohm, the calculated nonsense of Walter Sickert. But the talk – of art, books, politics and London gossip – was an education, and Gus knew he was meeting people who could be important for him.

It was Will, too, who introduced Gus to Wyndham Lewis, the student who'd thrilled to his appearance at the Slade. When Lewis first came to visit Gus at the small Fitzroy Street flat he'd borrowed from Michel, he heard the wails of a crying baby drifting down the stairs, followed by 'Biblical curses' from Gus. But if Lewis was unsettled to find his hero in so domestic a setting, he was still inclined to worship, and for several years he would sport the same style of broad-brimmed black hat Gus wore and would make a habit of picking up any drawings he'd thrown away, pasting them carefully into an album. Gus was exhilarated by the admiration, but he was also aware that Lewis was a potential rival force. He'd created a huge stir by getting himself expelled from the Slade for the crime of smoking in front of Fred Brown, yet he'd also been considered a talent – not only an exceptionally gifted draughtsman, but also a precociously original poet.

Gus enjoyed Lewis, his ambition as well as his satirical intelligence; he nicknamed him 'the Poet', giving that title to the first of many portraits he would draw and paint; and he particularly enjoyed talking to Lewis about books. Even at twenty, Lewis was better read than Gus – it may have been he who first introduced Gus to the Russian darkness of Dostoyevsky – and it was often their discussions of literature, the self and the soul that kept them drinking together at the Café Royal until closing time.

The Café, with its fading, red plush grandeur and its tolerance for customers too poor to afford more than a single glass of wine or crème de menthe, had become Gus's new favourite haunt. It was a place to see and be seen, walled with huge, age-spotted mirrors which threw reflections of the drinkers back on themselves, and Gus had become pleasurably aware that his was a reflection others watched. He liked having Lewis witness the stir he created when he arrived at the Café, the enthusiastic gathering of people around his table. Late at night, when he made his way home, his mind agreeably racing, his senses agreeably lulled, Gus didn't stop to think that Ida had been left on her own, yet again, and that the money he'd promised to save for finding them a larger flat had been spent, yet again, on drinks, both for himself and for all the friends who'd clustered around him.

In his mind, Gus considered himself an excellent husband. It was with only a touch of sarcasm that he reported to Michel how very staid and old fashioned he'd become, how much a man of 'beer, tobacco and slippers'.[2] And Ida rarely contradicted him. Her love for Gus was still the central fact of her life, he could still transform her day with his jokes and stories, his gift of a sketch, his promise to paint another portrait. She had also learned how irritable it made him to feel trapped in any way, realizing that freedom was oxygen to him, essential to his work. She tried not to rebuke him when he returned tipsy and laughing from a night at the Café Royal; she didn't complain about their cramped living space, simply counting herself lucky that they could afford a maid, who slept uncomplainingly in the kitchen. And, as she grew more pragmatic about managing Gus, she even accepted that there would be other women whom he would prefer to draw and paint.

Estella Cerutti, an Italian musician who lived in the flat below theirs, was the subject of a second portrait that Gus had submitted to the NEAC along with *Merikli*. In contrast to the elemental physicality he'd captured in Ida, Estella looked like a woman of the boudoir, her body both voluptuous and tightly corseted, her cheeks flushed with rouge, her hair intricately curled. To Gus, and to Ida, she was an embodiment of European worldliness: she played the piano, she had a wardrobe of dizzyingly elaborate outfits and she suffered from an interestingly fragile condition that demanded a regular supply of Turkish cigarettes. And, if Ida minded how frequently Gus continued to draw Estella, she felt unable to criticize because, by mid-autumn, she'd realized she was pregnant again, and, with her body thickening and little David still so demanding, she understood Gus's need for an alternative muse.

Marriage, she admitted to her friend Mary Dowdall, was starting to feel like a constant act of compromise, 'eternally fitting a square peg into a round hole and squeezing up one's eyes to make it look and feel a better fit.'[3] She and Gus had been arguing: the onset of winter, the short chilly days had made him irritable, and so too had the fact that Ida's mother was continually calling round, and continually questioning why they hadn't yet found better lodgings. Ida tried to appease everyone, yet sometimes she dared to imagine what it would have been like if she'd never got married – 'to live with a girlfriend & have lovers would be almost perfect', she confided to Mary.[4] Yet the new baby was due in March and, although he turned out to be another 'roaring boy', with the 'face of a Chinese pig', Ida felt her dreariness lift with the birth.[5] They named the baby Caspar (sometimes 'Capper') and he turned out to be much easier than David: he fed well, grew plump and, with the help of a temporary night nurse, he allowed Ida and Gus some unbroken sleep. For a few weeks, Ida could almost feel excited about her future – the weather was 'glorious', she was being visited by her family, by Gwen, and Gus, who turned out to love all new-born babies, was making special efforts to be attentive.

But then she discovered that, for months, the coquettish Estella, with her perfumed dresses and curves, had been more to Gus than a muse. It was possibly his first serious infidelity and neither of them knew what to do with it. Gus, once he'd been found out, was overwhelmed by guilt and indecision. He didn't want to hurt Ida, but he didn't want to be deprived of Estella. 'For days I have been inert and dejected', he wrote to Mary, admitting that he too had never realized how difficult marriage would be. 'I begin now and then to suspect its weakening – or perhaps it is that I am a weak member . . .'[6] Ida herself was too proud to beg; Gus had never pretended, she later wrote, to be anything but a man 'driven by his impulses', and she may well have hoped that Estella was simply too frivolous to satisfy him for long. All she could do, while she awaited some resolution, was hang on to her own dignity, for Ida despised jealousy, thought it the meanest, most belittling of weaknesses. She also knew full well that, if she gave in to it, and fought openly with Gus, she would humiliate herself. Several months later, after a particularly ugly row, she would confess to Mary, 'I made an ass of myself and Gussie is unmerciful to asses.'[7]

But the pressure of their unresolved situation wore away at Ida and, in June, she took the babies to see Winnie in Tenby. She loved her sister-in-law and she was particularly eager to see her now because, having failed to make progress with her music career in England, Winnie was about to join Thornton in Canada.* While they were together in Tenby, Winnie helped Ida to sew some new dresses, in which she would be able to compete with Estella's 'hundred lovely costumes' on her return. However, Ida had no idea that a far more significant challenge was awaiting her. Already Gus had begun his feverish drawing of Dorelia, and if he hadn't yet made love to her, he was dreaming of it, fantasizing about a secret wood where they could 'smoke and sleep and stop without being stared at'. So fast and powerfully did his feelings for Dorelia grow that, shortly after Ida's return, he was unable to hide them any longer. In a desperate gamble, he confessed everything to her, explaining how essential Dorelia had become to his happiness and his work, and asking if Ida, for all their sakes, would be able to accept Dorelia as a permanent part of their lives.

It was a brutal request, foisting on Ida the responsibility of whether they might all three coexist together, or be miserably apart. Yet, in truth, she had little choice but to tolerate this new affair. She could see that it was more than a passing infatuation – that, if Gus were pushed, he might even sacrifice her and the boys for its sake. Ida also wanted to believe that she herself could be strong enough, that her love for Gus and his art could be large enough, for her to accommodate another woman in their marriage.

There was no question, yet, of Dorelia sharing their home, only an acceptance of the frequency with which she would come to Gus's studio and with which he would visit her room. Ida willed herself to remain wise and tolerant, she even helped Gus shop for some accessories in

---

* Edwin may have tried to prevent Winnie from going by refusing to pay her fare, since Gwen had to lend Winnie some money for the voyage.

which he wanted to paint his new muse – white stockings and little black boots, and 'lots of silly things for her hair'. In a curious way, she was able to enjoy the novelty of Dorelia, who was so extraordinary to look at, so transparently devoid of artifice, so warm in her admiration of Ida herself and so obviously good for Gus.

But acceptance was still a bleak and lonely place. With Caspar barely three months old and David still clinging to her skirts, Ida felt like a shabby hausfrau, and she could do nothing about the jealousy that corroded her. To see the blaze of excitement with which Gus drew Dorelia, to discover that he was even teaching her to speak and write the Romani language, was horribly diminishing. Ida's humiliation was even more acute when she realized that she and Gus were now the subject of grim-faced discussion. 'I saw [Augustus] John last week,' Will told his brother Albert, 'and he doesn't seem to be pulling himself together as he should have done'.[9]

So ashamed was Ida of her ignoble misery that, for a while, she refused to speak of it. Gus, however, was conscious of his part in it and, torn between guilt and resentment, he began to feel treacherous longings for escape. It was a daily torment that Dorelia and her bed were only minutes away: 'I want to kiss you again all over your bare fiery body, when our faces touch my blood burns with a wild fire of love.' And sometimes, when the combined frustrations of Dorelia's proximity, Ida's unhappiness and the noise of the children all bore down on him, he simply had to get away. He went to Wales to see Sampson, to Liverpool to wave off Winnie when she sailed to Canada, and then to rural Berkshire to visit Ambrose McEvoy's brother Charles.

It was while Gus was striding through the countryside, relishing his release from the 'four mournful walls and . . . suffocating roof' of Fitzroy Street, that it suddenly occurred to him his problems might be solved by moving his family out of London.[10] He could imagine Ida at peace in a pretty rural cottage, reading and painting while the boys played outside; he could imagine himself spending half of his week in the city with Dorelia, then coming home to be a good husband and father. It was surely the cleanest way to manage their situation, and when he returned and proposed it to Ida, she had no real objection to make. Even though she liked London and most of her friends and family were there, the rooms in their flat were so cramped, the city was so dirty and so rife with gossip, that the idea of the countryside seemed almost idyllic.

She and Gus decided on Essex, which was only an hour and a half on the train from London, and now that the two of them were making plans together, they began to feel hopeful, energized. They also took it for granted that Dorelia would fall in with their arrangement. At the beginning of August, however, just as Ida was writing cheerfully to Michel about the progress of their 'house hunting', Dorelia announced she was making very different plans for herself. She told them, rather shockingly, that it no longer suited her to remain in Fitzroy Street as Gus's weekday mistress and muse; instead she wanted her own adventure and was going travelling with Gwen.

By this time Gwen, too, had been wanting to leave London. Even though she'd felt less isolated since meeting Dorelia, she'd become increasingly sure that the city wasn't good for her, or her work.

Back in March, Gus had persuaded her to show some paintings in an exhibition he'd been offered at the Carfax, but it was a decision she came to regret. Because she worked so slowly and doubtingly – was happy if she managed to paint just 'one beautiful square inch' in a day, Gwen had only two works she was ready to submit. When the exhibition opened, her own small pictures were, predictably, overshadowed by her brother's forty-five drawings, etchings and oils. Mortifyingly, her name was not even mentioned in the reviews.

Gus had been furious on her behalf, writing to Will that Gwen should have 'had the honours' and that the critics had been fools not to appreciate the beauty of her carefully achieved paintings. To him, they were 'rare blossoms from the most delicate trees' and he claimed they made him almost ashamed of his own 'professional industry'.[11] Yet, while his intervention was lovingly meant, it was difficult for Gwen to bear. She would never allow herself to be intimidated by her brother's success, nor think of herself as the inferior artist, but his eagerness to help, his actual power to help, was too reminiscent of his attempts to dominate her as a child.

Gwen was starting to believe that the rising clamour around Gus's career must always undermine her own unless she was able to put some distance between them. Her desire to leave London, though, was also driven by the consciousness that, while Gus had been packing his life with travel and people, her own had been stagnant for too long. She needed to do something large and decisive, and because she'd always wanted to see the art and the buildings of Rome, the idea came to her that she would go on a pilgrimage there, sailing to France and then travelling the rest of the way by foot. She would paint and draw, she would test herself on the open road. And, feeling that her own claim to Dorelia was still very strong, she suggested that the two of them might be pilgrims together.

'I have never seen [Gwen] so well or so gay,' reported Albert Rothenstein to Michel on 9 August, for Dorelia had agreed almost immediately to the idea. However deeply in thrall she was to Gus and his art, she was quite ready to take a break from the demands he made on her. If ever she missed one of their meetings or ignored one of his notes, Gus would exhaust her with a storm of reproach and she felt frankly uneasy about the new arrangement he'd proposed for her and Ida. She disliked being the cause of Ida's unhappiness and had little confidence that a move to Essex would make the situation more comfortable for any of them. To leave those complications behind, to go out on the road with Gwen was so much easier and more exciting. Dorelia had also long believed her life was determined by fate, and she reasoned, now, that if fate was offering her the opportunity of Rome, she would be wrong to resist. As for Gus, if their love for each other was equally pre-ordained, he would be waiting for her when she returned.

Gus, inevitably, saw things differently. He couldn't understand why Dorelia would inflict the pain of a prolonged separation on them both; he thought the whole idea of walking to Rome was 'cracked'. But now that Dorelia had made her decision, she and Gwen were as giddy as an eloping couple. In the middle of August, when they boarded the steamer for Bordeaux, carrying their clothes and their art equipment on their backs, all Gus could do was offer them a little extra cash for the journey, along with a pistol for their protection (which they refused).

Back in Fitzroy Street, Dorelia's absence pervaded everything. Gus missed her in his bed and no less sharply in his studio, where her half-finished portrait was still propped on his easel. Ida was miserable too, because she would have given almost everything to have boarded that steamer herself, to have been sailing away to freedom. Locked as they were in their private, lonely heartache, they each had powerful reasons for finding the letters that came from Gwen (and less frequently from Dorelia) alternately tantalizing and painful to read.

Many of those letters were subsequently lost, but Gwen was also writing regularly to Ursula Tyrwhitt, and enough of her correspondence survived to leave a graphic account of their travels. Initially, the journey went excitingly to plan. Gwen and Dorelia were walking south-east from Bordeaux, following the curves of the river Garonne. They were covering several kilometres a day, occasionally hitching rides on a farmer's cart, and foraging what food they could find from orchards and vines. At night, they found shelter under haystacks or in barns, and Gwen described how they never tired of watching the slow, beautiful fading of the light from the trees and hills. The two of them were making a little money, too, venturing into friendly-looking cafes where they would draw portraits for two francs apiece, or, chancing their luck, would offer to sing in exchange for a meal. Gwen boasted that on one occasion she'd dashed off five portraits in a single hour. 'What facility you have acquired,' Ida replied. 'You will come home with bags of money & bank notes sewn about you'. She imagined, with some sneaking pleasure, that Dorelia was rather less competent: 'I suppose she does an eye in 2 hours like Gwen Salmond.'[12]

Ida did, however, begin to suspect that Gwen's reports were edited: 'It's all so golden I can't believe you tell me everything'. There was no mention of blisters, heat, fatigue, or the inconvenience of keeping themselves clean. Even though they had the river for bathing, and for rinsing out the strips of rag they used for their monthly periods, it would have been difficult to wash and dry their clothes. The only problem to which Gwen would admit was the aggressive attention they attracted. Two young British women travelling alone through rural France were very noticeable, and one night, when they'd slept by a haystack, their luggage stacked up around them, they'd woken to find themselves surrounded by farmers and policemen. Even though they escaped being attacked or robbed on the road, they were often made to feel vulnerable. Drunk men, stumbling out of bars, would follow them, catcalling for sex; an innkeeper refused to rent them a room one rainy night because he assumed they were prostitutes.

Dorelia remained stoic, but Gwen fell prey to irrational fears. When she was woken at night by a noisy farm machine, she was convinced there was something 'monstrous' moving among the vines. When she and Dorelia were waylaid by an elderly shepherd, she was sure from the vehemence of his gestures that he meant to do them harm – until she realized he was simply offering them shelter for the night. It was 'a rather horrid sensation', Gwen confessed, to realize the tricks her mind was playing, and by the time they reached the small town of La Réole, about seventy kilometres into their journey, she was glad to pause.[13] La Réole, with its hilltop setting and wide river views, had long been popular with artists, and the women were treated with respectful interest. They were offered a warm stable for the night, given gifts of food, drink, posies of flowers, and they were also introduced to a young painter who, like them, was travelling around France. He was friendly and ready with advice, suggesting that, when the weather turned cold, they might divert to Paris and earn money for their journey from modelling. Gwen wasn't interested – she wanted to keep pressing on for Rome – but Dorelia apparently took note of the address where the young man would be staying.

Gus, meanwhile, was already begging for her return. He sent regular appeals to his 'Kameli Dorel', his 'Divine Ardor', pathetically describing his lovelorn state. 'I am getting into a weedy condition, my hair uncombed, my nails unpared, my teeth uncleaned', he wrote, and he complained of the 'inward fluttering' he suffered after hearing that Dorelia, despite her 'diet of wine and onions and . . . a burden of ½ a hundredweight odd', had actually been gaining weight. 'Your fat entices me enormously, I long to inspect it,' he groaned extravagantly as he told her how impatient he was to have her in his studio again.[14]

He also put pressure on Gwen. Although he hoped she was painting a portrait of Dorelia as 'wild as your travels', he suggested there were good professional reasons for her to cut her journey short.[15] The NEAC deadline was approaching for autumn submissions, he warned, and he was also hoping to tempt her with news of the art school which he and Orpen were planning to open in Chelsea. It was to be a 'bold enterprise', he boasted, 'a very respectable undertaking by which we expect to replenish our coffers.' Two adjacent studios in Flood Street had been found and, while he and Orpen were to do most of the teaching, several of their friends would also be involved. Michel and Will had promised their services as guest lecturers; Gwen Salmond had been drafted in as superintendent to the women students;* Jack Knewstub, brother of Alice and the beautiful Grace (to whom Orpen was now married), was to be secretary; and Edna Clarke Hall had signed up for classes. Orpen, on hearing news of Edna's interest, had shouted to Gus, 'John, the great are following, we shall succeed.'[16]

Gus hinted to Gwen that there could be a role for her too, but her only concern was the progress of her journey. The nights were turning chilly – sometimes she and Dorelia had to take turns in lying on top of each other to keep warm – and she wanted to reach Toulouse by the end of October. At that point, she thought it would be best to pause for the winter, and to allow themselves what she loftily called 'the bourgeois life of rooms.'[17]

Only Gwen could have described the one bare space that she and Dorelia rented in Toulouse as bourgeois; it contained little more than a bed, a table and two chairs. But it was large enough for her to unpack her easel, her canvases and tubes of colour, and to begin work on something more challenging than the chalk and charcoal sketches she'd been drawing of Dorelia on the road.

It was the room itself, and its lack of natural light, which also influenced the three oils Gwen painted over the winter. In *Dorelia by Lamplight at Toulouse*, Dorelia was reading at their table, and the golden lamplight which fell across her face, the dark shadows thrown up on the walls behind, gave the room an atmosphere of compelling intimacy. In Gwen's second painting, *The Student*, she revisited that theme, only this time a little more theatrically, with Dorelia standing rather seated, so that the lamp threw her features into more dramatic relief.

Dressed in a grey checked frock, her expression girlishly grave, Dorelia looked very different from the mercurial temptress of Gus's

---

* For the sake of respectability, Gus and Orpen had decided on separate classes for men and women, except for Saturdays, when 'a spirit of frivolity' would be allowed.

imagination. Only in the third of the Toulouse series, *Dorelia in a Black Dress*, did Gwen hint at her friend's seductiveness, making her gaze more mysteriously opaque and darkening the flush of her cheeks to echo the extravagantly pink bow attached to her dress.

Gwen was still under the spell of Dorelia's beauty, all three pictures were visual love letters of sorts, yet she made no attempt to disturb the even temper of their lives together. They drew during the day, in the evenings they read, and they were also devoting time and attention to their travelling wardrobes, washing, mending and adding what few frivolous trimmings they could afford. Dorelia's pink bow might well have been one of them, although she would recall, years later, that Gwen had always cared far more than she did about clothes – 'she always managed to look elegant, wasn't at all careless of her appearance, [and was] in fact rather vain.'[18]

Now that they had a settled address, letters from Gus and Ida were arriving more promptly and, with them, news of the move to Essex. Even without Dorelia, they had stuck to the plan, and in November had found a small, two-storey house for rent in the Essex village of Matching Green. It was not as pretty as Gus had hoped, its rooms were meanly proportioned, but it came with stables, an orchard, a garden, and it opened out onto the huge open space of the village green. Even with the hiring of a new live-in help called Maggie, Elm House felt infinitely more accommodating than anything they could afford in London.

For Gus, the clinching joy had been the gypsies who occasionally camped on the green, but, as he wrote to Gwen and Dorelia, the whole situation was pleasing to him. 'This village seems to be curiously beautiful . . . even in the wet of December when the green is flooded . . . at night the little lighted tenements are reflected in the water in a very grave and secret way.'[19] Ida, too, was moved by the tranquillity of their new home: 'It is lovely here, to go out into the quiet evening and see the moon floating above,' she wrote, and she enjoyed watching Gus as he made the best of their 'bald little house', hanging up their pictures and their canary cages, arranging the most comfortable of their chairs around the fire.

Yet the nerve endings of their marriage were still exposed, and both of them were impatient for the travellers' return. They made individually shameless appeals to Gwen's conscience – Ida reporting that little David was missing her, that he repeated her name – '*Gen*' – 'a great many times', and Gus begging her to send Dorelia home because he badly needed to finish her portrait.[20] To Dorelia herself, Gus reiterated his complaint that she was killing him, yet all their entreaties fell on stony ears. Gwen simply parcelled up some Christmas presents for Ida to distribute around the family, while Dorelia told Gus that, if he was really so desperate to see her, he could always come out to France. The simplicity of her logic floored him: did she want him just for a visit or did she expect him to stay? Both were impossible, and Gus, knowing he was cornered, replied with a provocatively erotic sketch of Dorelia, which he contrasted with a tender image of David. 'It's all very well talking about Toulouse,' he rebuked her, 'But there's the question d'enfants.'

Nor was it just the *enfants*, for, however genuinely Gus ached for Dorelia, he was engrossed in his new commuting life. He and Orpen had now opened their school and he was teaching there several days a week; he'd found a new studio, where he was working hard, and he was busy with Will and his friends. By the time he took the train back to Essex, Gus was overstimulated and tired. He was more than happy to lose himself in the peace of Essex and ready to enjoy his family. Even though the children could be exasperating, they were amusing too – David begging for pictures of the hyenas, cows and 'taegers' with which he was currently obsessed, and Caspar showing a formidable determination to start toddling, hauling himself around the furniture, making 'dents' in his forehead when he tumbled to the floor, and 'exclaiming "Mama" as if it were a kind of joke'.[21]

Travelling between two worlds, Gus kept his boredom at bay, and when Mary Dowdall came to visit the following March, she told her husband that Gus was being 'as good as gold'. He was in bed, nursing a mild head cold, playing tunes on his new melodium (a miniature accordion) and reading French novels. Then, when he came downstairs, he made Mary sit for him, drawing sketch after sketch with a 'tension and rapidity' that amazed her. 'He scraped and tore away . . . in the most marvellous way. I only saw one – too squirrelly and funny for description but beautiful.' By the time she left, Mary was convinced that the Johns' marriage was solid and that Gus himself 'was the sweetest natured person in the world.'[22]

Ida herself had been working hard to spread that perception. When Alice Rothenstein had berated her folly in allowing Gus his weeks of freedom in London, she'd sent back a dignified retort: 'In the first place I prefer being here. And Gus . . . enjoys being in London alone.'[23] But still there was much Ida could not admit to Alice. Daily life was hard in Elm House: oil lamps had to be trimmed and cleaned, fires laid, water boiled, children and pets all looked after. Even with Maggie's help, Ida had little time for reading and none at all for her art. 'If I do get half an hour I am certain to tear my dress and have to mend it or spill a box of pins or somethings.'[24] She was stuck in what she called the 'life of the lady slavey' and, by her calculation, if she were ever to paint seriously again, she would require the assistance of a cook, a cleaner, a maid and a nurse.[25]

Gus, as undomesticated as most of his peers, had little notion of what it took to run a house and even less desire to be told. Discussions about bills and repairs, problems with Maggie or the children, made him irritable – they represented all that was banal about 'moral living', and if Ida was ever tempted to explain that she too resented that banality, she also knew it would make him feel guilty, and there would be another row.

She was not yet thirty and it was sometimes inexplicable to her how quickly she'd gone from the brave ardent girl who'd believed she could claim 'everything', to the tired mother and housewife who was crushed by routine. At those moments, she was frightened of the power she'd ceded to Gus, 'c'est un homme pour qui mourir and literally I am sometimes inclined to kill myself,' she admitted to Mary, early in 1904.[26] Yet, without Gus, she was often lonely. Visitors from London were rare and, as the months passed, Ida retreated more and more into her own imagination. She invented a whimsical spirit companion called Friuncelli, and she fantasized alternative versions of herself, versions she called Anna, Ann, Susannah or Susan, to whom she gave bolder, freer lives than her own. Whenever she thought about Gwen and Dorelia and their adventures in France, Ida felt that depression was coming dangerously near.

*

But, out in Toulouse, those adventures were starting to pall. Gwen admitted to Ursula Tyrwhitt that Rome now seemed 'further away than ever' and that life was 'rather hard'.[27] She and Dorelia were running short of funds: they could no longer afford their Sunday visit to the public baths and had to wash their clothes in the now-freezing water of the Garonne; their restaurant meals had become rationed to one or two per week and most days they lived on little but bread, cheese and figs. 'I do nothing but paint,' Gwen sighed to Ursula, and, forgetting how disillusioned she'd become with London, she admitted how much she missed its galleries, its theatres, its crowds.

Perhaps it was the tedium and hardship of their days which also drove Gwen into the arms of a young, married, Frenchwoman whom she met in Toulouse. The relationship was briefly passionate and beautifully absorbing for Gwen, a reprieve from austerity. To Dorelia, though, it seemed badly misjudged. She thought Gwen had a dangerous tendency to be 'always attracted to the wrong people for their beauty alone' – and this Frenchwoman, although lovely to look at, was clingy and demanding.[28] She was even talking of leaving her husband for Gwen, and Dorelia, who found the woman's presence a grating intrusion, felt her own intimacy with Gwen under threat.

But that long winter in Toulouse had already made Dorelia question Gwen in other ways. At the start of their journey, she'd been willing to follow Gwen's lead in everything, accepting her decisions about how they would spend their money, how far they would walk each day. She had willingly shouldered the heaviest bags so that Gwen could save her energy for work. On their arrival at Toulouse, however, Dorelia began to wonder if there was not something 'hard and queer' in Gwen's character, an implacable core of selfishness. Gwen had promised they would take equal turns in modelling for each other, yet, so far, it had been Dorelia who'd done all the sitting. Even after she'd persuaded Gwen to hire a professional model to pose for them both, that arrangement had foundered when Gwen took an unreasonable dislike to the woman's 'vulgar red lips' and sent her away.[29]

Of course, Gwen was trying to save money, hoarding every centime for the resumption of their journey to Rome. Yet her parsimony grated on Dorelia, who longed for a night at the theatre, a decent restaurant meal, and, as time began to drag for her in Toulouse, as she chafed over Gwen's unsuitable affair, she began to wonder if she should abandon Gwen and make her own separate way to Paris, as the painter from La Réole had suggested.

But, sometime towards the end of February, Gwen acknowledged that she, too, had had enough of Toulouse and was ready to make a change. Even though she was still fully committed to the idea of Rome she could see that, if she and Dorelia diverted to Paris and replenished their funds with some modelling work, it could ultimately make their journey easier and faster.

When the two women eventually reached Paris it was early to mid-March, and they must have hitched several lifts on the way or risked precious francs on a train. On Gwen's suggestion, they went to Montparnasse, where they took rooms in Hotel Mont Blanc, a cheap lodging house on boulevard Edgar Quinet. It was close to the railway station and in a much rougher neighbourhood than rue Froidevaux: strays from the local dosshouse hung around doorways; the cafes smelt of cheap cooking oil and the streets stank of horse shit and drains. But still it had some of the magic Gwen remembered from her previous stay in the city; there was an excellent market at one end of the boulevard, the trees were already coming into bud, and the galleries and museums of Paris were waiting.

Montparnasse itself had become even more of an artists' *quartier*. Young men and women were arriving from all parts of France, Europe, even America, to profit from its cheap cafes and studios; there were now so many painters and sculptors in the area, in fact, that an informal *marché des modèles* was held on the boulevard Montparnasse to service their needs. Commercially, the arrangement made practical sense. However, for the models themselves, as they lined up on the pavements and waited to be hired, it had all the indignity of a cattle market, with the most beautiful and experienced allowed to charge three francs an hour, while those less desirable could ask only a third of the price. Dorelia and Gwen were, naturally, reluctant to expose themselves to such humiliation, and while Dorelia sought out their painter friend from La Réole to ask for assistance, Gwen chose to make a systematic tour of their neighbourhood, knocking on the doors of rooms she'd been told were artists' studios.

She'd assumed that her experience, both as a model and painter, would merit some respect, but her first round of enquiries brought only rejection and abuse. Doors were banged in her face, and out of the few men who expressed any interest, one tried to fondle her breasts – to check she was sufficiently 'developpée' [sic] – while another offensively badgered her to move in with him. Paris suddenly began to feel harsh to Gwen. However, just as she was close to giving up, she met with one of her old Slade friends, Constance Lloyd, and, through Constance, learned of a small network of female artists, kindred spirits who were able to offer modest fees for reliable models.

Once Gwen and Dorelia were both in work and starting to earn, their life in Paris took pleasurable shape. They went to the Louvre, the Jardin de Luxembourg, and lingered over the bookstalls along the banks of the Seine. They acquired a cat, a feral tortoiseshell which, despite being female, they christened Edgar Quinet, and eventually nicknamed Tiger. Although one of the other lodgers in their hotel, an English painter called Miss Hart, developed an intrusive crush on Gwen, she proved a useful source of professional contacts and soon the two women had amassed enough money for luxuries like the planning of their summer wardrobes. 'The room is full of pieces of dresses we are making', Gwen wrote to Alice Rothenstein. 'Dorelia's is pink with a skirt of new flounces. She will look lovely in it.'[30]

Gus, when he heard reports of their life, was confounded. 'What a surprise to hear from you in Paris', he wrote crossly to Gwen. 'I suppose you have willed yourself there.' He was gracious enough to send a list of people who might be useful to her, to ask what paintings she was seeing, but to Dorelia he wrote more importunately, telling her of the 'mighty canvas' he'd ordered in readiness for her return and describing the portrait he was planning to paint. Still there was no move from her, though, and when she wrote to Gus about her modelling work, and let slip that she'd been posing nude, he felt he would go mad with jealousy. 'You wicked little bloody harlot,' he wrote. 'You exhibit your naked fat body for money not for love. How much do you show them for a franc . . .? I am sorry that I never offered to give you a shilling or two for a look at your minj. That was all you were waiting for. I am sorry that I was so foolish to love you. Well if you are not a whore, truly tell me why not. Gustavus.'[31]

The minute he'd posted the letter, Gus was appalled. He prowled around Elm House, hating his own viciousness and convincing himself that Dorelia would never forgive it. He waited in vain for a response from his 'beloved Ardor', and, floundering in the depths of his terror and shame, he made himself intolerable to Ida. She, having spent the last few months at war with her own despair, could hardly bear to deal with Gus's; she could feel no pity for him, too, because, by a cruel stroke of timing, she had just discovered she was pregnant again. Another baby meant another manacle that chained her to the 'life of the lady slavey', and to Mary she agonized that the prospect made her feel, 'bored to extinction almost. Depression, it sits on my brow like lead.' Ida couldn't believe the 'pig-stye' her life had become and she fantasized to Mary that the two of them might go out to Paris themselves.[32] She pictured the room they could rent – above a restaurant and close to the Louvre – and she urged Mary to imagine all the deliciousness that awaited them: 'Think of the salads & the sun & blue dresses & waiters. And the smell of butter and cheese in the small streets.'[33]

All these pleasures spelled freedom for Ida, and the knowledge that, for her, at least, they were still out of reach, made her doubly impatient with Gus. Why, she demanded, did he not simply go out to Paris and confront Dorelia? If he needed to furnish himself with a more dignified reason for his trip, Gwen had just written about a 'magnificent' exhibition of medieval and early Renaissance French art at the Louvre, which she'd much recommended Gus should see.

For Gus, it was as though Ida had given him permission to act, and in mid-May he was writing breezily to Gwen of his intention to visit: 'I want to see you and the Primitiffs and that pretty slut Dorelia, she who is too lazy to answer my frequent and affectionate letters'.[34]

His tone was studiedly casual. But while Gus was already anticipating the joy of having Dorelia in his arms again and of soliciting her forgiveness, Dorelia herself was dreading his arrival. She'd been frightened by the violence of his reaction to her admission that she was modelling nude, and she barely dared contemplate what he might do or say when he discovered that the painter for whom she was posing (almost certainly the young man from La Réole) was also now her lover. His name was Leonard Brouke, he came from a small village near Bruges and, while Dorelia could see that his talent and personality burned far less brightly than Gus's, he appealed to her in other ways. He was single, he was comfortably supported by the income from his family's farm, and, above all he unequivocally adored her. Already he'd asked if she might go back with him to Belgium, and already she'd agreed.

Dorelia had not yet confessed anything of this to Gwen, not even her attachment to Leonard, and when Gus arrived in Paris her courage failed her entirely. Taking very little luggage with her, she slipped away from the Hotel Mont Blanc, leaving behind a note in which she claimed to have been called home urgently by her parents. So little reason was there to question her lie that Gus took the next convenient boat train back to London in order to meet Dorelia there; and when word then came that she was actually in Belgium, and with Leonard, the news was almost too shocking for either him or Gwen to believe.

Gus remained miserably in England, sending out reams of reproachful love poetry to Dorelia. These poems were all he could focus on, and he became so obsessed with perfecting them he started to bombard Dorelia with lists of pedantic corrections – 'the word ardent in the first sonnet I sent you should be changed to "nodding". Kindly make that correction.' Gwen, in Paris, was no less stricken by Dorelia's flight. For the last nine months, the two of them had shared everything, and it seemed incomprehensible that Dorelia could have kept so huge and treacherous a secret. Even Gus, in the depths of his own misery, was worried about Gwen and, knowing how she'd pined after losing Ambrose, he begged her to take care that she was eating properly and getting enough sleep.

Ida was equally concerned: 'Poor little thing,' she sympathized to Gwen. 'It is really hardest on you that she went. It was a *shame*. Did you overdrive her? I know you are a beauty once you start. But you are worth devoting yourself to, & she should not have given up.'[35] But, even as Ida criticized Dorelia's defection, she could sympathize with it too. She knew from her own experience how self-absorbed the two Johns could be, how much they demanded from those they loved, and she could understand how Dorelia might be drawn to a simpler soul like Leonard. She may also have been hoping, a little bit, that Dorelia would stay with Leonard and that she, Ida, would recover her place at the centre of Gus's life and work.

Hard experience, however, had taught Ida that her marriage could not magically be mended, that her 'child genius' of a husband would always need some other mistress, some other muse. It wasn't just the novelty of a different face or body he craved, rather the dazzle and dread of being in love with a woman whose beauty could transport him beyond the limitations of his own daily self. Dorelia, at least, had never been manipulative as a mistress, she'd never tried to steal Gus for herself, and the more clearly Ida was able to think about her own situation, the more evident it became her best chance of retaining some control was by ensuring that Dorelia came back to Gus. Between them, they might surely find a new arrangement, a new three-way marriage that would bind their lives permanently together.

As the plan burnished in Ida's imagination, she urged Gus to return immediately to Paris and begin the hunt for Dorelia. 'Mrs Dorel Harem must be with you,' she insisted.[36] She believed that her plan was not only rational, but noble and romantic: 'Dorelia is ours and she knows it. By god I will haunt her till she comes back.' And, as Ida urged Gus into action, she also experienced a sudden exalted renewal of feeling for him: 'I have discovered I love you', she wrote from Essex, 'and what you want I want passionately'.

Gus was moved by Ida's resolve and by her continuing power to surprise him, yet his own self-confidence had been shaken – so much so that he even asked Gwen whether, for the sake of Dorelia's 'worldly welfare', he ought to let her remain with Leonard. Gwen, however, was now as ardent as Ida in her desire to see the plan through, and wrote immediately to Dorelia, urging her to see the wonder of it all.

'Something has happened which takes my breath away, so beautiful it is. Ida wants you to go to Gussy, not only wants but desires it passionately . . . you are necessary to his development and to Ida's and he is necessary to yours.' As Gwen underlined the courage of what Ida had proposed, she urged Dorelia to be equally brave: 'These instincts are inspired by what is divine in us.' More callously, she suggested that Leonard, a mediocre painter with all the limitations of his bourgeois upbringing, could hardly be described as divine. 'I feel sorry for [him] but he has had his happiness for a time, what more can he expect?'[37]

'You know I love you,' Gwen added, 'you don't know how much'. But, although she advised Dorelia to take the first train to Paris and avoid any troublesome farewells with Leonard, Dorelia didn't come. Instead, she sent a letter in which she pleaded for Gwen's understanding, begging to be left alone to think and act for herself.

> You must know I love you all – I cannot say how much. You say I must be unselfish and brave. I must but not in the way you mean . . . Whatever I do there must be something false, let me choose the least false, the most natural. If I loved Gussie and you twenty times more – though I cannot love you more than I do, I would not come back . . . If I did what you wanted I think it would be the weakest thing I have ever done or could do. God, I'm tired of being weak, of depending on people, of being dragged this way & that by my feelings, of listening to everyone but myself. I must be free – I will be.[38]

To Gwen, who'd become so used to Dorelia's compliancy, this show of resistance was startling, and she was equally taken aback by the dignified letter that came from Leonard. He'd evidently read what she'd written to Dorelia, and scornfully demanded to know what she meant by suggesting he had already had his allotted share of 'Dor's' love. 'Do you think happiness is a thing that you take like a café after dinner, a thing that you enjoy a few times and something you can get sick of? . . . I am not some ordinary man who loves a girl because she is beautiful or whatever. I am an artist and I cannot live without her – I think that is clear.'[39]

But, if Gwen was reluctantly impressed by Leonard's letter, she wouldn't be budged by it. 'I know that Gussie and Ida are more parts of you than Leonard is for ever', she urged Dorelia, and Ida, writing from Essex, was adding her own extravagant pressure: 'Oh my honey let me say I crave for you to come here. I now feel incomplete and thirsty without you.' With a fantastical twist of irony, she promised Dorelia that the two of them would unite together in a state of 'wonderful concubinage'.[40] For poor Dorelia, morally harassed by Gwen, flustered by Gus's poetry and confused by Ida's flattery, this campaign was too much. Even though she wrote to Gwen to demand more time, she conceded she would probably end up 'giving in'.

To Gus, Dorelia's cautious offering spelled hope, and he set off for Belgium to track her down. She was still nervous, leaving an enigmatic trail of notes that took him from Antwerp to Brussels to Ghent; and at each city, each poste restante, Gus left his own messages for Dorelia, his excitement mounting, his emotions inflamed by the hunt. 'If I don't hear from you I will come to find you again . . . I will have you for myself . . . I have tears of love for you and yet I am not drunk . . . Sometimes I talk to you while walking along. All night I have strange dreams . . . I think of the portrait I shall paint of you. If anyone can understand you I can. Love, I know you – Know me. Know me.'[41]

Gus was in Ghent when word came from Dorelia that she would give one more week to Leonard and then come to him. He sent her an ecstatic sketch of himself racing towards her, his hat in his hand. On 1 August, he found her among the crowds at Bruges station, ready to be taken home.

From the evidence of their surviving letters, the final act to this drama was oddly subdued. Perhaps they were all exhausted. When Gus asked Gwen, in Paris, to forward the rest of Dorelia's things, there was only a modest register of triumph in his note. From Dorelia, Gwen received only the briefest of postcards enquiring, 'How is the cat?'; and out of the four of them, it was Leonard who showed the most emotion. Apparently, Dorelia had lacked the courage to explain that she was leaving him for good, and, in the middle of August, he suddenly appeared at Gwen's room, begging for news of his 'Dor' and vowing he could 'not live without her'.

Gwen was touched by Leonard's distress and finally ready to acknowledge how badly he'd been treated. 'I should write him a nice letter if I were you,' she urged Dorelia. 'He will get very ill otherwise I think.'[42] But she was already moving on from the whole affair and, as passionately as she'd campaigned to reunite Dorelia with Ida and Gus, she had no intention of rejoining them back in England. 'What is London like after France and how do you like being in the bosom of your family?' she wrote. Almost, there was a note of pity in her question.[43]

While Dorelia's life had been settled for her, Gwen's own future was still unfolding, and she couldn't really visualize it anywhere but Paris. The galleries, the streets, the cafes and the people all held her now, but even more decisive for Gwen was the new modelling work she'd found in the studio of Auguste Rodin. To be posing for one of the world's most celebrated sculptors was of course a momentous experience for her, infinitely richer and more creative than anything her lady artists could offer. Yet she was still more compelled by the relationship she was forming with Rodin himself. Even though he was thirty-six years her senior, an artist far beyond her in reputation and genius, he was starting to treat her with a flattering regard. And over the course of the summer, as Gwen basked in the warmth of his attention, in the joy of being singled out from the rest of his models, there were times when she felt that serving Rodin brought her far simpler rewards than struggling with her own art. There were even times when she dared to wonder if the kindness Rodin was showing her, if the awe and gratitude she felt in response, might also become a prelude to love.

Chapter Six

RODIN

'I was born to love'
GWEN JOHN[1]

It was Gus who'd first suggested that Gwen 'call' on Rodin. As teenagers in Tenby, the two of them had studied pictures of Rodin's work in magazines, had sensed there was something extraordinary in its weight and humanity. Gwen had also been struck by photographs of the man himself – his granite slope of a forehead, his Old Testament beard – and she had even woven imaginary meetings with him into the fantasies she'd spun of her future. Now, in Paris, she had her opportunity. Yet, while Gus had assured Gwen that Rodin would welcome her request to join his team of models – 'he loves English young ladies'[2], he wrote to her in March – the thought of turning up at his studio unannounced, of braving the great man's fame, was all too daunting for her.*

It may have been one of the women artists for whom Gwen sat who gave her the courage. Hilda Flodin, a Finnish sculptor and painter, knew Rodin well – she had occasionally worked with his team of studio assistants and had also been his occasional mistress. Miss Flodin (it would be a while before she became Hilda to Gwen) confirmed Gus's airy conviction that Rodin was always looking for new models, and, sometime in late April or early May, Gwen made her way to rue de l'Université, to the government-run marble depot where Rodin did much of his work.

Hidden from the road by two huge wooden gates, the Depot was like

---

* At the Paris Universal Exhibition in 1900, an entire pavilion was devoted to Rodin's art, 165 pieces, which amounted to the largest single showing of his works.

no other place in Paris – a vast cobbled courtyard, overgrown with moss and weeds, in which blocks of marble were roughly stacked. Along one side of the yard was a row of artists' studios, two of which were Rodin's, and when Gwen nerved herself to knock at one of them, she was ushered into a world of intimidating activity. Rodin was almost always surrounded by people as he worked – his team of assistants, perched on scaffolding or crouched over tables as they chiselled at works-in-progress, his secretary, with a clutch of papers, consulting over letters and dates, and often a group of half-naked women, ready to pose when required.

If Gwen froze for a moment, unable to make sense of this scene, Rodin had long experience with apprehensive new models. Very genial in his clay-spattered smock, he would always offer them a screen behind which to remove their clothes, and would always be tactfully professional when requesting them to demonstrate some poses. As a rule, Rodin preferred his women to be solidly built, their flesh the physical equal of marble and clay. But photographs taken of Gwen several years later show that her own body, though small, was flexible and strong. She was elegantly proportioned, with small high breasts, narrow hips, long muscled legs and a graceful neck – a woman who looked powerful in her nakedness.

Rodin liked to think of himself as a connoisseur of the female form. 'The whole of nature resides in the body of every model [for] those who are capable of seeing,' he wrote later, and what he saw in Gwen was evidently pleasing.[3] At the end of her short interview, he told her she had 'un corps admirable' and asked her to come back soon. There was no suggestion, yet, of her posing for a specific work, but Rodin liked to have a roster of women available to him, moving around his studio while he worked. He could devote an afternoon to making rapid drawings, or little clay maquettes – exercises in which he captured the particular twist, heft or flexion of the women's bodies. Sometimes, he used them only as a point of reference while working on larger pieces, observing how the light fell on their flesh, how their muscles bunched or the tendons stretched.

Gwen had been shocked at first by the sexual frankness with which some of the models displayed themselves, admitting she was 'too shy' to imitate their 'extraordinary poses'.[4] Yet she interested Rodin and, when he began to summon her more regularly to his studio, he seemed to find her conversation as admirable as her body. He liked to talk as he worked, reflecting on the books he was reading, the people he met, expanding his theories on nature, art, religion and the magnificence of the ancient Greeks. Gwen would have been thrilled simply to listen, but Rodin was curious about her life, wanting to know how she had come to Paris and what kind of artist she was. Even though Gwen winced at the clumsiness of her schoolgirl French, Rodin's manner was so easy and direct that her shyness eased. She asked if there were any documents in English she could translate for him; she learned passages from his favourite Greek plays, which she could recite as he worked. In August, when he asked to see some of her drawings and gave her one of his own in return, Gwen's joy was immense. Her disappointment was equally great when he summoned her to his studio one day and failed to appear: 'Cher monsieur, I don't know what to do this afternoon because you are not here. I want to come here at least one day a week for ever, just as you said, until I'm an old lady, by which time I'll be an artist, but if you told me you didn't need me any more I couldn't bear it. I'm worried about annoying you when you see me on Saturday because I'm not particularly amusing.'[5]

Saturdays were open days at the studio, and, even though there was no work for Gwen then, she often joined the crowd of journalists, art students and buyers over whom Rodin held court, so that she might see more of him. He was becoming the point around which she organized her life, although she was still very far from being obsessed by him. As she reported back to Dorelia, she believed she was painting 'better than ever', and Paris still felt full of interest and discovery. Every day, there were colours, textures, shapes that snagged her eye: faces glimpsed from a carriage, beggars, street vendors, girls in cheap finery, huge cart horses steaming from the weight of their burdens. And, despite the 'mauvaises types' who sometimes bothered her, who tried to comment on her drawings or buy her drinks, Gwen cherished being in Paris by herself. In the evenings, she liked to sit in the Jardin de Luxembourg: 'the sky is deep blue with some grey clouds,' she told Ursula Tyrwhitt, 'so beautiful with no soul there'. Alternatively, she walked by the Seine, where, in the deepening dusk, the lights of the passing riverboats reminded her of Japanese paintings. When other people stared at her, she imagined them pitying her for being 'all alone', wondering, 'What's she looking at, why is she there?' and these thoughts made her feel like the heroine of her own Parisian novel.[6]

According to Gus, their father, Edwin, evidently had some other, more melodramatic novel in mind when he learned that Gwen hadn't gone home with her brother, and he convinced himself that 'some dark plot' was detaining her in Paris. In his anxiety, he travelled over to find her, not knowing that Gwen had borrowed Constance Lloyd's flat for the summer and was no longer in her room at the Hotel Mont Blanc. 'He is a strange unique little man, all silver pink & black,' Gus wrote, when he reported how their father had asked a 'garçon' at the hotel to assist him in his search and had then invited the boy out to dinner.[7]

Now that he was sufficiently far away from Tenby, Gus could be rather charmed by Edwin's eccentricities. Gwen, however, felt only an automatic flare of irritation. She'd hoped never to be bothered by her father again, never to feel diminished by his fussy banalities. The life she was creating in Paris was meant to free her, definitively, from the past, and, much as she loved Gus, Ida and Dorelia, it was also meant to free her from them. They, too, carried the complications of family. And at the end of August, when Gwen got word that their lives were in trouble, her instinct was not to get involved.

It was Ida who'd buckled first from the strain of the new ménage. When Gus had brought Dorelia back from Belgium, she'd been determined to make it all work. 'We are not a *conventional* family,' she would insist to a beady-eyed Alice Rothenstein, who was eager to know exactly where everyone slept. Even though Ida was prepared to admit that their three-way marriage had cost the 'occasional heartache', she still believed it was both 'beautiful and possible' and she hoped that Will and Alice could be sufficiently 'large minded' to agree.[8]

Yet, the excitement, the secret satisfaction of her own nobility were hard for Ida to sustain, and within weeks the depression that had been shadowing her returned. She was heavily pregnant now and easily tired; her two little boys were getting on her nerves and, when Maggie took them to visit Edwin in Tenby, she realized, to her horror, that she was dreading their return. Marriage, motherhood, friendship, art had failed her. Or rather, Ida believed, she had failed them. By late summer, she was feeling so lost to herself that she told Gus they must work out a different arrangement. For her part, she'd decided it would be best for them all if Gus and Dorelia remained together, while she took the children out to Paris and found a flat close to Gwen in Montparnasse.

Gus was dismayed. He'd been so absorbed in the joy of having Dorelia back in his studio and his bed that he'd failed to notice the cracks in Ida's saintly facade. Now, when she confronted him, determined and pale, he could only panic. He swore blindly that of course he still loved her, that he still wanted her in every part of his life. However, when he wrote to Gwen with news of the crisis, his sympathy for Ida's 'moments of défaillances' – which he ascribed to her pregnancy – was undercut by the anger he felt. If Ida were to walk out now, he claimed, it would expose their whole ménage to scandal, it would 'belittle and vulgarise the affair'.[9] And evidently Gus assumed Gwen would agree, for his letter to her was clearly a prompt for her to add her persuasions to his.

In the end, Ida stayed. Gus promised that, once she'd had the baby, he would arrange for her to go on a long holiday to Paris, he would paint a new portrait of her, he would become more attentive. However, the letter Ida wrote to Gwen was grim: 'I regret not coming, but it is the only thing I could do – I asked [Gus] which he would truly prefer, and he said stay, so I could not come could I? I suppose I shall manage if I always remember he *does* want me here – it is only when I think he doesn't it becomes unbearable. I hope for a different life later on – I think it can only be postponed . . . Matching Green seems a grave now, but I live in hopes of a resurrection.'[10]

When Ida added that she hoped Gwen would not be too disappointed by the delay in her visit to Paris – 'You have Rodin and work and streets and museums' – she had no idea of how little Gwen wanted her to come, how reluctant she was to share her new life with Ida and expose her secret new feelings for Rodin. Yet she could not ignore the unhappiness in Ida's letter. For several weeks already, Ida had been begging her to visit, had sent extravagant reminders of their friendship – 'Little darling I am yours . . . for ever world without end' – and, sometime around late September, Gwen felt duty-bound to offer her support in person.[11]

Once she was in Essex, though, there wasn't much she could do, or say.

However passionately she'd first advocated for the 'divinity' of the ménage, she had no advice on how to make it work. The crush of family life in Elm House, the tensions between Gus and Ida were also quite intolerable and, although there had been some suggestion that Gwen might stay for a week or two, she manged only three days before announcing that Rodin needed her back in his studio. When Gus wrote to her shortly afterwards, 'You are evidently becoming indispensable, it must be indeed a pleasure to be of service to such a man,' his comment may have come with an ironic subtext of irritation and disappointment.[12]

There was also, in that comment, an implied mischief, for Gus was well aware that the services Rodin obtained from his models were often sexual. In late middle age the sculptor had become notorious for the number and variety of his affairs. One scandalized acquaintance reported that 'the whole of Paris was talking about the not very savoury details of his erotic adventures', and, according to the Duchess of Marlborough, who'd suffered his advances, any attractive woman was prey – 'Hands all over you', she complained.[13] Even though Rodin still lived with his common-law wife, Rose Beuret, she'd become little more than his housekeeper and had left him free to pursue any woman who was willing to be seduced by his fame and his charm.

Gwen apparently knew little or nothing of Rodin's promiscuity; to Gus, she wrote only about his kindness, his greatness of character. But, over the autumn, their relationship was becoming subtly more intimate. Rodin had begun to call Gwen 'Marie' (using her middle name, Mary, which he found easier to pronounce); she, in return, felt emboldened to address him as 'dear maître'. In the studio, as her poses became less tentative, her conversation more direct, she felt his attention becoming more exclusively focused on her. And it was sometime towards the end of the year or the beginning of the next that she received most wonderful proof of his regard. 'I am now at Rodin's nearly every day,' she wrote to Ursula. 'He has begun a statue.'[14]

That new statue was a memorial to Whistler, who had died in July 1903. The International Society of Sculptors, Painters and Engravers, of which Whistler had been founding president in London, had approached Rodin about creating some kind of commemorative statue. And, even though the formal details of the commission would not be settled until the spring of 1905, Rodin had already begun thinking about his approach and had already decided that, in preference to a portrait of Whistler, he would sculpt a more symbolic figure – the painter's Muse.

Gwen had told Rodin of her connection to Whistler, but he chose her to model for this statue, too, because she was flexible and strong. The pose on which he'd decided – the Muse ascending 'the mountain of fame' – would be physically challenging, requiring Gwen to curve her body forward while lifting one leg, steeply, like a dancer. Even with a support for her elevated foot, the long sessions during which she would have to hold that pose as Rodin worked on his preliminary studies would cause her muscles to cramp and her tendons to burn.

For Gwen, however, the discomfort of her body was nothing compared to the glory of seeing herself reinvented through Rodin's hands and his eyes. His speed as he fashioned his maquettes was extraordinary, as was the decisiveness with which he checked the proportions of her body with a measuring compass, with which his thick blunt fingers gouged, smoothed and chafed the clay. Gwen, who worked so meticulously at her easel, was awed by the casual confidence with which Rodin could slice off an ear, a nose or a breast that was wrongly positioned, jamming it back in a better alignment, making a new thumbprint for an eye, slashing a differently angled line for the mouth.

Her pleasure was even more exquisite when Rodin rewarded her with a grateful kiss or caress. He tended to be affectionately tactile with all his models, yet Gwen couldn't help but respond to his touch. And, when Rodin, curious perhaps to see how his little English model would react, led her into an anteroom one day and kissed her with a very deliberate thoroughness, she wrote afterwards that never before had she understood what the Irish poet, Thomas Moore, had meant by describing 'the sensations of mystery and intoxication' of a lover's first kiss.[15]

And so the affair began, with covert embraces in the studio and more leisurely trysts in Gwen's room. Nothing that she'd experienced in her previous, awkward relationships had prepared her for the responses Rodin awoke in her body, responses which she'd 'never thought of before'. He sometimes said that, at nearly sixty-five, he was too old for her, but she told him he was more beautiful and more vigorous than any young man she'd ever known. Needing to be beautiful for him too, she devoted hours to her appearance, brushing her hair repeatedly to make it shine, pinching her breasts to make them plumper, and squandering so much of her earnings on hats, gloves, jackets and dresses that Hilda Flodin pronounced her a proper 'coquette'. Her body engrossed her so entirely that, as soon as they'd finished making love, Gwen wanted more – when she told Rodin once that her little *affaire* (her vagina) was becoming sore, it was not a complaint but a boast.

'You are all that is beautiful and romantic in my life, all my days are so delicious,' she wrote, and she believed that, as mistress, muse, collaborator and pupil to Rodin, she was being refashioned by him, made sexually and spiritually complete.[16] But, of course, the affair was fatally unequal. However much Rodin enjoyed and admired Gwen – her excellence as a model, her seriousness as an artist, her unexpected combination of naivety and boldness in bed – he never regarded her as more than an intriguing *cinq à sept*, an enjoyable way to pass the couple of hours between leaving his studio and taking the train back to the Villa Brillants, his home in the Paris suburb of Meudon. Even during the first months of their affair, when he was assiduous in sending notes of affection to Gwen, setting times and places for meetings, he was also seeing other women. One of them was Eve Fairfax, an English socialite whose bust he'd first sculpted in 1901 and whom he was desperate to make his mistress. As Eve wrote, carelessly, 'unlike most other women I was not prepared to jump into bed with him', and the pain of her rejection kept Rodin in a state of far more passionate wanting than Gwen could ever provoke.[17]

Even if she'd been capable of toying with Rodin, Gwen would have considered it a betrayal of all she felt for him. It was he who'd inspired her joyous declaration, 'I was born to love', and while she never imagined that he would invite her to live with him, she fantasized about them going together to Rome, where they would eat their supper on a river bank, where she would wear the red dress he always liked, and where they would make love in the moonlight (which Gus had always said was most flattering to her).[18] For a while these dreams sustained Gwen in the first flush of her love, however she did begin to mind that her meetings with Rodin were always so closeted, that he would not even take her arm when they were out on the street. She also began to note that their afternoon trysts were becoming less frequent. Of course, Rodin was busy with his commissions, his clients and his professional travels. Yet it became hurtfully apparent to Gwen that he was no less busy with parties, soirées and meetings with admirers, trivial distractions which she considered demeaning to his greatness – and an obstacle to their love.

Tentatively, Gwen began to reproach Rodin, imagining that, if she could only persuade him to spend more time with her, she could return his mind to higher things. But he either ignored or dismissed her gentle criticisms and, by the summer of 1905, there were weeks when she saw very little of him, when he was abroad or at work on other commissions. Confusion and unhappiness began to crowd out the joy she took in Rodin, but she could not look to anyone for counsel or comfort, because she'd told none of her close friends or family about her affair.

In Paris, though, such secrets were difficult to keep, and Gwen was mortified when she realized that rumours of her relationship with Rodin had spread. The women for whom she modelled all seemed to know, and one of them, an Irish sculptor called Nuala O'Donel, took particular delight in tormenting her. Miss O'Donel had herself been infatuated with Rodin for years and, having been jealous of Gwen's success in attracting him, she now took vindictive satisfaction in her misery. She pressed Gwen greedily for details of the affair and, when Gwen remained silent, she turned vicious, mocking Gwen's appearance, her pretensions to being an artist, and accusing her of behaving like a schoolgirl with an adolescent crush.

Gwen's instinct was to turn her back on Miss O'Donel. She'd already come to despise certain aspects of the woman: the desperation with which she boasted of her aristocratic connections; the selfishness with which she insisted on detaining Gwen long after their sessions, bringing out her tray of sticky liqueur bottles, throwing herself theatrically back on her divan and demanding gossip. Yet, while Gwen grumbled that O'Donel was 'une femme méchante et lunatique aussi', she needed her, just as she needed her other lady artists. Apart from her friend Constance, with whom she'd resumed the old Slade habit of drawing and modelling together, and apart from the few people she saw in Rodin's studio, these women formed the extent of her Paris acquaintance.* Despite the streak of coarseness she saw in Hilda Flodin, Gwen had nonetheless come to appreciate Hilda's lively conversation when she accompanied Gwen (and her cat Tiger) on Sunday walks in the woods around Paris. Equally, despite the unsolicited kisses which the painter Miss Gerhardie tried to press on her, Gwen had come to enjoy their occasional evenings together, when they shared pastries and studied books on art.

These women were part of Gwen's tribe. She understood their struggles for independence, for recognition and success, and she was also dependent on their money. Rodin had been paying her generous fees while she'd been posing for the Whistler Muse, but those fees had begun to diminish over the course of the summer, when he'd reached a sticking point over how to position the Muse's arms, and by mid-September, when he put the statue aside, they'd dropped even more sharply.†

For Gwen, however, the reduction in her income meant little compared to the loss of her privileged collaboration with Rodin, which seemed also to signal a diminishing of his affections. He rarely made time to see her alone in the studio and came even less frequently to her room. He said he was busy, was feeling his age, but Gwen felt she'd been cruelly cast aside. 'What a life you give me now', she wrote, in uncomprehending reproach: 'What is it I have done to you mon maître? You know that my heart is profound'.[19]

Rodin's secretary, Renée Chéruy, claimed to have seen it all before. 'She became of course like many others, Rodin's mistress, and like many others he broke her like a stem of glass.'[20] But, wretched though Gwen was, she had chosen to love Rodin with every fibre of her being and she would not allow herself to be broken, nor would she let him go. Sometimes, she would sit in the cafe near his studio, hoping to catch a glimpse of him; sometimes, when he left to catch his evening train, she followed

---

* In 1905, Constance painted a study of Gwen, naked on a bed and reading a novel. It was an expression of their mutual respect – one female artist contemplating another.
† In his original conception, Rodin had envisaged the Muse holding some sort of emblematic object in her arms – a casket or a medallion of Whistler's face. Then, as his indecision mounted, he thought of leaving out the arms entirely, as an oblique homage to the *Venus de Milo*.

him down the street, apologizing awkwardly when he spotted her, urging him to think of her only 'as a petite feuille emporté par le vent'. Driven by longing and curiosity, she occasionally hovered near Rodin's Meudon home, wondering what kind of life he lived behind its showy turrets and stuccoed walls, and wondering what kind of relationship he had with Rose Beuret, on whom she once spied guiltily in the garden.

It didn't occur to Gwen that Rodin might consider her behaviour excessive; she simply believed she was keeping their relationship alive. Deprived of their conversations, she wrote letters instead, reminding her 'tender lover' of the happiness they'd shared, reiterating her dedication to him and his work. 'I get much more pleasure writing to you than I do from drawing,' she claimed, and although Rodin's replies were disappointingly brusque, some even written by his secretary, Gwen feasted on every small hint of affection. 'Heureuse, heureuse moi,' she wrote in her diary one night. 'J'ai reçu ce soir une lettre adorable de mon maître.'[21]

Someday, she believed, Rodin's love must return, and while she waited, she redoubled her efforts to make herself desirable. Worried about the weight she was losing (Rodin always complained when she was too thin), she bought new clothes to disguise her slenderness, splurging fifteen francs, an entire week's wages, on a velvet shawl. She devoted herself to the study of Rodin's favourite books, volumes of poetry by Baudelaire, Verlaine, Mallarmé, the philosophical writings of William James and Schopenhauer, and the two volumes of Samuel Richardson's novel *Pamela*, which Rodin had given her as a present (piqued perhaps by its mildly salacious account of the relationship between a young serving woman and her older employer).

So consumed was Gwen in the project of perfecting herself that, late in 1905, she even offered to give up her art for Rodin's sake. She told him that she'd once been as ambitious as anyone to have her 'place in the sun', but that she now wanted nothing more than to give him 'a heart without reserve, an infinite affection' – an affection she was willing to prove by sweeping his floor and buttoning his boots.

It was an extraordinary declaration. Gwen's work had always been the core of her life and she'd sworn never to follow Edna and Ida in becoming a slave to the man she loved. Yet she believed that Rodin was no ordinary man; he had liberated in her all that was most 'beautiful . . .

wild and eternal' and she saw no contradiction between the Gwen who'd fought to study art in London and Paris, who'd walked from Bordeaux to Toulouse, and the Gwen who now vowed to abase herself to Rodin's genius.

Rodin, in the face of this unswerving love, was irritated and confused; yet, the more he tried to curb Gwen, the more determinedly she clung. 'If you chide me do it gently as to a child', she begged. 'One day you'll have a woman you can be proud of, a woman without caprice and mechancété – if you can just be patient with me.'[22] Perhaps it would have been easier, and more compassionate, if Rodin had simply cut off all communication, but he cared for Gwen and thought he could modulate their relationship to a gentler, more rational affection. He may also have wanted to avoid the catastrophic rupture of his affair with the sculptor Camille Claudel, who had perhaps been the love of his life. Claudel's anguish when Rodin told her he could no longer support the intensity of their love had driven her half mad and she'd turned very publicly against him, accusing him of stealing her ideas and of conspiring to murder her.*

So, Rodin continued to make sporadic visits to Gwen's room and to write encouraging notes. 'You have great faculties of feeling and thought. Courage little friend. I am so tired . . . but I love your little body, so devoted, patient, and peaceful.'†[23] He begged her not to renounce her art, or at least to continue drawing, and he suggested he might even try to find buyers for one or two of her sketches. He urged her, above all, to take better care of herself and, having always felt a mild disgust for the noise and dirt of Hotel Mont Blanc, he said that, if she found herself more pleasant lodgings, he would pay the deposit and make a contribution towards her furniture and rent.

What Rodin regarded as calming intervention, however, Gwen interpreted as love, and, early in 1906, she went obediently in search of a new

---

* Rodin tried to assuage his guilt by offering Claudel financial support, but many, like her brother, considered him to be responsible for the disruption to her career and the deterioration in her mental health.
† 'Voux avez des grandes faculties de sentir et de penser. Courage petite amie, moi je suis si fatigué . . . mais j'aime votre petite corps si dévouée, patience et pas de violence.'

room. Number 7 rue Saint-Placide, she felt, was all that Rodin could ask. Although close to boulevard Edgar Quinet, it was in a quieter, more refined neighbourhood, and the room itself was very pretty, with fresh wallpaper, a red brick floor and a view over an airy courtyard. Once Gwen had hung up her pictures* and arranged her few pieces of furniture – a wicker chair, a small round table, a bed and an armoire with a full-length mirror – she wrote to Rodin of her contentment. 'It is so beautiful here when I've finished eating and everything is clean and tidy, a little fire in the grate, a few flowers on the mantlepiece . . . Every night I read the books you've given me.'[24] In deference to Rodin's fussiness, she became scrupulously tidy: sweeping, dusting and polishing, arranging potted ferns on the narrow plank that served as her windowsill, tying a pretty ribbon around Tiger's neck. In the past, Gwen had been so quick to disdain the bourgeois life of rooms. Now, when the rituals of housework were so intimately bound to Rodin, she found in them a soothing, almost sensual pleasure.

But, while Rodin approved of her room, he was still sparing in his visits. Every day, Gwen listened for his step on the staircase, the slow, heavy tread she recognized so well, and, fearful of missing him, she hurried through her shopping, reduced the hours in which she sat for her lady artists. Strung out with waiting, she tormented herself with images of Rodin in bed with other women. 'Jealous thoughts rise up in my heart, and the unreasonable desires,' she admitted painfully, and it often seemed to Gwen that the only way she had of reaching Rodin was by writing to him.[25]

Her letters had, in fact, been escalating in their frequency and force. She'd begun demanding Rodin's attention through a combination of supplication, anger and sexual provocation, reminding him, graphically, of the most intimate details of their lovemaking. So distasteful, so alarming was all this to Rodin that he'd tried to channel Gwen's correspondence onto more neutral ground, suggesting that she compose her letters in the form of a diary, following the model of Richardson's *Pamela* and focusing more on the 'daily events' of her life. Gwen, immediately

---

* Including the small engraving Rodin had given her early on in their relationship.

ashamed of the 'selfishness' and 'trivialities' with which she'd been bothering Rodin, had made an effort to obey. And, on 28 February 1906, she'd sent him the first of her 'Dear Julie' letters, addressed to an invented penfriend who lived, like her sister Winnie, in Canada.

That first Julie letter wasn't at all what Rodin had intended, for Gwen had recorded no 'daily events', only the emotions she'd felt when Rodin had summoned her to his studio, embraced her in the anteroom and then invited her to walk with him to the station. '[Rodin] said "Are you coming with me Mademoiselle?" (Because we were in front of the concierge) We walked side by side . . . having a most interesting talk. As usual he said he was old but for me he is young. When I got back to my room I went on my knees and gave thanks.'[26]

Once Gwen understood more clearly what Rodin required, her Julie letters did change, becoming lively with the detail of her own small world. She wrote about her neighbours in rue Saint-Placide: the woman who lodged in the room next to hers, who was visited by men at all hours and occasionally stole; the enormously fat, kind concierge, whose husband had taken a vicious dislike to Tiger. She described each one of her lady artists, her visit to the music hall with Miss Gerhardie, her walk in the forest with Miss Flodin and she reported on the birth of Tiger's three tiny kittens, two of whom she had to drown. Much as Gwen loved all cats, she knew that neither her concierge nor Rodin himself would appreciate a litter of them mewling around her room.

As Gwen grew into the rhythm of her Julie letters, she became proud of them. Her French was improving; she'd always been ashamed of her limited grammar and vocabulary, despairing to Ursula, 'there is so much to learn and it is so *disgusting* speaking and writing bad French'.[27] Even though she couldn't prevent her feelings for Rodin from breaking into her narrative (she told him it was much easier to write about their lovemaking, about 'his thumb' and her 'affaire', now that she had the cover of 'Julie'), he approved of her progress: 'Your little novel is very sweet and gracefully done, the style is something like *Pamela* and it pleases me very much.'* A year or two later, Gwen sent Rodin a small portrait of

---

* 'Votre petit roman est très gentil et gracieusement fait, le style est un peu celui de *Pamela* et me plait beaucoup'.

herself in which she was holding up a letter, ready to post; and there was a quality of steadiness, of quiet challenge, in her gaze which suggested that – in her writing, at least – she considered she'd become worthy of her maître.

But, entertaining and well composed though the Julie letters were, they were highly edited. It was only in the notes which Gwen drafted but never sent to Rodin, only in the private entries she'd begun to make in her notebook that she gave way to the hope and despair that still tore at her, to the jealousy that could sometimes feel, she wrote, like 'a mad rage, mounting from the heart to the brain'.[28]

By now, she'd confessed something of her situation to Winnie, who had sturdily advised her not to 'get soft' on Rodin, to concentrate on her work, even to visit Canada, where she herself had found a beau. Hilda Flodin also attempted to rally Gwen, but the bawdiness of her approach only made Gwen suffer more. One evening, when Hilda took the cigarette Gwen was smoking to light her own, she joked, 'You know that means I'm going to kiss your favourite lover.' And, even though Hilda retracted her tease, hastily assuring Gwen, 'I'm sure he does not want kisses from me,' the damage was done. Later, in her room, Gwen wrote a letter of naked pleading to Rodin: 'Oh mon maître, you are the whole world to me, *promise* me that if you love anybody else you won't tell me or if you kiss anybody else I'll *never* know about it.'[29]

However hard Gwen tried to discipline her emotions, her body betrayed her. At night, she had hauntingly erotic dreams of Rodin, which, as she confessed to him, made her wake to such a painful ache of desire, she had to do what 'only what Rodin should do'. Rodin himself claimed to be shocked by the idea of Gwen masturbating – so shocked, he instructed her to sleep with her hands crossed over her chest and suggested that she find other lovers with whom to satisfy herself.

For Gwen, this proposal was the most incomprehensible betrayal of all, and she turned on Rodin, furiously enquiring how he could possibly imagine she would want any man who wasn't him. In fact, during the twelve years in which Gwen loved Rodin, the only 'infidelity' she would ever permit herself was an encounter with Hilda – and even this was a kind of gift, a homage to her maître.

As Gwen described the event in one of her Julie letters, it had taken place after Rodin had asked her to meet him at Hilda's studio and had said it would excite him very much if he could make love to her while Hilda watched, and if he could then draw Gwen and Hilda posing naked together. Up until now, Gwen had had no direct experience of her maître's more epicurean tastes, having never been invited to the studio when the most willing of his models had posed for him with their legs splayed and genitalia exposed, had masturbated in front of him and, on one occasion, had danced for him dressed blasphemously in priests' robes. The thousands of erotic sketches Rodin made from these sessions were stored in a secret archive shown only to his most sophisticated clients. Gwen, however, didn't flinch from the mildly transgressive session which her maître had proposed. In fact, as she later told him, she was so aroused by it that, after Rodin had left the studio, she and Hilda had made love to each other. It had not been 'as good' as it was with him, she assured Rodin, but still it had been 'quelque chose'.[30]

And so Gwen existed on the scraps of Rodin's regard, yet, even though she suffered from his neglect, she could never imagine being without him. She claimed, extravagantly, that before meeting him she'd been nothing: 'I was a little solitaire, no one helped me or awoke me.'[31] And slowly, very slowly, she disciplined herself into accepting what little time and affection he could offer, and she convinced herself that, the more effectively she was able to moderate her passions, the 'more free and independent' she would become 'in the mind & heart'.

Often, there were periods when the effort of sustaining this detachment was so hard Gwen felt she was being wrenched out of shape. But, late in 1905, she found an ally – even a mentor, of sorts – in her suffering. The poet Rainer Maria Rilke had come to live and work with Rodin as his temporary amanuensis, and part of his duties may even have been dealing with Gwen's letters. Unlike the seasoned and cynical Chéruy, however, Rilke came to feel a special sympathy for her situation. He'd endured his own form of emotional torment when he'd been strung out between love for the painter Paula Modersohn-Becker and loyalty to his wife, the sculptor Clara Westhoff. And he'd emerged from that ordeal with the conviction that, however necessary it was to know the 'scattering' bliss of sexual and romantic love, it was even more essential for the writer or artist to 'save and gather' themselves for the discipline of creation. 'Only solitaries shall behold the mysteries', Rilke wrote, and he made it his quiet business to offer some version of that advice to Gwen.* Even though they met each other rarely, often by chance, Rilke wrote short encouraging notes to Gwen, lent her books on art and philosophy, and she found in him a wisdom and kindness without which she would have struggled to survive the diminishing of Rodin's love.

One consequence of Gwen's painfully acquired composure was, as Rilke hoped, the slow return of her art. Painting in oils was too difficult at first, and she may have been unwilling to spoil her new room with the mess of her jars, brushes and tubes of colour, with the acrid smell of turpentine. But drawing became her joy, and one in which she was trying to emulate something of Rodin's speed and vitality. She'd watched him sketching in the studio and had been awed by the ease with which he caught the essence of a pose, or a face, using just a few rapid strokes. His drawing, according to the critic Camille Macalir, was like a form of 'passionate writing', and, as Gwen tried to copy it, she felt the last vestige of Tonks' influence, his insistence on the anatomically clear and beautiful line, fall away.[32]

Mostly, she was using Tiger as her model and, working in charcoal, red chalk or pencil, sometimes with a thin wash of watercolour, she was trying, she wrote, to penetrate 'the mysterious soul that haunts the body of a cat', capturing Tiger as she was arched in an arrogant stretch, curled up in soft repose, or quick and delicate in play. They were exquisite, these sketches, and so assured that, when fifteen of them were discovered, posthumously, in Rodin's art collection, they were initially attributed to him.

Gwen was also starting to draw herself and her room in rue Saint-Placide. At first, her sketches took the form of a visual diary, moments in her day when she was reading a book or a letter, sewing by lamplight. Yet it was through these small domestic studies that Gwen eventually found her way back to painting. 'I am doing some views . . . with me as a figure doing something. They will be like Dutch paintings in subject',

---

* Rilke elaborated this philosophy through a series of posthumously published letters to the poet Franz Xaver Kappus.

she told Rodin.[33] The detail of these 'views' – the worn grain of Gwen's wicker chair, the quality of the sunlight coming through her window, the drift of breeze that lifted a curtain – all these brought something new to her work. While the life of her early self-portraits had been concentrated in her face and the set of her body, these little biographical interiors created a wider narrative. They told the story of Gwen's life in Paris. And, if they revealed nothing of the hours in which she felt her longing for Rodin like an illness, they had recorded something else that was no less true: the simple fact that Gwen had succeeded in making a life in Paris, that, even with very little money and with few professional connections, she had outsoared the dreams of the angry little girl who'd sat miserably alone in her Tenby bedroom, wondering when something 'of importance' would ever happen to her.

Chapter Seven

IDA

'Life is not only that coloured vista we see from tiptoe'
IDA JOHN TO AUGUSTUS JOHN[1]

Throughout Gwen's first years in Paris and her love affair with Rodin, she had resisted all her brother's attempts to coax from her the intimate details of her life. She'd kept her letters practical and short, and Gus, defeated by her reticence, had been forced to respond in kind, sending news of Ida, Dorelia and the boys, reporting on the changing seasons in Essex. For one brief period, however, during the autumn and winter of 1904, Gus had tried to push their correspondence onto a different level altogether, writing to Gwen as one artist to another and initiating what he hoped would be an exchange of ideas.

Gus was envious, when he thought of how his sister's knowledge and experience must be expanding through her association with Rodin. There had been moments in his career when he'd felt adrift in his own fitful impulses and had wished for a wiser artist to guide him. He'd all but outgrown Tonks and Steer, despite the affection he still felt for them; he was grateful to Will for his generosity, but he couldn't regard him as a mentor. In fact, as he grumbled to Gwen, he was feeling disillusioned with most of the London art world. 'Over here paltry little clubs and exhibitions agitate the artistic atmosphere,' he complained; the Royal Academy was nothing but a 'vast collection of wrong-minded stuff' and it seemed to him that, as factions hardened over issues of technique and style, the painters around him had lost all connection to what he called 'the old essential things, the unchanging instincts . . . the salt of life.'[2]

The letter Gus wrote to Gwen in October was perhaps the most personal expression of his belief in art that he'd ever committed to paper. He was trying to articulate for her the essence of what he'd learned from Rembrandt, his conviction that the artist's first duty was always to discover the core of truth within each of his subjects, whether those subjects be 'the old men who have the wisdom of age, the young people who have the folly of youth [,] middle aged people who have the passion & confidence of middle age . . . calm young virgins . . . agitated mothers.' He was also trying to express the connection he sensed between that fundamental humanity and the forces of nature. 'Larch trees and pine trees murmur the secret and insects with the deep note . . . and the rocks that push themselves through the earth'.[3]

This muddled but fervent manifesto was an overture from Gus, with which he was hoping to elicit some equivalent revelations from Gwen. When he informed her of his current progress in the studio, reporting with almost semaphoric brevity that 'Dorelia's face is a mystery', he was hoping that his sister, of all people, would understand the precise challenges of that mystery, and would sympathize with the doubts that were starting to unsettle him as he tried to finish his latest submissions for the NEAC show.

He was painting two portraits of Dorelia, wrestling not only with the familiar technical demands of light, colour and composition, but with the tug between observing and imagining. He was trying to go beyond Dorelia's face to an intimation of the sexual torment she'd made him endure during the year of her absence. In *Ardor*, he'd painted her with an almost diabolical succulence, exaggerating her plump, dimpled flesh, her dark eyes and cushioned mouth with a brio that was reminiscent of Frans Hals, but also making her barely recognizable as the bookish young woman whom his sister had painted in Toulouse. Gwen, if she'd seen *Ardor* and its companion piece, *Dorelia in a Feathered Hat*, would surely have disliked both portraits. If she responded to Gus's long manifesto, there is no record of her reply.

As Gus battled with his portraits, it was to Will that he confessed most fearfully the 'grinding see saw' of his doubts, the 'alternations of achievement, failure, impotence and power . . . under a studio light cold informal meaningless.'[4] Painting still came harder to him than drawing, and it must have been a relief to him when the critic Roger Fry, reviewing his portraits at the NEAC, seemed to grasp what he was attempting. Normally sparing with his praise, Fry declared that Gus had finally managed to transfer the 'masterly qualities' of his draughtsmanship onto canvas, that he had 'arrived at a control of his medium which astonishes one by comparison with his work a year or two back.'

However grandly Gus might have disparaged the smallness of the London art world, he needed its recognition. He was tremendously bucked by the conclusion of Fry's review: 'We hardly dare confess how high are the hopes of [his] future which his paintings this year have led us to form . . .'[5] He was flattered, too, when Fry brought Sickert to visit him at Elm House, and pleased that Rothenstein and Conder were inviting him to join the newly formed Society of Twelve, a group dedicated to reviving British traditions of etching and draughtsmanship.

As Gus was making professional strides, he believed his domestic life was also improving. He had kept his promise to include Ida more in his London life, and she admitted to Gwen how much it had improved her mood. 'It is nicer here now. I have been up to town with [Gus and Dorelia] and we are going again on Saturday . . . They . . . are very kind and when I do not think it is compassion I am happy enough . . . we are making curtains and cushions for [the] studio. I am making a black velvet toque with red feathers.' In late October, when the baby was born, the delivery was easy and little Robin (who was briefly burdened with the name Lorenzo Paganini) proved so good at sleeping and feeding, Ida recovered her strength unusually fast. The baby's arrival also seemed to steady the atmosphere because it gave Dorelia the chance to make herself useful, looking after the children and helping with the housework. 'Dorelia is so angelic', Ida acknowledged to Gwen. 'I have not a nurse and she does so much. Mr Paganini is so splendid and growing fast. He is very beautiful *of course*.'[6]

For Gus, it was enormously encouraging to see his two women getting on so well, to see his boys running free with their cats and dogs and the chickens. He could almost believe that the beautiful ménage of which he'd dreamed was finally making sense, that between them they'd managed to create their version of the authentic life.

But the idyll couldn't last. Ida was still at the mercy of her volatile hormones and, all too quickly, her euphoria over Robin's birth gave way to a slow, seeping depression. Even with Dorelia's help, there were days when she was crushed under the burden of running her family. 'What with babies' toothaches and a visitation of fleas (where from we do not know) I am fast losing my reason,' she told Alice. It was particularly hard on her, too, that Dorelia had just discovered she was pregnant and was beautifully glowing. To Will, Ida confessed that she feared she would never manage to escape the 'demon devil and windbag' of her own jealousy.[7]

She was lonely, as well, because her mother and sisters were so scandalized by the revolution at Elm House, they would only visit if Dorelia was absent. Ida had begged Gwen to spare her a few more days from Paris, but she'd heard nothing back. In a renewed appeal to Gus, she wrote him a long letter in late November, trying to explain what it cost her to keep their domestic arrangement afloat, her longing for him to appreciate all the compromises it required. 'Life is *not only* that coloured vista we see from tiptoe etc. Life is also a hard way covered with difficulties and the only thing is to make that our delight. What a science it is – & what an art and how much must be destroyed before one can begin to delight in it. I have been in the position of seeing the thing to do but not having the strength to accomplish it.'[8]

Gus wasn't blind to what he owed Ida, the generosity, intelligence and courage she brought to their marriage; yet, as he later admitted, he suffered 'a kind of moral impotence' when forced to acknowledge her goodness.[9] It was selfish, he knew, but it was always easier to duck his feelings of inadequacy, to escape back to London and into his work, to tell himself Ida was always low after having a baby and would soon recover. Because he was so often absent, Gus had no idea that, far from recovering, Ida was spiralling into a new and quite terrifying anxiety: 'Do you know what it is to sit down and be bounced up again', she asked Mary Dowdall, 'and for that to happen *continuously* so that you can't sit *anywhere*?' She began medicating herself with phenacetin, a powerful analgesic, to calm her nerves, but its effect was only to induce in her a paralysing apathy, an amputation of hope and will. 'Isn't it awful when even the desire to live forsakes one,' she mused drearily to Mary. 'I *cannot* see any reason why I should'; and she admitted how sometimes she felt drawn to the restful oblivion of laudanum.[10]

Mary, alarmed by the suicidal tone of Ida's letter, sent Gus a telegram which was sharp enough to get him on the next train to Essex. Ida greeted him with a dull indifference, which was shocking in itself, but it was only when he saw the draft of a second letter she'd been writing to Mary that he fully understood the danger she was in. 'I am a sickener,' Ida had written. 'As to the suicide. Why not? What a fuss about one's life which is really not valuable . . . I have lost all my sense of reason or right . . . It's so funny not to want to be good. I never remember to have felt it before. It is such a nice free feeling – criminals must be like that . . . Gus is adorable, only all he says is like sounds far away.'[11]

Gus begged Ida not to alarm Mary by sending this morbid report of herself, and swore he would find ways of making her happier. But, even now, his first instinct was to salvage his own conscience and, when he wrote to assure Mary that he was taking proper care of Ida, he was also anxious to explain that, complicated though his ménage might appear, it had nothing to do with him trying to 'épater les bourgeoisie', only with his belief they must all live according to the truth of their individual selves. He conceded that his own truth, especially his intemperate love for women, might be judged a 'congenital weakness', yet he'd read enough of Dostoyevsky and Nietzsche to believe that a man's character was his fate: 'one cannot erase the invisible hand,' he told Mary, 'to attempt that is pure folly.'[12]

Caught up in the force of his own arguments, Gus did not see how self-serving his letter must have appeared. He was convinced he was doing his best for Ida, not only by insisting that she take a recuperative break from the family, in London, but, on her return, by starting work on a double portrait of her and Dorelia. He knew how desperately Ida had missed modelling during the last couple of years; to pose for Gus had always allowed her to retain some sense of being an artist – as she once admitted to Gwen, she felt she would almost 'rather lose a child than the power of sitting'. However, this new portrait, well-intentioned though it was, only made the situation worse. Shortly after Gus began work on it, he realized the composition was all wrong and, unable to find a way of fixing it, his only solution was to leave Ida out. He honestly believed he was simply following the picture's logic, but Ida of course could only see a devasting affront in her erasure. So disillusioned was she by Gus, she went with the children to spend Christmas with her mother at a seaside hotel.

Perhaps Ida was practising for a permanent separation; perhaps she simply hoped to give the boys the chance of a happy Christmas. Yet she was still unsure what she wanted and, after several days of Ada's reproachful comments on her marriage and the children's restless noise, she began to long for Essex. She even began to long for Dorelia. Even though she'd often wished to see Dorelia 'at the bottom of the sea', the two of them had become sisters, of sorts, in their peculiar situation. When she wrote to send Christmas greetings to Dorelia, along with thanks for her present of a coat, she signed herself, both affectionately and darkly, 'Yours jealously enviously and adoringly, Ida Margaret Anne JOHN.'[13]

By the time Ida was back in Essex, she'd almost resigned herself to muddling on as before. In late March, she went cheerfully with Dorelia to help Gus move into his new London studio (just a few doors up from his old one in Flood Street). As the three of them shifted furniture and paintings, they were almost comfortable together. Yet, as Ida told Alice, their problems were still dangerously close to the surface, and there had suddenly been a '*terrific* flare up'.[14]

'The ménage was on the point of breaking up', she wrote, and the calmness with which Ida reported all this to Alice came from a certain satisfaction that, this time, it was Dorelia, not she, who was to blame. During the long winter months when Ida and Gus had been quarrelling and their future together had hung in the balance, Dorelia had become anxious about her own situation. She was midway through her pregnancy and there had still been no discussion about how she and her baby would figure in the household, about whether they would remain in Elm House or whether an illegitimate child would be a scandal too far. Once or twice, Dorelia had tried to broach her anxieties with Gus, but he'd waved them aside with his usual impatience, and she had begun to think that the only 'sane and sensible thing . . . to do' would be to strike out on her own. She would leave behind the mess of Gus and Ida's marriage and she would go back to Paris, where she imagined herself picking up the life she started over a year ago with Gwen.

Something must have happened in London that provoked Dorelia into admitting her plan, and, as Ida told Alice, with some relish, it had led to a furious row – 'Lord it was a murky time, most sulphurous'. Ida also admitted that the novelty of seeing Dorelia floundering in guilt and being on the receiving end of recriminations from Gus had given her a 'queer impersonal enjoyment', even more so her own self-appointed roles as peacemaker. Eventually, the row exhausted itself. Ida persuaded Dorelia not to do anything until the baby was born, and instructed Gus to show more consideration. 'We all 3 dined at a restaurant (which is now a rare joy)', Ida told Alice, '& drank wine, & then rode miles on the top of a bus, very gay & light hearted. Gus has been a sweet mild creature since.'[15]

But Ida would always try to put an optimistic slant on things to Alice, and the peace was more fragile than she indicated. Gus had actually been shocked and disappointed when Dorelia, his romantic, his intoxicating 'Ardor', had shown herself capable of such conventional concerns. He felt his love for her evaporating, along with his wonder at her beauty, and she, picking up on his coldness, grew untypically fretful. The atmosphere at Elm House became strained once more, and Ida, having lost all appetite for keeping the peace, again felt the temptation of laudanum 'very near'.

All three of them were becoming rather hateful to each other, but in May they had a visit from Mary Dowdall and – to Ida, at least – it seemed that Mary shone a sane and rescuing light onto the muddle of their life. 'The Rani is so human,' Ida wrote with awe, and under Mary's influence it became clear to her she must give herself time alone to think.[16] Announcing to Gus that she needed a 'rest cure', she arranged to stay first with the Rothensteins in London, then with Louise Salaman (now married to Edgar Bishop) in Oxford, and finally with Mary in Liverpool. Dorelia and Maggie could look after the children, she said. As for Gus, he could do as he chose.

Once Ida was gone, it became obvious to Gus how crucial she'd always been in holding the household together. Dorelia, over seven months pregnant, burdened with all three children and with her future still unresolved, was unable to cope and announced that she'd changed her mind about staying in Essex and wanted to leave for Paris as soon as possible. He, in a panic, wrote indignantly to Ida, hoping to shame her into returning home. But, this time, she would not be budged.

She was passionately preoccupied in puzzling out her own situation. And, because she'd given up trying to explain herself to Gus, it was to Dorelia – her sister, rival and fellow victim – that Ida sent a series of lacerating letters in which she tried to analyse how and why their 'wonderful concubinage' had failed: '[It was] because you meant to Gus all that lay outside the dull home, the unspeakable fireside, the gruesome dinner table, that I became so hopeless. I was the chain, you were the key to unlock it. This is what I have been made to feel ever since you came. Gus will deny it but he denies many facts which are daily occurrences – apparently denies them because they are true and he wants to pretend they aren't.'

'I tried not to be horrid . . . I tried to be jolly,' Ida wrote, but she pointed out that Dorelia and Gus had each, in their own way, made it impossible. Ida had attempted to get closer to Dorelia, but had never been graced with a reciprocal intimacy.[17] Gus, meanwhile, had refused to accept Ida's right to unhappiness, accusing her of being 'vulgar and insensible'. '[He] blames me entirely for *everything* now – I daresay he's right but when I think of some things I feel I suffered too much . . . I do not think it is likely Gus and I can live together after this – I want to separate – I feel sick at heart . . . I think he's a mean & childish creature beside being the fine old chap he is.'[18]

This was the furthest Ida had ever gone in admitting that Gus might be a seriously damaged and damaging man, and, in the first of her letters to Dorelia, she argued that the two of them should make their escape together: 'we have neither the peace of mind of a wife nor the freedom (or at least I haven't) of the mistress. We have the evils of both states for the one good which belongs to both – a man's company.' But, at the same time, Ida feared she lacked the necessary steel to abandon Gus entirely. She loved him still, she recognized that the qualities which made him intolerable were also those that made him quite magical. 'He's a poet and knows no more about actual life than a poet. This is sometimes everything when he's struck a spark to illumine the darkness and sometimes nothing when he's looking at the moon', she wrote, and it occurred to her that she would find it easier to leave him if Dorelia remained behind. Her letters shifted from sisterly conspiracy to brisk advice, assuring Dorelia that, even though Gus had left her alone to 'bottle up' her worries, even though his affections had apparently 'sunk to the bottom', such behaviour was to be expected from any man. As soon as the baby was born, she promised, Gus would be as 'stirred up with love as he'd ever been.'[19]

Gus saw none of these letters – they would make him 'wild', Ida wrote, when she instructed Dorelia to keep them hidden. He would, in fact, have been particularly injured by their accusations of neglect, because he'd been far more concerned than either woman realized with the question of where Dorelia should give birth. A maternity hospital was out of the question, it would be far too coldly institutional for his 'Ardor'; yet Elm House was almost as problematic because Ida was still so ambivalent about the forthcoming baby, wanting to be 'good' about it but unsure if she could 'manage it'. Gus recognized that Dorelia needed a refuge of her own, somewhere private and poetic, and it was around mid-May that he realized the obvious solution to their dilemma was to make use of the gypsy caravan which he'd recently bought from Michel Salaman.

Michel, who'd got married the previous year, had acquired the van for his honeymoon but had then left it parked in a remote spot on Dartmoor. It was still lying empty and Gus saw how thrilling it would be for Dorelia to have her baby there – a gypsy Madonna in the wilds of Devon. As this prospect began to glow in his imagination, he also saw how easily Ida and the boys might come down to Dartmoor once the baby was born, how easily he could set them all up in a couple of extra tents. A radical family, he decided, needed a radical way of living, and, energized as always by the making of plans, he wrote affectionately to Ida, telling her that 'a summer of camping' would be excellent for them all.

Ida, still in Liverpool with Mary, was rather impressed by Gus's decisiveness; she'd always fantasized about living outdoors, like Mowgli in her favourite Kipling novel, *Jungle Book*, and she accepted that this might be one last opportunity to salvage their ménage. To Dorelia, she sent a hesitant offer to come down early and assist with the birth: 'would you like me to . . . or would you like me to stay away.' Painfully candid, as always, she confessed that, if she did come, it would 'probably [be] because I don't like to be away from things.'[20]

If Dorelia responded to this awkward offer, her reply has been lost. Gus took her down to Dartmoor in late May or early June and the caravan looked very beautiful, parked in an isolated valley with wild ponies grazing and a fast-running stream. It didn't matter to Dorelia that there was only a wooden shelf in the van for a bed and a tiny stove for cooking. Nor was she troubled that the nearest village, Postbridge, was six miles away. Gus had intuited exactly the right place for her. And, even though he would have to leave her alone for a week or two, while he went up to Liverpool to paint a portrait, he was very good about settling her in, buying her provisions from the village and, in the event of her being bothered by questions, instructing her to say that she was the wife of a naval officer who was away at sea, and that Gus himself was her brother.

But Gus had only been gone for a few days when Dorelia went into labour. She'd miscalculated her dates, believing the baby was not due for another month, and her only option was to stumble through her contractions to the nearby pub. Someone, perhaps the publican or his wife, got her back to the caravan and summoned a midwife, and the first news that Gus and Ida received of the birth came in two brief telegrams, carefully composed in Romani, in which Dorelia informed them that the baby had been safely delivered and was a boy.

Ida travelled through the night to get to Dorelia. 'The babe is fine, a tawny colour – very contented on the whole', she told Mary, although she added with a sliver of triumph that Dorelia was 'having to use a breast pump thing' because 'her nipples [were too] flat on the breast.'[21] Gus arrived shortly afterwards, cock-a-hoop that his latest son had been born in such lyrical circumstances. He'd already drawn up a list of names, and Dorelia, far more susceptible to poetry than Ida, had chosen Pyramus – a name to which she would stick, except for the occasional shortening to Pyra.

Once the baby was feeding well, the other children were brought down by Maggie. Gus was still in a state of high excitement. He'd been busy acquiring the skills of a gypsy paterfamilias, learning how to dig peat for a fire, constructing a large sleeping tent out of blankets and rods. At first, he was disappointed by David and Caspar, who were inclined to grizzle for the toys and pets they'd left behind, but the two boys soon began inventing outdoor games for themselves. And, as Gus proudly observed how his children were adapting to life under canvas, he was even more beguiled by the changes in his wife and his lover.

Dorelia, wandering around the encampment with Pyramus in her arms, appeared fully restored to Gus, in all her beauty and grace. But it was Ida who looked transformed, her skin turning rosy and her energy revived. To Mary, she acknowledged that camping had indeed been 'a tonic': 'The air is soft as honey and strong as wine. I can work all day with joy & you know I hate it as a rule – in a bloody house. Here there are about 10 square yards to keep clean and tidy and beyond the moor & the sky.'[22]

Barefoot and strong, Ida was once again the wild spirit with whom Gus had fallen in love. One of his drawings that summer was among the most ravishingly romantic he'd ever done of Ida, her hair a tangle of curls, her back straight and stern as a dancer's as she held baby Robin in her arms. But everything inspired Gus. In *Caravan, A Gypsy Encampment*, he painted a scene from their family life, in which Ida and Dorelia were hanging up laundry and minding the children while he remained a shadowy background figure, standing in the doorway of the van. The scene was presented as though glimpsed by an unseen observer from inside the family tent, creating an effect both secretive and staged. And in the painting's deliberately roughened brushstrokes, its stark juxtapositions of colour, its abruptly foreshortened perspective, it went beyond anything Gus had previously attempted. To Michel, he wrote confidently that the boldness of his camping experiment had been a breakthrough for his work: 'I know now infallibly what is good painting, good imagination & good art.'[23]

But, even here, in this beautiful valley, where Gus was working so well and everyone seemed so robustly content, the marital peace was uneasy. Gus had vowed to divide his time and affections equally between both women. Yet his conscientious efforts had made Dorelia feel neglected, while Ida, always more complex, secret and ironic than Gus had ever fathomed, had judged this new, uxorious side of him to be little more than a charade. 'He is (or acts) in love with *me* for a change,' she reported to Mary. 'He is so afraid of making me jealous.'

Ida believed the situation between them all was ultimately 'impossible', but, at the same time, she told Mary it was 'so interesting and truth excavating.'[24] Observing Gus through the lens of her new detachment, she saw how extreme and fragmented his character could be, how possible it was for him to be 'a horrid beast & a lazy wretch & a sky blue angel & an eagle of the ranges' within the space of a single day. Even while Ida was pleased to see him intent on his work, she noted how idle he'd become around the camp. Most of the chores were falling on her, especially since Maggie had left for her own summer holiday, and, by mid- to late July, Ida was grumbling that she'd been working from six in the morning till nine at night, she'd been wearing the same dress for over a week and was suffering from 'a tyrannical backache and about 100 cuts and burns'.[25]

Gus, however, seemed to think the camp ran itself. Often, he sloped off to the pub in the evenings, or went away to London, where he claimed that Orpen needed his help in selling their school (which they'd discovered was harder, less profitable work than they'd imagined). Ida suspected he was seeing other friends, and possibly other women, and if, at the start of the holidays, she'd believed in her ability to insulate herself from disappointment and to look dispassionately at Gus, her detachment deserted her when she realized she was pregnant, yet again.

Neither she nor Gus had ever tried to control their apparently relentless fertility. Condoms existed, but they were crude and difficult to obtain. A vinegar-saturated sponge worked for some women, yet was unreliable at best. As for the traditional techniques of abstinence, or coitus interruptus, Ida believed, as did Gus and Dorelia, that they were an affront to spontaneity. Yet, if Ida didn't want to interfere with nature, she also wasn't ready for another baby, and out on Dartmoor she made 'violent efforts' to miscarry. Whatever she did – jumping up and down or dosing herself with a herbal abortifacient – had no effect, as she calculated with horror she must already be over five months pregnant. The reality of what this fourth baby would mean, in binding her more tightly to the 'half and half, timorous, supposed-to-be-restful sort of life' that her marriage had become, was terrifying to Ida, and once again she longed to be done with it all.[26]

The camp at least was coming to an end. A second, longer

commission was awaiting Gus in Liverpool, and it was only practical for Ida and Dorelia to take the children back to Essex. Gus, for his part, assumed that everything would now settle back to normal. As he sent home virtuous reports from Liverpool, of how he was finding his 'isolation very good for work', he imagined that Ida was now fully sympathetic to Dorelia and Pyramus remaining a permanent part of their family, and that Dorelia was now happy to stay.[27]

He had no notion, yet, of how deeply Ida feared a return to their old ménage, of how complicit Dorelia had become in her own resistance, and of how subversive a bond the two women had formed. The quality of their relationship had changed at the camp. Even though Dorelia had felt overlooked by Gus and Ida had felt overburdened, it had become natural for them to spend their evenings intimately together. They'd shared a confederacy of motherhood, chatting and playing chess while the children slept and Gus was off drinking at the pub. Then, as the weeks passed, they'd begun admitting to each other how much easier things were when Gus was altogether absent from the camp and was busy with his own affairs. They'd dared to wonder what it would be like if that arrangement could be made more permanent and, by the time they were back at Elm House, they were already starting to imagine new ways of managing their lives which no longer had Gus at their centre.

They decided that their best plan was to move to Paris together, with the children. Apartments in the city were still cheap and easy to find, they could earn money as models, and, while Gus would be free to visit any time he chose, there would be a much more rational distance between them all. They assumed, as they worked on the details of their plan, that Gus would see the beauty of it, for, while they didn't doubt his love for them and the boys, it was obvious that the family had become a distraction, a constraint on his work. As Ida wrote, by removing themselves to Paris, she and Dorelia would be giving Gus all the 'liberty of soul and calm of body' for which he was so obviously 'starving'.[28]

When Ida informed Gus of this scheme, however, he was aghast. Disruption terrified him when it wasn't of his own making; he'd had his childhood turned upside down by the death of his mother, and to be abandoned now by his wife and his lover was almost as traumatic. To each of the women he wrote separately, begging them to change their minds, yet the tone of his letters had been misjudged and their effect had only been to strengthen the women's faith in their plan.

To Ida, he'd made an appeal to her reason, insisting that any unkindness she had sensed in him had come only from the 'nervous aberrations' of his character. To Dorelia, however, he'd appealed to her heart, and, absorbed as he was in his own private fears, it didn't occur to Gus that the women would read each other's letters. Of course they did, and Ida, in particular, was so wounded by the passion with which he'd written to Dorelia, and by the pedantic tone he'd taken with her, she felt doubly justified in her decision to leave. 'With people one loves one does not suffer from nervous aberrations', she wrote to him stiffly.

Even in her anger, however, Ida wanted to be fair. She recognized that she and Gus had been so very young when they'd married, so very naive in believing they were embarking on an adventure together, so hopelessly ill-prepared for the compromises they would have to make.

'Dearest of G's', she wrote, 'I think it is because I love you that I see it . . . It has been a straining of the material for you and I ever to live together'. She told him that she still wanted only what was best for him and she promised that, if Dorelia changed her mind and decided to stay, she would be happy to go by herself to Paris. 'I am quite sure you will visit me and I will receive you oh my love. But do not let us any longer desecrate our love by bringing it into places where it is not.'[29]

But Dorelia didn't want to stay: 'I do not know if Ardor & I love one another – we seem to be bound together by sterner bonds,' Ida observed when she informed Gus that she and Dorelia were still committed to each other, and to Paris.[30] To convince him of her certainty, she said that she'd already begun clearing out Elm House and had already begun informing friends of the move, facing down objections from spikey Gwen Salmond that she and Dorelia could never live easily together, and staunchly rebutting accusations from Will and Alice that she was betraying her duty to Gus's work.

Ida was proud of the firmness with which she'd argued her case – 'Alice Rothenstein has at last shut up', she told Gus, but the confrontation with her mother was far more harrowing.[31] Ada Nettleship had always hated the life for which Ida had settled; she'd been beside herself when Dorelia had first moved into Elm House and had threatened to set the law on Gus. Yet, the notion of Ida actually leaving her husband, and in such a public way, was horrifying to her. She couldn't understand why, if there had to be a separation, it couldn't be managed more discreetly, and, with anguished tears, she warned Ida that, by moving to Paris, she would be condemning all of her Nettleship family to scandal.

Rarely had Ida been so tested; she was seven months pregnant, sailing away from her closest friends and opening an even wider rift with her family. Yet she wrote to Alice, 'The idea of change and life is like strong air to me – I can't look back at the stagnation'.[32] She knew that to stay in Elm House would kill all hope in her, and, faced with her courage, Gus could no longer argue against it. If he was honest with himself, he could see there were exciting prospects for him in this new cross-Channel arrangement: the chance to live both in London and Paris, the chance to have both his liberty and his family. It occurred to him too that, if Ada Nettleship and the two moralizing Rothensteins were so set against the plan, the least he could do was support it. 'I think you must all go,' he wrote to Dorelia, and he agreed to be back from Liverpool by late September to escort the family on their journey.

By the time they reached the Hotel Saint Pierre, where Ida had booked two large rooms at an 'excellent price', Gus was fully engaged with the adventure. Paris was still 'the Queen of cities' for him, and he cheerfully imagined himself renting a studio in Montparnasse, going to all the galleries, rooting out Gwen and finally getting an introduction to Rodin. When he wrote to Sampson, he boasted that, even though the crossing had been rough, Dorelia and the boys had been sick, and brave little Caspar had asked if they hadn't 'better go back', he had personally managed to 'get the family over here without mishap'.[33] Already Gus had forgotten his first shocked opposition to the Paris plan, already he'd half convinced himself that it had been his from the start.

Chapter Eight

CROSS-CHANNEL AFFAIRS

To celebrate his arrival, Gus bought a hat. It was soft brown plush, with an extravagantly jaunty feather, and he planned to wear it as he revisited the cafes and the Louvre. But a family apartment needed to be found and, since Ida was too pregnant to go tramping the streets, Gus was grudgingly obliged, he told Sampson, to 'go through the faithless formality of climbing several thousand stairs a day, and arousing a thousand suspicions, a thousand vague hopes'.[1] Within a week, though, he'd delivered the miracle for which Ida hoped: a three-roomed flat that overlooked a sunny courtyard, with sufficient space to hold their few bits of furniture – a table and chairs, a large bed for Ida and Dorelia to share, a couple of wooden boxes on rollers to serve as beds for the two older boys, and baskets for all the babies.

Number 63 rue Monsieur le Prince was close enough to the Jardin du Luxembourg for the children and the dog to play there every day. It bordered on Montparnasse, where the two women had first fallen under the city's spell. And it was also only a mile away from the studio Gus found for himself, in the garden of a small townhouse in rue Dareau. The light was good in the studio, there was birdsong and, as Gus laid out his painting things, he was flooded with the conviction that this new arrangement was what he'd needed all along. 'I must tell you how happy thoughts fill me just now', he wrote to Alice in mid-October. 'I begin to see how it is all going to come about – all the children and mothers and me.' Now that Gus no longer had the daily affront of the babies' noise, the responsibility for Dorelia and Ida's happiness, he knew he could not only love them all better, but embrace them in his work. 'In my former impatience and unwisdom I *used* to think of them sometimes as accidental and perhaps a little in the way of my art,' he told Alice: 'what a mistake – now it dawns on me they are, must be the real material and soul of it.'[2]

Any hopes Gus had entertained of including his sister in this new domestic harmony were disappointed, though. Gwen had grown even less communicative of late; her response to the news of Dorelia's new baby had been affectionate but almost callously offhand. 'I am so glad everything has gone well, & it is such a charming one, it seems to be a real gypsy. I should like to come over but I don't suppose I shall.'[3] And, although she brought round the gift of '3 very nice pictures' for the flat when she came to see them all, she made it clear there would be no casual dropping in and out; if there were to be visits, they were to be prearranged by postcard. So wary a distance did she maintain that, by the time Gus had to go back to London for work, he was almost ready to give up on her. 'Gwen persists in Paris,' he commented crossly to Michel; 'I suppose she prefers penurious liberty to social dependence. She has several pictures which she never shows anyone.'[4]

Ida and Dorelia did little better. Gwen rejected Dorelia's offer to model for her and rebuffed all Ida's attempts to exchange confidences. Neither of them yet knew about Rodin, and Ida, having no idea of why Gwen should be so private, was particularly hurt. 'Gwen John lives in Paris & we see her sometimes,' she would write to Meg Sampson the following July. 'Always the same reserved creature.'[5]

Ida had more immediate issues, though, than penetrating Gwen's reserve. On 27 November, she went into labour and gave birth to 'another beastly boy . . . a great coarse looking, bull necked unpoetical man, an unmusical commercial snoring blockhead.' He was called Edwin, after his Tenby grandfather, and at first he seemed as fussy as his namesake – colicky and reluctant to feed.[6] When David, Caspar and Robin all went down with measles, Ida might easily have been overwhelmed. Yet, already she felt like a different, much stronger mother.

Her life was certainly easier now – Gus had provided enough money for her and Dorelia to hire a maid, and, with the work of the flat divided between three of them, there were suddenly hours in the day when Ida could read and look at pictures again. Yet it was the simple fact of being in Paris and in control of her world which felt most liberating to her. She had recovered her ability to delight in the children, in the deliciously comical 'flow of monkey talk' with which one-year-old Robin was learning to speak; and she had recovered her greed for food.[7] As soon as she and Dorelia were able to find an elderly woman to mind the children in the evening, they often went out to eat in restaurants. 'I think we must be rich,' Ida wrote happily to Mary. '[We] saunter out, spend money to an outrageous extent . . . and we come in again and find absolute tranquillity – babies everywhere asleep and 2 virtuous little boys looking out of the windows . . . from a house built of chairs.'[8]

She was also delighting in Dorelia, explaining to Mary that the self-sufficiency, which had always aggravated her, now struck her as a form of saintliness. 'She is good as gold, cheerful, patient, beautiful to look upon, ready to laugh at everything and nothing.'[9] She began calling Dorelia 'Dodo', and a sketch which Gus drew of them in soft, red chalk expressed his own slightly awed pleasure in the friendship they were forming, the two women leaning close to each other and sharing the same slightly conspiratorial expression.

Will Rothenstein, who came to see them on his way through Paris, was shocked by the way they were living, with the children 'rolling around the floor as if in a slum family.'[10] But Will's disapproval only made Ida laugh. She'd longed for this simplicity when she'd been living in Essex, when she'd felt disapproving eyes and ears attuned to her every move. Here, in this cheap rented apartment, in this big anonymous city, she could do exactly what she pleased. She cut off her thick dark hair in what she hoped was a 'new womanish' style, she walked freely around the streets. To Meg Sampson she wrote, 'I've come to the conclusion that laughter is the chief reason for living.'[11]

Ida wished her family could appreciate her contentment. A week after Edwin was born, she wrote a long letter to her sister, Ursula, acknowledging that, while her situation in Paris might seem a 'frightening experiment' and a threat to her family's reputation in London, it was the only way she knew of living 'genuinely'. Dorelia, she insisted, was 'a very wonderful person – a child of nature – calm and beautiful'. However hard it might have been when Gus first fell in love with Dorelia, that pain was all in the past. 'It is a beautiful life we live now', Ida insisted to Ursula, 'and I have never been so happy.'[12]

In late January, there was a potential hitch in the happiness when their landlord, unable to tolerate the children's clatter, gave them notice to quit. Ida wrote to Gus, with some trepidation, to say that, out of the 'millions' of flats she'd viewed, the only one that suited was in the building to which his own studio was attached, but he told her she must take it. He was still lit up with the beauty of 'all the children and mothers and me' being together in Paris, and he'd forgotten how the incessant 'howling' and 'growling' of family life had so often disrupted his peace.[13]

Ever since his return to London, Gus's work had been going well. His submissions to the NEAC winter show had received an excellent review in the *Athenaeum*, which, in contrast to those who still balked at the rawness of his style and his subject matter, had grasped that his aim was not to shock. 'Mr John . . . may be perverse – at times he certainly is – but what he feels and sees he feels quite seriously and records with absolute simplicity'. Singling out one work in particular, the *Athenaeum* commented that *Mother and Child* had 'killed' all the other works in the show 'by making us realize that they lack this rarest of qualities, this inner life.'[14]

Shortly afterwards, Gus was approached by the British Museum, which wanted to buy some of his etchings and drawings. To his amazement, he realized he had a selection 'of about a 100' to show, while still having enough work to fill a solo exhibition at the Chenil, a new Chelsea gallery which he was helping to launch. There was also a good studio attached to the gallery, into which he could move; and now that he and Orpen were progressing with the sale of their school, it seemed to Gus that his professional life had rarely been so ordered.

Yet he was missing his family and missing Paris. Living on his own and subsisting on 'bad eggs and putrid dinners', he envied the easy, graceful domesticity that Ida and Dorelia enjoyed, and it made him think seriously about spending more time with them. On each of his visits, he'd felt more strongly that Paris could be his home. The cobbled streets of the Latin quarter, the alleyways of Montmartre, the little *bal-musettes* and seedy nightclubs – all spoke to him as London never had.

Like Gwen, he had got into the habit of sitting in cafes, watching and drawing 'the never-ending spectacle' of the streets around him.[15]

Through a new friend – the poet Maurice Cremnitz – he'd also been introduced to a circle of writers – the novelist Colette, the poets Paul Fort and Guillaume Apollinaire – who met regularly in the Closerie des Lilas cafe. Gus was greatly impressed by the writers' conversation – their impassioned opinions articulated in a colourful, often filthily idiomatic French, which he took pains to copy – and he could not help comparing his sophisticated new friends to those of his old London circle. Generous Will had grown irksomely pious, Michel was now solidly married, and no longer painting. Even Charles Conder had found a wife and reneged on his old buccaneering dissipation. As for his two oldest friends, Benjamin Evans seemed to have 'gone down the drain', while Ambrose McEvoy was drinking too much and, the last time they'd met, had been 'in a horrible condition, slobbering and wobbling and drivelling'. Gus was also reaching the limits of his friendship with Wyndham Lewis.[16] The quickness of the younger man's well-stocked mind, the lethal wit with which he dissected the characters of their mutual friends made him entertaining company. But his faults were becoming harder to ignore: the furtive lust with which he hankered after unsuitable women; the shameless way in which he borrowed money and the high-minded intransigence with which he refused to pay it back.

Gus had found other friendships – with Jacob Epstein, the rebarbative sculptor who was always good for a drink and an argument, and with Henry Lamb, a former medical student who was among the last intake of pupils at his and Orpen's dwindling school. Henry was talented and flatteringly inclined to worship Gus, imitating his drawing style, growing a beard and flourishing his own pair of gypsy earrings. He had an interesting girlfriend, too, in eighteen-year-old Euphemia, who seemed eager to behave as badly possible, especially with Gus. Yet London still lacked for him the glamour and stimulus of Paris, and, by early 1906, he began making serious plans to shift the balance of his life, trusting to the skill with which Ida and Dorelia had so generously managed to make room in Paris for both freedom and family.

Then, in the spring, he met Alexandra Schepeler. She was a typist at the *Illustrated London News* and, when Gus was first introduced to her (possibly by Frieda Bloch, her art student friend), he might easily have dismissed her as part of the young, vaguely artistic crowd which circulated around the pubs of Soho and the tables of the Café Royal. Yet there was something about Alexandra that mesmerized. It was partly her indefinable but exotic foreignness – handed down from her German father and Irish mother, from the childhood she'd spent in Russia and Poland – but it was also the promise of danger Gus saw in the sharpness of her cheekbones, the heavy-lidded seductiveness of her brilliant green gaze and in her carelessly entitled manner.

However much Gus revered Ida's intelligence or Dorelia's serenity, both women were encumbered, in his mind, with domesticity, especially now that Dorelia had fallen pregnant again. Alexandra – Alick – was just twenty-four, and she appeared to live principally for pleasure. When Gus asked her to pose for him, when he took her to bed, she didn't seem particularly interested in his art, nor particularly awed by his growing reputation. She chattered about her clothes, her cats, her books, her colleagues at work, and she was often elusive, refusing to see Gus as frequently as he wanted. The combination of her beauty and her insouciance only maddened his need for her. 'You are . . . one of those on whom I must depend – for life and beyond life. I am subjected to you – be loyal to your subject,' he wrote, and his imagination boiled with all the ways in which he wanted to draw Alick and make love to her. 'I have burst certain bonds . . . that bound my brain with iron and now my bewildered eye mixes dream with reality.'[17] When Gus looked at himself in the mirror, he saw a man scattered, undone by lust, and, in a self-portrait he etched that spring, his expression was savagely rumpled, his hair and beard flaring wildly around his face. He titled the portrait *Tête Farouche*.

Now, when family duties called him back to Paris, Gus was reluctant to go, and he counted the days to his return. Afraid that Alick might give up on him, he sent her a daily scrawl of everything he was thinking and feeling. He conjured elaborate sexual fantasies, in which he was peeping through a 'leafy screen or a key hole' while Alick 'gambolled [naked] like a 5-year-old', and he proposed ways in which Alick might pleasure herself. He even devoted paragraphs to the subject of his wardrobe, which he feared had taken on a life of its own: 'I have half a mind to get shaved and assume a bowler', he wrote, musing on how much simpler it would be to walk around the streets like an anonymous member of the bourgeoisie, but also how enjoyably shocking it would be to all his friends.[18]

No detail was too banal for Gus to share, but about Ida, Dorelia and the children, he was virtually silent. He might send Alick a drawing of David falling asleep over a half-drunk glass of lemonade, but the tenderness of the sketch was countered by the caustic irony of its caption: 'one of my kids opposite is enjoying my company in the following manner'.[19] Alick – his love for Alick, his pain at being separated from Alick – was all he wanted to write about, and in the full flood of his passion he could be as hectoring as Gwen. Alick, much like Rodin, was perplexed and exhausted by the tidal onrush of his letters, but when she gave up replying to them, Gus only sent more. 'Why don't I hear from you . . . my moon, my tender dove, rose of my soul . . . you darken my beautiful blue sky and dry up the waters of my content'.[20] Perhaps, if he hadn't been obliged to go so regularly to Paris, Gus might have tired of Alick, yet these periods of absence only made his desire more reckless. He must have sensed the moment would come when he would risk everything, but he was in so deep with Alick, he was unable to care.

Gus had a horror of secrets. The world in which he'd grown up had been shrouded in them, and now, even if he could thrill to the first clandestine rush of a love affair, the strain of keeping his emotions hidden almost always proved too much for him. He thought that the keeping of secrets was 'unnatural' as well as dishonest, and he disliked it even more when other people kept secrets from him. He particularly disliked it in Gwen, and now that he felt he should be seeing more of her in Paris, he was baffled by the walls of privacy she'd erected around herself.

Sometime in the summer of 1906, however, Gwen opened up to Gus and finally admitted the truth of her relationship with Rodin. To her, the confession felt enormous – she'd never exposed herself so nakedly to her brother's judgement, nor been so anxious for his support. Yet Gus himself was too shocked by Gwen's account to offer the understanding she craved. He could see nothing of beauty and grandeur in the love she described, only the folly of her submission to the whims of an old man's ego and the sacrifice of her youth and talent to an old man's art. So angry was he, in fact, that, rather than bringing the two of them closer, Gwen's confession became a trigger for one of their most prolonged and bitter rows.

Gus, in his genuine outrage at Rodin, his genuine concern for Gwen, begged her to end the affair and come back to London, where, he insisted, there were people who loved her and who wanted to support her work. Gwen, however, was only able to see blindness and arrogance in her brother's response. As she once admitted to Rodin, she had never forgotten the years when Gus had bullied her. They'd lodged in her memory 'like certain illnesses which recur in time' and, despite all that her brother had done for her and all the closeness they'd shared, she claimed there were still moments when she thought of him as her 'evil genius' and was afraid to be near him: 'I believe he will do me harm – perhaps without wishing to – if I do not avoid him.'[21]

Gwen had never actually planned to trust Gus with her secret. But, sometime in late June or early July, he'd asked her to come up to the Normandy coast, where he and the family were spending the summer. She, herself, had just lived through a nightmarish eleven days, during which she had lost her beloved Tiger and had believed her cat might be dead. And because she was left so weak from that trauma, she was not only feeling peculiarly grateful towards her brother when she joined him by the sea, she was far less vigilant about maintaining her guard.

For Gwen, the terror of Tiger's disappearance had been almost as excruciating as the loss of a child. She'd been returning from one of their Sunday walks in Meudon forest, when the cat had jumped out of the train and disappeared. For over a week, Gwen had searched, sleeping out at night in a little wooded copse, and it had only been fatigue that finally forced her back to her room. A letter from Rodin had been waiting for her, and Gwen trembled on opening it, yearning for her lover's sympathy. Yet there had only been a catalogue of complaints, as Rodin rebuked her for being obsessed with her cat, and for rushing around the countryside with no regard for her safety or health.

At that moment, Gwen was convinced she had not only lost Tiger, but alienated her maître's love. 'All is finished,' she wrote desolately to Rodin, 'I would like to live for longer but I will not be pretty and happy for you without my cat.'²² But, the following day, she received a note from a woman in Meudon who'd seen a cat matching Tiger's description. Gwen left rue Saint-Placide immediately, to camp out in the woman's garden and, three days later, was rewarded with the sight of a half-famished Tiger slinking out of the shrubbery. Her instinct then had been to keep her cat safely at home, but Tiger seemed so 'thin and nervous' and the weather in Paris had turned so hot that she decided she would take Gus up on his promise of 'some glorious swimming' and 'good sea air' in Normandy.

It had been the grit and dirt of an early London heatwave, meanwhile, that had first sent Gus out to France. He'd been feeling 'the dullest of all devils' and, with Lewis in tow, had found the remote fishing village Sainte-Honorine-des-Pertes, which had a camp of Piedmontese gypsies nearby and a community of 'wonderful sea women who collect shellfish, tall and quite prehistoric'. He'd wanted to bring Alick to this miraculous idyll, yet he knew it would be impossible to leave Ida, Dorelia and the boys for an entire summer, so his alternative plan had been to assemble the family at Sainte Honorine, while installing Alick and her friend Frieda at a convenient distance away, on the Channel Island of Jersey.

The summer was to be a seaside variation of his usual commute and Gus was confident of its success. He was attentive to his boys when they arrived, and David, who was usually so nervous in his father's presence, took to accompanying him on walks and climbing on his back when he went swimming. There were picnics and games: 'we have found a lovely place on the cliffs where we slide down. Gus goes down head first,' Ida reported to Meg Sampson, and she too was enjoying herself.²³ Lewis, who'd stayed on to rent a little house nearby, had set himself out to entertain, letting off fireworks, eying up the local girls and elaborating preposterous theories about his future. 'Today I laughed so much over the Poet's plans that I wept,' Gus told Alick. He had thought that Gwen would enjoy all this too. Yet, while she swam and walked barefoot on the beach, she was still overwrought from the drama of Tiger's disappearance. And, as she told Gus later, it had only been because she was so 'miserable' and 'crazy' that she'd trusted him with the truth about her love for Rodin.

She explained all this in the long letter she wrote to Gus once she was back in rue Saint-Placide. The row which her confession had triggered had been profoundly upsetting for her, and she needed him to understand how crushed she'd felt when he condemned her affair, how crushed she'd so often been, in fact, by his general high-handedness. 'We are so different! So different though our ages resemble. You have a great contempt for weakness. However there are people like plants who cannot flourish in the cold. I am one (and I want to flourish!) That is one reason why I have avoided you. Disapproval & snubs petrify me. It is not cowardice. If they were good for me I should know it and court them (in a way) but I know by experience they are not.'[24]

In writing to Gus, Gwen was painfully trying to correct the conclusions to which he had jumped at Sainte Honorine – that Rodin had been cruel to her, that her life in Paris had been made lonely and hard. On the contrary, she said, 'In my two years here I have had much love and pleasure & my mind has developed these last two years, my mind and body calming through it . . . What you call Rodin's insanity I call *adorable* weakness & sensibilité . . . as to my health and reason – don't fear for it. My mind does not totter except when I am feeling despair . . . My subterranean life was in Howland St . . . and I now see many more people . . . than I have ever.'

There was much more in the letter, parts of which verged into anxious incoherence as Gwen laboured under the stress of explaining herself, and as she questioned the very possibility of making herself clear to Gus – 'not from want of will but no words will express all or a part of the truth'. Yet the closing lines of her letter were beautifully candid, a simple expression of the love she still felt for her brother and the earnestness with which she longed for his sympathy: 'Chastise the others . . . but keep a place in your heart dear Gus a place of indulgence & tenderness, you will be much more than of "some use" to me, you will be a joy and strength if you do. Excuse the length and composition of this letter. It is from a little animal groping in the dark.'[25]

For Gus, this naked outpouring must have been difficult to read – he loved his sister and believed absolutely in her art, but he feared the extremes to which her wilful heart could take her. If he replied to her, though, if he acknowledged the justice of her criticisms, she didn't, apparently, keep his letter. And Gus himself had little enthusiasm for pursuing the discussion because, a few weeks after Gwen had left Sainte Honorine, he was lost in troubles of his own.

The heat of the summer had become oppressive and the holiday atmosphere had unravelled: the house was thick with flies, Lewis had become an annoying caricature of himself and Gus had been unable to work. It was too hot for him outside and too distracting in the house, where the older children were making their usual commotion and there was now the addition of a new baby.*

Dorelia had given birth to another boy, whom they named Romilly, and his birth was presumably straightforward, since it received no mention in any of the household's surviving letters. Presumably, with five children in the family, a sixth may no longer have seemed news. Yet it was unusual for Gus not to have commented on Romilly's arrival – to friends like Meg and John Sampson, he'd always sent fond reports of the other births – and the most likely explanation for his silence from Sainte Honorine was that the only arrival he cared about was Alick's, and she, outrageously, had stayed away.

Despite his stream of anxious enquires, despite the invitingly erotic sketch he'd drawn of himself, drink in hand, gazing lustfully at Alick's naked body, she'd preferred to go with Frieda on a walking tour of northern England rather than come to Jersey, as he'd proposed. Her correspondence, always uncertain, became alarmingly offhand, and Gus, terrified of losing her, wrote letters of maudlin self-pity. 'I sat in a garden the other day and wondered what there was in the world at all tolerable. I examined a tree attentively to discover any beauty in it – without success . . . I wonder why the devil I came here now – I curse myself and calculate the maximum number of years I have left to live.'[26]

This was a game Gus had often played with Alick, casting himself as the abject lover and her as the cruel mistress, but now there was nothing playful in his gloom. He felt himself numbed, trapped by misery, unable to read, work or even think, and he reached the point where it seemed his only possible escape was to make a full disclosure of his state to Ida

---

* The exact date of Romilly's birth is unknown, not only because no one wrote about it, but because Dorelia chose not to register it and Romilly himself never knew exactly when it was.

and Dorelia. He told them everything – about the depth of his love for Alick, about her importance to his art. Then, having thrown himself on their mercy, he may also have admitted to his half-formed plan of making a new change to their living arrangements, one in which Alick would come out to Paris and in which he too would spend more time in the city, so that he could divide himself equally between all three women.

After his confession, Gus felt giddy with irresponsible relief. 'I have thrown overboard all self-respect and am comfortable, free and on excellent terms with the devil', he wrote.[27] But he'd also cocooned himself in the kind of magical thinking he'd perfected as a child, simply refusing to consider that the most likely consequence of him telling the truth about Alick was to risk a final and complete alienation of Ida and Dorelia's love.

Dorelia was the most furious and hurt of the two. Despite all the ways in which Gus had disappointed her, she had never stopped trusting in the fundamental depth of their bond, and to hear him speak so passionately about Alick felt like a betrayal of all they'd shared. She told Gus she would have no part of his Parisian ménage à quatre and warned that, once they were back in rue Dareau, she would start looking for a new apartment for herself and her boys.

Ida's response was both more complicated and more bleak. She hadn't been particularly shocked by news of Gus's latest infidelity; she'd already endured his affairs with Estella and Dorelia, and had good reason to suspect there had been several others. Her anger with Gus and his women had now moved far beyond jealousy, to rage at the intrinsic selfishness of his character.

At the start of the holiday, he'd been delightful to them all – energetic, gay and attentive; yet, as soon as he'd fallen out of love with Sainte Honorine and slumped into his morbid depression over Alick, he'd behaved like a sullen and grouchy adolescent, his company impossible to endure. To Mary, Ida wrote, 'It's the mental state I don't understand', and, while she admitted that she was losing faith in Gus and in any future they may have together, she had just realized, to her horror, that she was pregnant again. Never before had Ida understood so acutely the trap that marriage and motherhood had become. 'I can't leave Gus and take his money and I can't keep the kids on what I have & if I left the kids I should not find peace . . . so I must stay as many another woman does.'[28]

When they all went back to Paris in late September, Gus was still convinced he could make his fantasy work. It all came down to finding the right places: a new flat for Dorelia, where her anger would surely cool; a tempting little apartment for Alick; and, for himself, a new studio at a more colourful address, 'some teeming street – where I can pounce on people as they pass, hob nob with Apaches and maquereaux [gangsters and pimps] and paint as I can.' As his imagination rioted with possibilities, he urged Alick to join him immediately. But, just as Gus had been wildly wrong in hoping for compliancy from Ida and Dorelia, he'd equally misread Alick. His sexy, carefree muse was a far more intelligent, practical woman than it suited him to imagine; she had friends, a job and her own independent life in London, and she was far too canny to sacrifice all these for an arrangement which sounded, on paper, so riskily improbable. It was so improbable, in fact, it was already becoming a public joke, with Lewis writing to his mother that 'John [would] no doubt end up building a city and being worshipped as the sole man there, the deity of masculinity'.[29]

When Alick made it clear she would not come to Paris, Gus went a little mad. 'I get fits of depression every two hours alternating with malign joy,' he told her, and rashly proposed they should forget about Paris and run away to somewhere new and exotic.[30] He picked destinations at random – Smyrna, Genoa or Bucharest – escaping into a fantasy of multiple irresponsible lives, but, when he came back to reality, he decided simply to go back to Alick in London. The relief of having settled on a plan sent him wheeling and gusting into poetry. 'I feel recurrent as the ocean waves, blue as the sky, ceaseless as the winds, multitudinous as a beehive, ardent as flames, cold as an exquisite hollow cave, generous and as pliant as a tree, aloof and pensive as an angel, tumultuous as the obscenest of demons.' When he finally held Alick in his arms, 'more adorable than ever', he told her that his soul had 'returned to its habitation'.[31]

Now, he was impatient for work – 'I have some 500 ideas for pictures in my mind – I absolutely must think out *at once*' – and he was encouraged by the letters coming from Ida, which made him believe she had decided, after all, to accept his affair with Alick: 'As to the love old chap, we all have our hearts full of love for someone at some time or other', she wrote, 'and if it's not this one it's the other one over there.'[32] What Gus did not guess from these letters, however, because Ida gave no hint of it, was that her acquiescence was simply a smokescreen – under its cover, she was now busy making plans to break free.

In Paris, Ida had been watching the admirable efficiency with which Dorelia had been establishing her independence. By mid-November, she'd found a new apartment in a 'lovely disreputable building' in rue du Château; she'd hired a childminder for Pyramus and Romilly and had got work as a model.* Even if Ida had to wait until her baby was born before making plans of her own, she had already begun to save for what she called her 'freedom fund', squirreling away cash from her household budget and using some money she was left by an uncle to buy a property in London which she could rent out to tenants. With careful saving, Ida believed she could be self-sufficient within less than a year. She could even imagine herself painting again.

Meanwhile, Ida continued to keep her secret beneath a veneer of distracting chatter. David and Caspar had started school, she told Gus; Edwin was not nearly 'so ratty'; she and Dorelia had been given supper by the 'nice and ugly and awkward' Constance Lloyd, and they'd also seen Gwen, who'd let slip that Rodin had made a small bust of her which was being shown at the Paris Salon.[33]

Ida wrote to Gus, too, about Winnie's imminent arrival. After two years on a horse ranch with Thornton, Winnie had grown tired of her brother's solitary ways and his resistance to her having 'beaus'. She had decided to strike out on her own, for the sunnier, more sociable prospects of California – but first she wanted to see the rest of her family, and, having visited Edwin in Tenby and Gus in London, she was concluding her tour in Paris. Ida, who was taking charge of the arrangements, told Gus that, in honour of Winnie's visit, she'd bought a new set of knives and forks and was getting them silver-plated.

In the past, such details would have bored him, but images of his two sisters, his wife and children all gathered together in Paris made him

---

* Dorelia's rent was a little expensive, at 300 francs a year, and she had to ask Gus to pay the deposit and sign the lease, since French law at that time prohibited women from managing large sums of money.

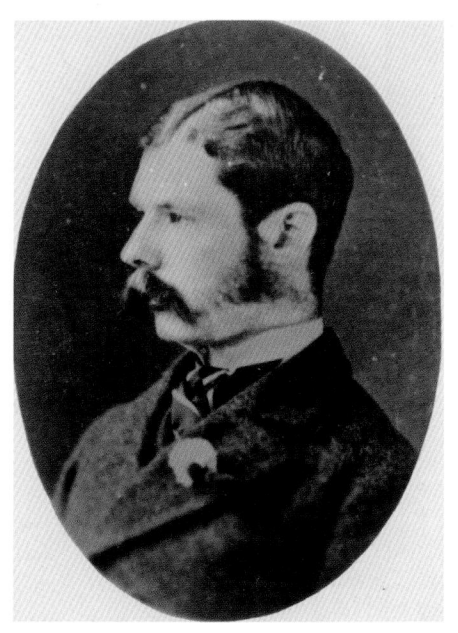
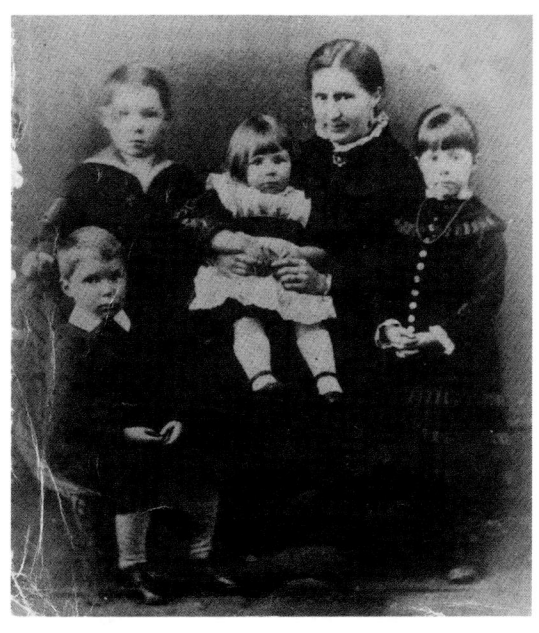

1. Gwen and Augustus John's father, Edwin John.

2. The four John children (left to right: Augustus, Thornton, Winifred and Gwen) with their nurse, c. 1880.

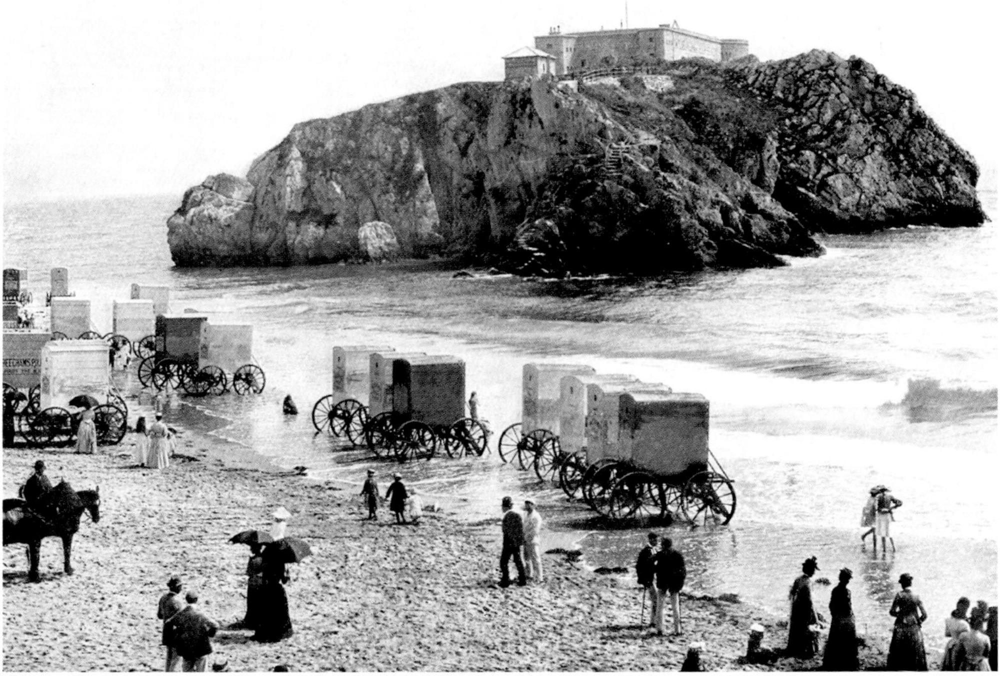

3. Tenby beach, c. 1890.

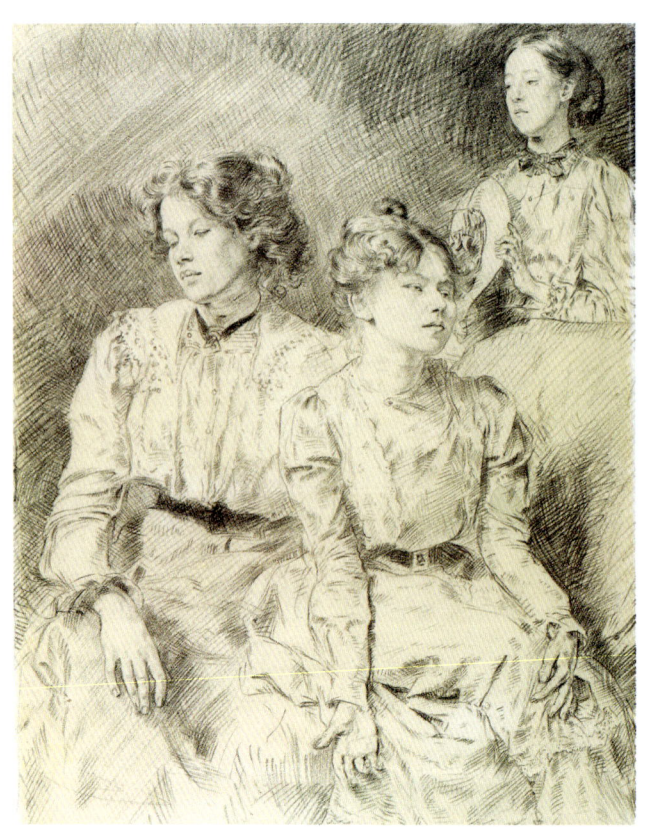

4. 'The talented and ornamental Slade girls' – Ida, Ursula and Gwen by Augustus John, 1898.

5. Drawings of Gwen by Augustus John, c. 1900.

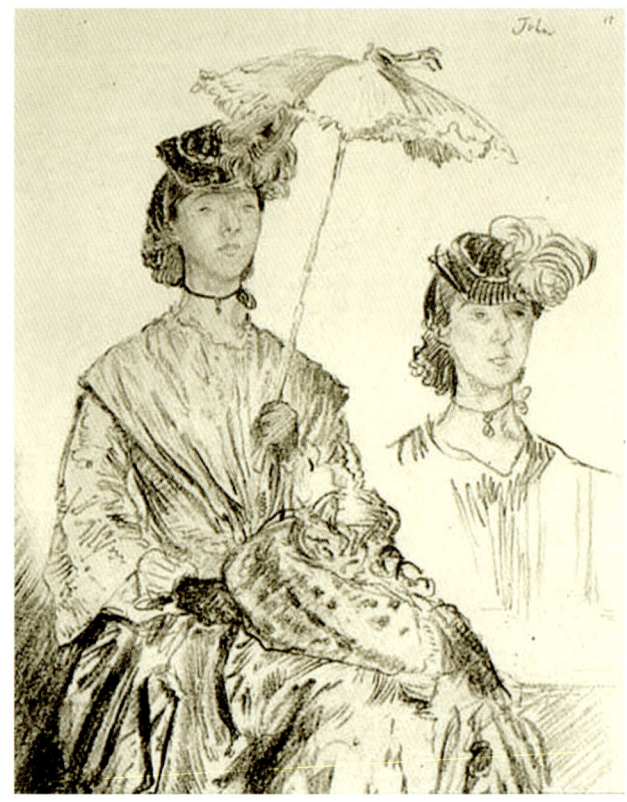

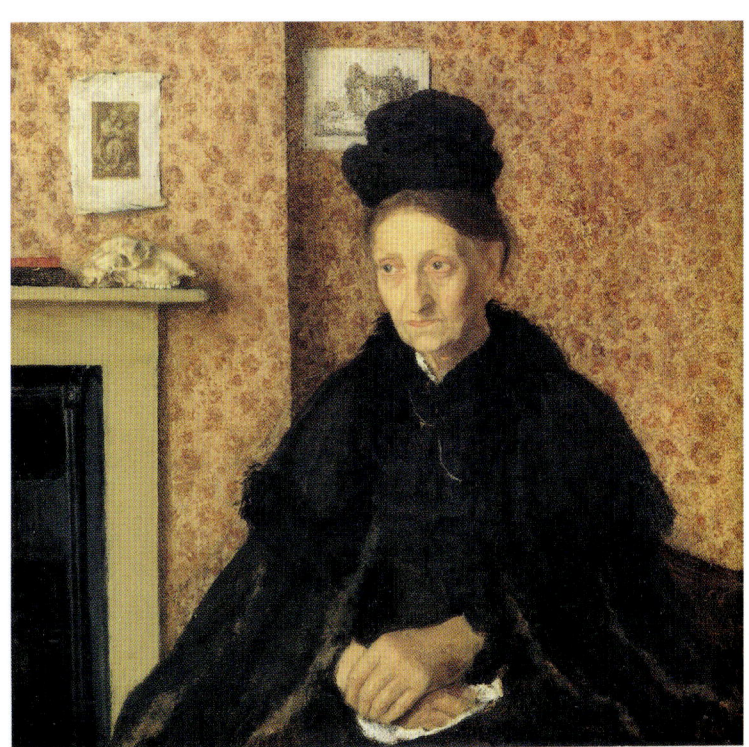

6. *Mrs. Atkinson*, Gwen John, 1898.

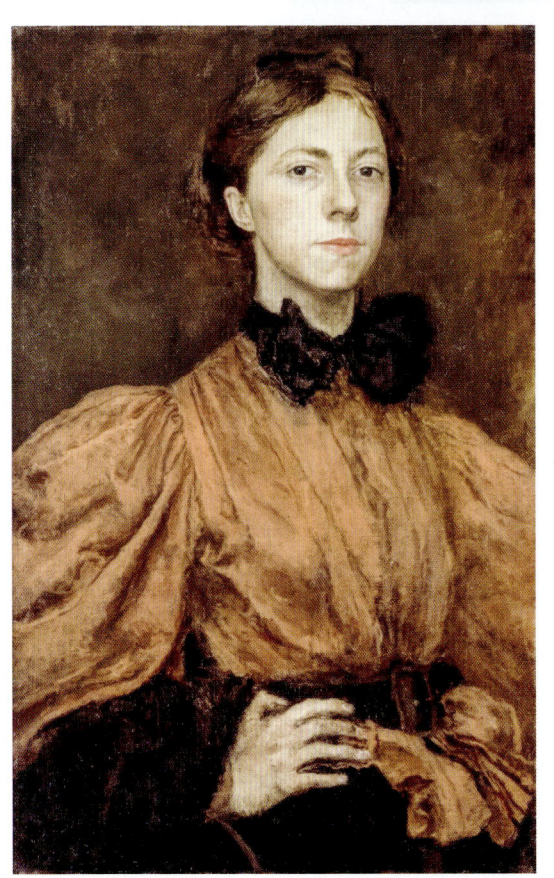

7. *Self Portrait*, Gwen John, 1899–1900.

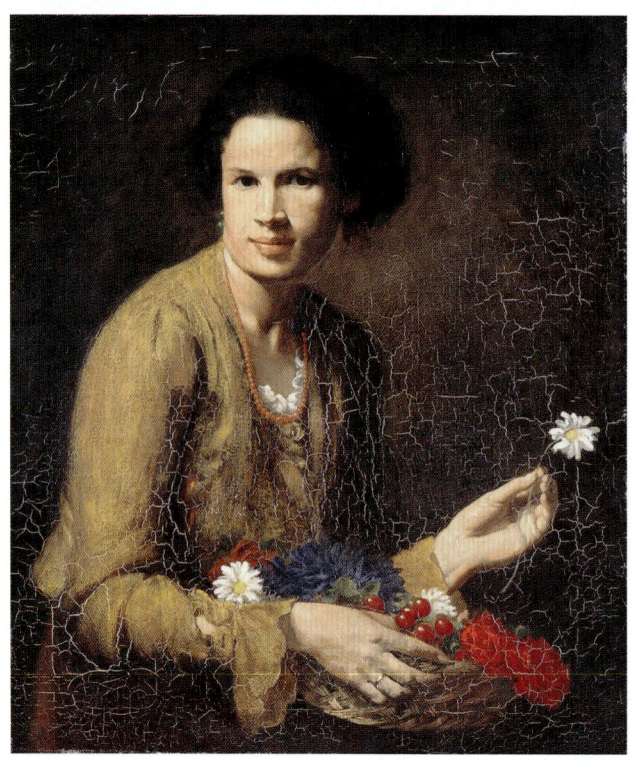

8. *Merikli*, Augustus John, 1902.

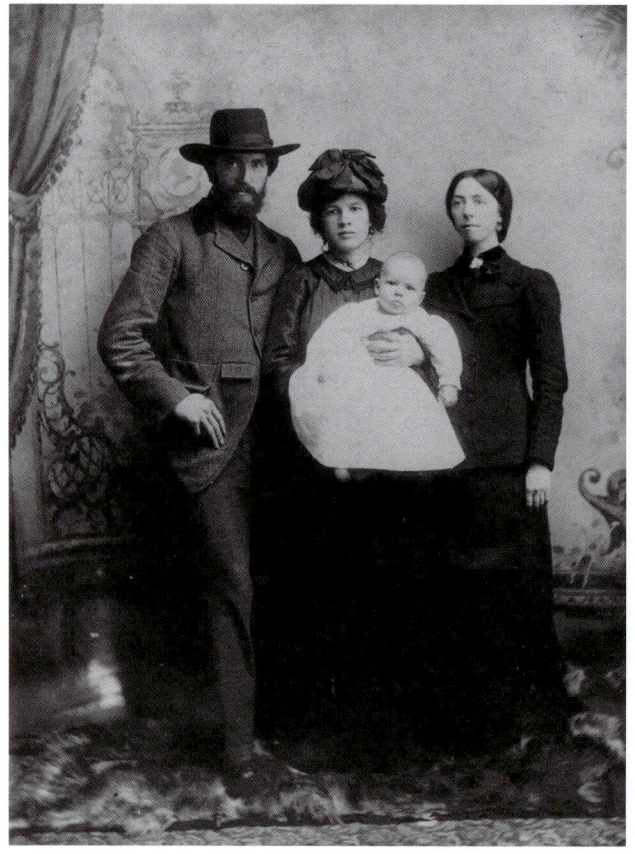

9. Augustus, Ida, Gwen and David John, Liverpool, 1902.

10. *The Student*, Gwen John, 1903–4.

11. Sketch at Matching Green with Elm House in the background, Augustus John, c. 1904–5.

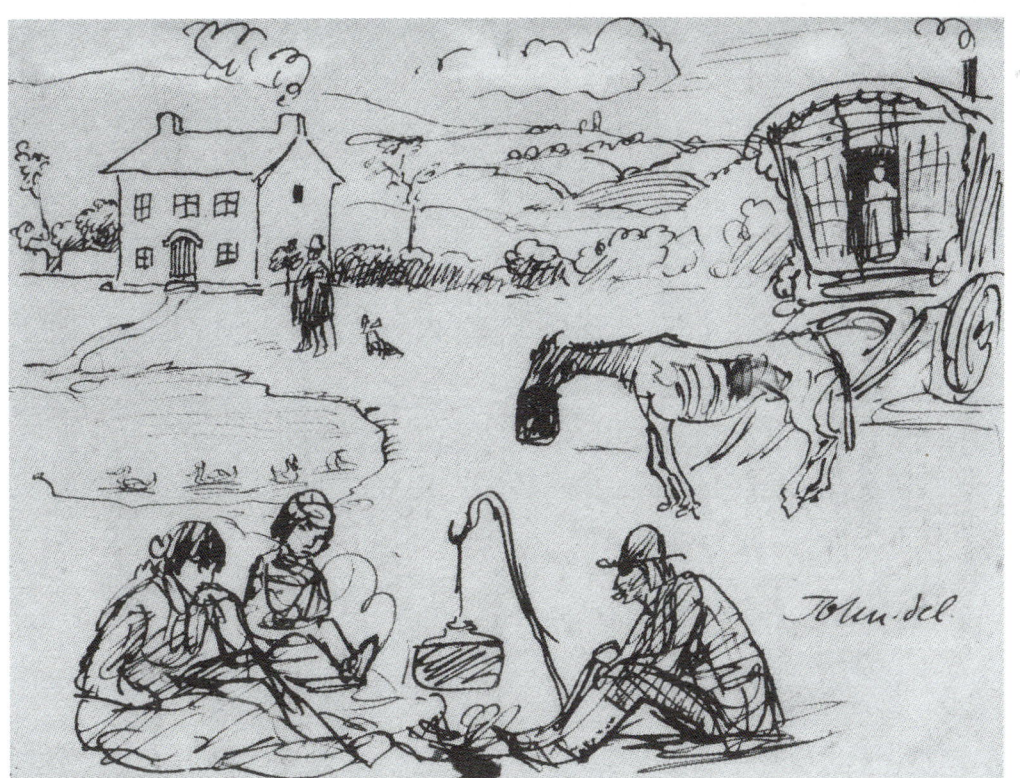

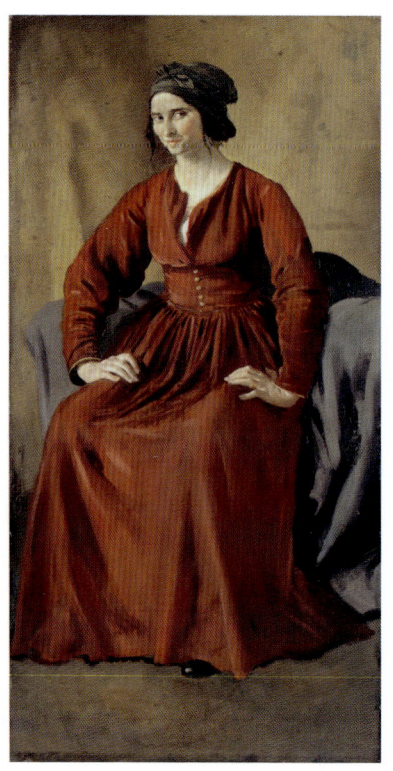

12. *Woman Smiling*,
Augustus John, 1908–9.

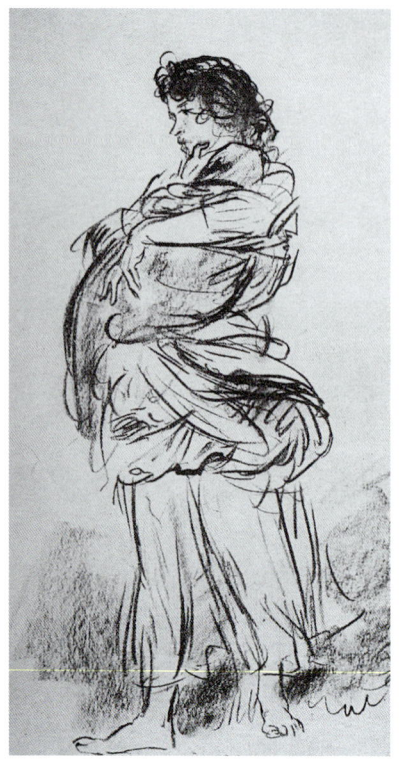

13. Sketch of Ida and Robin,
Augustus John, 1905.

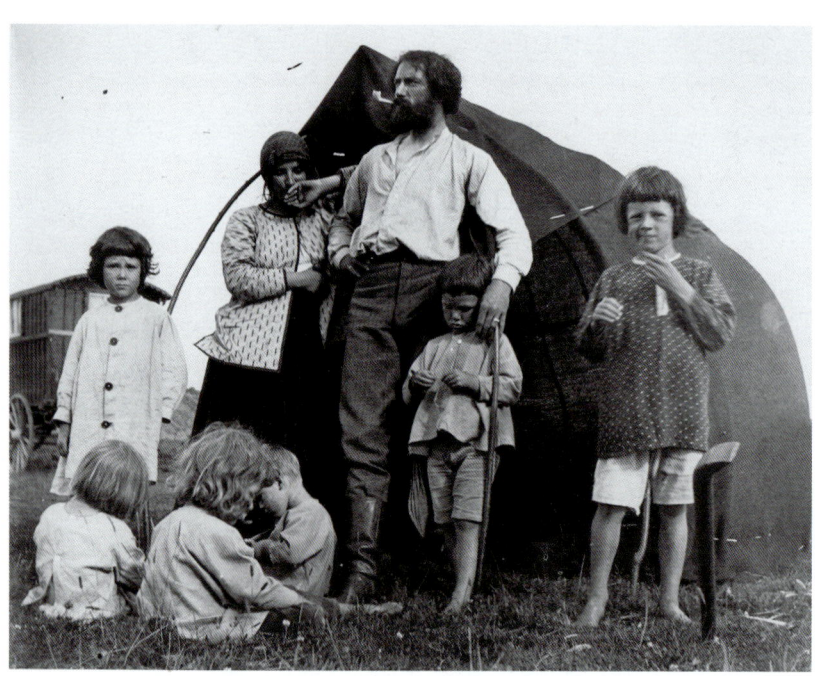

14. 'A dream of the nomadic life'; Augustus and his family, 1909.

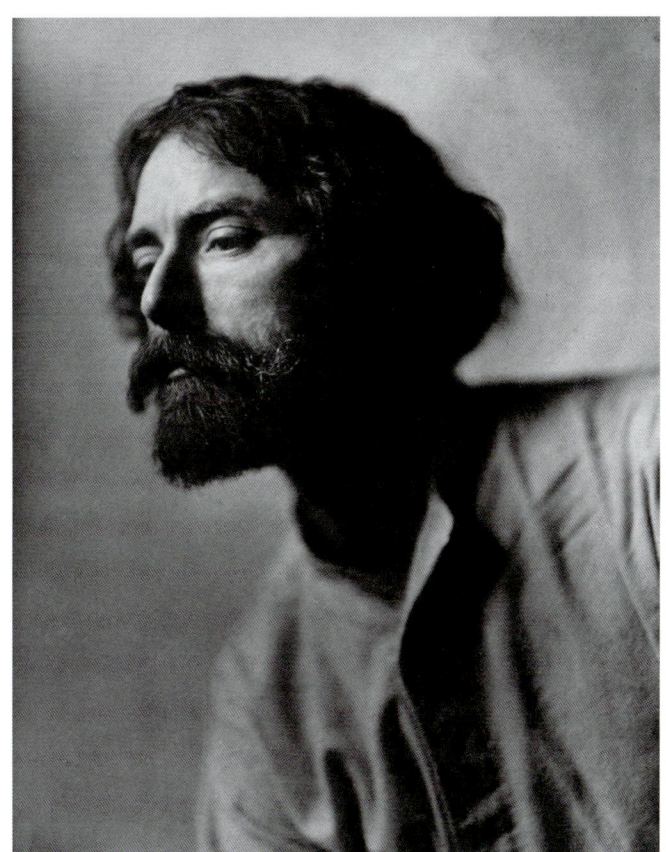

15. Augustus John, Jacob Hilsdorf, 1909.

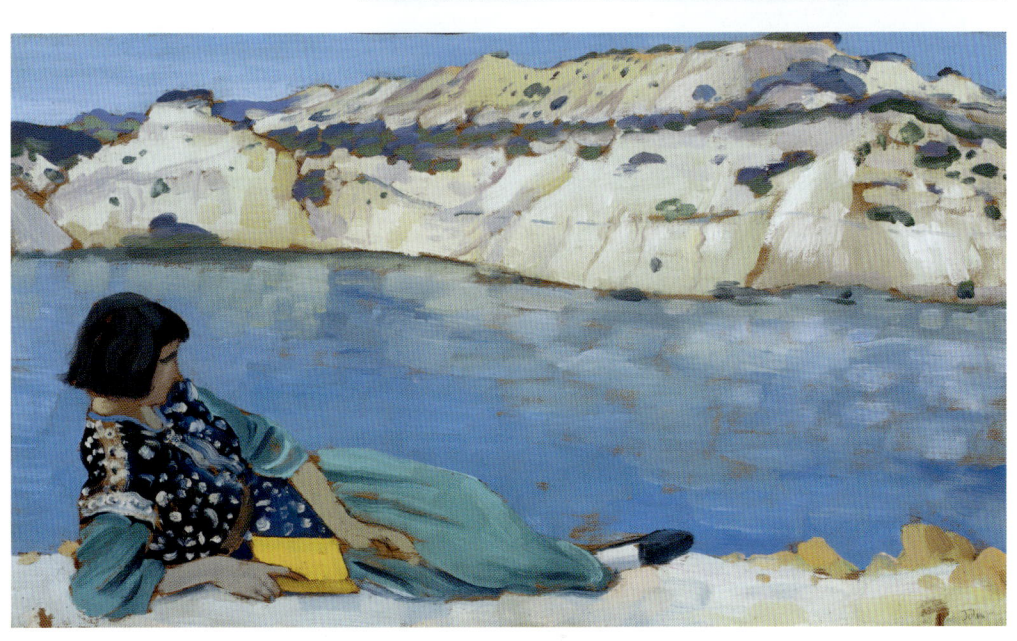

16. *The Blue Pool*, Augustus John, 1911.

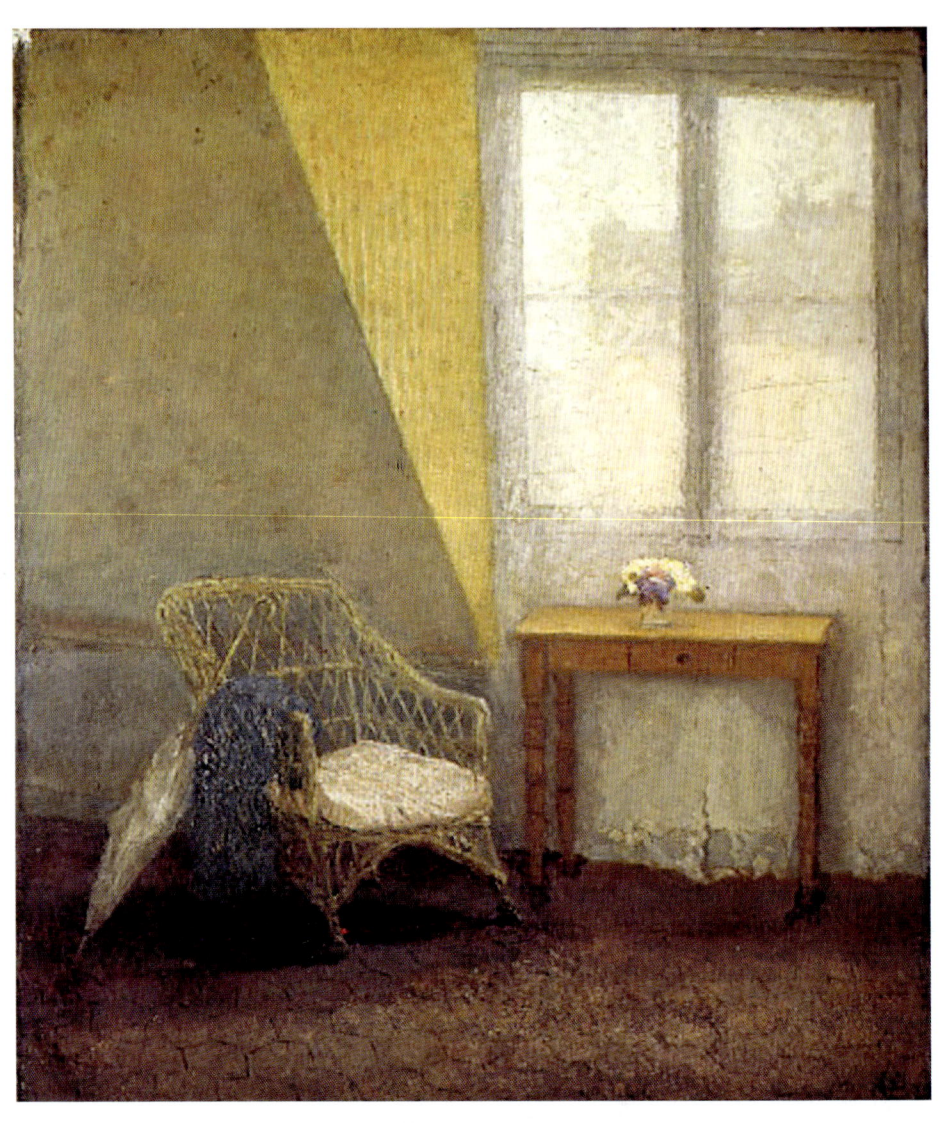

17. *A Corner of the Artist's Room in Paris*, Gwen John, 1907–9.

wistful. Adorable though Alick might be, his life in London was not comfortable. He was between studios again, moving from one 'beastly' borrowed room to another; reviews for his work at the NEAC winter show had been poor ('too insignificant to arouse even one's anger', wrote P. G. Konody[34]); and his stomach was unsettled, a sure sign of anxiety. He missed Ida's reassuring presence and, when he wrote to ask her advice on remedies for indigestion, he was disturbed by the near unsympathetic briskness of her reply.

Despite all their news and their chat, Ida's letters had become markedly cooler, they were no longer sprinkled with her usual whimsical endearments, and they worried Gus sufficiently to make him doubt the wisdom of all his recent actions. Alick might be scintillating, she might inspire him to confess things about himself he could never entrust to anyone else, but he recognized, now, that their love for each other was dependent on a fundamental fecklessness. It could never achieve the depth and permanence of his relationships with Ida and Dorelia; it would die if they set up house together. And, as Christmas approached and it was time for Gus to visit Paris, he was already starting to wonder how to mend the damage he'd done to his formerly beautiful arrangement.

To Dorelia, he wrote a loving overture, asking forgiveness and responding with self-righteous indignation to what must have been some caustic note from her: 'My Beloved Relia. I don't write to you without loving you or wanting to write. Believe this & don't suspect me of constant humbugging – who the Devil do you think I'm in love with! If you think I'm a mere liar, out goes the sun – I've been thinking strongly sometimes of clearing back over the Channel to get at you, you won't believe how strongly or how often.'[35]

To Ida, he forwarded cash for the Christmas meal, which she spent, extravagantly, on mistletoe, turkey, chestnuts, 'wonderful little cakes and punch au kirsch' and a *Père Noël* figurine, who was made to come down the chimney, 'bringing' presents for the children. David would not be present – Ada Nettleship had pleaded to have her oldest grandson with her at Wigmore Street – but there was still to be a crowd of them around Ida's improvised dining table: Dorelia, all the other little boys, Gwen, and also Wyndham Lewis, who was now renting a flat in Montparnasse.

Lewis was something of a bitter presence at that meal. He felt repelled by the overheated domesticity of the flat, deciding that Ida was 'much changed and no longer pretty'; that the children, confined indoors and spitting at each other in the bath, were an affront; and that Gus, in his sudden access of paternal enthusiasm, was in danger of castrating himself, and his art.[36] Yet Gus himself was so relieved to be among his family once more and so determined to regain their affection, he barely registered Lewis's sniping. In fact, he was positively cheerful when his stay in Paris had to be prolonged. David, at Wigmore Street, had fallen ill and Gus had to wait until his son was well before fetching him back home and then returning himself to London.

Gus also took advantage of those extra days to look for the studio he would need if he were to rebuild his life in Paris, and he was triumphant in his discovery of a ground-floor space to rent in a 'noble' town house, just off the boulevard Saint-Germain. The owners, intrigued to have a well-known artist for a tenant, were happy to let him convert the ground floor of their building into a kitchen, bedroom and painting area, and when a builder was found who could begin work immediately, Gus felt he was being practical, responsible, very adult. By the time he returned to London in mid-January, he was determined to push through the still-unresolved sale of his art school, and to start detaching himself from Alick.

Gwen apparently made no comment on these changes and reversals. Her five days in Sainte Honorine and her argument with Gus had made her even more protective of the distance she kept from her family. 'Silence is the element in which great things are formed,' she wrote in her notebook, a quote from Thomas Carlyle which reinforced all she had learned from Rilke about the potency of detachment.[37] She wanted to focus only on her work and on the works she might create with Rodin, and, late in the summer, she was joyfully vindicated when she was summoned by him to model again. One of the works he wanted to sculpt was a little portrait bust of Gwen herself, and it seemed so beautiful to her, in the purity of its moulding and in the serene but questioning expression he'd caught in her gaze, that she felt she was once again seen and loved by her maître.

He had, in fact, begun coming to her room more frequently, making love to her with more tender enthusiasm, and, if Gwen had been able to stick to her vows of self-reliance, that autumn might have been a period of contentment for her. But Rodin's visits and his lovemaking aroused her tearing hunger for him and the old vicious cycle set in, as Gwen poured out her heart in long letters of love and need, and Rodin retreated to an offended distance.

He may have been casting around for excuses when he told Gwen that he'd taken a dislike to her room in rue Saint-Placide, which he claimed was too stuffy in summer and too dark in the winter. And, while Gwen loved that room, she was so eager to please that she agreed to begin searching for another. It was late December 1906 – the fag end of the year – and, while Gus would have all the luck of finding his own new studio straight away, everything conspired against Gwen. The rooms she saw were either too mean and too chilly or too far beyond her budget, and when Rodin went travelling in early January, giving no word of his return, she was left to wonder drearily what she was trying to achieve.

A dull, depleted lassitude took over Gwen; she could hardly bother to dress herself except when she had to go shopping for food. Then Nuala O'Donel came knocking on her door, boasting that Rodin himself had requested her assistance in the hunt for a room. Gwen, galvanized as much by her dislike of O'Donel as by Rodin's concern, went back to her search, and eventually her fortunes changed with the discovery of a charming 'chambre de bonne' on the fourth floor of a classic eighteenth-century building, at 87 rue du Cherche-Midi. The neighbourhood was quiet and the room itself was almost picturesque – an attic with low sloping eaves and a window that overlooked a courtyard with a spreading tree.

When Gwen moved there, towards the end of February, she felt an immediate affinity with her room, an affinity that was almost spiritual. One morning, when she awoke at dawn and watched how the light filtered slowly through the darkness, she decided this was the hour when it was most beautifully itself. But then she thought it was 'prettiest' at noon, and, later that year, when she painted two small interiors of her rue du Cherche-Midi attic, she chose to show it lit by the midday sun.

Gwen never exhibited either version of *A Corner of the Artist's Room in*

Paris, and she never knew they would become two of her most widely loved works. Perhaps she saw them only as an experiment, a transitional project. Yet, at the time, she must have felt deeply absorbed in them, for they were painted with a detail so luminous, so alert that, even though Gwen did not paint herself into the room, it seems fully imprinted with the atmosphere of her presence.

In both versions of the picture, the compositional essentials look almost the same – the steep diagonal eave that cuts down one side of the space, the silvered light coming through the window, the small table and the wicker chair, which has a coat or dress draped over its arm. In one version, a rolled umbrella is balanced against the chair and a posy of flowers is on the table; in the other, an open book replaces the flowers and the window is ajar, the curtain lifting in the breeze. As an interior, it is beautifully complete, yet each of its precisely placed details – the book that looks so recently read, the flowers so recently arranged, the umbrella left so casually behind – also speak of Gwen herself. One can almost visualize her in this little attic corner, reading, drawing, waiting for Rodin, or setting out for a walk; in painting her room, it feels as though Gwen was also making a portrait of the self she'd created in coming to Paris, and in finding a space of her own.

The hopes Gus had entertained for his own new Parisian studio had meanwhile gone awry. When he returned to London in mid-January, he began to question the wisdom of shifting his base across the Channel. His best contacts were all in England; it would be difficult for him to build up an equivalent network in Paris. And when he began discussing with Ida the possibility of them living together again, he asked if she might consider doing so in London. With a disingenuous show of fastidiousness, he suggested that Paris was too insanitary and immoral a city for bringing up their boys; more convincingly, he promised Ida that he now had enough money to offer her a decent family house and proper domestic help, so that she would have all the freedom she wanted for her life and her work.

Gus still had no idea, of course, that the life Ida wanted was one in which she was physically and financially independent of him. She still loved him; she still acknowledged that he'd 'never pretended to be anyone other than he was', in his subjection to his impulses and desires; and she didn't want to push him entirely away. But she knew that their marriage could only be a losing battle between his needs and hers. When he wrote to outline his vision of them living together in London, she replied with what she hoped was a definitive rebuttal, reminding him of how badly they'd failed at marriage before, how risky it would be to make a second attempt.

But, while she pointed out how certain they were to start arguing again, how quickly the children would worry him 'to death', Ida found it harder to stand firm when Gus came back to Paris in early February. She was eight months pregnant and, even though the two older boys were in school and she had a new live-in nursemaid, Delphine, she was feeling like a 'bad-tempered lump' and believed she was failing all over again as a mother. She fretted particularly about David, confessing to Meg Sampson that he was growing into 'such a queer, twisted, many-sided kid. Horrid and lovely, plucky and cowardly – cruel and kind – thoughtful and stupid', and that he needed guidance from a firmer, wiser hand than her own.[38] It seemed to Ida that, if she couldn't even manage her children, she had little chance of holding out against Gus, and to Mary she wrote, with dull resignation, 'I feel duties beating little hammers about me and probably shall find myself padding about London in another ½ year – Damn it all.'[39]

Nothing was to be decided until after the baby was born. It was due in early March and Gus decided to remain in Paris. Work on his Saint-Germain studio had been completed and he wanted everybody to come and sit for him: Dorelia and Dorelia's sister, Jessie (who'd come to help mind the two little boys); Ida and her own four children. He was encouraged to linger in Paris, too, by the arrival of Henry and Euphemia Lamb, recently married, who brought entertaining disruption in their wake. Euphemia was angling to make herself notorious in Paris, setting her sights on Gus, on the occultist Aleister Crowley and other potential lovers. Henry, meanwhile, was showing signs of being smitten with Dorelia, and the writer Lytton Strachey, hearing rumours of these 'abominable' goings-on, was reporting that 'John and his ménage' had all been 'seen rolling down the boulevards drunk . . . The complications of their copulations became intense.'[40]

The rumours had been greatly exaggerated, and probably started by Euphemia, yet some ugly whisper of them must have reached Ida. To Alice, she wrote that it chilled her 'marrow' to think of being dragged back into the chaos of Gus's life and she wondered what kind of mother she was, to be bringing yet another baby into her unstable world.[41] Wearied by the hopeless circling of her thoughts, she decided to book herself into the local maternity hospital for the birth. She could stay for ten days, free of charge, and the strict visiting hours would give her respite from Gus's bounding expectations and from the children's demands. On the evening of 8 March, when her pains began, Ida packed her overnight bag, left instructions for Delphine and walked alone to the hospital. The baby came early next morning and, as predicted, it was another boy. 'I really admire him', Gus wrote proudly to Meg Sampson. 'He has a distinct profile and we called him Henry'.*

He and Dorelia had visited the hospital as soon as they were allowed, and their first glimpse of Ida, with Henry beside her, had seemed reassuringly normal. Within hours of his visit, though, Gus was told that Ida had developed an infection, a small abscess, and would have to be moved to another hospital for surgery. Ada Nettleship, who'd come over for the birth, didn't trust Gus to make the right arrangements, so, sweeping into action, she found a private hospital and 'one of the best men in Paris' to operate. To her daughters, she wrote confidently that, 'in 48 hours [Ida] will be quite out of danger'.[42]

But, when the surgeon investigated, it became clear the infection was not an abscess but acute peritonitis, and he could do nothing but dose Ida with morphine and then hope she could fight the infection herself.

Even now, Ada remained determinedly optimistic – Ida was blessed with a 'natural vitality', it all depended on her 'not giving way'. – and she threw her own formidable energy into managing the older boys, cleaning the flat and replanting the garden, which the children had dug into a mess of mud pies. However, the agitations of the last six months had weakened Ida, and when her temperature remained alarmingly high, even Ada admitted to panic. On 11 March, she sent an urgent message

---

* He was named after their favourite actor, Henry Irving.

to her daughters, asking Ethel to come to Paris but advising Ursula to stay behind in case Ida should be frightened by the sudden appearance of all her family.

Gus, by this time, was entirely stricken, and the ink-spattered note he sent to Meg was barely legible: 'Ida is most seriously ill after an operation. Excuse no more just now Yrs Gus'. As he sat by his wife's bed, fearfully alert to every hallucinating, shivering fluctuation of her fever, he was appalled by his own futility.[43] He was as powerless to save Ida's life as his father had once been to save his mother. On 13 March, he had a false moment of hope when Ida sat up in bed and loudly insisted she must leave the hospital and go to Dorelia's flat, where all she needed was a 'bottle of tonic wine, Cody's and an enema' to cure herself. But it was only the fever talking and, as she began to struggle fiercely with her sheets, Gus had to ask for extra morphine to calm her.

That night, he refused to leave her bedside, and afterwards told Mary, with a kind of awe, how strangely Ida had spoken to him in her delirium. There had been a heavy thunderstorm and Ida, who'd always 'adored stormy weather', had become very animated. 'How can I speak of her glittering smiles and moving hands', Gus wrote to Mary: Ida had had 'such charming visions', had said that she 'wanted to be a bit of the wind'.[44] She'd had moments, too, of childlike affection, when she'd tugged playfully at Gus's beard, asked him to rub her neck and tickle her feet. Early the next morning, she requested a sip of Vichy water and demanded that Gus join her in a toast. 'Here's to love,' she said weakly, and she had never seemed more heartbreaking to him – more valiant, ironic, romantic and true. But death was close and, at half past three in the afternoon, it came. The nun who had nursed her folded Ida's hands over a bunch of violets which Gus had fetched earlier and, at Ada's request, placed a crucifix and some lighted candles on the bedside table. 'C'était la destinée,' the nun said gravely, 'and we must believe it was the right thing for her'.

Arrangements then had to be made for Ida's body, but, while Ada and Ethel remained at the hospital, Gus's only instinct was to run. For four days he had sat and watched the slow extinguishing of Ida's 'beautiful spirit', and, as he later admitted, the relief of its all being over had filled him with a mad elation. Paris felt surreally alive to him, the sun was shining, the Seine was 'unbelievably fantastic like a Chinese painting' and he wanted to embrace every passer-by.[45] It was almost the same euphoria he and Gwen had felt when their mother had died and they'd run around the house shouting 'Mama is dead'. Even though Gus knew that grief would follow, and with it guilt, he could only feel glad that Ida and her 'poor dead beaten body' had been released to the world of her own dying visions – a 'land of miraculous caves', he told the Sampsons, 'where the air is pure & light enough for her to breathe in peace.'[46]

Chapter Nine

GRIEFS AND DUTIES

'I present a pretty spectacle of a paterfamilias'
AUGUSTUS JOHN TO URSULA NETTLESHIP[1]

It was Gwen who kept watch over Gus in the days after Ida's death, moving into his studio, where her quiet, watchful presence was a buffer against the onslaught of his grief. All of their former antagonisms, their fight over Rodin, had been displaced by the huge, intractable fact of Ida's loss, and Gus was deeply grateful that Gwen, as one of the few people 'who really knew Ida', would allow him to honour the courage by which his wife had lived.[2] He trusted Gwen not to falsify Ida's memory with sentimental platitudes and he also trusted her not to judge him when, unable to face the reality of what his life would now become, he went reeling around Paris on an extended drinking jag.

Dorelia was left to manage the boys – so young, they could barely comprehend what was happening to them – while Ada Nettleship took charge of the funeral. She had proposed, with a breaking heart, that Ida's body should be burned rather than buried, since Gus could not be trusted to look after a grave; but there was no report of her actual presence among the handful of mourners who gathered at the crematorium of Père Lachaise on 16 March 1907. Henry Lamb and Wyndham Lewis were there, but Gus had discouraged other friends from travelling over; Will Rothenstein's letter of condolence had been so lachrymose he'd simply ignored it, and Ambrose McEvoy, the one friend who had disobeyed orders and come to Paris, had 'the delicacy', Gus wrote, 'to keep drunk all the time and was perfectly charming.'[3]

Gus was drunk too, barely able to stand the idea of a priest intoning irrelevant words at Ida's funeral, barely able to credit that the urn of ashes he'd been handed was all that remained of his wife's beautiful, familiar body. Afterwards, an impromptu memorial was organized by Henry Lamb and, after that, Gus continued to drink, with Ambrose as his dogged companion. His behaviour was mystifying, even to those who knew him well. 'I can't tell if he is glad or sorry,' Lewis wrote, and Gus, at that moment, did not know himself.[4]

Of Gwen, there was apparently no mention – by Lewis or anyone else. The grief she felt was private – she shared Gus's revulsion for 'silly sentimental lamentations' – and it's possible she chose not to attend the cremation. Although she told Rodin that 'sadness had struck and [she] needed to be consoled', she advised him not to waste energy on writing to her brother.[5] A letter of condolence did come to her from Ursula Tyrwhitt, both touching and comfortingly direct: 'It's all so sad and I can only say how sorry I am. I've thought of you and Gus so often . . . It must be worse now, when one realizes every day adds to one's grief.'[6] But weeks would pass before Gwen could admit to Ursula the true extent of her feelings, the magnitude of her loss and, especially, her guilt. During these past two years, she knew she had not been careful of Ida. Consumed by Rodin, she'd blinded herself to her friend's unhappiness, had made herself, as Ida had written to Will, more 'mysterious flame like and impitoyable' than ever.[7] Now that Ida was dead, Gwen could only look back and mourn the braveness of her friend's character, her poetry and her honesty, and recognize that she had lost one of the truest touchstones of her life.

She was comforted a little by Gus's need of her, and by the little watercolour, *Sonnet*, which he painted around this time. It was a reimagining of her own early picture *Interior with Figures*, in which he had transported Ida and Gwen Salmond from their original Parisian setting to a sublimely romantic landscape of hills, rocks and windblown sky. It was a landscape with echoes of the golden-age Arcadias of Puvis de Chavannes, and was perhaps the closest to any heaven that Gus or Gwen could imagine for Ida.

By late April, though, Gwen no longer had Gus to share her grief – he needed to get out of Paris, to think about work and his future with his boys. She felt bereft of his presence, particularly as Rodin was busy and often abroad, and a portrait she sketched of herself that spring was an aching study in desolation – her hair hanging loose, her shoulders bowed, a haunted defencelessness in her face.

There were times when grief and loneliness made Gwen feel a little mad, and very vulnerable to danger: she believed that strangers were following her in the street, that a priest was trying to seduce her when his hand brushed against her arm on the tram.[8] In August, when she lost Tiger for a second time, she felt herself the victim of malign conspiracies. The leaflets she distributed, appealing for information, were desecrated with obscene puns about 'English pussy'; some of the people to whom she appealed were quite horrible, she thought, in insisting that Tiger must have died, while there were men who offered more enthusiastic aid but did so with 'strange gleams' in their eyes.

And, this time, there was no happy resolution to Gwen's search for Tiger; after several fruitless days of scouring shrubbery and woods, she was forced to accept she would never see her cat again. Back in her attic, she wrote a poem of mourning, her grief so profound she imagined herself following Tiger 'to the land of the dead'.

When she sent the poem to Rodin, however, hoping to make him understand the immensity of her loss, he dismissed her grief as hysterical, absurd. He punished her by keeping away, and this August was almost the lowest point of Gwen's year. At night, she was haunted by dreams of Rodin's former tenderness; at dawn, when she woke to the cold light of his indifference, she could hardly drag herself out of bed.

'I don't know when I can begin to live again,' she despaired to Ursula. But, although Gwen was often wretched in the months after Ida's death, she was not always so. Constance Lloyd and another new friend, a painter called Isabel Bowser, were both very kind to her, and it may have been their gentle influence which persuaded Gwen to attend a couple of painting classes at Studio Colarossi. Even Nuala O'Donel offered some help of sorts, inviting Gwen to model for a group of women who were on a sketching holiday outside Paris. While Gwen had taken the job mostly for the money, it had done her good to spend some time in the countryside, taking long bracing walks and eating home-cooked food.

It was Ursula, though, who was her best support. Their friendship had almost lapsed in the two years before Ida's death – when Ursula wrote to Gwen, she apologized for letting so much time slip past – but, in May or June, she came to Paris, intent on reconciliation. Her energy was boundless as she insisted on making the acquaintance of Gwen's neighbours and friends, as she organized outings to galleries, museums, restaurants and shops. She also demanded that Gwen take her to one of Rodin's open Saturdays, for she'd set aside her usual watercolours of landscapes and flowers and had begun sculpting a little terracotta head of Gwen, on which she was hoping to get Rodin's advice. Gwen herself must have had mixed emotions about taking Ursula to meet her maître, yet the visit passed off well. She was gratified by Ursula's open admiration for Rodin's work, even more by the nod of approval which he gave to her terracotta head. And the warmth Gwen felt on seeing her friend and her maître together had apparently prompted her to tell Ursula everything about her and Rodin's affair.

This time, she didn't regret her confession. Ursula was far more tactful than Gus had been, refraining from any comment on Rodin's behaviour, concentrating only on the importance of Gwen returning fully to work. She encouraged Gwen to show her what she'd begun painting and drawing that year and gently reminded her that an artist of her talents should not be earning her living by modelling but through the sales of her own work. After Ursula left, her words and her encouragement continued to resonate with Gwen, and it was around now that she probably started work on her two attic pictures, with their vivid expression of her Parisian life. It was now, too, that she found a new model to sit for her, and began painting her first portrait in oils since moving to Paris.

Chloe Boughton-Lee was the sister of Grilda, Gwen's contemporary at the Slade, and the two sisters had come to Paris for a season of painting. Although Gwen hardly knew Chloe, she saw something in her large ungainly features, in her expression of gentle diffidence, which appealed to her eye as well as her sympathy. When she asked Chloe to sit for her, she wanted to capture that diffidence, that tremor of uncertainty. She wanted to paint Chloe as though she'd been caught unawares, and, although it had been over three years since Gwen had painted Dorelia in Toulouse, the recent studies she'd been making of herself and her cat had all been giving her a mastery of movement and atmosphere. In the finished canvas, Chloe gazed out at the viewer without artifice or defence, her eyes vague and startled, her frock slightly rumpled, her hair hanging loose around her shoulders. It was a portrait that lived in the moment, and for Gwen it signalled a new register in her painting which would take her through a period of unexpected and often unsettling change.

By the winter of 1907–8, Gwen was feeling so much stronger in both her health and her work, she was developing a new acerbic confidence in standing up to Rodin. When he wrote to apologize for cancelling a promised visit, assuring Gwen that he still loved her and wished for her happiness, she retorted that he had 'a very strange way of showing it.'[9] She threatened to have nothing more to do with him unless his behaviour improved, and, to her slightly bewildered satisfaction, she discovered that this more caustic line of attack was very piquant to him.

'I have been very stupid in never scolding him enough,' Gwen wrote to Ursula the following summer. 'I see now that I should have done so much more – there is no one else but me to do it, everybody spoils him . . . I adore him & so it is dreadful to be angry with him – I see it must be so, though.'[10]

Just as Rodin was showing a renewed desire for Gwen, there was also a sudden flare of public interest in the Whistler memorial. In London, the International Society of Sculptors, Painters and Engravers had become concerned by the non-appearance of their statue and, early in 1908, had asked for a photograph to be sent. Rodin's Muse, in her massive nakedness and strangely bowed pose, was not at all what they'd imagined, and the committee were loud in their dismay. But, in Paris, the critics who were also shown the photograph were entranced: the Muse had 'a modern beauty equivalent to the most beautiful art of antiquity', wrote one, and another declared that the sensuous, sensitive curve of Gwen's back was 'one of the most astonishing things' he'd ever seen.[11]

A year ago, it would have meant everything to Gwen that her collaboration with Rodin was attracting so much praise. But, under the influence of her friends, she was learning to care more about the art she had made herself and the importance of having it seen. Rodin had done almost nothing to promote her work – his efforts to encourage her drawing had been motivated largely by his own self-interested desire to redirect her attention and her energy away from him. Had he acted differently, of course, had he used his vast influence to introduce her work to one or two of the smaller galleries or to one of the Salons, the shape of her career might have been different. Acknowledgement might have come earlier. But, for years, Gwen had wanted nothing from Rodin beyond his love, and it was only now, as she learned to hold herself a little apart from him, that she was ready to listen to the encouragement of her friends. 'Even your postcards give me energy and inspire me', she wrote to Ursula, and, in the spring of 1908, when Ursula came back to Paris, Gwen gratefully accepted her help in selecting two pictures for submission to the NEAC summer show.[12]

One was the Chloe portrait; the other was a more recent work, *La Chambre sur la Cour*, which had evolved from one of the studies Gwen had drawn of herself in her room at rue Saint-Placide. It was a quiet interior in which Gwen sat at her sewing, her profile dark against the sunlit window, her cat (still Tiger, at that time) curled up on the chair beside her. Ursula thought it very fine and, even though Gwen panicked about the practicalities of sending her work to London, she was already thinking about what she might do if they sold. During the winter, she and Ursula had talked about taking a large flat together in Paris. It had seemed a distant, expensive prospect then, for she knew that Rodin wouldn't care to subsidize the extra rent. Now, if there really was a market for her work, Gwen saw that the possibilities of her life might be very different.

As she waited for the show to open in May, Gwen worried that she was deluding herself into thinking either of her pictures would sell. But Chloe purchased her own portrait, while the poet Frances Cornford bought *Chambre sur la Cour* – and, even more encouragingly, Gwen was given her first serious review when *Studio* magazine singled out her Chloe painting as 'one of the greatest achievements in the exhibition'. More praise also came in a letter from Will Rothenstein – so enthusiastic, Gwen wrote, 'it took my breath away', and Gus too was beautifully quick to write, declaring both paintings to be 'simply staggering' and expressing outrage that they'd been priced at a derisory fifteen pounds, when he thought they could have fetched fifty pounds each.[13]

*

Gus's praise was important to Gwen – as she'd written to him two years earlier, she'd never been able to bear his 'snubs or disapproval'. Yet she was particularly glad to hear from him now, because, after the intimacy they'd shared in their grief for Ida, the two of them had drifted on their separate ways.

For Gus, the months after Ida's death had been a period of shattering strangeness, but also of difficult decisions. Once he'd emerged from the anaesthetizing effects of his drinking jag, he realized that plans had to be made for the children. In his mind he formed a hazy, hopeful vision of finding a large house in London where Dorelia might become mother to all seven boys. But, even if Dorelia agreed to such a scheme, he couldn't yet afford it. He had been neglecting his work, and the sum on which he'd been counting from the sale of his art school had never materialized. Jack Knewstub, who'd been secretary to both the school and the Chenil Gallery, had allowed the profits from one to be spent on the other. And, until Gus could enrich his account with some profitable commissions, he had no home, no security to offer his family.

When Ada Nettleship stepped in with her own proposal, Gus could only be grateful. Her principal concern was the three older boys, who'd been most obviously distressed by their mother's death, and while she judged that Edwin and baby Henry were small enough to remain for a while in Paris under Delphine's care, she was impatient to get David, Caspar and Robin back to Wigmore Street, the first two enrolled into school. She implied it would only be a temporary arrangement until Gus was back on his feet, and he had no reason, then, to doubt her word. She'd been such a strength to him during Ida's illness and death, he had come to feel a trust, even a sort of love for her.

'Dear Mother', he wrote to Ada shortly afterwards:

> It's so difficult to realize that Ida has gone so far away she was the most utterly truthful soul in the world and there was nobody like her.
>
> If she could only just come to sit and sit for me sometimes – I've never painted her – I thought I had so much time and began by getting at sidelights of her only, counting on doing the real thing in the end – she was such a big subject.

> If I hadn't been with her that night it would have been a thousand times worse – but she was so gay and spiritual – the world seemed too stuffy for her. She has found her own rare atmosphere now.[14]

So complete was the faith Gus placed in Ada, he could not guess that her plan was ultimately to get custody of all five of her grandsons. She had, however, been more appalled than he knew by the manner in which the boys were being raised. While she'd always loved Ida, she thought her weak as a mother, allowing her children to be dragged from one scruffily unsuitable flat to another, their manners unchecked, their hair uncut. She could only imagine what savages they would become if they were left to Gus. He might possess some boisterously endearing qualities as a father, but he had no patience, no domestic skills. In fact, Ada believed that, when she did eventually propose taking custody of the children, he would only argue against it as a matter of form and would be glad to be relieved of his responsibilities.

But Ada had underestimated Gus. Even though he had no immediate plans for his boys, they were his only link to Ida and he would not give them up, nor would he allow Ada to undercut Ida's most fundamental desire for her children to become intellectually curious and physically independent. A photograph sent from Wigmore Street, in which David, Caspar and Robin were scowling hotly at the camera in shorts, jackets, boots and wide-brimmed hats, was troubling evidence for Gus that Ada had already discarded the jolly, practical clothes Ida had made for her boys and was trussing them up like 'bourgeois Victorian prigs'. Gus wrote back to suggest that Ada should send them to stay for short periods of time with friends of his, like Edna Clarke Hall or Ambrose McEvoy, who could be trusted to keep Ida's influence alive. 'It is a pity to scatter them so,' he acknowledged, 'but one will know what to do later.' And, for Ida's sake, he also urged his mother-in-law not to discourage the children from talking about Dorelia, who, he warned, was going to be 'much in evidence in the future.'[15]

It was a shot across Ada's bows, but Gus was unable to do more. He needed to work, and he needed to be alone to think about the ideas that had been coming to him since Ida's death. As he'd admitted to Ada, he'd never known how to paint Ida while she'd still been alive; despite all the portraits he'd done of her, she'd remained too 'big [a] subject'. All he could hope for now was to paint her spirit, and search for a style to do it justice. His previous attempts at portraiture seemed hollow and inadequate, and, from his still limited knowledge of the new Parisian artists, he'd seen little to inspire him to a new direction. 'One feels these chaps have stumbled on something alive', he told Will, 'without being able to master it.'[16]

That April, when Gus left Paris, he wound his way north towards the Boulogne coast, and ended up in the little fishing village of Equihen. It was set in an austere landscape of empty rolling dunes, ramshackle fishing sheds and vast skies – a place, he thought, for serious reflection. 'I don't know that I feel really *wiser* through my sorrows,' he wrote to Alick, 'but at any rate I feel more knowing. I also feel curiously more myself.'[17] For weeks, he remained there on his own, making sketches of the fishing people, slowly letting his imagination work its way onto paper. 'I haven't got at it really', he told Henry Lamb in June, 'but my "head" still yields enchanting suggestions. In fact, call it what you will, [my head] is my best friend.'[18]

In July, Gus went briefly back to Paris, where he met the young Spanish painter Pablo Picasso. He'd already heard of Picasso, and his bold, precocious talent, and he may have asked Maurice Cremnitz to engineer an introduction. Their meeting, in a cafe, was friendly, and after Picasso asked Gus to show him some drawings, he invited him back to his own Montmartre studio, where he'd recently finished work on his most experimental painting, *Les Demoiselles D'Avignon*.

This huge canvas, with its ferocious concentration of sexual energy and fractured form, was like no painting Gus had seen – and he wasn't sure he liked it. Its five naked women, with their angled bodies and blank devouring gaze, were not his women, its argument with tradition was not his own. Yet it was painted by a man who was far more arrogantly sure of his vision than Gus, and he wanted to know more. Afterwards, when he looked through pictures from Picasso's earlier 'Blue' and 'Rose' periods, he found in them a style and sensibility which appealed more directly to his own; they had a poetry that reminded him of Puvis de Chavannes and he saw in them elements he could use.

After he left Paris and returned to Equihen, he began work on *A French Fisherboy* – a drawing of a barefoot youth with huge ears, etiolated limbs and eyes that burned in the hollows of his face. The boy could have been one of the beggars or drinkers, saints or lost souls from Picasso's paintings; he looked both biblical and contemporary, a figure outside time or place; and, in drawing him, Gus felt he was moving towards the imaginative freedom for which he'd been searching.

He wanted his family with him now, to figure in this phase of his work, and in late July he asked Ada to bring the three older boys from London, and Dorelia to bring the four younger ones from Paris. Already, he had several portraits in his mind, including one of Dorelia and Pyramus – who, at three years old, had grown into a blue-eyed cherub: 'the essence of a daisy', Gus thought, 'a divine little phrase from Shelley or Wordsworth.' The studies he drew that summer would find their way into *A Family Group*, a huge landscape in which Ida, holding baby Henry in her arms, stood together with Dorelia and three of the boys. Each of the figures was painted with loving accuracy, the children fidgeting, scowling, peeping shyly around their mothers' skirts. Yet the world they inhabited came direct from Gus's imagination, a blue abstract wash of valleys and hills, and, beyond them, a grey and gold flourish of mackerel sky.

There was a dreamy suspension in this 1908 work, a synthesis of the poetry Gus had seen in Picasso and Puvis de Chavannes. The poetry of his models, though, had been hard to access at first, for, when David, Caspar and Robin arrived in Equihen, they looked dreadfully unpaintable to Gus – suited and booted in their London clothes, and worryingly under the thumb of Ada's discipline. He made determined efforts to reclaim them, encouraging them to fill their bedrooms with frogs, grasshoppers, stones and driftwood, to strip off their clothes and swim naked in the sea. Ada herself, however, would not budge, for she was adamant in her determination not to leave her grandsons alone in Gus's care.

She claimed she was responsible for their welfare, and she plainly felt her concern was justified when Gus and Dorelia refused to consult a doctor about the eye infection that was spreading through the family and when the older boys, allowed to swim unsupervised in the sea, had to be rescued one day by a fisherman. While Ada informed her daughters she was trying to 'be nice' to Gus for the sake of the children, a series of photographs that were taken of him on the rocks at Equihen, striking absurdly classical poses and wearing nothing but an improvised loin cloth around his skinny hips, suggest how much of a provocation he was to her.

Towards Dorelia, whom she blamed for destroying Ida's life, it was even harder for Ada to be civil, and her hostility was impossible to contain when she learned that the pain and nausea from which Dorelia was suffering were the consequence of a self-induced abortion. It made Ada sick to the soul to think that such a 'child murderer' might one day be entrusted with her grandsons' care. And she might have felt sicker still had she known that one of the reasons why Dorelia may have chosen not to have this baby was her uncertainty about who had fathered it. It could have been Gus, but it could equally have been Henry Lamb, who, back in the spring, had become her lover.

Gus would defend Dorelia when he and Ada clashed bitterly over the morality of this abortion; he pointed out that Ida, too, had attempted to end one of her pregnancies and that he personally would 'have killed many an unborn child' if only it could have saved Ida's life.[19] Over the course of the holiday, he became furiously irked by his mother-in-law's high-handedness, her persistent self-righteous interference, and it may have been a quirk of malice that made him invite Henry and Euphemia Lamb to stay in Equihen.

Henry did not come, he was too deeply in love with Dorelia to be comfortable in such a situation, but Euphemia arrived in a state of glinting excitement, accompanied by her Swedish lover and wielding a knife, which she claimed she was ready to use on Dorelia, in revenge for the theft of her husband's affections. Just ahead of Euphemia had come Lewis, and, under the influence of his three ill-assorted guests and all the alcohol they consumed, Gus gave up almost every pretence of responsible fatherhood.

For Ada, her last shred of confidence in Gus was destroyed when she saw him in the company of 'these vile people'. He'd become 'hopeless – just one mass of selfishness – not thinking of anyone but his own desires.'[20] When he was hauled off to jail on charges of homosexuality – having been caught making love to Euphemia while she was dressed in men's clothes – Ada declared it was 'war to the knife'. By the time she went back to London, she was determined not to leave anything of Ida's behind, not only taking all five of the boys with her, but also the little urn containing Ida's ashes.

She made no further attempt to conceal from Gus her determination to gain custody of her grandchildren. As soon as he realized that she'd already begun taking advice on the matter, he wrote a sharp letter from Equihen, threatening to take back his sons unless Ada could show more respect for the spirit in which their mother had wanted them raised: 'Having been nearer to her than anyone else in the world', he wrote, 'I know best what [Ida] would have wished.'

Gus was aware, however, that he still had nowhere to take his boys, and he seized gratefully on the idea (floated either by him or by Ursula Nettleship) that Ursula should replace Ada in managing their care: 'If any consideration could move me to part with the children it would be the fact that *you* alone would have them. The immediate future has an unsettled aspect for me. Homeless penniless and lawless I present a pretty spectacle of a paterfamilias. But thanks to you things *begin* to look much more tractable'. He told Ursula that he trusted her to ensure his sons grew up to be 'brave intelligent and gay', admitting how shocked he'd been when they first appeared at Equihen. 'I really was beginning to fear I shouldn't recognise them in a year or so or they me.' And he begged Ursula to ensure that Dorelia remained part of their lives: 'she is a very rare and respectable being . . . I should like her always to continue to give the children the benefit of her honesty and simplicity and affection and help to dress them bravely too, as she knows how.' For his part, he promised that, even when he was ready to take back his sons, he would ensure they stayed close to their Nettleship family.[21]

'My greatest wish is to re-establish friendliness and patience all round,' he wrote. But Ada was in no mood for conciliation. She read through what Gus had written and tossed it aside, snorting that it was typical of his 'selfish introspection and gross ingratitude' and that it deserved to be met with 'a good slapping letter' from a lawyer.[22]

Decades later, Ida's sister Ethel would write to Caspar about the fight between her mother and Gus, and regret that there had been so obdurate a clash of personality and expectation. 'Gus being so young, & with so much fine feeling' had created a kind of 'wreckage', she wrote, when he'd come into collision with Ada's 'Victorian' family values, and the two of them made each other 'as selfish and passionate as they could be.' Ultimately, Ethel laid most of the blame on her mother. 'Gus really *tried* with [her] . . . and a wise elder woman could have done him no end of good . . . I think he longed for it, for his tremendous vitality and passions used to get the better of him. But mother only growled & scowled and complained'. In hindsight, it was clear to Ethel that Ada had not only failed to understand Gus but Ida too; she may have 'worshipped and spoilt' her oldest daughter, but she had never appreciated that Ida, with her determination to live a 'grand life . . . going full tilt', was always going to marry a man like Gus. 'I'm sure they none of them knew where they were heading', Ethel concluded, and it was clear to her that the real victims in this situation were not the adults but the children who were so tragically caught up in the fight.[23]

Gus, determined to win, was now focused on making money. Portraiture was still his main source of income – and, after Equihen, he went to Ireland, where he'd been commissioned to make an etching of the poet W. B. Yeats, as frontispiece for a new collected edition of his work. It had probably been Robert Gregory, a student at the Slade and the son of Yeats's friend and patron Augusta Gregory, who'd proposed Gus, and he'd been quick to accept the commission, not only for its eighteen-pound advance but for the promise of additional cash if he agreed to sketch members of the Gregory family.

In September, he arrived at Coole Park, an austere stone house, made beautiful by its woodland setting and by the flock of wild swans on its lake. He'd come in a rush, with only his paints, brushes and pencils, and the clothes he'd been wearing at Equihen. Lady Gregory professed some nervous surprise when he appeared in her drawing room dressed in an old fisherman's jersey, with 'all his luggage hanging from one finger', and Gus heightened her apprehensions when the long, formal meals at Coole House provoked him, once or twice, to flee the dining room and, in a fever of restlessness, go shinning up a tree or sculling across the lake.

But he was determined to fulfil this commission quickly and well. He'd already met Yeats briefly, in the houses of both Jack Nettleship and Will; he was ready to charm and be charmed, and, once he began work on his portrait, he was able to relax. He and Yeats drank whiskey together, and they reached what they believed to be a unique and mutual sympathy. 'He is most delightful, nobody seems to know him but me – unless it is the Gregorys,' Gus boasted to Alick, and Yeats claimed a similarly privileged insight: '[John is] the most innocent wicked man I have ever met . . . A good and well-behaved man. The only difference is in code.'[24]

Yeats had been nervous of sitting for Gus, knowing his reputation for 'making everybody perfectly hideous, beautiful according to his own standard', and he'd been relieved by the youthfully romantic image Gus had painted in his preliminary oil portrait.[25] The etching Gus then made, however, was much darker, with thickly scored lines and cross-hatchings which, according to Lady Gregory, made Yeats look like 'a tinker in the dock or a charwoman at a prayer'. She refused to sanction its publication and Yeats agreed. With almost priggish anxiety, he wondered what had inspired Gus to make this 'drunken unpleasant and disreputable' image of him when he was always so 'particular . . . never to appear unshaven [or] dissipated.'

But, once Yeats had recovered from the shock to his vanity, he found this etching strangely compelling; he thought Gus had captured something deeper than reputation or 'character', some wild, exiled part of his soul where he was most himself as a poet. The oil portrait now seemed to him 'fanciful', the etching rather 'wonderful', and he defended it stoutly, writing to his publisher that, 'all fine artistic work is received with an outcry' and recommending to friends that they should all get themselves drawn or painted by John.[26]

Gus himself was quite satisfied by the commission. The fee enabled him to rent a new studio in Fitzroy Street, from which he was able to set himself up for a winter of work, completing a portrait of Alick and working up the studies he'd made in Equihen and Ireland. With exhibitions organized at the Chenil, the Carfax and the NEAC, he was soon buoyantly in profit – 'I'm making millions,' he boasted cheerfully to Henry Lamb after having earned £225 from just one morning of sales. The critics were still divided. MacColl might celebrate the 'wild flame of life' in his drawings, while the sceptical *Athenaeum* considered some of his paintings to be 'nightmares' – either indifferent to technique or incapable of it. But his reputation was on the rise. An illustrated study of works by students and alumni of the Slade, published in 1907, identified Gus as one of the school's most masterly talents, and his name was spreading to more monied and more socially elevated circles. Hugh Lane, Lady Gregory's nephew, was interested in him, so too was Lady Ottoline Morrell, who would not only start recommending his work to her relatives and friends, but for several years would claim Gus himself as the project and love of her life.

Ottoline was a very shy woman, whose cold, stifling childhood had driven her to take refuge in poetry and art. She had dreamed, as Gwen and Gus had dreamed, of '[breaking the] bounds set by the world' and, because she had no artistic talent herself, she collected around her those who did.[27] Gus the untamed genius was exactly the kind of man she longed to know and, when she was first introduced to him, by Charles Conder, she was predictably mesmerized. His eyes, she wrote, 'were of that mysterious pale grey-green colour, more aesthetically and poetically perceptive than any of the darker and more definite shades.'[28] His voice, from the few remarks he uttered, sounded 'deep and melodious', while his hands were 'more beautiful almost than any man's hands I have ever seen'.[29]

Gus had barely registered Ottoline at the time. It was the spring of 1906, he'd just met Alick and was consumed by the complications of his cross-Channel life. When they met again in early 1908, however, at a dinner given by Ethel Sands, he'd been glad of their slight acquaintance. That dinner had seemed a miserable prospect – Ethel Sands was a painter, but also an ambitious hostess, and, while Gus knew she could be helpful to his career, he much disliked the prospect of being forced into a dinner jacket and put on show. He had been suffering from his regular winter attacks of indigestion and catarrh; he was grieving for Ida and was prone to 'terrible glooms and ennuis'. To Henry Lamb, Gus wrote, 'I can think of no one I want to see and am yet tormented by solitude'.[30]

But, seated beside Ottoline at dinner, Gus found her an unexpectedly kindred spirit: she spoke to him about Balzac, Dostoyevsky, the work of the French primitives, and, while he was often uneasy around sophisticated women, he was touched, even flattered by her enthusiasm. He was also frankly fascinated by Ottoline's appearance. Loomingly tall, with a beaky nose and a jutting jaw, she was, he wrote, a 'yard or two too long' and very far from what he considered beautiful.[31] Yet she dressed like no other woman he'd ever seen. As soon as she'd been old enough to decide her own wardrobe, Ottoline had instructed her dressmaker to create extravagantly romantic costumes, modelled on the wide crinolined skirts, the lace and ribbons of the past. These costumes had become Ottoline's armour and disguise, a deflection from her bony awkwardness, and Gus had recognized something of himself in her willingness, he wrote, 'to go over the top.'*

Shortly after Ethel Sands' dinner, Ottoline came to Gus's studio, accompanied by her husband, the Liberal MP Philip Morrell. They were interested in commissioning a portrait of Ottoline, even though, as they looked through Gus's work – stacked against walls, propped on easels – it seemed to them a bemusing confusion of styles. Another couple arrived – the painter Vanessa Bell and her art-critic husband, Clive. Ottoline knew them to be members of the 'Bloomsbury Group', a tight little circle of painters, writers and intellectuals – 'wonderfully remote beings' whose acquaintances she yearned to make; and when the Bells began exclaiming over the wonder of Gus's work and asked to buy a small picture of Pyramus, any hesitation Ottoline felt about having her own portrait painted was immediately shelved.[32]

The studies which Gus drew of her, lyrical pen-and-wash sketches which gave a sibylline elegance to her face, were amazing to Ottoline. She saw herself made beautiful through his eyes, and she could not stop thinking about him. 'The figure of this man, so questionably remarkable, living a life so completely different from anything I saw around me, haunted and disturbed me,' she wrote. Her life outside the studio became 'absurd' to her; she longed only for their meetings and she filled the days in between by writing ardent letters and searching out expensively thoughtful gifts – handsome editions of poetry, rings, scarves, concert tickets, and a replica of the enormous hat worn by Thomas

---

* Over time, Ottoline's wardrobe would grow bolder and more capricious: her crinolines spread wider, her heels became higher, her hats more extravagant and her use of cosmetics more startling. As Virginia Woolf would write savagely in her diary on 12 October 1918, she started to look as 'brilliantly painted and garish as a shipwreck'.

Carlyle, which even Gus admitted was not to be worn 'every day of the week – stupendous, it reduced even the rudest street gamin to speechlessness.'[33]

At first, Ottoline wouldn't dare admit how deeply in love she was. Although she and Philip had an open marriage, and Gus was notorious for his own affairs, she was afraid of exposing her feelings and being rebuffed. Gus, in fact, had seen clearly what Ottoline felt, but he too had been wary of acknowledging it. While he'd been tempted by several other women during the months after Ida's death, he knew that his battle to regain his children and to persuade Dorelia back to mother them all was dependent on him maintaining an appearance of virtue. An affair with the socially prominent Ottoline would be hard to conceal, and – more bluntly – he was not particularly attracted to her; she touched and intrigued him, yet he admitted that he found her 'rather awful to examine closely.'[34]

He hadn't, however, reckoned with the force of his own natural gallantry. On 25 May, when Ottoline wrote to convey her burning admiration for his art, to beg another session in his studio, Gus misjudged the enthusiasm with which he replied: 'If I had words to express the kind of excitement your words fill me with . . . Do not doubt I would be overjoyed to be "bothered" to draw you.' Five days later, when Ottoline came to his studio, she believed he was ready to receive her love. She told him how perfectly she understood his conflicted character – his 'ruthless animal gypsy side' and his 'simple nervous sensitive side'; she said how passionately she longed to soothe away his loneliness and how certain she was that their relationship could soar into something wonderful, lit by a 'creative flame' and bound by 'experiences of the soul'.

Gus was so moved, he felt compelled to make love to Ottoline, but as soon as she'd left the studio he regretted his mistake and wrote to tell her that they must never repeat it. 'When you were in my studio today I wished I could cry . . . with the delicatist and noblest woman loving me so infinitely beyond my deserts. Do you know what a horror I have of hurting a hair of your head and bringing a shadow into your thoughts?' He tried to warn her of his own faithless record. 'We *can't* go on thus, darling that you are'.[35]

Yet Ottoline was deaf to reasoning or danger. With Gus she felt transfigured, beautiful and free; she needed her Elffin, as she now began to call him, to realize her truest self. So, as Gus weakly allowed the affair to continue, all he could do was lower her expectations, try to convince her that their future together could only be that of intimate friends. 'You must know that I do care for you and how I hate to pain you but I see the inevitable . . . Forgive me . . . you are the most generous soul in the world and I the unworthiest.'[36]

Gus also never allowed Ottoline to forget that the woman with whom his real future lay was Dorelia. Throughout much of the winter and spring, he'd been visiting her in Paris, riding out long months of ambivalence during which she'd rejected his half-serious proposal of marriage and had threatened to go travelling around Europe with Henry Lamb. Gus had continued to press his own case, arguing for the practical logic of Dorelia joining him in London, the emotional logic of having all seven boys under one roof. Then, late in June, without any warning, she gave in. 'Dorelia has suddenly turned up here to help with the children,' Gus wrote to Ottoline. And, while he tried for her sake to moderate his relief, he informed her that, in celebration of this happy outcome, he was going to take Dorelia and as many boys as they could manage on a holiday to France.[37]

Gus sent immediate word of his plan to Ada, asking for David and Caspar to be brought round to Fitzroy Street the following morning, and apologizing for having to leave the three younger boys behind. Ada, of course, had no intention of relinquishing any of her grandsons and fired off a furious warning to Gus that she would have him arrested if he made any attempt to remove them. Inevitably, her threats inflamed Gus, and he informed Ada that, instead of two boys, he now demanded all five. 'Take your proceedings at once,' he taunted, 'but deliver up all my children in your charge by tomorrow morning.'[38]

It was an absurd confrontation and became even more so the following day. Straight after breakfast, Ada took the three oldest boys to London Zoo, planning to keep them hidden; Gus, however, coaxed one of her maids into revealing the ruse and, according to the farcical account he sent Lewis, he trailed her to the zoo, gave 'heated chase through the monkey house' and finally ran Ada to ground behind the pelicans' enclosure. Grabbing two of the boys, he bundled them into a taxi, swearing he would keep them hostage until she agreed to his demands.

There was no obvious way of resolving this stand-off, but in the end Gus offered up the concession of Henry. It may have occurred to him that a fifteen-month-old toddler would be hard to manage while the family were travelling around France, but he may also have been thinking, less selfishly, of Henry's best interests. Since coming to London, much of the little boy's care had been given over to Ida's unmarried cousin, Edith, and because she and the Nettleships were essentially the only family that Henry had known, Gus could see it would be kinder to let him stay where he was. No formal decision was made at first, but over time the arrangement became permanent: Edith became Henry's guardian and Gus would only see his youngest son for holidays.

By early July, he, Dorelia and the rest of the boys were in Paris. The city had never seemed so 'amazingly beautiful and brilliant', Gus reported back to Ottoline, and, as virtuous as his intention to devote himself to family had been, he was unable to resist that brilliance. He took himself off to the galleries, curious to know more of Picasso and the 'moderns'. He spent hours at a retrospective exhibition of Cézanne. And, in the company of a new friend, a gypsy guitarist called Fabio de Castro, he went to a night of flamenco. The harsh, keening melodies of the singers, the intent, undulating grace of the dancers were all so new and extraordinary to Gus that he felt as elated, as restless, as when he'd first met the gypsies at Cabbage Hall. He needed suddenly to be out on the road, and, as soon as he'd left Paris and taken the family to Cherbourg to look for some seaside lodgings, he set off walking on his own.

For two weeks, he tramped across the countryside, sleeping rough in ditches and barns, and narrowly avoiding arrest for vagrancy. He spent two 'very wonderful' days with a troupe of circus performers and, on his way back to Cherbourg, he met a convoy of Russian coppersmiths – a miracle of noise and colour, he told Will, 'like artists in a world of petits bourgeois'.[39] The desire to tag along with the Russians, to buy a couple of caravans and horses for himself and the family, was very strong, and, if Gus had had sufficient ready cash, he might have given in to it.

But he needed his funds to last out the summer, and he also needed to work. The Cézannes that he'd studied in Paris had affected him greatly: landscapes that had been whittled down to their elemental forms; portraits that were raw and awkward with life; and all of them painted with a control of colour that, as Gus told Ottoline, was 'more powerful than Titian's and searched for with more intensity'.[40] When Gus found rooms in the little fishing port of Diélette, it was that intensity for which he searched. The pictures he did that summer moved into a new register for him: David and Dorelia, painted in a windswept palette of greys and blues; a woman who stood on a clifftop of brilliant green, poised between a lowering sky and an electric, indigo sea.

That woman was Edna Clarke Hall, who, by an extraordinary coincidence, had come to Diélette on holiday with her husband. Edna's arrival had been emotional for Gus. Memories of Ida had come vividly alive to him, now he was with his boys, and to share those memories with Edna, one of Ida's dearest friends, was a bittersweet pleasure. The two of them spent long days together, walking and sketching, and they were often alone. Willie, who disapproved of Gus, chose to avoid his company, while Dorelia was occupied both by the boys and by Henry Lamb, who'd made a sudden appearance from Paris.

The situation was now becoming highly charged, and it so affected Gus that, once again, he nearly risked everything with Dorelia. One afternoon, when he was drawing Edna, his heart was so full that he kissed her. 'There was something very lovely about it,' Edna admitted, forbidden desire mixed with sorrow for all they had lost, but she believed Gus when he promised never to repeat it. A few nights later, however, when the adults all met at a local inn, Gus drank too much and, needled perhaps by Henry's attentions to Dorelia, he began singing to Edna – a loud, crassly amorous serenade, which was embarrassing for everyone.

Dorelia was so angry, she grabbed Edna's hand and ran with her back to their lodgings – she may even have thought about packing her bags and leaving Gus altogether. But she had made her own private consultation with fate when deciding to go back to him and she chose to let the incident pass. Gus himself was penitent and, when they returned to London in mid-September, he began a conscientious search for their new family home, eventually deciding on a large Georgian villa at 153 Church Street, in Chelsea, with a nearby patch of waste ground on which the children could play. He joked to Ottoline that he and Dorelia would become good 'bourgeois folk, with carpets and front doors and dining rooms'.[41] But more earnestly he told her that their own affair must stop. 'I love no one living more [than Dorelia] and in loving her I am loyal to my wife [Ida] and not else [sic].'[42]

To underline the seriousness of his intentions, Gus now signed off his letters to Ottoline as 'John'. It was, in fact, how he generally preferred to be addressed these days, even by those who were close to him. He was thirty, he relished the professional gravitas of his surname and, apart from Dorelia, there were very few people who called him Augustus, and only his siblings still used his childhood diminutive, Gus.

Even so, for Ottoline to have her Elffin recast himself as 'John' was the clearest possible signal of his altered feelings. It was hard for her to bear, and Gus often had to be stern in quashing her attempts to rekindle their affair. But he was never cruel and, as with many of the women he'd loved, he continued to value her as a friend. He went to her for advice about his children and his health, he made appeals to her generosity when trying to drum up support for Jacob Epstein and for other of his impecunious peers. Most wonderfully to Ottoline, he made her his confidante, sharing his thoughts about art, confessing his struggles; and she was able to compensate for the loss of his love by imagining herself in the role of his helpmeet, helping to guide him towards the greatness of which she believed him capable.

As the years passed, though, their friendship diminished, for the world in which Ottoline moved, with its parties and dinners and intricate social connections, was ultimately boring to Gus. And while she would find other artists and writers to love and to manage, he would find other patrons to help fund his career. Indeed, by the summer of 1909, Gus was already being courted by a rich American lawyer who possessed far more money and influence than Ottoline could ever command.

Chapter Ten

MONEY

Gwen and Gus had once thought that money was irrelevant; as students, they'd believed that all they needed was a roof over their heads, materials with which to paint – and their freedom. Edna recalled that Gus had been particularly scathing in his contempt for the rich: 'These ridiculous people who think you can't ride a horse unless you've got the proper clothes.'[1] Over time, the pressures of his growing family had obliged him to moderate his scorn and to court his wealthier clients for commissions. Gwen, however, had never wavered in her independence. Living alone, in her small basic rooms, she'd remained almost an innocent about money. And, in the summer of 1908, when she'd discovered that Rodin had taken a glamorous American for a mistress and was apparently being corrupted to a life of expensive pleasures, she felt it as a betrayal not only of her love for him, but of her belief in his essential greatness.

Claire de Choiseul had made no secret of her social ambitions when she first arrived in Paris. She'd used her money to buy herself a husband, an impoverished marquis; she'd adopted the brazenly fake title of 'Duchesse' and, on meeting Rodin in 1904, had been very intrigued by the possibilities of his fame. Even though Rodin had dismissed her, then, as a typically brash American, he'd eventually succumbed to the persistence of her attentions. Claire, in her early forties, was still very youthful – red-haired, with a round, supple body which she dressed in the latest fashions, a plump mouth and a liquid glance. Even more seductive to Rodin, she made him laugh.

To a degree that Gwen had never accepted, Rodin was feeling his age. He'd become tormented by fears of impotency, both in bed and in the studio, and Claire, with her naughty anecdotes, her extravagant frivolities and her American ways, had made him feel young and vigorous again. By the spring of 1908, he was seeing so much of her that the marquis was suing for divorce. By this time, too, Rodin had all but relinquished to Claire the control of his finances, his diary and his public image.

Claire did love Rodin, but she loved even more the prestige she could gain as his mistress. While she might never achieve the status of Yonkers-born Winaretta Singer – who, as the Princesse de Polignac, held court over the most prestigious cultural salon in Paris – she could still make herself very visible on Rodin's arm. To better enhance that visibility, however, she needed Rodin to circulate more energetically, to be more welcoming in his studio to the rich and the titled, and above all she needed him to be rich.* During the five or six years in which Claire was his mistress, she persuaded Rodin to raise the price of his works so steeply that his annual income went from 60,000 francs to 400,000.

Gwen, who'd been kept apart from so much of Rodin's life, knew nothing of the Duchesse until one of her lady artists, perhaps Nuala O'Donel, enlightened her. She hardly dared believe it until, one day in July 1908, she was summoned to Rodin's studio and saw a bust he was sculpting of Claire. It showed her laughing, her head tilted back, her mouth opened wide, and to Gwen it evoked hideous, mocking images of this woman in bed with her maître. At night, she had terrible dreams – of Rodin surrounded by crowds and beyond her reach, of herself becoming paralysed, unable to speak or move. She no longer dared go into Rodin's studio in case Claire was there, but she often loitered outside, hoping to catch sight of her maître when he left at the end of the day.

One afternoon, Gwen was keeping watch when Rodin emerged

---

* Among the rich and the titled to visit his studio were the king of England, Gabriele D'Annunzio and Theodore Roosevelt's wife.

through the gates of the Depot – but, to her dismay, he was arm in arm with a woman who was plainly the Duchesse. She was wearing an expensive green velvet coat with an elaborately decorated hat, and seemed to Gwen the epitome of all she most feared – a brilliant, worldly rival who 'wore bright colours and [was] loud'.[2] Far more grievous to her, though, was Rodin's demonstratively affectionate manner with Claire, out in the street. He'd never been so free with Gwen herself, and feeling suddenly that she'd been taken for a fool, she ran out of the doorway where she'd been hiding and raged at him blindly, a torrent of jealousy and reproach.

It was the end of everything, she believed, and she composed a dramatic farewell note, swearing to Rodin she would never accept another sou from him, and would wear her misery in 'thin cotton rags' for the rest of her days.[3] Yet, although Rodin was furious with Gwen for embarrassing him in public, he wasn't going to let her go. She was important to him as a model (he might need her again for his Whistler Muse), but he also felt genuine ties of affection and duty. Once his annoyance had subsided, he made deliberate attempts to woo back her trust: visiting her room, solicitously enquiring about her health and finances, trying to find her additional modelling work.

Gwen wanted to resist. She was out when Rodin first called at rue du Cherche-Midi and she sent a caustic reply to the note he left, asking why he dared assume she would always be waiting for him, wondering scornfully what his 'petite amie' would say. Later, she gave him a nude picture of herself, which was nothing like the lyrical, compliant offerings she'd drawn in the past. It was roughly done, with patches of bare canvas, and with the dark smudge of her pubic hair standing out aggressively against the pallor of her skin. It also showed Gwen in the act of drawing, so that, rather than posing herself for Rodin's appreciation, she was simply standing with her feet solidly planted on the floor, her gaze intent on the sketchbook in her hands.

But love was too ingrained for Gwen to maintain her distance and, by the winter, she was seeing Rodin once or twice a month, clinging to any small gifts of tenderness he might bestow. There was sufficient contact between them to worry Claire; even though she could hardly regard this odd, mousy Englishwoman as a serious rival, she could see that Gwen had a sensibility and a talent which she herself lacked. The following autumn, when Rodin moved into a new studio space in the centre of Paris, Claire was determined to keep Gwen away.

The Hotel Biron was a large eighteenth-century mansion, set in rambling grounds off the rue de Varenne. It had been purchased by the government and designated for transformation into an expensive apartment building, but, until work could begin, it was being rented out. Matisse had a teaching studio there, Isadora Duncan choreographed her dances in the long gallery upstairs, Jean Cocteau had one of its rooms and so too did Clara Westhoff, Rilke's wife. Clara had actually been the one to recommend the Hotel Biron to Rodin, and Rilke had encouraged the idea, imagining that Rodin would enjoy being part of a young creative community, something like the artists' colony in Germany where he and Clara had first met.

The Duchesse, however, had other ideas. She wanted to create an 'enchanted abode' out of the four ground-floor rooms which Rodin agreed to rent, setting aside one of them as a reception room where she could entertain on his behalf. As soon as the (expensive) renovations were done, Claire became very busy in throwing parties at the Hotel, entertaining guests with her highly coloured anecdotes, and dancing vivaciously to the records Rodin played on his newly acquired phonograph.

Rodin was lost in admiration: 'When she dances she is bathed in light, my light, the pulsations of my heart, which also beats time.'[4] Others, though, were alarmed by Claire's hold over him, believing he'd 'lost all sense of right and wrong in submitting to her greed for pleasure and profit.'[5] Rilke found it particularly offensive that Rodin, once a proud man of the people, had allowed himself to be tamed by Claire into a Parisian dandy, his rough grey crewcut coiffed into a helmet of curls, his beard trimmed and brilliantined, his suits expensively tailored, his square, workmanlike hands concealed in 'gloves the colour of fresh butter.'[6]

Rilke was also distressed by Claire's arrogance as she appointed herself gatekeeper of Rodin's studio. Back at the Depot, students, models, friends and journalists had often dropped in unannounced – it had been the aspect of Rodin's generosity Rilke most admired. At the Hotel, however, Claire would admit no one to Rodin's presence unless by prior invitation – and, if Rilke found her protocol morally objectionable, for Gwen it was a disaster. The one time she tried to visit Rodin, she was sent away by the concierge and, when a summons finally came for her, early in 1910, it was through a coldly officious note which had almost certainly been written by Claire.

In fact, Claire had organized the whole of Gwen's visit with the intention of inflicting maximum humiliation. She was waiting at the door of the Hotel when Gwen arrived, demanding to see her note of invitation; she then accompanied Gwen into Rodin's studio, where she remained throughout the session. It was impossible for Gwen to talk openly with Rodin, or to exchange even the smallest token of affection. Exposed as she was to Claire's haughty, malicious scrutiny, Gwen felt herself reduced to a model for hire. As a final insult, when Gwen was putting on her clothes to leave, Claire offered her a banana and a packet of bonbons, then, with poisonous sweetness, said that, if ever Gwen needed work, she knew of some Americans who were in search of a model.

Rodin didn't like what he saw and afterwards he wrote with apologetic tenderness to Gwen: 'Courage petite amie. I love your little heart so devout patient and without violence.' He was even more contrite when he learned Gwen had been writing to him regularly at the Hotel and that her letters had been intercepted by Claire. In a tacit gesture of complicity, he proposed that she write to him only at the Depot, where he still went occasionally to work.[7] This at least was some small crumb of comfort, some small triumph over Claire, but it was very small. Only later, when the Hotel Biron became the Rodin Museum, would Gwen achieve public ascendancy over Claire. A magnificent bronze of the Whistler Muse would then hold court on the Hotel's back terrace while the only trace of Claire's presence would be in a small display of black and white photographs, showing a plump, smiling woman in a large hat.

Yet, even while Gwen was being crushed by Claire, the momentum of her painting was gathering force. Early in 1909, she found a new model, a young Englishwoman called Fenella Lovell, who lived in creative squalor in Montparnasse and offended Gwen with her boasts of all the famous men who'd both hired and admired her – among them, Gus and Rodin. Fenella had 'a pretty face' but 'a horrid character', Gwen fumed to Ursula.[8] Yet there was something about her – the tension in her skinny body, the sensuality of her small sullen mouth, the bruised shadows around her eyes – that stirred Gwen to a reluctant desire and an equally reluctant pity. She saw a vulnerability in Fenella that chimed with her own, and – influenced perhaps by her recently discovered interest in Picasso and Modigliani – Gwen shifted her style of painting towards a new, and harsher, intensity of expression.*

The two portraits she painted of Fenella, *Nude Girl* and *Girl with Bare Shoulders*, were an exploration of distortion. Gwen elongated the lines of Fenella's body so that her neck appeared too frail to support her head; she exaggerated the angles and hollows of Fenella's face and muted her flesh to dull white pallor, contrasting it against the seedy, greenish radiance of the background colour.

The effect was erotic, haunting, tragic and angry – Wyndham Lewis wrote later that Gwen had painted a woman who seemed 'painfully galvanised by something underneath which we are not shown . . . an Eve after the Fall.'[9] However, during the twelve months in which Gwen worked on these portraits, the excitement that gripped her was undercut by alarm. Sometimes this new direction in her work looked so irredeemably 'ugly' she wondered if her dislike of Fenella had warped her judgement. Sometimes its intensity quite frightened her.

She was also painting against a backdrop of personal difficulty. On top of the distress she was suffering over Rodin and Claire, her health was erratic and she was also forced to change her lodgings because the concierge at rue du Cherche-Midi had said she needed the attic for herself. Although Gwen found a new room easily enough, at 6 rue de l'Ouest, it never felt more than serviceable to her, never like a home. And, unsettled as she was by the disruption of the move, in July 1910 she also had to endure a visit from her father.

It had been almost a decade since Gwen last saw him and, during that time, she had hardly bothered to write him more than the occasional card. Edwin, though, had remained stubbornly anxious about her well-being and, having missed her back in 1904, he was very determined now in tracking her down at her correct address.

Inevitably, the few days of his visit were a disappointment for him and

---

* Although Gwen would not meet Picasso until 1921, he exhibited in Paris in 1904 and 1905, and his work was on regular display at his dealer's gallery.

a vexation for Gwen, who felt obliged to show her father around the city, all the while enduring his litany of concerns about the filth of the streets, the poverty of her room. 'For that I have been tired out & unable to paint for days,' she grumbled to Ursula. She was convinced that Edwin had only come to Paris so that he could boast to his neighbours afterwards, convinced too that, if he'd genuinely been worried about her, he would have shown it by helping her 'materially' – forgetting that, the last time she'd seen Edwin, she'd sworn never to accept any more of his money.[10]

It was all bogus, Gwen thought, this sentimental faith in family to which her father clung, and she swore to Ursula that she personally was done with it. 'I think if we are to do beautiful pictures we ought to be free from family conventions and ties. I think the family has had its day. We won't go to heaven in families now but one by one'.[11] Despite the doubts and disruptions in her life, ideas for pictures had been coming to Gwen throughout this year. She'd been working hard to fix them on paper and canvas, and, while part of her had wanted to resist this compulsion ('I am quite frightened at my coldness towards painting which gets worse and worse', she told Ursula), she knew she was working towards something important. 'I cannot imagine why my vision will have some value in the world – and yet I know it will.'[12]

In May, when she'd sent her two Fenella portraits to the NEAC, Gwen had worried they might be too ugly to sell, yet it was this same ugliness which still fascinated her, as her work progressed towards a more expressionist way of seeing and painting. In *Woman Sewing*, she used an attenuated line and a thin, almost sulphurous palette to create the image of a middle-aged seamstress, faded from years of labour. In a second portrait of Chloe, painted at speed in September, she returned to a more classically representational approach, yet she was still pushing her style and playing with it. In the exaggeratedly startled tilt of Chloe's head, in the flecks of red, grey, yellow and brown that flared like anxiety over Chloe's skin, Gwen gave raw and vivid expression to her friend's sensitivities.

In this portrait's freedom of line and colour she could also have been influenced by Cézanne. Gwen's initial appreciation of the painter may well have been sparked by Gus; it may equally have been directed by Rilke, who believed that 'Only a saint could be as united with his God as Cézanne was with his work'. Yet for a while Cézanne was an important model for Gwen, and it was, above all, the boldness of his paintings she admired – the physical vitality of his brushstrokes, the audacity with which he left patches of his canvas bare, the confidence, too, with which he chose to paint multiple variations of a single subject, rather than striving for one perfect result. For Gwen, painting had nearly always been anxious physical labour, and the most fundamental lessons she learned from Cézanne were not only about technique but courage.*

It became her mission and her joy to 'lay things down with decision', and she was building on techniques which she'd recently discovered that allowed her to work with even greater rapidity and assurance. She was using tracing paper to make copies of her drawings so that she could vary them at will, playing with the tones, the relationship between figure and background. She was adding white gouache to the watercolour she laid over some of those images ('like painting with oils only quicker') and at one point she was boasting to Ursula that she had five self-portraits on the go. 'One must paint a lot of canvases and probably waste them', she decided.[13]

The start of the Fenella portraits had led Gwen to a period of accelerated transition. Ideas and discoveries were now tumbling into her work and they were giving her the strength to see how she might survive her relationship with Rodin. 'I have been thinking of painting a good deal lately,' she told Ursula in the summer of 1910. 'I think I shall do something good – if I am left to myself.'[14] And the timing could not have been better for Gwen when, that same summer, she received a letter from the American lawyer and art collector John Quinn, offering not only to buy some of her work, but proposing a modest form of financial patronage that would allow her to focus even more intently on her art.

It had been Gus, still eager to encourage his sister's career, who'd been behind the approach. The previous year, he'd painted Quinn's portrait,

---

* Gwen would shortly be impressed by what the painter Maurice Denis wrote about the 'mystique of the unfinished in Cézanne's work'. Denis saw an element of spirituality in the rapid dabs of colour and the empty spaces of Cézanne's art, and interpreted them as a form of humility before Nature and God.

urged on by Yeats, who, like a number of writers and artists, had benefited much from Quinn's generosity and legal advice. Gus, on first meeting Quinn, had been unimpressed. Unable to see beyond the Wall Street suit, the impeccably starched shirt and conservative tie, he'd painted an unflattering parody of what he imagined the typical 'Yankee' to be. '[John] painted me as though I were the referee or umpire of a baseball game or the president of a street railway company with a head as round and inexpressive and under-developed as a billiard ball', admitted Quinn.[15]

But Quinn was game in his devotion to modern art and, far from being insulted by his portrait, he offered to become Gus's patron, proposing to pay him an annual stipend on top of any paintings he might buy. Gus was amazed at such largesse and didn't hesitate to accept. 'He's offered me 250 a year for life,' he told Dorelia, 'and I can send him what I like. He's a daisy and will do much more than that.'[16]

Quinn did. The following year, he raised the stipend to £300, offering another annual £200 if Gus would act as his European agent, introducing him to other artists of interest. It was the promise of a steady income, as well as the scale of the sum (the equivalent now of around £60,000), which made this intervention so miraculous to Gus, freeing him from the money-making commissions that wasted too much of his time, allowing him to concentrate on the lyric experiments he wanted to paint.

For a while, Quinn was also more than a financial Good Samaritan to Gus. They corresponded regularly with each other, and Gus, impressed by Quinn's depth of knowledge about artists and art, began looking to him for counsel and direction. Shortly after they'd met, Gus wrote to tell Quinn about his latest enthusiasm: 'I am quite ready to say goodbye to oil painting,' he said, explaining that he'd decided he now wanted to paint with tempera and to switch from canvases to frescos.[17] Quinn, partly concerned with protecting his own investment, was horrified by the idea and wrote back immediately to advise against so rash a change of direction, and Gus was almost humble in his gratitude for Quinn's guidance. 'I suffer from being unduly impressionable and often forget the essential continuity of my own life. What you say is true that one is apt to despise one's own facility – whereas one should recognize it as a road to mastery itself. I shall keep your letter and read it over whenever I feel off the track – *my own track*. It will be medicine for me who am occasionally afflicted with intellectual vapours.'[18]

For the first two years of their arrangement, Gus continued to believe he'd found a mentor as well as a patron in Quinn, a wisely objective voice who would 'keep me up to the scratch'. He'd outgrown Will – 'I have known him too long,' he told Ottoline – but he sensed that Will was outgrowing him too, since he was becoming less generous with his hospitality and money.[19] Having once shed tears of joy over Will's letters of praise, he now wanted to force an end to their relationship, and, although he accused himself of 'base ingratitude', Gus felt that the only way he could be free of Will was by behaving as badly as he knew how.

The speed with which he ran through his friends was, he recognized, a fault in him. 'I can never find my perfect man,' he admitted, conscious that there always came a point when he saw his friends' virtues as faults, when he started to feel trapped by their presumption to know him, and to resent the claims they made on his time. Lewis, who'd already seen himself replaced in Gus's affections by Epstein, Henry Lamb and others, was now maliciously entertained to see how Quinn was staking his own claim to Gus, 'recklessly attaching John with the strings of his purse.'[20] It was obvious to Lewis that Quinn not only wanted a piece of Gus's art, but, like so many others, hoped for a vicarious involvement in the dramas of his life. He predicted, correctly, that the relationship wouldn't last, and, by the summer of 1911, Gus was already starting to buck against the yoke of his own obligations.

A driving holiday he took with Quinn in France was made uncomfortably fractious because Gus had sold off a painting, *The Way Down to the Sea*, which he'd already promised to his patron. Even though Gus had known he was violating the terms of their agreement, he'd been annoyed when Quinn rebuked him, had felt the man was becoming too arrogant in believing he could control Gus through his dollars. To Will, he complained that Quinn was turning out to be the worst kind of American, one in whom 'Money had literally taken the place of brains and character.'[21]

But, in July 1910, Gus was still marvelling at the reach of Quinn's generosity and he wanted his sister to benefit as well. Quinn had actually seen something of Gwen's work at the NEAC, two years previously, and had made a bid for *La Chambre sur la Cour*. When he'd learned it was sold, he'd gone fruitlessly in search of others to buy, so, when Gus suggested that he write directly to Gwen and propose an arrangement a little like his, Quinn was already well disposed to the idea.

The offer he made was initially modest, little more than a statement of his readiness to pay a thirty-pound advance on any painting she would be willing to sell. To Gwen, however, the overture felt momentous, both in its promise of a steady income, but also in its challenge to her own very private relationship with her art. To expose herself to the taste and wallet of an American stranger felt like a wholly different matter from sending off the occasional picture to the NEAC. And she worried that she didn't have anything that was good or impressive enough to suit Quinn.* As she mentally surveyed the works she had recently painted, she wondered if the nude portrait of Fenella would do; Gus, intuiting Gwen's uncertainty and very anxious for her not to lose this opportunity, offered to get the picture photographed for Quinn so that he might judge it for himself. In less than a fortnight, however, Gwen herself had decided against the Fenella portrait, and by mid-August she was writing apologetically to Quinn to say that she would prefer to paint him something new: 'Please let me do as I wish . . . I desire to send you a picture I like very much myself.'[22]

Months passed, though, and still Gwen couldn't commit herself. On Christmas Day, she was writing guiltily to Quinn, 'I have been working but I am not yet satisfied.'[23] He was gallantly quick to reassure: 'Do not worry a particle in regard to my picture. Take your time with it.' With almost pompous tact, he insisted it was his delight to associate with artists like her, who were treading new ground rather than 'travelling over the beaten path . . . which generations before have learned to appreciate and value.'[24]

Gwen might have offered Quinn her second, recently completed portrait of Chloe; when she eventually sold it to him in 1914, he would admire it terrifically. Yet she was already moving beyond that first wave of experimentation and was revisiting some of the influences that had

---

* Gwen also disliked the ornate gold frames in which he liked to hang his acquisitions, dreading that her own modest canvases would be swamped by 'hollow gilt'.

moved her in the past. A recent exhibition of Rembrandt and the Dutch masters had made her notice afresh their attention to the detail and beauty of ordinary things, had made her dislike the element of decadence in her Fenella pictures. The work she was now thinking of sending to Quinn was a quietly glowing interior in which a young woman stood leaning against a desk, an open book in her hands, face half illuminated in a shaft of sunlight. The room, with its simple furniture, was recognizably Gwen's, but the woman, she told Ursula, was copied from a 'sweet-faced vierge' painted by Durer, who was, almost certainly, his *Madonna of the Pear*.

Gwen's anxiety to please Quinn had undermined her determination to be more spontaneous in her work, 'to paint a lot of canvases and probably waste them'. She devoted most of the winter and spring of 1911 to *A Lady Reading*, and even then, she felt unsure of its quality, sending it to Ursula for a first opinion. Ursula's response, though, was unhelpfully puzzled. She was confused by the woman's identity – was she meant to be Gwen? – and unsure of her pose – was she meant to be seated or standing? Tentatively, Ursula wrote to ask if the ambiguity was intentional – 'artistic' in some way – and while Gwen had snapped irritably in response – 'Wasn't artistic meant to be good?' – Ursula's queries had further eroded her confidence.

It was impossible now to send this picture to New York. And, in November, Gwen was still so doubting of herself that, when Quinn came out to Paris in the hope of seeing her, she took pains to avoid him, telling him afterwards that she'd been away from home and that she hadn't received the messages he sent.

Even though they had been writing to each other for over a year, the idea of meeting Quinn was quite terrifying to Gwen. As she'd recently explained to Ursula, she still trembled at the prospect of encountering anyone new; the effort it cost her to interpret their behaviour, to adapt herself to their expectations was so great it could 'affect' her, she said, 'beyond reason.'[25]

Yet Quinn refused to be put off by Gwen's elusiveness; instead, he wrote to send her another advance, this one of fifty pounds. Guilt and gratitude rushed over her in equal measure: 'It is so good of you to offer me another commission. I have felt this year, sometimes, that I have been taking advantage of your generosity . . . it requires a quiet mind for me to paint, and I found myself in debt. I am not in want of money now'.

She did, however, have a painting she felt able to send, a second version of *A Lady Reading* which she'd retitled *A Girl Reading by a Window*. It was apparently a response to Ursula's reservations, since the girl was quite clearly seated and her features were recognizable as Gwen's own; yet there were other changes – a lightening of the palette, a sharpening of the room's detail, a bow in the girl's hair – which Gwen may have thought pleasing to Quinn. The original version might have resonated with a more interior life (Gwen had been delighted by Ursula's report that a friend had found it almost Dostoyevskian), but when she sent it first for exhibition at the NEAC it was well reviewed. 'I don't quite know what that means,' she wrote disingenuously to Quinn. 'However I have heard from several artists who can really judge it, that it has given them pleasure to see it, and I know it expresses something of what I felt.'[26]

Gwen still waited until the following spring before getting the painting shipped, and because it was delayed in transit and she didn't hear back from Quinn, she feared it had been an unspeakable disappointment. Defensively, she wrote to him, 'I know a little more what I want to do [now] I will send a better picture than the other.'[27] But Quinn was delighted when it eventually arrived. 'People who see it always ask me if there are others,' he told her, and he proposed a new arrangement, paying her a fixed stipend, in quarterly instalments, in return for two or three pictures a year. 'Not to monopolise your work,' he wrote judiciously, '[but] I think we both might be the gainers from it.'[28] Already, he said, he had placed a 500-franc advance with Brentano's bookshop in Paris and had arranged for the Chenil in London to deal with the shipping arrangements on Gwen's behalf.

Quinn had rightly anticipated that she would hesitate over his offer. 'It will be good for me to have money regularly,' she replied nervously. 'But I am not sure at this moment whether my pictures will be any good.'[29] Nevertheless, after two years of corresponding with Quinn, Gwen was coming to regard him almost as a friend. He might have been the most powerfully influential man she knew, friend and advisor to figures like W. B. Yeats, Ezra Pound, James Joyce, T. S. Eliot, Eric Satie and Guillaume Apollinaire, a much-admired campaigner against the censorship laws in America. Yet, in all his dealings with Gwen, he never made her feel inferior or stupid; on the contrary, he made a point of deferring to her. He sought her opinion on his acquisitions (she congratulated him on buying a Puvis de Chavannes) and he asked for information about the latest developments in Paris. Flattered and stimulated, she reported on a new play by D'Annunzio and on the paintings of Henri Rousseau, which she'd seen hung at the Salon des Indépendants. Most of the exhibition she dismissed as the ravings of 'mad people', but Rousseau, she believed, had a natural genius; 'at fifty years old, he felt he must paint and so he painted, not knowing at all how to paint. His pictures are very remarkable . . .'[30] Quinn, on her recommendation, would buy five of Rousseau's works.

The trust which he placed in her also made Gwen readier to defer to his judgement as he began promoting her work more extensively. In 1913, he proposed putting two of her paintings – *A Girl Reading* and a new work, *A Woman in a Red Shawl* – into the monumental show of modern art he was helping to organize at the Armory in New York. Three hundred artists were being represented, among them Cézanne, Rodin, Puvis de Chavannes and, inevitably, her brother. A year or two earlier, Gwen would have flinched from so public an exposure, yet her courage was growing. She asked Quinn if, after the Armory, he might arrange a one-woman show for her, which would give a 'better impression' of her work.[31] She told him, too, that he should be giving more consideration to her drawings: 'I have been doing [them] for a long time . . . [they] must be done because I feel so much inclined to do them and I learn for my pictures in doing them. The subjects keep on presenting themselves.'

Of course, Gwen still fell prey to chronic self-doubt and was never easy about sending her art out into the world. She was feeling her way, she told Ursula, and she believed that, if her 'vision' was ever to gain 'some value', it was because she was 'patient and *receullie* in some degree', and was able to work at her own private pace.[32] Deadlines and pressure over sales could still feel like a threat to her, and even Quinn's most tactful probing could sometimes provoke her to complain that he knew 'nothing about painting' and was only interested in money.

She was echoing some of her brother's ungracious hostility, but, unlike Gus, she always came back to a recognition of what Quinn was doing for her. He was freeing her from the drudgery of modelling, he was allowing her to buy better materials, a larger easel to replace the small travelling one she'd been using for years. Above all, he was providing her with a benevolent buffer against the fickle demands of the art market and the whims of clients. Such generosity would be a gift to any artist, but it was especially crucial to Gwen as she followed the private thread of her vision. When Quinn died, in 1924, she would feel the loss so acutely that, for weeks, she could barely work. 'If I painted it would be to finish some things which were going to John [Quinn]', she wrote, 'and it gives me pain'.[33]

Chapter Eleven

SEARCHING FOR ARCADIA

'The bourgeois of all countries are alike. Vain, pretentious, silly, soft, timid, senile puerile impudent – ugly'
AUGUSTUS JOHN[1]

If Quinn and his money had given Gwen the security to work in peace, to Gus they'd given the promise of living his life more largely. Six months before meeting Quinn, when he'd first moved his family into their Chelsea home, he had fallen and broken his collarbone. He'd been unable to paint, fallen prey to 'nerves and glooms'.[2] And, as he'd whiled away his convalescence reading Dostoyevsky's *The Possessed* and books on Roma culture, he'd been overwhelmed by the belief that his life – his real life – lay elsewhere. 'I feel acutely what I am missing all the time shut up in my studio', he wrote, 'all the sights & delights of the high road or any road.'[3]

The road's siren call had resonated through the epic painting which Gus had just completed of Dorelia, in which he'd portrayed her as a gypsy, a sensual earth mother – sitting with her legs akimbo, her hands planted firmly on her thighs, the brazen colour of her crimson dress reflected in the glint of sexual mischief illuminating her face. He'd made her an embodiment of the freedom for which he longed, and the critics had seen something of that when they'd reviewed *Smiling Woman* in February.* C. J. Holmes had thought it 'fierce disquieting and emphatic', while Roger Fry was almost euphoric: 'Here for once is a figure without any of the social pretence, the veils and subterfuges of modern life. It is character seen with

---

* It was shown in an exhibition of female portraits, mounted by the International Society, and was one of the largest Gus had attempted, measuring 196 cm by 98.2 cm.

the uncompromising frankness of the Middle Ages. This woman is essentially modern but she belongs nonetheless to the fifteenth century.'[4]

But the timeless 'gypsy Gioconda' whom the critics admired was not quite the Dorelia with whom Gus was living. She was restless, unhappy; the burden of looking after a large London household of emotionally unsettled children was taking its toll and, as the grey winter of 1909 slid reluctantly towards spring, Gus longed to take her away. He looked back to the summer on Dartmoor, four years earlier, and remembered, or thought he remembered, how happy a time it had been – the boys running wild, Dorelia sharing her contented motherhood with Ida, and work coming so easily to him. That gypsy summer had given Gus a glimpse of Arcadia and he saw no reason why he shouldn't recreate it – not simply by setting up camp for Dorelia and the boys, but by taking them travelling, living the life of Whitman's 'Song of the Open Road', with 'The long brown path before me leading wherever I choose.'

The caravan which Gus had bought for that summer was still parked on Dartmoor, and in March he had it transported to Wantage, in Oxfordshire, where it was overhauled and repainted a brilliant sky blue. He then drove the van himself to the Surrey village of Effingham, riding an elderly black hunter, with his friend, the architect John Fothergill, as his companion. To Ottoline, he wrote that his 'dream of the nomadic life' was shaping up nicely, and once back in London he began ordering up the rest of his equipment: a second caravan (painted canary yellow), blankets and poles for the fashioning of tents, a cart and some additional horses. A young groom, Arthur, was found to manage the animals; Dorelia's younger sister, Edie, agreed to help with the children; and, by late June, they were all ready to drive through England, wherever chance or Gus's own whims might direct them.

His first destination was to be the racecourse at Epsom, where he was expecting to find a large encampment of gypsies in readiness for the Derby season. Gus had been looking forward to practising his Romani, to being acknowledged as a citizen of the road, and he was furiously disappointed when there were no gypsies to be seen. A recent clampdown on the rights of travellers had included a ban on all gatherings at the Derby. And, while Gus had been sufficiently prudent to secure letters of introduction, arming himself against any 'corrupt policemen' or 'supercilious landlords' who might interfere with his journey, he still felt the Roma's persecution as his own. In a mood of righteous defiance, he parked his family convoy right next to the racecourse and made a grandstanding speech of protest when the police moved in to evict them. The following day, he was hugely gratified to see that he'd made headline news in the local press.[5]

The battle and the publicity all gave a tremendous moral lift to the vagabond experience when they resumed their travels. To Ada (who must have been horrified), Gus wrote with provocatively blithe enthusiasm: 'It's great fun . . . the boys have never looked better'. But in truth, the children were sometimes terrified. While Gus was seated astride one of the horses the family were inside the vans, packed in amongst the provisions and camping equipment. So heavily burdened were the vans, so rudimentary their brakes, they went barrelling down the slightest incline at breakneck speed. Gus, however, remained deaf to the children's screams, urging them onwards, as they continued north-east through Hertfordshire and then on to Cambridge, where he found them a pretty camping spot on Grantchester Meadows, just outside the city.

Here, he was planning to pause for a month. The horses, which had been pulling two heavy vans for ten or fifteen miles each day, needed rest, but Gus himself had work to do, painting the classical scholar Jane Harrison in her rooms at Newnham College. He'd needed this commission to replenish his funds, for, although he'd been painting well and profitably in London (including a fine, sardonic portrait of the painter William Nicholson), he'd spent most of his savings on furnishing the gypsy convoy. In fact, before meeting Harrison, he'd assumed the portrait would have nothing more than commercial value for him. The world of academia had always repelled Gus slightly, and he'd imagined that Harrison herself would embody its worst characteristics – that she would be bloodless, aloof and very disposed to look down on his own more limited education.

Gus, however, had typically rushed to judgement, for Jane Harrison was the opposite of bloodless. Now in her late fifties, she had travelled the world on her own, she had passionately fought her ground on issues of politics, religion and feminism; when her friends had persuaded her to sit for her portrait, hoping to lift her out of a recent depression, she'd welcomed their suggestion of Augustus John, whom she knew had a preference for painting those 'who have lived hard.'[6]

The two of them got on tremendously well. Gus was charmed by Harrison's utter lack of vanity as she posed for him, lying carelessly sprawled on her chaise longue, chain-smoking cigarettes and holding brilliantly animated conversations with her fellow classicist, Gilbert Murray, who wandered in and out of the room. There was, Gus thought, a 'beautiful humanity' between the two scholars and, while he gave full weight to Harrison's own academic authority, emphasizing the strong, clever lines of her face, the heavy book on her lap, he also captured her freedom of spirit, painting her in loose, semi-impressionistic brushstrokes and exaggerating her colourful dishevelment as she lay on her couch, one shoe half kicked-off to reveal the darning on the heel of her stocking.

Harrison adored her portrait. 'I look like a fine distinguished prize fighter who has had a vision and collapsed under it . . . it seems to me beautiful,' she wrote.[7] But, although this commission had been a pleasure for Gus, it hadn't dissuaded him from his essential distrust of academia, and, during the four weeks he spent in Cambridge, his only other contact with the university was through one of its students, the beautiful and soon to be published poet Rupert Brooke.

Brooke was part of a young group of men known loosely as the Neo-Pagans. In 1909, as Britain's industrial cities were expanding and rural traditions were being eroded, there were clusters of romantic idealists who resisted change – the Georgian poets, who wrote of lost pastorals; the urban bohemians, who found poetry in garrets; the collectors of folk songs; the potters, weavers and vegetarians; and the members of the newly resurrected Gypsy Lore Society. Augustus John, in his art and his life, seemed to Brooke the beating heart of this resistance; earlier that year, when he'd seen Gus's work at the NEAC, he'd been 'faint with passion'. The sudden manifestation of his hero in Cambridge, with his 'chief wife, a very beautiful woman' and a tribe of 'brown wild bare boys . . . dressed, if at all, in lovely yellow, red or brown tattered garments', now seemed to Brooke almost heaven-sent.[8] He visited the camp many times, taking the family punting, playing with the boys, bringing his fellow Neo-Pagans along too. The glamour Gus had for those young

Cambridge men can be seen in a photograph which was taken that summer, which shows him squatting, savant-like, on his haunches, pipe in his mouth, sandals on his dusty feet. 'We cause a good deal of astonishment in this well-bred town,' he wrote to Ottoline, with some complacency.[9]

Yet, although Gus would not admit it, his dream of the nomadic life was starting to tarnish. Weeks of variable weather, of smoking fires and slightly charred meals, of boisterous children and recalcitrant horses, were taking their toll, and he'd come to regret Arthur the groom, who was truculent and lazy. In Cambridge, Arthur had taken to spending most of his time in the city's pubs, and one evening, when Gus went out drinking with him and explained they would shortly be on the move again, Arthur had turned mutinous and said he wasn't ready to leave. The two of them had ended up brawling on the pavement – and Gus, to his fury, had come off worst, his face bloody and bruised, one eye almost swollen shut.

A day or two after the fight, Ottoline came to visit, eager to see for herself the pastoral idyll which Gus had been describing in his letters. She was shocked by the still-battered state of his face, embarrassed by his clumsiness in managing the horse and cart when he met her at the station, but she was even more upset by the squalor of the camp itself, which seemed to her nothing but a huddle of weather-stained tents and vans, squashed into the corner of a 'melancholy sodden meadow'. There was no hot meal to welcome her, bubbling over a fire, only an apple and a crust of bread for lunch. Regretting the thin muslin gown in which she'd dressed for the visit, which gave her no protection against the chill fenland wind, Ottoline spent most of the day marching up and down to keep warm, waiting impatiently for the 'cheerless' day to end.[10]

Finally, with a very bolshie Arthur back on duty, Gus led the convoy north towards Liverpool. He had another commission waiting, to paint his friend Harold Chaloner Dowdall, who'd recently been elected Lord Mayor. While he'd been hoping to impress the Dowdalls by arriving at their house on horseback, he was running late and would have to go by train. So, on a drab piece of wasteland just outside Norwich, he helped the others pitch camp, leaving strict instructions for Arthur, while promising that he, himself, would be back within a fortnight.

But time was always elastic for Gus, however good his intentions. Once he was in Liverpool, staying with the Dowdalls, he thought he must see Sampson, who was on a research adventure in Wales. Their reunion was euphoric, too euphoric, for Gus lost his head. He drank too much, offended Sampson by trying to seduce one of his staff and got into a pub brawl with some of Sampson's gypsies. When he eventually limped back to the Dowdalls' house, it was so late, he had to spend the night in the park.

He'd already stayed away from his family longer than he'd promised, and his return was further delayed by having to go down to London and meet Quinn (of whom he knew little, at this point, beyond the generous price he was willing to pay to be painted). Over five weeks had passed by the time Gus made his way back to Norwich, and, with Arthur having spent most of that period in the pub, rather than assisting with the children and chores, the camp had fallen into filthy disarray. Gus was so angry with himself and his groom, he felt duty-bound to sack Arthur, but it was a self-defeating gesture because without Arthur the family were stuck, unable to travel any further and unable to return home.

Eventually, they thought of Charles Slade – the brother-in-law of Dorelia's sister Jessie – who lived on a farm close by. Slade couldn't have been kinder when Gus telegrammed for help, escorting the family to his farm and offering them a field on which to camp. But the rot had now set in. In a series of photographs Slade took of the Johns, the tired adults and filthy children all stared, grim and unsmiling, at the camera. The horses had become variously ill or lame, the boys went down with whooping cough and, towards the end of September, even Gus had to admit he'd be 'damn glad' to get back to London.

Yet, if the gypsy experiment had run its course, it had yielded good work for him. Out on the road, he'd had daily opportunities to sketch his family – the littlest boys in their dimpled infancy, the older ones at play – and he'd drawn a particularly exquisite likeness of Dorelia, detailing the heavy-lidded elegance of her gaze, the slant of her cheekbones, the beauty of her character. Throughout most of the summer, she had heroically lived up to her image in *Smiling Woman*, and now that Gus had met Quinn, and had been promised his generous support, he believed there would be a limitless future for him and Dorelia, one in which they would find new ways of living their vision of the authentic life.

But the larger Gus's dreams, the more disappointments he seemed fated to endure. During that autumn, the first assault came from the critics, who hated his portrait of Dowdall. Gus's hopes had been high for that painting; he'd seen it as an opportunity to develop the new ironic style in which he'd been playing with references to the portraiture of the past. He'd painted William Nicholson in the guise of an aristocratic dandy, wearing a high-collared velvet coat and flourishing a gilded cane; he'd painted Jane Harrison on her couch with a sly hint of the classical odalisque; and he had thought it 'great sport' to maximize the full mayoral glory of Dowdall's portrait, to detail 'all the jewels and sword hilts', the tricorne, the chain and fur-trimmed cloak. As an additional enhancement, Gus had also decided to include the mayoral sword-bearer, Mr Smith. But Smith was short and plump, Dowdall tall and lean, and Gus had been unable not to make a joke of the men's comically mismatched proportions.

When the painting was unveiled, first at Liverpool's Walker Gallery, then at a series of smaller venues, it was condemned as cruel parody, the mayor depicted as a lanky Don Quixote and Smith his fat and foolish Sancho Panza. The northern press competed to denounce it as 'the worst drawn, worst painted modern artwork ever shown', and while Gus retorted airily that Liverpool should have been grateful that he'd included Smith in the picture 'at no extra cost', he was badly shaken by the furore of these 'stupid, disgusting and unnecessary' attacks.[11]

On top of professional adversity, there was trouble at home. Dorelia had developed worrying symptoms – vaginal bleeding and abdominal cramps – and Gus, haunted by Ida's fatal infection, begged her to see a doctor. She, however, was convinced that she'd simply fallen pregnant again, that her symptoms were those of an early miscarriage and required no medical attention. Of course, her obstinacy terrified Gus, and, as he argued with Dorelia over doctors, the mood at Church Street became grimmer still when Robin contracted scarlet fever and they all had to be confined at home. Everyone was bored and cross under quarantine, but Gus was driven to a violence that frightened him as he shouted at Dorelia and lashed out at the boys. 'I don't seem to be cut out for family life', he wrote miserably to Quinn. 'The crisis which takes place at least weekly leaves me less and less hopeful as regards this ménage. It is a great pity as I am fond of the missus and she of me.'[12]

These weekly rows were particularly difficult, too, because Gus and Dorelia quarrelled so rarely and they did it so badly. In the past, they'd depended on Ida and her articulate honesty to tease out the logic of all their conflicts; without her, they struggled to explain themselves. Gus did his best, composing careful notes to Dorelia: 'You know how mercurial I am, veering from Heaven to Hell and torn to pieces by emotion or nerves or thoughts'. He wanted a resolution – 'I can't help thinking we *can* go on better than we have been by using our wits' – but, when he slipped into blaming Dorelia for 'exhibiting a quite false aspect' of herself, their fights only grew more rancorous.[13]

Something had to shift, and for Gus it was always easier to contemplate a change in his physical circumstance. He began to wonder if he should move out of Church Street to a nearby studio, where he would be able to remain close to the family without 'the day-to-day test' of constant exposure. But, once he'd allowed himself to imagine that first small act of separation, he felt a longing for even greater distances, a longing which was then heightened for him by the disappointing experience of his next painting commission.

The previous month, he'd been asked to paint two large murals for the wealthy art collector Hugh Lane, and eager ideas had come to him for decorating the walls of Lane's Chelsea mansion with 'vast' fantasies of gypsies and travellers. Lane, however, wanted to see immediate results, and Gus's enthusiasm soured as he complained to Ottoline that the man was a philistine, interested only in getting Gus's 'quickest and convenientist' work. His contempt gathered force when, coming home to discover that 'the lovely gypsy girl' who was modelling for Gus had brought along friends for an impromptu party, Lane threw them all out.[14]

This prissy, mean-spirited attack by Lane seemed proof to Gus that the London art world had lost its soul. He told Lewis he could hardly breathe, and would die unless he could find some other place where 'life is more stable and beautiful and primitive and one is not bound to be in a hurry.'[15]

His art, his family, his dreams of liberty all seemed on the point of implosion, and Gus was afraid of doing something irreparably reckless.

Then, early in January 1910, the first of Quinn's cheques arrived – and with it, a solution. The sum was large enough for Gus to keep paying his bills at home while he took himself abroad for what Ida would have called a 'rest cure' of his mind and soul. He'd always wanted to go south – to the landscape of Provence, where Cézanne had painted; to the art galleries of Florence and Rome. All he needed were some weeks alone, to walk and think and draw, and he came to an agreement with Dorelia that, once her symptoms had settled, she would join him in the spring, bringing with her the three youngest boys and leaving the older ones in school, under the Nettleships' care.

By mid-January, Gus was already in Avignon, and already feeling that the 'foetid plague spot of England' was far behind.[16] He continued on to Arles, travelling by train and by foot, wearing 'the largest pair of boots in the world' and getting more enjoyably filthy by the day – 'you could almost grow mushrooms in my vest', he claimed.[17] This part of France was more ancient, more austere than any Gus had seen, 'so beautiful – a chain of rocky hills quite barren except for olives here and there', and he was sketching it all – the landscape and the tough, handsome people who worked it.[18] To Dorelia, he sent evocative descriptions, transparent with his wonder, and told her he was already imagining their reunion – perhaps among the sand dunes of the Camargue, or in a precipitous hilltop village he'd seen, 'built among billows of rocks'. He was in love with her again, thinking only of the qualities that 'never [fail] to bowl me over'.

Upon reaching Marseilles, however, his fond imaginings were cast aside by the excitement of meeting a group of Russian gypsies. 'Beautiful people,' he exclaimed to Ottoline, 'I cannot tell you how they affect me'. Gratefully, he accepted their invitation to stay at their camp, where he tried, unsuccessfully, to draw them ('they never look the same when they are posing') and scribbled down examples of their dialect to send back to Scott Macfie, who was secretary of the recently reformed Gypsy Lore Society.*[19] When the Russians invited him to travel on with them

---

* Macfie was the principal force in reviving the Society in 1907.

to Milan and to join the annual gathering of Roma clans, Gus was lost in flattered delight.

But he had yet to see any of the Italian art which he'd promised to study. Resisting the lure of the Russian convoy and making arrangements to meet them in Milan, he took the train down to Genoa, from where he planned to embark on a tour of some galleries and churches – 'a week should do it', he predicted briskly to Ottoline.

Genoa almost put him off making that tour – it was 'crawling' with 'swarms' of the 'bourgeoisie'. But once he reached Tuscany and Umbria, Gus saw the folly of his arrogance. The landscape, with its intricate folding of vines, cypresses and hilltop villages, seemed to him beautifully 'unchanged since the 14th century' and the art quite incredible in its profusion. Florence was too much for him – he could do little more than wonder at Botticelli's *Primavera*, 'lovely beyond compare' – but he lingered for nearly two weeks in the smaller places, studying the frescos of Luca Signorelli and Pietro Lorenzetti in Orvieto, the Giottos in Padua, the Byzantine mosaics in Ravenna, and Piero della Francesca's 'majestic Christ rising from the tomb' in Arezzo.[20]

Here, in a world far removed from the 'petty upsets' of London, Gus believed he had found the essence of a European tradition, a line of beauty which extended from the early Italians to himself. A little while later, he wrote to Quinn, 'My imagination and sense of reality seem to be just twice as strong as it was before – and no exaggeration. I tell you frankly and sincerely I feel nobody dead or alive is so near the guts of things as I am at present. What is surprising together with this infallible realism, my sense of beauty seems to have grown, simultaneously.'[21]

But still the gypsies were calling, and Gus travelled up to Milan to find the field where they were assembling. It was the largest camp he'd visited: twenty enormous tents pitched within a circle of caravans, a gorgeous pandemonium of men, women, children, dogs and horses. Yet he managed to locate the Russians and, on their recommendation, was made guest of honour at the singing and feasting with which the clans were about to celebrate their reunion.

That celebration went on for a full day and a night, and to Gus it seemed that he'd been shown the essential soul of Roma culture, 'the rarest and most unattainable thing in the world.'[22] The men, dressed in silver-beaded tunics, played music of hallucinatory wildness – complex rhythms beaten out on copper drums and accompanying melodies of fantastical ornateness. As the sound swelled to fill the tent, the women, in scarlet blouses, with gold coins threaded through their hair, began to dance, moving together in a ritualized quivering shimmer that seemed to Gus both religious and orgiastic.

When he stumbled out into the real world, he took the train to Marseilles and, still reeling from the wonders of his experience, it seemed to him that every street was yielding 'some marvellous face' to draw. 'I feel ready to live here,' he told Dorelia. Yet, even in the middle of his elation, it was starting to dawn on Gus how little he'd heard back from Dorelia beyond the few bald notes with which she'd forwarded bills and sent news of the family. At first, he was simply hurt by her silence – as he'd proudly informed Quinn, he'd been keeping himself celibate until he saw her again. But then it occurred to him that he should be alarmed, that Dorelia might finally have decided to give up on him, that she might have no intention of coming to France. Suddenly afraid, Gus sent her a flurry of telegrams, asking for reassurance.

He was right to worry, for there was much that Dorelia hadn't told him. While he had been comfortably cured of all his 'bad humours', she had become the victim of Wyndham Lewis's continuing possessiveness over Gus. Lewis had spread vicious rumours around London that Dorelia was trying to trap Gus into marriage, an accusation so maliciously far from the truth, the injustice had made her gasp. It had also made her bitter towards Gus himself, and when she'd discovered that she hadn't, in fact, had a miscarriage, but was now three or four months pregnant, she'd hesitated about telling him the news.

She probably hoped, even now, that she might lose the baby, but by February she felt obliged to inform Gus they were expecting another child. He was relieved to hear from her, and tried to feign enthusiasm in his reply: 'Splendid news I hope it will be another boy'. Yet, in an unusually candid letter to Quinn, he confessed his extreme anxiety: 'God knows I've got plenty of kids as it is and worst of all Dorelia is not in robust health. Her insides bother her.' He'd done his 'best', he said, to persuade her they should start using birth control, if only to safeguard her health, yet she'd continued to argue, as Ida had done, that it was 'interfering with nature'. He took comfort at least from the fact that she'd agreed to come out to France, where he hoped she would 'get strong'.[23] And, when Dorelia arrived in early March, accompanied by the three little boys and her new friend, Helen Maitland, Gus had to admit that she looked 'incredible' – her stomach delicately rounded, her face veiled against the sun.

Gus met the family off the train at Arles and escorted them on to Martigues, a pretty fishing town of tall spires and brightly coloured cottages, where he hoped they could stay until the end of the summer. There was a suitable house for rent, the Villa Sainte Anne, which stood high amidst pines and rocky terraces and overlooked the Étang de Berre – a vast lagoon whose water, in sunlight, turned a startling blue. There was a room in the house that would do for Gus's studio and a garden for Dorelia to tend, with wild thyme and lavender, a row or two of vines, a little orchard of fig, olive and almond trees. Sometimes a crowd of gypsies came past, and sometimes they stayed, dancing and singing 'at any hour of the day'. The children were free to play outside, and photographs taken at the villa show them squatting happily in the dust, huddled together in whispers, sword fighting with sticks, and wearing nothing but headscarves and boots.

For Gus, this life in Martigues held the promise of a southern Arcadia, and when the three older boys came out for Easter, he needed to paint them as part of it, making small portraits in the style of the Italian Renaissance, in which their faces were framed by a stylized landscape of olives, pines and amethyst cliffs.*

But it was also those trees and cliffs Gus needed to paint. In the past, he'd been suspicious of landscape art – put off, perhaps, by the amateurs who'd descended on Tenby every year. He'd thought there was something 'indecent' about painting a landscape without really knowing it, 'like button-holing a complete stranger.'[24] Now, it became his project to master 'the secrets of the Midi' and, harnessing up the family's newly acquired donkey, he explored deeper into the terrain, adjusting his eye

---

* He may also have seen portraits that Cézanne painted of his son Paul, which were similarly simple close-ups of the child's face, placed against a single background colour.

to the southern light that made perspectives sharper and colours more intense. He waited several weeks before he was ready to commit to paint, and his first experiments were with colour – streaks of green to approximate the scatterings of herbs and shrubs, a spectrum of blues to reflect the pale spring turquoise of the sky, the depths of the distant sea. He was still thinking about Cézanne, and also learning from him to look for the deep strata of the landscape, to see it in more geometric form.

Here, in this ancient unspoiled part of France, Gus felt his identity becoming more lucid, his control of his work more secure, his concentration fixed. Yet his weeks of celibacy had left him physically restless, and, because Dorelia's 'insides' were still bothering her, he began slipping out to the brothels of Marseilles, which, he cheerfully told Scott Macfie, were reputed to boast a 'fine assortment of Mediterranean whores'.[25] He had the tact to concoct an excuse for Dorelia – guitar lessons with some 'gitano pals' – yet, to a degree that foxed him profoundly, his trips to Marseilles were affecting him with a novel and very sour sensation of guilt.

In the past, Gus had always regarded sex with a prostitute as the most basic of human transactions – an exchange of money for physical release – and one that was also irrelevant to his finer feelings for Dorelia, or any other woman he loved. Now, he seemed to have developed a moral conscience and, as he laboriously wrote to Macfie, he couldn't understand what was causing his 'last neglected unbroken religious chord to vibrate with such . . . terrifying sonority.'[26] He wasn't a Christian, he didn't believe in the sanctity of marriage, he scorned the cheap illusions of romantic love and he'd always taken the view that a whore, who charged '20 sous la pusse', was more honest than most of the human race, because she understood the fundamental truth that 'intimacy doesn't really exist except to reveal the untransversable gulf that can isolate two souls.'[27] Any concerns for the 'whore' herself, and whatever pain or degradation she might suffer, were not, apparently, part of his moral calculation. Gus was generous with his money, and the women he paid were skilled at making him feel good about himself.

From Macfie, there was no reply to Gus's Dostoyevskian ramblings, and he didn't choose to share them back at the Villa Sainte Anne. Dorelia's friend Helen could be strict about sex: even though she herself was having an affair with Henry Lamb, in full knowledge of Henry's continuing devotion to Dorelia, she was quick to criticize any behaviour in men that she considered careless, entitled or cruel. Towards the end of spring, when Henry came out to Provence, Helen flinched from his suggestion that they should all meet up with Ottoline and Philip Morrell. Complicating the histories that already lay between Gus and Ottoline, Dorelia and Henry, was the short but intense affair that Henry had had with Ottoline. When Henry sent an anticipatory cartoon to Helen, of himself as a busy sexual bee buzzing around the others, he came very close to offending her.*

There was a meeting of sorts, in southern France, although it was only between Gus, Dorelia and Ottoline. They'd agreed to visit Chateau Noir in Aix en Provence, where Cézanne had lived and worked, and where some of his pictures were still on display. Even though the journey, by donkey and trap, would be long for the pregnant Dorelia, for Gus it would be a pilgrimage. And the hours he spent at the chateau, studying Cézanne's work in the landscape and light that had inspired him, strengthened Gus in the hope and belief that his own art was undergoing a transformative change.

Ottoline, pleased to be with Gus for this uplifting experience, had planned for them to look around Aix the following day. To her confused irritation, though, he sloped off to a cafe to drink. She was starting to wonder about Gus: 'He seems curiously unaware of the world,' she noted in her diary, 'too heavily laden and oppressed with boredom to break through and to realize life.' Dorelia, she decided, was part of the problem. She was beautiful, of course, even with her swollen belly and dusty, sandalled feet, but, while she'd served Gus well as a muse, she seemed too passive, too intellectually unformed to challenge him. As Ottoline fretted over the time Gus was wasting in Aix, drinking with 'a little untidy waiter . . . and a drunken box-maker from the street nearby', she grieved for her own missed chance of guiding him to his proper greatness – 'a greatness', she wrote, 'to equal Michelangelo, Cézanne or Van Gogh'.[28]

---

* Helen would go on to marry the Russian mosaicist Boris Anrep, whom she would then leave for Roger Fry.

Gus admitted to his own weaknesses, his self-indulgences, his deplorable 'wool gathering', acknowledging as much to the poet Arthur Symons: 'I wish I had been born with more method in my madness.'[29] But there was a rhythm to his work, and, just as Rodin had needed to relax in the voluptuous shallowness of Claire, so Gus needed the release of what Ottoline could only scorn as his intellectual slumming.

After Aix, he was too keyed up to work, so he accepted an invitation to visit the writer Frank Harris, who was summering in Nice. Harris was a beefy drunk who took pride in his own competitively bad behaviour, and Gus was hoping for some boozy fun. But perhaps he was more fastidious than Ottoline allowed. The three days he spent in Nice were 'mighty queer', he wrote, for Harris appeared to be engineering some kind of odd, sexual scenario between Gus, his wife and his secretary. Both women, Gus thought, were flirting in a bizarrely unnatural way, and he was so afraid of falling victim to some sort of trap, he simply ran away, slipping out of his bedroom just before dawn.

Back at the Villa Sainte Anne, however, he still felt the unpleasantness of this 'mad, infected' visit, his head hurt and he was cross with everyone. Helen decided it was time for her to join Henry, assuring Gus that Dorelia's pregnancy was progressing well and that she no longer needed another woman's care. But Helen's optimism was horrifically misplaced. On the morning of 1 May, Dorelia went into premature labour, and the baby, a girl, was stillborn. She then began haemorrhaging quantities of blood, perhaps because of a displaced placenta. But the transfusion she needed was not available in rural France in 1910, and the Martigues doctor could only maintain her blood pressure through injections of salt water. For twenty-four hours, her life hung in the balance, and Gus relived all the agony of Ida's death as he sat by Dorelia's bed, watching her slip in and out of consciousness. Even when the bleeding stopped, she remained frighteningly weak, and Gus telegrammed an urgent plea for Helen and Henry to come back and help.

The next few weeks were awful. Helen and Henry did what they could, but the little boys were hard to control, Helen's cooking played havoc with Gus's digestion and the southern heat affected everyone. By the time the older boys came out in August, Gus was desperate to regain the cool green shade of the British countryside. But then, just as he was on the point of leaving, the Provençal landscape recast its spell. The earth had been baked to an intense, red ochre, the fierce sunlight and the cutting shadows had brought out the bare bones of the terrain, and suddenly Gus saw how it all had to be painted. In his impatience to get it down, he worked on small wooden boards prepared with a transparent primer, onto which he drew a few guiding lines before applying the paint. He ignored detail, working instead in brilliant blocks of yellow, green, grey and blue with which he tried to capture the heat, the harshness, the purity and majesty around him. If there were people in these landscapes, they were similarly abstracted, their faces featureless ovals, their clothes rectangles of colour.

Even in his more representational pictures – of Dorelia, of gypsies, of the children – Gus worked with the same elemental force. One of the most sublime pictures he did that summer was of his three smallest boys bathing naked in the lake, a tender concentration of chubby limbs and bottoms, of pink infant flesh set against limpid blue. To Quinn he wrote, 'What I have been about here is rapid sketching in paint and I can say (with some excitement) that it is only during the last week or two that I have made an absolute technical step . . . I want to live long.'[30]

Of course, this 'absolute step' had come out of a long period of thinking and looking at other painters' work. But, in London, in late November, when Gus put fifty of his Provençal studies on show at the Chenil, it was widely agreed that his art had undergone a definitive change. *The Times* was uncertain of its value, arguing that there was 'neither nature nor art in many of these queer, clever, forcible but ugly and uncanny notes of form and dashes of colour.'[31] The *Athenaeum*, however, wrote enthusiastically of John's new 'scientific approach towards decorative colour'.[32] And Laurence Binyon, in the *Saturday Review*, judged the Provençal studies to be among the most expressive works Gus had ever painted, the portraits especially having 'a primitive energy, powerful and unaccountable like life itself . . . A tall woman, leaning on a staff, a little boy in scarlet on a cliff edge . . . a woman carrying bundles of lavender, they seem creatures of the infancy of the world.'[33]

*

These were the terms in which Gus wanted his work described, and the public, sharing the critics' enthusiasm, bought up most of the pictures, paying up to fifty guineas apiece for the little wood panels.

Yet, while the reviews and the profits were both 'excellent', Gus wrote, there had been a troubling shadow cast over his show, from an exhibition that had opened three weeks earlier at the Grafton Gallery in Mayfair.

'Manet and the Post Impressionists'* was the project of Roger Fry, who'd become evangelical in his support for the European painters, mostly French, who were breaking revolutionary ground with their development of what Fry described as 'expressive' form'.† For his show at the Grafton, Fry had sourced about a hundred of these painters' works, most of which were unfamiliar to the British public.‡ When the show opened on 8 November, the turbulent, saturated colours of Van Gogh and Gauguin, the brilliant decorative flatness of Matisse, the vibrating life force of Cézanne and the haunting distortions of Picasso had burst onto the London art scene with a force that was both hallucinatory and divisive.

In support of the show were the young and progressive. Vanessa Bell declared that it had acted on her like a lightning strike, a galvanizing recognition that it was possible to 'say things one always felt instead of trying to say things that other people told one to say'. Against the exhibition were the older generation and the majority of critics, who condemned it as 'a handful of mud', a 'huge practical joke organised by Paris at the expense of our countrymen.'[34]

'It is war to the palette knife', quipped the *Manchester Guardian*, and Gus, who went to the exhibition twice, was unsettled by the controversy, unable to take sides.[35] The Cézannes were predictably 'marvellous', the Picassos 'wonderfully fine, full of secret beauty of sentiment', and he admired a 'stunning self-portrait' by Van Gogh.[36] But Matisse, he decided, was an 'ingenious charlatan', and he sensed, perhaps unfairly,

---

* When Fry had been casting around for a suitable title, he'd coined the term 'post impressionism' and, imprecise though it was, it stuck.
† Clive Bell would later label that concept as 'significant form'.
‡ It included twenty Van Goghs, twenty Cézannes and thirty-seven Gauguins.

that Fry had been opportunistically provocative in stirring up discord, not only among the British public but among the artists as well.

Gus had always tried to insulate himself from the bickering of art-world politics, and from the market tendency to brand artists by label and style. But detachment was hard for him now, when the Grafton divide was pushing everyone to identify themselves as either conservatives or moderns. His own Provençal paintings could easily have been hung at Fry's show; the following year, a critic would praise his ability 'to suck the essence from a Cézanne landscape, from a Gauguin savage' and make it his own.[37] In 1912, when Gus exhibited *Mumpers* (his finally completed commission for Lane), it was hailed as 'the first mature masterpiece of Post-Impressionism'.[38] And when he was invited to participate in a second post-impressionist show, his principal reason for declining was the poisonous atmosphere of its organizing committee.

Yet, while Gus had found a deep affinity with the European avant-garde, he'd only taken elements that were useful to him, and there were critics for whom his work remained too romantic in its instincts, too eclectic in its technique to be counted as modern. One writer in *The Times* had argued that the 'most extreme works of Mr John [were] as timid as the opinions of a Fabian Socialist compared with those of a bomb throwing anarchist'.[39] And the formerly loyal Fry was now openly regretting that Gus had isolated himself from the 'comradeship and rivalry that exists in Paris' and was unable to push 'his mode of expression to the same logical completeness.'[40] Vanessa and Clive Bell, who'd been eager visitors to Gus's studio in 1908, now thought his work sentimental and, in 1913, would sell their portrait of Pyramus to raise money for a Cézanne.*

Gus waved off the complaints; to Quinn, he mocked Fry as a 'gifted obscurantist', joking that if he were shown 'a gilded turd in a glass case he would [hail it] as a cataclysmic genius'.[41] But still he felt a shifting of the ground. For almost a decade, he'd been hailed as the rising genius, the enfant terrible of British art. His astounding facility, his bohemian

---

* The uncertainty of his place in the art world was signalled by the offer made to Gus, in 1912, to join the Camden Town Group, a collective of London painters, dominated by Sickert, whose signature was a grimy urban realism.

flamboyance, his scrapes with the law had made him the 'Wonder of Chelsea'. Without fully acknowledging the truth to himself, Gus had grown dependent on his notoriety. He might deplore his life becoming fodder for the popular press, each new exhibition studied not only by critics but by gossip columnists in search of scandal, yet, however foolish the publicity, it had been proof that he was seen, that he mattered, that he was at the forefront of things. Now, at the age of thirty-two, Gus was being cast as the timid Fabian, irrelevant to the stirrings abroad.

The whole world, it seemed to Gus, was moving too fast. During the year of the Grafton divide, there had been miners and dockers on strike, militant suffragettes mobbing the prime minister. Motor cars had been appearing on the streets, women had been discarding their corsets and the first American-style nightclub had opened in London. There had been a mood of defiance, a call for liberty, and, while Gus could sympathize with its spirit, he was uneasy with much of its expression. He hankered after unspoiled landscapes rather than cocktails and jazz, after gypsy caravans rather than motor cars, and he cared more about the preservation of the old ways than the advancement of modern democracy. Early in 1911, when the walls of the Church Street house had again begun to close in, when he and Dorelia had been quarrelling so badly that he'd run away to Paris for Christmas and she'd disappeared for a week with Henry Lamb, he made the decision to move his family out of London. Dorelia hated the city, and it seemed to Gus, if he could find somewhere remote and beautiful for them to settle, some English equivalent of the Villa Sainte Anne, he might still hold onto his dream of the authentic life.

When he first proposed the idea to Dorelia, he had only the vaguest idea of where they might go. But he knew some people, the Everetts, who lived in rural Dorset, and, sometime in early March, they wrote to inform him of a house that was available for rent. It was called Alderney Manor and, although it was only one storey high, it had eight good-sized rooms and was wonderfully isolated, set in sixty acres of private grounds, which merged into the wildness of heath, marshland and pine.

It sounded so perfect to Dorelia, she wanted to take it immediately; but Gus, unusually cautious, insisted on a preliminary inspection.

Katherine Everett had offered to take them, and, when they appeared in her driveway, a 'vivid' little group with a donkey and two of the littlest children in tow, she was convinced they would approve her choice – for Alderney Manor was not so much a house as a bungalow with the aspect of a fairy-tale castle.[42] Lying at the end of a dark rhododendron drive, it was a confection of pink stuccoed walls, pointed gothic windows and a castellated parapet. And, while it had been badly neglected and would require months of work, it seemed very affordable to Gus, its owner, Lady Winbourne, having declared she was 'so tickled to have a clever artist' for a tenant, she was willing to let it for fifty pounds a year.[43]

While they were waiting for the renovations to be done, Gus spent much of the spring and early summer in north Wales. He'd recently met the young Welsh artist James Dickson Innes, who, having spent a formative period in Provence, had returned to his roots, discovering that the mountainous Welsh landscape, with its dramatic changes of light and weather, was an even more inspiring subject for him than France. He'd invited Gus to join him there in the remote valley of Nant Ddu, and Gus agreed it was the 'most wonderful place' he'd ever seen. He felt no professional rivalry for Innes as the two men tramped the countryside, drawing and painting together. He admired Innes's 'swiftness of decision', the 'jewelled' sureness of his palette – artistically, it was the most collaborative relationship he'd known since sketching with Gwen as a child. And the more time he spent in Innes's company, the more Gus came to love this intense young man with his melancholy clown's face. They drank together riotously and they chased after local girls – apart from the weeks when they were joined by Dorelia and Euphemia Lamb, with whom Innes was now fathoms deep in love. But the touchstone of their bond, with each other and with Wales, was the brooding majesty of one particular mountain, Arenig Fawr. Following the example of Cézanne and his devotion to Mont Sainte-Victoire, Innes had drawn and painted Arenig over and over again, at different hours of the day, in different weathers. Quickened by his influence, Gus too had deepened his experiments with colour and form, and, between the two of them, they transformed the dour tradition of Welsh landscape painting into something playful and modern. When they were joined in Wales by the

Australian painter Derwent Lees, their work was so jointly prolific it would come to be identified as the Arenig school.*

The untrammelled beauty of Provence and Wales had electrified the way in which Gus saw and painted landscape, but, when the family moved into Alderney in late summer, he found a different, more domestic inspiration. Although Henry Lamb had predicted Dorelia might become 'overgrown in such isolation', it was here that she found her true form of expression, and she conferred a magic on the house and the grounds. She repainted each room at Alderney in a brilliant palette of yellows, browns and reds; she hung pictures, scattered cushions, placed vases of wild and cultivated flowers on every surface. Outside, she planted a vegetable garden; over the years, she learned how to keep chickens, cows and bees, how to make butter and harvest honey. And, dressed in the intricately printed and colourful clothes she sewed for herself, her hair bound up in a gypsy scarf, her long silver earrings dangling, Dorelia became the presiding spirit of the place.

Many young women would admire Dorelia's style and try, unsuccessfully, to copy it. The children, however, were becoming old enough to find it a hideous embarrassment. Romilly would pray urgently to God to make his mother wear 'proper clothes' when she came to his school, and he and his brothers would pray even more urgently for deliverance from the rustic, brightly coloured smocks and breeches Dorelia continued to make for them, blithely ignoring their urgent requests for the jolly anonymity of trousers and jerseys.

Gus had no truck with his children's shame; he believed they were growing up exactly as Ida had wanted, dressed in their smocks, learning how to cut wood, collect eggs and help with the animals. And, even though there would be times when family life in Alderney became as confining to him as it had been everywhere else, he would always be conscious of the beauty Dorelia had created there – a beauty he could never have imagined in the grim mausoleum that had been his childhood home.

The pictures Gus painted of Dorelia during their first months in

---

* Landscapes by the three men would be hung together by John Quinn in the New York Armory Show of 1913.

Dorset were irradiated with his love for her and with the pleasures of their move. In *Dorelia in the Garden of Alderney Manor* she was a column of vibrant colour, dressed in shades of blue and peach and set against a background of jungle-green spikes, earthy stripes of brown, pink and grey. In *The Blue Pool*, painted near the flooded claypit that was close to the house, she was his dreamier, quieter muse, cradling her pregnant belly (she had, to Lamb's despair, become '*enceinte*' again) and – in the most beautiful of the picture's two versions – lying on the grass, a book in one hand. The heat and colour of this painting, the baked silver grey of the distant cliffs, the indigo blue of the pool below, the heavy afternoon drowse of sunshine owed as much to Provence as they did to southern England. For the moment, it was as though Gus, in the calm of his domestic and creative contentment, had at last found Arcadia at home.

Chapter Twelve

SEARCHING FOR RELIGION

'God your lover is waiting for you.'
GWEN JOHN[1]

The Christmas before Alderney, when Gus had fled to Paris to escape the escalating tensions in Church Street, he'd gone looking for Gwen. He hadn't spent any time with her since Ida's death and he wanted to see for himself that she was well. But she was not in her room at rue de l'Ouest, nor could her neighbours tell him where she might be, for Gwen had also felt a longing to leave the city, and, unbeknownst to Gus, had just signed the lease on a modest flat in the hilly, rural suburb of Meudon.

For months, Gwen had needed more space. Now that she was painting regularly again, her room had become cluttered with her equipment: her brushes, glues and primers, the wooden strainers for stretching her canvases. She'd had cravings to wake each morning to birdsong, to sleep without the city clattering around her. And, now that Quinn would be making regular boosts to her income, she'd realized she could afford to keep on her little Paris room as a studio, while looking for a more peaceful refuge elsewhere.

Meudon had possibly been recommended by Isabel Bowser, who'd lived there for a while. But it had long been popular with painters, who'd come for its cheap rents, its clear light, its leafy streets and its proximity to the centre of Paris – just a six-and-a-half-mile journey by riverboat or train. For Gwen, there was also the draw of Rodin, who still returned to Meudon most nights, and whose loss she could bear more easily through the knowledge that he was sleeping close by, and through the hope that the two of them might accidentally meet on their morning commute.

It was late in 1910 when Gwen wrote to Ursula of the flat she had found in the steep and beguilingly crooked rue Terre Neuve: 'It only costs 45 francs every 3 months . . . It is the top storey of an old house . . . there are three rooms and a little kitchen and heaps of cupboards & a grenier [attic].'[2] The washing facilities were minimal – Gwen would still have to use the public baths on Sunday afternoons – and her modest collection of furniture looked sparse in the extra space. Yet it was, she told Ursula, 'my little joy'. Perched high in her flat, she could look out over trees in one direction and over to Paris in the other, the distant dome of Sacré-Coeur shining white in the winter sun. Even more fantastic were the views from the Observatory Terrace, a wide, open plateau at the top of rue Terre Neuve. People came to the Observatory from miles around to see the whole of Paris laid out below, but Gwen preferred to leave its manicured pathways for the forest that lay beyond – a dense 1,200 hectares of chestnut, oak, wild cherry and pine, with a scattering of lakes and picnic spots. She had often gone to Meudon forest for her Sunday excursions, bringing home bunches of wild flowers to decorate her room. Now, it was her pleasure to go there in all seasons and all weathers. To Ursula, she would write of her joy in tramping through the 'dark and rain' one November evening: 'it was lovely walking through the fallen leaves. I picked up a bundle of wood for my fire, there was much wind too.'[3]

Just as Alderney was to become Gus and Dorelia's first settled home, so 29 rue Terre Neuve was Gwen's. Just down the hill was a row of little shops – a butcher, barber and baker – and at the bottom was the pretty station, Meudon val Fleury, from which she caught her Paris train. She felt rooted in the place, given substance by it, and her notebook entry of February 1911 was replete with confidence and calm:

Live largely and deeply do not be afraid
Don't be a poor little worldly frightened worried thing!
Don't expect anything more from love
A beautiful life is one led, perhaps, in the shadow, but ordered regular harmonious.[4]

With conscious pride of ownership, Gwen urged Ursula to come and stay: 'you shall have a lovely bedroom with sun coming in early and no street noise.'[5] The two of them still had hopes of living and working together someday, and for Gwen it was to be something of a betrayal when, two years later, Ursula accepted a marriage proposal from her second cousin, Walter Tyrwhitt. But even if Ursula did not come to Meudon, Gwen was far from alone. In addition to the family of cats she'd acquired, there was Isabel, with whom she'd fallen into the habit of swapping books and going to shops and galleries – and with whom she'd also discovered another bond: that Isabel was sister-in-law to Gus's close friend Arthur Symons.

Also in Meudon was an English painter called Ruth Manson, who lived alone with her small daughter, Rosamond. A sturdy, physically affectionate woman, Ruth became Gwen's closest painting companion for several years. They sat for each other (it was almost certainly Ruth who took the photographs of Gwen posing nude), they went on painting holidays together on the Breton coast, and Ruth and Rosamond became sufficiently like family for Gwen to offer them a room in her flat when they were made temporarily homeless.

For almost the first time since Fitzroy Street, Gwen felt she was part of a community. She made particular friends of some of her neighbours: the Joly sisters, who were the daughters of her landlady; an elderly couple, Monsieur and Madame Gervais; and a frail young woman called Angeline Lhuisset. Although she needed to guard her privacy still, Gwen developed a fond, if dispassionate, interest in the people who lived and worked around her. She liked to pause and chat with the women who were shopping and talking in the street, she learned the names of their children, and, in return, she was accepted by Meudon with a tolerant curiosity. Mademoiselle John might have been eccentrically unmarried, she might have been paint-stained and have kept odd hours, yet she often gave money to charity, she patronized the local shops and she was seen almost every Sunday at Mass, in the parish church of Saint Martin and Saint Blaise.

'I am in love with the atmosphere of Meudon church,' Gwen would write, 'and the people who go to church here have a charm for me.'[6] These people, in fact, became a new subject for her work; sitting discreetly at the back of the church, Gwen began making small rapid images of the worshippers around her – the women in their fur-trimmed Sunday coats, the quiet-faced nuns and the rows of orphans in their care, little girls in pinafores, who delighted Gwen as they bent earnestly over their prayer books or exchanged furtive whispers.* The drawings she made were often little more than roughly drawn marks, but they brought her joy; and, during her first year in Meudon, Gwen also moved from simply observing her fellow parishioners to becoming a member of their congregation, a convert to the Catholic faith.

For years, Gwen's ideas about religion had been tainted by the rantings of her evangelical aunts, by the timid, conventional piety of her father. She'd never imagined she would willingly attend a church or a chapel again. When she'd come to Paris, she'd been surprised to learn that Rodin, for all his agnosticism, went often to Notre Dame, claiming to enjoy the familiarity of Mass, as well as the sublimity of the architecture and the music.

It had been the hope of meeting Rodin which had first drawn Gwen to Notre Dame as well, but over the years her hostility towards religion had begun to shift. In the summer of 1908, she'd been given a book by Rilke, a volume of letters written by a young Portuguese nun who'd been seduced and abandoned by a French officer and had eventually found consolation in God. The letters touched Gwen. 'They come down to us from several centuries ago, they are very beautiful and simple like a bird singing', she told Ursula. 'Unhappy love, *naturellement*.'[7] And she was equally moved by Rilke's gentle hope that, in following the nun's example, she too might find some spiritual relief from the heartbreak of her affair with Rodin. Rilke was no longer a Christian, but he did believe there was a higher power which guided the universe, and he seems to have urged Gwen, now, to look to that power and find in it her own calm centre of acceptance.

His counsel had helped Gwen before, and so, throughout the turbulent months of 1909 and 1910, when she was raging over her displacement by Claire, when she was thrilling to the new intensity of

---

* They were housed in the Orphelinat Saint Jospeh.

her work, she was trying to meditate and find stillness in her thoughts. Perhaps her Chapel background was stronger than she believed, for at times she framed her meditation in religious terms, addressing some of her private jottings to 'JC' (Jesus Christ) and urging herself to rise above despair or self-doubt with informal acts of prayer: 'Ask God to help you. Keep his commandment; Do not be depressed by the idea of falling short – you can go some distance'.[8]

When Gwen moved to Meudon, though, and became a regular worshipper at Mass, those unformed religious impulses became clearer, more compelling to her. She began to see a grandeur, a mystery in Catholicism, which had been missing from the chapel in Tenby; she began to anticipate the joy of submitting herself to an all-powerful God – her own mortal god, Rodin, having proved so fallible. And her cravings for some higher form of guidance and love had been heightened, too, because, three or four months after moving to Meudon, she'd been assaulted by what she bleakly described in her diary as her 'Great Depression'.

She didn't elaborate on its cause. Possibly it was some new cruelty of Claire's, possibly it was exacerbated by the weeks of illness she'd been suffering, debilitating migraines followed by a bout of bronchitis. It's also conceivable that she'd been affected by the suicide of her former employer Nuala O'Donel, who had given up on her disappointing life and, alone in her marble-walled apartment and among her worn velvet gowns, had switched on the gas and turned her face to the wall. Even if Gwen left no comment on the tragedy, she could not have been unmoved by it. Miss O'Donel had been a constant in her life; she had provided work, company, a rivalry of sorts and, despite her volatile and occasionally spiteful moods, she'd been central to the sisterhood of artists who'd first eased Gwen's way into Paris.

Also, death, in itself, was always acutely upsetting. The losses of her mother, her cat, of Ida, had all become linked for Gwen, each grief feeding off the other. That spring, when Thornton appeared in Paris, hoping to see his sister during a short visit home, he was alarmed by her morbidly depleted state. He sounded the alarm to Edwin, who wrote immediately to beg Gwen to come home, and to Gus, who, equally swiftly, offered help. Gwen was grateful – 'My dear Gus, I am touched by your gentle solicitude. I think too it would be wise to shake off this funeste fatigue'[9] – but she was frightened by the depths to which she'd sunk and she knew she needed more assistance than either of her brothers could offer. In May, she wrote in her diary that the only way she could see of casting out the 'sin' of her misery was to entrust herself to the mercy of God.

For the rest of the year, Gwen disciplined herself to pray 'incessantly' and, in early 1912, she approached the curé of Saint Martin and Saint Blaise, asking for the formal instruction that would prepare her for entry to the Catholic Church. The relief was wonderful. After years of battling with herself, Gwen could imagine nothing more beautiful than giving herself over to a God who had the power to 'arrange my life . . . tell me what to say, what people to talk to', and who would never abandon her as Rodin, Ambrose, even her mother had done.[10] So pure was her desire for submission, she briefly considered leaving Paris for an isolated spot, where there could be no disruption to her devotions.

Instead, Gwen went to Mass almost every day and paid regular visits to the Mother Superior at Meudon convent. In her notebook, she wrote with joyful anticipation, 'God your lover is waiting for you'; and, as the date of her First Communion approached, she sensed her belief growing stronger: 'I have chosen to be God's spiritual child. I will ask God to make me faithful to the life I have chosen . . .'[11]

Just as love for Rodin had once changed her world, Gwen believed that her new-found faith would direct the course of her work as well as her life. She may already have attempted her first religious painting with *A Lady Reading* (which the art historian Alicia Foster has interpreted as an image of the Annunciation, the sunlight falling on the Lady's face symbolic of the Angel Gabriel who came to the Virgin Mary). In September 1912, when Gwen wrote to Ursula, she intimated that her vocation for art and for religion were starting to merge: 'I think I may never have anything to express except this desire for a more interior life'.[12]

But finding a correct balance between the two remained a confused and troubling issue for Gwen. She had been very distressed when her curé had advised her that sketching in Mass was wrong, a distraction from prayer; yet, even as she'd argued against his directive, had defended the necessity of her work, she had worried that the professional ambitions which Quinn had reawoken in her, the renewed passion for work might be an offence against the teachings of the Church. As early as November 1911 she was writing that the worry of selecting and sending her pictures for exhibition in London was making her 'feel further from God'.[13] And the following autumn, when she made a list of the faults she needed to correct in herself, they all, in some way, led back to her art.

> Too much vanity
> Too much care for material things
> Too much sensual reverie
> Too much care for the opinion of the world
> Too much criticism of others
> Too much uneasiness about work in life[14]

Gwen tried to tell herself that her only goal, now, was simplicity – 'not caring for the opinion of anyone, not afraid of obscurity or contempt' – yet not even God could make her simple.[15]

Her need to reinvent the world through colour and form was still as powerfully present as her faith. And it was her curé, perhaps bowing to the obvious, who proposed she might begin solving her dilemma by painting a picture for the Meudon sisters. They had talked of wanting a new portrait of Mère Poussepin, the nun who'd founded their order back in the seventeenth century. The only image they had of her was the little black and white print on their prayer cards, which had been taken from a much earlier painting and which the curé assumed would be quite straightforward for Gwen to copy.*

Well intentioned as the curé was, however, he knew little about art. It was possible for Gwen to glimpse something of Mère Poussepin's character from her image on the prayer-card image, the maternal curve of her smile, the serene merriment of her gaze. But Gwen had always drawn and painted from life, she'd always depended on feeling the specific heat and tone of her subject's presence. Her portraits had also

---

* The Meudon nuns were a chapter of the Sœurs de la charité dominicane de la Présantation de la Saint Vierge de Tours.

evolved too far beyond the art of simple representation for her to be content with making a replica. If she were to penetrate to the 'interior life' of Mère Poussepin and capture her soul, Gwen knew she could only do so by going deeper into her own technique.*

The challenge of painting the nun's picture would take her over seven years. Because the nuns wanted a portrait for each of the convent's rooms, she would make several different versions, often complaining bitterly of the time she was wasting. Yet, however hard the labour and the 'falling short', this portrait became a crucible of experiment for Gwen.

Working on a larger scale than before, she was searching for the truth of Mère Poussepin by altering the tone, the texture, the spacing and the pose with each different version. She was exploring a new palette – a quietly luminous spectrum of greys, yellows and whites – and she was refining her new method of 'painting dry', adding chalk to the paint and the canvas primer, using a stippling of short, rapid strokes. The culminative effect was to make the space of the portrait both shallower and more abstract, so that Mère Poussepin, in all her lively detail, seemed almost to float in the canvas – a seventeenth-century nun suspended in an early modernist painting.

The process of repetition, which Gwen had already begun in her drawing, was becoming almost an end itself, an act of meditation, a way for her to think through her ideas. In addition to the portraits of Mère Poussepin, she was painting several of the young Meudon nuns, one of whom she found particularly intriguing, with 'something in the little face, a little sulky and sad.'[16] She was also working with a new model, a young woman from Meudon, whose pale oval face, modest demeanour and simple fall of dark brown hair conveyed an exceptional quality of stillness. It was this quality, perhaps, that made Gwen paint her new model dozens of times. Some of the pictures were grouped into series, categorized by the colour of the dress the woman wore, or by the object she held in her lap – a book, a letter, a piece of sewing, and sometimes a cat, whose solid weight seemed to anchor the woman in her own quiet space. There was a steady evolution through all of them, though, as Gwen,

---

* Gwen had recently been affected by an assertion made by Maurice Denis, that the 'Christian truth' of a picture must lie not only in its subject but in its approach.

making nuanced changes to each of the portraits, worked to achieve more of what interested her now – not so much a physical representation as a capturing of emotional atmosphere.

The Meudon model was almost a secular sister of the nuns, in fact the contemplative style in which Gwen painted these portraits might suggest that she herself had reached an equivalent calm. Despite her vows of discipline and renunciation, however, Gwen was still far from subduing her old greedy hungers – for love, for beauty and for experience. On the day of her First Communion, she panicked about all she was expected to sacrifice: 'I have felt momentarily a fear of losing the world I know, as if I should be losing something of value'.[17] She knew that, however diligently she prayed, she could never curb her delight in a new dress, in a word of praise for her work. Even though she knew that the heaven and hell which Rodin had made of her life were a perversion of Christian theology, she could never imagine erasing him from her life.

If anything, her attachment had deepened, because, in the summer of 1912, he'd finally broken with Claire after learning that she had tried to frame his secretary for stealing. According to *The New York Times*, everyone was glad to see the back of her and her 'monopolising [of] the sculptor's affairs', and at first Rodin himself had been relieved. Claire's relentless animation, her relentless pursuit of profit and publicity had all begun to exhaust him.[18] Yet, without her vitality, he also began to feel the full weight of his seventy years, and, to Gwen's delight, he began seeking out her company again. He summoned her to the studio from time to time, invited her to ride in the car that now drove him into Paris, and occasionally he returned to her bed. In his need of her, he became even more precious to Gwen, and her happiness was sometimes too painful to bear: 'perhaps, *mon maître cheri*, it was you coming to my room to make love to me that has made me feel as if I am dying'.[19]

If Gwen could never think of abandoning Rodin, she was grateful to him, too, for the acceptance he showed of her new religious faith, his appreciation of how much stronger she was through its support. The approval of those she loved was important to her. Ursula, whom she'd feared might be sceptical, had been kind. 'You have given me so much encouragement,' Gwen wrote with gratitude, 'you seem to agree with my decision to live as much as I can in a way that I have collectedness of my thoughts'.[20] Winnie had also given her blessing. She believed that Gwen, like all of their family, had been cursed with an 'overdevelopment of the subjective mind,' that she had 'to look out not to overbalance'; and, having become interested in Christian Science herself, she could only admire Gwen's willing submission to the teachings of the Catholic Church.

Thornton, so elusive and withdrawn as a child, was equally sympathetic to his sister's new faith. Ever since he'd visited Gwen in Paris he'd been corresponding with her more regularly and become interested in her efforts to strengthen herself through prayer. He too was developing his own quiet habits of meditation and, on Gwen's advice, had begun reading Dostoyevsky's *The Idiot*, whose saintly protagonist, Prince Myshkin, she wrote, made her 'tremble'.[21]

From Gus, however, there could be no such sympathy. He had turned his back on religion years ago; like Gwen, the shaming theatrics of the evangelical aunts, the mealy-mouthed piety of his father had left him with a dread of the Church. And when he eventually learned of his sister's conversion, he found it incredible that she, who'd always despised hypocrisy and false sentiment, should now willingly submit to the mumbo jumbo of Catholic priests – more incredible still that she could attempt to elevate doctrine over beauty and passion. Even after her death, he would not accept it, writing that, while Gwen had 'attempted to cultivate the *saînte indifférence* recommended by some of her spiritual guides, success on these lines was hardly to be expected while such a heart as hers continued to beat.'[22]

Gwen, anticipating his reaction, had told Gus nothing of the first steps she'd taken towards the Church during the early summer of 1911. And her silence had hardened over the winter, as the two of them had become drawn into one of their most unhappy quarrels. After Gus had moved his family into Alderney, he'd wanted Gwen to visit – he was proud of his new house and he thought the countryside would do her good after her recent depression. She, however, had been too deeply absorbed in her new Meudon life to make any move; she'd fobbed off his repeated invitations with such vague promises for the future that, in the end, he'd grown tired of her prevarication and had even given up bothering to write.

This, for Gwen, was something new. There had always been periods when their correspondence had lapsed, when Gus had been travelling, busy with work or a new affair. But he'd always got back in touch, and Gwen wondered now if he was playing some kind of childish game. She continued, pointedly, to write to him; in February 1912, she sent him the catalogue of an Italian Futurists' show she'd seen in Paris, asking for his opinion on whether the work was as amusing as she'd thought, and whether it showed some evidence of 'great talent'.[23]

Still there was no reply, and, in early March, when Gwen realized that Gus had failed to forward an urgent letter from the NEAC, she was livid. To Ursula, she complained that, while she'd been fully intending to visit her brother at Alderney, she had no intention of doing so now. 'For months he has been ignoring my letters. I don't feel inclined to stay with him! I don't think I shall ever go . . .'[24]

It was a harsh reaction, and also a dishonest one, for Gwen was now so deep into her religious instruction, her attendance at Mass, she wouldn't have considered leaving Meudon even if Gus had been writing to her. Among the many faults for which she so willingly castigated herself – emotional weakness, material vanity – Gwen rarely thought to question her quickness to criticize others. There was a streak of ruthless self-absorption in her still, a lack of charity and of self-awareness. And, in her readiness to blame Gus now for his apparent neglect, Gwen was also forgetting the frequent gaps on her own side of their correspondence, the barriers she had tried to erect between her life and his.

From the depths of her righteous irritation, Gwen also had no idea that there was a terrible reason for her brother's silence. In late February, when she'd been so cross about his lack of response to her Futurists letter, Gus had been sick with worry. Dorelia had been nearing the end of her pregnancy, and he was nagged by memories of her near-fatal haemorrhaging. Then, suddenly, his beautiful Pyramus had developed a drastic infection, which their doctor had diagnosed as meningitis. Even Gus knew how fatal this could be, and, having failed to get a specialist down from London, he could only hover in despair as his most angelic child, his 'daisy', lay racked in fever and pain.

Dorelia had been willing herself not to go into labour so that she could nurse her little boy. On 8 March, when her pains began, she allowed herself to be moved into a separate room, where, without serious difficulty, she gave birth to a 'big nice girl'. It was the daughter for whom Gus had always longed, but joy was impossible as Pyramus slipped into unconsciousness. 'I do not think he will outlive today,' he scrawled wretchedly to Sampson on 12 March. 'He was indeed a celestial child and that is why the gods take him.' By the evening, Pyramus was gone.[25]

Gus had no priest to counsel him, no faith on which to offload the burden of his sorrow, and what followed, he admitted to Quinn, were 'awful days'. For some reason, Pyramus was cremated at Woking, about eighty miles away, and Gus went there alone to collect his child's ashes. He had just asked Ada for the return of Ida's and it was 'stupefying', he wrote to Sampson, to have 'one more urn for my collection – the mind refuses to contemplate such a fact.' So mortally afraid was Gus of facing the 'real hell' of his loss that, when he left his train at Poole, he completely forgot the tragic little urn, which was stashed away in the luggage rack, and he had to arrange for it to be delivered to Alderney later that day.

It was almost impossible for him to speak directly of his grief. To Ottoline, he sent an anguished parody of a birth and death announcement, 'dearest friend le roi est mort vive la reine'.[26] His note to Ada was punitively abrupt: 'Pyramus died and a girl baby has been born. All the boys are extremely well.' And, as he withdrew behind a wall of silence, Gus admitted to Quinn how grateful he was that Dorelia, too, was mourning in deepest privacy. 'I must say the missus behaves throughout as I think few women would, with amazing good sense and a splendid determination not to give way to the *luxury* of the expression of grief.'[27] The baby, who was named Elizabeth but always called Poppet, was a 'godsend', a new life and a distraction for them all. 'The loss of so lovely a child as Pyramus is quite unnerving', he wrote to Meg Sampson. 'Let us hope that the little girl may be the second beauty of the world.'[28]

But the facade of stoicism behind which Gus and Dorelia retreated was damaging to everyone. Despite Gus's claims that the family were 'extremely well', the boys had just suffered a second bewildering death, and they needed to be comforted. Gus, however, had little aptitude for the task, and no language for it. He'd found it easy to love his children as babies, so newly formed and so tactile, but the older they grew, the more inhibited he became about showing his affection. His second daughter, Vivien, born in 1915, would recall, years later, how the idea of 'parents *fondling* their children' seemed abhorrent to Gus. Caspar would concur, 'He was not really warm hearted, a tremendously difficult fellow to understand for a kid, I don't think he ever understood himself.'[29]

Relations between parents and children were still quite formal in England in 1912, but Gus, in his inability to console his own children over the loss of their brother, was laying down the same bedrock of resentment he'd once felt for his own father. He was also allowing his relationship with Dorelia to drift. The strength she had shown over Pyramus's illness and death, and her subsequent ability to immerse herself in the running of the house, had made Gus so grateful, he hadn't realized the gulf that was opening up between them, even in bed. 'I want to live with you . . . but I don't like imposing myself,' Gus would write awkwardly to Dorelia.[30] And, as always, when his life reached an impasse, his response was to create a diversion, a physical change of scene.

Early in the summer, he took the family to Wales, to a cottage in the isolated Nant Ddu valley where he'd painted the previous year, and from there he set off, alone, to Ireland. He went first to Dublin, the city of pubs, where he was chauffeured around in style by his host, the garrulous surgeon and bon viveur Oliver St John Gogarty, and fed quantities of whiskey to 'float the intellect'. Gogarty was 'such a mad hatter', Gus reported back to Dorelia, and he was quite relieved to move on to the rural tranquillity of County Clare. Here he was staying with the writer Francis Macnamara, who took him to the Aran Islands, remote rocky outposts which were still among the wildest parts of Ireland. The people who lived on the islands subsisted as they always had, on fish and island cattle, burning kelp for fuel; to Gus, they seemed to exist in a world away from his own troubled demons, indifferent to the passing of the centuries. Even their speech seemed to him the most exquisite dialect he had ever heard, 'slow ornate and somewhat archaic'.[31]

He resolved to return to the islands to set up a studio and paint. Meanwhile, having escorted his mulishly bored family back to Alderney, he returned to Wales, staying first at Chirk Castle to work on some commissioned portraits and murals, then on to Nant Ddu for some painting with Innes, and finally to the old mining village of Tan-y-grisiau, where he rented a cottage with two new companions – the composer Joseph Holbrooke ('the funniest man I have ever met') and the illustrator Sidney Sime.[32]

All of this travelling, which had begun as an escape from death, had finally rekindled Gus's appetite for work. From Wales, he told Dorelia he was 'full' of it, and, for the next twelve months, he continued tracking backwards and forwards to Wales, still obsessed by the mountains and by the extraordinary shifts of colour he saw when a haze of rain gave way to a brightening of sunshine. He took out a new cockney model, Lily, whom he posed as he might have done Dorelia, standing barefoot in the grass. To Quinn, he would rejoice that the panels he painted in the landscape around Tan-y-grisiau were among the best he'd ever done.[33]

His energy seemed unfailing: after Wales, he wintered in Provence; in the summer of 1913, he was in Paris, looking at art and bar-hopping with Epstein, Innes and Derwent Lees. Down in Alderney, he was painting the children, ignoring their protests as he ordered them to sit still. One frowning, belligerent portrait of Robin was particularly sublime, the little boy's face almost filling the picture, ruddy, cross and irreducibly alive. Up in London, he started work on *Lyric Fantasy* – his second frieze for Hugh Lane. The painting's dreamily choreographed figures owed something to Botticelli's *Primavera*, but they were also an elegy for Gus's two lost loves: little Pyramus, blond, exuberant and playing a drum, and a shawled, beatific Ida, keeping watch over the children with Dorelia.

The results of his energy were everywhere – at the Chenil, the NEAC, the Society of Twelve; at a new gallery called the Goupil and also at the National Portrait Society (who would elect him president in 1914). When his *Mumpers* frieze was shown in November 1912, it was considered by *The Times* to be the 'best he had ever painted'. In February 1913, when Quinn arranged for his work to be hung at the New York Armory Show, Gus was represented by thirty-six paintings and drawings – only one other painter had more. The painter Paul Nash would remember him as one of the three 'larger than life-sized personalities' who dominated London at the time – the others were Jacob Epstein and the stage designer Edward Gordon Craig.[34]

Gus would have liked to share more of his travels with Dorelia and he would have liked to paint her. But the lonely friction of their grief hadn't eased – twelve months after Pyramus died, Dorelia was still telling Ottoline she couldn't bear to speak of it. And, even though Gus sent her regular assurances of love while he was away – 'You may be sure I want you a great deal more than any other damsels' – he had, of course, found plenty of 'other damsels' who were happy to take Dorelia's place in his bed.

It seemed to Gus now that his love of women was a force beyond his control: to Alick Schepeler, he would describe it as 'a sort of paranoia or emotional hailstorm', explaining that, as soon as he was attracted to one woman, the 'impression' she made on him would be 'immediately obliterated by the next girl's, irrespective of its importance.'[35] He did not, apparently, consider that his insatiable need for love and sexual excitement might be linked to the void that had been opened up by his mother's death. But he did try to justify it in other terms. Sometimes, he elevated it to the level of existential epiphany. 'The dirty little girl I meet in the lane has a secret for me communicable in no language estimable at no price, momentous beyond knowledge, though it concerns but her and me'.[36] Sometimes, he would justify it as the logical consequence of being an artist, a man whose work made him go in search of beauty, 'the authentic thrill'.

There were also periods when Gus could feel a queasiness of disgust, a weariness with his own promiscuity. But mostly he found it too easy to believe he was entitled to it all. Men applauded him and many women chased after him. Frida Strindberg, second wife to the Swedish playwright, became so possessively crazed after one brief encounter with Gus that, for two years, she stalked him around Europe threatening to kill either herself or him. And Dorelia, who could have suffered most from his affairs, was now all but resigned. When one infatuated young woman came straggling down to Alderney, Dorelia impressed the friend who happened to be visiting with the calmness of her response, dispatching the young woman back to the station and simply commenting, 'I'm not going to have Augustus' girls here when he is not present'.[37]

There was an element of fatalism in Dorelia's poise; she'd accepted that Gus, with all his faults, was her destiny. But she also had the support of Henry's continuing devotion, and when she was alone, he often came to stay. A closeness, almost like marriage, had developed between them, and the drawings Henry made of Dorelia, working in the garden at Alderney or lying in bed, had now replaced the Arcadian pictures which Gus had painted only two years earlier.

Gus was glad of the relationship with Henry; it eased any guilt he might have felt about his own infidelities, and he recognized that the younger man could give Dorelia things he could not. But he also knew that, if he hurt Dorelia too badly, Henry would be ready to take her away, and that knowledge made him worry a little about the danger of leaving her too long alone. He decided, on impulse, to build a new home for Dorelia in London, so that he could include her in more of his life. And when he learned that the piece of waste ground near Church Street, where his children used to play, was now being sold off as building plots, he walked straight into a nearby pub and asked if there was an architect present who could design him a house.

Extraordinarily, there was: a Dutch man called Van-t-Hoff, who said he was willing to draw up some plans straight away. The plot itself was not large, but the design which the Dutchman proposed seemed 'charming' to Gus: a tall narrow house, with a curving wooden staircase copied from Rembrandt's home in Amsterdam, and a large studio at the back, with a romantically sloping ceiling, two fireplaces and good northern light. Gus, excited as always by new places, believed that 28 Mallord Street would be another fresh start. 'How glad I will be to live more quietly,' he mused to Quinn, imagining how well he would paint at the house, his intimacy with Dorelia restored.[38]

But Mallord Street was doomed to disappoint. It took a year and a half to build, going far beyond the promised budget of £2,200, and the delay and expense ran Gus ragged. He felt plagued by the lawyers, decorators and builders, who seemed to produce problems for him to solve every week. 'I can't be rushing all over London and paint too,' he complained to Dorelia. But he got little sympathy from her, since of course she had never asked for the house. London had become an anathema to her, with its dirt, noise and gossip; and the futility of Gus's hopes for a shared life in Mallord Street was symbolized by the little roof garden he'd requested Van-t-Hoff to incorporate. Overshadowed by neighbouring buildings, poisoned by winter smog, none of the plants that Dorelia might cultivate there could possibly survive.

Although she did make occasional, reluctant journeys to London – 'your appearance at the Café Royal caused a great sensation', Gus applauded – Dorelia never thought of Mallord Street as a home.[39] Even Gus tended to regard it only as somewhere for him to work or throw parties and it took a very different place, Lamorna Cove in Cornwall, to help ease the friction between them. Gus took Dorelia down in early 1914, to visit Laura and Harold Knight, who'd established a painting colony there. The company was 'excellent', Gus thought, and, for almost the first time in two years, he was able to get Dorelia to sit for him again. A study he made of her, down by the rocks at Lamorna Cove, was thought gorgeous by Laura Knight: 'He never did anything better'.[40]

Gus had also been trying to heal the rift with Gwen. Even in the harrowing aftermath of Pyramus's death he'd found time to worry about her, telling Meg Sampson he wished she would 'take a change' from her solitary life in Paris.[41] By September that year, he'd begun renewing invitations for her to visit Alderney. But Gwen, who may or may not have learned about Pyramus's death, remained fixed in her determination not to oblige. She was annoyed by Gus's persistence and wrote crossly to Ursula that 'there is no reason in visiting a man who is not sympathetic to one – even if one has no nerves it is a waste of time.'[42]

Yet Gus refused to give up and, in the summer of 1913, when he went to Paris with Epstein and the others, he hoped to see her. He wanted to talk to her about the art he was seeing, about the two primitive-looking stone heads he'd bought from Modigliani, about their mutual joy in Cézanne, their shared reservations about Matisse. And, while neither of them left an account of any meeting, an entry in Gwen's notebook suggested that she had agreed to one – and had been bracing herself for it: 'Do not be afraid to meet those you love after a long absence, you need not be afraid to have your hands empty, to make them sad and chilled, to discourage them.'⁴³ Perhaps she had been anticipating some fresh dispute with her brother, possibly some row over her religious conversion, yet Gus must have been tactful, because, over time, there was a gradual mellowing in Gwen's attitude.

Early in 1914, she made a point of alerting Gus to the three works she was sending to Quinn, via the Chenil, and which she wanted him to see.* Encouraged by her overture, he was quick to reply – 'Thank you for letting me know about the pictures. Quinn will be very happy to have them. He has often asked me if there is a chance of having more of your work.'⁴⁴ And he also seized that moment of conciliation to remind Gwen that the agreement she had with Quinn was not exclusive; there were 'plenty of others who want to have your things' he wrote, adding that she could depend on him, as her brother, to organize sales and exhibitions of her work back in London.

In scattering these breadcrumbs of professional opportunity, Gus may have been hinting for Gwen's own return to London – certainly he was hoping for a visit to Alderney. Made cautious by the past, however, he did not press, treating Gwen almost as though she were one of her feral cats, and would come to him in her own good time.

But, six months later, the situation became suddenly urgent. The assassination of Archduke Franz Ferdinand by Serbian nationalists, and the consequent unravelling of international relations, had brought the great powers of Europe to the brink of war. So fast did the situation deteriorate that, by 3 August, the combined forces of France, Britain and Russia were pitched against those of Austria and Germany.

Paris was almost certain to become a battle zone (as it had been forty years ago in the Franco-Prussian war), and Gus was sure that Gwen, who rarely read a newspaper, had little idea of the danger she might face. She would not realize how fast her situation could deteriorate, how serious the possibility was of her becoming trapped in Meudon and of her cheques from Quinn and the family trust being blocked. On 4 August, he wrote a long letter, outlining all his concerns: 'I wonder if you are going to remain in Paris . . . I hope not. You will have to suffer great

---

* One of the three was her 1910 portrait of Chloe, which Quinn greatly admired.

hardships . . . food will be awfully dear and most likely communication will be stopped, and in any case sending money over will be difficult if not impossible . . . It is not too late to come back here'.[45]

Willing Gwen to appreciate the gravity of the situation, he explained that he'd looked at the timetables and discovered that, while there were still two trains running daily from Paris to England, there was no guarantee of how long that service would continue. It was important for her to act fast, and, if she was afraid of travelling alone or unable to manage her luggage, he would come out to help. She might prefer to stay in London or go to one of her friends, but there would always be room for her at Alderney.

'Let me know what you decide and if I can help you in any way. With love Gus', he concluded. Yet, however persuasively he tried to write to Gwen about the dangers she faced, he knew she was almost certain to remain in Meudon. The attachments she'd formed to her church, to her nuns and her neighbours, the love that still bound her to Rodin – all these were stronger than any warnings he might make about hardships and bombs. When he wrote to warn Dorelia that he'd invited Gwen to stay with him, he added, with helpless exasperation, 'but of course she won't.'

Even in war, she would 'go her own way'.[46]

Chapter Thirteen

THE GREAT WAR

'Dear Gus, Your letter gave me great pleasure and still does, thank you for it, dear love. You tell me things too I didn't know and put it clearly'
GWEN JOHN TO AUGUSTUS JOHN[1]

Gwen took two and a half months to respond to Gus's offer – months that left him anxiously dangling – but she'd been touched by his concern, keeping his letter close, reading and rereading it many times. When she did eventually write back, her detailed reply was the start of an unusually intimate period of correspondence in which Gwen was more candid with Gus than she'd been for years.

She admitted that her situation had been bad, especially during the early weeks of the fighting, when a million German troops had advanced on Paris, and when their planes had taken control of the skies, bombing the streets and sending down blizzards of pamphlets to urge surrender. Even though the raids had become less frequent by the time Gwen wrote to Gus, the Germans were still flying planes over Paris, letting loose the occasional bomb to keep the city in a state of fearful submission. Gwen told Gus that, the day before yesterday, there had been 'a good many victims'. Grimly, she added, 'They hit children generally.'[2]

Meudon had so far escaped the bombing, although, in the first wave of panic, the mayor had considered evacuation and several of Gwen's friends, including Ruth Manson, had fled. At that point, she too had come close to leaving, but, as she'd explained to Ursula, she hadn't wanted to desert her adopted city. 'I suppose I am rather contrary, every day after seeing the Gare Montparnasse crammed & luggage & cattle trains loaded with frightened people I felt more and more disinclined to go.'[3] Even though she'd been required to register as a foreign national and had to endure three 'dreadful' days of queuing, Gwen had wanted to stand with the French, who now seemed to her 'wonderfully philosophic' in the face of potential catastrophe. Now that she'd lived so long among them, she couldn't imagine returning to England, which had, she realized, 'become quite a foreign country to me.'[4]

Paris, however, felt like a broken city to Gwen when she decided it was safe for her to resume work in her studio. On her way to rue de l'Ouest, she passed bombed and blackened buildings, streets pitted with craters; often, she had to shoulder her way through crowds of soldiers, many of them aggressively flirtatious in their hunger to grab one last kiss from a woman before they were sent to the front.

Despite her daily petitions to God, her earnest attempts to find some 'spiritual beauty' in war, Gwen was developing a bitter hatred towards the enemy, who seemed intent on destroying all she held dear: 'It will be a step in civilisation,' she wrote to Gus, 'to put a check on this brute force!'[5]

And yet the war energized Gwen – excited her, even. She begged Ursula to forward copies of the English *Times*, whose news was less heavily censored than the press in France; in return, she sent a detailed diagram of the defence fortifications around Paris and told Ursula how much she too wanted to become part of the war effort. Despite the precarious state of her income, she had already started to donate money to refugee charities, and now, despite her reluctance with strangers, she decided to volunteer her services as a translator and guide for the English-speaking soldiers arriving in Paris.

These men needed her, she explained later to Gus. The officers kept losing their luggage '& sometimes their servants', while the lower ranks had no idea of how to behave: 'They take what they want in the shops, they say *souvenir* and put things in their pockets . . . they seem like boys they talk like boys even the older ones.'[6] But Gwen was still proud of the British for 'stepping up to the mark', and when Meudon began to take in the wounded and she was able to help the Catholics among them to confess, she told Ursula how glad she was of the work. 'They are so pleased to be spoken to and I find them so charming.'[7]

Gus, reading her letters, was inclined to believe that his sister had undergone a quite startling change. She was not only taking charge of soldiers, she was frequenting cafes and striking up conversations with strangers – among them, she wrote proudly, a gypsy whom she'd met in the Rotonde. Gus egged her on: 'I wish I was in the Rotonde too [with] a couple of *grogs Americains* to neutralise the cold'; he urged Gwen to introduce herself to Modigliani, who also drank at the cafe, and to Beatrice Hastings, a correspondent for *The New Age*, whose war coverage he recommended. Very eager to see Gwen herself, he promised he would 'dash over' soon; meanwhile, he sent news of Alderney. 'Ici tout va bien, surtout la petite fille. The children . . . are all flourishing & Dorelia too . . . We have several visitors who tell us all sorts of news. I hear most startling tales about myself often when I go to town – but of course they are never authentic. Dorelia wants me to tell you she is sending you over a dress.'[8]

As always, Gus sent volleys of questions and advice. 'Do you manage to work? Don't let yourself get frozen dearest. Take exercises.' Yet Gwen no longer minded her brother's interference. The drama of the war had wiped away the tensions between them, especially as Gus was even more gripped by the conflict than Gwen. 'The Germans seem to be fighting desperately with up to now no particular success,' he wrote jubilantly to her in late October. 'It is true what you say – the British soldiers are all boys, not to say babes, but very pugnacious and capable ones.' Unlike some of his acquaintance – Ottoline and the writers and painters of Bloomsbury – Gus had been roused to a vehement patriotism; he'd believed uncritically the reports of German barbarism, had celebrated the British and French as defenders of a righteous cause. Watching the 'damn fine' sight of 1,500 men marching along Regent Street, he'd even been convinced of the ennobling effect of war – 'It ought to do people a world of good. I'm sure this country will benefit' – and he was half spoiling to enlist himself.[9]

Yet, while Gus briefly volunteered for the home defence effort – or at least was seen by Ezra Pound to be drilling enthusiastically one day with the Artists Rifles Regiment at Burlington House – his military ambitions went no further. A soldier's pay could never support two households and seven children – soon to be eight, since Dorelia was pregnant again – and Gus admitted to Gwen that his 'establishment would go bust' if he left them all for the front.

He also felt responsible for her, as her brother, and in mid-December he managed to wrangle a ticket to Paris and catch Gwen at work in her room on rue de l'Ouest. At first, he was dismayed by her apparent poverty. Even though the weather had turned bitterly cold, the fire in Gwen's studio was pitifully inadequate, and, under questioning, she admitted her Meudon flat was little warmer, and she was sometimes too cold to sleep. Yet, while she looked thinner, a little paler perhaps, she insisted she was eating well, and was receiving parcels of good, thick clothes from Ursula. Even more importantly, she seemed to Gus, during the short time of his visit, to be significantly less anxious and withdrawn than he'd seen her in a while.

One surprising reason for this, Gus learned, was that Rodin was no longer in Paris. The sculptor had been wildly, selfishly agitated at the start of the war, demanding to know what the authorities had planned to ensure his safety. When Gwen was summoned to his Meudon home on 4 September, a privilege she'd never been accorded before, she feared some crisis in his mental health. Yet, as she approached the Villa Brillantes, she was informed that the master was no longer in residence, that he and Rose Beuret were leaving for England. And, as Gwen grappled with the implications of this news, a horse-drawn cart came racing down the drive, piled up with Rodin's boxes and trunks.

Later in the day, she learned that the only reason she'd been invited to the Villa was to collect a one-hundred-franc note Rodin had left for her, and, for a moment, the knowledge that he'd abandoned her, that he'd paid her off in some way, had cut deep. But the war, and Gwen's determination to be part of it, had cauterized the shock. She simply found out where Rodin had gone, just outside London, and wrote a short, loving note, in which she thanked him for the money and recommended books for his spiritual comfort.* He replied with a reassuring fondness: 'Tell me what you're doing I shall read your news with great pleasure. With all my heart, your friend Rodin who thinks of you'.[10]

---

* It was in Epping Forest and Tonks visited him there to draw his portrait.

He continued to write and send money, but the cheerfulness that Gus observed in Gwen was prompted not so much by the warmth of Rodin's letters as by his physical absence from her life. For the first time in a decade, she was no longer referring all her thoughts and emotions back to her maître, no longer framing her days around the possibility of seeing him. His absence brought a lightness and, with that lightness, a terrific capacity for work. Even as Gwen was making progress with the portraits of her nuns and her young Meudon model, she had also embarked on two other projects: the portrait of a much younger girl, *La Petite Modèle*, and a study of her Meudon sitting room.

In all of the four versions Gwen painted of *Interior*, her own presence was as alive in the room as it had been in her attic paintings, her tea things and her newspaper spread out on her table as if she'd only just got up and walked away.* But the quality of the air and the light were different. There was no window to let in the Paris sunshine, and the furniture, the corner of the fireplace, were all made to appear fractionally too close to each other, as though the room had huddled itself together and had become a refuge from the danger outside.

This interior was as evocative of Gwen's life during war as the attic had been of her early years in Paris. Yet, however closeted the feel of the room, the confidence with which Gwen painted it was resilient with energy, with experiments in perspective, with blocks of stippled colour and gradations of tone. The exigencies of war, the imperative to seize the moment had accelerated the development of her work, and, by 1917, Gwen was writing breezily to Ursula, 'I think there will come a time when we will never paint for a few hours without doing something. A picture for every sitting or a part of one. At present I, at any rate, do so many canvases to be thrown away.'[11]

Gus had had little progress of his own to report when he went to see Gwen in December. The outbreak of war, however stimulating, had made him pessimistic about work. 'No one will want luxuries like pictures for a while,' he predicted to Quinn, and he was unsettled by the

---

* The three alternate versions of *Interior* were titled *The Brown Teapot*, *The Teapot* and *Study for The Brown Teapot*.

speed with which the art world had started to fragment.[12] Many of the men he knew were enlisting, signing up for home defence or, like Henry Lamb, volunteering to drive ambulances in France. Even Tonks had abandoned the Slade, joining a medical team at a prisoner-of-war camp in England, before going out to serve as an orderly at a Red Cross hospital in Marne.

Innes and Derwent Lees were lost to Gus, too, although it was not the war that had taken them. Innes was carried off by the tuberculosis with which he'd been diagnosed in 1908 (a diagnosis he had recklessly ignored), while Lees was exhibiting signs of the schizophrenia which would have him committed to an asylum in 1918. Grieving for the loss of his familiar world, uncertain whether to follow his peers to the front, Gus had admitted to Gwen back in October that his concentration was shot: 'It seems impossible to work consistently during all this.'[13]

He was worried, too, that his imagination would be starved. Now that German U-boats were patrolling the seas, he could no longer make his regular escapes abroad. So frightened was he of stagnating in England, he began to experience pains in his head and his legs that were like the physical effects of incarceration. Yet he needed to work, for the discipline as well as the money, and in wartime, at least there was always a demand for portraits.

In May, he was sent a second invitation by Lady Gregory, this time to paint the playwright George Bernard Shaw. He'd been eager to accept, having always admired Shaw's polemics, and saluted him as a fellow disrupter, so he was disappointed at first by the posturing, pontificating way in which Shaw was holding court at Coole House – 'a ridiculous vain object in knickerbockers', he told Dorelia. Once he began work, though, Gus warmed to the man, and relished the challenge of painting him – the energetic jut of his beard, the bushy profusion of his brows, the authoritarian glint of his eye. These features were so familiar to Gus, they were difficult not to caricature, yet they were also so expressively mobile, they were hard to pin down. He made six attempts in just over a week, only three of which he considered worth saving. Shaw himself bought one of them, for £300, and, while he accepted it was not the most flattering likeness, he claimed that now he'd been 'done' by Rodin and John – the artists he most admired – his days of posing were over.

Shaw's portrait dominated the NEAC show that summer, but it lacked the inward force of Gus's other submission, *The Orange Jacket*. This portrait of an unnamed woman was made arrestingly modern by the deceptively casual slouch of her pose, her keen but private stare, and also by the strength of Gus's palette, the rumpled, peachy tones of the woman's oversized jacket set against blocks of green, blue and grey. Not since *Smiling Woman* had he painted a female subject with such ambiguity and power. He may even have been at work on it when, in March 1915, he assured Dorelia that he'd overcome his doubts about painting his way through the war: 'I was never more confident and never felt more capable – I will succeed in shedding the last skin and scale and emerge the naked artist, a thousand times stronger for the struggle.'[14]

That belief took Gus back to Ireland in the autumn, to the port of Galway, where he planned to collect impressions for a large-scale frieze – 'a grand marshalling of the elements . . . troops of women and children, groups of fishermen, docks wharves the church, mills, constables, donkeys, widows, men from Aran . . . etc perhaps with a night sky and all illuminated by the light of a dream.'[15] But this Galway frieze was also to be Gus's escape from the war, his clinging to the Arcadian past of his imagination. The triptych on which he began work at home – a picturesque marketplace, a sylvan wood and travelling musicians – gave no intimation of the fighting across the Channel, nor of the escalating divisions in Ireland which would lead to the bloody uprisings of 1916. As one critic later noted, Gus had gone 'looking for peasants' in Galway 'when the peasants had ceased to exist'.[16]

By now, the war had all but lost its glamour for him. The casualty lists were soaring, Zeppelin bombs were falling on Britain and the nation's patriotism was being overtaken by a mood of febrile fatalism. When Gus was in London, he preferred to concentrate only on his own work and his own pleasure. Many nights there were parties, and many were given by him. The painter Dora Carrington recalled one riotous event which Gus held in honour of his favourite barmaid: 'a charming character, very solid with bosoms and a fat pouting face', Carrington wrote, whom Gus, as 'drunk as a King Fisher', had pretended to seduce: 'It was wonderful to see John kissing this fat Pussycat and diving his hand down her bodice. Lying with his legs apart on a divan in the most affected attitudes.'[17]

When Gus wasn't giving parties, he was prowling the city. London under blackout was almost thrilling to him, its darkness illuminated only by the ghostly blue headlamps of passing cars, by the wavering fingers of searchlights in the sky. Behind the shuttered windows, however, the pubs, the cafes, the restaurants and hotels still roared, and Gus had become particularly attached to the Eiffel Tower in Soho. Rudolf Stulik, its Austrian proprietor, was a gifted chef, but his clientele was also part of the attraction – Arthur Symons, cadaverously melancholic; rich, beautiful and scabrous Nancy Cunard; brittle and witty Ronald Firbank. Warmed by a long evening of wine, tobacco and talk, Gus would often end up paying everyone's bill, his mood far too lordly and free to worry about Dorelia's anxieties as she presented him with the latest accusing sheaf of bills.

In the exhilaratingly fluid, uncertain atmosphere of wartime London, it was easy for Gus to spend money, and easy for him to have sex. It often felt as though the last vestiges of Victorian restraint had been blasted away, as lovers – soon to be parted by the war – embraced openly in the streets. Iris Tree, a young Slade student who was very dear to Gus, was generous in the sexual comfort she offered to officer friends.* In her diary, she wrote that love, for her generation, had become nothing more than a 'brief fulfilment before the terrible sacrifice.'[18]

Gus, who was hardly part of the sacrifice, enjoyed all the rest. Helen Maitland recalled one Mallord Street party where he appeared to be making half ironic, half hopeful advances to virtually all his female guests, slurring dreamily, 'When shall I see you again? You know how much it means to me, I never cease thinking of you. Relax a little and inspire your poor artist with a kiss.'[19] In March 1917, a fundraising revue was staged in Chelsea, themed around the artists who'd been resident there, and the legend of Gus and his women had a starring role. The 'John Beauty Chorus' – composed of female Slade students – sang

---

* Tree's generosity would, however, cost her six abortions over the next decade, the last of which almost killed her.

loudly and satirically of their role in the creation of the wicked, successful Augustus John:

> John! John!
> How he's got on
> He owes it, he knows it, to me.[20]

Dorelia put up with most of it, though at times she was severely tested. In 1914, when Gus got one of his models pregnant, he was so worried about the money she was requesting to support herself and the baby that Dorelia proposed keeping the child down at Alderney.* Gus felt her saintly practicality as a rebuke to his own vast carelessness and, by way of penance, he briefly took up yoga, which he confidently informed Ursula Tyrwhitt was 'an excellent method of restoring oneself physically and spiritually.'[21] Yet he sensed Dorelia withdrawing from him again. 'I'm blest if I see why you think I *pretend* to want you,' he wrote, with guilty awkwardness. In March 1915, when Dorelia gave birth to their second daughter, Vivien, Gus was loving and attentive as he assisted at the delivery. The strain, however, persisted. Dorelia had become anxious about the rising cost of running their family and house in wartime. There was, too, an additional fractiousness at Alderney, arising from the difficulties between Gus and his three oldest boys.

The confusion of their early childhood years, shuttled between Gus and the Nettleship family, had left its mark on those boys, but so too had Gus's own erratic parenting, his alarmingly sudden switches from jokey exuberance to infuriated rage. Robin had become the most emotionally embattled of the three and his deliciously childish 'monkey talk' had long given way to hostile silences, in which he seemed to be trying to blank out his father. His two older brothers, meanwhile, wanted simply to leave home. David, who was musically gifted, had begged to become a boarder at Westminster School in London, one of the elite 'mouldy' English institutions Gus chose to despise.[22] Thirteen-year-old Caspar, more shockingly, was planning to enrol as a Royal Navy cadet. Had Ida

---

* The model was a music student called Norah Brownsword, and the daughter Gus fathered would grow up to be an artist herself.

been alive, she would have understood. Even when Caspar was little, she'd predicted he would 'go, morally, straight ahead . . . he is one of those people who [has] a business and knows it'.[23] But Gus, who'd dreamed of trapping beavers in America at a similar age, was unable to comprehend why any boy of his would want to exchange the freedoms of Alderney for a military establishment. He argued fiercely against it, and, years later, Caspar recorded the wound he felt at his father's disparagement: 'I had no encouragement at home. I felt a lonely outcast'.[24]

It was Dorelia who, in the end, persuaded Gus to let Caspar go; it was Dorelia, too, who urged him to see David whenever he was up in London. If she was resetting the terms of her relationship with Gus, she was, in her own quietly detached way, keeping the family together. When visitors came down to Alderney – some of them seeking refuge from the war, some from their own domestic problems – the household still seemed like an oasis. Francis Macnamara's four children, who were often farmed out to the Johns after Francis had abandoned their mother, would remember it as a place of picnics and pranks, of sleeping four in a bedroom and splashing naked in the pond.

As Gus disengaged from the war, his letters to Gwen became more intermittent, but her own patriotic certainties were also under siege. She was terrified by rumours that Germany was poised to invade Britain, and nagged Ursula for regular reassurances that her friends and family were safe. Ursula replied as chattily as she was able: Albert Rothenstein, having changed his name to the marginally less Germanic Rutherston, had tried to enlist, but had failed his military board; the government had ordered all the 'best' paintings to be removed from the National Gallery in case they were bombed; and Ursula herself was in Oxford, teaching French to convalescent soldiers. But it was hard for Ursula to maintain her cheerful facade because the teaching work felt brutal to her – its sole purpose to equip the men with a few useful phrases before they went back to the front and faced the enemy all over again.

Ursula found she no longer wanted to talk of the men's heroic sacrifice, now that she'd seen what shrapnel and steel could do to young flesh. And Gwen, too, had suffered the same reaction when, at Quinn's persuasion, she'd gone to visit his friend Maude Gonne. Maude had recently returned from several months as a volunteer nurse on the Pyrenees front, and Gwen told Quinn that she'd been 'frightened and chilled for days' after hearing how Maude had helped to ease the most severely injured soldiers into death, while patching up the rest so that the 'poor mangled creatures . . . may be sent back to the slaughter'.

Only months had passed since Gwen had been applauding these soldiers in their fight to save the civilized world; now, she wondered to Quinn what kind of civilization could endure if 'all the young art and intellect was being killed in the trenches.' She felt it was her moral duty never again to look away from the wounded who were appearing in ever greater numbers around Paris. 'It is heart-breaking to see the maimed in the street and it is still more heart-rending to see a [group] of the blind. A man goes before and cries "Faîtes place! faîtes place" and the poor men follow holding on to one another'.[25]

She took comfort that no one close to her was fighting. Thornton had attempted to enlist in the Canadian army, but had been rejected because of a broken foot and was now working at a munitions factory in London. He wrote to Gwen quite often, describing occasional trips down to Alderney, where he struggled to talk to Gus but was 'good friends' with little Poppet, however he also confessed how much he hated his work. Always a loner, an outdoors man, it was hellish for Thornton to be stuck at a conveyor belt, hemmed in by the crush and the noise of other men. 'It is an abomination,' he told Gwen, 'but there is nothing to do but hang on grimly. I try to do as much as I can with as little thought of rewards as possible. I know I am not liked.'[26]

Winnie, at least, was happy – safe from the war, giving violin lessons and learning to square dance. She had recently married, and in November she gave birth to a baby girl. Her reports to Gwen were ecstatic: 'she is *perfect*, with a little round face . . . dark hair blue eyes and tiny hands with very long fingers'. Kisses were sent from both sides of the Atlantic. Yet, as Gwen exchanged news about family, she was sparing with information about herself. She told no one, not even Gus, that Rodin had eventually returned to Paris in late 1915, and that, shortly afterwards, he had suffered a major stroke, leaving her in an agony of worry. Only later, when she was apologizing to Quinn for not sending him some work, did Gwen admit she had been 'suffering from a grief for weeks'.[27]

Her grief and worry had been all the more acute because Rodin was being nursed very strictly at home at the Villa Brillantes, and she'd been unable to see him. Her own health, meanwhile, had not been good; the winter had brought on her now annual bout of flu and, with her already meagre income now straitened by wartime inflation, she didn't always have enough money for food and fuel. She went foraging for wood in the forest, dragging it back down to rue de Terre Neuve; she commandeered a corner of the library at the Bon Marché store in Paris, where she could read and draw. But, at night, when she lay shivering under blankets, she struggled to focus her mind on meditation and prayer.

Gwen was too proud to admit her difficulties – although Quinn had a pretty good idea of them. In March 1916, when she managed to send over her first wartime package of work, he insisted on paying her extra, and was cross when she demurred. The curé at Meudon was also worried about Gwen; observing how thin she'd become and how regularly she was troubled by chest infections, he suggested she might try her hand at some more profitable work, proposing that sketches of the Allied war generals might find a ready market.

If anyone else had proposed such a project, Gwen would probably have rejected it out of hand, yet she revered her priest, would later describe him as her 'spiritual lover'. Obediently, she began work on six charcoal and wash portraits, working from photographs she'd cut out of newspapers, and, to her pleased surprise, the work came easily. She'd drawn very few men since her life classes at the Slade, yet the challenge of capturing the broad impassive presence of General Mangin, the nervous energy of General Sarrailh was interesting and, she thought, educational. She sent all six drawings to Quinn and was so confident of his enthusiasm, she asked if he would help her to sell them in New York, suggesting an individual price of 150 francs (about six pounds) and promising that more would be following soon.

Quinn, however, was dismayed by Gwen's new venture. He could see little life or imagination in the drawings and was offended by her sudden enthusiasm for profit. When he told Gwen that he would take no more of her generals beyond the six she'd already sent (and which he privately planned to give away), she was unreasonably disappointed, sniping to Ursula, 'My faith in his judgment is not very strong now.'[28] But Ursula was even more blunt in scolding Gwen for wasting her time on 'such stuff', and eventually she put the generals aside, announcing to a very relieved Quinn that she was now going back to painting 'what I like'.

It was summer, and, as Gwen walked the dappled forest pathways and the green streets of Meudon, her anxieties about Rodin, about money and the war all started to lift. 'Oh what a world is open to us when our mind is in peace! A world of eternal things', she wrote.[29] In September and October, she ventured on two short trips to the Breton coast, the second with Ruth Manson and her daughter. To swim in the sea again, to feel the crunch of sand between her toes, to look out over new horizons was a benediction for her, and it stayed with her long after she returned to rue Terre Neuve as a promise of better times. Two parcels came from England – a grey silk blouse, a skirt, coat and velvet cap from Ursula, and an elegant fur muff from Chloe – and Gwen gloated over them gratefully: 'What a wonderful influence on the mind clothes are . . . I am like a butterfly coming out of a chrysalis'.[30]

Ideas for work were hatching, too. As she pressed forwards with her painting, she was drawing intensively – multiple studies of people, landscape, flowers and cats, in which she was making new experiments with colour, form and emotional affect. She was also developing a private shorthand to keep track of her ideas:

Treatments: the blob. The 2nd and 3rd line. dry painting
   Note: in 2nd 3rd line the masses lighter. When the masses are to be dark, treatment is not 2nd 3rd line
   Portraits, cats: dry painting the masses put in first but as much together as possible lines & masses. the line of equal value with the mass
   Dark motives Night street. Twilight Street. Night forest Twilight forest. In church eve. sands at night with fish boxes. grey dress on a brune
   Rule for tones Find *first* the tones of the principal point.[31]

Barely comprehensible to anyone but herself, there was both poetry and confidence in Gwen's jottings. The anxieties she'd felt about combining her work and her faith had subsided and she was now confessing to

Ursula that it seemed a 'weakness' in her to have done so little 'exhibiting' for so long. She was impatient to submit some work to the NEAC and also to get herself known in Paris, suggesting to Ursula that they might even hold a joint exhibition in the city.

The possibility of exhibiting again, in London and Paris, had become real to Gwen because, in the spring of 1917, America finally entered the war. At last, an Allied victory began to look feasible – and, with it, a return to normal life. 'I speak to very few people so I know very little,' Gwen told Quinn, but she assured him there was now a 'courage and energy', a 'lifting of helplessness' among the French. To Gus, she wrote of her renewed pride in the British troops: 'Everybody I speak to praises them'.[32]

Gwen's own quiet buoyancy was reflected in the series of paintings she began that year, which she eventually titled *The Convalescent*. They showed a seated woman, supported by cushions, with a set of tea things placed within easy reach on the table beside her. Yet they were more than a literal depiction of convalescence, for Gwen was searching for a quality in the light, a stillness in the space which would give the image a larger resonance, a suggestion that the world too might shortly be allowed to recover from its own grievous illness.

In Britain, there was a similar upsurge of hope, although Gus was struggling to feel it. The excesses of his London life had given way to an inevitable reaction of disgust. 'I feel horribly alone,' he wrote, and, according to the writer Katherine Mansfield, who saw him at the theatre one night, he looked 'haggard', a lost soul: 'Everything exhausted and finished, great black rings where the fires had been, and not a single fire even left to smoulder'.[33] Gus was ashamed of the time he'd been squandering, and ashamed of what he'd been recently painting. After reaching for the poetry of his Galway frieze, he'd got stuck in the reliable rut of portraits. Several had been commissioned to raise money for war charities, and as a consequence their subjects had become progressively more grand – men in power, like David Lloyd George and First Sea Lord Admiral Fisher, and women in high society, like Cynthia Asquith, daughter-in-law of the Liberal prime minister.

Gus knew he was veering into dangerously facile terrain and, by

November 1917, when he was given a solo show at the Alpine Club in Mayfair, he was almost ready to agree with the long, tough review that appeared in *The Times*. While that review was quick to acknowledge him as 'the most famous of living English painters', arguably in possession of 'a greater natural gift . . . than any other', it also pointed out that few of his recent works could be judged 'entirely serious works of art'. The review continued, 'He has much to express and he has a brilliant machinery of expression; but [his works] are cut off from each other and the result is unrest, blind experiment, a bewilderment that becomes ferocious and occasional gleams of enchanting beauty and sincerity. He remains at the mercy of Heaven-sent moments, and the danger is that they will become rarer'.[34]

Gus understood that he couldn't pin the blame entirely on the war. There were artists, mostly younger than him, for whom it had been a brutal source of inspiration, and for Lewis it had even been savagely timely, giving force to the new art movement, Vorticism, which he had helped to found in 1913. Leapfrogging over cubism and Futurism, Vorticism was violently anti-Romantic; in its brash colours and jagged geometries there was a new generation's embrace of industrialism, jazz, the fractured urban world. In early 1914, the movement had been given political teeth with the launch of *Blast*, a magazine Lewis edited with Pound, in which the two of them had been ruthless in their denunciations of establishment figures, enemies of the modern. They had even turned on Roger Fry, although Henry Tonks had the distinction of being both 'blasted' and 'blessed'. And, in 1915, they also targeted Gus – declaring that his genius had 'prematurely exhausted' itself and that he was in danger of becoming 'an institution like Madame Tussauds'.

Gus had actually punched Lewis after reading this attack, but later he'd felt obliged to concede that its 'thrusts at me were salutary and well deserved'.[35] He knew he had not been painting well and he could also see that the war required from him a deeper, more committed response. However well it suited him to mock 'the cubists Voodooists Futurists and other boomists', he was conscious that their art was more honestly attuned to the current carnage, to the smashing of moral certainties, than anything he had yet produced.[36]

In November 1916, Gus had made one dutiful attempt to engage with the war when he'd accepted a commission from the Ministry of Information to make a print for its morale-boosting publication *British Efforts and Ideals*. He had done his best, producing a violently allegorical warscape in which a small child was seated, calmly building with bricks. He called it *The Dawn*, and he hated its sentimentality, knowing it was an image that could never have been produced by anyone with personal experience of a battlefield.

Although Gus now loathed the war, he'd become sickened by his own civilian status. Conscription had been introduced in early 1916; Lewis was serving as a gunner in France, Robert Gregory was a fighter pilot with the Royal Flying Corps; and, in the autumn, when Gus was summoned before the Military Board, he was more than ready to take his turn. He wanted to be part of the experience which seemed to be defining the lives of so many, and the bluntness with which he was rejected, on account of his deaf ear and recently fractured knee, was utterly mortifying. He felt it as an insult to his courage and vigour. Yet, when he attempted another route to the front, as an official war artist with the British Army, even that was blocked, because the Propaganda Bureau would only send painters, photographers or filmmakers to France if they had already been deemed fit and ready to serve.

Even though Gus made regular petitions, pulled every powerful string he knew, his efforts with the British authorities all failed and in the end, it was Max Aitken, the Canadian-born newspaper magnate, who got him to France. Aitken, now Lord Beaverbrook, had set up the Canadian War Memorials Fund in November 1916, with the aim of commissioning art from a Canadian perspective. Having formed the opinion that Gus was the 'greatest artist of our time, and possibly of any time', Beaverbrook was now willing to use all his influence to get him an honorary commission with the Canadian Armed Forces.

This, to Gus's great gratification, came with the rank and pay of a major, and, in late October 1917, he was very full of himself when he purchased his new khaki uniform, splendidly accessorized with leather gloves, spurs and riding boots laced to the knee. 'I am told I look very beautiful,' he wrote, and he made a point of wearing his uniform to the opening of his Alpine Club show. Lytton Strachey, one of the most committed of the Bloomsbury Group pacifists, was archly horrified. 'Major

John looked decidedly colonial . . . a dwindled creature, with clipped beard, pseudo-smart . . . the darling of the upper classes.'[37] But Gus was deaf to criticism, caring only about getting out of London and purging his black humours of frustration and guilt. In mid-December, when his travel orders came through, he hosted a farewell party at Mallord Street ('the wildest orgy London had seen for many a year'), and he was still reeling from drink when he took the boat train to Boulogne, in northern France. His official brief was to produce a large frieze of war impressions, which would hang in a memorial building in Canada. His private hope was to find some kind of artistic and moral redemption.[38]

Arriving at the Canadian HQ, however, Gus had a sudden freezing of apprehension. He'd expected privation, but his first billet, a cold, cramped hut he had to share with another man, was dismayingly primitive and 'impossible [for] work'. He'd expected, also, to be faced with scenes of destruction, but when he was first driven around the Canadian front, a twenty-mile stretch between Bethune and Arras, it looked to him like hell. The green fields of this once-fertile corner had been churned to a sea of foul, sticky mud, and its villages shelled so ruthlessly, he wrote, that only a few 'blackened spires', a few 'shattered trees' were left standing above 'the general ruin'.[39]

He had no choice but to adjust. Shortly after his arrival, a hard frost fell, etching the mud, the gun emplacements, the barbed wire and the tanks into a remote and silvery abstraction. Gus could not help but see beauty in it: 'All is glittering at the front, amidst great silence the guns reverberated,' he told Arthur Symons; and when he witnessed his first Canadian assault, he could not help but be thrilled. 'German divisions repulsed with colossal slaughter! I saw a wonderful show last night when we discharged five thousand gas drums at the Boches followed by an intense bombardment.'[40]

'Things,' he reported jubilantly to Dorelia, 'are getting interesting here.'[41] His mood had been boosted, too, by his transfer to a far superior billet – two rooms in a large villa that overlooked the relatively unscathed town of Aubigny-en-Artois. One of the rooms was spacious enough to function as a studio, and already Gus had found some Canadian soldiers who were willing to pose, as well as locating a 'remarkable place' for the setting of his war frieze: 'a ruined chateau converted into a battery position with towers and a river running through it'.[42] To Tonks, who was now working as a British war artist, Gus admitted how 'overjoyed' he was to be seeing action at last.

He had, however, envisaged his war adventure in privately heroic terms and his emotions were mixed when Lewis appeared in Aubigny as another beneficiary of Beaverbrook's Memorial Fund. The two of them had barely met since their fight over *Blast*, yet, for three weeks, they were to be companions, sharing the same billet and car. They made the best of it, getting carousingly drunk each evening in Aubigny's one decent restaurant, but their rivalry was still close to the surface, as Lewis boasted of his superior combat experience, and Gus made sarcastic enquiries about how Lewis planned to make his Vorticism intelligible to his Canadian paymasters. One day, when their driver veered too close to the fighting and they were in danger of being caught by exploding shells, Gus would not allow Lewis to see his fear. As their car raced away from the scene, he drawled, 'Well no one can say we haven't been *under fire*, can they – what!'[43]

The rivalries of the art world had travelled a long way from London, and Gus was also on the defensive when he encountered William Orpen in Paris during a brief period of leave. Relations between the two men had already cooled, each a little stung by the other's success – Orpen, the wittily finessed portrait painter; John, the unreliable genius. Gus was also aware that Orpen was already far ahead of him as a war artist, since he'd been coming out to France since April 1917.

Their meeting in Paris hadn't even been of their own choosing, but had been arranged by Beaverbrook when he'd invited them to enjoy an evening 'of special entertainment' which he'd organized for some Canadian officers. It was to be a lavish supper, in the company of some 'highly recommended' prostitutes, and it would almost kill the last vestiges of friendship between Orpen and Gus.

Neither of the two men had liked the fact that they'd been set up for an expensive orgy, but while Orpen had walked out in disgust, Gus had felt in some way responsible to the women and to Beaverbrook. Afterwards, he wrote that it had only been a 'curious' combination of 'melancholy' and 'desperation' that had led him to grab hold of one of the women and 'plank her on the table'.[44]

He'd judged himself for doing so, almost as harshly as he'd judged Orpen for being a cowardly 'low lick spittle' and abandoning the scene. But the decadence of the evening also rankled with Gus because he'd begun to feel serious qualms about his place in this war. Compared to the soldiers who were manning the guns, driving ambulances, rebuilding bridges, defusing mines, his own presence seemed hardly to make sense. He wondered if it was even possible to make art out of the desolation and chaos of the front: 'So much contradiction is necessary,' he told Will.[45] And, when he realized that his first instinct, now, when visiting a battleground was to note how 'a good sun makes beauty of wreckage', he wondered what that said about him as an artist, let alone as a man.[46]

As Gus nagged away at the morality of his art, he also recognized how ill at ease he was with most of the soldiers. He'd drawn dozens of them, had made genuine attempts to befriend them, yet his officer's rank and his privileges – his driver, his comfortable bed, his access to decent food and drink – had set him apart. More awkward still was the fact that he'd been given permission to keep his beard, and, because only the king of England had been afforded the same right, Gus was frequently mistaken for royalty by the younger soldiers and, as Lewis reported, had become 'a constant source of anxiety and terror wherever he went'.[47]

Divisions of class, Gus realized, were even more rigid here than in civilian life, and his first impression that the army was full of 'excellent fellows' had been undercut by the weary realization that it was run by a coterie of the rich and entitled and serviced by men who, for all their courage, were often wretchedly 'illiterate'. As he fell out of love with the army, Gus also came to loathe his surroundings. The officers' restaurant at Aubigny had lost its charm, and recent manoeuvres meant the town itself had changed – its once pretty streets now 'continuously traversed by troops and transports'. Wistfully, he told Dorelia that, on his most recent visit to Paris, he'd bought some cheap reproductions of Cézanne, Renoir and Van Gogh to remind himself that another life existed.

Home tugged at Gus, and while he still signed off his letters with witty cartoons of himself, saluting in his army greatcoat, he'd all but stopped reporting his impressions from the front. He only wanted news of family: of David, who'd given up his hopes of becoming a professional pianist; of Robin, who wanted to take the entrance exam for Winchester school;

of little Henry, who was now a precocious eleven-year-old and whose last letter to Gus had been written with an affectedly adult style he found both amusing and faintly revolting. Most of all, he wanted reassurance from Dorelia, who'd been angered by rumours of his reckless behaviour during the couple of days he'd been allowed back to London. 'It shows that you are like everybody else,' Gus grumbled, 'capable of believing any tale about me.'

Doubting his work, out of sorts with Dorelia, feeling like 'a fish out of water' among the men, Gus recognized he was becoming frighteningly adrift from himself.[48] He tried to explain his state to Cynthia Asquith, who, having forgiven 'the rough and disagreeable' pass he'd made while painting her, had become something of a confidante. She herself was prone to depression and Gus trusted her to understand the 'curious state' in which he was finding himself. 'I watch myself closely without yet being able to classify myself. I evade definition – and that must mean I have no character . . . I am alone in what they call the "Chateau" in this dismal little town . . . When out at the front . . . I wander among bricks and wonder if those shells will come a little nearer.'[49]

Gus was closer to a breakdown than he realized. In the middle of March, when an officer addressed some vaguely insulting comment to him, he hardly knew what he was doing when he physically lashed out at the man and knocked him unconscious. This, in the army, was deemed criminal assault, and it was only Beaverbrook's determination to keep his Memorial Fund free from scandal that allowed Gus to avoid a court martial. Instead, he was shipped back to England and instructed to start work on his war frieze. Yet, although he was conscious of being gifted a lucky escape, it seemed that his 'utter mental confusion' only worsened once he was home. He felt a sick burden of guilt, both at his ignominious exit from the war and at his relief in escaping its perils and its brutalities. Images of the front came back to haunt him, leaving him speechless, 'doubting the reality of my own existence'. And, as Gus trekked aimlessly between London and Dorset, neither the bustle of the city nor the domestic calm of Alderney felt like home. To Dorelia, he wrote simply, 'There is no one I can be with for long.'[50]

*

One other shaming consequence of this ending to Gus's war was his inability to keep the promise he'd made to Gwen, to visit when he was next on leave. He had never stopped worrying about his sister's wellbeing, but it was of crucial concern to him now, because when he'd last managed to see her the previous December, when he'd been freshly outfitted in his major's uniform and breaking his journey from London to the Canadian HQ, he had found Gwen in a terrible state, not only half-starved in appearance but on the verge of emotional collapse.

Just a few weeks earlier, on 17 November 1917, Rodin had died, and Gwen had been utterly unprepared for his loss. She had never wanted to accept that her maître was growing old; even after enduring the shock of his stroke, she had managed to convince herself that his strength, his lust for life must return. The letter she wrote to Rodin in May 1916 (her last known correspondence with him) was warm with assurances that they would meet very soon, and the small profile sketch she drew of him was that of an agelessly wise, commanding man. She had no idea then how ill Rodin was, his mind wandering, his breathing laboured. Nor did she know that his lawyers, anticipating his further deterioration, were persuading him to marry Rose Beuret and legalize her status.

A forlorn little ceremony had taken place on 29 January 1917 at the Villa Brillantes – the house so cold that the elderly, infirm couple had to be shuffled back to bed as soon as they were married. Rose died just a fortnight afterwards. Rodin, however, hung on and because Gwen still knew little of his weakened state, when the news finally reached her, nine and a half months later, that Rodin had died from congestion of the lungs, she had no defences in place.

'I don't know now what I am going to do,' she wrote to Ursula, her handwriting almost illegible with pain.[51] There was no one with whom Gwen could mourn; her place in Rodin's life had been so secret, so small, that she was not invited to his funeral, and if she hovered near the public memorial that was held for him at Meudon, she would have found little comfort from the formal pageantry of it all – the honour guard of territorials, the speeches from civic officials.

Her friends and family all worried – Ursula wrote immediately and Thornton tried to get over to see her. He couldn't secure the necessary travel papers, though, and in the end it was Gus, in mid-December, who came to Gwen. Even though he'd been on his way to the front, at the command of his new Canadian paymasters, he'd managed to get permission for a detour to Paris, to purchase some art supplies, and so was able to track Gwen down at her studio on rue de l'Ouest.

Afterwards, he told Dorelia that he thought his visit might have done 'some good'. Gwen had looked pitifully bleached with grief, and very frail, when he'd first arrived. Yet she said she was pleased to see him, she accepted his invitation to dinner, and when she asked him to come out to Meudon the following morning she seemed to become a little more animated, walking on the Observatory Terrace with Gus and listening with mild interest to his news.*

Despite this small improvement, though, Gus was still very anxious about Gwen. She seemed only half-present to him, deep in her struggle with grief; he could see she wasn't eating enough and he was appalled by the condition of her 'comfortless garret'. Even though she assured him she could always find wood in the forest, she had only lit one meagre fire in her sitting room, which barely cut through the cold.

Harsh with worry, he reported back to Dorelia that 'for some bloody mystical reason' Gwen was deliberately neglecting herself. 'The Lord knows how she spends her days. Perhaps one might send out a Jaeger blanket as she admits the cold keeps her awake at night.'[52] Once again, he urged his sister to come back to Alderney, or at least get away to the sea, but Gwen said she was in no state to travel, and Gus, who was due to report to the Canadians, could do no more for her. He had eased his conscience, then, with the promise to return to her in the spring, but, once he was thrown out of the army, he was, of course, unable to keep his word.

For all his brotherly concern, however, Gus had only a limited understanding of Gwen and when he'd seen her in Meudon, still grieving over Rodin, he'd been unable to see that the 'bloody mysticism' he so deplored was actually her strength and her support. While his own instinctive response to death, to any form of crisis, was always to run

---

* To his embarrassment, he had to borrow money from Gwen to pay the bill because he was still awaiting his pay.

away, Gwen survived by looking inwards. During the long winter of 1917–18, she had made herself a daily schedule of meditation, housework and prayer. 'Give up your art and everything you have to [God]', she wrote, and by the end of February, she was so much recovered she was able to assure Ursula that she was 'nearly normal' again.[53] She was even able to rise to a little professional bitchery over a British art magazine, *Colour*, which Gus had sent. Having conceded that Gus's own featured works were quite good – 'They want something, which perhaps will come soon!' – she dismissed the rest of the magazine as 'dreadful', and one more reason why she never wanted to see 'any English pictures again'.

Soon, she could tell Ursula she was well enough to paint: 'I feel as if I have been ill for a long time and am getting better'. The world outside, though, was lurching back into horror for on 21 March, the Germans had launched a new offensive against Paris, and the city was under siege.* On 29 March, when Gwen wrote to Ursula, she reported, 'we have two dangers now, from the *avions* and the *canon à longue portée* [long-range artillery]', and she admitted that, earlier in the day, when she'd been queuing for food at the market on boulevard Edgar Quinet, a shell had exploded nearby: 'The noise is not very deafening but there is no mistaking it for anything else.'[54]

That shell had also convinced Gwen she could no longer brave her studio. It took her several journeys by train and cart to move all her equipment from rue de l'Ouest back to Meudon, although even in the suburbs her safety wasn't assured, for, while German guns were trained only on the centre of Paris, German bombers were roaming more widely. People were once again fleeing Meudon, and Ruth Manson begged Gwen to go with her to Brittany. Yet still she refused to leave: she felt loyal to her little community, she believed there was refuge enough in her familiar routines of work and church, and she had no notion then that the siege of Paris would continue for another five months, and that

---

* German forces and German morale had been fortified by Russia's withdrawal from the Triple Alliance in November 1917 – the new Bolshevik government now committed to waging its war against forces still loyal to the deposed Tsar.

the spring and summer during which she remained confined to Meudon would be the most gruelling period of her war.

At night, when the sirens started to blare and Meudon's one anti-aircraft gun went into frantic action, it was impossible to sleep. There was a cellar at 29 rue Terre Neuve where the residents were meant to shelter, but crouching in the musty darkness, listening to the 'uneducated talk and nonsense' of her neighbours was all but intolerable for Gwen. Sometimes, she preferred to remain in her bedroom, staring out at the 'lights of the *avions*'; sometimes, she went to shelter with nearby friends. The walk to their house was an ordeal, though: 'The bushes have dark shadows and look as if there were *mauvais sujets* hiding in them to spring out on me as I pass,' she told Ursula, and those same terrors infected her fitful sleep: 'I dreamed last night that I was pursued by the Boches . . . and tried to hide under the leaves but they were never thick enough and I was always discovered.'[55]

'It has been a dreadful time for me sometimes,' Gwen admitted. 'I am so tired because of the loss of sleep.'[56] Yet fear and fatigue had also sharpened her appetite for life. She took pleasure in noting the flowers and the trees as they unfurled into summer, she admired the stoicism of her neighbours as they chatted and queued for food, and she explained to Ursula how much she'd come to love the lively charm of the all-clear signal when it floated up to her from the centre of Paris: 'a *beloque* . . . a gay little tune . . . is played on something like an auto which passes through the streets. After the *beloque* the church bells are rung.'[57] Ursula herself sent regular gifts of clothes and news from home. 'Your letter is a joy to me', Gwen wrote, and she was happy to hear also that Thornton had been transferred to a shipwright's yard in Gravesend. He was now much more contented and he sent Gwen a copy of the *Rubaiyat* by Omar Khayyám, illustrated with some of his own drawings, to celebrate the change in his fortunes.

Finally, when the siege was broken and the Germans were in retreat, Gwen was ready to go back to Brittany. Ruth and her daughter were staying in a tiny fishing hamlet close to the village of Pléneuf, and there would be little space or privacy for Gwen, since the lodgings were already being shared with another mother and child. Yet the weeks she spent at Pléneuf were the happiest she'd known since the start of the war. She felt almost reckless with health, exploring the miles of unspoilt coastline whose rocky coves reminded her of the wilder stretches of Pembrokeshire. She swam at least once a day, plunging into rolling breakers; she took solitary walks over the cliffs, glorying in the wide skies, the chasing clouds; and often she returned at night to stare at the moon's reflection on the darkly moving sea.

Gwen also had an enormous energy for work. The local children delighted her, and she persuaded several of them to pose for her, using charcoal or the point of a fine brush to capture each gauche, fidgety little body and wary gaze. She was drawing the landscape, too, experimenting with delicate washes and streaks of colour to approximate the weathered greys of the cottages, the subtle greens of the hedgerows and fields, the misting effect of sunshine and spray. It felt to her as if she was on the brink of expressing exactly what she saw and felt, and when she sent six of her Brittany drawings to Quinn, she asked him to evaluate them as a group, explaining how they enhanced and amplified each other. He wrote back to express his admiration, and passed on the opinion of his artist friend, Walter Kuhn, that Gwen's draughtsmanship was now superior to her brother's. He added that, if she were able to send him an additional three drawings, he would pay her 800 francs (thirty-two pounds) for the set.

Quinn almost hadn't received any of her drawings, though. When Gwen returned to Paris at the beginning of September, the station at Montparnasse had been heaving. Disoriented by the crowds, she lost her trunk and, during the two fraught days in which she searched among 'thousands' of other missing items, she imagined that, not only her clothes and painting equipment would be lost, but her entire Brittany portfolio. The chaos had been a 'nightmare', she told Ursula, yet, for most of those who'd been crowding through Gare Montparnasse, it had been a wonderful relief. On 6 September, the enemy alliance had requested negotiations for an armistice and the Parisians who'd fled their city were now returning home.

Gwen had not believed it, at first. But when sections of the German navy mutinied, on 3 November, events moved very fast: the Austro-Hungarians started suing for peace, revolutionaries in Germany forced the abdication of the Kaiser and, just eight days later, on 11 November, the church bells rang out across Europe to signal the final end of the war.

To Quinn, Gwen wrote of the 'wild joy' and the 'touching scenes' she'd witnessed in Paris, yet otherwise her account of Armistice Day was muted.[58] Perhaps, as the city had partied, she simply preferred to go back to Meudon and give thanks with her priest and fellow congregants. But it's also possible she had already begun to look forward, beyond the war and the celebrations, to what her own future could be. During the last fourteen years, Gwen's life had been focused on Paris and on Rodin, and while she'd been transfigured by those years, had discovered so much about herself, the time she'd spent in Pléneuf had convinced her she was ready for change. She felt she must go back there, perhaps for a very long time, and already she had written to Ursula of her plan. 'It is strange of you advising me to stay in Brittany the same time as I felt I ought to and decided to. I am going back there in about two months. The day before I came away I saw an old chateau with some wonderful rooms in it. They are very cheap and I think I should be alone there . . . I am going to write and take them.'[59]

Chapter Fourteen

THE PEACE

> 'My dear Gwen
> I trust you to believe that my infrequent letters don't mean that I don't think of you very often . . . Since you wrote, Peace has arrived. London went mad for a week and Paris too I suppose. Do you manage to get any work done . . . now that [the war] is over one will work better I hope'
> AUGUSTUS JOHN TO GWEN JOHN[1]

While Gwen had detached herself from the armistice celebrations in Paris, Gus had revelled in London's madness, carousing the streets with a group of tipsy land girls and ending up at the Adelphi Hotel, where, courtesy of the art collector Montague Shearman, a party was in full swing. Writers, painters and stars from Diaghilev's Ballets Russes were all dancing together, the millionaire Henry Bond sat at the pianola, stripped to his vest, and, when Gus appeared in his major's uniform, even Lytton Strachey cheered.

For several days, Gus was euphoric, gloating at the defeat of the Boches. But, once the city had quieted and Britain was left to count its losses, his mood grew dark again. He didn't believe the war had been conclusively won. 'The allied powers will have to be careful or Germany will be stronger than ever,' he wrote presciently to Gwen – and, while she was already making plans for her future, he felt marooned. 'Rather dreadful', he admitted, 'that feeling of wanting to go somewhere and not know where. I spend hours of anguish trying to make a move – in some direction.' He still couldn't speak of it clearly. Even though he'd confessed something of his malaise to Cynthia Asquith, it now went deeper than his shame at being ejected from the war. It was his failure to redeem that shame through his art.²

His commissioned frieze had seemed so promising when he felt recovered enough to start work. He'd blocked out a choreographed sweep of scenes from the front – officers on horseback, marching groups of infantry, stretcher bearers and fleeing refugees, and, although some of it was drawn from imagination, the rest he'd witnessed first hand and he believed it carried the truth of personal experience. When Virginia Woolf saw one of his preliminary studies for *Pageant of War* at the NEAC, she thought it 'knocked everything else out'.³

Once Gus began layering on the first wash of paint, however, using an evocatively reduced palette of khaki and grey, his confidence faltered, and, as the months passed, he couldn't bring himself to complete the work.* He was working on other, smaller paintings, elaborating on the sketches he'd done at Aubigny. But already his impressions were growing stale, and he'd had to copy the three soldiers in his painting *Fraternity* from a propaganda postcard circulated by the *Daily Mail*. Although this painting had its own lively spirit of camaraderie, although a preliminary showing of *Pageant of War* provoked the normally sceptical P. G. Konody to claim it would 'rank with the mightiest achievements of European art', Gus remained unconvinced.⁴ It was impossible for him not to feel that his months as a war artist had been a failure of spirit, a waste of time. After Gus died, the frieze was privately sold, and was only restored to Canada in 2011, when it was hung at the War Museum in Ottawa.

He didn't know how to move on from that failure, but in February an offer came from the government, inviting him to join Orpen as official artist at the Peace Conference in Paris. Gus admitted to Sampson it would be 'No small job!' to paint the proceedings of the conference, making art out of grey-haired men seated around large tables. But he was flattered by the challenge, determined to succeed. With living expenses of three pounds a day, potential fees of £3,000 for group pictures, £500 for individual portraits, the commission promised rich financial reward, the equivalent, now, of many thousands of pounds.

---

* It was initially titled *Canadian Opposite Lens – Winter 1917–18* and Beaverbrook would never see its completion.

He'd also been told he could travel to Paris by plane, an adventure for which he'd been longing ever since he wrote to Gwen the previous year about how easy it would become to visit her, 'One will soon be able to fly in 2 or 3 hours'.[5]

Thick smog forced Gus to make do with the usual boat train, yet Paris, on his arrival, was a blaze of light. The opening of the conference had signalled a season of entertainments. Aristocrats, socialites and international celebrities had flocked back to the city, and Gus found himself at the centre of it all. One of the conference delegates was Jose-Antonio de Gandarillas, the Chilean painter, playboy and powerbroker, with whom Gus had a slight acquaintance; and when Gandarillas insisted on him using the luxury apartment next to his own at 60 Avenue Montaigne, Gus had little option but to attend the almost nightly parties where his host gathered 'le tout Paris' to dance and sniff cocaine.

'Gandarillas leads a lurid and fashionable life,' Gus grumbled to Cynthia, yet he was surprised to discover he was enjoying himself. The men at the parties were interesting, the women 'loved a bit of fun', and all of them seemed tremendously warm in their appreciation of Gus himself.[6] 'Quickly I lost all feeling of constraint,' he recalled, and to one of the guests at least he seemed 'easily the most picturesque personality' in the room.*

Work had to be his focus, though. He commandeered a studio for himself with good high windows, and, while he had no idea yet how to paint scenes from the conference, he was racing through a quantity of portraits. Generals, statesmen, judges and prime ministers all came to sit for him, as did the desert hero T. E. Lawrence – very splendid in his Arab robes. The aristocrats sought him out too, and, by early spring, both the Marchesa Luisa Casati and the Duchesse de Gramont were competing to have their portraits painted.

Gus felt a particular obligation to the Duchesse – a 'warm tender even fragile heart' – who'd offered him a small apartment after Gandarillas had left Paris. But it was Luisa Casati – rich, beautiful and highly strung – who'd caught his imagination when he'd first glimpsed her at a

---

* Lloyd George's secretary, Frances Stevenson.

thé dansant. A tall, slender figure, dressed entirely in black, her flaming hennaed hair topped by a towering headdress of velvet and antique gold lace, she'd made every other woman look 'somewhat rustic', Gus thought. When he asked for an introduction, he discovered that Luisa's personality was even more remarkable than her appearance. She was not only a fabulously generous patron of artists, she aspired to become a work of art herself. She paid a fortune to designers, to outfit her with outrageously decorative costumes, and the parties she gave at her Venetian palazzo, surrounded by her menagerie of cheetahs, monkeys and parrots, were notorious for their theatrical excess.

Luisa, in her reverence for beauty and the imagination, was an extreme, and very wealthy, version of Ottoline, and like Ottoline her extravagance masked a profound shyness. Gus thought he saw an odd 'child of nature' beneath Luisa's artifice, and for a short time they were lovers. In one of the two Paris portraits he painted, she was posed in a rare state of physical dishevelment, a glint of mischief in her kohl-ringed eyes – 'very hot stuff', thought T. E. Lawrence.[7] But Luisa was too addicted to the theatre of seduction, and Gus too simple and straightforward as a lover for them to be compatible for long, and after Paris they drifted into an erratic friendship.

One day, when they were lunching in London with Ronald Firbank, Luisa proposed they should all sail together to America immediately. She would pay for everything, she said, and to Gus her extraordinary disregard of money was as fascinating as it was absurd. He stayed loyal to her, though, after the money ran out, after Luisa had exhausted her fortune on ever more fabulous parties and costumes (gowns made of swansdown that moulted as she moved, or constructed, cubist-style, out of electric light bulbs and wire). When she ended up in a one-bedroom flat in London, Gus would be among the small group of friends who supported her with occasional gifts of money and practical help.

But, even at the start of their affair, Luisa was only bearable to Gus in limited doses, and Paris itself began to wear thin. He paid a couple of nostalgic visits to Montparnasse, but was embarrassed by how incongruous he'd become in his gleaming major's uniform. Disgusted, a little, by the ease with which he'd been co-opted to the establishment Gus was made even more queasy by the politics of the conference, whose mission to shape a more peaceful and equitable world was fast disintegrating into a naked jockeying for power. The British contingent were 'showing signs of despair,' he told Dorelia, 'all except LL G who looks bursting with satisfaction'.[8]

Even his efficiency as a portrait painter was making Gus uncomfortable. 'I think I have acquired more common skill or is it that I have learned to limit my horizons merely,' he worried to Cynthia. Towards the end of his stay, he gave up the parties, preferring to walk alone by the Seine and contemplate a return to his proper art. He tried to contact Gwen, but she had disappeared from Paris and left no forwarding address. It was only in August, after Gus had returned home, that he learned she'd been staying all these months in her chateau at Pléneuf.

As Gwen had told Ursula, she'd discovered the chateau by chance at the end of her holiday with Ruth. She'd gone out for one last walk and had spotted a pair of immense wrought-iron gates, behind which lay an apparently deserted building. The grey-shuttered windows, the single turreted tower, the overgrown garden thrumming with butterflies and bees had given the place an air of secret enchantment. And when Gwen made enquiries at the farm next door and was told that the Chateau Vauclair was available for rent, she fell deeper under its spell. Looking around the interior, she could see traces of some former opulence in the chandelier that still hung in the salon, the assortment of stately stiff-backed chairs. Yet there was nothing oppressive in that opulence, and when Gwen learned how cheaply she could rent a couple of its rooms, she knew immediately she would return.

It was early January by the time she did, yet, even in the dead of winter, when the ground was frozen and cold winds tore at the leafless trees, the chateau hadn't lost its poetry. Nor was Gwen afraid of its isolation. The farmers next door were friendly, their chickens pecking around in the chateau's grounds; the shops of Pléneuf were only an eight-minute walk away and there was regular Mass at the parish church. Later that year, Ursula would confide how hard it had been for her to adjust to the ending of the war. 'For such a long time one's thoughts were full of fears for other people and all the frightfulness'.[9] For

Gwen, however, alone in her chateau, the transition to peace had felt entirely natural.

'You must leave everybody and be alone with God', she wrote. Yet it was work more than prayer that occupied her days.[10] She bribed the small daughters of her neighbour to sit for her – offering them a few centimes and the promise of a china doll from Paris. Odette, the oldest of the two, with her sharp eyes, rosebud mouth and tight little plaits, appeared most often in Gwen's drawings, her little sister Simone was too inclined to giggle when she saw Gwen squinting through her fingers to estimate the proportions of the girls' features and limbs. There was also a farm boy who sat for Gwen, and the picture she drew of him, his ears protruding awkwardly from his close-cropped hair, his hands sticking out from his ill-fitting jacket, was both simple and perfectly complete.* Gwen had always said she didn't want children herself, and she drew these Pléneuf boys and girls with an unsentimental eye. Yet she portrayed them too with all the tenderness she had brought to her sketches of the Meudon orphans. Just as Gus had found a near-infallible touch when painting and drawing his family, some of Gwen's most affecting images were those she was making of children.

Rarely had she felt so attuned to her surroundings, so close to her vow of 'living fully within oneself', as she did in Pléneuf now.[11] She sat by the sea, noting how her mood responded to the rhythm of the waves; she walked every day, collecting firewood, picking ferns and grasses to decorate her room. A family of stray cats came to live with her, curling up by the stove as Gwen read patiently though her small library of books – Bertrand Russell, Thomas Aquinas, Catherine of Siena.

But in late February came news that the owners were putting Vauclair up for sale, and even though Gwen tried to convince herself that it shouldn't matter where she lived, the blow fell hard. She'd already come to think of Vauclair as home and to anticipate the greening of the landscape in spring, the first bracing swims of the summer. The sale, however, progressed slowly, and the eventual buyer, a cattle merchant named Bourdin, took his time in deciding what he wanted to do with the

---

* The pose in which Gwen drew the farm boy, his hands clasped mutely in front of him, may have owed something to Picasso's *Child with Dove*.

property. By the time Gwen had to go to Paris, in July, to deal with some paperwork for Quinn, she'd begun to hope that Bourdin was regretting his purchase. She had also begun to wonder if Gus, with his mysterious access to funds, might buy the chateau instead, and when she sent him a postcard in August to explain where she'd been living, she was preparing the ground for her campaign.

Gus was pleased to hear that Gwen had been out of Paris and, mistakenly believing she was still at Vauclair, he bought a guidebook and suggested he might visit. 'Are you with friends, how long shall you stay? . . . I have never been to Brittany and long to go.'[12] He was still reacting against the frenetic pace of the Peace Conference; to Cynthia, he wrote, 'I want to dig myself up and replant myself in some corner where no one will look for me. I know I shall be able to paint better'.[13] And, intrigued by Gwen's enthusiasm for Vauclair, he was tempted to agree that one of those 'lovely . . . old French chateaus . . . would just suit us'.[14]

He was unable to think of buying it immediately, though. The Paris conference had been less lucrative than he'd hoped; the challenge of painting its proceedings had defeated him, and he'd even been asked to pay back some of the – excessive – expenses he'd charged.* He was also worried about his boys, who, with the exception of Caspar, were still unsettled and still costing him money. David, undecided about his music, was now asking for private tuition in drawing; Edwin, too, was wondering about art school; while Robin, having spent two terms at Malvern College, was refusing to return and was simply hanging around Alderney, silent and hostile. As Gus admitted to Gwen, his expectations were now pinned on Henry, who, at twelve years old, was becoming 'exactly like Ida and such an intelligent and charming creature'.[15]

In mid-September, though, Gus was writing more hopefully that his 'debts and responsibilities' were lifting. He'd been invited to the Normandy resort of Deauville, to paint Lloyd George, and, because there were others in the prime minister's party who were 'clamouring for portraits', he was expecting to make good money. He and Dorelia were

---

* He did so by selling off his painting *Fraternity* to the Imperial War Museum.

also planning to look at a college in Rouen which he thought might suit Edwin and Robin, his two most difficult boys, and, with that in mind, he was already wondering how he and his family would organize their time if he went ahead with the purchase of Vauclair. He would need to keep a studio in London – 'my marketing place at the present' – and Dorelia would be reluctant to let go of Alderney, but he still thought they could make excellent use of the chateau. He told Gwen he wished she were still there, so that he could come out from Deauville and see it.[16]

Spurred by Gus's enthusiasm, Gwen wrote to the Pléneuf *notaire* to enquire whether Bourdin would be agreeable to a sale, and the news was both good and bad. Bourdin *was* willing to sell, but wanted 50,000 francs (£2,000), which was more than double the price he'd paid. Even for Gus, that sum was too high, especially given the expense and inconvenience involved in travelling between Pléneuf and London. Although he hated to disappoint Gwen, he told her the plan would have to be put on hold.

Had it been otherwise, the chateau might have become a shared second home, which might, conceivably, have brought the two of them closer. Already they had overcome some of their underlying differences. Gwen was now as re-focused on her work as Gus could wish, and was actually in the process of submitting nine drawings and one of her nun portraits for exhibition at the Salon d'Automne, her first public showing in Paris. Gus, meanwhile, was showing an even more earnest desire to escape from the clamour of his celebrity, to live and paint more like Gwen. When he wrote to her from Deauville, he was very nostalgic for the innocent years of his early career, for the time when he hadn't yet become harried into painting the famous and the rich. 'One of the finest things I've seen for a long time', he told her, 'was a group of old gentlemen friends playing cards in a cafe. I should love to paint them.'[17]

But, although there was a renewed sympathy between Gus and Gwen, they were both in their early forties and very set in their ways. Intimacy was only easy for them in limited doses, and, if the chateau had been bought, it would more probably have become a battleground rather than a bridge. However carefully they might have tried to divide its rooms and stagger their periods of residence, the still-inescapable hubbub of Gus's world and the austerity of Gwen's would surely have provoked them to a mutual exasperation, and they may well have quarrelled their way to some irrevocable split.

As it was, Vauclair remained an abstract possibility. Gus, alarmed by Gwen's talk of going to a moneylender, suggested she approach Quinn. 'Why doesn't [he] buy it? . . . He could then give it you and come and stay there sometimes'. This possibility had already occurred to Gwen, in fact, for at the beginning of October she wrote a long letter to Quinn, preparing her approach with wistful descriptions of Vauclair's poetry. 'It has a beauty of its own, rather sad . . . the gardens are beautiful, too; of course all grown sauvage now, but that gave them more charm to me. The people who bought it were cattle merchants and so not used to thinking of what is beautiful . . . They are rather afraid of living there, I think because of the solitude and are going to do so only two months in the year . . . they would sell it to me not dear at all, and I think I shall live there again some day.'[18]

Four days after Gwen wrote that letter, however, all thoughts of the chateau were driven away by news that her friend Isabel Bowser had died. Gwen had known for months that Isabel had cancer, and had been angered by her rejection of conventional treatment: a zealous convert to Christian Science, Isabel had insisted that faith rather than medicine would cure her. Yet, just as Gwen had refused to admit the gravity of Rodin's decline, she hadn't expected Isabel to die, and the shock of her grief was intensified by the guilt she felt at having seen so little of her friend during the time she'd been caught up with her chateau. She hadn't even finished the painting which she'd promised to Isabel as a gift. It was one of the *Convalescent* series, and Gwen was tormented by the ironic joke she'd planned to make on presenting it to Isabel – that 'it didn't matter about the title because no doubt she had been cured by Christian Science'.[19]

Gwen's friends and family all rallied round, knowing how broken she would be after yet another loss. Chloe sent comforting packages of books, clothes and English tea; she urged Gwen to seek comfort from her Mother Superior, her priest having been moved to another parish. Gus was equally solicitous: 'I regret Vauclair . . . I'm afraid you'll not be happy at Meudon after this loss of your friend . . . Do not for God's sake allow it to make you morbid . . . you have too much sense and esprit.'[20]

He begged her to keep on working and pressed her gently to send some pictures to London, 'where a number of people long to acquire them.' One of that number was Arthur Symons, who now wrote to Gwen to express his admiration of some drawings he'd recently seen of hers, and his appreciation of the friendship she'd given to Isabel. 'I adore your devotion for [her] – those awful Christian Science people killed her as you knew by instinct.' He added that he and his wife Rhoda (Isabel's sister) would very much like to meet Gwen when they were next in Paris, and he urged her to take 'all possible care' of herself. 'One has to live and with that one's art'.[21]

In gratitude for Arthur's compassion, Gwen sent him a drawing, *L'enfant with poupée*, which he promptly wrote back to declare a 'miracle of strange beauty'. However, during the first unravelling weeks of Gwen's bereavement, it was to one of Isabel's other sisters, Nona Watkins, that she turned. The two of them barely knew each other, but, to Gwen, Nona appeared to possess near-mystical powers of empathy. 'My mind is suffering often,' she wrote, 'and suddenly I hear your words "my dear, dear Gwen." Nona, what angel made you say it. Nona when you look at me so thoughtfully and write to me you don't know what you do.' She thought Nona was like a 'sculptor' as she modelled the 'lovely form' of their intimacy, and the allusion to Rodin was not accidental, for the love Gwen had started to feel for Nona had turned suddenly and shockingly physical.[22]

It had been years since she'd wanted a woman this way and she barely knew what to do with herself. 'I didn't want to love again a human being but only God,' she wrote miserably, convinced that her feelings went against every teaching of her Church, and that Nona, who was married, could never reciprocate them.

Yet something had come loose in Gwen and, in the delirium of her desire, she wrote a series of desperate letters to Nona: 'I need you . . . I am a beggar at your door I know that now. I know I wrote "I don't ask for your tenderness" but only let me speak to you'.[23]

Some of those letters were never sent, and Nona herself was careful to manage Gwen, addressing only the issue of her grief as she counselled her to try to remember the millions who'd suffered similar bereavement in the war. Bleakly, Gwen promised to obey. 'I will try to be brave because you tell me to . . . it is my only nourishment because all the other things I knew before have gone away now from my memory.'[24] And eventually she managed to wrench her emotions back under her control.

There was no more mention of Nona, yet Gwen was still very weak, her equilibrium fragile. Early in January 1920, when she went to visit Constance Lloyd, the sight of her friend's dear familiar features, coupled with the warmth of her embrace, had aroused in Gwen the same shockingly transgressive need as Nona's kindness had done.

She was horrified by her own wickedness and made awkward excuses to leave, yet, back home in Meudon, she was helpless against the feverish scenarios that played out in her mind as she planned how she and Constance might make love. 'Let her draw you to her and kiss your hand . . . later you can kiss her more willingly with love and you can later still put your arms around her knees and kiss her giving yourself . . . Be like two girls.'[25] Gwen knew her fantasies were a sin and she prayed to be rid of them: 'Oh god who hast helped me in the past, oh help me now'. Yet, even in the middle of her repentance, she was imagining how she might impress Constance with the intensity of her 'striving'.

Constance almost certainly remained ignorant of Gwen's feelings, and it's unclear whether Nona was fully aware of the passion she'd aroused. Although Gwen might believe herself lost to reason, adrift on the flood of her sinful desires, she had actually become more skilled at managing herself. Back in the autumn, when she'd felt racked with grief for Isabel and with love for Nona, she'd also been dealing quite competently with the Salon d'Automne (who had accepted her submissions and were proposing to make her an '*associataire*'), and she had only broken focus on her art for a very short while.

'Work through suffering has another quality, not necessarily inferior to work through tranquillity,' she thought.[26] During the autumn and winter, Gwen was making a diligent rediscovery of colour, allowing herself to expand into a brighter spectrum of greens, pinks, yellows and browns, but all the while making precise annotations of the effects each colour produced. With the same steady invention, she was still working with her Meudon model, trying to paint her way deeper into what she called the woman's 'atmosphere' or 'strangeness', and learning how much more likely she was to find that atmosphere by refining out all unnecessary detail from her art. The relationship between figure and space, the alchemy between tones, were the issues that interested her now, and, as the faces in her paintings became sketchier, the expressions of her models more opaque, Gwen would eventually move so far beyond ordinary definitions of portraiture that she would tell Ursula she no longer approached her models as individuals, but as an 'affair of volumes'.[27]

In another compartment of her life, Gwen was also still thinking about her chateau. Quinn had been very taken with her descriptions of Vauclair and, in the spring of 1920, he was serious about making an offer. He imagined himself playing host in his own rural salon and thought he might persuade Arthur Symons and his wife Rhoda (who was a former actress) to take up permanent residence as caretakers. Eager to know more about the chateau, he wrote to Gwen for exact details about the number and condition of its rooms, the state of its access roads, its distance from the nearest town. He promised to send her a camera with which she could take pictures when she next visited Vauclair – 'Snapshotting in the country is rather amusing,' he said.

Gwen, however, was dismayed by Quinn's plans. Even if he were to set aside a private space for her, she could not agree to him bringing all his friends to Vauclair, even less to installing the Symons. 'It is not practical,' she wrote firmly. 'I have heard it is his [Arthur's] great pleasure to spend his time often with literary and artistic friends in London. He would be too lonely at Vauclair and his wife would not stay there three days, no, not one. I don't know her but my friend was her sister and so I know what she is like.'[28]

Gwen hadn't forgotten Arthur's kindness to her the previous autumn, but, in January, she'd received a letter from Rhoda that made her shrink from further contact.

> Gwen – I'm Rhoda I feel as if I know you, Nona and Isabel have told me so much of you and I feel Gwen that I love you, because of your wonderful self and because of your understanding of – and love of – Isabel.
> Someday I want to talk with you about her.
> Always your friend if you will let me be so Rhoda [29]

The idea of this emotionally noisy woman invading the sublime quiet of Vauclair was appalling, and Quinn, sensing Gwen's disquiet, let the subject rest. The Symons themselves, however, were not so easily dropped. On 21 May, Arthur wrote to send Gwen the gift of some of his poetry, together with the announcement of his and Rhoda's imminent arrival in Paris. 'Shall we call on Saturday morning to see your paintings and drawings,' he proposed, 'and then descend into Paris where you can show us certain places you know better than we do.'

It was a note that allowed no escape, and Gwen awaited their arrival with dread, already resenting the time she would waste. But, when they appeared in Meudon, she found them unexpectedly lovable. Arthur, tall and stooped, was a marvellous conversationalist, talking to Gwen about his friendship with Gus, his meetings with Rodin, and about the Pembrokeshire countryside where he'd also grown up. As for Rhoda, Gwen admitted she was not at all 'what I imagined an actress to be'.[30] She was disarmed by the candour with which Rhoda talked about her own, sometimes difficult, relationship with Isabel, and she was pleased by the perceptiveness with which Rhoda commented on her work, observing that art was rather like acting: 'the more one discovers in oneself to express . . . the more technique one requires to express it.'

'It has been a happiness meeting them', Gwen wrote afterwards to Quinn. 'The winter and spring with their troubles seem to have really passed for me. It is lovely here.'[31] Arthur and Rhoda had irradiated Paris for her and so easy had she felt in their company that, with uncharacteristic enthusiasm, Gwen had accepted their invitation to come and visit them in England later that year.

Rhoda, like many other women, had developed a proprietorial fascination with Gwen and wanted to make a project of her. 'I take as much interest in your progress – both your artistic progress and your material one as I do my own,' she wrote, and promised that everything would be made perfect for Gwen when she came to stay, with a room set aside for her work, a cook and a cleaner to take care of her. 'You know Gwen you're too tired after doing your housework to draw,' Rhoda scolded, adding that there was no question of her even paying for her travel. 'Do you think we would *dream* of your coming all the way over from France to *be* with us at your expense. No my dear.'[32]

Gus, who had been pressing Gwen to visit for years, was offended when he saw the Symons at the opera one night and was told of their plans for his sister's visit. Brusquely, he informed them that they knew nothing of Gwen and that they would find her a difficult guest – prickly about her privacy and likely to be ungrateful. To Gwen herself, Gus wrote a sharp little letter. '[Rhoda] told me you were coming to stay at their cottage in Kent. I am glad you have decided to take a change although I wish you had agreed to stay with us . . . where there is more room and we would have made you quite at home; also I think you would have liked to see something of the children.'[33] Family, he implied, ought to matter more to Gwen than the whims of friendship; he himself was about to take Dorelia and the children to Tenby. 'It will be nice to see again some of those familiar places . . . I wish you were coming too.' As for the Symons, he warned Gwen that she would soon find the couple 'troublesome' as friends: 'Although I like [Arthur] I find it difficult to support his company for more than 5 minutes'.

Arthur had in fact become difficult for Gus long before the issue of Gwen's visit. They had met in 1903, and Arthur had joined the ranks of men to whom Gus seemed almost godlike: 'so full of lust and life and animality, so exorbitant in his desires, in his vision that rises from his eyes.' For a while, Gus had admired Arthur too, had enjoyed the reams of poetry he dedicated to him. But, in 1908, Arthur had a severe mental breakdown which left him prone to morbid hypochondria, and the sympathy Gus tried to feel for his friend had become frayed by his own impatience. He'd also begun to mind that Arthur was no longer so ready with his compliments, nor so quick to revere Gus's genius, and, by June 1920, there was a history of touchiness between them.

It was Rhoda, though, who was most energetic in the rivalry over Gwen. She made blatant attempts to divide her from Gus, passing on the criticisms he'd made of her, along with rumours of his drinking: 'don't for heaven's sake say I said so but I heard he had delirium tremens 3 weeks ago'.

Gwen's response, however, was wary. She had enjoyed meeting the Symons, they had inspired her to wonder if it was time for her to be a little 'less shy if possible'. As she confided to Quinn, 'I like being alone but I don't pretend to know how to live. And sometimes I think everything I do is wrong'.[34] Yet she didn't care for Rhoda's gossiping about Gus, nor did she appreciate the bossiness with which Rhoda exhorted her to fix a date for her visit, telling her to 'Buck up and write a few lines there's a good soul'.

Instead, she spent August with Ruth, in Pléneuf, perhaps casting wistful eyes at her chateau. And on her return to Paris she could not think of planning a trip to England because she had to prepare herself for the alarming visit of Quinn's close friend and mistress, the writer Jeanne Robert Foster.

Jeanne, a woman of considerable beauty and charm, as well as literary talent (she was soon to be made American editor of the *Transatlantic Review*), was often very helpful to Quinn in his dealings with artists and clients. He'd asked her to go to Paris and try to form a friendship with Gwen, because, even after a decade of dealing with Gwen, he remained perplexed by her and her reluctance to part with her art. When he'd offered to raise her stipend to £750 for a guaranteed three-year period, she'd tried to caution him against making so firm a commitment, because her work might change and he might no longer want it. Frustrated in his desire for more of Gwen's pictures, and influenced in part by what he'd heard from Gus, Quinn had formed the impression that she was a complete recluse – 'very shy, almost impossible to help and liv[ing] in the greatest poverty'.[35] Nor had Gwen challenged that impression when, in response to Quinn's news that Jeanne would be coming to Meudon, she wrote, 'I have never met a poetess nor any woman writer. I am tortured by shyness with strangers.'[36]

On 14 September, when Jeanne appeared at rue Terre Neuve, the encounter was almost as tortured as Gwen had predicted. Jeanne was told by one of the neighbours that Mademoiselle John was not at home, so she went upstairs to the flat, intending to slip a note through the door. Gwen, however, *was* at home, at work on a painting, and when she heard a noise on the landing and looked to see who was there, her mortification was absolute. Jeanne had once been employed as a fashion model and was still gorgeously dressed, her skirt fashionably narrow, her neck adorned with ropes of ivory beads. Gwen – hair unbrushed and wearing her old painting clothes – felt ambushed by this vision of elegance. And while Jeanne apologized profusely, saying she would go to the

Observatory Terrace and wait while Gwen changed, Gwen was unable to prevent herself muttering rudely to Jeanne that Quinn had instructed her to 'behave decently' otherwise she 'probably wouldn't'.

But Jeanne simply smiled, and when Gwen joined her for a turn around the Terrace, her anger calmed and she invited Jeanne back to her flat. It was then, as they drank tea together in the fading light and looked through some of Gwen's work, that Gwen gave in to Jeanne's charm and, under gentle questioning, began to talk about herself, her work, her dealings with the Parisian art scene. She confessed her dislike of Matisse, whom she considered shallow and vain – he'd boasted once of having 'squeez[ed] all the juice' from the contemporary art market, 'leaving only the rind and the dried pulp' for the rest.[37] She also talked about Quinn. He had sent a second camera over when the first had failed to arrive and, as Jeanne patiently explained how it worked, Gwen was suddenly struck by the thoughtfulness of the gift. Searching for some of Quinn's letters, she read parts of them aloud, tearful now at their kind generosity. By the end of the afternoon, Gwen had not only agreed to see Jeanne again, but to consider the idea of painting her portrait.

Jeanne herself had been deeply moved by their meeting. In a seven-page letter to Quinn, she wrote, 'I loved her at once with real affection. Here is a woman brave enough to live a touching spiritual reality every day of her life. All the pathetic dramatization of life has fallen away, she is real.'[38] She herself was deeply interested in mysticism and was quick to correct Quinn's image of Gwen as a strange and impoverished hermit. The flat was beautifully 'monastic', she wrote, its modest furniture elegantly arranged and perfectly functional, with a small library of books lined up on the shelves, an easel in one corner and a single drawing of Gus's pinned to the wall. As for Gwen being shy, Jeanne thought that an absurd simplification of a personality which seemed to her both complex and fierce. 'She is perfectly poised, a great lady in a way, bitter towards the average person, determined to get her own way, proud, savagely proud yet childish, very affectionate, wanting love yet refusing it'.[39] Even her voice, Jeanne noted, expressed the paradoxes of her nature – 'wavering' at first, but then punctuated by 'contralto notes of a fantastic determination to live as she pleases'.

Jeanne's powers of observation were acute. From this single meeting, she intuited that Gwen's reluctance to sell her work was not only motivated by self-doubt, but by the fact that her pictures were as necessary to her as the 'air she breathed' – it pained her to let any of them go. However, the confidence Jeanne felt in having got the true measure of Gwen was thrown by their second meeting, a fortnight later. They had agreed to have lunch in a restaurant, but when Gwen arrived, very late, she was highly agitated, so close to tears she could barely speak. A few days earlier, her former curé at Meudon had hanged himself, apparently unhinged by the death of an older nun who'd been like a mother to him; and, as far as Jeanne could make out, when Gwen had gone to see her priest's body, she'd been so affected by the tragedy of his suicide, she'd imagined she was in some way culpable. She blamed herself for losing contact with him, even more for failing to live up to the spiritual standards he'd instilled in her: 'I have become corrupted and depraved,' she despaired, and she told Jeanne she wished she were dead.

Gwen was so distraught about the scale of her imagined sin, it took all of Jeanne's tact to calm her. But, by the end of the afternoon, she was talking dreamily of more normal things, memories of her mother and of Winnie, whom she'd always thought 'quite wonderful with a practical instinct for life.'[40] And, when the two of them left the restaurant, they were holding hands and making plans for when they would next meet.

From this point on, their intimacy was established and they saw each other almost every day. They went to the Salon d'Automne to see Gwen's latest submissions, to the Meudon convent to see the Mère Poussepin portrait which Quinn was now hoping to buy. They also scoured the galleries for works by Marie Laurencin, whom Quinn thought might be paired with Gwen for a New York show. He'd told Gwen that she and Laurencin were the only two women he knew 'who did not try to paint like men', and although it was an obtuse compliment – Quinn would never offer Gus or any other man an exhibition on such terms – Gwen apparently took no offence. She knew nothing of Laurencin's work, she told Quinn, but was happy to go in search of her paintings. She was even happier, perhaps, to see that none were on show.

With each new encounter, Gwen found it easier and easier to talk

18. *Nude Girl*,
Gwen John, 1909–10.

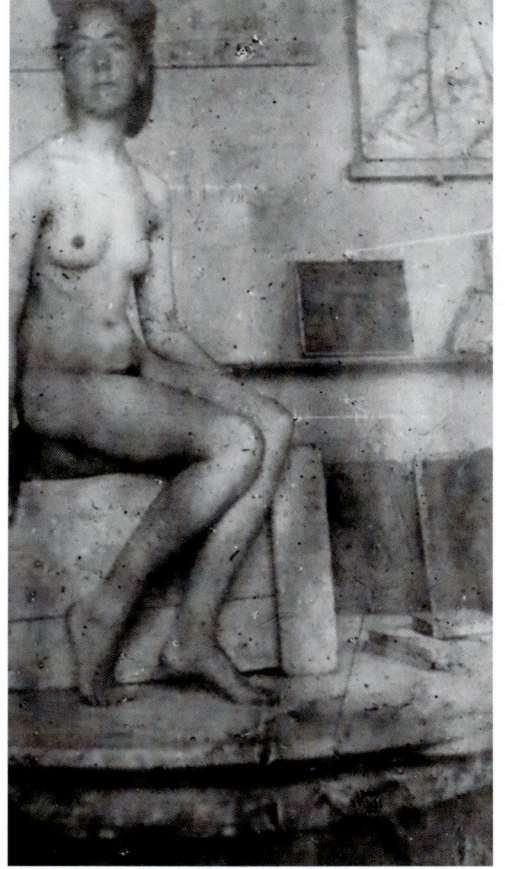

19. Gwen posing nude,
possibly for Ruth Manson,
c. 1911.

20. *Self-portrait*, sketching,
Gwen John, c. 1909.

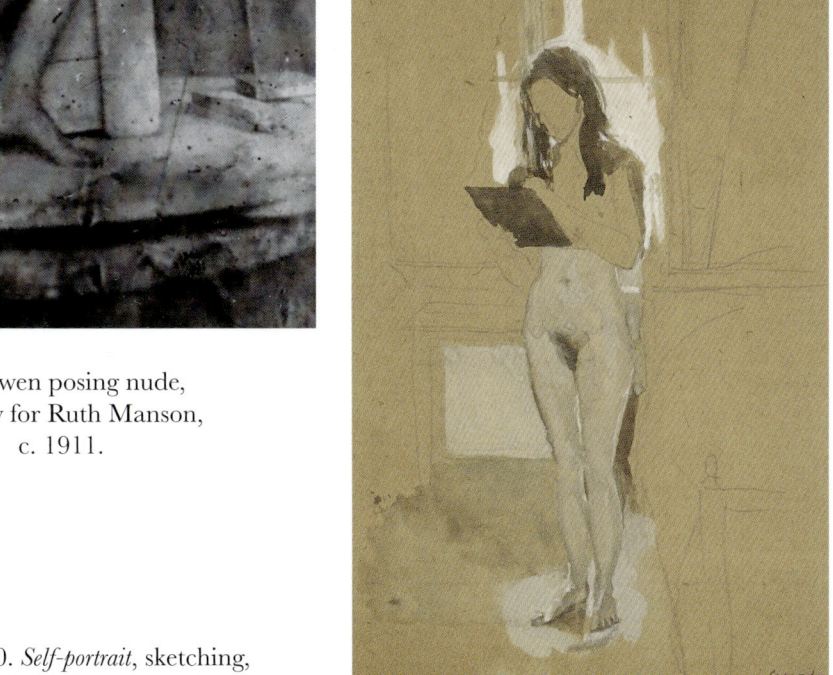

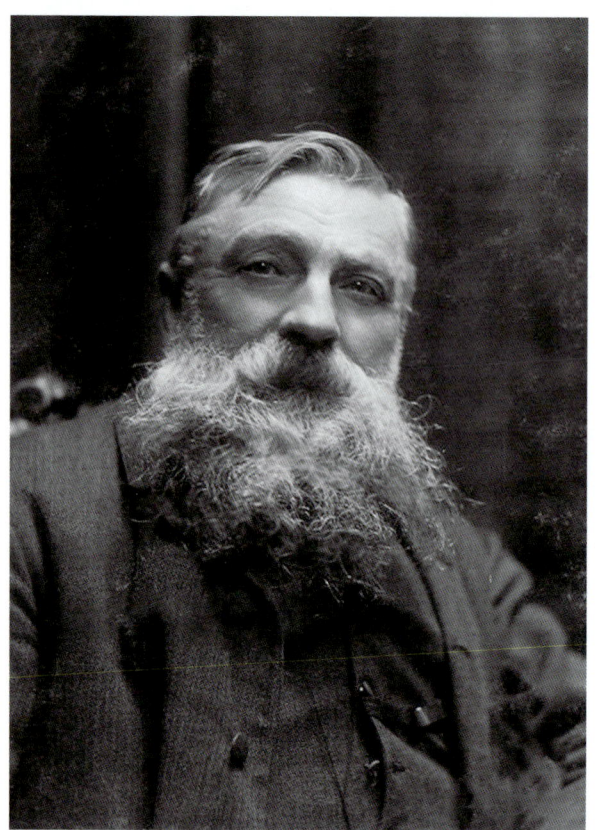

21. Auguste Rodin.

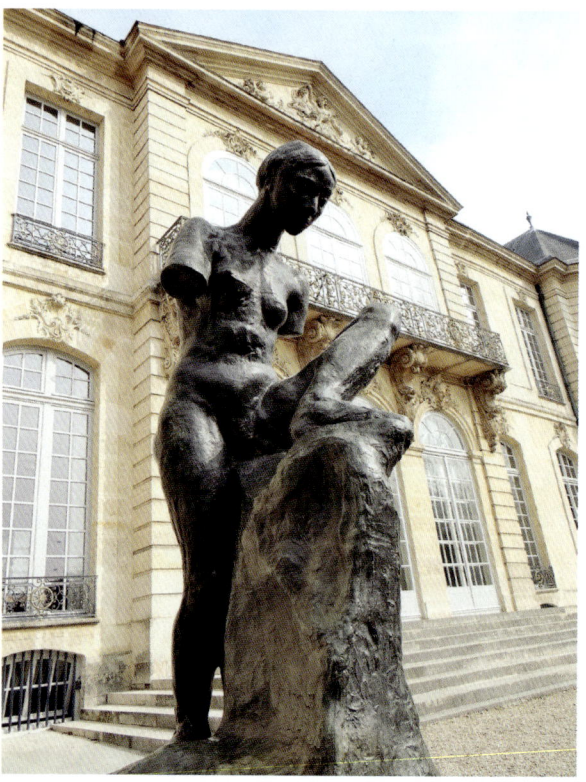

22. *Whistler's Muse*, Auguste Rodin, c. 1908.

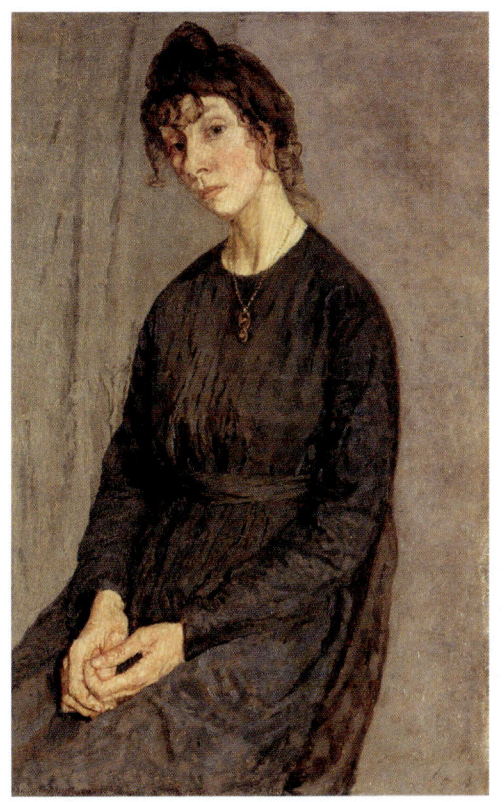

23. *Chloe Boughton-Leigh*, Gwen John, 1910.

24. *Interior*, Gwen John, 1915–16.

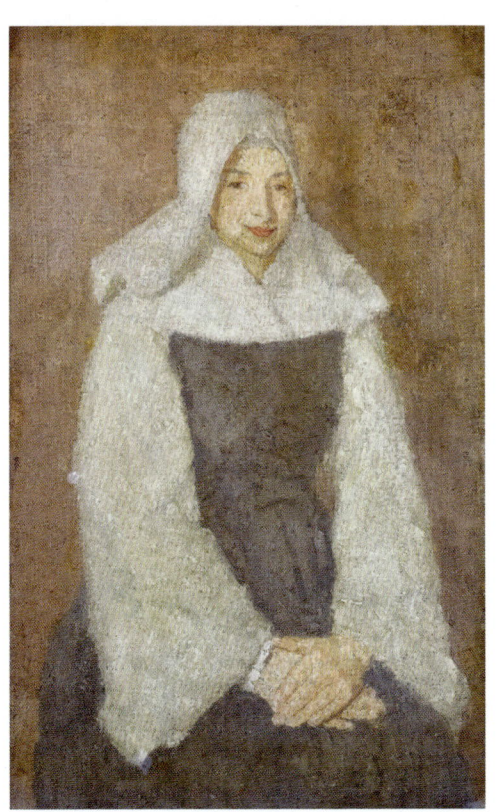

25. *Mère Poussepin*, Gwen John, c. 1913–20.

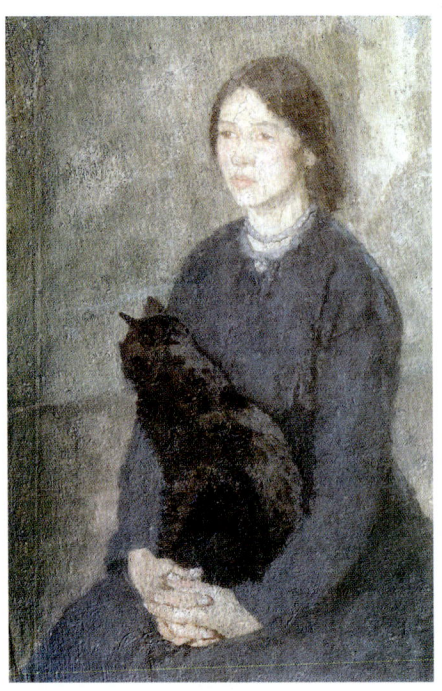

26. *Young Woman Holding a Black Cat*, Gwen John, c. 1919–early 1920s.

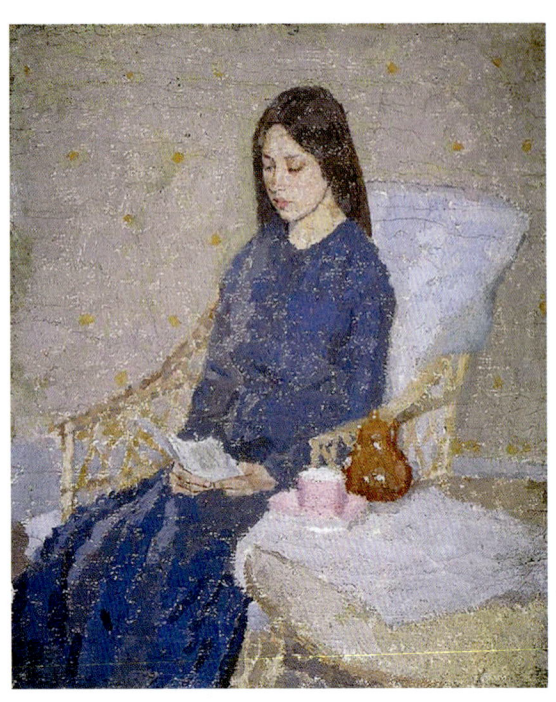

27. *The Convalescent*, Gwen John, c. 1923–4.

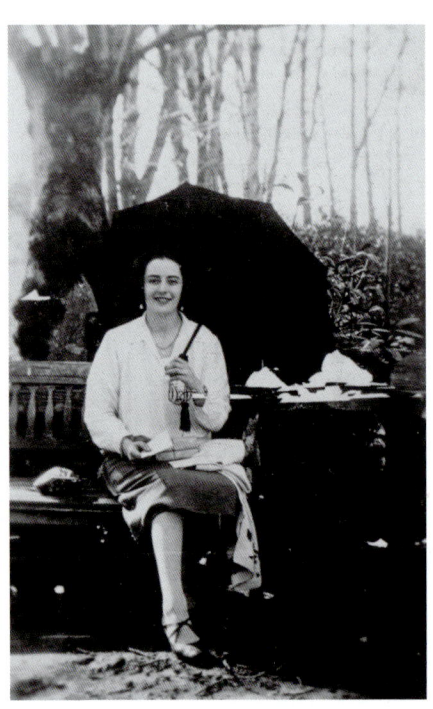

28. Jeanne Robert Foster.

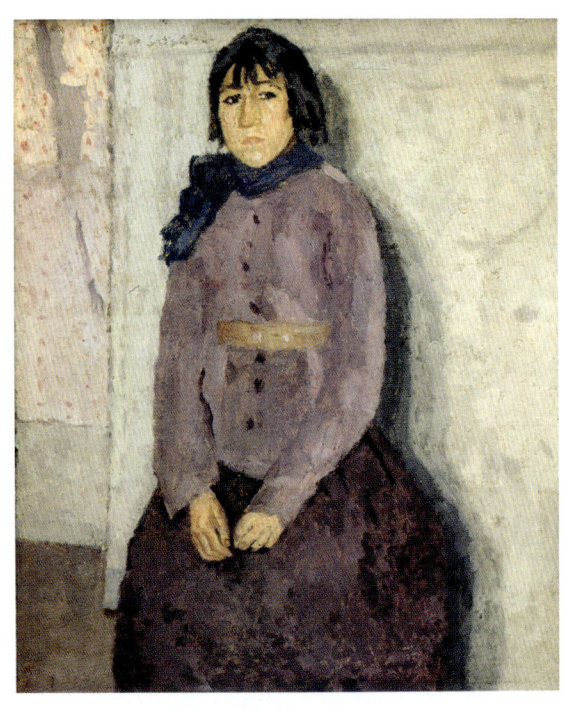

29. *Girl with a Blue Scarf*, Gwen John, 1923–4.

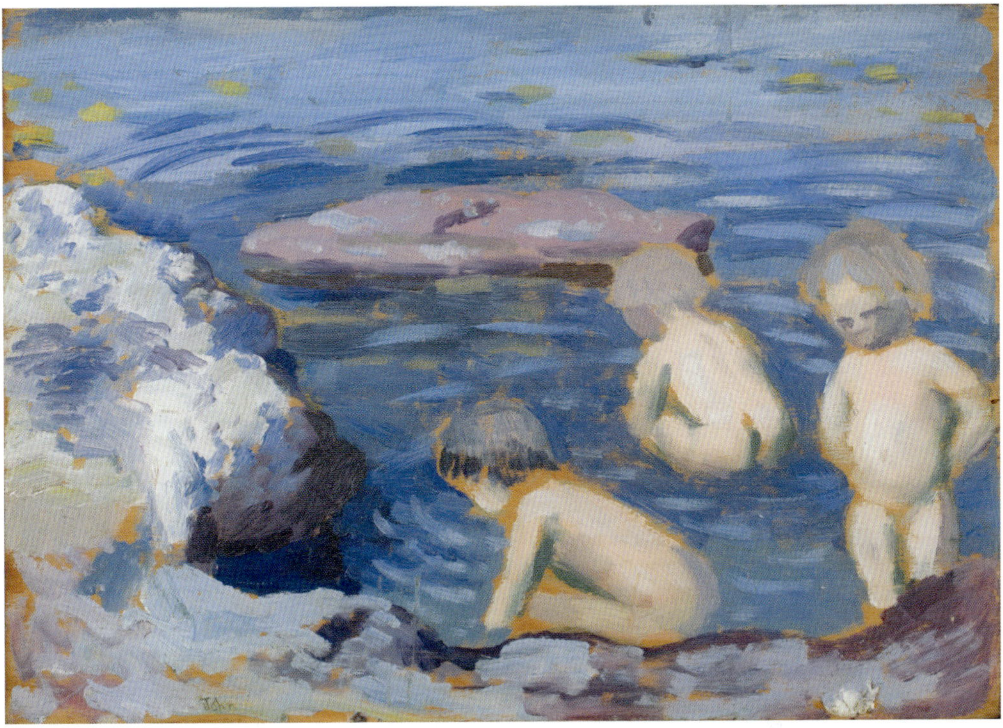

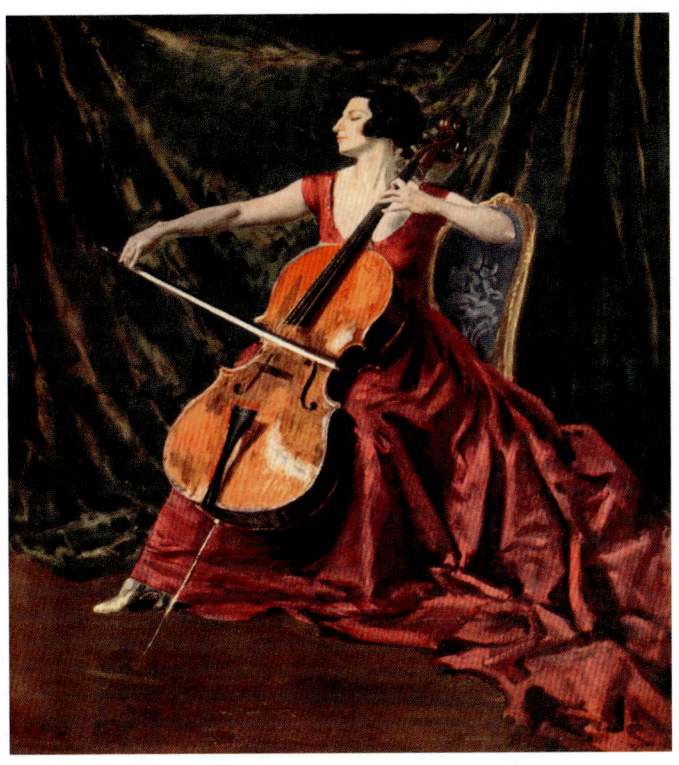

30. *Three Children Bathing*, Augustus John, c. 1910.

31. *Madame Suggia*, Augustus John, 1920–3.

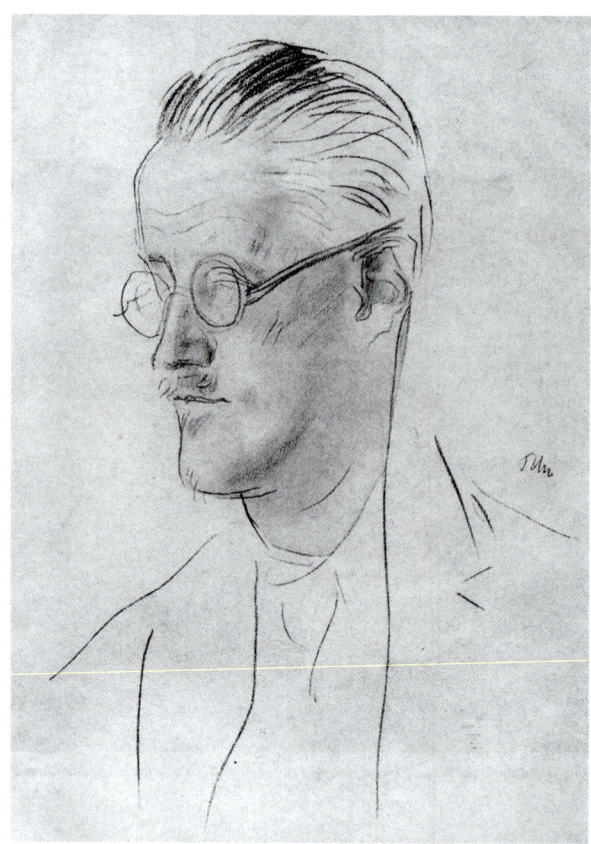

32. *Portrait of James Joyce*,
Augustus John, 1930.

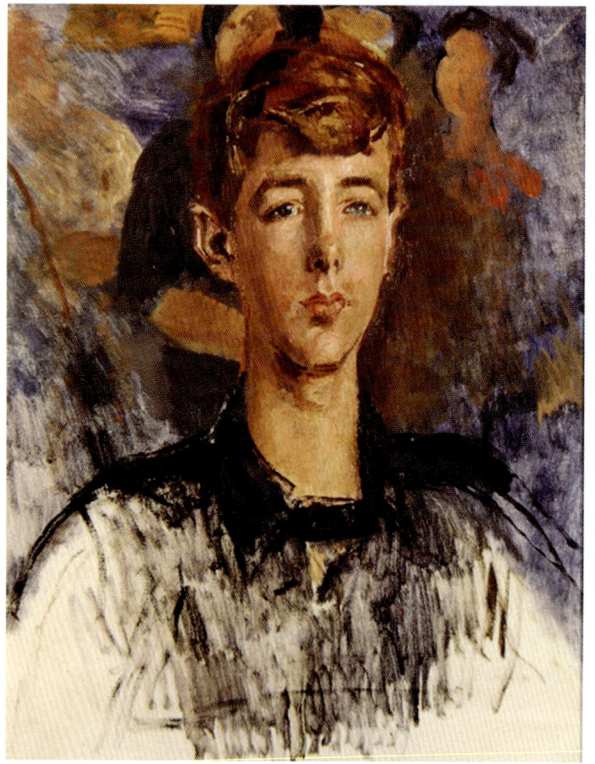

33. *Portrait of Tristan de Vere Cole*,
Augustus John, 1951.

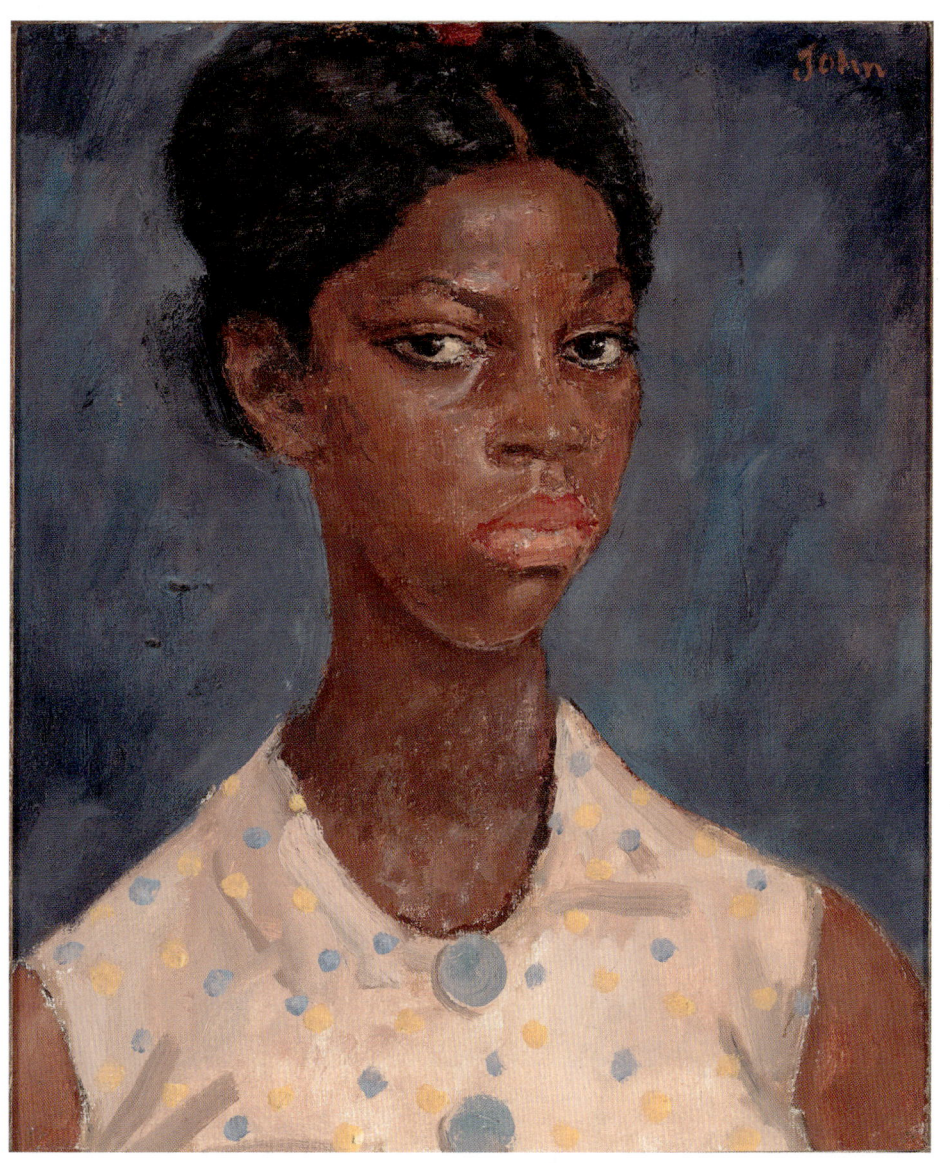

34. *A Jamaican Girl*, Augustus John, 1937.

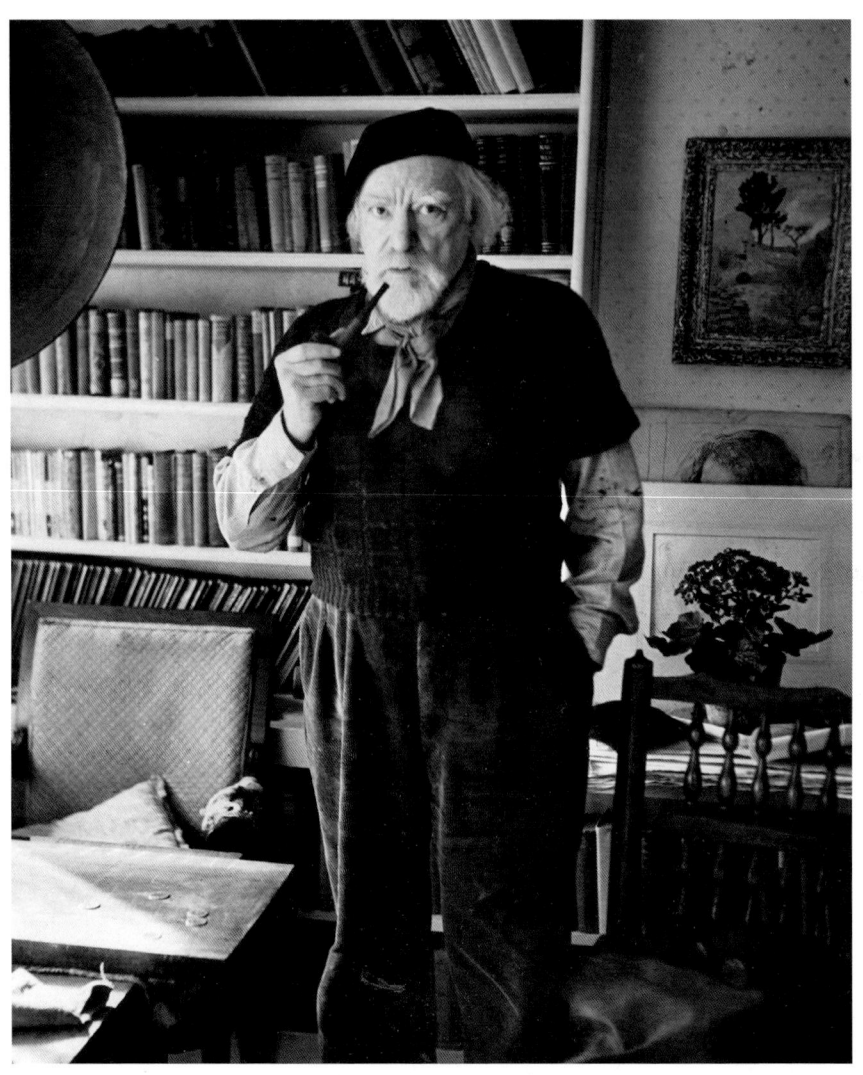
35. Augustus John at Fryern Court, 1959.

to Jeanne, so much so that she began to take subtle control of their relationship. She played on Jeanne's sympathy, exaggerating her early struggles with poverty; she gave a dramatic account of her difficulties with Gus, whom she blamed alternately for being neglectful and interfering. Jeanne, who had no idea of the push-pull vehemence of Gwen's relationship with her brother, had no reason to question the truth of her stories. But, even if she had, she was now being drawn so deeply into Gwen's way of seeing and thinking, she could not have contradicted her. 'Miss John's mind is extraordinarily fluid,' she wrote to Quinn. 'She flows into that which is nearest. She is more myself than I am.'[41] One day, when Gwen was talking about the portrait she might paint of her, she produced a faded pink corduroy jacket and flowing plaid skirt which she thought Jeanne ought to wear. They were more artistic, she explained, than Jeanne's Manhattan outfits and they would suit her far better. Jeanne, who was so very famous for her style, could only humbly concur.

The women had become so close, it was difficult for Jeanne to leave, and she remained in Paris until 1 December. Gwen was miserable to see her go; she had come to love Jeanne, even though she'd been careful not to overreach the boundaries of their friendship. But Jeanne promised to return in the summer, and, in the afterglow of her visit, Gwen found herself drawing and painting with an extra joy. 'I am in my work now – in the harmony or the "atmosphere" or whatever it is called', she told Jeanne.[42]

She was looking at the cubist paintings of Albert Gleizes, was experimenting with more geometric forms of her own in her search for the effect of 'strangeness'. As she painted steadily through the winter, she felt she could have continued for months, but she was still being pestered by Rhoda and, in June, she felt obliged to make her long-delayed visit to the Symons' cottage in Kent.

It was the first time Gwen had been in England for almost two decades, however she left very little record of her three-week stay beyond the few affectionate sketches she drew of Arthur. She made no attempt to visit Alderney, but she did have dinner with Gus when the Symons took her up to London, perhaps to see her Fenella portrait at the Tate.

He was looking handsome, she thought, with his hair shorter and his beard trimmed, and there was family news to share – about Winnie, who'd given birth to her second child; about Thornton, who was mining oil shale in Newfoundland; and about their father, whom Gus had just visited, and who was in sprightly good health. They didn't apparently discuss the vexed issue of the Symons, but they did have a difficult conversation about Quinn, who had finally broken off all his dealings with Gus. He'd lost patience with the non-delivery of too many paintings, but he'd also been persuaded by his artist friend Walter Khun that years had passed since he had seen the best of Gus's art and that it would be far more satisfying and profitable to concentrate on collecting Gwen – the other John.

Gwen, on hearing about the quarrel from Gus, was distressed; she didn't want to think too badly of Quinn, preferred to believe that he'd been given malicious advice by Khun. But still she felt he had behaved shabbily to Gus, and that feeling coloured her perceptions of her patron when, just a couple of weeks later, she finally met him in person.

Quinn himself had become impatient to see Gwen at last, to get a more complete sense of what she was working on – and of what she might be keeping hidden from him. He'd additionally wanted her to meet his friend the art dealer Henri-Pierre Roché, and having been foiled by Gwen in his last attempted visit, he decided not to warn her in advance when he and Roché came calling. In his unannounced arrival at rue Terre Neuve, however, Quinn had miscalculated badly, for Gwen, ambushed yet again in her old painting dress, felt furiously embarrassed. She was crosser still when, having slipped from the room to change her clothes, she returned to find Quinn and Roché already in the act of looking through her work, and Quinn already picking out the drawings he wanted to buy, including her sketch of the little Pléneuf boy, which she'd earmarked as a gift for Ursula.

At that moment Gwen almost hated her patron for his pushy American entitlement. 'He thinks he has the right to it all,' she wrote crossly to Ursula, and it took all of Quinn's tact to win back her trust.[43] He was carefully courteous when he went with her to the Meudon convent to negotiate the purchase of her Mère Poussepin portrait – 'a beautiful cool thing', he enthused – and he made a generously charitable donation to the nuns and to the orphans in their care. Afterwards, he drove Gwen into the city, wanting her opinion on the three new Picassos he'd bought, and explaining the account he proposed to open for her at the New York Equitable Trust Company, which would simplify the transfer of his money. This, finally, was the Quinn Gwen had come to admire through their correspondence, and she was equally touched by the day he organized for her and for Jeanne (of whom she'd yet seen very little), taking them both on a picnic in Meudon forest, on a tour of the palace at Versailles and for dinner at an expensive restaurant.

Afterwards, Quinn told Jeanne that he believed Gwen had really come to care for him, and to a degree she had. Yet she had also been counting the days until he left, because she was then going to start work on Jeanne's portrait and, for two weeks, would have her friend exclusively to herself. Rooms had been taken for Jeanne at the Villa Calypso in Meudon, so that she could conveniently come to rue Terre Neuve for two or three sessions each day. And, as Gwen looked forward to the long hours during which she could gaze uninterruptedly at Jeanne, to the evenings in which they could talk quietly together, she imagined their intimacy growing daily more golden and more profound.

Yet, while the portrait had promised so much, it turned out to be a cause of uneasy contention. Jeanne, who'd been excited to see Gwen at work and curious about what insights she might gain, was dismayed by how slow and exacting she proved to be. 'I have posed for drawings in every corner of her studio but she has not begun to paint,' Jeanne grumbled to Quinn. 'She makes a drawing of me in the morning light, in the afternoon she makes another drawing before tea. After tea she does another one. I have not seen any of them. She is impatient if my pose grows still, and she says she had rather not do me at all if I am going to pose.'

It was difficult for Jeanne to know what Gwen meant by posing or not posing. Only when Gwen instructed her to remove her jewellery, to loosen her hair and arrange her body in a certain way did she realize she was meant to look more like Gwen herself. 'I felt the absorption of her personality as I [sat]', Jeanne wrote – conscious, yet again, of the curious power Gwen had for getting deep beneath her skin.[44]

But, just as Jeanne thought she understood what Gwen wanted, that the portrait was starting to progress, Gwen suddenly called a halt to their sessions, explaining that she had pictures to get ready for the Salon d'Automne. And while she agreed to come to the tea which Jeanne had arranged to meet the poet Ezra Pound and his wife, Gwen did not appear at all that day.

Afterwards, she apologized, explaining that she'd got lost in her work. But, from this point on, Gwen began to put a slight distance between herself and Jeanne. It's possible she was irked by the eagerness with which Jeanne had pressed her to meet the Pounds – had felt it as a betrayal of their own closeted intimacy – but she was fearful too of her growing feelings for Jeanne. During the long days they'd been spending together, Gwen had begun to struggle with the same, dangerously importunate desire she'd experienced with Nona and Constance. And while she had tried to channel that desire into the concentration of her painting, an entry she made in her notebook, after Jeanne returned home, suggests the agonized effort it had cost.

It was a chaotic kind of prayer, apparently addressed both to Jeanne and to God, in which Gwen begged for assistance in subduing her treacherous heart: 'Don't abandon me I will never leave you. My lapses will not be taken into account and my works will be a prayer for you and me. My lapses will not be taken into account but god will look into my heart and see my love and submission. You say you will be my love . . . I would be disobedient if I didn't strive. I must finish my work. He and she may be pleased to see me brave. Don't look in the past. Tell him everything. Wait for his answers and advice'.[45]

If Jeanne had guessed at the battle in Gwen, her own letters remained steadily affectionate, describing the 'vividness' with which she remembered her time at Meudon – 'your talk, your face, the drawings, the flowers' – and suggesting that, next year, they might go travelling together: 'I should love to take you gypsying, wherever you would like to go'.[46] Gradually, in Jeanne's absence, Gwen recovered her calm; she steadied herself through prayer and, setting aside Jeanne's portrait (which she would never finish), she returned to less agitating work. As she waited through the winter for Jeanne's return, Gwen wrote to Ursula of her conviction that she must always grow stronger through suffering. 'One of the things that gives me most pleasure is the crowing of the cock here. It tells me of long quiet days of work and other happiness.' Although the weather was freezing and there were 'acacia leaves of frost over the window even when the fire was lighted', she told Ursula that it still felt like spring: 'Me I'm like a plant that was dying or nearly dead and begins to grow again. How almost unbelievable, and what a joy it is to live.'[47]

Chapter Fifteen

GOOD INTENTIONS

G us had also felt the promise of change with the start of the new decade. He'd been told that the catarrh which clogged his breathing and exacerbated his deafness every winter might also be the source of his depressions, and, in the spring of 1920, he agreed to an operation on his sinuses, which he confidently believed would restore him to his 'normal self'.[1] He had even more confidence in the new portrait he'd started, of the imperiously talented cellist Guilhermina Suggia, a portrait which he dared to believe might atone for all the time he'd wasted during the last five years.

Suggia was a handsome woman, but it was her musicianship that inspired Gus's faith in this commission. When she came to sit for him at Mallord Street, she agreed to play while he worked, selections from the six Bach suites, which he was soon able to whistle from memory. Others who sat for Gus would comment on the physical effort he put into his portraits, breathing heavily, smoking as he paced the studio. Suggia, however, recalled only the buoyancy with which he walked in time to the Bach, rising up on tiptoe when he was particularly pleased by some detail he'd mastered.

The beauty of her playing had certainly powered Gus through the initial studies he made. In one early charcoal sketch, the intensity of Suggia's expression, as she'd leaned in towards her cello, had made the sound of the music almost visible. Yet once he began painting, Gus wanted perfection too much, and the more time he devoted to the portrait, the more elusive it became. He painted and repainted, changing the colour of Suggia's dress from gold, to white, to a deep ruby red, then swapping to a larger canvas, six feet high and nearly six feet wide. Edwin Hudson, the magazine publisher who'd commissioned the portrait as an engagement present for Suggia, lost interest, but Gus would not let it go. It was not only a technical challenge but a personal contest, in which his stamina, his powers of empathy and imagination, his very credibility as an artist were at stake.

In 1923, when he'd extracted over eighty sessions from Suggia, he had to accept he was done. Suggia herself was 'more delighted' than he'd dared hope, and the portrait, in its scale, its spectacular boldness of colour, was unquestionably compelling. Even its composition was unusually finessed, invoking the patterns of Bach's music through the series of zigzags that connect the angles of Suggia's limbs to the plunging neckline of her dress, the V-shaped folds of the background drapes, and the spots of light which travelled diagonally from the polished wood of her cello up to the luminous tints of her face.

Yet, for all the care Gus had lavished on the picture, all the high romantic drama he'd extracted from Suggia's pose, it lacked the immediacy, the inwardness of his preliminary studies. It was almost too much of a spectacle and, when it was shown at the Alpine Club, a review in *The Burlington Magazine* complained that Gus had lost his gift of spontaneity. While his recent paintings were 'nothing if not sensational', they were, in this critic's opinion, 'mostly . . . too "thin" to satisfy for long or repeatedly . . . The design lacks something of solidity, the colour of seriousness, the handling of feeling. The people's faces are extraordinarily well noticed but their deeper character is never probed.'[2]

This was a harsh condemnation, excessively harsh, and as Gus tried to ignore the anxiety that wormed in his gut, he vowed to set aside the commissions, at least for a while. On Dorelia's advice, he began to paint flowers and plants; down at Alderney, he bribed his two small daughters with lumps of sugar to model – his children still capable of eliciting his most unfaltering work.

But, while Gus was trying to keep the world away, the world was demanding more of him. In 1917, *The Burlington* had declared that 'Augustus John [has come] to stand for modern art', and during the 1920s his fame extended into popular culture. Versions of Gus appeared in novels and plays – badly behaved painters with beards, broadbrimmed hats and trails of adoring women. Restaurants where he dined named dishes after him: *Entrecote à la John*. To be painted by John became its own mark of success, and even as Gus tried to resist the commissions, they were too profitable to ignore, as actors like Tallulah Bankhead and Gerald du Maurier lined up with airmen, socialites, bankers and tennis players to sit for him.*

At least he was able to whip through them fast, because his painting methods had accelerated during the war, and he was now applying his colour thick and dry, leaving parts of the canvas uncovered. He prided himself, still, on painting the truth of his subjects, so much so that millionaire Lord Leverhulme, on seeing himself portrayed as a coarse and puffy-faced philistine, returned the portrait to Gus with its head cut off.[†] Yet the work kept coming and Gus knew he was in danger of becoming the thing he'd always despised: a painter for hire. He might complain bitterly to Ada Nettleship, 'I don't find it at all amusing to paint stupid millionaires when I might be painting entirely for my own satisfaction'.[3] Yet, by the end of the decade, when Virginia Woolf went to one of his exhibitions, she walked out in disgust. 'You can't conceive the vulgarity, banality coarseness and commonplaceness of those works', she told her sister, Vanessa Bell, 'all costing over 400 and sold in the first hour.'[4]

Even loyal Will Rothenstein was ready to admit that 'Augustus John whose brain was once teeming with ideas for great compositions had ceased to do imaginative work'.[5] Yet still there were individual portraits of beauty and power, portraits in which Gus still reached for the 'salt of life' in his subjects, and among the best of them was his 1923 painting of Thomas Hardy, at the writer's Dorset home.

Gus, who'd been taught to love Hardy's poetry by John Sampson, was moved both by the privilege of painting him and by the 'affection [and] almost complete understanding' which developed between them.[6] Even

---

* When Anthony Blunt analysed the Suggia portrait a decade later in *The Spectator* (27 May 1938), he wrote 'one grows tired of the over-emphatic gesture before one has finished admiring the brilliance of the drawing and the brush work'. At the time, however, it sold almost immediately, and two years later was acquired for the Tate.

† Leverhulme's reaction created a ruckus of debate over legal and artistic rights, which rumbled right across Europe.

though the portrait he painted made Hardy look every one of his eighty-three years – his hands gripping onto the lapels of his old-fashioned suit, his skin wrinkled and mottled, his jowls hanging loose – the affinity Gus felt for the man was present in every small feature, the nervous sensitivity of Hardy's long delicate hands, the high querying arch of his brow and the particular gravity of his gaze – reaching out into distance, yet veiled in private thought.

'I don't know whether that is how I look or not but that is how I *feel*,' Hardy commented, and he claimed that Gus's portrait meant far more to him than his recent nomination for the Nobel Prize.[7] Gus wanted to do a second, more thorough version, but it was the speed with which he'd painted Hardy that had kept the portrait so true. As with the study he made of Lord Baden-Powell, and the delicately observed sketch he drew of an adolescent boy, Gus was now producing his best and most humane works when he could resist overthinking them.

But even in the finest of his portraits he was making fewer and fewer discoveries. Little more than a decade earlier, Gus had been searching for his place among the European moderns, taking Cézanne as his master, absorbing elements from Picasso and Gauguin; as late as 1920, the *Manchester Guardian* had still been describing him as 'the untamed lion of art'.[8] Now, with each successive wave of the avant-garde – Vorticism, expressionism, abstraction, art deco and surrealism – Gus was left further and further behind.

Despite his insistence that he would never become so conventional, so comfortable in his work as to accept election to the Royal Academy, he was even compromising on that, becoming an associate R.A. in 1921 and a full member in 1928. To Gwen, he justified his changed position on the grounds that it would give their father so much pleasure; to Ursula Tyrwhitt, he said it had been a purely pragmatic move, forced on him by the shortage of exhibition spaces in London. Post-war rent hikes had been brutal to the gallery scene – the Grosvenor was now a cinema, the Grafton a dance hall, and the Academy, Gus claimed, had become the 'cheapest and probably the best place to show'.[9] Even so, he knew he would have to fight to convince his more radical peers that he hadn't betrayed himself. He protested that some of Britain's greatest painters – Gainsborough, Hogarth, Turner and Constable – had graced the Academy and that it was sentimental to measure an artist's integrity by the wretchedness of their life and by the degree of their official neglect: Cézanne himself had longed for the Légion d'honneur, he said, while Van Gogh had 'dreamed of electric light, hot and cold water w.c.'s and general comfort anglaise'.[10]

Yet, for all his desire to be seen as one of the 'insurgents' still, Gus was allowing himself to become more gentrified by the year. The 1920s were turning into a decade of gorgeous consumption as the economy bounced back from its post-war slump. Shiny new goods were available for those who could afford them, and Gus was giving in to their allure. He was starting to adorn himself with silk shirts and brightly fringed scarves, a dazzling check suit, an overcoat of the best Harris tweed; having always dreamed of travelling the world by gypsy caravan, he fell under the spell of the motor car. His first was a two-seater Buick which he'd swapped for a painting in 1920 and which, after one half-hour lesson, he drove everywhere. The speed was intoxicating (especially once he learned how to move out of first gear) and so too was the danger. Gus had little care for the appearance of his Buick, the odd dent or scratch acquired from recklessly overtaking another motorist, swerving too near a tree, or – most perilously – falling asleep at the wheel and driving through the iron gate of a churchyard, were a small price to pay for the joy of racing free on the open road.

That road was often the route between Alderney and London. The city glittered for Gus, and however much he regretted the speed with which it was being modernized – the music halls and street markets replaced by cinemas and department stores – the pulse of the capital was irresistible. Invitations for parties and dinners came to him constantly by post and by telephone; while he was wary of the London hostesses who vied for his presence in their smart drawing rooms, he was often agreeably surprised by the people he met – amusing aesthetes like the composer Lord Berners and more serious-hearted young men like Evan Morgan (soon to become Lord Tredegar).

The parties Gus hosted himself were a mix of his new London set and his old pre-war crowd. There were all kinds of sexual transgression – the impressionable young painter Christopher Wood reported dramatically that an evening at Mallord Street had turned into 'the most dreadful orgy

I have ever seen'.[11] There were drugs too, and, while the electric rush of cocaine had little appeal for Gus, he was briefly entranced by marijuana, the 'Indian herb' to which Iris Tree introduced him early in the decade. He was astounded, he recalled later, by the speed with which it took him from deliriously disinhibited laughter to a state of transcendent clarity. 'I was permitted to see my companions in a new and unearthly life,' he wrote. 'The girls became radiant with more than human beauty, exciting in me emotions of an intensity surpassing those of sex. In the silence one seemed to hear the tick of the clockwork of the universe and voices reached one as if from across the frozen wastes between the stars. Ping! A shifting of the slates of time and space.'[12]

Gus might well have become a habitual user had he not smoked an incautious amount of marijuana one day and discovered how fast the visions could tip into paranoia – a 'panic indescribable', he admitted, which left him 'silent and solitary like a ghost'.[13] Far safer was the more familiar drug of sex, which had never been more easily available. The young women whom Gus met in the twenties, with their fashionably shingled hair, their short skirts, shiny silk stockings and crimson mouths, behaved with a boldness, a freedom that made his own generation's rebellion seem tame. Gus, in his forties, might have been thickening around the waist, his beard slightly grizzled, his eyes beginning to pouch, yet he found plenty of bright young things who were eager to share his bed.

Few of these sleek and strenuous girls held any mystery for him, though, and, in a moment of shame, or fatigue, Gus confided to Mary Dowdall that none came close to replacing Ida: 'having lost her one simply tries all the others in rotation – I've nearly reached the limits'.[14]

But he hadn't, of course, reached any limits. Gus was becoming even more restless, even more susceptible in his search for the ideal lover and muse; his affairs, too, were becoming even more disruptive and damaging, and one of the most persistent of his mistresses, Eve Fleming, came close to destroying his relationship with Dorelia.

Eve was the attractive, wilful and wealthy widow of the former MP and financier Valentine Fleming, and she had ambitious plans both for her four teenage sons and for her own social elevation. When she met Gus, however, sometime at the start of the decade, she fell so recklessly in love, became so obsessed with the idea of bearing his child, that she was ready to flout the terms of her inheritance and persuade him to marry her. Gus himself wanted nothing of this, but there was a force in Eve that both excited and cowed him. When she drove down to Alderney, to whisk him away for sex, Gus willingly allowed himself to be whisked.

As Eve grew more demanding, Gus wanted to end the affair, yet she muddled him so much he couldn't see a way to extricate himself. In one ludicrous moment of desperation, he actually thought his only solution was to marry Eve, get her pregnant, then obtain a divorce. Dorelia, however, naturally found that notion both insulting and contemptible, and she made it very clear to Gus that, if he pushed her any further, she would leave him for Henry Lamb.

Dorelia had already come close to acting on that threat, had once or twice packed her bags, but she had stronger ammunition now because Henry had recently bought a house in nearby Salisbury, which was ready and waiting for her. There had to be some other, less dangerous way, Gus felt, for satisfying Eve, and over the winter of 1922–3, he believed he'd been gifted an easy solution.

A decade earlier, when they'd moved to Alderney, Gus had hired a tutor for the boys, a dreamy, good-looking young graduate called John Hope Johnstone. The lessons had been useless, Hope Johnstone had no idea of how to teach small children, but he'd remained in contact with the family, and, in 1921, Gus had invited him back as companion and mentor to the apparently unteachable Robin. With him had come Chiquita, his teenage girlfriend, and when Gus asked Chiquita to model for him, when their painting sessions eventually and all too predictably led to sex, Chiquita had fallen pregnant.

The affair itself had been a wretched lapse of judgement. Despite the enthusiasm with which Chiquita had taken off her clothes and posed for Gus, waving around her cigarette holder and chatting about the boys she'd known, she was only seventeen, still a girl. When Gus made love to her, the whisky smell of his breath and the chafing of his beard had erased any glamour she'd seen in him – at forty-four he'd seemed suddenly old and rather horrible. Yet, even when Chiquita realized that Gus had got her pregnant, she would not accept his offer to pay for an abortion, and instead she gratefully accepted Dorelia's invitation to remain in Alderney until after the birth.

Chiquita's future, as an unmarried mother, would be far less protected though, and when Gus ventured the idea of Eve adopting the baby (who would at least have his genes, if not hers), Chiquita was at first persuaded to agree. 'It was a very drastic time but I was too young to be unhappy', she later recalled, acknowledging how easily swayed she had been.[15]

As soon as the baby was born, however, in March 1923, Chiquita changed her mind; the baby was a girl and, once Chiquita had named her Zoe, once she had cradled and fed her, she knew she could never give her up. She left for London, and, having found a foster family to care for Zoe for part of the week, she began earning her living as a photographers' model. This should have been the end of the matter, except that Eve was still fixated on having the child and one day she simply collected Zoe from her foster family and drove her up to north Wales.

Gus, who was travelling abroad and receiving the news by letter, mistakenly assumed Chiquita had relinquished Zoe voluntarily, and he gratefully proposed paying her twenty pounds for the baby and a weekly one-pound allowance for herself. Chiquita, of course, demanded the return of her child, and she and Eve began a legal tug of war into which Gus, complaining and frustrated, was dragged. 'There is no peace for a *man* at all', he grumbled to Mary Dowdall, but he got no sympathy from anyone because, even though Eve had behaved monstrously, it was he who'd first set the whole grubby business in motion.[16]

Eventually, in the spring of 1925, Eve did get pregnant. By now, sufficient time had passed for her to accept that Gus would never marry her, so she discreetly closed up her London house and 'took a long cruise', from which she returned with Amaryllis Marie Louise Fleming in her arms. The baby, she claimed, was adopted, her mother dead and her father untraceable, and Amaryllis would have to wait until she was twenty-three to learn the actual truth. She would despise Eve, then, for lying to her, just as Zoe would turn on Chiquita when she too learned the real identity of her father. Gus, however, would emerge unscathed:

after a brief humming and hawing, he would be chuffed at having two beautiful new daughters to claim, and flattered by their eagerness to know him.

But, at the time, the women and the babies were becoming a distraction and a pressure for Gus. Often it seemed that he was devoting more energy to his private life than to his work, and early in the decade, when his commissions and commitments were already threatening to spin out of control, he hired a secretary to come and live at Mallord Street, so that his professional affairs, at least, might acquire some order. She was Kathleen Hale, a twenty-two-year-old art student who would later make her name as the author and illustrator of *Orlando the Marmalade Cat*, and to Gus she seemed a wonderfully efficient force. Drawings which had lain in careless, stained profusion around his studio were rescued by Kathleen and put into portfolios; bills were paid, letters and invitations answered.

As she worked to keep some of Gus's chaos at bay, Kathleen also helped stave off his glooms when he was stalled in his work. She joined him for games of shove ha'penny or chess at the pub, and once, out of curiosity, she allowed him to make love to her. When he tried for a second time, though, she laughed him away; she was neither spellbound by Gus nor offended by him, and he liked her for that. He respected her work as well, encouraging her to exhibit her drawings and to use his own contacts to advance her career. To Dorelia, who had never seen Gus in a comparable relationship, it could sometimes seem as though Kathleen was more of a wife and companion to him than she.

But, while Kathleen recalled with great affection 'the silly fun' of their pub games, the striking panache with which Gus wore his 'best silk shirts and wonderful wide brimmed hats', she remembered him principally as a man in abiding conflict with himself. He was often irritable, 'poised to take things the wrong way' and unable to speak openly about the things which mattered most to him. 'I always felt that there was more to Augustus than he could ever express', Kathleen wrote, 'and though he appeared inhibited he seemed to me to be always trying to break through tremendous frustration – as if there was a volcano inside him that might erupt at any moment.'[17]

Of course, the operation on his sinuses had done nothing to alleviate the true source of his darkness, which his daughter Vivien would later identify as his 'two black dogs: one his shyness, the other his despair.'[18] And Gus did despair. The extravagance of his life, the weakness for women and parties, had undermined every good intention he'd formed to become more like his sister, to recuse himself from the world and just paint. When his frustration became too much, he simply travelled, looking for places that might make him feel 'fresher and more myself'.[19] Back in the spring and summer of 1922, he'd been in Barcelona, admiring 'Gitanas [of] flashing beauty and elegance', and then in Madrid, where, exploring the galleries of the Prado, he'd realized that his 'passion for Goya was boundless' and that 'Velasquez [was] much greater and more marvellous than I had been in the habit of thinking'.[20] The El Grecos were disappointing, he thought, yet, on returning to his studio he found that they had stuck in his memory, little synapses of possibility to be chased in his own art.

Gus needed these new impressions to keep his imagination fired, and, when they failed, he was disproportionally let down. After the war, he still went regularly to the Villa Sainte Anne, sometimes on his own, sometimes with Dorelia and the girls, but the landscape no longer held its mystery. Although there were picnics, Saturday evenings at the local cafe, paintings done of the family, Gus could not ignore the cars that were now parked in the square, the new houses that were being built among the rocks and pines. By 1928, the modern world had so encroached on Martigues, he felt he could no longer bear to see it again.

The country which aroused his most turbulent expectations and disappointments was America. As a small boy, obsessed with cowboys and Indians, Gus had longed to go to the States, and, in 1923, when he was invited to Pittsburgh to judge submissions for the Carnegie Institute International Exhibition, he had extravagant hopes of travelling out to the Wild West, of setting up camp in the prairies, of taking a boat down the Mississippi. On 28 March, he set sail on the SS *Olympia*, taking pains to dodge the rich Americans who begged for portraits, but finding enjoyable company with Arthur Conan Doyle, who told him 'startling things about the spook world'. Often, he stayed up on deck, mesmerized by the immensity of the ocean and 'its ever moving yet never changing pattern of foam'. And when he first saw the thrusting New York skyline appear over the horizon, his hopes of America were very high – there was, he wrote, 'a new excitement in the air, a feeling of adventure.'[21]

A mob of journalists and photographers were awaiting his arrival, swarming onto the boat with a volley of questions and a blaze of magnesium flash bulbs. Gus had long been a name in America; his tremendous showing at the Armory exhibition had created a market for his art, and his reputation had been swelled by the gossip travelling over from Britain. Yet, while he'd become accustomed to some attention from the press, the audacity of New York journalists was new to him, and, when he'd eventually disembarked and passed through customs, Gus felt the same disorienting assault of brashness in the city. To ten-year-old Poppet, he wrote, 'there are railways over your head in the streets and the houses are about a mile high . . . The policemen chew gum and hold clubs to knock people down. The people . . . eat clams and fried chicken . . . and waffles with maple syrup. They drink soda ices all the time, the rich drink champagne and whisky for dinner and go about with bottles of gin in their pockets.'[22]

Apart from the few days in which he was fulfilling his obligations to the Carnegie Institute in Pittsburgh, Gus spent most of his time in New York, where the parties, dinners and interviews, the irresistibly lucrative commissions, left him no chance of escaping to the prairies. He began to tire of Manhattan, the honking of traffic, the glare of the shops, and his initial heightened sense of adventure gave way to a deepening moral distaste for the peculiar combination of puritanism and greed in the American sensibility. He was horrified by the recently introduced prohibition laws – a kind of punitive hypocrisy, he thought, which did little to prevent the rich from getting 'all the liquor' they wanted, while imposing unaffordable fines on the poor. From out of his hotel window, he could see a 'stupendous scintillating sign advertising Wrigley's chewing gum', and this seemed to him symbolic of the obscene gap between America's vulgar wealth and 'the poor bewildered multitudes seething aimlessly below'.[23]

His contempt spilled over to the people he painted, who cared only about the cachet of his signature. To Dorelia, he was particularly bitter about one of his clients, 'a pretty complacent [woman] with hideous little boys [and] a horrible and most expensive house'.[24] The only part of New York Gus unequivocally enjoyed was Harlem, where a 'handsome negress, gay, frank and quick witted' showed him around the neighbourhood and took him to nightclubs which were crammed with dancers 'brilliant beyond description'. The population of Harlem reminded him of the European 'gitanos', and he held it against the national character of America that almost no one he met in Manhattan could comprehend his enthusiasm.[25]

But America paid extraordinarily good money for his work, and Gus would return two more times. On each visit, he still hoped he might catch some remnant of the country he'd once imagined – from his childhood reading of cowboy and Indian books, from his adolescent reverence for Whitman's poetry. Instead, he came away feeling more English than ever. In 1928, when he was in Massachusetts, painting Governor Alvan T. Fuller and his family, news came over the radio that the singer Al Jolson had lost his son. The entire Fuller tribe wept in sympathy, and Mrs Fuller, observing Gus's stony face, asked reproachfully, 'have you no children of your own?'[26] All he could mutter was, 'Yes, too many' – not only because he was affronted by this mawkish display of emotion, but because he thought the governor had not been nearly so tender hearted when approving the death sentences of Sacco and Vanzetti, the two Italian anarchists whose recent trial had been a legal disgrace. As for acknowledging to Mrs Fuller the death of his own son, Pyramus – nothing would have induced Gus to share that private grief.

He did find sympathetic friends in America, though – writers and painters with whom he would correspond for the rest of his life – and, on his very first visit, he also made peace with John Quinn. By 1923, their professional and financial relationship was long over, yet the two of them were still bound by their relationship with Gwen. When Gus invited Quinn and Jeanne Foster to his New York hotel, he was hoping to hear news of his sister, and he was moved by what they reported. Quinn had clearly been busy in promoting Gwen's career, having put five of her paintings into the 'Seven English Modernists' show which he'd organized at the Sculptors' Gallery in New York.* Jeanne also appeared to be a loving influence, and when she told Gus of her plans to take Gwen away to the coast that summer, he offered to organize their lodgings, wondering even if there might be rooms to rent at Vauclair.

The most certain evidence that his sister was well, however, were the pictures Quinn brought to show Gus – pictures that told him how steadily and surely Gwen's vision was evolving, her early realism dissolving towards a quieter abstraction.† Quinn's support meant that Gwen's work was becoming known to a widening circle of admirers in America, but in England, too, her reputation was growing. In 1922, the *Manchester Guardian* had published a seminal article which addressed the historic neglect of female artists and directly challenged the Royal Academy over its failure to elect any women since the original two who'd been among its founding membership in 1768. The paper had proposed a list of candidates for the Academy to consider, and among them was Gwen – a painter, the article said, of 'rare and distinguished works'.[27]

In Paris, there was also a shift in the culture. Marie Laurencin, Sonia Delaunay and Tamara de Lempicka were among several of the women gaining recognition for their art during the course of the decade. And, according to Jeanne, 'everyone had heard of [Gwen]'. By 1923, she'd had three showings at the Salon d'Automne and her works had also been hung at the Société des Artistes Français, at the Salon des Beaux Arts (where the art dealer Manouray so admired one of the *Girl in Blue* series, he asked Gwen to 'name her price') and at the newly founded Salon des Tuileries – 'a lovely place for pictures,' Gwen told Quinn, with 'a lovely light', adding with pride that she'd been considered too prestigious to submit her work to a selection jury.‡

Showing at these salons had become a positive pleasure for Gwen; she invited friends like Constance to the opening vernissages, and she took

---

* That show also included works by Lewis, Epstein and Gus himself. Quinn wrote to tell Gwen that her own paintings, especially the nun portrait, had been 'much admired'.
† The naked Fenella, *Lady Reading*, and her first of the two Chloe portraits.
‡ The Salon had to withdraw their offer of associate membership, however, because Gwen was not a French national.

a curious interest in some of the other exhibiting artists. With each year, she was growing more assured of her place within the Paris art scene, and more knowing in her assessment of her peers. Picasso and his post-war cubism had ceased to interest her – although she acknowledged, a little sardonically, to Quinn that she understood it remained a good investment for him. In 1921, when Gwen encountered Picasso at his dealer's gallery, she attached no real importance to their meeting. She was far more engaged with artists whose technical experiments had some spiritual resonance for her – the sombrely expressive landscapes and intimate war drawings of André Dunoyer de Segonzac, the gentler cubism of Albert Gleizes, the religious depths of Maurice Denis.

It was important for Gwen to look at the art of her peers and take from it what interested her – yet she was rarely swayed as deeply as Gus could be by their influence. She was describing herself as 'God's little artist: a seer of strange beauties, a teller of harmonies. A diligent worker', and learning to overcome her doubts by switching her focus away from herself to whatever it was she was painting or drawing. 'Instead of this sudden discouragement and sadness', she wrote, 'take up your mind in a leaf, a flower, a simple little form and find its form, take it into your possession as it were'.[28]

Her productivity delighted her. 'I am quite in my work now and think of nothing else,' Gwen told Quinn in the spring of 1922. 'I paint till it is dark and the days are longer now and lighter, and then I have supper and then read about an hour and think of my painting and then I go to bed. Every day is the same I like this life very much.'[29] She was painting views from her flat, small atmospheric studies of houses, people and trees. The following year, too, the style of her portraits began to shift. She'd found a pair of new models, darker and more forceful than her Meudon sitter, and one in particular, a heavy-set woman in a reddish-purple dress, had a truculent energy that inspired Gwen to an almost combative approach, sketchier brushstrokes, more swaggering streaks of colour, a more monumental weighting of figure and space.

Form and technique were always the foundation of Gwen's thinking about art, but so too was her inward life – and, during this period, the changes in her work may conceivably have been fed by the emotions of anger and frustration she was starting to feel towards Jeanne.

Jeanne had always warned Gwen that she would never be able to devote as much time and energy to their friendship as she would like. In addition to her writing and editing, she had personal responsibilities at home: an invalid husband, an emotionally fragile sister, both of whom required her care. She was also worried about Quinn, who was becoming unusually withdrawn and more than usually worried about his health. Although their relationship as lovers had always been discreetly guarded, it had been almost as close as a marriage. Now, Jeanne was afraid that something had broken between them. 'Things are the same with us,' she confided unhappily to Gwen, 'only now there will never be a future together. I shall go on loving him and he will never know that he does not love me, *nor that I know he does not*.'[30]

Gwen had accepted that Jeanne would often be too busy to write to her, but she had trusted to her promise that they would meet every summer in Paris. In 1922, when Jeanne sent word that she was too ill to travel, Gwen had been distressed not to see her friend, worried for her health, but her concern had quickly turned to anger when she received well-meaning assurances from Quinn that Jeanne's condition was not as serious as initially feared. Rushing to judgement, Gwen believed Jeanne had been exaggerating her illness and, recalling all the times Rodin had claimed sickness as an excuse not to see her, she decided that Jeanne could no longer be trusted.

She stopped writing to her, and it was only after six months of silence, when Jeanne sent a loving apology and described how debilitating her illness had been, that Gwen was shamed into sending a reply. She was still wary, though, and she implied in her letter that Jeanne had been culpable in allowing her to expect too much from their intimacy: 'I think I understand you more than when you were here. I can think of you without myself coming forward.'[31] In her notebook, she counselled herself to trust only in God and in July 1923, when Jeanne and Quinn were both back in Paris, Gwen apparently took the decision to stay away. 'You are free only when you have left all,' she wrote. 'Leave everyone and let them leave you. Then only will you be without fear.'[32]

She was unable to ignore the two Americans, however, when they returned in September. Quinn took a picture of Gwen sitting with Jeanne and Henri-Pierre Roché on the wall of the Observatory Terrace.

And, if the stiffness of her expression spoke mostly of her dislike of being photographed, the tone with which she wrote to Quinn afterwards was distinctly constrained, acknowledging that while she had been pleased to see him, his busy arrangements had been too much for her, especially the dinners and the soirée they'd attended at the studio of the sculptor Brâncuși. 'I am not accustomed to parties, they were lovely but I am not used to them and I like other things we did better.'[33]

Quinn's arrangements had also left little time for Gwen to be alone with Jeanne, and, once he'd left Paris, the two women had only a few unsatisfactory days together. Jeanne was as attentive as always, taking Gwen out to lunch and finding a dentist to treat the infected tooth that had been plaguing her. However, she was still not well in herself. Her recent illness, her continuing worries about her husband and Quinn had all depleted her strength; most distressingly, they had blocked her ability to write. One reason why Jeanne was not staying longer in Paris this time was that she needed to be by herself and was planning to spend the rest of the autumn on a tour of Ireland and England.

To Gwen, she apparently confided little of this, and when Jeanne eventually wrote to her, around Christmas, Gwen had become so angered by all the time that had elapsed, she waited several weeks before sending a reply. The tone of her letter was childishly punitive: 'I was distressed that morning at saying goodbye to you in the taxi and I missed you very much for a long time. But when you made no sign for such a long time I stopped thinking of you. I hope you will come in the spring but I don't love you so much now.'

Everything in Gwen's letter was ungracious and cross; she complained about the time and money she'd wasted on the dentist Jeanne had recommended, about the three 'boring' afternoons she'd had to spend with the mistress of Ford Madox Ford, who'd apparently come to Meudon on Jeanne's advice. She was so quick to take offence, so slow to forgive, she was even insulted by a proposal Jeanne made that they might collaborate together on a book of fairy tales, with Gwen illustrating Jeanne's text and taking a half share of the profits. Haughtily, Gwen replied that, while she would do the drawings with 'great pleasure', it made her 'sad' and 'offended' that Jeanne would raise the issue of money. Having not yet received the gift of clothes Jeanne had sent from New York, a fur jacket and silk blouse, she considered herself poorly treated.[34]

'I am very much troubled that I have lost a part of your love. It was and is very precious to me,' Jeanne replied hastily, and it took several more letters and a suggestion that Gwen might like to come out to her 'little den' in Manhattan, where they could have 'tea and cakes in bed', before Gwen was ready to relinquish her grudge.[35] Quinn, however, had already regained his place in her affections. Early in 1924, she had sent him five of her drawings and three paintings, and she was moved by his intimate letter of thanks. It was addressed to 'my dear Gwen' – breaking the habit of fourteen careful years during which they'd mostly been Miss John and Mr Quinn to each other – and it beamed with enthusiasm for the new Rousseau picture he'd acquired. It was *The Sleeping Gypsy* – 'one of the greatest paintings done in modern times', he thought – and he sent grateful thanks to Gwen for having first brought Rousseau to his notice.

Her own reply to 'dear John' was equally fond. She promised that she had a 'good many drawings' to send, a painting which 'was almost done' and some interesting news about events in Paris. That news, she said, would have to keep for her next letter, though – 'so that I can bring this [one] to the post now'.[36]

Gwen had no presentiment then that there would be no next letter. Neither Jeanne nor Quinn had intimated that the symptoms which had begun troubling him two years earlier had recently been diagnosed as liver cancer, and it was only to her diary that Jeanne was now recording the agonizing speed with which Quinn was declining, 'his face a mask of pain . . . his poor body a skin swelled with water'.

The end came on 28 July, but Gwen, who'd been away in Brittany, still knew nothing of his death until a letter of condolence came from Ursula. She was appalled by her own ignorance. 'Is it really true John Quinn is dead? Is it a mistake?' she replied shakily. 'I feel very unhappy and must write a note to Mrs Foster.'[37] Memories of her patron came back to her with painful clarity – his generosity to her, his pride and joy in the art he collected, his enjoyment in putting people together. When she learned that her own pictures had been among the few Quinn had wanted to look at during his final weeks, she was so moved she could barely imagine herself working again.

But, as acutely as Gwen felt the loss of Quinn, she could not help but refer it back to herself. When she wrote to beg Jeanne to come and be comforted in Paris, she was already imagining how their intimacy could flourish: 'you will see how I love you and have never ceased to though I pretended (because I was hurt).'[38] When Jeanne replied that she couldn't possibly travel, and wished only to die along with Quinn, Gwen continued to press her claims. In anticipation of Jeanne's arrival, she even began to plan improvements to her flat, repainting her walls in bright Fauvist colours of salmon pink and apple green, and retrieving some of the furniture she'd left with Ambrose McEvoy's father over twenty years ago.

Then the question of money arose, which complicated everything. Quinn had led Jeanne to understand she would inherit a good part of his estate, and she in turn had assured Gwen that she would continue to honour his arrangement with her. But Quinn had died before updating his will, and when Gwen learned that Jeanne had been left almost nothing, she was torn between concern for her friend and panic about her own financial future. Jeanne, even in the middle of her own wretchedness, still felt responsible, suggesting she could help Gwen with New York sales of her work 'for my own sake, and because I love you and want you to go on with your painting'.[39] Quinn's sister, Julia Anderson, who'd been the main beneficiary of the will, was also troubled and offered to take on the role of Gwen's American agent. In the end, however, it was Gus to whom she turned.

In early September, Gwen wrote to inform him of her situation, stressing her particular worry that she still had work owing to Quinn and was unsure, now, how to deal with his estate. Gus replied immediately, and his advice seemed to Gwen wonderfully clear. He told her she need only offer one or two pictures to settle her debt to the estate (adding that Quinn had been undervaluing her work for years); he also cautioned against using either Jeanne or Julia Anderson to manage her American sales, pointing out that they lacked experience and might charge her fees. But, above all, he wanted to offer his own services to Gwen, to persuade her that he was the most trustworthy person to look after her career.

Knowing his sister, however, and the agitation she must be suffering, Gus recognized that he ought to make his arguments directly; so, towards the end of September, he came out to see her, taking a room at the Villa Calypso. As so often when Gwen really needed her brother, she forgot all the grudges she'd held and listened to him trustingly as he explained how easily she could match the income she'd received from Quinn by switching her focus to exhibitions and sales in London. He thought that London, in fact, was the better market for her, and said that, if she could put together an album of her drawings for him to show around to his contacts and friends, she would quickly appreciate what prices she could command.

'Your visit was very wonderful. It gave me courage and still does . . . It gives me joy that you want my drawings', Gwen wrote to Gus afterwards, and, with unusual decisiveness, she made up an album for him, which she was able to hand over to his son Robin, who happened to be passing through Paris with John Hope Johnstone.[40] Gus was impressed: 'I didn't think you were going to give me so many. I am so delighted to have them. They seem even better than I thought.' Ten days later, he sent news that he'd already shown her drawings 'to several people' who were 'full of admiration' and ready to buy.[41]

Five years ago, when Gwen had asked Gus to purchase Vauclair, it had been his practical generosity to which she'd appealed. But now that Quinn was dead and Jeanne seemed unwilling to come to Paris, Gwen had lost two of the people on whom she'd most depended, and it was now also love and comfort that she sought from her brother. During the few days she spent with Gus in Meudon, sharing memories of Quinn and discussing the future of her own career, Gwen was soothed by his loyal affection. And, even though she didn't feel guilt, precisely, about all the times she had disparaged and dismissed him, she wanted to show her gratitude. That autumn, thirteen years after Gus had first invited her to Alderney, she gave him an (almost) definitive promise to visit.

'Oh Yes!' she wrote. 'I am getting ready (in my mind) to come to stay at your home'.[42]

Chapter Sixteen

ALTERED MOVES

'You make your own life. Let it be consciously
with *fearlessness*'
GWEN JOHN[1]

In Meudon, when Gus had been offering to organize Gwen's sales in London, he'd also proposed an exhibition and wondered, a little sentimentally, if they might hold one together. It would be a mark of their new closeness, and he was keen to press the advantages of the Chenil Gallery, which, under the direction of his friend Jack Knewstub, was soon to be reopened as a centre for all the arts, with the addition of a small concert hall, a library, a restaurant and meeting rooms. Gus, with a flourish of ironic ceremony, had laid the foundation stone for the gallery's new extension; he'd promised several of his works for its permanent collection and he'd attracted the support of several wealthy patrons. Some of the old Slade gang would also be involved – McEvoy, Orpen and Rothenstein – and this was yet another reason, he thought, why the Chenil would be a sympathetic platform for Gwen.*

Caught up in the pleasure of Gus's company and the warmth of his support, Gwen allowed herself to go along with his proposal. But once he'd left Meudon, she started to see more of its dangers and difficulties. If she were to share an exhibition with Gus, the scale and celebrity of his work would surely overwhelm hers. And, even if she insisted on a solo show, she suspected he would try to make it too grandiose an event for

---

* The New Chenil was unfortunately ahead of its time, and Knewstub lacked the drive and the acumen to make it work. In 1927, he would have to declare himself bankrupt, and would fall out badly with Gus when he refused to bail him out.

her taste. As she fretted over the implications of the exhibition, Gwen began to wonder if it would be safer to take charge of it herself, and even to think she might revisit her idea of collaborating on a show with Ursula.

Her friendship with Ursula had suffered a number of vicissitudes since she'd first had that idea in 1917. Gwen knew that she herself had been somewhat neglectful, preoccupied with her chateau, her grief over Isabel, her excitement over Jeanne. But she felt even more strongly that Ursula was at fault, that she'd become much less attentive to Gwen since her marriage. While her husband, Walter, in the language of the day was a 'confirmed bachelor', he'd also turned out to be an excellent companion to Ursula. 'Fortunately and by a great piece of luck I am not unhappy', she had written dryly to their old Slade friend Edna.[2]

In contrast to Edna herself, whose talent had bowed to her husband's expectations, and to Gwen Salmond, who'd married the painter Matthew Smith and found that his art took automatic precedence over hers, Ursula had enjoyed all the freedom and support for which she could wish, and every summer had been taken by Walter on painting holidays in Europe.

Ursula sent postcards to Gwen, but otherwise her correspondence had been skimpy, and Gwen had been quick to feel slighted. When Ursula managed a brief visit to Paris in the early summer of 1924, it had ended sourly. She and Gwen had planned a farewell meeting, but had muddled the arrangements, and Gwen, thinking she'd been left in the lurch by Ursula, was ready to believe their friendship might be over. Then Quinn had died, and Ursula had been very staunch in her support, writing Gwen sweetly solicitous letters and sending her a jacket in her favourite cerulean blue. She'd also offered to sell one of the paintings Gwen had given her, *Dorelia in a Black Dress*, and give back all the money. But it was the resumption of their regular communications about work that mattered most to Gwen. 'It is consoling to talk to an artist after all this time,' she wrote in February 1925, and she imagined that Ursula would be equally receptive when, at the beginning of June, she wrote to outline her idea of them sharing a modest London exhibition – 'I think little shows are much nicer than big ones. Big ones are so tiring and stupid'.*[3]

But Ursula was unexpectedly resistant. She told Gwen that an exhibition, big or small, would be too much of a financial risk for her; she didn't have enough work to show and she was convinced that her own watercolours would be overshadowed by Gwen's more experimental oils. In essence, her worries were similar to those Gwen had felt about collaborating with Gus, and they provoked Gwen to the same hectoring impatience she disliked in her brother. 'I don't understand about the exhibition,' she snapped at Ursula in June. 'Can't you get enough things together . . . It won't take many.'[4]

As Gwen cajoled and reproached, she also admitted flippantly to Ursula that she hadn't yet told Gus about their prospective exhibition. 'He may be offended if we have it without his patronage as he is offended at everything I do or don't,' she wrote.[5] Gus himself was travelling with Dorelia that summer and was not only under the impression that Gwen was still fully compliant with his Chenil plan, but also thought she was intending to visit Alderney very soon. 'We sent you a wire hoping to see you in Paris and persuade you to come back here with us', he wrote to her in June, 'but I suppose you were away . . . We would so love you to come. You would like our Siamese cats I think.'[6]

Gus may never have known about Gwen's hopes for a rival show, because Ursula remained stubbornly opposed to participating in it, and, when the Chenil began pressing Gwen for decisions about dates, she was obliged to give way. At Christmas, when she wrote to thank Gus for the gift of some earrings, her letter was warm with sisterly gratitude. 'I thought my time for earrings was over but these are so lovely I must wear them. If you don't like them on me when you see me I shall exchange them for something else.'[7] She sent season's greetings to all the family, reiterated her promise to come and see them, and added that Meudon was very beautiful to her at the moment. 'The little road down from my house has been covered with snow and ice, now it is covered with pale brown, yellow ochre leaves'.

---

* Gwen thought they might approach the Leicester Gallery, or ask for one of the smaller rooms at the Chenil.

But, once it was decided that her show was really happening, that it would open on 1 June 1926, Gwen's gratitude gave way to worry. She fretted about all the logistics involved: about shipping her pictures to London, about asking for loans of paintings she'd previously sold, about how to manage the publicity. 'My exhibition is a right mess', she despaired to Ursula, begging her to write a 'charming "little" foreword' for the catalogue and to deal with a magazine editor who wanted an interview.[8] Gus had been wintering in Provence, so could be of little practical help, and Gwen was perversely cross when he announced that he wouldn't be exhibiting any of his work along with hers. He wasn't particularly proud of his most recent paintings; more disinterestedly, he wanted the focus to be exclusively on Gwen. She, however, could only visualize the terrifyingly empty spaces that would be left on the Chenil's walls without her brother's work, and, at the end of March, she was still panicking that she had 'only about eight little tiny paintings to send'.[9]

It was only by a hair's breadth that Gwen met the Chenil deadline, assembling a total of twenty paintings, two dozen drawings and four albums. The private view of her show was on 30 May and several of her friends were present. Among them was Michel Salaman, who, after years of silence, had recently written to Gwen about a painting he'd bought of hers. It was part of a series in which she had posed her Meudon model as a pilgrim, wrapped in a grey cloak with a crucifix held loosely in her hand, and the inward fervour of the image had reminded Michel of Gwen herself, and had made him regret the loss of their friendship.

'There is so much to say after all these years, so much that can't be said,' he wrote, and Gwen, who'd trusted so much of her younger self to Michel, was moved by his candour. 'I am so happy you have a painting of mine,' she replied. 'Do not mind about unwritten letters future or past. Artists understand things sometimes don't they and I shall . . . I don't think we change but we disappear sometimes. You disappeared for a long time'.[10] She felt she would like to see Michel, to meet his wife Chattie, and she promised that, when she came to London for her private view, she would accept his invitation to visit.

But when the moment came, Gwen stayed away. To be placed in the spotlight of her own show, to be coerced into meetings with buyers and critics, even to be faced with old friends, had come to seem so much of an ordeal to her that she was convinced it would take her 'months to recover'.

And so Gwen missed the most successful exhibition of her life. Several of her pictures sold, and ripples of interest spread. The Tate paid £200 for the loan of *Dorelia in a Black Dress* – informing Gwen that the public were 'most enthusiastic about your work . . . and increasingly so'. The Manchester Art Gallery hung three of her works; the following year, her paintings were seen in Toronto and Vienna; and the Ferargil Gallery in New York, alerted by a retrospective exhibition of Quinn's collection, would shortly express interest in giving her a one-woman show.[11]

In addition to the sales and the loans, Gwen also had the joy of two long and sensitively appreciative reviews which appeared in *Country Life* magazine. They were written by Mary Chamot, a curator at the Tate, and they were eloquent in their analysis of Gwen's style. Chamot noted the influences of Vermeer and the Slade, as well as Cézanne and the European moderns, which she considered ran deeper in Gwen's work than her brother's.* But Chamot also admired the unique route Gwen had taken, through and beyond her influences. '[She] cannot be called an Impressionist, there is far too much delineation in her work far too much monumental design . . . there is certainly no lack of force behind all the softness . . . but it is curious to see how this delicious sense of softness increases as the artist develops her technique from a low to a miraculously high key of tint. The last paintings are so light, with such delicate contrasts that they appear as though through a haze'.[12]

Chamot's articles were a fine, scholarly tribute, but no less moving to Gwen was the praise that came from her brother and her friends. 'Dear Gwen', wrote Will Rothenstein. 'What a rich past, what a sure and sensitive present. It is as though you once fought against Augustus's flaming and undisciplined genius and have now an exquisite peace and perfume . . . Those cool nuns with their quiet and beautiful hands – the remembrance of them has been with me all day.'[13]

---

* Chamot's articles were titled 'Gwen John; an Undiscovered Artist' and 'The Johns'. Gwen herself had signalled her debt to Cézanne by including a quote by André Derain in her catalogue which spoke of the artist's 'power to suggest connections between ideas and objects', his ability to capture 'sensation'.

From Michel Salaman came an even more poetic appreciation:

> I felt far more keenly than I hitherto had done the great beauty of your later work. It was indeed a chastening joy to stand among the pale quiet songs of yours – like listening to the still music of the harpsicord [sic] – only there is nothing antique or archaic about your works, they are so intensely modern in all but their peacefulness. My thoughts went back to our youth with its aims and its hopes and you seemed to be the only one of that eager band who had been utterly faithful to those aspirations, who not only had not failed them but achieved more than we dreamt of . . . it has made me prize that picture I had from you more than ever.[14]

For Michel to admire not only the beauty of her works but the discipline of their creation was almost too much for Gwen: 'I have been trying to find something in myself to merit your praise but I cannot find anything at all', she replied.[15] Yet, even now, when her show had been praised by everyone who mattered to her, Gwen lacked the courage to see it for herself. Her pictures were her children, so much a part of herself that to sell them was hard enough; to see them exposed to public scrutiny was worse. She needed to be alone, to absorb the astonishing, unsettling pleasure of her success, and, even though she'd given a firm promise to Gus that she would come to Alderney in the autumn, Gwen didn't feel strong or steady enough to take that plunge until mid-December.

Dorelia had sent a fur coat and elaborate instructions for the journey, for she and Gus were aware that, even now, Gwen's courage might fail and she might be unable to face the enormity of seeing them together at home, with all their family. They would have liked to ensure that she had some privacy during her visit. But, because she'd delayed it for so long, it would be approaching Christmas by the time she arrived and the house would already be busier than usual, with guests dropping in and out and a flurry of seasonal preparations.

The few days Gwen spent with Gus and his family were certainly difficult. She was so flustered by mealtimes, by the chatter and the arguments, that she had to ask to eat alone, in her room. To read, to meditate, let alone work was impossible. Yet she was genuinely glad to be there. It had been years since she'd seen Dorelia (who was now Dodo to almost everyone), and she was curious about all the children. Robin she'd met most recently, when she'd entrusted him with her drawings; David, too, had sought her out when he'd been passing through Paris. But the younger ones had all been babies when she'd seen them last, and Poppet and Vivien she'd never met.

Out of all her nieces and nephews, it was twenty-two-year-old Edwin and twelve-year-old Vivien who interested her most. They both had aspirations to paint, and Vivien would remember how pleased they were by Gwen when she took their ambitions seriously, telling them, 'You have to work and work'.

In other ways, though, the children found Gwen difficult to make out. She seemed so elderly to them, with her nervous reclusive habits, yet also quite oddly girlish. Vivien, who was observant for her age, was fascinated by the tears that came to Gwen's eyes whenever the conversation excited her, and the peculiar way she muddled her English and French. Most surprising was the closeness between this small shy aunt and their domineering father. Gwen looked exactly like Gus, Vivien wrote, 'a miniature version'; and, as the two of them talked together about family, about Thornton, who was finally coming out of his shell and talking of marriage, about the curious longevity of their own father in Tenby, the children noticed how Gwen was also one of the very few people who still called Gus by his childhood name, and to whom he seemed oddly to defer.[16]

It had taken Gus sixteen years of cajoling, frustration and anger to lure his sister to Alderney, and he was gratified to see her take her first wary steps back towards family life. So satisfied was he by the visit, he was sure he could build on its success, and, the following spring, he believed he had found a way of drawing Gwen even closer.

There had been an agreement between him and Dodo that, when the lease on Alderney came up for renewal, they would look for their own house to buy; and they had found it in Fryern Court, a gracefully English property that was set in large encircling grounds on the edge of Hampshire's New Forest. Fryern was not only larger than Alderney, with a spread of outbuildings and a wooden studio for Gus, it came with the additional attraction of a pretty thatched cottage, just under a mile away, which was coincidentally up for sale as well.

Yew Tree Cottage would be perfect, Gus thought, as a second home for Gwen, putting her within easy walking distance of him and Dodo, while offering her all the privacy she required. In late March, he wrote to her cautiously, asking if she would accept the cottage from him, as a gift; and, to his absolute astonishment, she said yes, stipulating only that she would pay him back the £500 purchase price in whatever instalments she could manage. From then, events moved fast. Dodo told Gwen she'd done a close inspection of the cottage and was certain it could be 'made delightful without much money'. There was a pump in the scullery, she reported, the trees in the orchard promised to be 'full of apples', and, even before the sale was completed in May, she'd taken the liberty of moving a dresser into the kitchen, hanging up one of Gus's pictures and taking measurements for curtains.[17]

'I'm very glad,' Gwen replied, and said she would come to see her cottage as soon as she could. There were paintings she had to finish, however, arrangements to be made for feeding her cats (who required a diet of fresh fish heads and soft meat pâtés for the oldest and most toothless), so it was late in July when she eventually arrived. Her delight, though, was all that Gus had hoped. 'My cottage is *lovely!*' she told Ursula. 'I looked in through the windows and saw a lovely dresser and the ground is bordered on one side by lovely little fir trees.' Its walls needed whitewash and Gwen hoped that Ursula might have some unwanted 'things' to help with the furnishing, yet to Alice Rothenstein, always the upholder of high domestic standards, she sent a confident promise: 'I'm not going to be so *sauvage* in the future'.[18]

That future remained on hold, though, after Gwen decided she wanted some of the partition walls taken down to create extra space and light, and after it was discovered the roof was in need of repair. She went back to Meudon while the work was being done, leaving Dodo to order her a new bed and mattress ('£5.10s!' Gwen exclaimed) and to take delivery of Ursula's donations – bed linen, an elderly carpet and a counterpane. When she returned in mid-August, Gwen was optimistically hopeful that the cottage would be ready. However, there were still too many builders, too much dust for her to contemplate moving in, so she had to go back to Fryern. And although she'd assured Ursula, just a short while earlier, that she didn't mind 'seeing Gus now or that family', the three and a half weeks which Gwen spent with them all were so fraying to her nerves, she began to lose all confidence in her move.

As usual, she found it hard to defend herself against the constant noise, against the comings and goings of so many people, and she was terrified by the recklessness of Gus's driving when he took them down to the sea. But the principal cause of her misery was Henry, the youngest of Gus's boys, who had just arrived for his summer visit. He was very different from the other children: at the instigation of his guardian, Edith Nettleship, he had attended a Jesuit boarding school and was not only better educated than the rest of his siblings, but had discovered a vocation for the priesthood. This, for Gwen, should have made him sympathetic company, except that Henry had embraced his faith with a provocative intellectual arrogance. He was currently trying to make a convert of his father, and the knowing casuistry with which he argued his case, assuring Gus that he had nothing to lose by accepting God's truth, and everything to gain, was completely sickening to Gwen. Tearfully, she berated Henry for his cynicism and told him how wrong he was to reduce religion to the level of a 'business transaction.'[19]

Arguments were always terrible for Gwen. 'My mind is not strong enough to keep its harmony when any difficulties and obstacles come', she told Ursula.[20] When Henry Lamb came to Fryern, he was shocked by the strain he saw etched on her face, which made her look, he thought, like 'a little old lady'. Gwen had promised Gus that she would stay until her cottage was ready, that she might remain there until Christmas. But, by early September, she had already fled back to Meudon.

The relief of finding her little apartment waiting for her, everything in its place, was immense. Gwen needed the security of her own four walls as profoundly as Gus needed escape, and it would be months before she was strong enough to imagine herself going back to Hampshire and taking possession of Yew Tree Cottage. She was there for a couple of weeks in the spring of 1928, however, organizing her few bits of furniture and some things she'd brought over from France. Ursula, to whom she wrote warmly about the 'beauty' of her cottage and its 'exquisite' surroundings, was quite ready to believe that Gwen would be spending more time in England; and Gus, much gratified by his sister's show of enthusiasm, was also hopeful it might signify her willingness to consider herself part of the family again.[21]

He'd already been encouraged in that hope by the interest Gwen had started to take in his son Edwin. Earlier that year, Edwin had moved to Paris to study at one of the art academies, and Gwen had met him several times in cafes and galleries. She had enjoyed talking to him about art and been interested in his opinion of her work – 'Don't think about my feelings in telling me, but be straightforward', she would always insist. Over time, she'd begun to feel almost maternal towards her 'dear little boy (whom I admire very much)' and even to feel she had a duty to correct his faults.[22] Edwin could be slippery over money, and arrogant too. He would later infuriate Gwen by dismissing her admiration of Georges Rouault, only to change his mind when he heard some older students praising the painter's work. 'Nearly always my opinions are met thus by Edwin and in a few weeks he comes to me with the same opinions as if newly discovered,' Gwen wrote irritably to Ursula.[23] But, even in her crossness, she saw much of herself in her nephew – his social awkwardness, his thin-skinned passions and uncertainties – and she particularly sympathized with his struggle to establish himself against the forcefield of his father's talent.

Gus himself had never got the measure of Edwin. As a child, his moods had swung unaccountably between sulkiness and clowning; as an adult, he pained Gus with his stubborn determination to paint. Perhaps it was some atavistic rivalry in Gus, but he genuinely believed that his son lacked the talent to succeed, and he could not bear to see how obsessively hard Edwin was driving himself in Paris, and how 'extremely negligent' he was becoming of his health.

Yet, even as he worried grimly to Dodo that Edwin was becoming as 'cracked as his aunt', Gus was glad of the unexpected relationship that had developed between them, and hopeful that it would be another link to bind Gwen more tightly to him and Dodo. His expectations, however, would slowly be eroded, for those few weeks Gwen spent at Yew Tree Cottage in 1928 were also to be her last.

It was never a deliberate decision. The following year, Gwen was telling Ursula that sometimes she wanted to be at her cottage 'very much', implying that it was only her work and her cats that kept her away. She was eager for other members of the family to make use of it too: her father, when he came down to Fryern, and Winnie, if she brought her family to England. Yet there were secrets in her life now, secrets so vivid and consuming that Yew Tree Cottage was becoming almost an abstraction to Gwen, a pleasant possibility that grew more distant with every year.

Gwen had first become aware of Véra Oumançoff in 1923, when Véra and her Russian-Ukrainian sister Raïsa had moved to Meudon, with Raïsa's theologian husband Jacques Maritain. Rilke had written to recommend the trio to Gwen, as devout but cultured Catholics whose company she would enjoy. Yet, although they had interested her when she watched them in church – Jacques, refined and angular; Raïsa, a fierce dark contrast to her sister's plump fairness – they had seemed too intimidating for her to initiate an approach. And it had taken the shattering news of Rilke's death from leukaemia, late in 1926, for Gwen to overcome her shyness.

Rilke had remained crucially important to Gwen. Even though he'd left Paris and the two of them had rarely corresponded, she still thought of him as her spiritual guide, as the friend who'd seen her most clearly in her unhappiness, as the teacher who'd instructed her in the creative power of solitude. When she heard of Rilke's death, she wanted desperately to pray for his soul, to commune with his spirit. Yet she didn't know if there was a correct formula for such a prayer, and, in the extremity of her grief and uncertainty, she found the courage to follow Jacques, Raïsa and Véra home from Mass the next morning and ask for their help.

They were very good to her. Observing her distress, they invited her into their house, where they spoke to her gently for hours. Véra was particularly kind, and when Gwen tripped and burned herself awkwardly on one of the newly lit paraffin lamps, she gathered Gwen up in a soothing embrace. That moment, however, flipped a dangerous trigger in Gwen, as the pain of her injury, the rawness of her grief, the ineffable comfort of Véra's arms, all merged into a jolt of desire. It was the same treacherous desire that had disoriented her so badly with Nona, Constance and Jeanne. And it was so powerful in Gwen, that when Véra suggested the two of them might get to know each other better, that they might walk and talk after church, it was impossible for her not to believe that Véra had intuited her feelings – and to hope she might respond.

Rationally, Gwen knew that such a hope was impossible. Everything she'd learned so far about Véra had suggested she was a woman of unassailable piety. When she was younger, Véra had worn hair shirts next to her skin, had sprinkled bitter powder, as a penance, on her food; even now, she spent hours on her knees each day in meditation and prayer. Véra claimed, in fact, to have a direct personal communication with God and, in the face of such formidable holiness, Gwen understood she must try to elevate her own emotions to a higher plane.

But the demands of her body and her heart were too strong. When Véra offered to act as her counsellor and confessor, inviting her to send weekly accounts of her spiritual struggles, the letters Gwen wrote to Véra turned swiftly to declarations of love, to expressions of wanting and need. 'Part of my heart imprisons me, I will die of hunger or be suffocated,' she wrote, her passions as naked on the page as they had ever been with Rodin. She begged Véra to look kindly on her love, to call her by her middle name, Marie, just as Rodin had done. Reckless of Véra's disapproval, she began calling at her home on rue du Parc, following her to the shops and asking to carry her parcels.[24] She knew her behaviour would be judged excessive, even sinful, and she prayed to Rilke's spirit for guidance. 'I accept to suffer always, but Rilke! hold my hand! You must hold me by the hand! Teach me inspire me, make me know what to do. Take care of me when my mind is asleep you began to help me you must continue.'[25]

Yet, often, Gwen felt utterly lost to her obsession, so lost she had to remove herself physically from Véra's proximity, taking long walks deep into the forest, sometimes sleeping there all night, her mind slipping into the hallucinatory states she often suffered at moments of extreme emotional stress.

Véra herself had been a little slow to grasp the nature of Gwen's devotion, but once she did, she was stern in her efforts to quash it. 'Yes, I said that you could write to me if you felt the need but do you really need to write to me almost every day? I think not and I even think it is injurious to your soul for you are becoming too attached to a fellow creature who you hardly know . . . I know you have strong feelings but they should be turned towards Our Lord and our Lady.'[26] She insisted that Gwen must limit her letters to one a week and only call at the house when Jacques was holding his Monday discussion groups. When she signed off her letters, 'croyez chère Mary à mes sentiments affectueux en Notre Seigneur Jésus', Véra believed she was drawing Gwen, and their friendship, back to the true path of God.

All this was unfolding as Gus was making his offer to buy Yew Tree Cottage for Gwen, and it may have been Véra's strictness that made Gwen warm to the idea of being closer to her brother. But then it was love for Véra that kept drawing her back. She was trying to control herself, apologizing to Véra for writing so many 'bad things'. However, even in her contrition, as she offered to kiss Véra on her 'knees' and her 'sleeve', she could not disguise the longings behind her gesture of penitence. When she begged Véra to treat her with compassion, her language was that of a tormented lover: 'I think the soul in purgatory must feel like me. I don't live calmly like you and the rest of the world'.[27]

Gwen was also petitioning Véra to show some interest in her art, claiming wildly and untruthfully that no one had ever offered her a useful critique of her work. Yet, in this, her expectations were equally dashed. Véra had already expressed her disapproval of Gwen sketching in church and had made no response to the letter in which Gwen tried to explain that her drawing, like all her art, was a discipline as necessary as prayer.

'I do it as I do my housework, because it has to be done. The only difference is that my painting is more tiring and more difficult and also sometimes gives me little surprise now that I understand the Technique better. But the pleasure is so rare that it doesn't count. I sometimes enjoy seeing the things but that's before thinking about them as drawings or pictures.'[28]

A more intellectually curious woman than Véra would surely have engaged with Gwen's letter, with the subtleties she was trying to articulate. But Véra could only value art that was obviously religious in theme. When Gwen tried to entice her deeper interest by giving her some drawings each week, Véra rarely gave these offerings more than a cursory glance before shoving them into the back of a cupboard. Years later, they would be discovered there, dozens of Gwen's subtly rendered studies of flowers, ferns and the Meudon congregation, studies that Gus could have sold in London for a total of hundreds, even thousands, of pounds.

Eventually, Véra's ruthlessness had its effect and Gwen came to see her friend not only as cold but as fraudulent, even coarse – concluding that her vaunting claims to spirituality were based on 'millions of little lies'.[29] She was especially disgusted by Véra's avid requests for gossip about her brother and his circle – as Gus himself would observe, 'it caused [Gwen] anguish of mind to discover that pious people can be just as stupid insensitive and vulgar as everyone else'.[30] By the spring of 1930, when Jacques announced there would be no more Monday meetings at their villa, Gwen had all but extinguished her passion for Véra. Two years later, when Jacques, Raïsa and Véra left Meudon for good, she barely cared.

But, if Gwen had fallen out of love with Véra, it was also because she'd given her heart elsewhere. Sometime in 1928, she began talking about her art to the recently appointed curé at Meudon, hoping to elicit from him the interest that Véra had withheld. At first, Canon Piermé was at a loss – knowing little about painting, he wanted to know why the colours in Gwen's pictures were so 'misty'. But he was kind, making it clear to Gwen how much he enjoyed their conversations, and, later that year, their relationship began to shift onto more intimate ground than congregant and priest. They began to meet privately in the forest, and, the following year, when the canon was transferred to the parish of Champney-sur-Marne, twenty-five kilometres away, their meetings continued in the woods near his church.

Together, they tumbled into a fraught but thrilling muddle of desire, frustration and religious ardour. Gwen begged the canon to use her intimate name, Marie; she confessed she was unable to stop thinking about him, and he, in return, was clearly obsessed by her, making slippery attempts to conceal his desire under the cloak of his priestly authority. 'I shall call you my lover instead of worshipper,' he wrote grandly, 'it's equal to me provided that my lover loves me as a worshipper. Come my little lover and kiss the feet of your master, who kisses you tenderly . . . I have very well understood your letters, continue.'[31] The affair almost certainly remained unconsummated, but, by the end of

1929, it had become sufficiently intense for the canon to take fright. He begged Gwen to destroy all his letters, to forget all she'd felt for him; and, if she was confused and unhappy at first, she understood there could be no future for them. In her last letter to the canon, she told him that she missed him all the time, but hoped he would keep this farewell note as a memento of their love.

Love for Véra, which had blurred into this brief but transgressive relationship with her priest, had been enough to detain Gwen in Meudon, but it was a third love affair which was to keep her there permanently. In the summer of 1927, just after her first happy viewing of Yew Tree Cottage, she had been walking down a secluded street in Meudon and noticed a plot of land for sale. Even though it lay behind a wall and locked iron gates, she could see that it was an enchantingly ragged Eden, a sloping half-acre of green in which the boughs of mature lime trees spread over a tangle of shrubs and wild flowers and over a huddle of wooden buildings – two small sheds and a larger one, a *hangar*, that was elevated on low stilts.

In its surprising wildness, 8 rue Babie reminded Gwen of Vauclair, and it caught at her heart and her imagination no less fiercely. She could imagine herself living and working there, perfectly undisturbed, yet with her church and her shops a short distance away. Even though she'd just sent seventy-six pounds, almost all of her savings, to Gus as her first instalment on Yew Tree Cottage, she felt she was fated to own this plot. The sale price was 65,000 francs, and Gwen would spend over a year simply working out how she could manage to raise it. But her timing was lucky; the French currency was in a freefall of devaluation. In late 1928, when she asked Chloe for a loan of £590, that sum was now worth over 70,000 francs, and by early 1929 the plot was hers.

She called it her 'ground', and at first she couldn't regard it as anything else. Chloe's loan had covered little more than the sale of the land and the lawyer's fees, and the only work Gwen could afford was basic – boarding up holes in the *hangar*, raising the height of the enclosing brick wall and laying down paving stones, around which she hoped the weeds and flowers, would 'pousser a leur fantasie'.[32] When spring arrived, she spent long days in her new kingdom – sketching, reading, playing with the cats, and camping there when the nights were warm.

Gwen told very few people about her ground, which she was anxious to keep secret from Gus. He was already inclined to get cranky about her non-appearance at Yew Tree Cottage and she could fully imagine his hurt when he discovered all her money and interest were now invested elsewhere. She didn't even discuss her new purchase with Ursula, beyond dropping hints that she had 'another secret to tell'.[33]

The two of them had, in any case, lapsed into another period of coolness, with Gwen distracted by Véra and her priest, while Ursula was having to nurse both her husband and herself through illness. In June 1930, when Ursula had come out to Paris to see Gwen, she'd been called home almost immediately by another crisis in Walter's health. She had left some compensatory gifts for Gwen at a department store, but Gwen had somehow not been informed. 'Ursula Tyrwhitt is *always* rude,' she carped untruthfully to Constance; and to Ursula herself she sent a slightly chilly note: 'I'm so disappointed, but I suppose it's your duty not to disappoint Walter?'[34]

Ursula's reply was heroically poised: 'These last two years have been clouded over. Had you seen me in Paris I could have told you and you would have understood why I never wrote.'[35] She loved and admired Gwen enough to accept her self-absorption and her thin-skinned sensitivities; tougher, more pragmatic – in every way more nimble – Ursula was not inclined to nurse grudges. Yet, even though the breach was healed and Gwen was once again sending news of herself to 'dearest Ursula', she waited another few months before entrusting her friend with the secret of her 'ground'.

In 1931, however, it became public news. The estate of the Johns' maternal grandfather, Thomas Smith, was being wound up, and Gwen's share would amount to two lump sums of £200 and £750. Not only could she pay off her debts to Chloe and Gus, she could also afford to start making her *hangar* more habitable. Old Edwin was predictably bewildered when he learned how she wanted to spend her inheritance – 'it is the only certain source of income which you have,' he protested, begging Gwen to invest it more sensibly.

Even Chloe had raised objections. She'd seen Gwen the previous year when she and her sister had been in Belgium looking at the Rembrandts in Londerzeel. Gwen had agreed to join them – a rare outing for her, these days – but the trip had not been a success. She'd been unwell, plagued by debilitating stomach cramps, a persistent eye infection and flu, and she had obviously been disoriented by the change of scene. It now seemed to Chloe that, even if the *hangar* was made weatherproof, it could not be a suitable home, and she urged Gwen to think of building a comfortable new house on the sunny side of the plot. 'I am sure it would be far better for your health'.[36]

The person on whom the news fell hardest, though, was Gus. When he finally learned that Gwen was planning to live in 'a shed, in a wilderness of wasteground,' he thought it madness – proof of his sister's inability to organize her life with any rational regard to her well-being; proof, too, that she'd never been serious about Yew Tree Cottage. It was a rebuff to every sincere effort he'd made with her – although, even in the middle of his hurt, he felt a certain exasperated awe. A quarter of a century ago, he and Gwen had lived together in squalid flats, had subsisted on beer, bread and nuts – and, in some way, their poverty had been a badge of their integrity. Although Gus did not consider himself rich, he was aware of how comfortably upholstered his life had become, and of the artistic compromises he'd made to fund it. Even as he ranted over the absurdity of Gwen's plan, he could imagine the disdain with which she would shrug away his objections, regarding them as confirmation of his own 'absence of sensibility and . . . fundamentally bourgeois state of mind'.[37]

There was no direct confrontation between them, no deliberate severance of ties. Gwen couldn't bring herself to let go of Yew Tree Cottage, and while she willingly agreed to the idea of an old friend of Gus and Dodo's, Fanny Fletcher, using part of the cottage to run a summer tearoom, she ignored all her brother's requests to sell it back. The cottage was her most solid link to family, a link that was still important to her, even though her correspondence with Fryern was becoming more and more erratic, and even though it was Dodo, increasingly, with whom she was in closest contact. By the start of the 1930s, it was Dodo, not Gus, who was sending Gwen news of Poppet's engagement to a young scientist, of Edwin's surprising marriage to a young woman named Betty. And even in matters concerning Gwen's work, it was Dodo who began taking charge of the arrangements, writing in 1933 to urge

Gwen's agreement to a second London show. 'Augustus' agents are anxious to have one & I think you ought to, you have many admirers here.'[38]

Occasionally, Gus would propose calling in on Gwen when he and Dodo were driving through France; occasionally, he would ask her to come back and see them in Fryern. But these exchanges were becoming a polite formality, a token of family connection. To Gus, it seemed that his sister was withdrawing into an ever more unreachable solitude – her life confined to her ground, her church, her work and her cats. Although Gwen did make one brief return to England, in the spring of 1931, it was to see Edith Nettleship, who was dying. Henry had written to tell her of the uncomplaining piety with which his guardian was facing death, and Gwen, greatly moved, had felt duty-bound to visit. She didn't go to her cottage, though, nor make contact with Gus. And, although neither of them could have known it then, those few weeks in 1928 when Gwen had taken possession of Yew Tree Cottage were almost certainly the last time she and Gus ever saw each other.*

---

* Despite the occasional proposals Gus made to call in at Meudon, there is no solid evidence of him ever doing so.

Chapter Seventeen

THE BLOODY DECADE

'The worst spell of my bloody life. My life seems to become more and more complicated'
AUGUSTUS JOHN[1]

Over the years, Gus had often surprised himself with the importance he attached to family, and when Gwen had drifted away from him and from Yew Tree Cottage, his irritation had been layered with a deep and personal hurt. Yet there were other, broader reasons for the distance that was once again dividing Gus from his sister – for his own life was now in trouble.

Money, as always, was part of it. Fryern had been an expensive purchase and it was an expensive house to run. Dodo had made it beautiful – each room painted a different colour, each surface crammed with flowers, pots and curious objects. There were drawings and paintings by Gus and Gwen; a watercolour of Edwin's; a scattering of works by Eugène Boudin, Charles Conder, Henry Moore and Matthew Smith. One of the Modigliani stone heads, bought by Gus years ago in Paris, now stood amidst a clutter of umbrellas by the front door, bearing the weight of a potted cactus.

Cecil Beaton, a notoriously malicious judge of other people's homes, thought Fryern the true 'dwelling place of an artist': 'Its beauty was all in the atmosphere', he wrote, and in tribute he would draw a charming sketch, *Mrs John's Window Sill at Fryern Court*, in which a sunlit collection of vases, pots and flowers, a bust of Dodo herself, were set against views of the leafy grounds.[2]

Beaton was one of many visitors to Fryern, and together they ate up money. When Gus was in a mood to entertain, he was masterful at conjuring up a party, or presiding over long meals at the oak dining table. Many guests would recall his garrulous munificence as he ordered more wine to be bought up from the cellar, his laughter growing louder with every bottle, his anecdotes more floridly outrageous. After dinner, he would call for the furniture to be cleared for dancing, for friends to strum an accompaniment on the piano or guitar while he led the way in a boozy jig. On some of the wilder evenings at Fryern, Poppet recalled that the whisky was poured out 'in half-pint glasses' and that the grounds became a car park as more and more guests arrived.[3]

But staff were required for all this hospitality – two gardeners, two more women to help in the kitchen – and Gus became trapped in an ever more vicious circle of accepting commissions to meet his bills. He knew he was losing his way; it was years since he'd known the excitement of starting work on a 'supreme picture'. By the end of the 1920s, he was so prone to depression and self-disgust that the household began to dread his arrival back from London: 'Daddy has returned to the scene,' wrote Vivien, 'so it will be gloom gloom gloom.'[4]

Although Gus would not admit it to himself, he was also becoming a drunk. 'I find my fellow creatures very troublesome to contend with without stupéfiant,' he admitted, and the fizz and roar of the 1920s had been dangerous for him, as it had been for so many others.[5] Although he'd run scared of hashish, he'd consumed quantities of alcohol – not only wine and beer, but his lethally favourite tipple of a double rum and brandy. He had convinced himself he was master of his own consumption: 'I drink in order to become more myself,' he claimed, and with the first few glasses he could believe this was true.[6] As alcohol blurred the edges of his irritations and his shyness, as it soothed away the frustrations of his working day, it could also make Gus believe he had years still ahead of him to paint the next great work and achieve the next authentic adventure.

But, despite his large frame and thickening waist, Gus had a comparatively low tolerance of alcohol; by the end of the decade, he was experiencing bouts of dizziness, tremors of the hands and uncontrollable rages, during which he became so physically violent, he was capable of punching out a cigarette on a man's face. When the black mist had cleared, he would be mortally ashamed, yet he couldn't accept he had a problem. Everyone around him drank, and some to far greater excess – Gus was always greatly entertained by the painter Nina Hamnet as she made her wavering progress around the bars of Fitzrovia, 'mysteriously appearing to be in more than one place at a time'.[7] He tried to convince himself there must be some other cause for his rage and his shakes – his mercurial temperament, perhaps, his deafness, or even his persistent catarrh. Obstinately, he undermined Dodo's attempts to keep him sober at Fryern, bringing out the drink as soon as any visitor arrived so that, as Dodo complained wearily to Ottoline, 'in one evening . . . all of my good work is undone.'[8]

By March 1930, however, even Gus had become seriously alarmed. He wondered if he'd developed some sinister 'nervous condition' and asked Ottoline, who had a history of physical and psychological disorders, to recommend a doctor. Unhesitatingly, she replied that the new man she'd been seeing had done wonders. 'Dr Cameron . . . is the only really honest doctor I have found,' she avowed in her spidery handwriting. 'I beg of you dear John to see him . . . These are the orders of your faithful old friend.'[9]

Cameron was a quack, however, expert in pandering to wealthy clients. Even though drink was so obviously the root of Gus's problems, he offered the more acceptable diagnosis of an overtaxed system – a 'depletion' of the nerves, liver and stomach, which could easily be resolved with a month's rest cure. Gus, credulous and comforted, told Ottoline that Cameron had 'put his finger on the spot at once' and, declaring that he already felt ten years younger, he admitted himself into Cameron's recommended clinic.[10]

Preston Deanery Court, in Northampton, was everything Gus would ordinarily despise, hideously ostentatious, with footmen who served vitamins on silver platters. He had to endure a strict vegetarian diet and an 'electric belly waggler' to reduce his paunch. But he submitted obediently to it all, and, when Ottoline arrived at the clinic for her own short course of treatment, he was very proud to show off his 'newly-etherealized form'.[11]

It was the enforced break from alcohol, of course, that made Gus feel so well, and when he came home from the clinic, claiming he was 'a giant refreshed', Dorelia did what she could to sustain his improvement.

If they were eating out together, she would surreptitiously empty his glass; at home, she kept their alcohol under lock and key. But, once Gus was away from Dodo's vigilance, he was starting to drink almost as heavily as before. T. E. Lawrence, who saw him in London in 1932, looking seedy and bloodshot, wrote with melodramatic horror – 'John is in ruins'.[12]

Gus did mind what he saw of himself in the mirror. He'd never regarded himself as particularly vain; the energy he'd devoted to his appearance had always been more about creating a stir, a visual effect. For most of his life, he'd taken his beauty for granted, another piece of physical good fortune to add to his excellent balance, his stamina and strength. Now, when his physical luck was deserting him, the chagrin of witnessing his own alteration into a slack and coarsened stranger was one more reason for Gus to rage over the general 'bloodiness' of things.

Yet, shackled though he was to his aging, fallible body, Gus was still assaulted by hailstorms of lust, by dreams of the next perfect woman. In 1933, he began an affair with Mavis Wright, a waitress turned photographer's model who was to be the last great love of his life. Mavis was tall, blonde and glamorous, forthright and fun, and when Gus had first met her he'd wanted her very badly. His old friend and rival, the prankster Horace de Vere Cole, had already claimed Mavis, though, and married her, so Gus had only felt free to make his move when a failed business gamble forced Horace to leave the country.

'I absolutely must paint you soon or die,' he told Mavis. His portraits of her were actually dreadful – vapid and sentimental – yet the love Gus felt was genuine.[13] Mavis, in bed, was more skilled and straightforward than any woman he'd known, and he felt almost young again as he signed off his letters 'Yrs stiff and strong'. She knew how to tickle his imagination with stories about her past (her mother, she claimed, had been stolen away by gypsies); she had dazzling ways with cosmetics and clothes. And she regularly kept Gus in a state of delicious suspense, disappearing for days at a time so that he was left to compose 'tasty poems' for his 'sweet honey bird', to draw erotic pictures of her with her legs spread wide, and to write love letters begging extravagantly for her return.[14]

In March 1935, when Mavis gave birth to his child (a boy whom they named, preposterously, Tristan Hilarius John de Vere Cole), Gus wanted to keep both mother and baby close. Mallord Street had just been sold to bring in some much-needed income, so he had to take them both down to Fryern, hopefully telling Dodo how much she would enjoy Mavis, who was 'really a good wench and has a good deal of gumption'. The experiment did not go well. Even though Dodo was not in a position to refuse Gus – Henry Lamb had given up waiting for her, had gone away and got married – she made it plain how strongly she disapproved of Mavis, whom she considered noisy, manipulative and shallow.

However, the reason why Mavis herself didn't choose to stay long at Fryern was her hope that Gus could be persuaded into offering her a more settled future. In 1936, she tried to force his hand by placing one-year-old Tristan into a children's home and going down to Cornwall, where, she claimed, there was a man who wanted to marry her. But it was the loss of Tristan, with whom he'd become unexpectedly besotted, that most upset Gus. Rather than responding as Mavis had hoped and offering his own proposal of marriage, he simply insisted on removing his infant son from the children's home and bringing him back to Fryern.

In this, he'd had no argument from Dodo. Tristan was growing into a tractable, pretty child, very easy to love, and she had plenty of staff to help with his care. 'Everybody covets him,' Gus boasted, and because it suited Mavis to have her freedom restored, a new arrangement developed by which Gus would keep Tristan at Fryern, as his semi-adopted son, and would keep Mavis in London as his mistress. Even when Mavis managed to secure herself a new husband, the archaeologist Mortimer Wheeler, and Gus was jealous enough to propose a duel, the arrangement continued as before. Tristan would eventually spend more time with his mother, but he still came to Fryern for his holidays. So close did the attachment remain that, in 1944, when a Pathé news crew came to Fryern, it was Mavis who was filmed sitting for Gus, Tristan who was shown reading quietly with his father. Dodo chose not to be featured at all.*

---

* Ten years later, when Mavis shot one of her lovers, Lord Vivian, after a jealous argument, Gus was staunch in his support, attending her trial and visiting her in Holloway prison.

Gus would never stop loving Mavis for her wicked resourcefulness, for the pleasure she gave. Yet, even in the 1930s, when the affair was at its height, she wasn't enough. Once, when he was attempting to justify his promiscuity to D. S. MacColl, he claimed that his continuing need for women was entirely bound up with his art, with his need to sustain the 'illusion of beauty' so essential to his work. And while he could concede how self-serving his argument must sound – 'From this you may perceive my soul is sick' – he felt no real sense of compunction, no urgency for reform.[15] Even if he hadn't been so widely indulged in his affairs, he had long convinced himself that he'd never been knowingly cruel to any woman, that no one had been harmed.

But some of Gus's women had been harmed, especially the youngest and most defenceless, like Chiquita. And, during the 1930s, he would do real damage, when he had affairs with both of the two younger daughters of his friend Francis Macnamara. Brigit and Caitlin were both vulnerable girls; during much of their childhood, they'd been shuffled, along with their other two siblings, between numerous houses and friends, allowing their promiscuous father and unhappy mother to pursue their own separate affairs. They had come to depend on Alderney and Fryern as a respite from their chaotic lives, and even to regard the Johns as their surrogate family.*

Caitlin, the most angry and insecure of all the Macnamara children, had initially had a teenage crush on Caspar. Eleven years her senior, very handsome in his naval uniform, he had seemed to her a figure of romance and authority; and, in early 1930, when she was just fifteen, Caitlin was determined to make him her lover. According to her own highly coloured memoir, she twice attempted to seduce him, first during a moonlit picnic, then when she slipped into his bedroom wearing her most revealing nightdress. But Caspar had no desire to make love to such a child, and Caitlin's mortification, when he turned her down, would trigger a series of events that led her, eventually, to Gus.

Wanting to remove herself entirely from Caspar's orbit, Caitlin persuaded Vivien to run away with her to London. The two girls – close in

---

* That Gus had briefly been rumoured to be Caitlin's biological father was another indication of the confusing world in which she had been raised.

age – had dreamed together of becoming professional dancers, and Caitlin convinced Vivien that, once in the city, they could easily take classes and find work on the stage. Caitlin may also have been hoping to stir up a drama in her wake, although back at Fryern, when their disappearance was discovered, Gus and Dodo were not seriously alarmed. Vivien was actually one of their more responsible children and they only had an hour or two of mild anxiety before a telegram arrived with news that Vivien and Caitlin were staying safely with Ida's sister, Ethel Nettleship.

Dodo's response to Vivien's escapade was also bolstered by her fatalism, which had grown even stronger with time. She frequently came to a decision, now, by dangling a ring from a thread – if it swung from left to right, she would read that as an affirmation, a negative if it swung in a circle – and she thought it was important to trust Vivien to follow her own path. Gus, too, chose to believe there was little cause for concern: he himself had been barely older than Vivien when he first arrived in London, and he was, in any case, convinced that her fantasy of a stage career would soon exhaust itself and she would return to her long-held ambition of studying art.

He was right – by the end of the year, Vivien was enrolled at the Slade. Caitlin remained more determined, though, and having immersed herself in a world of classes and auditions, having managed to pick up a minor role or two in musicals, she might have easily been lost to Gus's view. But Caitlin had discovered that theatre people were often impressed when she dropped the name of Augustus John at parties and stage calls, and, once she realized how useful he might be to her, she began calling round to his London studio, flirting with him and angling to be painted.

Gus should have recognized the danger, he should have acknowledged that Caitlin, who was still only sixteen, was testing her powers of attraction, a flaunting but inexperienced girl. He was, however, too intrigued by her blond curls, her pink and white prettiness, too flattered and exhilarated by her youth, and, without any apparent qualms, he took his 'little seraph' into bed.

The affair, such as it was, continued for five years. It was always intermittent; after Caitlin gave up the stage in 1932, she went abroad for a time, and Gus too was travelling. Yet, whenever they were together, Gus fully believed their relationship was mutual, and fun. He gave pocket money to Caitlin, he took her to expensive restaurants, he provided her with useful contacts. And, even though he saw that she was still angry with the world, in a state of 'perpetual disgust', he assumed this was nothing more than teenage angst. As Caitlin snuggled and giggled with him, as she relished the attention she received in his company, Gus half-believed that she loved him; and the portraits he painted of her, posed in sensual invitation, were a register of how deep his delusion went.

Caitlin's own account was brutally different. Years later, she would recall Gus as a monstrous old goat, a rapist, even, who'd stolen her virginity and all but destroyed her capacity for sexual pleasure. Gus would be dead by the time Caitlin made her most bitter denunciations, and the friends who came to his defence would argue that her memory had become warped over time, that her accusations of rape were a fantasy. But Caitlin's own family and friends would equally maintain there was no fabrication; and, however disputed the facts of the affair, it is impossible, now, not to regard Gus's role in it as a shameful dereliction of his responsibility. However gauchely manipulative Caitlin may or may not have been with him, however helplessly he may have believed himself in thrall to her beautiful vitality, the hard truth remains that she'd been little more than a child, a very damaged child, when he seduced her, and, in that, he was guilty of abuse.

That same failure of judgement told against Gus when he began making love to Brigit Macnamara, despite the fact that Brigit was both stronger and much more practical than her younger sister. Down at Fryern, where Brigit spent much of her time, she'd long made herself happily useful to everyone, especially to Dodo whom she helped with the animals and the garden; around 1935, when she first graduated from posing for Gus to being his lover, she felt none of the disgust that Caitlin would claim. Brigit's own scattered recollections of Gus were, in fact, only of pleasure, and her older sister Nicolette would remember how comfortable she seemed with him, how 'an intonation, pause, movement of Brigit's hand would be answered with a smile from Augustus that started slowly all over his face and faded in his beard.'[16] The portraits Gus painted were also a celebration of that ease, for, in contrast to the false, pouting sensuality he projected onto Caitlin, he allowed Brigit to look like her robust, laughing self, dressed in dungarees and with a tankard of beer in her hand.

But, if Brigit was far from being a victim of Gus's middle-aged lust, she may still have been marked by it. Most of the affair was conducted at Fryern where Dodo, if she realized what was going on, made no comment. According to Vivien, Dodo always had 'a mysterious way of disappearing when anything troublesome cropped up', a mysterious way of not seeing what she didn't want to see.[17] However, even though Brigit could slip into Gus's studio without any fuss, even though the habits of silence and the averted gaze were now so entrenched at Fryern, the fundamental secrecy of this affair may have scarred Brigit. After it was over she became increasingly solitary in her habits, she never married, and, later in life, the closest relationships she formed were with animals and small children.

Gus saw nothing wrong at the time. The restfulness he found in Brigit, the steadiness and warmth of her character, were deeply consoling; and these qualities became especially important when his affair with Caitlin began to unravel, and when he realized that he, himself, had precipitated its ending.

Early in 1936 Gus had introduced Caitlin to the young Welsh poet Dylan Thomas and, still deluding himself that his 'little seraph' was contentedly loyal, he had no reason to suspect that the two young people had, as Caitlin later recorded, fallen immediately 'into bed'.[18] For several months she managed to keep Gus in ignorance of her affair. But in July, when she accompanied him to Wales, to stay with the novelist Richard Hughes, Dylan chose to go to Wales as well, to see his friend, the painter Fred Janes. When a plan was made for them all to meet up for a trawl of the local pubs, this seemed to Caitlin an opportunity ripe for disclosure. Emboldened by drink, she began to embrace Dylan openly in the back seat of Gus's car, and he, unable to contain his rage at the blatancy of her behaviour, stopped the car at the nearest pub, then, letting fly with his fists, knocked Dylan to the ground.

Hughes thought Gus looked blurry, a little strange, when he returned from this drama, while Caitlin seemed very smug, like 'a cat that's been fed on cream'.[19] Apparently, she had relished being fought over by the two men, and for a while she continued to stoke their rivalry. But, fundamentally, she'd set her heart on Dylan and, in July 1937, she married him. Gus pined a little: 'I spent some time combing out the London Pubs in the hopes of finding you & getting you back for a bit to finish that picture, which I rather bank on'.[20] However, once he'd been invited to be godfather to the couple's first child, he conceded that his role had switched from lover to provider, and, whenever he visited them in the 'frightful squalor' of their rented cottage in Laugharne, he would deliberately leave money in the pockets of his coat for them to steal.[21]

Gus was also reconciled to the loss of Caitlin because Dylan at least was a poet. Although he would dismiss *Under Milk Wood* as a sentimental travesty of Welshness, he recognized there was a genius in the younger man. He relished his sensuous feel for the melody of words, even more, perhaps, he admired his willingness to live on air, his drinking, his combativeness, his talent for mischief. In Dylan Gus saw a blithe capacity for rebellion that he himself had lost, and, in one of the two portraits he painted, he gave to Dylan the unsettling charm of some fallen choir boy, the innocence of his snub-nosed features and exuberant curls undercut by the scintilla of malice in his smile, the sardonic intelligence of his pale blue gaze.

Even though Gus had told MacColl he needed women for his work, his better portraits, these days, were often of men. In the summer of 1930, he revisited Ireland and painted two more versions of Yeats. The first, rather 'gay and whimsical', glossed over the poet's sixty-five years; the second, in which he sat with a rug over his knees, had been more honest. Yeats's hair was a nimbus of white, his eyes, behind thick reading glasses, had a shadowing of melancholy. The two men had talked to each other about their mutual dread of aging: it was hard enough, Yeats admitted, to accept the physical 'marks of time', much worse to realize how weakly he'd given in to his own vanities, his own self-delusion. 'My character is so little myself that all my life it has thwarted me,' he mourned, and in that regret Gus must surely have recognized himself.[22]

That same year, he was also in Paris to draw James Joyce. He'd been asked to contribute an illustration for *The Joyce Book*, a publication which featured thirteen poems, each one with an accompanying musical text. Time was short – Gus apologized to Gwen that he'd be unable to get over to Meudon – and some of his sketches were little more than a few spare lines. Joyce, profoundly short sighted, quipped that they were so minimal, so very 'School of Paris', he could hardly see them. Yet he admired the drawings very much, especially a three-quarter profile in which his half-blind gaze had something dark and inward, like a visionary, a seer. Six years later, when Joyce used this sketch for the cover of his first edition of collected poems, he told Gus it was 'the one thing in the volume which is indispensable.' Eventually, it would become one of the most iconic representations of Joyce, appearing on later editions of *Ulysses*, reproduced as a postcard and illustration for magazine articles.

Other portraits Gus drew, of Joseph Hone and Theodore Powys, had that same imprint of empathy, that connection with aging men who still lived vividly in their minds. The 'GREAT painting', however, continued to elude him. In 1935, when a fire broke out in the studio at Fryern, Gus felt, almost stoically, that few of the canvases destroyed were a serious loss. His art had become stuck, and, unlike Gwen, who could probe so narrowly into the fundamentals of her subject matter and technique, his own jaded imagination seemed to require ever more provocation. Years had passed since he'd been able to paint the same landscape over and over again; years had passed since his family had reliably inspired him to paint the lyric fantasies that mattered so much to him.

In 1929, when the void in his studio had become particularly frightening, Gus had been persuaded to work briefly for the stage. Sean O'Casey wanted him to design the second act of his anti-war play, *The Silver Tassie*, and, while Gus demurred that he knew nothing about the theatre, he realized that the imagery O'Casey wanted from him – 'a grisly jagged battlefield', a ruined chapel with a stained-glass window of the Madonna – could all come from the drawings he'd brought back from the front.*[23]

Having accepted the commission, the initial work was easy – the physical labour of constructing and painting the set was left to professionals. The central task, however, of painting the stained-glass Madonna onto a

---

* O'Casey was also a good friend. Gus enjoyed the playwright's roistering Irishness and celebrated it in a pair of portraits, which O'Casey himself found 'uncanny powerful embarrassingly vivid'.

huge piece of oiled silk had to be his, and for weeks Gus procrastinated, apprehensive of being put on the spot. Finally, he did the painting in a concentrated two-hour burst; and, when it was hoisted into place and the stage lights were switched on, he was rewarded with one of the more unexpectedly pleasing moments of his career. On the stage, his work had acquired an astonishing radiance and power. Swaying very slightly as the crew and cast broke into spontaneous cheers, Gus believed he'd found himself a new métier.

He was keen for more and, the following March, he agreed to work on the designs for a new ballet, *Pamona*, collaborating with the brilliant young talents of choreographer Frederick Ashton and composer Constant Lambert. The invitation had come from Lydia Lopokova, the fleet and witty Russian ballerina whom Gus had once painted (allegedly terrifying her with his 'pouncing hands'), and he was looking forward to starting work, both for the creative camaraderie of the studio and the proximity to attractive dancers. But his alcoholic shakes had become too seriously disabling and he'd been forced to put himself in the hands of Dr Cameron. Although other approaches were made from the theatre, he would have to wait several years for one that appealed.

This came in a commission to design both sets and costumes for J. M. Barrie's biblical drama *The Boy David*. Barrie was now a distinguished man of letters and Gus thought it would be an amusing honour to work for the old boy, a pleasure to re-immerse himself in the buzz of production meetings and rehearsals. But he really didn't know what he was doing: the costumes he designed were so uncomfortable to wear, they had to be reworked by professionals, while the set he conceived – a glittering waterfall coursing through rocks – was so ambitious that the actors could barely navigate their way across the stage.

Gus was not present for the opening night in Edinburgh, and was saved from the embarrassment of seeing the cast stumble around his set. Nor did he know about the hurriedly enforced changes that were then made to his designs. In November 1936, when he attended the play's London premiere, he expected to receive all the plaudits he'd enjoyed for *The Silver Tassie*; instead he was faced with the violation of all his ideas – his waterfall abandoned, his 'dark and lowering' skyscape replaced by a dreary backcloth, and his magnificent rocky landscape reduced to a scattering of boulders. Stalking out of the auditorium, Gus swore never to work in the theatre again.

If the inspiration Gus found from the stage was fleeting, his travels, too, were providing diminishing returns. The modern world, with its newly built hotels and highways, its scourge of 'detestable day trippers' had started to encroach on what remained of his wild and favourite places. In 1932, when he went to Mallorca, enticed perhaps by reports of the idyll Robert Graves had found on the island, he discovered that, even here, the developers had moved in, with their 'screeching rock drills and general banging of machinery'.[24]

He came back to England 'feeling like death' and pronouncing Mallorca 'not paintable' at all. Perhaps it was the violation of the mountains and seascapes which then drove Gus to Venice the following August, with the hope that this city of light, water and stone would still prove as paintable as it had been for centuries.* At first, he believed it would be so. The liquid beauty of the city's canals, its gloriously listing palazzos, its cacophony of swifts and church bells were all 'wonderful', and, like generations before him, he submitted willingly to the fairy-tale extravagance of the Piazza San Marco, with its latticework palace, its soaring campanile and its crowds of 'promenaders [who] emitted a low murmuring as if a thousand secrets were being whispered'.[25]

But the spell didn't hold. Compared to the teeming variety of Marseilles, Paris, even London, Venice seemed fundamentally dead to Gus, a place to which he'd arrived 'a few centuries late'. He might have felt differently had he travelled there in the foggy silence of winter, but at the height of the summer season there were tourists everywhere and he was continually running into the kind of 'bores buggers and bums' he tried to avoid at home. He was infuriated by the extortionate cost of everything, and he lashed out at Vivien, whom he'd asked to come with him to 'keep an eye on the money', but who was having far too much fun being flirted with and taken out to parties.[26]

---

* His work had been exhibited at the Venice Biennale the previous year, but he apparently didn't attend.

Even the art disappointed. With his guidebook in his hand, Gus trekked conscientiously around 'all the famous paintings', yet, while he could admire the abundance of Titians, Tintorettos and Tiepolos, they didn't speak to him. The joy of recognition that he'd felt on seeing his first Giottos and Fra Angelicos in Tuscany, the confidence with which he'd been able to think of himself as their rightful descendant, as part of a great European tradition – all that seemed lost. Venice made Gus feel old, wrung out, and that consciousness of passing time became even more acute to him when he eventually risked a return to Provence.

It was Dodo who'd tempted him back. In 1936, she had gone on her own to southern France, possibly to see Poppet and her husband, who summered there, and during her visit Dodo had found a modest stone farmhouse – or *mas* – for rent near Saint-Rémy-de-Provence. 'I couldn't resist it,' she told Gus after signing the lease, and, when he came out the following summer, he was no less excited. The *mas* was surrounded by the same landscape that had burned into his brain during his first discovery of Provence, and he wanted immediately to paint it. But the magnificence of the rocky Alpilles, the austere beauty of baked red earth, of silvery olive trees and infinite sky inspired nothing new in him. Wryly, he commented to a neighbour that, while 'these hills deserved a real painter', it was no longer him.[27]

All that Provence could give Gus now was a melancholy register of how much he'd lost, how little he could regain. But he may have been seeing the landscape through unsettled eyes, for, earlier that year, he'd travelled to Jamaica, and the extremes of its beauty and its violence still lived with him.

He'd been prompted, half-frivolously, to embark on this trip when an occultist he'd consulted claimed to see 'a journey to one of the colonies' in his future; but it had principally been his own malaise that drove Gus to set sail in February 1937, taking with him Dorelia, Vivien, Brigit and two-and-a-half-year-old Tristan, who entertainingly 'imagined himself to be captain of [the] ship'.[28]

The voyage was stormy, with much crashing of crockery and flooding of cabins, and when they docked in Kingston, Gus was almost ready to turn back. The city, he wrote, was 'aesthetically repellent and prostituted to tourists', and he was as disgusted by the filthy slums into which the black population had been corralled as by the suburban villas of the wealthy whites. But, once he'd hired a driver to take them deeper into the island, Jamaica came alive. The sequinned emeralds and blues of the hummingbirds, the tropical scarlet of the frangipani flowers, the lush oily greens of the vegetation were colours he had never seen, and he felt the 'wonderment of Columbus' as he and the family were driven through 'tumultuous peaks and ridges . . . fairy woods . . . perpendicular cliffs and rushing torrents'. There were abominations, even outside Kingston – soulless modern constructions and impoverished shanty towns – but there were also villages where woodcarvers continued to practise their traditional craft, where communities came together in spinning, chanting rituals that made Gus believe he was witnessing the genuine 'pageantry of native life'.[29]

He needed to get his impressions down on paper, and, after a month, he sent the family back to England so that he could draw and paint undisturbed. 'I am working with a quite remarkable renewal,' he told Mavis. Yet, the more Gus experienced of Jamaica, the more it troubled him. Often, when he went into a village to look for models to draw, he was treated with hostility – his white skin, his obvious wealth, his driver and his car all making him look like a man who worked for the government or the police. While he wished he could live more authentically, swapping his hotel room for a hut 'made of mahogany and plantation leaves', Gus had to accept that a huge chasm of race and privilege existed between him and those he called 'the natives'.

He was shamed by that chasm and, when a series of demonstrations broke out across the island, with impoverished black workers protesting over wages and conditions, Gus asked to meet with some of their leaders, wanting to know more about the exploitation they'd endured. He wanted to help, and, with his easy rush to romanticize, he imagined putting his money and his reputation at the service of their cause. Yet he knew he was impotent, he knew that the only material assistance he could offer the islanders was to pay extra generous fees to those who sat for him – and that knowledge gave him pain.

Jamaica changed Gus in this way. It tempered his fantasy with political irony, it made him acknowledge that the reality behind his own Arcadian dream of the simple life was one that most people struggled to escape. There were blind spots, still, in his attempts to re-educate himself: the crassness with which he joked to Mavis about the 'innumerable dusky beauties' he wished he could 'sample'; the colonialist condescension with which he talked about Jamaican culture as belonging to the 'childhood of the world'.[30] But the conflicting emotions which the island aroused in Gus – the wonder and the outrage – left a powerful imprint on his art. Back in his studio, he worked up the studies he'd made, painting a series of portraits which, at their best, were more vital and more questioning than anything he'd attempted in years. The light and the colours of the island had influenced his palette: the skin tones of the young black woman in *A Jamaican Girl* were a precisely observed fusion of coral, cinnamon, petrol blue and white. But the power of the portrait lay in the model's demeanour, the glint of wary defiance in her gaze, the stubborn set of her lips, the pride of her elegantly modelled face and neck. There was a story, here, of a black Jamaican woman posing for a foreign white male, and, in that tension, Gus painted a reflection of his own ambiguous relationship with the island itself.

The Jamaican series was exhibited at Tooths Gallery in May and June the following year. Some older work was included in the show, and sales were excellent, earning Gus what would today amount to tens of thousands of pounds. Praise came from the usual quarters, and even from Wyndham Lewis, who, writing in *The Listener*, argued that the 'beauty and squalor' of Gus's Jamaican portraits showed a thrilling return to form. These 'African' faces, with their 'blistered skins' and 'twisted lips' and 'mournful' eyes, came closer, Lewis argued, to expressing 'the tragedy of this branch of the human race' than any pictures of a 'more literary . . . intention.'[31]

Such enthusiasm from Lewis might have been surprising to Gus, given their long years of mutual sniping. However, their friendship had just been rekindled, because the Royal Academy had wilfully rejected one of Lewis's finer portraits (of T. S. Eliot) and Gus, in protest, had resigned his own membership, stating that, 'Nothing that Mr Lewis paints is negligible or to be condemned lightly'.[32] His words had been widely reported and Lewis had then repaid the compliment by announcing that, in losing the membership of Augustus John, 'a Titan among the minnows', the Academy had been exposed as an institution of 'gigantic platitudes'.[33]

The controversy had briefly become very public and very lively; it had felt like the old days, when Gus and Lewis led the ranks of the insurgents together, and it had almost certainly played a role in Lewis's enthusiastic review of the Tooth's Gallery show.

Other critics were not so kind, however. Clive Bell thought that even the most successful paintings in the show had 'the air of a fluke', evidence that Gus had 'never developed the intellectual powers of composition that are the mature test of an artist's ability'.[34] Anthony Blunt, in *The Spectator*, was apparently more graceful in acknowledging that Augustus John disappointed only because he forced 'one . . . to judge by the highest standards'. Yet Blunt could hardly have been more damning in his ultimate assessment: 'Everyone is agreed on the fact that Augustus John was born with a quite exceptional talent for painting – some even use the word genius – and almost everyone is agreed that he has in some way wasted it.'[35]

Almost the same conclusion was reached by *The Times*, who regretted that so 'great a natural talent for painting, possibly the greatest in Europe, should have been treated so lightly by its possessor'.[36] Perhaps the cruellest register of Gus's decline was the indifference, even contempt, with which he was now viewed by the young. In 1909, Rupert Brooke had almost fainted with the emotion of seeing his work, but three decades later, the poet Geoffrey Grigson was ready to dismiss Gus as 'a vulgar art-school technician with a provincial mind'.[37] Even if Dodo was able to hide the worst of the reviews, they only echoed what Gus had long feared in himself. It wasn't only illness and the violating effects of the modern world that made him look back on this decade as 'the worst spell of my bloody life'; it was the slow seeping away of his powers, the shallowness of the groove into which his art was settling.

The children, too, had continued to bother him, perhaps even more so now they were grown up. While he was counting on Vivien to stick to her art, he was disappointed in Poppet, who'd got married at the age of eighteen and had settled for becoming a 'hausfrau'.* Gus mourned the

---

* The Slade disappointed Vivien, but she transferred from the Slade to the Euston Road School, under Victor Pasmore, and then to a Paris academy.

waste of his daughter's lively intelligence, although his regret was also complicated by the extreme possessiveness he'd always felt towards his daughters. When Poppet was fifteen, holidaying with the family at Villa Sainte Anne, she'd worn lipstick to a local dance and Gus had reacted with all the pomp and indignation of a Victorian papa, ordering her to wipe her face clean. She had been brave enough to confront his hypocrisy, to point out the obviousness of his double standards, and so too had Vivien, when he'd objected to her flirtatiousness in Venice. But the girls never quite lost their terror of him. Vivien was thirty when she became engaged to a haematologist named John White, but she admitted to her brother Edwin that she was terrified of breaking the news to their father: 'I just don't feel it in me! Can't see the way, feel like . . . keeping it dark for a year or two'.[38]

The two oldest boys, at least, were professionally employed. David now played the oboe and had found work with the orchestras of Covent Garden and Sadler's Wells. He'd married, becoming a parent to his first daughter, Anna, in 1932, and these developments all seemed to steady his confidence. Caspar, meanwhile, was rising through the ranks of the navy, and even though Gus was still inclined to disparage his son's career, he could at least applaud Caspar for becoming the most financially independent of his boys.

It was hard to imagine how the others might earn a decent living. Romilly, having studied at Cambridge, had fallen under the influence of Francis Macnamara and was writing a book on religion and philosophy which Gus could barely understand. Edwin was still painting in Paris, although, for one brief moment in 1930, he'd brought joy to Gus's heart by coming home to London and taking up boxing. As 'Teddy John of Chelsea', Edwin had scored seven successive wins, and while Gwen had been appalled at her favourite nephew taking up so 'brutish' a sport, Gus had enjoyed it terrifically. Suddenly, his truculent, maladroit son had made sense: 'I like him immensely he has become a tall hefty fellow full of confidence humour and character.'[39] But then Edwin had changed his mind, going back to his art and leaving Gus to fret over his son's misguided choices and to continue paying his bills.

Most bewildering to him was Robin, who appeared to have made a vocation out of doing and saying as little as possible. He was living abroad – in Spain, then Florida – but his occasional appearances at Fryern were a misery. 'He hardly utters a word and somehow radiates *hostility*,' Gus told Mavis. 'I fear I shall reach a crisis and go for him tooth and nail. This happened once here and I soon floored him on the gravel outside – most unpleasant I assure you. I fear he may be slightly mad for he seems to live or just exist in another and quite unpopular world. I feel I must soon make myself horrid and cut off his allowance. He may then see fit to modify his philosophy of life. But it will end our relationship for ever. If only he had a good heart, he could sponge off me indefinitely.'[40]

But these disappointments were nothing to the agonizing sense of waste Gus suffered when Henry, his once golden child, was found washed up, drowned, on a Cornish beach in 1935. Out of all Ida's boys, Henry had been born with the most haunting physical resemblance to his mother, and had inherited most of her questioning intelligence. Gus had been maddened by Henry's teenage vocation for the priesthood, his determination to hobble himself with 'beastly vows of chastity and poverty', but he'd also been intensely worried when Henry, having suffered a series of crises over his faith and his sexuality, had thrown over his training to go and live and work among London's poor. 'He is as mad as a hatter,' Gus wrote to Ursula Tyrwhitt with baffled alarm, 'studying dancing for which he has no aptitude and the price of vegetables, neglecting his person and showing utter indifference to social conventions.'[41]

Then Henry had fallen in love. Olivia Plunkett Green, a clever, rather frantic party girl who'd recently converted to Catholicism, had offered him a heady, if confusing, combination of flirtation and piety; and when Henry had borrowed a cottage for them to stay in Cornwall, he'd been hoping finally to make love to her. Instead, he received a six-page letter from Olivia, explaining why sex must be impossible for them. 'I never knew how anti-birth control I was', she wrote. And Gus never knew what was in Henry's mind when, on the evening of 22 June, he bicycled down to the sea for a solitary swim. As soon as he learned his boy was missing, Gus went straight down to Cornwall, but the police and coastguards were preparing him for the worst. He could barely acknowledge to himself the horror of having to wait for certain news. 'I'm here searching for my blessed son who's gone and fallen into the sea,' he told Mavis; 'I have no hope of finding him alive. His corpse will come to the surface after nine days. A damn shame you are not hereabouts . . . he was a brilliant and strange youth.'[42]

On 5 July, when Henry's body did finally surface, it was Gus's appalling duty to make the formal identification. Years later, he wrote stiffly that, although the body 'was without a face from the attentions of birds and crabs I was able to identify it all the same'.[43] The drowning was ruled accidental, a tragic fall as Henry had been scrambling down to the beach, and that view was corroborated by Henry's former tutor, Father D'Arcy, who wrote to assure Gus that Henry, during their last meeting, had appeared much more stable and was 'beginning to recover that spontaneous & happy character with all its brilliance, which he himself had seemed at one time to choke.'[44] Yet, while Gus had no choice but to accept the coroner's verdict, he never lost the fear that Henry had killed himself, that the Johns' 'ancestral strain' of melancholia had driven him to suicide. As with the death of little Pyramus, he tried to bury his grief, responding with terse, even flippant thanks to the letters of condolence. To Michel Salaman, however, he admitted the vastness of his sorrow: 'as Ida's last child I thought of [Henry] as somehow compensating for her loss . . . but now . . .' He could not finish the sentence.[45]

One of his other links to Ida, Ada Nettleship, had already gone. Over time, Gus had become more accommodating to his mother-in-law, and in December 1932, when Ada was dying, he went with two of his sons to sit with her. Even though she was barely conscious, Gus spoke tenderly to her, recounting stories from his and Ida's past, and Ursula Nettleship thought his attentiveness was very touching – a 'good memory to treasure up', she wrote.

It was the loss of friends, though, which marked this bloodiest of decades for Gus. John Sampson, his Romani guru, had died in 1931, and Gus had wept openly as he'd presided over a ceremonial scattering of Sampson's ashes. 'It's a ghastly blow for me', he told Meg, 'for the Rai was so much a part of my life'. To Sampson's son Michael, he wrote, 'there is no one with whom I have quarrelled . . . more often and no one whose loss I feel more.'[46] Five years later, Horace de Vere Cole died, and when Gus took Mavis to the funeral, he hoped against hope that it would turn out to be one of his friend's more ghoulish pranks, that the coffin lid would be thrust aside and a 'well-known figure [would] leap out with an ear splitting yell'. He and Horace had goaded and ruffled each other for years, had competed over the same women, but there had been a complicity between them, a mutual sense of life's absurdity that Gus had found in no one else.[47]

Then, in April 1938, came news that Ottoline was gone. Gus had last seen her in 1936, when, despite the cancer that was wasting her body, she'd been determinedly splendid in canary yellow and black lace. He'd wanted to paint her, but Ottoline had refused, and instead he'd given her one of his small pre-war panels. 'God you have made me so happy, I can hardly believe it,' she wrote in thanks and she still clung to Gus as her 'dear good friend.'[48] Ironically, it may have been her revered Dr Cameron who'd hastened her death; an opportunistic peddler of the new drug Prontosil, he'd prescribed a course of treatments for Ottoline which were lethally above the recommended dose.

For years, the one person who had seemed to defy death was old Edwin. Throughout his eighties, he'd remained spry and alert, content with his own small pleasures and his shyly cultivated friendships. However ill-suited he'd been to raising his children, he had tried to hold them all together: he had rarely complained of how little he saw them and had kept them informed of each other's news, sending cuttings that might interest them, or a *Punch* cartoon of Gus. But, with every winter, Edwin had admitted to worsening bouts of bronchitis, and in the spring of 1938, he'd taken longer than usual to recover. On 7 April, just shy of his ninety-first birthday, he'd informed his housekeeper he was retiring to bed for an afternoon nap, and once there his heart must have given out. A short while later, she heard him calling out, 'Good bye Miss Davis, good bye.' By the time she reached Edwin, he was gone, as polite and careful in death as he'd been in life.

Gus, who was the only sibling within reasonable distance, had to take charge of the funeral, going up to Tenby with Caspar. He'd often joked about his father's persistent longevity, but he felt the loss of him now, and was distressed when he learned the 'flabbergasting' worth of Edwin's estate – £50,000, the modern equivalent of over a million pounds. It seemed to Gus both comic and unbearably poignant that Edwin had remained so stuck in his frugal ways – even to the end, Gus told Mavis, 'he always tore his note paper in half so to economise'.

Yet, touched though he was by Edwin's death, Gus didn't think to tell Gwen about it for several days. His note, aside from one fond observation that the last of their father's letters had been written in 'exactly the same firm and elegant character we have been accustomed to for so long', was briskly practical, informing Gwen of the instructions left in Edwin's will that his estate should be divided equally between his four children.[49] Given the efforts to which Gwen had always gone to avoid their father, Gus had no reason to believe she would care much about his death. Nor, given the drifting apart of their own relationship, did he imagine that Gwen would care about the melancholy that had stolen over him as he'd stood beside Caspar at the windy little graveyard at Gumfreston Chapel, watching his father's coffin being lowered into the ground. Gus had no way of knowing, then, that, even if Gwen had wanted to attend Edwin's funeral, her own health had become so frail the journey would have been beyond her.

Chapter Eighteen

MORTALITY

'Don't think (as before) to work for years ahead – & the
number possible – you work for one moment'
GWEN JOHN[1]

B y the start of the 1930s, sickness had become Gwen's familiar, and she may not have registered how severe her annual attacks of flu and stomach cramps, her minor infections and migraines had grown. If she was suffering from some kind of genetic condition – coeliac, Crohn's or lupus – she could have been entering a more critical phase; or, by the middle of the decade, as biographer Sue Rose has speculated, she may have been developing cancer of the stomach or bowel. Yet no diagnosis was attempted. Although Gwen did ask for Chloe's advice on whether she should make a will, she refused to waste her time or her money on doctors. She believed that her illness had a rhythm of its own, with periods of sickness followed by months of remission, and, even by the spring of 1938, when she'd become so weak that the journey into Paris was almost beyond her, Gwen was still trusting to prayer to speed her recovery.

Her patron saint, in illness, was Thérèse de Lisieux. A young nun, who'd died of tuberculosis in 1897, Thérèse had been canonized in 1925 for the exceptional piety with which she'd borne her suffering, and among Gwen's most cherished possessions was a photograph of the saint as a child, posed for the camera with her little sister. She used it as a prayer card to direct her thoughts, but she drew it, too, over and over again, dividing her paper into a grid of squares, filling each one with a tiny image. It became for her both an exercise in picture-making and an act of meditation – the images accumulating like beads on a rosary.

Even when Gwen's symptoms were in remission and she was well enough to resume something of her normal life, she was careful to hoard her resources, and throughout the last decade of her life she made a habit of setting aside periods of '*retrait*', when she saw almost no one but her neighbours and her cats. A badgering note had arrived from Rhoda Symons, in August 1931: 'What has become of you? Won't you send us a little word? I think I'll write a line to the illustrious "Gus" asking for your address [but] Arthur says it's useless and hopeless!'[2] And it was intrusions like this which had made Gwen renew all her vows to detach herself from everyone who fatigued and unsettled her, and to lay down stern commands to herself that there must be no more:

1 sitting before people, listening to them in an idiotic way
2 undergoing their influence – being what they expect – demand
3 by fear flattering them
4 valuing too much their signs of friendship
5 Thinking too often of people.[3]

'Aloneness,' she wrote in 1932, is 'nearer God nearer realité.'[4] But, if Gwen was unburdening herself of unwanted company, it was not only for the sake of her health and her religion, but also for work. In April 1928, she had told Ursula how close she was getting to understanding the essence of her art: 'I feel more than ever on the point of knowing how to express things, in painting.' Always cautious, she admitted it could be 'months or years perhaps' before she reached that point.[5] Yet she may have sensed, even then, that her time was limited, for she was accelerating the pace at which she worked, at which she was adopting and discarding ideas.

Early in the decade, she was wondering what she could take from the boldly figurative visions of Chagall and Rouault; subsequently it was the analytic cubism of André Lhote to which she was drawn. Lhote's theories on colour were particularly interesting to her and she was studying them in relation to her newly acquired chromatic wheel, an elaborate circular chart, designed by the chemist Michel Chevreul, which laid out 'seventy-two hues' in a graduated spectrum, a visual shortcut to understanding all their contrasting, and complementary, interactions.*

The fruits of Gwen's thinking, her reading and her observations were now being channelled into hundreds of small drawings, similar to those she made of Sainte Thérèse. Some were little more than pencilled doodles, a dot for an eye, a dark scribble for a coat or dress; some were more detailed – coloured gouache studies of plants or street views. She was still searching for the quicksilver line between her eye, her hand and her subject matter, searching for the 'simple form' that would contain the emotion, the truth of the moment. And although there was no point at which Gwen made the decision to give up painting in oils, the last decade of her working life was almost entirely taken up with making these rapid explorations in colour and form, these little images that were also for her a form of prayer – 'the transformation of your sins your faults'.[6]

One of the very last portraits she began was at the request of Louise Salaman (now Bishop), who'd written in October 1928 to say how often she still thought of Gwen and their days at the Slade. She was coming to Paris with her daughter Bridget and hoped that Gwen would not only see them, but also consider painting Bridget's portrait.

For the sake of the past, Gwen agreed, but, while she grew fond of Louise's daughter, the work of the portrait felt even harder than before. Her eyesight was bothering her, she ached from the strain of spending long hours at her easel, and, as soon as Louise and Bridget left Paris, she put the portrait aside. She said there was a problem with painting the hands, which she was trying to solve. As that problem continued to puzzle her, though, she became less interested in solving the hands, and her thoughts shifted instead towards an analysis of what the fundamental elements of portraiture now meant for her.

She listed them in her notebook:

1 The strange form,
2 The pose and proportions

---

* Along with Chevreul's book *The Law of Simultaneous Colour*, published in 1839, the chromatic wheel had influenced not only the work of his peers, but the subsequent generation of impressionists.

3 The atmosphere and notes, the tones
4 The finding of the forms (the sphere – the hair the forehead the cheek, the eye . . .)
5 Blobbing
6 The sculpting with the hands.[7]

Yet, she did not use her analysis to finish the portrait. There were long periods, now, when thinking about something carried almost the same weight for Gwen as doing it, and this act of deferral had become part of her strategy for keeping the world at bay. As long as she could imagine herself returning to Yew Tree Cottage, as long as she could plan to send work for Gus to sell, she would not feel the pressure to act. Similarly, when the Ferargil Gallery in New York had first made their approach to her in 1929, Gwen had believed herself quite genuine when she wrote to the director Frederic Newlin Price to confirm her interest in having a one-woman show.

The realities of what that might entail remained quite abstract to her, and Gwen was deeply flustered when the gallery wrote to her in July 1930 to confirm that they planned to hold her exhibition the following spring, and to advise her that one of their representatives, Maynard Walker, would be coming to Meudon to make a preliminary selection of her art. To Ursula, Gwen panicked that she would have to work 'from the first glimmer of light till dark every day' to get her pictures in a state of readiness for Walker, and, feeling her usual anxiety about strangers, she warned him she would only be able to spare an hour of her time.

In fact, Walker rather charmed Gwen when he arrived at rue Terre Neuve. He looked carefully and respectfully through her stacks of work and his tone could not have been more reasonable when he asked if she could find ten more pictures to add to the thirty he thought suitable for exhibition, and if she could possibly get them all shipped to New York by November.

Walker clearly believed his visit had gone well. Afterwards, he wrote warmly to Gwen, 'if everything else in Europe disappointed me I should still be repaid for my long journey by that one brief hour in which I came to know more of you and your art.'[8] He also believed there was no real reason to doubt that the November deadline would be met.

Yet November came and went, and Gwen had still done nothing about assembling and shipping her work. To Newlin Price she explained that she'd been sidetracked by the urgency of drawing the view from her window, before it was spoiled by some new apartment buildings; apologetically, she assured him she was ready to make a start. To further convince him of her 'good intentions', she listed the titles of some paintings she'd asked her friend Chloe to track down, which she believed were in storage at the Warren Gallery in London. Even more persuasively, she told him that she'd just begun work on a new series, *Girl by a Window*, which she thought he might like.[9]

The girl in this series was seated by a window, her face in profile, a half-open book on her lap. Gwen had painted so many young women like this, except here she had simplified the image to a pattern of plain and forceful curves – the heavy fall of the girl's skirt, the scalloped edge of her collar, the dome of her hat, the seat of her chair. One of the six versions was painted in oil (the last known oil of Gwen's career), while the others were a mix of oil and gouache, but the palette was the same – a spectrum of browns to which she had introduced two singing notes of colour, the green of the window frame and the airy blue of the girl's hat. The effect of the picture was simultaneously one of solitude and bright expectation, of emotion in transition. 'The drawing is the discord,' Gwen wrote in her notebook. 'Paint the atmosphere & it's compl[e]mentary'.[10]

But Newlin Price would never get the chance to see this series, nor any of Gwen's other promised pictures. She simply lacked the energy to get her work crated up for New York, and she had no appetite for what would follow – the decisions to be made over the contents of her catalogue, the bothersome requests for interviews (what New York journalists might have made of Gwen is hard to imagine). Even though Gwen would still consider herself bound to the Ferargil and would engage with later discussions for a show, she was simply letting the idea of it float. At her core, she'd long ago decided it was no longer necessary to send her pictures out into the world – they were only for herself and for God.

The New Life
God has taken me.
To enter into Art as one enters religion.[11]

*

But, even though Gwen was retreating deeper into her own private world, she was far from being a recluse. Her Mother Superior – who'd recently retired to a convent at Joigny – had counselled her to 'seek happiness by creating joy around you', and she still valued her little community of friends. There might be fewer visits with Ruth Manson (who was now a grandmother) and with Constance (who was now spending part of her year in England), but Gwen was still very close to her neighbour Angeline Lhuisset, the two of them exchanging sympathetic news of each other's illnesses. When Angeline's seven nieces and nephews were tragically orphaned, Gwen sent letters of condolence to each of them, along with presents of cash and lottery tickets.

At rue Babie, there was also a middle-aged woman living opposite Gwen who became a good friend. As a neighbour, Louise Roche was unusually tactful, unusually quick to intuit whether Gwen was in a mood for conversation or needed to be left alone. Louise also had a far more sophisticated idea of Gwen's work than most of the Meudon community. An embarrassing awkwardness had developed when the local *boulangère* had tried to commission a painting from Gwen, having no idea of the prices she could command. Gwen herself had been too fearful of causing offence to refuse, and it was Louise who extricated her from the dilemma. One morning, when the two women were buying bread together, Louise observed the blanched expression on Gwen's face when the *boulangère* enquired about the progress of her painting. She returned to the shop the following day and quietly asked the woman how much money she was expecting to pay. When the latter replied 'maybe 150 francs for a nice flower painting', Louise informed her that Mademoiselle John's works often sold for over 1,000 francs. The woman gaped, saying she certainly wouldn't 'broach the subject again'. And Gwen, hearing of her rescue, kissed Louise gratefully on both cheeks, whispering, 'What a favour you've done me'.[12]

This was one of several episodes which Louise later recorded in her unpublished memoir about Gwen. She was not uncritical – she deplored Gwen's lack of concern when one of her cats killed a pair of nesting birds in Louise's garden. But she was very acute, especially when noting the shifting forces in Gwen's nature – the shyness and the pride, the vulnerability and the matter-of-factness. Once, when she asked Gwen about her quickness to take offence, Gwen shrugged and said, 'yes but I wouldn't be an artist without that'. On another occasion, when Louise observed that Gwen seemed more upset by the death of an elderly neighbour than that of the recent Pope, Gwen gave a 'long frank challenging burst of laughter' and replied, 'I knew her, I didn't know the Pope at all, they'll soon find another Pope'.[13]

Louise Roche's memories, so ordinary but so telling, were a register of the day-to-day life Gwen was leading, when her health allowed. Other people could still engage her sympathy and curiosity, and, in November 1933, she was very pleased when her nephew Edwin came back to Paris to resume his studies. Their relationship had almost been broken by his short-lived boxing career; as Edwin had admitted to his brother Henry, he'd been shocked by the degree of Gwen's contempt for the sport and hurt by the apparent withdrawal of her affections. 'Our meetings were few and far between and more often than not my communications by letter remained unanswered.'[14]

Yet, when Edwin had wanted advice about whether to resume his studies in London or Paris, it was to Gwen he'd written, and although she refused to comment – 'one can't judge for another. You must live where you would like to live' – she was glad when he decided on Paris. She warned him that she might be on one of her '*retraits*' when he arrived and might not be able to see him for '1 or 2 months', but she was warm in her promise see him for dinner as soon as she 're-surfaced'.[15]

Gwen, in late middle age, had started to enjoy the ideas, the energy of the young. Sometime around 1929, Gus had put her in touch with a school friend of Henry's, a clever young Catholic called Tom Burns, whom he considered to be a steadying influence on his son and whom he may have hoped might be equally steadying for his sister. Despite the thirty-year age gap between them, Gwen and Tom did, for a while, become lively and affectionate correspondents. It was to Tom that Gwen confided her disillusionment with Véra, her realization that Véra's piety was all based on lies. And it was through Tom that she also drew closer to Henry himself, and was able to look beyond her nephew's former brashness to the clever and sensitive man he'd become. She and Henry began writing to each other about religion, family and art, and Gwen evidently confided in him when she was puzzling over her portrait of

Bridget Bishop and the unresolved problem of her hands. 'I liked so much what you said,' Henry wrote back. 'Saw daddie . . . Told him re the hands'.[16]

If Gus had an opinion on the hands, it wasn't recorded. In December 1932, he sent a snappish note to Gwen, pointing out how long it had been since she'd written, wondering if she was ever going to make good her promise to visit. 'I hope you will come . . . I have been rather ill lately.' Gus had been unwell, of course, with his shakes and his rages, yet, even in the middle of his irritation with Gwen, it was impossible for him not to worry about her and the state of her income and health.[17] The following year, he would try to rouse her into agreeing to another London show, and even succeed in getting her to send over five preliminary pictures.

But it was Dodo who was in charge of the actual arrangements, Dodo who was doing most of the letter-writing. In 1936, when Gwen wanted those five pictures returned to Paris, it was Dodo to whom she made the request – although the affectionate but distracted tone of her letter showed how scattered her correspondence had become:

> Dearest Dodo
> Thank you so much for sending a telegram to Gus to send the pictures. I'm rather late in thanking you, 1st because I didn't get your card till weeks after you wrote it, it was put in somebody else's letter box, 2nd because of being so hurried.[18]

So prolonged were the silences between Gwen and Fryern that no evidence remains of any communication between them over the tragedy of Henry's drowning. Perhaps Gus sent a telegram, perhaps Gwen wrote words of condolence – but, if so, neither was saved.

Gwen's most intimate correspondent for most of this period was still Ursula. There were sometimes lengthy breaks between letters, when Ursula was travelling or when Gwen's health was bad – in the winter of 1935, she had a fall and fractured her hand, which left her unable to write or draw – but, in July 1936, Ursula came out to Paris and their friendship felt as secure as it had ever been. Gwen was feeling unusually strong that month, so strong she was even able to discuss with Ursula the possibility of accompanying her to Italy in the autumn. During the week or ten days of their time together, they went to restaurants and galleries, and to a couple of classes with André Lhote, from whom Gwen felt she 'learned so much' about atmosphere and colour, about the expressive '*passage* [of tones] from the dark to the fair'.[19] Even on the days they didn't meet, the two women sent notes to each other. After Ursula had gone home, Gwen couldn't bear to think that anything had marred the visit. There had been one small fracture of discord, and she wrote anxiously to repair it: 'At the Dôme you interrupted me and I couldn't say what I wanted to. I felt a sort of *angoisse* and showed it and you looked sorry as if it was your fault. It wasn't your fault . . . I showed that impatience and *angoisse* because I have the *habit* of it.'[20]

Ursula's visit had reminded Gwen how precious their friendship could be, and it had made her suddenly impatient with herself and the narrowness to which her world had shrunk. She'd allowed herself to become too limited in her work, she thought, and vowed to enrol for a full term of classes with Lhote. 'I'm tired of not knowing how to realize my little paintings (realize is Cézanne) I think finish would be a better word in my case,' she told Ursula.[21]

In this rekindling of her ambition and energy, Gwen even felt ready to engage with Newlin Price again over discussions of her New York show. He was proposing to send someone else to meet her, a woman this time, called Mary Sullivan (perhaps they thought a '*she*' would not be so 'terrifying', Gwen joked), and she intended to prepare seriously for the visit. Having written to Dodo to request the return of her five paintings, she selected twenty of her more recent colour-wash drawings, which she thought sufficiently finished to show.

But the flare of her enthusiasm had been quenched almost as suddenly as it had arisen. In August, Gwen was again very sick, with 'an interior chill, a lot of pain and fever', and she wrote unhappily to Ursula that she thought her trip to Italy would be 'impossible, perhaps for ever'.[22] She had recovered sufficiently by mid-September to agree to Sullivan's visit, to talk to her about the Slade (where Sullivan had studied) and about Quinn (whom Sullivan had also known quite well). But she was too weak to make any more promises about her exhibition. By the winter, her stomach cramps and her chest infections were so debilitating, she couldn't even imagine such an event, let alone create any new work for it.

Gwen would not admit it to herself, nor to anyone else, but this deterioration in her health had been exacerbated by her decision to move out of rue Terre Neuve and live full time in her *hangar* at rue Babie. Early in July, she'd ordered some rudimentary structural improvements: new boards hammered onto the *hangar*'s roof and walls, internal partitions erected to create a small kitchen and bedroom at the front, with a studio area at the back. At Chloe's begging, she'd even bought a paraffin stove. But when she moved into the *hangar* in late autumn, that stove could offer little protection against the chill and damp. However much Gwen wanted to think of herself as the sturdy young woman who'd walked miles every day and slept rough in haystacks and forests, she had just turned sixty and was frequently very unwell. She assured Ursula she was taking care of herself with a sustaining new drink – 'malted barley grains boiled in water and drunk with milk like a *café au lait*' – but her system was buckling. In March 1937, when Michel Salaman's son, Michael, asked to meet her in Paris, she had to tell him she had 'la grippe the real [one] fever etc' and was unable to see anyone.[23]

The warmer weather brought some respite, and, in June, Gwen was well enough to receive another visit from Maynard Walker. He'd left the Ferargil to set up his own small gallery, and he'd written to Gwen in the hope of exhibiting some of her work. She was worried about her obligation to Newlin Price, but she'd liked Walker on their previous meeting and was willing to let him come and see her work again.

For Walker, this encounter was, in some ways, as inspiring as his first. 'She gave me tea underneath those great brooding trees at the back of that wild garden,' he wrote afterwards. 'We talked of Proust and saints and sinners and angels and painters . . . I came away filled with the wonder of her spirit and the keenness of her intellect'.[24] He apparently saw nothing to concern him about Gwen's health; he was, however, extremely alarmed by the state of some of her paintings, which were stacked up in her sheds and barely protected by oilcloths: 'the little place she now lived in was far from weatherproof,' he recorded, 'there were sad signs that moisture had got into some of the canvases and damaged them.'

When he repeated to Gwen his earnest desire to show her work to the world, he may have been hoping to rescue at least some of it from further deterioration. Her only reply, however, was the gift of a small picture, for which she refused any payment.

The summer's remission was short; in September 1937, when Gwen attempted to visit an exhibition at the Musée d'Art Français Ancien, she could barely stagger through the gallery, admitting to Ursula it was painful just to stand. Even now, though, her pride and her resistance to fuss made her reluctant to confess the severity of her condition, not only to Ursula but to her family. Edwin was no longer in Paris to witness her decline, because he'd moved back to England, and the only person with whom Gwen seriously broached the issue of her health was Thornton. Over the years, they had come to recognize how temperamentally alike they were in their oblique, awkward ways of dealing with the world; they had also started to compare notes on their physical maladies. Thornton too was a victim of stomach cramps, although his were milder than Gwen's, and early in 1937 he had written to recommend a daily dose of linseed oil – a 'miracle' cure, he believed – and to reassure Gwen that their family had always been fundamentally tough, and that, once she got though her suffering, she would be 'all the stronger'.

Thornton did start to wonder, though, if Gwen was being entirely open with him about the state of her health. While he accepted that secrecy might be 'a valuable aid and force' in conserving her strength, he tried to warn against taking it to extremes, suggesting that it could be hurtful to those who loved her and wanted to help.[25] Gwen herself was sometimes troubled by the fading of contact with her family, and especially with Gus. When Maynard Walker came to Meudon and said he would be going next to London, she asked him to contact her brother on her behalf and let him know that she was well.

It was an odd request to make, since Gwen could so easily have written to Gus, but perhaps it was becoming too difficult for her to find the appropriate words. The following April, when Gus wrote to inform Gwen of their father's death, it could have been a moment for reminiscing about the past, for exchanging confidences, or for renewing promises of future communication. A different kind of family might have been brought closer by the loss of a parent, however difficult that parent had been. Yet, even with Thornton, there was no intimate exchange on the subject of Edwin's death. His letter to Gwen was as practical as Gus's had been in focusing on the terms of the will, and Gwen's reply to Thornton made little reference to family, was principally concerned with a book she was sending him about the rise of religious cults.

But there were more and more days when it was an effort for Gwen to write anything. Just after Edwin died, Ursula made a lightning visit to Paris and Gwen apparently managed to see her once or twice. Afterwards, she was also able to write to Ursula about a new range of paint colours she liked and about the technique she'd devised for remembering them.

She listed some examples in her letter: '*Rouge Phénicien* is the colour of what we call wild geranium. The stems are dark crimson the leaves seemed dipped in pale crimson just now . . . *Cinabre vert* is the green ball holding the snowdrop petals'.* Yet, while there was a delicate poetry in the detail of Gwen's list, the note which accompanied it was terse and almost disjointed. Dispensing with her usual fond address to 'Dearest Ursula', Gwen had simply launched into the note with a bald set of instructions: 'Press very firmly, not on temple but down sides of eyes *plûtot*. Elbows supporting body, when doing the back of ears tilt head forward and down'.[26] It's possible she was simply picking up on some earlier conversation she and Ursula had had about the easing of headaches, yet it is hard not to visualize Gwen, at her little table, trying to massage away her pain as she wrote.

This was her last surviving letter to her closest friend, and, although Gwen may have written others, she was retreating deeper and deeper into her illness. She remained fixed in her determination to endure, modelling herself on the admirable Sainte Thérèse who'd remained stoically impervious to the tuberculosis that had wasted her, refusing to sleep in a bed or heat her room. This same grit of stubbornness had

---

* The paints were from her favourite brand, LeFranc.

always been Gwen's strength, and it helped her now to sit through Mass, to keep herself tidy, to make crabbed attempts to draw and write. But according to Louise Roche, who was watching her decline with helpless anxiety, Gwen was killing herself – she was 'treat[ing] her body as though she was its executioner . . . to go to a doctor inconvenienced her, to take solid nourishment inconvenienced her.'[27]

The last year of Gwen's life was recorded only in fragments. In September 1938, she sent a cheque for fifty pounds to Winnie, and already she may have been thinking of divesting her funds, since she hinted that a larger sum was to follow. She sent Christmas greetings to Chloe with apologies for her silence – 'you must have thought I was dead'. In February 1939, she wrote to thank Thornton for his last two batches of news about his wife and baby daughter. 'They gave me joy as always,' she told him, explaining that she'd been too unwell to reply, but was now improving just a little – 'as you see from my being able to write.'[28] In May, she heard from Dodo on the vexed issue of Yew Tree Cottage. Dodo wanted to give the cottage to Fanny Fletcher, whose health was now poor, and if Gwen would agree to sell it back, Dodo said she would send over the money in instalments, adding that it would simplify things financially if they could make the cottage look like a gift and not a sale. Clearly, Dodo had no idea of how ill Gwen was; earlier that year, when Vivien had been passing through Paris and had tried to call in at rue Babie, she'd reported back that Gwen had been ill with flu and unable to see her. Casually, Dodo told Gwen that she too had been laid low but was much better now, and she hoped Gwen was also recovered.

Ursula, too, had a very incomplete picture of Gwen's decline. During the spring, she'd been travelling in Morocco, sending back descriptions to Gwen of palm trees and pink, walled towns; on her return in June, she'd bundled up a large parcel of clothes for her. The scribbled note that accompanied Ursula's parcel – 'I am very glad you are painting' – suggests Gwen had remained very sparing with the truth; Ursula certainly had no idea that the clothes she'd sent over to Meudon – suits, blouses, dresses, a hat and corselette – would get pitifully little wear. Over the summer, Gwen was sicker than she'd ever been – sick enough to start accepting that whatever was wrong could no longer be remedied by endurance and prayer. On 10 September, she contacted a lawyer in

Meudon for advice about drawing up her will. Then, through an extraordinary act of fortitude, she took the train to Dieppe.

Even during the last years of her illness, Gwen had hoped she might brave a journey back to the sea; she'd never stopped missing the bracing joy of waves and salt air, the spiritual lift of open horizons. In 1934, when Chloe had proposed they might meet each other in Dieppe, she'd got as far as writing down the train times and keeping them tucked inside the cover of her notebook. To attempt that 200-kilometre journey now, with two difficult changes of train, must have taken all her strength; yet there was an urgency to Gwen's decision which was sharpened not only by the heightened sense of her own mortality, but by the fact that Europe was once again at war.

There was little that Gwen wrote in her letters or her notebook to suggest she'd taken any real notice of Hitler's rise to power or of his bellicose designs on Europe. She'd lived through one conflict and had little energy to engage with the threat of another, especially one she might not live to see. On 3 September, when France and Britain declared war on Germany, there had been a flurry of panic in Meudon, as people once again prepared to leave. Yet, when Gwen caught the train to Dieppe, in the middle of September, she'd made no plans for anything more ambitious than an overnight stay. She'd packed no luggage and had made no arrangements for the care of her precious cats.

But the effort of the journey had been too much for her. By the time Gwen reached Dieppe, she was in a state of collapse and was rushed to the Civic Hospital. She remained sufficiently alert to ask for a lawyer, and Jean Jousset, who came to her bedside, stated later that she'd requested him 'to draw up her last will and testament', and made other 'various instructions'. The legal note which Jousset sent to the family was, however, all they knew of Gwen's final hours. She died at 8.30 on the morning of 18 September, a tiny elderly woman in a foreign city. And because there was no one to take an interest in her, the cause of Gwen's death was left unspecified on the death certificate, and the details of where and when she was buried were lost.[29]

The French authorities were obviously overwhelmed at that point, as the nation mobilized for war – hospitals were being placed on high alert, communications and travel were fraught. But, for the family, the mystery of Gwen's death remained cruelly unresolved. Years later, they would learn that she'd been buried first at Cimetière de Janval, in a suburb of Dieppe, but that her body had then been moved to make room for the graves of soldiers who'd been killed in the subsequent fighting. No one could tell them the new location. Gus would make an attempt to track it down, very much wanting to mark his sister's grave with a headstone or a sculpture of his own design. Yet, in death, as in life, Gwen remained frustratingly out of reach.*

The grief Gus experienced was hard and confused. He and Gwen had grown up together, as artists as well as children, and they'd shared certain fundamental things with each other. Now that she was dead, and their intimacy could never be recovered, he mourned the years that had been wasted in wrangling and misunderstanding. He blamed himself for the times Gwen had thought him a bully, for the times he had scorned the choices she'd made. But loss, guilt and anger took on a new and uglier twist when he learned it was Edwin, not he, whom Gwen had chosen as heir and executor of her estate.

For Gwen, that decision may well have been pragmatic. She'd grown fond of her nephew in Paris, had sympathized with his battles to assert himself as an artist; even though she had only her modest savings, her rue Babie plot to bequeath, she may have felt that he, out of all the family, had greatest material need. But, in leaving Edwin her art, her truest legacy, she was delivering a blow to Gus, not only because he'd personally made so many efforts to support her career, but because he was convinced that Edwin – who now lived with his wife and baby son in the remote Cornish village of Mousehole – had none of the necessary contacts or skills to ensure it was properly managed. As Edwin discovered when he travelled out to rue Babie in late September to organize the transportation of Gwen's things, she had left all her papers and

---

* The Janval cemetery had been used as a burial ground for Commonwealth soldiers in the First World War and, after the massive losses of spring 1940, some two dozen civilian bodies were relocated to accommodate the new military graves. Even though Gwen's body had been among them, Janval remained her last known resting place; in 2015, a memorial plaque was attached to the wall of the cemetery.

artworks in a daunting jumble – 'a mass of beautiful drawings in various mediums, pencil, gouache, water colour, charcoal etc, along with some water damaged paintings and her notebooks and letters'.[30]

To sort through that legacy, to get the damaged canvases restored and organize their exhibition and sale – this, Gus believed, could have been his own final duty to Gwen. When the crates from rue Babie were eventually unpacked and the secret riches of her life came spilling out, he was pierced with anguish and awe. There were letters to Rodin, Rilke, Jeanne, Nona and Véra; notebooks filled with spiritual reflection and minute annotations of art. 'Astonishing how she cultivated the scientific method,' Gus commented to Vivien, and now that he was able to look through the full evolution of Gwen's work – 'the secret message she whispered in such precious terms' – he admitted he was 'flummoxed' by their beauty and humbled by their rigour: 'I feel ready to shut up shop'.[31]

He urged Edwin to organize an exhibition for Gwen, conscious that there might be little time before London became a target for Hitler's bombs. 'It will be a satisfaction to show [her paintings] without dreaming for a moment their exquisite reticence will excite the multitudes,' he wrote, and he offered to take charge of the necessary work – the repairing and re-stretching of damaged canvases, as well as the mounting and framing. He reminded Edwin, too, that, as executor of the estate, it was up to him to decide which works should be kept and which could be sold: 'There will be a number of people apart from her old friends who will wish to acquire some of them'.[32]

A small show did take place in 1940, at the Wildenstein Gallery in Bond Street, which was too modest to provoke much conflict between father and son. A larger memorial exhibition, six years later, however, became a battleground, starting with Edwin's decision to appoint Francis Matthiesen, the London gallerist, to represent Gwen's art and take charge of the show. Gus had personally expended a massive amount of time and money to ensure it would be as inclusive as possible, tracking down galleries and private collectors on both sides of the Atlantic to ask for loans of Gwen's work. Over two hundred pictures were eventually hung in Matthiesen's gallery, ranging from her early student copy of the Metsu painting to some of her late views of Meudon. But still Gus considered Matthiesen had made very poor decisions, both in the works he'd excluded from the final cut and in the pictures he'd selected to illustrate the catalogue. It was all very 'ill chosen', he roared in an angry letter to Edwin: 'A self-portrait from the Tate over which I took some trouble is not shown.' Most exasperating for Gus, however, was Edwin's refusal to take any initiative in the affair: 'While this fiasco has been arranged I presume you have been conspicuously absent in your Mousehole.'[33]

Gus had at least got his way in writing a foreword to the exhibition catalogue, reworking an essay on Gwen that he'd prepared for *The Burlington Magazine* back in 1942: 'I don't fancy a stranger writing about her somehow,' he'd told Edwin.[34] Yet, the larger issue of whether there should be a fuller biography of Gwen's life and career was starting to provoke a much uglier clash of wills. An early proposal had come from the Pleiades Press to publish a short critical monograph, illustrated with reproductions of her work. That proposal had been made in the middle of the war and had been left to hang; but the 1946 exhibition, coupled with the discovery of some correspondence between Gwen and Rodin, which had been filed away at the Musée Rodin, had reawoken the publisher's interest. In a long, careful letter to Edwin, the Pleiades editor, a Mr Ranks, explained they now had ideas for a longer book, nothing 'sensational', but one that allowed readers to 'understand what [Gwen] was aiming for', drawing on interviews with her friends and peers, and offering a critical analysis of her art.

Ranks wanted to commission a professional writer, and Edwin thought that was right; Gus, however, was still unable to tolerate the idea of a stranger meddling in his sister's life and insisted, if there was to be a book, it should be written by him. 'I am the sole person living who is fitted for the task,' he argued, while also admitting to Edwin it would feel like an act of atonement. 'I blame myself continually for having even appeared to be unkind to her at times.'[35]

His confident claim to have known Gwen better than anyone was undercut, however, by his mysterious ignorance of basic facts. When Edwin asked for the exact date and place of Gwen's birth, Gus was forced to confess, 'I only know she was about 2 years older than me. We can find out at Haverfordwest where I think she was probably born.' His confidence in writing the book was also starting to falter. It would be a very 'great labour', he conceded, saying he would 'gladly retire' if Edwin could find someone 'better equipped'. But none of Edwin's suggestions were acceptable; when he floated the idea of Romilly's new wife, Katy, a professional writer and translator, Gus dismissed it angrily: 'She knows nothing of Gwen, [and] I don't fancy making her my confidante'.[36]

So the bickering continued; Gus felt so deeply that it was he who had principal rights and responsibilities to Gwen's life that he could only regard Edwin's ideas as intolerable intrusions. Their letters degenerated into the rancorous hurling of insults and into mutual accusations of obstruction and arrogance. 'I had no idea that my last communication re the book was going to arouse so foul an exhibition of bad taste (and worse) as your last letter displays,' spat Gus in response to one of Edwin's more bitter recriminations.[37] And, even after Ranks gave up on the project, defeated by the rages and the delays, the arguments persisted well into the mid-1950s, as Gus and Edwin both felt a book should be written, but could not agree on its form or its author. At one point, Wyndham Lewis put himself forward, proposing a double biography of both Gwen and Gus. But, in the end, it was Winnie who called a halt. Both she and Thornton had been dragged into the rows, yet, as Winnie pointed out, the squabbling over Gwen's biography had ignored the fundamental fact of who she was. 'There is no one in the world who would be more averse to having her private life made public,' she wrote, with dignified distaste. 'Gwen would wish to be forgotten. I think I knew her better than anyone else ever did and now I know this to be true I can't see what good it would do to her memory . . . Thornton feels the same way. Please be truly great and have mercy.'*[38]

The book was dropped and, for a while, Gwen did have the posthumous peace for which Winnie had begged. Lewis, when reviewing the memorial show at Matthiesen's, had described Gwen's life as 'chaste and bare and sad'; he had speculated about why she'd kept herself 'so isolated from the influences of the age'.[39] For several decades, this was the image of Gwen that Edwin, more passively, encouraged. During the few

---

* Gus remained very anxious about the most sensitive of Gwen's letters to Rodin. Edwin had entrusted them to Will and Alice's son, John Rothenstein, who was now director of the Tate, and Gus wrote several times to ensure they were locked up in a safe, away from prying eyes.

short years he'd known his aunt in Paris, he had seen how private she'd become with her art, regarding her pictures as prayers, not as objects to be bought and sold. And, for Edwin, it became his own form of vocation to protect Gwen's work, to sell as little of it as possible and eventually to bequeath it as a collection to an institution like the National Museum of Wales. As Edwin's niece, Rebecca John, wrote later, 'He guarded her work as if he owned her'.*[40]

Of course, there were exhibitions. The Matthiesen gallery mounted two more in London; Faerber and Maison, who took over the estate in 1964, held another that year. The work was featured in a number of touring shows and group exhibitions, and in 1968 the National Museum of Wales mounted a major retrospective. Yet, although Gwen hadn't been forgotten, her reputation remained modest, overshadowed by her brother, and it wasn't until the late 1970s, when the young and ambitious gallerist Anthony d'Offay took over from Faerber and Maison, that public perceptions began to shift.

D'Offay, a genuine admirer of Gwen's art, was frustrated by how little of it was in circulation, both at home and abroad. He persuaded Edwin that, even if the National Museum of Wales were to take charge of the collection, most of it would moulder away unseen, especially those pictures which were part of an extended series. Gwen's legacy would be better served, he felt, by allowing more of her work to be sold to 'people who knew [it was] precious and rare.' Edwin, who was now living alone in Wales, solitary and unwell, was swayed by d'Offay as he'd never been by his father. Caroline Cuthbert, who worked at the gallery, recalled how moved she was by the exhibition which d'Offay organized in 1976 – 'at the dinner [afterwards] he ended by singing to us all, very emotionally'.[41]

Edwin died two years later, and he didn't witness the efficiency with which d'Offay organized the spread of Gwen's reputation, linking up with the New York gallery Davis and Langdale, mounting a second,

---

* So closely did Edwin come to identify with Gwen, he went to live for a while at rue Babie. As he aged, he grew more and more like her, living on his own in a remote part of Wales. 'Absence rather than presence makes the heart grow fonder', he wrote to Caspar, when refusing a Christmas invitation. Towards the end, he even gave up painting.

larger show in 1982. Within a very short period of time – shockingly short to Rebecca John, who'd always regarded her great-aunt as a 'family secret' – Gwen was drawn into the mainstream of British art history. The 1985 retrospective *Gwen John: An Interior Life* toured from London to Manchester to Yale; two years later, the gallerist and scholar Cecily Langdale published a detailed critical study of the work and a catalogue raisonné; as prices for Gwen's art rose exponentially, journalists, historians and biographers began scouring the archives for material on her life.[42]

Gus would not live to see Gwen's posthumous fame, but he could claim to have been first to predict it. In the autumn of 1939, when he'd begun looking through the crates of his sister's work and realized what strange and beautiful treasures they contained, he'd commented, with sentimental gloom, 'In 50 years' time I will be known as the brother of Gwen John.' He had understood then how focused she'd been as an artist, how sure the line of development from her poised early portraits to her luminous, dappled canvases, to her final postage-stamp scribbles. He'd been struck all over again by the force of her discipline and the disgrace of his own scattered energies. 'I feel ashamed of wasting my time, thinking that life could last almost for ever,' he wrote. Yet it was not only Gwen who'd spurred Gus to reform. That autumn, as Poland fell to Germany, as the rest of Europe waited to see where Hitler would strike next, Gus could no longer cling to the illusion of his own immortality. He was sixty-one years old, his sister was dead, and the world in which he lived might soon be going up in flames.

Chapter Nineteen

A NATIONAL TREASURE

'I want a good 20 years or more to do
something respectable'
AUGUSTUS JOHN[1]

In the years leading up to the war, Gus had become an angry consumer of news. He'd railed against the spread of fascism in Europe, 'the bastard Franco', the 'old Schicklgruber' Hitler; he'd been an early joiner of the Artists' International Association, denouncing the 'philistine barbarism' of the Nazis, and he had shared the world's alarm as German troops marched into Austria and the Sudetenland.[2] Yet, as closely as he'd been following the bulletins on his wireless, Gus was unable to believe there would be another all-out war. In July 1939, when he and Dodo motored down to Saint-Rémy-de-Provence with Vivien, Tristan and Chiquita's daughter Zoe (now openly acknowledged as a John), Gus had packed the two family cars with enough luggage to stay for at least three months. By the time they reached the sun-scorched calm of their *mas*, the crisis negotiations between London, Paris and Berlin seemed a world away. One afternoon, drinking at a cafe with the artist André Derain, Gus had watched with almost idle curiosity as a group of newly uniformed soldiers began milling around the square, and had agreed with Derain that all this talk of war was 'un blague.'[3]

His insouciance was alarming to at least some of the children. In late August, Poppet made a series of emergency phone calls, concerned to know what arrangements her parents had made for returning home. She was infuriated to learn they had none. 'Mom and Pop . . . seemed to be in the dark about the international situation so I told them there was a man called Hitler who seemed to want a lot of things,' she wrote crossly to Edwin.[4] But, while Gus made a show of annoyance at having his summer disturbed, he knew Poppet was right to push. By the time he and Dodo had packed up the *mas*, he conceded that the threat was 'all too clear'; the neighbour to whom they entrusted their keys was touched by the 'pale smiles' with which they bade farewell to their house, as if fearing it might be years before they returned.

Still Gus refused to be panicked. Breaking the drive at Orléans, he took Vivien and Zoe out dancing, attracting a crowd of 'the jolliest girls'. When they reached Le Havre on 2 September and were told that the last available boat was about to sail, and was only accepting foot passengers, his mood remained bullishly jaunty. He bribed a couple of dock workers to winch up his cars, and waited until the very last moment before boarding himself. Dressed in a loud checked overcoat, waving a bottle of Châteauneuf-du-Pape in his hand, it was his symbolic gesture of allegiance and farewell to France – 'a magnificent exit,' Vivien dryly recalled, 'if one hadn't already been overdosed with similar rich occurrences'.[5]

The family reached Fryern late that night. The following morning, Gus retreated as usual to his studio, where he was working on a portrait of Zoe. At eleven o'clock, he came back to the house to sit with his family as Chamberlain announced the news that Britain was at war. Then, without comment, he turned off the radio and went back to work. Twenty-five years earlier, Gus had wanted to join his country's fight. Now, he could only think of it as a 'foul and bogus philosophy of violence'. To a friend, he wrote, 'I don't see what I can do but go on painting.'[6]

And it was real painting he wanted to do, painting that was sprung from his imagination. He started work on an epic romance, *The Tinkers*, or *The Little Concert*, which was set in an idealized Provençal landscape of mountains and cobalt sea views, and showed a trio of travelling musicians entertaining a group of peasants. It had the same choreographed feel as the *Pageant of War*, except the figures were bound together by music, not violence; as Gus freely admitted, it was 'as remote as possible from the world we precariously live in'. Essentially, *The Tinkers* was an elegy to his own past: the musicians and their antique instruments, the peasant women in their tall Welsh hats had all been retrieved from his earliest memories; the unsullied landscape was his youthful dream of Arcadia; and the young woman and her baby, at the painting's centre, was yet another incarnation of Ida.[7]

But escape from the war was only possible in the studio. When the Germans marched on Paris in June 1940, Gus was stricken: 'I can hardly bear to think of those monsters overrunning France'.[8] He was worried, too, for his children. His grown-up sons were serving in various branches of the military, and although his daughters were further removed – Vivien volunteering with the Red Cross, Poppet working in an army canteen, Zoe (an aspiring actor) and Amaryllis (a professional cellist) both entertaining the troops – the deadly reach of the Nazi bombers meant no one was reliably safe.

It was Edwin, though, who provoked his darkest anxieties. At the outbreak of war, Gus had assumed his son would try for an officer's commission, that he would aim for the benefits of a reasonable pay grade and the chance of a comfortable billet. Edwin, though, had chosen to enlist in the lower ranks of the military police, claiming that he lacked the right educational background for an officer's training, and this, to Gus, had seemed provocatively perverse.

He and Edwin had already begun spoiling for a fight over the issue of Gwen's legacy; now, they were openly at war. Edwin accused Gus of snobbery, of dismissing ordinary soldiers as 'dirt'; he also pointed out bitterly that, if Gus had wanted him to sport an officer's stripes, he should have provided him with a better education. Gus was outraged by these 'monstrous accusations': 'You . . . wax sarcastic about your educational disadvantages, an idée fixe with you. Forget it for god's sake', he wrote.[9] As the battle continued, letter by letter, insult by insult, Edwin was badly outgunned by his father, who picked apart each of his attacks with merciless pedantry. 'What's eating you? What I objected to was the tone of the second half of your last letter where you became definitely offensive. I replied accordingly. Your second letter shows your reasoning faculties are still in eclipse'.[10]

But Gus loathed this feud and was frightened by the deep disabling anger he saw in his son. When his own temper cooled, he offered intermittent gestures of reconciliation; in one of his letters, he suggested that the reason they fought so much was because they were so alike in their 'delicate' sensitivities – it was a shared form of 'neurotic inversion', he claimed (a term he'd got from the Russian philosopher Berdyaev). He tried to organize 'beer time' with Edwin whenever his son was passing through London, and when Edwin's wife and small baby came to visit Fryern, he was effortlessly courteous.

There were many visitors to Fryern, as there had been to Alderney during the previous war. It was distant enough from the southern ports to be safe from German bombs and its kitchen was generously stocked with produce from Dodo's garden and with food parcels sent by American friends. In addition to the families and friends, the waifs and strays, they also took in some evacuees, but the five bewildered London children who appeared in May 1940 did not, apparently, stay for long.

Gus himself was often absent. Although the Pathé news crew who came to Fryern in 1944 showed some footage of him pottering in the garden, he was spending long periods in London, working on portraits at his Tite Street studio. Some were official commissions of military men, including General Montgomery, who came to sit for Gus in 1944. Fresh from his heroic victories in the Desert War, Montgomery looked 'as tense as a hunting dog on a shoot', a 'queer combination of massiveness and delicacy'. Gus hoped to do something interesting, but the General was an impatient model and became incensed by what he saw as Gus's slipshod approach, dropping cigarette ash onto his palette and dabbing at his canvas in a kind of lurching dance. From what Montgomery could see of the portrait, it seemed a bizarre representation, his right ear was 'not in its proper place', and when Gus turned up for one of their sessions with a broken rib, having taken a fall the previous night, he could not contain his disgust. 'Who is this chap? He drinks, he's dirty. I know there are women in the background.' Conscious of Montgomery's disapproval, Gus lost courage – 'I feel his presence through the back of my head' – and he begged George Bernard Shaw to come and make diverting conversation. By the end, he thought he'd captured some truth in the portrait, but Montgomery loathed it, commenting only that it wasn't at all the 'kind of likeness' a man would want to pass on to his son.[11]

Harsh though the General had been in his dismissal of Gus, he hadn't been wrong about the drinking. This war, like the first, had made alcohol even more of a necessity to him; it blotted out the horror, induced illusions of well-being, and it also offered the physical camaraderie of fellow drinkers. Even when there were air raids, Gus would always prefer the refuge of a local pub or hotel bar to the smells, the dirt, the sheer human litter of public shelters. To those who drank with him, he came to be a comforting landmark of the war – an 'oaktrunked maestro', Dylan Thomas called him, while to Chips Channon he was a 'force of nature' and to Norman Douglas he was 'the last of the Titans'. In the summer of 1944, when the new Nazi flying bombs made the days as dangerous as the nights, Gus would refuse to be budged from his routines; according to one of the models he painted, he remained at his easel 'utterly unperturbed as . . . the bombs buzzed overhead. They might have been blue bottles for all he cared'.[12]

Yet Gus was not so much brave as fatalistic. While the skies boiled red over London, while buildings collapsed into rubble, he chose to regard death as a lottery: either his number would come up, or it wouldn't – and there were moments when he felt he didn't care. The war had tainted so many of his pleasures: travel was impossible, most of his friends were dispersed and, although Montgomery suspected there were women, sex too had become difficult for Gus. Legend might claim that he had fathered dozens of children, that when he walked through Chelsea he would pat the head of any passing infant in case it was one of his, but, now in his mid-sixties, he was enduring moments of mortifying impotence.* Mavis, with her frank sexuality, could still be relied upon. 'I cannot forget that last marvellous embrace, a real wonder, how was it possible,' he gratefully exclaimed.[13] Yet she was not always in town and Gus was perpetually anxious she might abandon him: 'I was getting so morbid thinking you had had enough or too much of me and had gone away from me,' he wrote to her in the spring of 1943. 'I don't want to see anybody but you, let alone paint.'

And it was painting, inevitably, that was coiled at the heart of his gloom. He had repeated his mistake of the previous war, allowing himself to be distracted by portraits. One night, the young artist Michael

---

* Officially, Gus fathered thirteen children, although there were a handful of others who grew up in the belief, or hope, they might be his.

Ayrton spotted Gus weaving through the blackout with tears coursing down his face; assuming he'd come from some showdown with a woman, Ayrton persuaded him into a taxi and tried to tease him out of his despair. Gus was beyond comfort, though, and, still weeping, he muttered over and over again to Ayrton, 'My work's not good enough, my work's not good enough.'[14]

This was the anguish that had dogged him for decades, and if Gus half hoped for a bomb to put an end to it all, he was equally afraid the war would rob him of his last chance to redeem himself.

Yet, to those who didn't know him well, his career seemed to be flourishing. The war, and its accompanying wave of cultural patriotism, had given a huge lift to his reputation. His works had been very prominent in *British Painting from Whistler*, an emblematic exhibition which had opened at the National Gallery in November 1940. The National had also mounted a show of his drawings, which Herbert Read – better known for his championship of the avant-garde – had praised as 'an astonishing record' of Gus's draughtsmanship, arguing that it was 'doubtful if any other contemporary artist in Europe could display such virtuosity and skill.'*[15]

In 1941, the drawings shown at the National Gallery were reproduced in a handsome publication; three years later, John Rothenstein edited a second collection of his work, for Phaidon, which ran to three editions in just two years. And all this was evidence that Gus, the delinquent 'marvel of Chelsea', was on his way to becoming a national treasure, was already being described by some as the grand old man of British painting.

There was some reassurance for him in this eminence, even if he wept for the loss of his old youthful powers. Gus had, in fact, been getting progressively grander with age, all trace of his provincial Welsh origins left far behind. At the start of the war, there had been talk of a knighthood, talk in which he'd been frankly interested, and when he heard that it might strengthen his case if he were to do the respectable thing and marry Dodo, he was being only half ironic when he went down on one knee to propose.

---

* The exhibition ran for several months, surviving two rounds of bomb damage. It also featured several pictures of Gwen's.

She, however, was too cross even to laugh. She'd given over her life to Gus and his art, had shared his belief in authentic living; to marry now, for the sake of a title, felt to her like a travesty. Gus could hardly object to Dodo's refusal, but he did mind being deprived of his honour, and he was tremendously pleased when, in 1942, he was offered the far more distinguished Order of Merit. 'It is the rarest of all orders,' he wrote proudly to Winnie, and he wished their father were still alive to see it. While he was careful not to flaunt his new title, he did make a strict point of correcting anyone who failed to add the crucial *OM* when addressing a letter to him.[16]

Finally, on 8 May 1945, the war in Europe was over. It had wasted five and a half years, Gus wrote, 'immobilising me for a devil of a time'. But he also felt a 'whiff of spring in the air, a gleam of blue sky', and, late the following summer, he and Dodo were able to return to Provence and to their *mas* at Saint-Rémy.[17]

Here, too, the war had left its mark. The local children looked rickety from years of rationing, and soldiers had broken into the *mas* and stolen some paintings. Yet the landscape had endured, as had the community, and when Gus went to drink in his local cafe, he felt the old illusion of beauty steal over him. 'Ensconced with a medicinal pastis or a glass of wine I achieved that agreeable sense of detachment in intimacy . . . I noted the grouping of the figures, the relationship of the heads; and sometimes I would be rewarded by the apparition of a face or a part of a face, a gesture or conjunction of forms which I recognised as belonging to a more real and harmonious world.'[18]

With that restoration of confidence, Gus could again believe there was life in his painting. He began work on a new lyric fantasy, a triptych based on the legend of Sainte Sara l'Egyptienne – a gypsy woman who was said to have been present with the three Marys at Christ's crucifixion and to have sailed with them to Saintes-Maries-de-la-Mer, the seaside capital of the Camargue.* Over the centuries, a shrine had been erected to Sara at Saintes-Maries and she had become patron saint of the Roma

---

* These were the Virgin Mary, Mary Magdalen and Mary of Clopas.

in France. Gus himself may have witnessed the pilgrimage the gypsies made each year, to bathe in the sea with Sara's statue, a semi-pagan ritual which may have influenced one section of his triptych, which showed a chorus of ecstatic women, angelically haloed yet sensuously naked.

'At last I feel myself interested only in work and feel always on the brink of discovery,' Gus wrote. A recent portrait he'd painted of Tristan, his beloved last child, had been a small treasure of observation and form. In the subtly elongated modelling of Tristan's head, the dreamily secretive cast of his eyes, he had captured a world of adolescent narcissism and vulnerability. Gus was still able to reach for something fresh, even in portraiture, but, in late 1952, he also made a brief but exuberant detour into sculpture.

A young Italian woman called Fiore de Henriques had come to Fryern to make a bust of him, and watching her at work as she moulded her clay had roused Gus to a captivated wonder. He'd begged for some basic tuition and had made several busts, of Dodo, Tristan and Yeats. To Jacob Epstein, the experiment had never looked convincing, it was too obviously the handiwork of a painter: 'sensitive but you could stick your finger through it.'[19] But Gus had believed in it and he found it fantastically exciting to go to the foundry and watch his work being cast into bronze – in January 1953, he announced to a journalist that 'a new phase in my history has opened up'.[20]

If there were distractions from work, they were becoming more serious, more political, than the romantic diversions of his past. His experiences in Jamaica had stirred him to become a more active champion of causes.* During the war, he'd campaigned for the release of German and Austrian refugee artists who'd been interned as enemy aliens; in his recently elected role as Secretary of the Gypsy Lore Society, he had also written to MPs and journalists to voice his alarm over the travelling restrictions which had been imposed on Roma families.

After the war, as more and more gypsies were corralled into urban

---

* After his return to London, Gus even had the vague idea of setting up a 'Jamaica House' that would provide some aid to the impoverished black workers by promoting sales of their crafts and produce.

wasteland, Gus kept up his campaign, declaring it was 'one of the shames of the modern world' that governments should take such brutal measures against the Roma people, who had 'enlivened and ornamented our countryside since the fifteenth century'.[21] But the countryside itself was also becoming a cause for Gus. He'd been grumbling for years about the insidious spread of roads and houses into the places he loved; now, in the post-war period, he claimed this spread had accelerated into an 'explosion of grey and concrete' which was laying waste all that remained of rural Britain. Even though much of the new building was necessary to rehouse a bombed and displaced nation, Gus considered it indefensibly hideous, 'a mixture of a concentration camp and a Butlins'.

Perhaps if he'd survived to the end of the 1960s, Gus might have found some common cause with the activism of the hippy generation and their repudiation of the capitalist-industrial world. Instead, he looked to the past, to the writings of the nineteenth-century social reformer Charles Fournier. Fournier was a utopian anarchist, a radical opponent of all centralized systems of power, and his vision of a world divided into small self-governing communities chimed deeply with Gus's own cherished romance of Arcadia. He saw in Fournier's vision a message for the modern age, a voice which spoke for the importance of safeguarding the old rural ways, for ridding the landscape of its 'monstrous industrial towns', and, during the 1950s, he became Fournier's enthusiastic apostle, recommending his writings to journalists, composing lengthy articles of his own for a local magazine, *The Delphic Oracle*.[22]

In Fournier's vision of a decentralized world, Gus saw not only an argument for beauty, but also for peace. The death toll from the recent war and from the atomic bomb which had so hideously forced its conclusion had convinced Gus that armed conflict could no longer be justified. By the late 1940s, he'd begun to immerse himself in the 'thrilling pacifism' of Bertrand Russell, and he became a loyal supporter of Russell's Campaign for Nuclear Disarmament. There were days when the international news was so depressing that Gus thought humanity deserved to be blown to 'a different planet'. His commitment to CND remained absolute, however, and on 17 September 1961, he struggled up to London to join its mass occupation of Trafalgar Square. Physically frail, and acting against doctor's orders, Gus sat down stiffly among the other protestors, declaring loudly that he was willing 'to go to prison if necessary'.[23]

If Gus worried that time was running out for the world, he half admitted it must eventually run out for him, and he began to think it would be fitting to leave some kind of account of his life. He'd had publishers chasing after a memoir for years, and, as early as 1930, he'd signed a contract with Jonathan Cape, confidently informing Henry Lamb that, 'We should all write autobiographies,' now. Writing had always been as necessary an outlet for him as it had been for Gwen, and having always been so prolific in his correspondence, in his penning of articles and poems, Gus imagined that producing a memoir would be equally enjoyable, requiring nothing more than the stringing together of his best ideas, along with some of his most 'side-splitting anecdotes'.

Yet a book presented far harder challenges, of course, and for years he shied away from making a start, pleading the excuse of travel, illness or work. In early 1941, he was presented with a simpler alternative, when Cyril Connolly invited him to write a series of short autobiographical essays for *Horizon* magazine. And he might never have got around to the memoir itself had he not taken deep offence with the biographical essay John Rothenstein had written for his 1944 book about Gus's work. So flawed and factually inaccurate did the essay seem to Gus that he felt honour-bound to correct it, and to publish his own full account of his life.

By 1949, he thought he was ready to begin; he had the eighteen *Horizon* essays as raw material and a 'tactful prodder', assigned by Cape, to help edit them into shape. But still the process proved agonizing to Gus. He very much wanted to prove himself as a writer, to show himself worthy of the authors like Whitman and Dostoyevsky who'd formed him, and of the contemporary novelists, Sartre and Camus, who interested him now. But he'd set himself unreachable standards, and as soon as he'd sent off a chapter to his editor, Daniel George, he would be plagued by indecision. 'I cannot write the simplest sentence without at once thinking of a better one,' he apologized, as he begged for his manuscript to be returned.[24]

In the end, George simply 'forgot' to send the chapters back, and, in 1952, the memoir, *Chiaroscuro*, was at last ready for publication. Or it was as ready as it could ever be. Despite the obsessive care which Gus had taken over the cadence of his sentences, the shaping of his paragraphs, he'd been unable to organize his material into a coherent narrative. After the opening chapters, in which he covered his childhood and his years at the Slade, he had simply let his story off the leash and had wandered so freely across themes and decades that his memoir read more like a scrapbook of reminiscence. In the face of this utter disregard of chronology, it may have been Cape who insisted on the pre-emptive subtitle *Fragments of Autobiography*.

Haphazard as the reminiscences were, however, some of them were finely done. Gus wrote with wit and feeling when he recalled himself as a teenager, naively fascinated by the impact of a new Catholic priest in Tenby whose 'knowing smile and mincing gait' seemed to earn him 'a good many converts, especially among the girls.'[25] He vividly remembered his travels, his first visit to Galway, entranced by the 'cries of fish-women', or his joy in the landscape of north Wales, where 'the slow drama of the sky unfolded itself . . . the mountains shifted and the illumination changed'.[26] He also devoted a long and detailed chapter to Gwen, describing moments from their shared childhood and their years at the Slade, correcting any notion that she might have been the lesser sibling by stressing the force of her 'talented and original' spirit, her 'lofty pride and implacable will'.[27]

It was on the strength of such memories that *The Guardian*, among others, declared Gus 'a writer of genius'. Crammed and disordered though *Chiaroscuro* was, its descriptions of journeys to extraordinary places, of meetings with remarkable men, read almost like a fairy tale to readers in grey, post-war Britain, while Gus himself seemed like a survivor from a more fabulous past – 'a giant', one critic wrote, 'covered with the dust of a falling world'.[28]

Yet, for readers who resisted its charisma, the memoir was a disappointment. Much of its writing was actually laboured, its paragraphs struggling for air, its sentences knotting into over-elaborate metaphor and straining after literary effects. But a far more fundamental failing was its lack of honesty. Within its 285 pages of anecdote, reminiscence and aperçu, there was, as Cyril Connolly observed, almost nothing of the 'hard truth'. There was no reference to the deaths of Ida or Pyramus, while the short memorial of Henry was stiffly facetious. Gus had also edited out his struggles with alcohol, his battle to retain care of his children, and, in writing about Gwen, he'd given no hint of their complicated, mutually hurtful relationship, no hint that Gwen had ever hated her brother to the point of calling him her 'torment', her 'evil genius'.

Gus was conscious of the gaps and evasions, and in the closing pages of *Chiaroscuro* he offered up a terse defence of his right to privacy. 'I am not accustomed to lay bare my heart to the first comer or indeed anyone'.[29] Yet, even where he did make one admission of regret, acknowledging the 'sad lack of system' that had led to all 'the ruined canvases which encumber my studio', it read more like a theatre of ruefulness. It made no mention of the effort it had cost Gus to go into the studio some days and face up to his fear of failure.

Wyndham Lewis was particularly frustrated by all that Gus had concealed. He wrote about *Chiaroscuro* for *The Spectator* and, in a passage that was deleted from his otherwise flattering review, he claimed that 'everyone would [have been] delighted to look into [John's] heart . . . so great a heart as his is surely the concern of everybody.'[30] In private, Gus also admitted that his 'horror of showing emotion', his need to conceal himself 'under a show of bravura & high-spirits' had become a habit too strong to break.[31] Seven years later, when Caitlin Macnamara published her own memoir, *Leftover Life to Kill*, Gus was awed by her candour: 'As a self-portrait it is an absolute knock out. Unlike me she cannot avoid the truth even at its ghastliest.'[32]

Therapy, so beloved of his American friends, but rather despised by Gus, might have helped him to speak more frankly about himself. But when he felt buffeted by his rages and his impulses, when he felt the prisoner of his own inhibitions – above all, when he found himself muttering fearfully, 'I'm just a legend I'm not a real person at all' – Gus despaired that there was less and less of a self of which to speak.[33]

Although he would start work on a second memoir, *Finishing Touches*, it would be even more insubstantial than the first.*

But Gus would not allow any other writer near his life. In 1951, the journalist and historian Alan Moorehead had offered himself as a prospective biographer, and Gus, still in the middle of writing *Chiaroscuro*, had thought it might be useful to have someone else to help untangle his muddles over facts and dates.† It was only when he read an early draft of Moorehead's biography that he realized it would be so very personal. He was genuinely shocked by the material Moorehead had sourced from interviews with his colleagues and friends, and even more disgusted by the writer's own commentary. 'Wrong . . . Liar', he scribbled angrily over the manuscript, and he sent it back with a furious dismissal: '*All your statements of fact are wrong . . . Your own observations I found quite incredibly out of place. I refuse to authorise this effort of a biography*'.[34]

Gus couldn't and wouldn't recognize himself in what Moorehead had written, but his disgust may also have come from the fear of having his life set in stone. He needed to believe there were more chapters to be written, more epiphanies to be had. In 1953, when he was offered the accolade of a one-man show at the Royal Academy, it mattered desperately to him that it would present him as a still-creative force. 'References to my early work sometimes make me sick as if I had done nothing since,' he grumbled; in the months leading up to the show, he barely left his studio.[35] 'I am working desperately – even at night I repaint and resculpt *agonisingly*', he told Amaryllis.[36] But time was against him. When the exhibition opened in March 1954, with 460 works on show, it was the early pictures that dominated, the drawings of Gus's youth that were celebrated for their 'freedom, sureness, versatility and sheer voluptuous

---

* This second volume offered no more insight into Gus's relationship with Gwen, although it did pay her a careful tribute: 'Few on meeting this retiring person in black, with her tiny hands and feet, soft almost inaudible voice and delicate Pembrokeshire accent, would have guessed that here was the greatest woman artist of her age or, I think, of any other'.
† As Moorehead discovered early on, Gus had a poetic – or wilful – approach to chronology, preferring to 'look at the past like one large painting – all dates present simultaneously'.

achievement', the pre-war panels which were admired for their 'radiant Tennysonian' poetry'.*[37]

Gus chose to be happy: 'I have had a wonderful press,' he said and Dodo, who'd borne the brunt of his nerves, confessed 'it was such a relief to see Augustus really pleased'. But the reviews had come with the now-familiar caveat that his early and extraordinary potential had never been realized. According to *The Times*, Gus had partly been a victim of history, born several centuries too late for the particular nature of his talents to thrive. But there was an implication, too, that Gus had also been born with the wrong personality – that he was simply too 'great a man . . . to practise the painter's slow and nine-tenths mechanical art.'[38]

Gus may have doubted that the critic's use of 'great' was complimentary, but he couldn't deny his own lack of method, which was still thwarting his hopes for the Sainte Sara triptych. He continued to do battle, adding and subtracting elements, redrawing outlines in chalk, splashing on gold and silver paint. Some footage that was filmed in his studio, during the mid-1950s, showed Gus looking very vigorous in his painting smock and beret, discoursing energetically about his work. Yet his vision for the triptych had receded, and his horror of failure had grown. Often, he returned to Gwen's pictures, 'peer[ing] at them fixedly, almost obsessively', as though trying to decipher the methods by which she'd overcome her own 'fear of falling short' – her probing into fundamentals, her painting of multiple versions of a single image. But he could not absorb her secrets now and he would fall back defeated, muttering, 'What the hell do I know about art?'[39]

Throughout this decade, too, the faltering in Gus's confidence had been stalked by problems with his health. In 1950, he and Dodo had been forced to give up their *mas*, acknowledging that the effort of packing up the car and driving through France had become too hard and that the stiffening in Gus's joints, the loss of his old easy grace had made it difficult for him to navigate the rocky Provençal terrain. Four years later, Gus was confronted with more brutal evidence of his decline when he had to undergo surgery on his prostate and bladder. Afterwards, he

---

* The exhibition ran for two months, attracting nearly 90,000 visitors (including a stick-thin Luisa Casati who came to look at the portrait of herself).

boasted ironically of his miraculous powers of recovery, and claimed to be looking forward to his first taste of air travel when he and Dodo took a convalescent holiday in Spain. But the operation had shaken him more than he realized. Romilly, who drove Gus and Dodo to London Airport, saw suddenly that his parents had grown anxious and old – both of them spooked by the milling crowds, the unfamiliar hustle of departure boards and travel desks. 'Augustus was glaring angrily at me for having got them into this fearful situation while Dodo, thinking I was about to desert them, cried out in anguish, "don't leave us, don't leave us".'[40] Even when they arrived safely at their Spanish hotel, Gus was still 'weak as a cat', the local wine made him dizzy and the landscape seemed too dauntingly 'superb' for him to paint.

Travel, for so many years his addiction and his joy, had become a fearful thing to Gus, and he would only risk going abroad one more time, in 1956, when Matthew Smith, the painter and former husband of Gwen Salmond, took him to Aix for an exhibition of Cézanne. Everything had been organized – tickets, currency, hotels – yet, while the exhibition had been 'wonderful' and Gus had been able to visit Poppet and her husband at their Provençal house in Opio, he had wanted only to be at home – finally understanding what Gwen had felt when she'd kept herself so cocooned in her Meudon life.

He had needed to get away from Provence too because, wonderful though the Cézannes had been, they had reinforced his own feelings of impotence. 'Painting seems more mysterious than ever, if not utterly impossible', he lamented to Matthew Smith.[41] As he continued to wrestle with his Sainte Sara canvas, he admitted, 'This working from the imagination is killing me. I find myself so variable that sometimes I lose all sense of identity and even forget my name'.[42] When he was very low, Gus looked back to the time when he and Dickson Innes had been in north Wales together, euphoric with the belief that they were reinventing landscape painting. He wondered even now if he could return to those mountains in Wales, to find a new house and recover the soul of his art. But Dodo could not be persuaded to make another move. So, with the triptych still unfinished, Gus retreated back to the easier work of portraits.

Most were mediocre, some frankly bad, his images of women now tending towards a generic doe-eyed sentimentality. Anthony Bertram wrote dismissively that Gus no longer seemed 'to have any profound interest in his sitters, or [to have achieved] any certain method of expressing such interest'.[43] And yet there were still exceptions. Portraits of his contemporaries – 'old buffers' like Thomas Beecham, Walter de la Mare and Gilbert Murray – were poignantly and personally evocative. John Cowper Powys was awed by the final drawing Gus did of him; it was, he wrote, 'simply of my very soul'.[44]

The humiliations and frustrations of age were softened, just a little, by the mellowing of Gus's relationships with family (even though that mellowing stopped short of him ever being called Grandpa by his growing tribe of grandchildren). He and Edwin still argued – as late as 1961 they'd found fresh dispute in some new drawings of Gwen's which had come to light, and which each suspected the other of having known about in secret. Yet, in general, Gus had become less critical of his children, less inhibited in his affections and more inclined to accept them for who they were.

David, by now, had abandoned his music career and had married for a second time; yet, as father to his own three daughters, he had become far less nervous around Gus. Even when his second marriage ended and his wife Simone moved in to help Dodo with the house, there was no lingering awkwardness. In 1960, when Gus was interviewed for the television programme *Face to Face*, David sent fond assurances to 'Dear Daddy' that he'd 'come off really well' in the interview and that he'd seemed 'completely natural. Most affecting'.[45]

Gus's relationship with Caspar had also improved. For years, he'd belittled his son's career and been cool towards his wife Mary (whom Caspar had married in 1944), claiming unkindly that he always used to hide in his studio whenever they came to Fryern. Yet, as Caspar had risen to extraordinary levels of distinction – Knight Companion of the Order of the Bath, Admiral of the Fleet, then First Sea Lord – Gus had come to feel a certain awe of his son. It was a small tragedy for them both that his acknowledgement had arrived so late, yet it had allowed Caspar to finally forgive the chaos of his childhood, and to concede the disciplined struggle behind Gus's success – 'He worked harder than anyone'. Even though Caspar, like most of his siblings, refused to trade on the family name, he could now speak of his father's career with pride and would be very severe with anyone who tried to describe Gus and his life as bohemian. It was a lasting regret to Caspar that, just as he was learning to talk openly with his father, Gus himself was becoming even more chronically deaf and the two of them had to communicate in bellows.[46]

Even Robin, the most distant of the boys, had attempted some sort of reconciliation with Gus. Mostly, he kept himself at a remove from the family, drifting through jobs and thinking about philosophy and art (according to Edwin, with whom he was in closest contact, he did nothing but gaze 'at a pot of marmalade'[47]). When *Chiaroscuro* had been published in 1952, Robin had written an unexpectedly warm letter to Gus – 'I often long very greatly to see you and the others . . . There is such an enormous amount I can learn from you' – and, with that gesture, he'd gone a little way to filling the silence between them.

Gus no longer had the fire in his belly for quarrels. He grumbled about Robin's financial dependency and wished his son could find some 'rich woman' to look after him (Robin did in fact marry in the late 1950s). But he stoically continued to pay Robin's allowance, just as he continued to support clever, charming and literary Romilly, who was always going to earn more from his casual labouring jobs than he did from his poetry. He was pleased that Poppet, for her third husband, had chosen an artist, Willem Pol. 'Thank god there is a painter in the family,' he wrote in 1952 – although, a few years later, his satisfaction might have come to irk Vivien when she began painting again, acquiring a modest reputation for her domestic interiors and scenes from provincial life.*

The two other daughters, late additions to the family, were easiest for Gus to admire. Zoe was showing admirable 'gumption' (his favourite compliment) in pursuit of her acting career, and he was very proud of Amaryllis, who was now an exceptionally fine cellist and showed proof

---

* Vivien's work would feature in several group exhibitions at the Royal Academy and she would exhibit with the London Group. Gus's illegitimate daughter Gwyneth Johnstone, born in 1914, also became an artist.

of his own forceful genes in her volatile temper and auburn hair.* She indulged and adored him in return. In 1960, when Gus wrote to her about painting her portrait, the tone of his letter might have been judged crass, even outlandish by an outsider; to Amaryllis, it reflected only their private code. 'Do you like babies? I adore them! If you should ever feel the urge to produce one, just give me a nudge and I will do my best, even if it took all my might to collaborate successfully. Such an experiment might prove more effective than catching you on the hop with a paintbrush.'[48]

Even in his late seventies and early eighties, Gus needed to believe himself capable of loving and of arousing love. His last serious affair had been in 1950, when a young art student had shown herself miraculously responsive to his attentions. Out of sheer gratitude, he'd declared he would give up everything for her – his family and Fryern – and he'd felt himself hideously wronged when his children had ordered him to go and stay with Poppet and recover his senses. His mood had been awful, vicious and self-pitying, and when he'd started to take out his misery on Dodo, Poppet had turned on him with disgust. The cold articulate force of her rage had stopped Gus in his tracks – 'I didn't know you had it in you', he'd said with grudging admiration – for, however much it maddened him to be thwarted in any way, he enjoyed a good fight with a critical adversary. Sometimes, Gus thought he'd never been criticized enough.

After that brief melodrama, the 'troublesome condition' of his prostate and bladder had temporarily quashed his interest in sex. He'd taken comfort in companionable meetings with friends and with former lovers, like Alick Schepeler, with whom he had pleasurable chats about books, friends and the state of their health. But, while William Empson thought Gus had become 'a ghost of his former self', the old hungers could still flicker, and thoughts of Mavis, 'the old cow', could still tear his heart. When he went up to London to paint (using a studio in Charlotte Street, which was, coincidentally, the same one he'd rented on leaving the Slade,

---

* One of Amaryllis's early teachers had been Guilhermina Suggia, although she had been less impressed by the cellist than Gus.

over half a century ago), he kept a love poem tucked in his pocket on the off chance of encountering some attractive young woman.

'He seems to set a terrific pace,' commented Mavis bluntly. 'I wonder how the old boy doesn't drop dead in his tracks.'[49] Even in the spring of 1959, when Gus was eighty-one, he could still assure Zoe that the warm weather was having its reliably enlivening effect, 'with me at any rate [it] reawakens one's dormant energy and one begins to experience a kind of second childhood with all its courage'.[50] When the mood was on him, he could still be the centre of any room. 'He had a marvellous sense of style,' thought the painter Lucian Freud, and that October, when Gus went to Tenby to be awarded Freedom of the Borough, he carried the occasion with his old panache.

He'd worried, beforehand, about making that trip, about the length of journey and about what he would feel on returning to his childhood town. Two decades had passed since he'd buried his father there. Yet the beauty of the coast and the Pembrokeshire countryside had brought back a rush of comic and bittersweet memories, and Gus had felt buoyed with eloquence as he'd entertained a packed town hall with stories of his youth. Afterwards, when he signed the Freedom Roll and the audience rose to sing 'For He's a Jolly Good Fellow', tears of pride, regret and nostalgia had sprung to his eyes.

Tenby was the last ambitious journey Gus would attempt. Towards the end of that year, his body began to shut down; his hearing and eyesight were deteriorating fast and the arthritis in his hand was complicated by a persistent tremor. Trips up to London became difficult and, while he continued to work down at Fryern, he had to break off for regular rests. By eight o'clock in the evening, he was ready for bed, taking his pipe, his books and his supper tray up to his room. He listened to his wireless, fiddling with the dials as he scoured the *Radio Times* for programmes of interest. When eventually he fell into a fitful doze, his pipe was often still dangerously smouldering, his beret still on his head.

Aside from the radio, one of Gus's most reliable sources of entertainment was the post. He had accumulated a wide international network of clients, lovers and friends over the eight decades of his life, and he remained a vigorous correspondent. Even if his handwriting had grown crabbier with age – almost unrecognizable from the exuberant scrawl of his youth – he had, if anything, become even more generous, ready to give money and encouragement to those who asked for it, in regular contact with fellow artists, buyers, writers, ready to lend support to his dearest political causes.

But the post could also bring bad news. Several of Gus's friends had died some years ago – Mary Dowdall, Will Rothenstein and Francis Macnamara – and those losses were cruelly accumulating. In 1953, Gus had been 'much cast down' by the death of Dylan Thomas, and he was unnerved by that of Alick Schepeler, who died in 1956, just weeks after retiring from her job at *The Illustrated London News*.[51] In 1957, Alick was followed by Luisa Casati, who finally joined the spirits with whom she'd long believed herself in magical communion, and, a much greater grief to Gus, by Wyndham Lewis.

There had been a period of extreme coldness between them just after the war. Gus had thought Lewis a coward for sitting out the conflict in America; he'd also thought Lewis a fool when he'd returned home, boasting of having been some kind of political 'big shot' in the States. In 1951, however, a tumour in his pituitary gland had robbed Lewis of his sight, and Gus had felt only loyalty to 'my old friend and enemy'. He was careful to sustain their old combative banter, but equally careful to look after Lewis, encouraging him to keep on writing, and making sure that, when they went out for dinner, Lewis's food had been cut up for him in advance.

Lewis had been one of the more stimulating, romantic influences of Gus's youth, challenging him to read, think and write more adventurously. Apart from Dickson Innes, and Conder perhaps, he'd had fewer comparable companionships with painters, but, during the mid-1940s, he'd become close to Matthew Smith after inviting him to Fryern to recover from the deaths of both his sons in the war. As the two men had painted each other's portraits and talked about work, Gus had come to place great trust in Smith's judgement. And when he too died, in 1959, it was for Gus as though the last of his intellectual and artistic peers had gone.

There were periods, now, when these multiplying losses, these reminders of mortality made the world intolerable to Gus. The slightest irritation – a bad bottle of wine, an incautiously voiced opinion, an intrusive phone call – could provoke him to disproportionate rage. Dodo inevitably bore the brunt of it. An elegiac series of photographs which Cecil Beaton took of them in the gardens of Fryern in 1960 – Gus in his beret and Dodo in her Chinese sun hat – gave no indication of the gulf between them. The more patiently and meticulously Dodo tried to care for Gus, the more humiliatingly he felt his age. 'One is far too much at the mercy of other people,' he complained. 'I shall never get used to it.' The revenge he took on Dodo could be vile. He sniped at her for being illiterate and stupid, and he developed an insane snobbish malice about her background, writing to Robin that she had come from 'a stinking cockney breed' and congratulating David on being 'a true born Nettleship' and therefore free from the taint of 'fishy' McNeill genes.*[52]

But Gus knew that his quarrel was not with Dodo, but with the hideous advance of his own dereliction. 'Hell seems nearer every day. I have never felt so near it as at Fryern Court', he wrote, and querulously he complained of his obligation to 'pretend to work away gaily and enjoy my worldwide renown.'[53] Ironically, that renown was expanding in proportion to his own decline – honours were coming to him from America, France and Belgium, journalists from newspapers, radio and television were begging for interviews. Gus, in his early eighties, had become more than a national treasure, he was a fabulous relic, and while it reassured him to know he was not forgotten, he was conscious that, with every new headline, every column inch, his life and his work were being more deeply subsumed into legend. The only proof of greatness he really wanted was from painting, and, while he'd announced in a 1957 interview that he wanted to live for 'another 100 years', Gus could no longer pretend there was any real work left in him.[54]

In May 1961, he was forced to send a melancholy note to Charles Wheeler at the Royal Academy, confessing that their plan for a public unveiling of his Sainte Sara triptych could never be realized – 'it would be a disappointment for you and perhaps a disaster for me'.[55] Gus had continued to hold out intermittent hopes for the painting and continued to believe it might be the masterpiece of his late career, but in the

---

* Ethel Nettleship died in 1961, anxious for her nephews to know that she regretted having no money to bequeath them. Her sister Ursula died in 1968.

end it had defeated him. He might have felt some bitter relief had he known that, shortly after his death, vandals would break into his studio and cover the three giant panels with graffiti and splashes of paint. An honest end, he might have thought, for a failed piece of art.

All of Gus's remaining stamina now was focused on portraits, 'lesser handier things'. Even if the lines of his drawings were shakier, they could still be true, and a sketch he made of Dodo, her body gracefully erect, her white hair and wrinkles enhancing the lovely planes of her face, may well have been his way of apologizing for his cruelty. The last of his portraits in oils, however, had been a fiasco. It was of Beaton – a work he'd begun in 1960 – and, when Gus tried to return to it in early 1961, his hands were shaking so badly as he stabbed at the canvas, his sense of colour so awry, that Beaton found their sessions excruciating. Worst of all for Beaton was having to listen to Gus's muttered assurances that the portrait was going to be the 'best I have painted'.

To Beaton, Gus seemed almost senile, and by the summer he was experiencing episodes of real confusion. The children were taking it in turns to assist with his care, and one night, when Zoe was at Fryern, Gus came stumbling up to her bedroom, still wearing his beret and carrying a torch. 'Thought you might be cold,' he mumbled, and heaved himself, wheezing, on top of her. Zoe could see her father was in some altered state and she simply held him in her arms as he continued to mutter, 'Can't seem to do it now, I don't know'. Eventually, when he was calm, she led him back to his bed.

Between the confusion, Gus had periods of perfect clarity, but these were crueller still, sharpening his sense that he was now 'a lost soul', marooned in the wreckage of his body. To Poppet, he wrote, 'I have been struck deaf and dumb so that the silence here is almost more than I can bear.' And, while he wanted to believe he might recover if he were taken to some warmer, brighter place, he knew he was deluding himself. He was too ill to travel and, besides, he asked, 'where is there to go?'[56]

In the end, Gus was released from his misery by the rapid onset of illness. A cold he'd caught in early autumn developed into a chest infection, and, in his fever and his weakening state, he was able to let go of his bitterness. To Dodo and Vivien, who were sharing the work of nursing him, he was sweetly compliant, apologizing for being a blundering nuisance and begging them not to exhaust themselves. By 30 October, his heart was failing, and, even though he still attempted to haul himself out of bed and sit in his favourite armchair, he was clearly approaching the end, his breathing laboured, his speech hesitant and wandering.

David had also come down to Fryern and, that evening, he took it in turns with Dodo and Vivien to keep watch over what they knew must be Gus's final hours. Almost the last words he spoke were a delirious rambling about a picture he thought he'd just done, a painting of a beautiful town. Perhaps it was his version of the 'miraculous caves' which Ida had hallucinated as her own end approached. Early the next morning, when Dorelia called out to the others that Gus had gone, David was very comforted to see how peaceful his father looked, 'His face . . . very fine, calm and smoothed out, in death.'[57]

The funeral service at Fordingbridge Church was small, and Gus was buried modestly at the nearby cemetery, the name on his gravestone carved in plain Roman letters. Groups of gypsy mourners came privately to pay their respects, one of them leaving a wild rose and commenting simply, 'The first time I've seen you take a back seat, old Rai. Here is a wild rose from a wild man.' But, in every other respect, Gus's death was a public event. While Gwen still lay in an unmarked grave on the other side of the Channel, her reputation in the hands of a diminishing number of connoisseurs, Gus was memorialized in a slew of mostly reverential obituaries: *The New York Times* acclaimed him not only as 'the grand old man of British painting', but as 'one of the greatest in British history'; *The Daily Telegraph* described his death as 'the close of an era'; and, although *The Times* attempted a note of toughness, remarking that perhaps 'his fame [was] not as secure as it ought to be', the collective tone was expressed by the critic Richard Hughes, who described Augustus John as 'a man in the 50 megaton range'.[58]

A memorial service was held in London early the following year, at St-Martin-in-the-Fields, and Lord David Cecil delivered an emotional address in which he recalled his own last meeting with Gus. 'It was a fine July evening. We sat for perhaps half an hour. Nothing very serious was spoken of. Augustus, genial, friendly, Jove-like, was in light-hearted mood and told us tales of his past, picturesquely and also with a delightful mischief. But, as we drove away, my friend said to me "we have had a very rare experience, we have been with a great man."'

That perception of greatness would linger for a while, and Gus's art and his life story would remain very marketable. In 1961 and 1962, Christie's organized two large sales of the works which were still in the family's possession; in 1972, the National Gallery of Wales purchased over 1,000 drawings, 110 paintings and 3 bronzes; several significant exhibitions were held; a television documentary was made. Five years after Dodo's death, in 1969, Michael Holroyd published the first of his two-volume biography. But, as *The Times* had predicted, Gus's reputation was not secure. His death had prompted a run on his work, much of it the late, mediocre portraits which he'd never intended for public view.*
And, over the years, as the force of his living personality was replaced by stale, second-hand anecdote, there was less and less to divert attention from the shortcomings of his art. By 1978, the critic Richard Shone was ready to ask the damning question of whether Gus's brilliance had simply been a fiction, spun out of charisma and circumstance. 'Was he really that good? What was it that seduced so many into making comparisons which strike us now as ludicrous – that his drawings bear comparison with Michelangelo's, his etchings are as fine as Rembrandt's, his paintings superior to Gauguin's.'[59]

In 2004, when the Tate mounted a joint retrospective of both Gwen and Augustus's work, Gwen's reputation had all but eclipsed his. She'd caught hold of the public imagination not only as an artist, but as a woman who'd lived, loved and worked by her own independent choices – at a time when such independence was rare. Yet she'd become fascinating, too, because she'd embraced a life of such mysterious rectitude, a rectitude which, in contrast to the highly documented dramas of her brother's career, had left her story so tantalizingly punctuated with silences and gaps, and so open to interpretation by the biographers, novelists and poets who'd begun writing about her.

Gus, of course, had always insisted that he and Gwen were fundamentally alike in their scorn for society, their ache for love. He'd claimed

---

* When Dodo and the children had sorted through the mass of work in Gus's studio, they'd chosen to burn the very worst of it.

it was the loss of their mother, their father's ineptitude, which had shaped them both. But he'd also stressed that other, happier elements in their childhood had been no less formative, especially the freedom they'd been given to roam around the countryside, to stare at gypsy camps, to swim in wild places, to read and paint.

As he'd written in his memoir, it was that freedom which had allowed both him and Gwen to imagine other lives. 'The messages of earth and changing sky . . . the example of the nomads, our desultory but voracious reading and unfettered daydreams all conspired to stir up discontent and longing for a wider free world than that symbolically enclosed by Tenby's town walls; we craved for Art Liberty Life, perhaps Love!'[60]

And it was perhaps in their craving for those great, capitalized wonders, in their need to reach beyond their own limits, that the Johns were most alike as siblings. Even when Gus appeared to be squandering his talent, to be settling for the easiest options, he was still always reading and thinking, still mustering his hopes for the next epic work, the next pure adventure. Equally, even when Gwen appeared to have withdrawn from her art and to have renounced her professional ambitions, she was still engaged in the act of creation – refashioning herself into a lover who was worthy of Rodin, into a Catholic who was worthy of God.

When David Cecil gave his memorial speech for Gus, he said, 'No one who knew him can dissociate the artist from the man. The grandeur of the one is the grandeur of the other.' Maynard Walker, on first meeting Gwen, had celebrated her in almost identical terms, as 'a very great woman, a very great artist.' The Johns could be difficult – ruthless, selfish, petulant and stubborn. But Ida, who'd endured so much from them, would also believe that they lived and worked at a higher tilt, and for higher stakes, than anyone she knew. She had a theory, she once told Mary Dowdall, that the vast majority of the human race, however talented or brilliant, were in some way '2nd rate'. She included herself, and even her beloved Rani, in this: 'You and I dear are puddings – with plums in perhaps – & good suet – but puddings.' In fact, Ida told Mary, she knew of only two people who uniquely transcended her rule: 'in my conception of things Augustus is essentially 1st rate . . . As to women, I know only one firster & that is Gwen John'.[61]

NOTES

All correspondence to and from Gwen and Augustus John is held at the National Library of Wales (NLW), unless otherwise specified.

Copies of letters to and from Augustus John which are held in other archives can be found in Michael Holroyd's Research Papers, also at NLW.

Letters from Gwen John to Auguste Rodin are held at the Musée Rodin in Paris.

For ease of reference, I have selectively indicated other sources where the letters are cited or reprinted in full, including the selected edition of Ida John's letters published by Michael Holroyd and Rebecca John, and the selected edition of Gwen John's letters and unpublished notebooks by Ceridwen Lloyd-Morgan.

INTRODUCTION

1. Thomson, Belinda, 'Gwen John', *The Burlington Magazine*, February 1986, p. 163.
2. Tickner, Lisa, 'Augustus's Sister', *Gwen John and Augustus John* (London: Tate Publishing, 2004), p. 23.

CHAPTER ONE

1. John, Augustus, with Holroyd, Michael (ed.), *Augustus John: Autobiography* (London: Jonathan Cape, 1975), p. 25. (This is an amalgamated edition of *Chiaroscuro* and *Finishing Touches*, hereafter referred to as *Autobiography*.)
2. Gwen John in a draft letter to Véra Oumançoff, undated, 1928, cited in Boyd Haycock, David, *Brilliant Destiny: The Age of Augustus John* (London: Lund Humphries, 2023), p. 19; John, Augustus, *Autobiography*, p. 24.

3 John, Augustus, *Autobiography*, p. 3.
4 Thornton John in a letter to Augustus John, 3 February 1959, cited in Holroyd, Michael, *Augustus John: The New Biography* (London: Vintage, 1997), p. 28.
5 John, Augustus, *Autobiography*, p. 36.
6 Ibid, p. 20.
7 Langdale, Cecily, *Gwen John* (New Haven and London: Yale University Press, 1987), p. 4, and John, Augustus, *Autobiography*, p. 27.
8 Gwen John in a letter to Véra Oumançoff, n.d.,1928, cited in Boyd Haycock, *Brilliant Destiny*, p. 19.
9 John, Augustus, *Autobiography*, p. 43.
10 Gwen John in a draft letter to Auguste Rodin, n.d., 1908–9, cited in Boyd Haycock, *Brilliant Destiny*, p. 22.
11 John, Augustus, *Autobiography*, p. 422.
12 Ibid, p. 33.
13 Ibid, p. 283.
14 John, Edwin, *Evening Standard*, 19 January 1929, cited in Holroyd, *Augustus John: The New Biography*, p. 28.
15 Cited in Boyd Haycock, *Brilliant Destiny*, p. 23.
16 John, Augustus, *Autobiography*, p. 58.

CHAPTER TWO

1 Henry Tonks in a letter to Ronald Gray, 11 January 1901, cited in Holroyd, Michael, *Augustus John: The New Biography* (London: Vintage, 1997), p. 40.
2 Boyd Haycock, David, *Drawn from Life* (London: Paul Hoberton, 2018), p. 38.
3 Roe, Sue, *Gwen John: A Life* (London: Vintage, 2002), p. 19.
4 Boyd Haycock, David, *Brilliant Destiny: The Age of Augustus John* (London: Lund Humphries, 2023), p. 28.
5 John, Augustus, with Holroyd, Michael (ed.), *Augustus John: Autobiography* (London: Jonathan Cape, 1975), p. 50.
6 Holroyd, *Augustus John: The New Biography*, p. 79.
7 *The Times*, 20 April 1894, cited in Boyd Haycock, *Brilliant Destiny*, p. 26.
8 Roe, p. 14.
9 Chitty, Susan, *Gwen John: 1876–1939* (London: Hodder & Stoughton, 1985), p. 37.
10 Tickner, Lisa, 'Augustus's Sister', *Gwen John and Augustus John* (London: Tate Publishing, 2004), p. 33.
11 Foster, Alicia, *Gwen John: Art and Life in Paris and London* (London: Thames and Hudson, 2023), p. 19.

12 Boyd Haycock, *Brilliant Destiny*, p. 34.
13 Ida Nettleship in a letter to Edna Waugh, 30 December [1895], reprinted in Holroyd and John (eds.), *The Good Bohemian: The Letters of Ida John* (London: Bloomsbury, 2018), p. 31.
14 John, Augustus, *Autobiography*, p. 57.
15 Foster, p. 214.
16 Boyd Haycock, *Brilliant Destiny*, p. 35.
17 Holroyd, *Augustus John: The New Biography*, p. 53.
18 Ida Nettleship in a letter to Edna Waugh, n.d. [August 1898], Holroyd and John, p. 61.
19 Holroyd, *Augustus John: The New Biography*, p. 43.
20 Foster, p. 27.
21 Ida Nettleship in a letter to Edna Waugh, 17 April 1896 and 1 January 1896, Holroyd and John, p. 35 and p. 33.
22 Gwen John to Dorothy (Dorelia) McNeil, n.d. [June] 1904, and Lloyd-Morgan, Ceridwen, *Gwen John: Letters and Notebooks* (London: Tate, 2004), p. 33.
23 John, Augustus, *Autobiography*, p. 283.
24 Ibid, p. 276.
25 Ibid, p. 319.
26 Ibid, p. 12.
27 Boyd Haycock, *Brilliant Destiny*, p. 47.
28 Holroyd, *Augustus John: The New Biography*, p. 54.
29 Ida Nettleship in a letter to Ada Nettleship, n.d., spring 1987, Holroyd and John, p. 58.
30 Holroyd, *Augustus John: The New Biography*, p. 65.
31 Ibid, p. 66.
32 John, Augustus, *Autobiography*, p. 55.
33 Holroyd, *Augustus John: The New Biography*, p. 68.

CHAPTER THREE

1 Ida Nettleship in a letter to Michel Salaman, autumn 1898, Holroyd and John (eds.), *The Good Bohemian: The Letters of Ida John* (London: Bloomsbury, 2018), p. 69.
2 Holroyd, Michael, *Augustus John: The New Biography* (London: Vintage, 1997), p. 56.
3 Ida Nettleship in a letter to Ada Nettleship, 18 September 1898, Holroyd and John, p. 69.
4 Ibid.

5   Ida Nettleship in a letter to Michel Salaman, n.d., [autumn] 1898, Holroyd and John, p. 69.
6   Ida Nettleship in a letter to Ada Nettleship, n.d. [autumn] 1898, Holroyd and John, p. 71.
7   Spencer, Robin, *Whistler* (London Studio Editions, 1994), p. 132.
8   Boyd Haycock, David, *Brilliant Destiny: The Age of Augustus John* (London: Lund Humphries, 2023), p. 73.
9   John, Augustus, with Holroyd, Michael (ed.), *Augustus John Autobiography* (London: Jonathan Cape, 1975), p. 78.
10 Gwen John in a letter to Ida Nettleship, n.d., [December] 1898, Holroyd and John, p. 75.
11 Ida Nettleship in a letter to Ada Nettleship, n.d., [January] 1899, ibid.
12 John, Augustus, *Finishing Touches* (London: Jonathan Cape, 1964), p. 79.
13 Gwen John in a letter to Augustus John, n.d., [summer] 1906.
14 Holroyd, *Augustus John: The New Biography*, p. 45.
15 Boyd Haycock, *Brilliant Destiny*, p. 51.
16 Holroyd, *Augustus John: The New Biography*, p. 58.
17 O'Keefe, Paul, *Some Sort of Genius* (London: Jonathan Cape, 2000), p. 32.
18 Boyd Haycock, *Brilliant Destiny*, p. 83.
19 Gwen John in a letter to Michel Salaman, n.d., [March] 1899.
20 Boyd Haycock, *Brilliant Destiny*, p. 59.
21 John, Augustus, *Autobiography*, p. 63 and pp. 433–4.
22 Holroyd, *Augustus John: The New Biography*, p. 78.
23 Ibid, p. 81.
24 Ibid, p. 83.
25 Ibid, p. 84.
26 Ibid, p. 86.
27 Ibid, p. 87.
28 Boyd Haycock, *Brilliant Destiny*, p. 71.
29 Ibid.
30 Gwen John in a letter to Michel Salaman, 22 May 1902.
31 Ibid.
32 Holroyd, *Augustus John: The New Biography*, p. 84.
33 Ida Nettleship in a letter to Augustus John, 9 September 1899, Holroyd and John, p. 79.
34 Holroyd, *Augustus John: The New Biography*, p. 89.
35 Ethel Nettleship in a letter to Caspar John, 27 June 1951.
36 Holroyd, *Augustus John: The New Biography*, p. 89.
37 Ida Nettleship in a letter to Dorothy Salaman, 13 October 1899, Holroyd and John, p. 80.

38 Ethel Nettleship in a letter to Caspar John, 27 June 1951.
39 Holroyd, *Augustus John: The New Biography*, p. 89.

CHAPTER FOUR

1 Holroyd, Michael, *Augustus John: The New Biography* (London: Vintage, 1997), p. 89.
2 Ibid, p. 96.
3 Boyd Haycock, David, *Drawn from Life* (London: Paul Hoberton, 2018), p. 15.
4 Holroyd, *Augustus John: The New Biography*, p. 97.
5 Ibid, p. 107.
6 Augustus John in a letter to William Rothenstein, 4 September 1901.
7 Ibid.
8 Quoted in Holroyd and John (eds.), *The Good Bohemian: The Letters of Ida John* (London: Bloomsbury, 2018), p. 96.
9 Holroyd, *Augustus John: The New Biography*, p. 101.
10 John, Augustus, with Holroyd, Michael (ed.), *Augustus John Autobiography* (London: Jonathan Cape, 1975), p. 70.
11 Holroyd, *Augustus John: The New Biography*, p. 104.
12 Ida John in a letter to Alice Rothenstein, n.d., [April] 1901, Holroyd and John, p. 89.
13 Holroyd, *Augustus John: The New Biography*, p. 107.
14 Ida John in a letter to Ada Nettleship, 16 October 1901, and Ida John in a letter to Jack Nettleship, 24 December 1901, Holroyd and John, pp. 98–100.
15 Holroyd, *Augustus John: The New Biography*, p. 110.
16 Ibid.
17 Ida John in a letter to Ursula Nettleship, 21 January 1902, Holroyd and John, p. 112.
18 Holroyd, *Augustus John: The New Biography*, p. 114.
19 Ida John in a letter to Alice Rothenstein, n.d., [spring] 1902, Holroyd and John, p. 105.
20 Ibid.
21 Augustus John in a letter to William Rothenstein, 16 April 1902.
22 Augustus John in a letter to Dorothy (Dorelia) McNeill, n.d., cited in Holroyd, *Augustus John: The New Biography*, p. 129.

CHAPTER FIVE

1. Holroyd, Michael, *Augustus John: The New Biography* (London: Vintage, 1997), p. 129.
2. Ibid, p. 119.
3. Ida John in a letter to Mary Dowdall, n.d., [March 1903], Holroyd and John (eds.), *The Good Bohemian: The Letters of Ida John* (London: Bloomsbury, 2018), pp. 112–13.
4. Ibid.
5. Ida John in a letter to Michel Salaman, n.d., [March 1903], ibid, p. 116.
6. Holroyd, *Augustus John: The New Biography*, p. 125.
7. Ida John in a letter to Mary Dowdall, n.d., [October 1903], Holroyd and John, p. 128.
8. Holroyd, *Augustus John: The New Biography*, p. 126.
9. Ibid, p. 133.
10. Ibid, p. 134.
11. Ibid, p. 135.
12. Ida John in a letter to Gwen John, n.d., [August / September 1903], Holroyd and John, p.123.
13. Roe, Sue, *Gwen John: A Life* (London: Vintage, 2002), p. 39.
14. Augustus John in a letter to Dorelia McNeill, 3 November 1903.
15. Roe, p. 40.
16. Boyd Haycock, David, *Brilliant Destiny: The Age of Augustus John* (London: Lund Humphries, 2023), p. 88.
17. Roe, p. 40.
18. Foster, Alicia, *Gwen John: Art and Life in Paris and London* (London: Thames and Hudson, 2023), p. 58.
19. Augustus John in a letter to Gwen John and Dorelia McNeill, n.d., [December] 1903.
20. Ida John in a letter to Gwen John, n.d., [December 1903], Holroyd and John, p. 142.
21. Ida John in a letter to Alice Rothenstein, 15 February 1904, Holroyd and John, p. 151.
22. Cited in Holroyd and John, p. 153.
23. Ida John in a letter to Alice Rothenstein, 12 December 1903, Holroyd and John, p. 134.
24. Ida John in a letter to Alice Rothenstein, n.d., [December 1903], Holroyd and John, p. 138.
25. Holroyd, *Augustus John: The New Biography*, p. 142.

26 Ida John in a letter to Mary Dowdall, n.d., [January 1904], Holroyd and John, p. 142.
27 Gwen John in a letter to Ursula Tyrwhitt, n.d., [early 1904], Lloyd-Morgan, Ceridwen, *Gwen John: Letters and Notebooks* (London: Tate, 2004), p. 28.
28 Holroyd, *Augustus John: The New Biography*, p. 149.
29 Chitty, Susan, *Gwen John: 1876–1939* (London: Hodder & Stoughton, 1985), p. 60.
30 Holroyd, *Augustus John: The New Biography*, p. 149.
31 Ibid, p. 150.
32 Ida John in a letter to Mary Dowdall, n.d., [April / May 1904], Holroyd and John, pp. 161–2.
33 Ibid.
34 Augustus John in a letter to Gwen John, 16 May 1904.
35 Ida John to Gwen John, n.d., [July 1904], Holroyd and John, p. 178.
36 Holroyd, *Augustus John: The New Biography*, p. 157.
37 Gwen John in a letter to Dorelia McNeill, n.d. [June / July] 1904, Lloyd-Morgan, p. 30.
38 Cited in Holroyd and John, p. 177.
39 Ibid, p. 178.
40 Ida John in a letter to Dorelia McNeill, n.d., [June / July 1904], Holroyd and John, p. 176.
41 Cited in Holroyd and John, p. 176.
42 Gwen John in a letter to Dorelia McNeill, n.d., [August] 1904, Holroyd and John, p. 179.
43 Holroyd, *Augustus John: The New Biography*, p. 163.

CHAPTER SIX

1 Holroyd, Michael, *Augustus John: The New Biography* (London: Vintage, 1997), p. 48.
2 Augustus John in a letter to Gwen John, 28 March 1904.
3 Roe, Sue, *Gwen John: A Life* (London: Vintage, 2002), p. 54. Rodin's quote is from *Les Cathédrales de France*, a loose collection of his drawings and reflections published in 1914.
4 Foster, Alicia, *Gwen John: Art and Life in Paris and London* (London: Thames and Hudson, 2023), p. 77.
5 Gwen John in a letter to Auguste Rodin, Musée Rodin, cited in Roe, pp. 51–2.
6 Roe, p. 53.
7 Augustus John in a letter to Gwen John, September 1904.

8   Ida John in a letter to Alice Rothenstein, n.d., [October] 1904, Holroyd and John (eds.), *The Good Bohemian: The Letters of Ida John* (London: Bloomsbury, 2018), p. 185.
9   Augustus John in a letter to Gwen John, 29 September 1904.
10 Ida John in a letter to Gwen John, n.d., [September] 1904, Holroyd and John, p. 181.
11 Ibid.
12 Augustus John in a letter to Gwen John, 28 October 1904.
13 Grunfeld, Frederic V., *Rodin* (London: Hutchinson, 1987), pp. 513–14.
14 Gwen John in a letter to Ursula Tyrwhitt, n.d., [late 1904 or early 1905], Lloyd-Morgan, Ceridwen, *Gwen John: Letters and Notebooks* (London: Tate, 2004), p. 37.
15 Roe, p. 56.
16 Ibid, pp. 56–7.
17 Grunfeld, p. 459.
18 Holroyd, *Augustus John: The New Biography*, p. 48.
19 Gwen John in a letter to Auguste Rodin, n.d., Musée Rodin, cited in Grunfeld, p. 481.
20 Ibid, p. 480.
21 Roe, p. 74.
22 Gwen John in a letter to Auguste Rodin, n.d., Musée Rodin, cited in Roe, p. 69.
23 Holroyd, *Augustus John: The New Biography*, p. 162.
24 Gwen John in a letter to Auguste Rodin, Musée Rodin, cited in Langdale, Cecily, *Gwen John* (New Haven and London: Yale University Press, 1987), p. 29.
25 Gwen John in a letter to Auguste Rodin, n.d., Musée Rodin, cited in Roe, p. 69.
26 Gwen John in a letter to Auguste Rodin, 28 February 1906, Musée Rodin, cited in Grunfeld, p. 482.
27 Gwen John in a letter to Ursula Tyrwhitt, n.d., Lloyd-Morgan, p. 38.
28 Holroyd, *Augustus John: The New Biography*, p. 217.
29 Gwen John in a letter to Auguste Rodin, n.d., Musée Rodin, cited in Roe, p. 59.
30 Ibid, p. 76.
31 Ibid, p. 75.
32 Grunfeld, p. 185.
33 Gwen John in a letter to Auguste Rodin, n.d., Musée Rodin, cited in Roe, p. 73.

CHAPTER SEVEN

1   Ida John in a letter to Augustus John, n.d., [November] 1904, Holroyd and John (eds.), *The Good Bohemian: The Letters of Ida John* (London: Bloomsbury, 2018), p. 194.

2 Augustus John in a letter to Gwen John, 24 October 1904.
3 Ibid.
4 Augustus John in a letter to William Rothenstein, n.d., cited in Holroyd, Michael, *Augustus John: The New Biography* (London: Vintage, 1997), p. 165.
5 *Athenaeum*, 19 November 1904, p. 700.
6 Ida John in letters to Gwen John, 29 September 1904 and 22 November 1904, Holroyd and John, pp. 183–4 and p. 188.
7 Holroyd, *Augustus John: The New Biography*, p. 168.
8 Ida John in a letter to Augustus John, n.d., [November] 1904, Holroyd and John, p. 194.
9 Cited in Holroyd and John, p. 254.
10 Holroyd, *Augustus John: The New Biography*, p. 176.
11 Cited in Holroyd and John, pp. 197–8.
12 Holroyd, *Augustus John: The New Biography*, p. 224.
13 Ida John in a letter to Dorelia McNeill, n.d., [December] 1904, Holroyd and John, p. 199.
14 Ida John in a letter to Alice Rothenstein, 27 March 1903, Holroyd and John, p. 201.
15 Ibid.
16 Ida John in a letter to Alice Rothenstein, n.d., [late May or early June] 1905, Holroyd and John, p. 205.
17 Ida John, in letters to Dorelia McNeill, n.d., [late May to early June], Holroyd and John, pp. 206–12.
18 Ibid.
19 Ibid.
20 Holroyd, *Augustus John: The New Biography*, p. 182.
21 Ida John in a letter to Mary Dowdall, n.d., [June] 1905, Holroyd and John, p. 219.
22 Ibid.
23 Holroyd, *Augustus John: The New Biography*, p. 184.
24 Ibid.
25 Ida John in a letter to Mary Dowdall, n.d., [July] 1905, Holroyd and John, pp. 224–5.
26 Ida John in a letter to Alice Rothenstein,19 August 1905, Holroyd and John, p. 228.
27 Quoted in a letter from Ida John to Alice Rothenstein, 23 August 1905, Holroyd and John, p. 231.
28 Ibid.
29 Ida John in a letter to Augustus John, n.d., [late August or early September]1905, Holroyd and John, pp. 234–5.

30 Ibid.
31 Ibid, p. 235.
32 Ida John in a letter to Alice Rothenstein, n.d., [August] 1905, Holroyd and John, p. 227.
33 Cited in Holroyd and John, p. 241.

CHAPTER EIGHT

1 Holroyd, Michael, *Augustus John: The New Biography* (London: Vintage, 1997), p. 193.
2 Augustus John in a letter to Alice Rothenstein, 16 October 1905, cited in Tickner, Lisa, 'Augustus's Sister', *Gwen John and Augustus John* (London: Tate Publishing, 2004), p. 36.
3 Gwen John in a letter to Dorelia McNeill, n.d., [June or July] 1905, Lloyd-Morgan, Ceridwen, *Gwen John: Letters and Notebooks* (London: Tate, 2004), p. 38.
4 Holroyd, *Augustus John: The New Biography*, p. 196.
5 Ida John in a letter to Meg Sampson, n.d., [summer] 1906, Holroyd and John (eds.), *The Good Bohemian: The Letters of Ida John* (London: Bloomsbury, 2018), p. 266.
6 Ida John in a letter to Meg Sampson, n.d., [November or December] 1905, Holroyd and John, p. 243.
7 Ida John in a letter to Ursula Nettleship, 6 December 1905, Holroyd and John, p. 246.
8 Holroyd, *Augustus John: The New Biography*, p. 195.
9 Ibid, p. 194.
10 Cited in Holroyd and John, p. 242.
11 Ibid.
12 Ida John in a letter to Ursula Nettleship, 6 December 1905, Holroyd and John, p. 246.
13 Holroyd, *Augustus John: The New Biography*, p. 195.
14 *Athenaeum*, 21 October 1905, cited in Boyd Haycock, David, *Brilliant Destiny: The Age of Augustus John* (London: Lund Humphries, 2023), p. 113.
15 John, Augustus, with Holroyd, Michael (ed.), *Augustus John: Autobiography* (London: Jonathan Cape, 1975), p. 83.
16 Boyd Haycock, *Brilliant Destiny*, p. 116.
17 Holroyd, *Augustus John: The New Biography*, pp. 210–14.
18 Ibid.
19 Augustus John to Alick Schepeler, undated.
20 Holroyd, *Augustus John: The New Biography*, p. 213.

21 Gwen John to Auguste Rodin, undated, Musée Rodin, cited in Holroyd, *Augustus John: The New Biography*, pp. 160–1.
22 Gwen John draft letter to Auguste Rodin, undated.
23 Ida John in a letter to Meg Sampson, n.d., [June / July] 1906, Holroyd and John, p. 268.
24 Gwen John in a letter to Augustus John, n.d., [summer] 1906.
25 Ibid.
26 Augustus John in a letter to Alick Schepeler, n.d., [summer] 1906, cited in Holroyd, *Augustus John: The New Biography*, p. 218.
27 Ibid, p. 219.
28 Ida John in a letter to Mary Dowdall, n.d., [summer] 1906, Holroyd and John, p. 267.
29 Holroyd, *Augustus John: The New Biography*, p. 220.
30 Ibid.
31 Ibid, p. 221.
32 Ida John in a letter to Augustus John, n.d., [autumn] 1906, cited in Holroyd and John, p. 227.
33 Ida John in a letter to Augustus John, n.d., [November] 1906, Holroyd, *Augustus John: The New Biography*, pp. 278–9.
34 Boyd Haycock, *Brilliant Destiny*, p. 125.
35 Augustus John in a letter to Dorelia McNeill, n.d., cited in Holroyd, *Augustus John: The New Biography*, p. 224.
36 O'Keefe, Paul, *Some Sort of Genius* (London: Jonathan Cape, 2000), p. 75.
37 Gwen John, notebook, n.d.
38 Holroyd, *Augustus John: The New Biography*, p. 226.
39 Ibid, p. 227.
40 Boyd Haycock, *Brilliant Destiny*, p. 130.
41 Holroyd, *Augustus John: The New Biography*, p. 228.
42 Ada Nettleship in a letter to Ursula and Ethel Nettleship, n.d [10 March 1907].
43 Holroyd, *Augustus John: The New Biography*, p. 231.
44 Ibid, p. 233.
45 John, Augustus, *Finishing Touches* (London: Jonathan Cape, 1964), p. 46.
46 Cited in Holroyd and John, pp. 295–6.

CHAPTER NINE

1 Augustus John in a letter to Ursula Nettleship, n.d., autumn 1907, cited in Holroyd, Michael, *Augustus John: The New Biography* (London: Vintage, 1997), p. 253.
2 Holroyd, p. 235.

NOTES

3   Augustus John in a letter to Mary Dowdall, March 1907.
4   Holroyd, *Augustus John: The New Biography*, p. 234.
5   Ibid.
6   Ursula Tyrwhitt in a letter to Gwen John, n.d., [March] 1907.
7   Ida John in a letter to William Rothenstein, n.d., [December] 1906, Holroyd and John (eds.), *The Good Bohemian: The Letters of Ida John* (London: Bloomsbury, 2018), p. 280.
8   Roe, Sue, *Gwen John: A Life* (London: Vintage, 2002), p. 95.
9   Ibid.
10 Gwen John in a letter to Ursula Tyrwhitt, 1 June 1908, Lloyd-Morgan, Ceridwen, *Gwen John: Letters and Notebooks* (London: Tate, 2004), p. 43.
11 Cantal, Lucien in *Action Française*; Blanche, J-F in *Grand Revue*, cited in Roe, p. 100.
12 Gwen John in a letter to Ursula Tyrwhitt, 29 May 1908, Lloyd-Morgan, p. 43.
13 Gwen John in a letter to Ursula Tyrwhitt, 1 June 1908, ibid.
14 Augustus John in a letter to Ada Nettleship, n.d., [spring] 1905.
15 Holroyd, *Augustus John: The New Biography*, p. 238.
16 Augustus John in a letter to William Rothenstein, April 1907, cited in Holroyd, *Augustus John: The New Biography*, p. 240.
17 Holroyd, *Augustus John: The New Biography*, p. 236.
18 Augustus John in a letter to Henry Lamb, 13 June 1907.
19 Augustus John in a letter to Ada Nettleship, n.d., [autumn] 1907.
20 Ada Nettleship in a letter to Ursula Nettleship, n.d., [autumn] 1907, cited in Holroyd, *Augustus John: The New Biography*, p. 252.
21 Augustus John in a letter to Ursula Nettleship, ibid, p. 253.
22 Ada Nettleship in a letter to Ursula Nettleship, 2 September 1907.
23 Ethel Nettleship in a letter to Caspar John, 27 June 1951, cited in Holroyd and John, p. 309.
24 Boyd Haycock, David, *Brilliant Destiny: The Age of Augustus John* (London: Lund Humphries, 2023) p. 139.
25 Ibid.
26 Holroyd, *Augustus John: The New Biography*, p. 245.
27 Ibid, p. 261.
28 Ibid.
29 Miranda Sawyer, *Ottoline Morrell* (London: Sceptre,1993), p. 114.
30 Boyd Haycock, *Brilliant Destiny*, p. 142.
31 Holroyd, *Augustus John: The New Biography*, p. 261.
32 Boyd Haycock, *Brilliant Destiny*, p. 143.
33 Holroyd, *Augustus John: The New Biography*, p. 263.
34 Ibid, p. 277.

35 Augustus John in a letter to Ottoline Morrell, 30 May 1908.
36 Augustus John in a letter to Ottoline Morrell, 17 June 1908.
37 Holroyd, *Augustus John: The New Biography*, p. 273.
38 Ibid.
39 Ibid, p. 281.
40 Boyd Haycock, *Brilliant Destiny*, p. 164.
41 Holroyd, *Augustus John: The New Biography*, p. 278.
42 Ibid, p. 267.

CHAPTER TEN

1 Boyd Haycock, David, *Brilliant Destiny: The Age of Augustus John* (London: Lund Humphries, 2023), p. 23.
2 Roe, Sue, *Gwen John: A Life* (London: Vintage, 2002), p. 95.
3 Chitty, Susan, *Gwen John: 1876–1939* (London: Hodder & Stoughton, 1985), p. 76.
4 Grunfeld, Frederic V., *Rodin* (London: Hutchinson, 1987), p. 490.
5 Ibid, p. 488.
6 Ibid, p. 593.
7 Auguste Rodin in a letter to Gwen John, 28 February 1910.
8 Gwen John in a letter to Ursula Tyrwhitt, 30 September 1909.
9 Wyndham Lewis, 'The Art of Gwen John', *The Listener*, 10 October 1946, p. 484.
10 Gwen John in a letter to Ursula Tyrwhitt, n.d., [summer] 1910, Lloyd-Morgan, Ceridwen, *Gwen John: Letters and Notebooks* (London: Tate, 2004), p. 57.
11 Ibid.
12 Gwen John in a letter to Ursula Tyrwhitt, 4 February 1910, Lloyd-Morgan, pp. 52–3.
13 Gwen John in a letter to Ursula Tyrwhitt, 15 February 1902, Lloyd-Morgan, p. 49.
14 Gwen John in a letter to Ursula Tyrwhitt, n.d., [summer] 1910, Lloyd-Morgan, p. 57.
15 Holroyd, Michael, *Augustus John: The New Biography* (London: Vintage, 1997), p. 300.
16 Ibid.
17 Augustus John in a letter to John Quinn, 18 December 1909.
18 Holroyd, *Augustus John: The New Biography*, p. 301.
19 Augustus John in a letter to Ottoline Morrell, 24 April 1909.
20 O'Keefe, Paul, *Some Sort of Genius* (London: Jonathan Cape, 2000), p. 94.
21 Augustus John in a letter to William Rothenstein, September 1911.

22 Gwen John in a letter to John Quinn, 18 August 1910, Lloyd-Morgan, p. 59.
23 Gwen John in a letter to John Quinn, 25 December 1910.
24 John Quinn in a letter to Gwen John, January 1911.
25 Gwen John in a letter to Ursula Tyrwhitt, 7 August 1911, Lloyd-Morgan, p. 68.
26 Gwen John in a letter to John Quinn, 28 November 1911, Lloyd-Morgan, p. 73.
27 Gwen John in a letter to John Quinn, 5 August 1912, Lloyd-Morgan, pp. 75–6.
28 John Quinn in a letter to Gwen John, 16 August 1912.
29 Gwen John in a letter to John Quinn, 19 November 1912, Lloyd-Morgan, p. 77.
30 Gwen John in a letter to John Quinn, 22 August 1911, Lloyd-Morgan, p. 69.
31 Gwen John in a letter to John Quinn, 20 February 1913, Lloyd-Morgan, p. 79.
32 Gwen John in a letter to Ursula Tyrwhitt, 4 February 1910, Lloyd-Morgan, p. 52.
33 Gwen John in a letter to Jeanne Robert Foster, n.d., [August] 1924.

CHAPTER ELEVEN

1 Boyd Haycock, David, *Brilliant Destiny: The Age of Augustus John* (London: Lund Humphries, 2023), p. 20.
2 Augustus John in a letter to Ottoline Morrell, 13 January 1909.
3 Augustus John in a letter to Robert Gregory, n.d.
4 *The Burlington Magazine*, vol. 19, 1909, p. 17.
5 Holroyd, Michael, *Augustus John: The New Biography* (London: Vintage, 1997), p. 284.
6 Boyd Haycock, *Brilliant Destiny*, p. 172.
7 Holroyd, *Augustus John: The New Biography*, p. 285.
8 Ibid, p. 286.
9 Ibid.
10 Boyd Haycock, *Brilliant Destiny*, p. 171.
11 Holroyd, *Augustus John: The New Biography*, pp. 291–2.
12 Augustus John in a letter to John Quinn, 18 December 1909.
13 Holroyd, *Augustus John: The New Biography*, p. 307.
14 Augustus John in a letter to Ottoline Morrell, 4 December 1909.
15 Augustus John in a letter to Wyndham Lewis, 4 December 1909.
16 Augustus John in a letter to Dorelia McNeill, 17 January 1910.
17 Holroyd, *Augustus John: The New Biography*, p. 311.
18 Augustus John in a letter to Dorelia McNeill, 17 January 1910.

19 Augustus John in a letter to Ottoline Morrell, February 1910.
20 Holroyd, *Augustus John: The New Biography*, p. 311.
21 Augustus John in a letter to John Quinn, 3 March 1910.
22 John, Augustus, with Holroyd, Michael (ed.), *Augustus John Autobiography* (London: Jonathan Cape, 1975), pp. 150–1.
23 Augustus John in a letter to John Quinn, 3 March 1910.
24 John, Augustus, *Autobiography*, p. 225.
25 Holroyd, *Augustus John: The New Biography*, p. 319.
26 Ibid, pp. 319–20.
27 Ibid.
28 Ibid, p. 321.
29 Ibid, p. 337.
30 Augustus John in a letter to John Quinn, 25 August 1910.
31 *The Times*, 5 December 1910.
32 'Mr Augustus John's Provençal Studies', *Athenaeum*, 10 December 1910.
33 *Saturday Review*, 10 December 1910, p .747.
34 Holroyd, *Augustus John: The New Biography*, p. 328.
35 *Manchester Guardian*, 18 November 1911.
36 Holroyd, *Augustus John: The New Biography*, p. 342.
37 Boyd Haycock, *Brilliant Destiny*, p. 184.
38 *Observer*, 24 November 1912.
39 Holroyd, *Augustus John: The New Biography*, p. 330.
40 Boyd Haycock, *Brilliant Destiny*, p. 183.
41 Augustus John in a letter to John Quinn, 10 February 1911.
42 Holroyd, *Augustus John: The New Biography*, p. 360.
43 Ibid.

CHAPTER TWELVE

1 Gwen John, notebook, October 1912.
2 Gwen John in a letter to Ursula Tyrwhitt, n.d., [November] 1910, Lloyd-Morgan, Ceridwen, *Gwen John: Letters and Notebooks* (London: Tate, 2004), p. 62.
3 Gwen John in a letter to Ursula Tyrwhitt, 18 November 1911, Lloyd-Morgan, p. 71.
4 Gwen John, notebook, February 1911.
5 Gwen John in a letter to Ursula Tyrwhitt, n.d., [November] 1910, Lloyd-Morgan, pp. 61–2.
6 Gwen John in a letter to Jeanne Robert Foster, 2 February 1925.
7 Gwen John in a letter to Ursula Tyrwhitt, 30 July 1908, Lloyd-Morgan, p. 47.

8   Gwen John, notebook, n.d., 1910.
9   Gwen John in a letter to Augustus John, n.d., [spring] 1911.
10 Gwen John, notebook, n.d., cited in Roe, Sue, *Gwen John: A Life* (London: Vintage, 2002), p. 136.
11 Gwen John, notebook, October 1912 and 12 February 1913.
12 Gwen John in a letter to Ursula Tyrwhitt, 4 September 1912, Lloyd-Morgan, p. 76.
13 Gwen John, notebook, 19 November 1911, Lloyd-Morgan, p.71.
14 Gwen John in a letter to Ursula Tyrwhitt, 5 October 1912.
15 Ibid, 18 October 1911.
16 Gwen John in a letter to Michel Salaman, 3 June 1926, Lloyd-Morgan, p. 151.
17 Gwen John, notebook, February 1913.
18 *The New York Times*, 16 September 1912.
19 Gwen John in a letter to Auguste Rodin, Musée Rodin, cited in Roe, p. 149.
20 Gwen John in a letter to Ursula Tyrwhitt, 4 September 1912, Lloyd-Morgan, p. 76.
21 Foster, Alicia, *Gwen John: Art and Life in Paris and London* (London: Thames and Hudson, 2023), p. 57.
22 John, Augustus, with Holroyd, Michael (ed.), *Augustus John: Autobiography* (London: Jonathan Cape, 1975), p. 109.
23 Boyd Haycock, David, *Brilliant Destiny: The Age of Augustus John* (London: Lund Humphries, 2023), p. 198.
24 Gwen John in a letter to Ursula Tyrwhitt, 7 March 1912, Lloyd-Morgan, p. 74.
25 Holroyd, Michael, *Augustus John: The New Biography* (London: Vintage, 1997), p. 389.
26 Augustus John in a letter to Ottoline Morrell, 25 March 1912.
27 Augustus John in a letter to John Quinn, 9 March 1912.
28 Augustus John in a letter to Meg Sampson, 25 March 1912.
29 Caspar John, in *Augustus and Gwen: The Fire and the Fountain* (documentary), BBC Wales, 1975.
30 Augustus John in a letter to Dorelia McNeill, n.d., [summer] 1912.
31 John, Augustus, *Autobiography*, p. 109.
32 Holroyd, *Augustus John: The New Biography*, p. 395.
33 Augustus John in a letter to John Quinn, September 1913.
34 Boyd Haycock, *Brilliant Destiny*, p. 195.
35 Augustus John in a letter to Alick Schepeler, 2 February 1918.
36 Holroyd, *Augustus John: The New Biography*, p. 372.
37 Ibid, p. 374.
38 Augustus John in a letter to John Quinn, 13 May 1913.
39 Holroyd, *Augustus John: The New Biography*, p. 400.
40 Ibid.

41 Augustus John in a letter to Margaret Sampson, 25 March 1912.
42 Gwen John in a letter to Ursula Tyrwhitt, 4 September 1912, Lloyd-Morgan, p. 76.
43 Gwen John, notebook, 29 August 1913.
44 Augustus John in a letter to Gwen John, n.d., January 1914.
45 Augustus John in a letter to Gwen John, 4 August 1914.
46 Holroyd, *Augustus John: The New Biography*, p. 401.

CHAPTER THIRTEEN

1 Gwen John in a letter to Augustus John, 13 October 1914, Lloyd-Morgan, Ceridwen, *Gwen John: Letters and Notebooks* (London: Tate, 2004), p. 91.
2 Ibid.
3 Gwen John in a letter to Ursula Tyrwhitt, 7 September 1914, Lloyd-Morgan, p. 88.
4 Gwen John in a letter to Ursula Tyrwhitt, 1 December 1914.
5 Gwen John in a letter to Augustus John, 13 October 1914, Lloyd-Morgan, p. 91.
6 Ibid.
7 Gwen John in a letter to Ursula Tyrwhitt, 27 September 1914, Lloyd-Morgan, p. 89.
8 Augustus John in letters to Gwen John, 24 October and 25 December 1914.
9 Augustus John in a letter to Gwen John, 24 October 1914.
10 Auguste Rodin in a letter to Gwen John, September 1914.
11 Gwen John in a letter to Ursula Tyrwhitt, 10 April 1917, Lloyd-Morgan, p. 98.
12 Augustus John in a letter to John Quinn, 19 October 1914.
13 Ibid, 24 October 1914.
14 Augustus John in a letter to Dorelia McNeill, 5 March 1915.
15 Ibid, 17 October 1915.
16 Boyd Haycock, David, *Brilliant Destiny: The Age of Augustus John* (London: Lund Humphries, 2023), p. 219.
17 Holroyd, Michael, *Augustus John: The New Biography* (London: Vintage, 1997), p. 421.
18 Mackrell, Judith, *Flappers* (London: Macmillan, 2013), p. 69.
19 Holroyd, *Augustus John: The New Biography*, p. 415.
20 Ibid, p. 423.
21 Boyd Haycock, David, *Drawn from Life* (London: Paul Hoberton, 2018), p. 84.
22 Augustus John in a letter to Gwen John, 17 September 1919.
23 Ida John in a letter to Alice Rothenstein, n.d., 1903, Holroyd and John (eds.), *The Good Bohemian: The Letters of Ida John* (London: Bloomsbury, 2018), p. 136.

24 Holroyd, *Augustus John: The New Biography*, pp. 387–8.
25 Gwen John in a letter to John Quinn, 17 March 1916.
26 Holroyd, *Augustus John: The New Biography*, p. 405.
27 Gwen John in a letter to John Quinn, 17 March 1916.
28 Gwen John in a letter to Ursula Tyrwhitt, 3 August 1916, Lloyd-Morgan, p. 96.
29 Gwen John, notebook, August 1917, Lloyd-Morgan, p. 97.
30 Gwen John in a letter to Ursula Tyrwhitt, 18 May 1917, Lloyd-Morgan, p. 99.
31 Gwen John, notebook, 6 October 1917, Lloyd-Morgan, p. 102.
32 Gwen John in a letter to John Quinn, 11 July 1917, and to Augustus John, 22 June 1917.
33 Katherine Mansfield in a letter to Ottoline Morrell, August 1917, cited in Holroyd, *Augustus John: The New Biography*, p. 431.
34 *The Times*, 21 November 1917.
35 Boyd Haycock, *Brilliant Destiny*, p. 208.
36 Holroyd, *Augustus John: The New Biography*, p. 418.
37 Ibid, p. 430.
38 Boyd Haycock, *Brilliant Destiny*, p. 221.
39 Ibid, p. 221.
40 Holroyd, *Augustus John: The New Biography*, p. 432.
41 Augustus John in a letter to Dorelia McNeill, 21 January 1918.
42 Ibid.
43 Boyd Haycock, David, *Augustus John and the First Crisis of Brilliance* (London, 2024), p. 224.
44 John, Augustus, with Holroyd, Michael (ed.), *Augustus John: Autobiography* (London: Jonathan Cape, 1975), p. 370; see also Holroyd, *Augustus John: The New Biography*, p. 433.
45 Boyd Haycock, *Brilliant Destiny*, p. 225.
46 Holroyd, *Augustus John: The New Biography*, p. 434.
47 Ibid, p. 433.
48 Ibid, p. 434.
49 Ibid.
50 Augustus John in a letter to Dorelia McNeill, n.d., [April] 1918.
51 Gwen John in a letter to Ursula Tyrwhitt, 22 November 1917, Lloyd-Morgan, p. 102.
52 Holroyd, *Augustus John: The New Biography*, pp. 436–7.
53 Gwen John in a letter to Ursula Tyrwhitt, n.d., [February] 1918, Lloyd-Morgan, p. 103.
54 Gwen John in a letter to Ursula Tyrwhitt, 29 March 1918, Lloyd-Morgan, p. 104.
55 Gwen John in a letter to Ursula Tyrwhitt, 19 May 1918, Lloyd-Morgan, p .105.

56 Ibid.
57 Ibid.
58 Gwen John in a letter to John Quinn, 12 November 1911.
59 Gwen John in a letter to Ursula Tyrwhitt, 6 September 1918.

CHAPTER FOURTEEN

1 Augustus John in a letter to Gwen John, 12 November 1911.
2 Holroyd, Michael, *Augustus John: The New Biography* (London: Vintage, 1997), p. 439.
3 Boyd Haycock, David, *Brilliant Destiny: The Age of Augustus John* (London: Lund Humphries, 2023), p. 226.
4 *Colour*, September 1918.
5 Holroyd, *Augustus John: The New Biography*, p. 439.
6 John, Augustus, with Holroyd, Michael (ed.), *Augustus John: Autobiography* (London: Jonathan Cape, 1975), p. 265.
7 Mackrell, Judith, *The Unfinished Palazzo* (London: Thames and Hudson, 2017), p. 117.
8 Holroyd, *Augustus John: The New Biography*, p. 441.
9 Ursula Tyrwhitt in a letter to Gwen John, 17 September 1919.
10 Gwen John, notebook, 8 January 1919.
11 Roe, Sue, *Gwen John: A Life* (London: Vintage, 2002), p. 184.
12 Augustus John in a letter to Gwen John, 20 August 1919.
13 Holroyd, *Augustus John: The New Biography*, p. 443.
14 Augustus John in a letter to Gwen John, 20 August 1919.
15 Ibid.
16 Augustus John in a letter to Gwen John, 17 September 1919.
17 Ibid.
18 Gwen John in a letter to John Quinn, 6 October 1919.
19 Gwen John in a draft letter to Nona Watkins, n.d., [October / November] 1919, Lloyd-Morgan, Ceridwen, *Gwen John: Letters and Notebooks* (London: Tate, 2004), p. 111.
20 Augustus John in a letter to Gwen John, n.d., [October] 1919.
21 Arthur Symons in a letter to Gwen John, 27 October 1919.
22 Gwen John in a letter to Nona Watkins, n.d., [October] 1919; see also Roe, p. 189.
23 Gwen John in a draft letter to Nona Watkins, 1 November 1919.
24 Gwen John in a draft letter to Nona Watkins, n.d., [November] 1919.
25 Roe, p. 192.

26 Gwen John, notebook, May 1921, Lloyd-Morgan, p. 118.
27 Gwen John in a letter to Ursula Tyrwhitt, n.d., 1936.
28 Gwen John in a letter to John Quinn, 4 April 1920, Lloyd-Morgan, pp. 113–14.
29 Rhoda Symons in a letter to Gwen John, 20 January 1920.
30 Gwen John in a letter to John Quinn, 15 June 1920.
31 Ibid.
32 Rhoda Symons in a letter to Gwen John, 29 June 1920.
33 Augustus John in a letter to Gwen John, 25 June 1920.
34 Gwen John in a letter to John Quinn, 18 July 1920, Lloyd-Morgan, p. 115.
35 Chitty, Susan, *Gwen John: 1876–1939* (London: Hodder & Stoughton, 1985), pp. 157–8.
36 Gwen John in a letter to John Quinn, 10 July 1920.
37 Roe, p. 204.
38 Ibid, pp. 203–4.
39 Ibid.
40 Ibid, p. 205.
41 Ibid, p. 207.
42 Ibid, p. 208.
43 Gwen John in a letter to Ursula Tyrwhitt, n.d., [August] 1921, Lloyd-Morgan, p. 121.
44 Roe, p. 219.
45 Gwen John, notebook, 17 October 1921.
46 Jeanne Robert Foster in a letter to Gwen John, 28 February 1922.
47 Gwen John in a letter to Ursula Tyrwhitt, n.d., [December] 1921, Lloyd-Morgan, p. 122.

CHAPTER FIFTEEN

1 Augustus John in a letter to Ottoline Morrell, 14 March 1920.
2 *The Burlington Magazine*, 1923, pp. 259–60.
3 Holroyd, Michael, *Augustus John: The New Biography* (London: Vintage, 1997), p. 453.
4 Boyd Haycock, David, *Brilliant Destiny: The Age of Augustus John* (London: Lund Humphries, 2023), p. 230.
5 Holroyd, *Augustus John: The New Biography*, p. 462.
6 John, Augustus, with Holroyd, Michael (ed.), *Augustus John: Autobiography* (London: Jonathan Cape, 1975), p. 152.
7 Holroyd, *Augustus John: The New Biography*, p. 465.

8 *Manchester Guardian*, 23 October 1920.
9 Holroyd, *Augustus John: The New Biography*, p. 476.
10 John, Augustus, *Autobiography*, p. 257.
11 Holroyd, *Augustus John: The New Biography*, p. 447.
12 John, Augustus, *Autobiography*, p. 201.
13 Ibid.
14 Holroyd, *Augustus John: The New Biography*, p. 461.
15 Ibid, p. 459.
16 Ibid, p. 461.
17 Ibid, p. 446.
18 Ibid.
19 Ibid, p. 484.
20 Ibid.
21 John, Augustus, *Autobiography*, p. 180.
22 Augustus John in a letter to Poppet John, 28 April 1923.
23 Holroyd, *Augustus John: The New Biography*, p. 490.
24 Augustus John in a letter to Dorelia McNeill, 17 April 1923.
25 John, Augustus, *Autobiography*, p. 184.
26 Ibid, p. 195.
27 *Manchester Guardian*, 25 April 1922.
28 Gwen John, notebook, 8 February 1922 and [August] 1922, Lloyd-Morgan, Ceridwen, *Gwen John: Letters and Notebooks* (London: Tate, 2004), p.124 and p. 128.
29 Gwen John in a letter to John Quinn, 27 March 1922, Lloyd-Morgan, p. 126.
30 Jeanne Robert Foster in a letter to Gwen John, 8 February 1922.
31 Gwen John in a letter to Jeanne Robert Foster, 6 December 1922, Lloyd-Morgan, p. 129.
32 Gwen John, notebook, 7 July 1923, Lloyd-Morgan, p. 130.
33 Gwen John in a letter to John Quinn, 29 September 1923, Lloyd-Morgan, p. 131.
34 Gwen John in a letter to Jeanne Robert Foster, 20 February 1924, Lloyd-Morgan, p. 132.
35 Roe, Sue, *Gwen John: A Life* (London: Vintage, 2002), p. 233.
36 Gwen John in a letter to John Quinn, 24 March 1924.
37 Gwen John in a letter to Ursula Tyrwhitt, n.d., [August] 1924, Lloyd-Morgan, p. 134.
38 Roe, p. 236.
39 Ibid, p. 241.
40 Gwen John in a letter to Augustus John, 1 October 1924.
41 Augustus John in letters to Gwen John, 18 and 29 October 1924.
42 Gwen John in a letter to Augustus John, 1 October 1924, Lloyd-Morgan, p. 137.

CHAPTER SIXTEEN

1 Gwen John, notebook, cited in Roe, Sue, *Gwen John: A Life* (London: Vintage, 2002), p. 305.
2 Holroyd, Michael, *Augustus John: The New Biography* (London: Vintage, 1997), p. 552.
3 Gwen John in a letter to Ursula Tyrwhitt, 2 June 1925, Lloyd-Morgan, Ceridwen, *Gwen John: Letters and Notebooks* (London: Tate, 2004), pp. 141–2.
4 Gwen John in a letter to Ursula Tyrwhitt, 6 June 1925, Lloyd-Morgan, p. 142.
5 Ibid.
6 Augustus John in a letter to Gwen John, June 1925.
7 Gwen John in a letter to Augustus John, 23 December 1925.
8 Gwen John in a letter to Ursula Tyrwhitt, 7 April 1926, Lloyd-Morgan, p.150.
9 Gwen John in a letter to Michel Salaman, 31 March 1926.
10 Gwen John in a letter to Michel Salaman, 17 January 1926, Lloyd-Morgan, p. 149.
11 Charles Aitken in a letter to Gwen John, 8 November 1926.
12 Mary Chamot, 'Gwen John: an Undiscovered Artist', *Country Life*, 19 June 1926.
13 William Rothenstein in a letter to Gwen John, 1 June 1926.
14 Michel Salaman in a letter to Gwen John, 1 June 1926.
15 Gwen John in a letter to Michel Salaman, 3 June 1926, Lloyd-Morgan, p. 150.
16 *Augustus and Gwen: The Fire and the Fountain* (documentary), BBC Wales, 1975.
17 Dorelia McNeill in a letter to Gwen John, 12 April 1927.
18 Gwen John in a letter to Ursula Tyrwhitt, 23 July [1927], Lloyd-Morgan, p. 152, and Chitty, Susan, *Gwen John: 1876–1939* (London: Hodder & Stoughton, 1985), p. 203.
19 Chitty, p. 181.
20 Gwen John in a letter to Ursula Tyrwhitt, 23 July 1927, Lloyd-Morgan, p. 151.
21 Gwen John in a letter to Ursula Tyrwhitt, 4 April 1928, Lloyd-Morgan, p. 161.
22 Gwen John in a letter to Edwin John, 26 October 1929.
23 Gwen John in a letter to Ursula Tyrwhitt, 17 March 1930, Lloyd-Morgan, p. 169.
24 Roe, p. 253.
25 Gwen John, notebook, 19 April 1927, Lloyd-Morgan, p. 151.
26 Véra Oumançoff in a letter to Gwen John, 20 May 1927.
27 Gwen John in a draft letter to Véra Oumançoff, n.d.; see also John, Augustus, with Holroyd, Michael (ed.), *Augustus John: Autobiography* (London: Jonathan Cape, 1975), pp. 279–80.
28 Gwen John in a draft letter to Véra Oumançoff, [July / August] 1927, Lloyd-Morgan, pp. 154–5.

29 Gwen John in a letter to Tom Burns, cited in Roe, p. 273.
30 John, Augustus, *Autobiography*, p. 283.
31 Canon Piermé in a letter to Gwen John, n.d., 1929.
32 Roe, p. 268.
33 Gwen John in a letter to Ursula Tyrwhitt, 14 June 1930.
34 Gwen John in a letter to Ursula Tyrwhitt, 30 June 1930, Lloyd-Morgan, p. 167.
35 Ursula Tyrwhitt in a letter to Gwen John, n.d., [July] 1930.
36 Roe, p. 295.
37 John, Augustus, 'Gwen John', *The Burlington Magazine*, October 1942; and see Chitty, p. 175.
38 Dorelia McNeill in a letter to Gwen John, 11 January 1933.

CHAPTER SEVENTEEN

1 Holroyd, Michael, *Augustus John: The New Biography* (London: Vintage, 1997), p. 521.
2 Ibid, p. 498.
3 *Augustus and Gwen: The Fire and the Fountain* (documentary), BBC Wales, 1975.
4 Holroyd, *Augustus John: The New Biography*, p. 501.
5 Ibid, p. 508.
6 Ibid, p. 504.
7 John, Augustus, with Holroyd, Michael (ed.), *Augustus John: Autobiography* (London: Jonathan Cape, 1975), p. 399.
8 Holroyd, *Augustus John: The New Biography*, p. 5.
9 Ottoline Morrell in a letter to Augustus John, 31 March 1930.
10 Holroyd, *Augustus John: The New Biography*, p. 506.
11 Ibid, p. 508.
12 Ibid.
13 Ibid, p. 527.
14 Ibid, p. 525.
15 Augustus John in a letter to D. S. MacColl, 14 January 1945.
16 Holroyd, *Augustus John: The New Biography*, p. 529.
17 Ibid, p. 535.
18 Ferris, Paul, *Caitlin: The Life of Caitlin Thomas* (London: Pimlico, 1995), p. 55.
19 Ibid, p. 61.
20 Ibid, p. 72.
21 Augustus John in a letter to Dorelia McNeill, September 1938.
22 Holroyd, *Augustus John: The New Biography*, pp. 509–10.
23 Ibid, p. 518.

24 Ibid, p. 512.
25 John, Augustus, *Autobiography*, p. 234.
26 Ibid, pp. 234–6.
27 Holroyd, *Augustus John: The New Biography*, p. 522.
28 Augustus John in a letter to Mavis de Vere Cole, 10 March 1937.
29 John, Augustus, *Autobiography*, pp. 295–6.
30 Ibid, p. 299.
31 *The Listener*, 25 May 1938, pp. 1105–7.
32 O'Keefe, Paul, *Some Sort of Genius* (London: Jonathan Cape, 2000), p. 383.
33 Ibid.
34 *The New Statesman and Nation*, 4 June 1938, pp. 952–3.
35 *The Spectator*, 27 May 1938, p. 96.
36 *The Times*, 12 May 1938.
37 Holroyd, *Augustus John: The New Biography*, p. 517.
38 Vivien John in a letter to Edwin John, n.d.,1945.
39 Augustus John in a letter to Henry John, n.d., 1930; see also Holroyd, *Augustus John: The New Biography*, p. 539.
40 Augustus John in a letter to Mavis de Vere Cole, n.d.; see also Holroyd, *Augustus John: The New Biography*, p. 535.
41 Holroyd, *Augustus John: The New Biography*, p. 545.
42 Augustus John in a letter to Mavis de Vere Cole, [June 1935]; see also Holroyd, *Augustus John: The New Biography*, p. 547
43 John, Augustus, *Autobiography*, p. 239.
44 Father Martin D'Arcy in a letter to Augustus John, 28 June 1935.
45 Holroyd, *Augustus John: The New Biography*, p. 547.
46 Ibid, p. 549.
47 Ibid, p. 550.
48 Ottoline Morrell in a letter to Augustus John, 26 December 1937.
49 Augustus John in a letter to Gwen John, 16 April 1938.

CHAPTER EIGHTEEN

1 Gwen John, notebook, 1932, Lloyd-Morgan, Ceridwen, *Gwen John: Letters and Notebooks* (London: Tate, 2004), p. 179.
2 Rhoda Symons in a letter to Gwen John, 16 August 1931.
3 Gwen John, notebook, 26 April [1932].
4 Ibid, 18 January 1932.
5 Gwen John in a letter to Ursula Tyrwhitt, 4 April 1928, Lloyd-Morgan, p. 162.
6 Gwen John, notebook, 23 November 1931, Lloyd-Morgan, p. 128.

7   Ibid, March 1932, Lloyd-Morgan, p. 177.
8   Maynard Walker in a letter to Gwen John, 16 July 1930.
9   Gwen John in a letter to Frederic Newlin Price, 1 February 1931.
10 Gwen John, notebook, 15 January 1931, Lloyd-Morgan, p. 176.
11 Ibid, 13 March 1932, Lloyd-Morgan, p. 177.
12 Roe, Sue, *Gwen John: A Life* (London: Vintage, 2002), pp. 268–70.
13 Ibid.
14 Edwin John in a letter to Henry John, 17 October 1932.
15 Gwen John in a letter to Edwin John, n.d., [November] 1933.
16 Roe, p. 291.
17 Augustus John in a letter to Gwen John, 18 December 1932.
18 Gwen John in a letter to Dorelia McNeill, 21 September 1936.
19 Gwen John in a letter to Ursula Tyrwhitt, n.d., [July / August], Lloyd-Morgan, p. 184.
20 Ibid, 22 July 1936, Lloyd-Morgan, p. 183.
21 Ibid, 30 August 1936, Lloyd-Morgan, p. 185.
22 Ibid.
23 Roe, p. 186.
24 Langdale, Cecily, *Gwen John* (New Haven and London: Yale University Press, 1987), pp. 116–18.
25 Roe, p. 300.
26 Gwen John in a letter to Ursula Tyrwhitt, n.d., [spring] 1938, Lloyd-Morgan, p. 187.
27 Langdale, p. 119.
28 Gwen John in a letter to Thornton John, 16 February 1939.
29 Jean Jousset in a letter to Edwin John, 20 September 1939.
30 Edwin John in a letter to Maynard Walker, autumn 1939, cited in Langdale, p. 130.
31 Holroyd, Michael, *Augustus John: The New Biography* (London: Vintage, 1997), p. 557.
32 Augustus John in a letter to Edwin John, 16 December 1939.
33 Ibid, 11 September 1946.
34 Ibid, 4 March 1946.
35 Ibid.
36 Holroyd, *Augustus John: The New Biography*, pp. 572–3.
37 Augustus John in a letter to Edwin John, 27 December 1946.
38 Winifred John in a letter to Augustus John, 3 March 1956.
39 Boyd Haycock, David, *Brilliant Destiny: The Age of Augustus John* (London: Lund Humphries, 2023), p. 235.
40 John, Rebecca, *Thinking the Plant* (London: Pimpernel Press, 2020), p. 34.

41 Interviews with the author, 2024.
42 John, Rebecca, *Thinking the Plant*, pp. 34–5.

CHAPTER NINETEEN

1 Holroyd, Michael, *Augustus John: The New Biography* (London: Vintage, 1997), p. 557.
2 Ibid, p. 561.
3 John, Augustus, with Holroyd, Michael (ed.), *Augustus John: Autobiography* (London: Jonathan Cape, 1975), p. 288.
4 Poppet John in a letter to Edwin John, 1 September 1939.
5 Holroyd, *Augustus John: The New Biography*, p. 522.
6 Ibid, p. 563 and p. 557.
7 Ibid, p. 558.
8 Augustus John in a letter to William and Alice Rothenstein, 15 June 1940.
9 Augustus John in a letter to Edwin John, May 1940.
10 Ibid, 24 April 1940.
11 Holroyd, *Augustus John: The New Biography*, pp. 559–60.
12 Ibid, pp.561–2.
13 Ibid, p. 527.
14 Ibid, p. 563.
15 *The Burlington Magazine*, December 1940, p. 28.
16 Holroyd, *Augustus John: The New Biography*, p. 565.
17 Ibid, p. 573.
18 John, Augustus, *Autobiography*, p. 290.
19 Boyd Haycock, David, *Drawn from Life* (London: Paul Hoberton, 2018), p. 113.
20 *The Sunday Times*, 18 January 1953.
21 John, Augustus, *Autobiography*, p. 359.
22 Holroyd, *Augustus John: The New Biography*, pp. 575–7.
23 Ibid, pp. 578–9.
24 Ibid, pp. 568–9.
25 John, Augustus, *Autobiography*, p. 30.
26 Ibid, p. 107 and p. 252.
27 Ibid, p. 275 and p. 283.
28 Holroyd, *Augustus John: The New Biography*, p. 569.
29 John, Augustus, *Autobiography*, p. 305.
30 *The Listener*, 20 March 1952.
31 Holroyd, *Augustus John: The New Biography*, p. 563.
32 Ibid, p. 570.

33 Holroyd, Michael, *Augustus John: The Years of Innocence* (London: Heinemann, 1974), p. 54.
34 Holroyd, *Augustus John: The New Biography*, p. 584.
35 Ibid, p. 585.
36 Augustus John in a letter to Amaryllis Fleming, 17 January 1954.
37 *The Sunday Times*, 14 March 1954.
38 *The Times*, 13 March 1954.
39 Holroyd, *Augustus John: The New Biography*, p. 597.
40 Ibid, pp. 588–9.
41 Ibid, p .590.
42 Ibid, p. 598.
43 Boyd Haycock, *Drawn from Life*, p. 29.
44 Holroyd, *Augustus John: The New Biography*, p. 595.
45 David John in a letter to Augustus John, 16 May 1960.
46 Caspar John, in *Augustus and Gwen: The Fire and the Fountain* (documentary), BBC Wales, 1975.
47 Augustus John in a letter to Mavis de Vere Cole, October 1957.
48 Augustus John in a letter to Amaryllis Fleming, 1960.
49 Holroyd, *Augustus John: The New Biography*, p. 581.
50 Augustus John in a letter to Zoe Hicks, 9 March 1959.
51 Augustus John in a letter to Amaryllis Fleming, 11 November 1953.
52 Holroyd, *Augustus John: The New Biography*, p. 583.
53 Ibid.
54 Ibid, p. 592.
55 Augustus John in a letter to Charles Wheeler, 9 March 1961.
56 Holroyd, *Augustus John: The New Biography*, pp. 598–9.
57 David John in a letter to Robin John, 20 November 1971.
58 Boyd Haycock, *Drawn from Life*, p. 11; and Holroyd, *Augustus John: The New Biography*, p. 600.
59 Richard Shone, 'The Augustus John Exhibition at Cambridge', *The Burlington Magazine*, 1978, pp. 869–71.
60 John, Augustus, *Autobiography*, p. 38.
61 Ida John in a letter to Mary Dowdall, n.d., [May / June] 1904, Holroyd and John (eds.), *The Good Bohemian: The Letters of Ida John* (London: Bloomsbury, 2018), p. 169.

BIBLIOGRAPHY

PRINCIPAL ARCHIVES

National Library of Wales, correspondence and personal papers of Gwen and Augustus John.
National Gallery Wales, artworks of Gwen and Augustus John.
Tate Britain, London, transcriptions of selected correspondence of Augustus John.
Musée Rodin, Paris, correspondence between Auguste Rodin and Gwen John.
New York Public Library, correspondence of John Quinn.
Houghton Library, Harvard University, Cambridge, Massachusetts, correspondence of William and Alice Rothenstein.

CATALOGUES

Gwen John:
Gwen John at Anthony d'Offay Gallery, London, 1976 and 2000.
Langdale, Cecily, and Fraser Jenkins, David, *Gwen John: An Interior Life* at Barbican Gallery, London, Barbican Publishing, 1985.
Augustus John:
Augustus John at Hazlitt Holland-Hibbert Gallery, London, London and New York, Hazlitt Holland-Hibbert, 2004.
Boyd Haycock, David, *Drawn from Life* at Poole Museum, 2018 and Salisbury Museum, 2019, London, Paul Hoberton Publishing, 2018.
Boyd Haycock, David, *Augustus John and the First Crisis of Brilliance* at Piano Nobile Gallery, London, 2024.

Frazer Jenkins, David, and Stephens, Chris (eds.), *Gwen John and Augustus John* at Tate Gallery, London, Tate Publishing, 2004.

BOOKS

Boyd Haycock, David, *Brilliant Destiny: The Age of Augustus John*, London: Lund Humphries, 2023.
Chitty, Susan, *Gwen John: 1876–1939*, London: Hodder & Stoughton, 1985.
Ferris, Paul, *Caitlin: The Life of Caitlin Thomas*, London: Pimlico, 1995.
Foster, Alicia, *Gwen John: Art and Life in Paris and London*, London: Thames and Hudson, 2023.
Grunfeld, Frederic V., *Rodin*, London: Hutchinson, 1987.
Higgie, Jennifer, *The Mirror and the Palette*, London: Weidenfeld & Nicholson, 2021.
Holroyd, Michael, *Augustus John: The New Biography*, London: Vintage, 1997.
Holroyd, Michael, *Augustus John: The Years of Innocence*, London: Heinemann, 1974.
Holroyd, Michael, and John, Rebecca (eds.), *The Good Bohemian: The Letters of Ida John*, London: Bloomsbury, 2018.
John, Augustus, *Chiaroscuro: Fragments of Autobiography*, London: Jonathan Cape, 1952.
John, Augustus, *Finishing Touches*, London: Jonathan Cape, 1964.
John, Augustus, with Holroyd, Michael (ed.), *Augustus John: Autobiography*, London: Jonathan Cape, 1975 (amalgamated edition of *Chiaroscuro* and *Finishing Touches*).
John, Rebecca, *Thinking the Plant*, London: Pimpernel Press, 2020.
Langdale, Cecily, *Gwen John*, New Haven and London: Yale University Press, 1987.
Lloyd-Morgan, Ceridwen, *Gwen John: Letters and Notebooks*, London: Tate Publishing, 2004.
Londraville, Richard and Janis, *Dear Yeats, Dear Pound, Dear Ford: Jeanne Robert Foster and Her Circle of Friends*, Syracuse: Syracuse University Press, 2001.
Mackrell, Judith, *Flappers*, London: Macmillan, 2013.
Mackrell, Judith, *The Unfinished Palazzo*, London: Thames and Hudson, 2017.
Nicholson, Virginia, *Among the Bohemians*, London: Penguin, 2003.
O'Keefe, Paul, *Some Sort of Genius: A Life of Wyndham Lewis*, London: Jonathan Cape, 2000.
Roe, Sue, *Gwen John: A Life*, London: Vintage, 2002.
Rothenstein, John, *Augustus John*, London: Phaidon, 1944.
Sawyer, Miranda, *Ottoline Morrell*, London: Sceptre, 1993.
Sturgis, Matthew, *Walter Sickert: A Life*, London: HarperCollins, 2005.
Tamboukou, Maria, *In the Fold Between Power and Desire: Women Artists' Narratives*, Newcastle-upon-Tyne: Cambridge Scholars, 2010.
Taubman, Mary, *Gwen John*, London: Scholar Press, 1985.

INDEX

Alick *see* Schepeler
Alpine Club, Mayfair 248, 249, 283
Amaryllis (daughter of Augustus and
    Eve) *see* Fleming
Anderson, Julia 299
Apollinaire, Guillaume 139, 190
Arenig school 212–13
Armory Show, New York 191, 213n,
    228, 292
Arthur (groom) 194, 197, 198
Artists' International Association 361
Asquith, Cynthia 247, 253, 260
Athenaeum 138, 170, 208
Ayrton, Michael 365–6

Baden-Powell, Lord 285
Bankhead, Tallulah 284
Beardsley, Aubrey 26, 57
Beaton, Cecil 319, 381, 382
Beaverbrook, Max Aitken, Lord 249,
    251, 253
Beecham, Thomas 376
Beerbohm, Max 80
Bell, Clive 172, 209n, 210, 335
Bell, Vanessa 172, 209, 210, 284
Berners, Lord 286
Bertram, Anthony 376
Beuret, Rose 107, 112, 254
Binyon, Laurence 208
Bishop, Bridget 343–4, 348
Bishop, Edgar 126
Bishop, Louise *see* Salaman

Blast 248, 251
Bloch, Frieda 140, 143, 145
Bloomsbury Group 172, 236, 249
Blunt, Anthony 284n, 335
Bond, Henry 260
Boudin, Eugène 319
Boughton-Leigh, Chloe
    appearance 160–1
    modelling for Gwen 160–1, 184
    portraits 160–1, 162, 184, 188, 232n, 294n
    relationship with Gwen 246, 268, 315,
        316–17, 341, 345, 350, 353–4
Boughton-Leigh, Grilda 160, 316
Bowser, Isabel
    beliefs 268, 269
    death 268, 269, 270, 302
    family background 217, 269, 271, 272
    Meudon life 215
    relationship with Gwen 159, 217, 268–9,
        270, 302
British Museum 24, 138
Brooke, Rupert 196–7, 335
Brouke, Leonard (met in La Réole) 88, 94,
    96–100
Brown, Fred 24, 32, 34, 53, 80
Brownsword, Norah 242
The Burlington Magazine 283, 357
Burns, Tom 347

Cabbage Hall, gypsy encampment 71, 73, 175
Café Royal 80–1
Cameron, Dr 321, 330, 339

Canadian War Memorials Fund 249, 251, 253
Carfax Gallery, Piccadilly 56, 85, 170
Carlyle, Thomas 172–3
Carnegie Institute International Exhibition, Pittsburgh 291, 292
Carrington, Dora 240
Casati, Luisa, Marchesa 262–3, 374n, 380
Cecil, Lord David 383, 385
Cerutti, Estella 81–3, 146
Cézanne, Paul
  ambitions 286
  exhibitions 175, 191, 209, 375
  influence on Augustus 176, 201, 205, 206, 209–10, 231, 252, 285, 375
  influence on Gwen 184–5, 231, 305, 349
  influence on Innes 212
  landscapes 176, 201, 206, 210
  portrait of son 204n
Chamot, Mary 33, 305
Channon, Chips 365
Chelsea Art School 88–9, 91, 131, 138, 139, 150
Chenil Gallery
  Augustus's exhibitions 138, 170, 208, 228
  finances 163, 301n
  Gwen's exhibition 301, 303–5
  reopening 301
  shipping Gwen's work 190, 232
Chéruy, Renée 111, 117
Chiquita 288–9, 324, 361
Choiseul, Claire de 178–82, 207, 218, 219, 223
Clarke Hall, Edna (Waugh)
  character 29, 30
  Chelsea Art School 89
  engagement 37
  marriage 51, 112, 302
  memories of Augustus 40, 178
  relationship with Augustus 176
  relationship with Gwen 77
  relationship with Ida 30, 35, 164, 176
  Slade studies 28–30, 37, 40
  wedding 51
  work 28–9, 30–1, 37, 40, 76
Clarke Hall, William (Willie) 37, 51, 76, 176
Claudel, Camille 113
Cole, Horace de Vere 322, 338–9

Cole, Mavis de Vere (née Wright, later Wheeler)
  birth of son Tristan 322–3
  death of Horace 338
  Fryern visit 323
  letters from Augustus 332, 333–4, 337, 340
  marriages 322, 323
  relationship with Augustus 322–4, 365, 378–9
  trial 323n
Cole, Tristan de Vere (son of Augustus and Mavis) 322–3, 332, 361, 368
Colette 139
Conder, Charles 54, 57–9, 60–1, 68, 122, 139, 171, 319, 380
Connolly, Cyril 370, 372
Cornford, Frances 162
Cremnitz, Maurice 139, 165
Crowley, Aleister 153
Cunard, Nancy 241
Cuthbert, Caroline 359

Daily Telegraph 383
D'Arcy, Father 338
Davis and Langdale gallery, New York 359–60
de la Mare, Walter 376
de Vere Cole *see* Cole
Delaunay, Sonia 294
Delphine (live-in nursemaid) 153, 163
Denis, Maurice 185n, 222n, 295
Derain, André 305n, 361
Diélette 176
Dodo *see* McNeill (Dorelia)
d'Offay, Anthony 359–60
Dorelia *see* McNeill
Dostoyevsky, Fyodor 75, 80, 124, 171, 193, 224, 370
Douglas, Norman 365
Dowdall, Harold Chaloner 70, 73, 197–8
Dowdall, Mary
  appearance 70
  background 70
  death 380
  letters from Augustus 82, 124, 155, 287, 289
  letters from Ida 82, 83, 92, 96, 123–4, 129, 130–1, 137, 146, 153, 385

relationship with Augustus 70, 91–2, 124, 197–8
relationship with Ida 70, 96, 126, 128
Doyle, Arthur Conan 291
du Maurier, Gerald 284
Dudley Gallery, Piccadilly 53

Elder, Miss (Slade teaching assistant) 29
Eliot, T. S. 190
Empson, William 378
Epstein, Jacob
  friendship with Augustus 139, 177, 187, 228, 231
  New York exhibition 294n
  social status 229
  view of Augustus's sculpture 368
Equihen 165–8, 169, 170
Estella *see* Cerutti
Evans, Allen 17–18
Evans, Benjamin
  Amsterdam trip 43
  friendship with Augustus 26, 38, 64, 139
  Slade studies 26, 31
  studio plans 44
Everett, John 25, 33, 40, 59
Everett, Katherine 212
Everett, Mrs Aurelia
  Augustus and Ida's honeymoon 66
  landlady of 21 Fitzroy Street 33–4, 59
  Salvation Army 33–4
  Slade studies 33
  summer picnic 34, 42
  Swanage boarding house 56, 60, 61, 66

Fabio de Castro 175
Faerber and Maison 359
Fairfax, Eve 109
Ferargil Gallery, New York 305, 344, 345, 350
Firbank, Ronald 241, 263
First World War
  American entry 247
  armistice 259, 260–1
  Augustus's experiences 236–7, 238–9, 240–1, 249–53
  casualties 240, 243–4
  conscription 249
  German advances on Paris 234–5, 256–7
  Gwen's experiences 234–6, 243–4, 256–7

home defence 236, 239
London life 240–1
medical services 239, 244
outbreak 232–3
wounded men 243–4
Zeppelin bombs 240
Fisher, Admiral 248
Fleming, Amaryllis (daughter of Augustus and Eve) 289–90, 363, 373, 377–8
Fleming, Eve 287–9
Fletcher, Fanny 317
Flodin, Hilda 102, 109, 111, 115, 116–17
Fort, Paul 139
Foster, Alicia 220
Foster, Jeanne Robert
  appearance 274
  career 274
  death of Quinn 298–9
  finances 299
  health 296
  portrait by Gwen 279–80
  relationship with Gwen 274–7, 279–80, 295–9, 300, 302, 311, 356
  relationship with Quinn 274, 293–4, 296, 299
  visiting Augustus in New York 293–4
Fothergill, John 194
Fournier, Charles 369
Freud, Lucian 379
Fry, Roger 121–2, 193–4, 206n, 209–10, 248
Fuller, Governor Alvan T. 293

Gandarillas, Jose-Antonio de 262
Gauguin, Paul 209, 210, 285, 384
George, Daniel 370–1
Gerhardie, Miss (painter) 111, 115
Gleizes, Albert 277, 295
Gogarty, Oliver St John 227
Gonne, Maude 243–4
Gordon Craig, Edward 229
Gore, Spencer 40, 54
Goupil Gallery 228
Grafton Gallery 209–10, 211, 285
Gramont, Duchesse de 262
Gregory, Augusta, Lady 169–70, 171, 239
Gregory, Robert 169, 249
Gregory family 169–70
Grigson, Geoffrey 335

420 INDEX

Gwen John: An Interior Life (touring exhibition) 360
Gypsy Lore Society 70, 196, 201, 368

Hale, Kathleen 290
Hamnet, Nina 321
Hardy, Thomas 71, 284–5
Harris, Frank 207
Harrison, Jane 195–6, 199
Hart, Miss (painter in Paris) 95
Hastings, Beatrice 236
Hatch, Ethel 23, 27–8, 34
Haverfordwest 8–12
Head, Edward 19–20
Hicks, Zoe (daughter of Augustus and Chiquita)
  birth 289
  career 363, 377
  custody 289
  father's old age 379, 382
  French holiday 361, 362
  paternity recognized 289, 361
  portrait by Augustus 362
  wartime work 363
Holbrooke, Joseph 228
Holmes, C. J. 193
Holroyd, Michael 384
Hone, Joseph 329
Hope Johnstone, John 288, 300
Horizon magazine 370
Hudson, Edwin 283
Hughes, Richard 327, 383

Innes, James Dickson 212–13, 228, 239, 375, 380
International Society of Sculptors, Painters and Engravers 107, 161

Janes, Fred 327
John, Alfred (uncle) 9, 12, 46
John, Anna (daughter of David) 336
John, Augusta (Smith, mother) 3, 8, 9–12, 156
John, Augustus (Gus)
  Amsterdam trip 43
  appearance 2, 11, 17, 22, 23, 25, 34, 39–40, 42, 50, 54, 55, 58, 65, 67, 68, 70, 135, 140, 171, 197, 247, 249–50, 252, 260, 286, 287, 290, 320, 322

Arenig school 212–13
armistice celebrations 260
belief in art 121
biography 384
birth 10
birth of daughter Amaryllis 289
birth of daughter Poppet 226
birth of daughter Vivien 242
birth of daughter Zoe 289
birth of son Caspar 82
birth of son David 74
birth of son Edwin 136
birth of son Henry 154
birth of son Pyramus 129–30
birth of son Robin 122
birth of son Romilly 145
birth of son Tristan 322–3
camping in Ireland 38
camping on Dartmoor 129–31, 194
Canadian Armed Forces wartime position 249–52, 253, 255
caravan holiday with Dorelia and children 194–5, 196–8
career 1–2, 4, 40, 68–9, 85–6, 91
cars 286, 309, 374
character 2, 3, 5–6, 40, 58, 59, 64, 81, 82, 92, 124, 127, 131, 141, 146, 170, 173, 205, 229–30, 255–6, 290–1, 372, 380–1, 385
Chelsea Art School 88–9, 91, 131, 138, 139, 150
Chenil Gallery role 301
childhood 2–3, 7–8, 10–15, 385
CND membership 369–70
commissioned murals 200, 228
commissioned portraits 54–5, 172, 195–6, 228, 247, 261, 282–4, 364
commissioned stage designs 329–31
custody battle with mother-in-law 174–5
death 1, 382–3, 384
death of father 339–40, 351–2, 379
death of Ida 3, 155–6, 157–8, 167–9
death of mother 11–12, 156
death of sister Gwen 355
death of son Henry 337–8
death of son Pyramus 225–6, 232, 293, 338
diving accident 39–40

INDEX

drawing 3, 7, 10, 17, 19–20, 24–5, 31, 40, 56, 68
drinking 61, 157–8, 176, 206, 240, 273, 320–2, 364–5
drugs 262, 287, 320
education 3, 4, 13, 16–20
Equihen stay 165–8
exhibitions 1, 53, 56, 76, 77, 85, 138, 149, 170, 208, 248, 301–2, 303–4, 334, 366, 373–4, 384
Face to Face interview 376
fall from ladder 73
family background 8–10
fatherhood 74, 91, 164, 166–9, 195, 198, 199, 226–7, 242–3, 310, 335–7, 363–4, 365n, 376–8
finances 4, 5, 25–6, 31, 44–5, 50, 53–4, 56, 59, 68, 73, 163, 169, 170, 178, 186–8, 201, 230, 241, 261, 292, 319–20
French holiday with Dorelia and children 174–6
French holidays 60–1
friendships 26, 31, 40, 41, 139, 187, 217, 272, 273, 293
funeral 383
Gwen's exhibition 356–7
gypsies 10, 14, 39, 42, 70–1, 73, 75, 90, 128, 129, 143, 175, 193, 194, 195, 200, 201–2, 202–3, 211, 286, 367–9, 383, 385
handwriting 379–80
health 16, 39–40, 56, 59, 60, 73, 91, 149, 171, 193, 249, 273, 282, 291, 320–2, 330, 348, 374–5, 377, 379, 382–3
home in Alderney Manor, Dorset 211–14, 216, 224–5, 226, 228, 229–30, 236, 242–3, 244, 253, 266–7, 283, 288–9, 306–7, 324, 364
home in Church Street, Chelsea 176, 199–200, 211, 215, 230
home in Elm House, Essex 90, 91, 92, 96, 107, 122–3, 125–6, 128, 132–4
home in Fitzroy Street 66, 68, 80, 84–5, 86
home in Fryern Court, Hampshire 307–9, 311, 319–21, 323–7, 329, 336–7, 362, 364, 368, 376, 378, 379–83, 362, 363–4, 380, 381

home in Mallord Street, Chelsea 230–1, 241, 250, 282, 286–7, 290, 323
home (*mas*) in Saint-Rémy-de-Provence 332, 361–2, 367, 374
influences on 25, 31–2, 43, 55–6, 59, 69, 166, 176, 205, 206, 285, 369–70
Italian tour 202
Jamaica visit 332–4, 368
letters to Dorelia 78, 79, 88, 90, 91, 95–6, 97, 100, 132–3, 149, 186, 201, 203, 227, 233, 240, 242, 250, 252–3, 255, 264, 292–3
letters to Gwen 90, 91, 96, 102, 105, 106, 107, 120–1, 232, 233, 236–7, 239, 260, 266, 267, 268, 273, 299, 300, 303, 340, 348, 351
letters to Ida 42, 64, 65, 66, 132–3, 167–9
Liverpool Art School teaching post 68–9, 73–4, 76n
Liverpool commissions 131–2, 197
Liverpool lodgings 70, 73, 74
London life 25–6, 29, 53–4, 80–1, 149, 286–7
London lodgings 20, 22, 27, 33–6, 40, 59, 61
Mallorca visit 331
marriage 2, 5, 64–5, 66, 68, 90–2, 105–7
Martigues stays (Villa Sainte Anne) 204–8, 291, 336
memorial service 383–4, 385
music 91
name 177
New York visit 292–3
Normandy holiday 57
obituaries 383
old age 374–83
Order of Merit 367
painting 25, 31–2, 60
Paris Christmas 149–50
Paris life 138–9
Paris Peace Conference 261–4
Paris plans 146–7, 150
Paris visits 50, 58–9, 96–7, 237
Provence stays 206, 228, 304, 332, 361–2, 367
Quinn's patronage 186–8, 193, 198, 201, 278
quoted 193, 361

John, Augustus (cont.)
  reading 75, 80, 91, 124, 193, 369, 370
  relationship with Ada (mother-in-law) 42, 64–5, 163–4, 166–9, 174–5, 338
  relationship with Alick 139–41, 143–7, 149, 378
  relationship with Brigit Macnamara 324, 326–7
  relationship with Caitlin Macnamara 324, 325–8
  relationship with Chiquita 288–9, 324, 361
  relationship with Dorelia 2, 78, 79, 83–4, 86, 95–7, 99–100, 125–6, 146, 149, 174, 176–7, 199–200, 203, 211, 227, 366–7, 378, 381
  relationship with Estella 81–3, 146
  relationship with Euphemia Lamb 167
  relationship with Eve Fleming 287–90
  relationship with Ida 40–2, 43, 64–5, 79–81, 92, 96, 106, 107, 123–4, 146, 149
  relationship with Kathleen Hale 290
  relationship with Luisa Casati 262–3, 380
  relationship with Maria Katerina 60–2
  relationship with Mavis 322–4, 338, 365, 378–9
  relationship with Ottoline Morrell 171–4, 177, 206–7, 321, 339
  relationship with Quinn 186–8, 278, 293–4
  relationship with Sampson 70–1, 72, 84, 134, 135, 145, 198, 226, 261, 284, 338
  relationship with sister Gwen 3–4, 5, 16–17, 34–5, 39, 56, 120–1, 136, 141–5, 157, 162–3, 224–5, 231–3, 237, 238, 254–5, 267–8, 273, 277, 299–300, 306–10, 313, 316, 317–18, 319, 348, 355–6, 384–5
  relationship with Ursula Tyrwhitt 36, 38–9, 40, 41
  relationship with Wyndham Lewis 80–1, 139, 167, 187, 203, 248, 251, 334–5, 380
  religious views 224
  reputation 2, 5–6, 140, 170–1, 210–11, 283–4, 292, 366, 383, 384
  response to Gwen's travels with Dorelia 88–9
  response to Ida and Dorelia's Paris plans 132–4, 135
  reviews 56, 77, 85, 121–2, 138, 149, 170, 198, 208–9, 210, 248, 283–4, 334–5, 366, 372, 373–4, 376
  Royal Academy membership 285–6, 334
  Sainte Honorine holiday 143–6
  sales 56, 138, 170, 187, 209, 239, 384
  secretary 290
  sex life 43, 55, 59, 60, 205, 229–30, 240–2, 287, 365, 378
  Slade scholarship 31
  Slade demonstration to life-drawing class 55–6
  Slade studies 3–4, 22–5, 31–2, 40, 44–5
  Slade Summer Competition prize 44–5, 50
  Society of Twelve 122, 228
  studios 45, 52, 54, 66, 68, 91, 135, 138, 149, 150, 152, 153, 170, 364, 378–9
  Swanage honeymoon 66
  Swanage visits 56, 60
  teenage years 18–19, 371
  Tenby Freedom 379
  Tenby visits 44–5, 72, 273, 339, 379
  travels in Europe 201–4, 291, 375
  US visit 291–4
  Venice visit 331–2
  view of Gwen biography 357–8
  view of Gwen's work 360, 371
  view of London art world 120, 122, 200
  violence 197, 198, 253, 320, 327
  wartime experiences (WWI) 236–7, 238–9, 240–1, 247, 248–52, 253
  wartime experiences (WWII) 361–5, 367, 368
  wedding 64–5
  works
    Ardor 121
    Athaliah 71
    The Blue Pool 214
    bust of Yeats 368
    canvases destroyed by fire 329
    Caravan, A Gypsy Encampment 130
    copy of Watteau 31
    The Dawn 249
    Dorelia in a Feathered Hat 121
    Dorelia in the Garden of Alderney Manor 214

drawings of Gwen 34–5
drawings of Joyce 328–9
essay on Gwen's work 357
etchings 69, 169–70, 384
A Family Group 166
Fraternity 261, 266n
A French Fisherboy 165–6
Galway frieze 240, 247
A Jamaican Girl 334
Jamaican portraits 334
landscapes 204–5, 208, 212–13, 375
late portraits 375–6, 382, 384
Liverpool sketches 69
Lyric Fantasy frieze 228
memoirs (*Chiaroscuro, Finishing Touches*) 36n, 370–3, 377, 385
Merikli 79–80
Moses and the Brazen Serpent 44–5, 55
Mother and Child 138
Mumpers frieze 210, 228
An Old Lady 54–5
The Orange Jacket 239
Paris Peace Conference portraits 261–3
poems 66n, 97, 322, 370, 379
portrait of Alick 170
portrait of Baden-Powell 285
portrait of Beaton 382
portrait of Brigit 327
portrait of Caitlin 326–7
portrait of Dowdall 197, 199
portrait of Hardy 284–5
portrait of Jane Harrison 195–6, 199
portrait of Joseph Hone 329
portrait of Lloyd George 247, 266
portrait of Michel 61
portrait of Montgomery 364
portrait of Pyramus 172, 210
portrait of Quinn 185–6
portrait of Shaw 239–40
portrait of Suggia 282–3, 284n
portrait of Theodore Powys 329
portrait of Tristan 368
portrait of William Nicholson 195, 199
portraits of Dorelia 79–80, 121, 198, 213–14, 231, 382
portraits of Dylan Thomas 328
portraits of Ida 31, 79–80, 163, 228
portraits of Yeats 169–70, 328

Provençal studies 208, 210
Sainte Sara triptych 367–8, 374, 375, 381–2
sculpture 368
self-portraits 67, 140
sketch of Ida and Dorelia 137
Smiling Woman 193–4, 198, 240
Sonnet 158
stage design (*The Boy David*) 330–1
stage design (*The Silver Tassie*) 329–30
Tête Farouche 140
The Tinkers (*The Little Concert*) 362–3
war frieze (*Pageant of War*) 250–1, 253, 261, 362
The Way Down to the Sea 187
writings 370
John, Betty (wife of Edwin, daughter-in-law of Augustus) 317, 355, 364
John, Caspar (son of Augustus and Ida)
appearance 164, 166, 324
birth 82
career 242–3, 266, 336, 376
character 243
childhood 84, 91, 129–30, 134, 376
custody issues 164, 166, 167–9, 174–5
education 148, 163
grandfather's funeral 339–40
grandmother's care 163–4, 166
health 136
marriage 376
mother's death 163
relationship with Caitlin 324
relationship with father 227, 243, 376–7
John, Clara (aunt) 12
John, David (son of Augustus and Ida)
appearance 164, 166
birth 74–5
career 252, 336
character 153
childhood 82, 84, 91, 129–30, 143, 153
Christmas with grandmother 149
custody issues 164, 166, 168, 174–5
education 148, 242, 266
fatherhood 336, 376
father's death 383
grandmother's care 163–4, 166, 167–9
health 136, 150
marriages 336

John, David (*cont.*)
  mother's death 163
  music 242, 252, 266, 336
  painting by father 176
  photographs 76, 164
  relationship with father 143, 242, 243, 376, 381
  relationship with Gwen 307
  sketch of 141
John, Edwin (father)
  appearance 10, 105
  Augustus's diving accident 39
  career 9, 12
  character 3, 9, 10, 13
  childhood 9
  children 10, 11
  death 339–40, 351–2
  education 9, 16
  fatherhood 3, 10, 13–16, 18–20, 27, 35, 46, 50–1, 184, 219, 316
  finances 12, 20, 51, 83n, 184, 316, 339–40
  funeral 339–40
  grandchildren's visit 105
  hobbies 46
  holiday house in Broad Haven 10
  home in Haverfordwest 8–9, 11, 12
  homes in Tenby 12, 45n, 46
  Ida's visit 72
  marriage 8, 9, 10
  Paris visits 51, 105, 183–4
  relationship with women as a widower 19
  visited in Tenby 72, 105, 148, 278
  wife's illness and death 8, 10–12
  will 339–40
John, Edwin (son of Augustus and Ida)
  birth 136, 137
  boxing 336, 347
  childhood 148, 163
  custody issues 168
  death 359
  education 266–7, 310
  executor of Gwen's estate 355–6
  exhibitions of Gwen's works 356–7, 359
  fatherhood 355
  Gwen biography question 357–8
  letter from Poppet 361–2
  marriage 317, 355
  mother's death 163

  painting ambitions 307, 310, 336, 347
  Paris studies 347, 351
  protection of Gwen's work 359
  relationship with brother Robin 377
  relationship with father 310, 336, 356–8, 363–4, 376
  relationship with Gwen 307, 310, 336, 347, 355, 359n
  wartime experiences 363
  works 319
John, Frederick (uncle) 12
John, Gwen
  appearance 11, 27–8, 32, 34–5, 51, 67, 76, 90, 103, 109, 158–9, 237, 307, 309
  biography 357–8
  birth 10, 358
  Brittany stays in Pléneuf 257–8, 259, 264–5, 274
  brother Augustus's visits 237, 254, 255, 300
  brother Thornton's visit 219, 224
  career 2, 4, 85–6
  cat Mudge 14
  cat Tiger 95, 111, 114, 115, 118, 142–3, 159, 162, 219
  cats 217, 232, 246, 265, 308, 311, 315, 318, 342, 346, 354
  character 2, 3, 5–6, 19, 38, 58, 93–4, 102, 273, 275–6, 316, 342, 346–7, 371, 385
  Chateau Vauclair purchase question 265–8, 271–2
  childhood 2–3, 7–8, 10–15, 18–19, 385
  death 1, 354–5
  death of father 340, 351–2
  death of Ida 157–8, 219
  death of Isabel 268–9
  death of mother 11–12, 156, 219
  death of Quinn 192, 298–9, 302
  death of Rodin 3, 254–6, 268
  depression 219–20
  draughtsmanship 258
  drawing 3, 7, 10, 15, 19, 28, 118, 246, 343
  education 3, 4, 15–16, 20–1
  exhibitions 1, 53, 85, 184, 187, 190, 191, 221, 267, 293–5, 303–5

INDEX

exhibitions after her death 1, 356–7, 358, 359–60, 366n, 384
family background 8–10
finances 4, 29, 45–6, 47, 49, 50–1, 53, 83n, 87, 93–4, 95, 111, 113, 162, 178, 180, 185, 188–90, 192, 215, 232–3, 245, 274, 299–300, 315, 316–17, 340, 353
friendships 29–31, 159–60, 217
grave 354–5, 383
health 12, 183, 219–20, 245, 297, 317, 341–2, 348, 349–54
home in Fryern (Yew Tree Cottage) 308–9, 310–11, 315, 317, 318, 319, 353
home in Meudon (rue Terre Neuve) 215–19, 245, 246, 257, 274–5, 278, 279, 299, 309, 344, 350
home in Meudon (*hangar* in rue Babie) 315–17, 346, 350, 353, 355–6, 359n
ideas for work 246
influences on 32, 183, 184–5, 188–9, 305, 342, 349
Le Puy holiday 62
letter to Ida 51
letters to Augustus 143–4, 219–20, 225, 232, 234, 235, 236, 299–300, 303
letters to Dorelia 98–9, 100, 104, 136, 348
letters to Rodin 111, 112, 114–17, 142, 151, 161, 237, 358n
Liverpool visit to Augustus and Ida 75–6
London life 53
London lodgings 27, 29, 33–5, 52, 56, 59–60, 144
Melville Nettleship Prize for Figure Composition 45
Meudon life 217–18
modelling 51, 52, 94–7, 101, 110, 159
modelling for Rodin 101, 102–4, 107–8, 111, 150
painting 32–3, 118, 246, 343
painting holiday in New Quay 72
Paris Christmas 149
Paris life 101, 104–5
Paris lodgings
  rue Froidevaux (Cold Veal Street) 47, 48, 52

Hotel Mont Blanc 94, 97, 105, 113
rue de l'Ouest 183, 215
rue du Cherche-Midi 151–2, 183
rue Saint-Placide 114, 151
Paris stay with Dorelia 94–7
Paris stay with Ida and Gwen Salmond 45–52
Paris studies 49–50, 159
Quinn's patronage 188–9, 190, 293–4, 300
quoted 102, 301, 341
reading 72, 118, 150, 218, 224, 265
relationship with Ambrose 62–4, 66–7, 72, 97
relationship with brother Augustus 3–4, 5, 16–17, 35, 39, 64–5, 66–7, 75–7, 120–1, 136, 141–5, 150, 157, 162–3, 219–20, 224–5, 231–3, 234, 237, 254–5, 267–8, 277–8, 299–300, 317–18, 319, 348, 355, 371–2, 385
relationship with brother Thornton 219, 224, 254, 351–2
relationship with Canon Piermé 314–15, 316
relationship with Constance 95, 105, 110, 159, 270, 280, 294, 311, 346
relationship with Dorelia (Dodo, Dorothy) 77–8, 85, 89–90, 93–4, 98–9, 136, 306–7, 317–18, 348, 353
relationship with 'Elinor' 38, 57
relationship with father 3, 19, 27, 46, 50–1, 72, 105, 183–4, 219, 316, 340
relationship with Frenchwoman in Toulouse 93–4
relationship with Ida 50, 66–7, 75–6, 97, 106–7, 136, 158
relationship with Isabel 159, 217, 268–9, 270, 302
relationship with Jeanne 274–7, 279–80, 293–4, 295–9, 300, 302, 311, 356
relationship with Louise Roche 346–7
relationship with Meudon curé 220, 221, 245, 276
relationship with Michel Salaman 56–7, 62, 63, 75, 304, 306
relationship with nephew Edwin 307, 310, 336, 347, 355–6

John, Gwen (cont.)
  relationship with nephew Henry 309, 347–8
  relationship with niece Vivien 307, 353
  relationship with Nona 269–70, 280, 311, 356
  relationship with Quinn 189–92, 278–9, 298–9
  relationship with Rodin 2, 4, 103–4, 108–10, 111–18, 136, 141–4, 150–1, 158–62, 178–82, 215–16, 218–20, 223, 233, 237–8
  relationship with Ruth Manson 217, 246, 256, 257, 274, 346
  relationship with sister Winnie 18–19, 34, 36, 63, 116, 224, 244, 276, 311, 353, 358
  relationship with Ursula 158, 159–60, 162, 189–90, 217, 223–4, 237, 245–6, 247, 257, 278, 302–4, 308, 316, 348–9, 352, 353
  relationship with Véra 311–14, 315, 316, 347, 356
  religion 2, 217–21, 223–4, 225, 309, 341–2, 345–6
  reputation 5–6, 294, 359–60, 383, 384
  reviews 162, 183, 190, 305–6
  Sainte Honorine visit 141–5, 150
  sales 53, 162, 188–9, 258, 294, 305, 346
  sexuality 18–19, 37–8, 57, 93, 117, 269–70
  Slade student life 3, 29–31, 33–6
  Slade studies 3–4, 21, 27–8, 32, 45
  studies with Whistler at Académie Carmen 49–50
  studio in rue de l'Ouest 215, 235, 237, 255, 256
  Swanage seaside holiday with Augustus 56–7
  teaching 77
  teenage years 18–19
  Tenby summer life 45
  Tenby visits 72
  Toulouse stay with Dorelia 89–90, 93–4
  travelling with Dorelia 85, 86–8, 89–90, 94
  visiting Augustus and family 106–7, 306–7, 308–9
  visiting England 277, 318
  wartime experiences in France 234–6, 243–4, 247, 256–7, 258, 264
  wedding of Augustus and Ida 64, 66–7
  will 354, 355–6
  works
    attic paintings 151, 160, 238
    Brittany drawings 258
    The Brown Teapot 238n
    catalogue raisonné 360
    La Chambre sur la Cour 162, 188
    The Convalescent 247
    Convalescent series 268
    copy of Metsu painting 32, 356
    A Corner of the Artist's Room in Paris 151–2, 160
    Dorelia by Lamplight at Toulouse 89
    Dorelia in a Black Dress 90, 302, 305
    drawings of Pléneuf boys and girls 265, 278
    L'enfant with poupée 269
    Girl by a Window series 345
    Girl in Blue series 294
    A Girl Reading by a Window 190, 191
    Girl with Bare Shoulders 183, 184
    Interior 238
    Interior with Figures 48, 77, 158
    A Lady Reading 189, 190, 220, 294n
    Landscape at Tenby with Figures 7–8, 35
    notebooks 116, 150, 216, 220, 231, 280, 296, 343–5, 354, 356
    Nude Girl 183, 184, 188, 294n
    La Petite Modèle 238
    poems 159
    Portrait Group 35, 48
    portrait of Bridget Bishop 343–4, 347–8
    portrait of Jeanne 277, 279–80
    portrait of Mère Poussepin 221–2, 276, 278
    portrait of Mrs Atkinson 32–3
    portraits of Chloe 160–1, 162, 184, 188, 232n, 294n
    portraits of Fenella 182–3, 184, 185, 188–9, 277
    portraits of Meudon model 222–3, 238, 270, 304

portraits of nuns 221–2, 238, 267, 276, 278, 294n
portraits of Winnie 35, 36, 49, 53
Self Portrait 52–3
Self Portrait in a Red Blouse 67
self-portraits 48–9, 115–16, 118–19, 158–9, 160
sketches of Allied generals 245–6
sketches of cat 118, 160
sketches of interiors 118–19
The Student 89–90, 121
studies of flowers, ferns and the Meudon congregation 314
Study for The Brown Teapot 238n
study of Ida 48
A Woman in a Red Shawl 191
Woman Sewing 184
John, Henry (son of Augustus and Ida)
appearance 266, 337
birth 154, 338
character 266, 337, 338
childhood 163, 166, 175, 253, 266
custody issues 168
death 337–8, 348
death of guardian 318
education 309
friendship with Tom Burns 347
guardianship 175, 309, 318
letter to father 253
love for Olivia 337
mother's death 163
relationship with father 309, 372
relationship with Gwen 309, 347–8
religious views 309, 337
John, Ida (Nettleship, wife of Augustus)
appearance 40–1, 48, 79–80, 130, 137
ashes 158, 168, 226
birth of Dorelia's baby Pyramus 129–30
birth of son Caspar 82
birth of son David 74
birth of son Edwin 136
birth of son Henry 154
birth of son Robin 122
character 92, 123, 140
Christmas with mother 125
death 3, 154–6, 383
depression 94, 96, 123

engagement to Clement Salaman 37, 41
family background 30, 42
father's illness 75, 76–7
finances 47, 68, 136, 148
Florence trip 41
friendships 30, 37, 45, 46, 176
funeral 157–8
health 123–4, 154–5
home in Essex (Elm House) 90, 92, 107, 123, 125, 126, 128, 132, 133–4
home in Fitzroy Street 66, 68, 80, 84–5, 86
honeymoon 66
letters to Augustus 64, 120, 123, 133, 147–9
letters to Dorelia 99, 125, 127–9, 132
letters to Gwen 87, 91, 97, 106, 122
marriage 2, 5, 66, 90–2, 105–7
modelling 124
motherhood 74–5, 82, 106
Paris life with Dorelia and children 134, 136–9
Paris life with Gwen John and Gwen Salmond 46–8, 51–2
Paris lodgings (rue Dareau) 138
Paris lodgings (rue Monsieur le Prince) 134, 135–8
Paris plans 106, 132–3
Paris studies 45, 49n
plans for independence 148, 152
portrait by Gwen 48
portraits by Augustus 31, 79–80, 163, 228
pregnancies 72–3, 82, 96, 105, 128, 131, 134, 135, 146, 153, 166
relationship with Augustus 35, 41–2, 64–5, 81–3, 92, 98, 105–6, 107, 123–5, 127–8, 130–1, 132–3, 146, 152–3, 385
relationship with Dorelia 83–4, 99, 122–3, 125, 127–8, 132–3, 137–8
relationship with Gwen 30, 31, 35, 45–6, 50, 53, 63, 86–7, 97, 106–7, 136, 385
response to Augustus's affair with Alick 146
'rest cure' away from Elm House 126–9
Sainte Honorine holiday 143, 145–6
Slade studies 30, 41, 44
Tenby visits 72–3, 83
wedding 64–5
works 72

John, Katy (wife of Romilly) 358
John, Mary (wife of Caspar) 376
John, Poppet (Elizabeth, daughter of
        Augustus and Dorelia)
    birth 226
    childhood 244, 292, 307
    engagement 317
    house in France 332, 375
    letters from father 292, 382
    marriages 332, 335–6, 375, 377
    parties at Fryern 320
    relationship with father 335–6, 375, 378
    response to war threat 361–2
    war service 363
John, Pyramus (son of Augustus and Dorelia)
    appearance 166
    ashes 226
    birth 129
    childhood 132, 148
    death 225–6, 227, 229, 231, 293, 338, 372
    portrait 172, 210, 228
John, Rebecca (daughter of Caspar) 359, 360
John, Robin (son of Augustus and Ida)
    appearance 164, 166
    birth 122
    childhood 137, 242
    custody issue 164, 166, 168
    drawing of 130
    education 163, 252, 266–7, 288, 300
    grandmother's care 163
    health 136, 199
    marriage 377
    mother's death 163
    portrait 228
    relationship with father 242, 336–7, 377, 381
    relationship with Gwen 300, 307
John, Romilly (son of Augustus and Dorelia)
    birth 145, 148
    career 377
    childhood 213
    education 336
    marriage 358
    relationship with parents 375
    writing 336, 377
John, Thornton (brother)
    appearance 11

birth 10
career 278
career plans 14, 20
character 11, 16, 224, 244
education 16
fatherhood 353
father's death 352
Gwen's biography plan 358
health 12, 351
life in Canada 20, 83, 148
marriage 353
marriage plans 307
mother's death 10–11
Paris visit 219
relationship with sister Gwen 219, 224, 254, 351–2
relationship with sister Winnie 148
war service 244, 257
John, Vivien (daughter of Augustus and
        Dorelia)
    art training 335
    birth 227, 242
    career 377
    childhood 307
    father's death 382–3
    French holiday 361–2
    Jamaica voyage 332
    relationship with father 227, 291, 320, 331, 335–6
    relationship with Gwen 307, 353
    relationship with mother 327
    running away to London 324–5
    Slade studies 325, 335n
    war work 363
John, William (grandfather) 9, 12
John, Winifred (Winnie, sister)
    appearance 11, 36
    Augustus's diving accident 39
    Augustus's wedding 64
    birth 10, 11
    career 244
    character 18, 36, 276
    childhood 8, 11, 13–16, 19
    death of mother 11–12, 156
    education 15–16
    finances 83n, 353
    letters from Augustus 64, 66, 367
    life in Canada 83, 84, 115, 116, 148

London lodgings 35–6
marriage 244
motherhood 244, 278
music studies 15, 35–6, 53
Paris visit 148
portrait by Augustus 36
portraits by Gwen 35, 36, 49, 53
relationship with brother Augustus 39, 148
relationship with brother Thornton 148
relationship with Ida 72, 83
relationship with sister Gwen 18–19, 34, 36, 63, 116, 224, 276, 311, 353, 358
religion 224
Tenby life 72
Tenby visit 148
view of Gwen biography plan 358
Johnstone, Gwyneth (daughter of Augustus) 377n
Jonathan Cape 370, 371
Jousset, Jean 354
Joyce, James 190, 328–9

Khun, Walter 278
Knewstub, Alice *see* Rothenstein
Knewstub, Grace *see* Orpen
Knewstub, Jack 89, 163, 301
Knight, Harold 231
Knight, Laura 231
Konody, P. G. 149, 261

Lamb, Euphemia 139, 153–4, 167, 212
Lamb, Henry
  affair with Helen Maitland 206
  affair with Ottoline 206
  appearance and background 139
  friendship with Augustus 139, 187
  girlfriend Euphemia 139
  Ida's funeral 157–8
  letters from Augustus 165, 170, 171, 370
  marriages 153, 323
  relationship with Dorelia 153, 167, 174, 176, 206, 211, 213, 214, 230, 288, 323
  view of Gwen 309
  war service 239
Lane, Hugh 171, 200, 228
Langdale, Cecily 360
Laurencin, Marie 276, 294
Lawrence, T. E. 262, 263, 322

Lees, Derwent 213, 228, 239
Lempicka, Tamara de 294
Leverhulme, Lord 284
Lewis, Percy Wyndham
  biography proposal 358
  Blast magazine 248, 251
  death 380
  health 380
  Ida's funeral 157–8
  letters from Augustus 174, 200
  Paris life 149–50
  poetry 80
  reading 80
  relationship with Augustus 80–1, 139, 167, 187, 203, 248, 251, 334–5, 380
  review of Augustus's Jamaican portraits 334–5
  Sainte Honorine holiday with Augustus 143, 145
  Slade studies 55–6, 80
  spreading rumours about Dorelia 203
  view of Augustus 55, 80, 147, 150, 252
  view of *Chiaroscuro* 372
  view of Gwen 358
  view of Gwen's work 183
  view of Quinn 187
  Vorticism 248, 251
  wartime experiences 249, 251
  works exhibited 294n
Lhote, André 342, 349
Lhuisset, Angeline 217, 346
The Listener 334
Liverpool Academy of Art 73
Liverpool Art School 68–9, 73–4, 76n
Lloyd, Constance
  appearance and character 148
  friendship with Gwen 95, 105, 110, 159, 270, 294, 346
  Gwen's feeling towards 270, 280, 311
  painting of Gwen 111n
  Paris life 95, 105, 148
  Slade studies 95
Lloyd George, David 247, 262n, 264, 266
Lopokova, Lydia 330
Lovell, Fenella 182–3, 184, 185, 188–9, 277

Macalir, Camille 118
MacColl, Dugald (D. S.) 56, 68

McEvoy, Ambrose
   Amsterdam trip 43
   appearance and character 26
   camping holiday 38
   Chenil Gallery role 301
   drinking 139, 157–8
   Ida's funeral 157–8
   marriage 63
   relationship with Augustus 26, 38, 43, 44, 139, 157–8, 164
   relationship with Gwen 35, 38, 49, 62–3, 97, 220
   Slade studies 26, 31
   wedding of Augustus and Ida 64–5
McEvoy, Charles 84
McEvoy, Mary (Spencer Edwards) 62–3, 75
Macfie, Scott 201, 205
Mackenzie, Irene 15, 39
Mackenzie, Mrs (teacher) 15
Macnamara, Brigit 324, 326–7, 332
Macnamara, Caitlin 324–8, 372
Macnamara, Francis 227, 243, 324, 336, 380
Macnamara, Nicolette 324, 326
McNeill, Dorelia (Dodo, Dorothy)
   abortion 166
   appearance 77, 89–90, 196, 204, 206, 213, 382
   background 77
   birth of daughter Poppet 226
   birth of daughter Vivien 242
   birth of son Pyramus 129–30
   birth of son Romilly 145
   caravan holiday with Augustus and children 194–5, 196–9
   care of children after Ida's death 157, 166, 174, 194, 201
   care of Chiquita 289
   character 137, 140, 325, 327
   Chateau Noir visit 206
   death 384
   death of Augustus 383
   death of Ida 157
   death of son Pyramus 226, 227, 229
   drawing 87
   Equihen stay 166–7
   finances 87, 93, 95, 148n, 241, 242
   flight to Belgium 97–8
   French holiday with Augustus and children 174–6
   health 199, 201, 203, 207, 225
   home in Alderney Manor 211–12, 213–14, 216, 306–7
   home in Elm House, Essex 122–3, 125–6, 128, 132–4
   home in Fryern Court 307–8, 364
   home (*mas*) in Saint-Rémy-de-Provence 332, 361–2, 367, 374
   Ida's illness and death 154–5, 157
   Jamaica voyage 332
   Lamorna Cove visit 231
   letters to Gwen 308, 317–18
   London life with Augustus and children 194
   marriage proposal by Augustus 366–7
   Martigues stay 204–7
   modelling in Paris 95–7, 148
   name 79, 137
   old age 375
   Paris Christmas 149
   Paris life with Ida and children (rue Monsieur le Prince) 134, 136–9
   Paris lodgings (rue du Château) 148
   Paris plans 132–3
   Paris stay with Gwen 94–7
   plans for childbirth 128–9
   portraits by Augustus 79–80, 121, 193–4, 198, 213–14, 231, 382
   portraits by Gwen 89–90, 302, 305
   pregnancies 123, 125–6, 140, 203–4, 214, 225236
   relationship with Augustus 2, 5, 78, 79, 83–5, 86, 95–7, 100, 125–6, 146, 174, 176, 199–200, 203, 205, 211, 227, 230–1, 242–3, 283, 287–8, 290, 321–2, 381
   relationship with Gwen 77–8, 85, 89–90, 93–4, 98–9, 136, 236, 306–7, 317–18, 348, 353
   relationship with Henry Lamb 153, 167, 174, 176, 206, 211, 213, 214, 230, 288, 323
   relationship with Ida 83–4, 99, 122–3, 125, 127–8, 132–3, 137–8
   relationship with Leonard Brouke 96–100
   response to Augustus's affair with Alick 146

Sainte Honorine holiday 143, 145–6
stillborn daughter 207
Tenby visit 273
Toulouse stay with Gwen 89–90, 93–4
travelling with Gwen 85, 86–8, 89–90, 93–4
McNeill, Edie 194
McNeill, Jessie 153, 198
Maggie (live-in help at Elm House) 90, 92, 126, 129, 131
Maitland, Helen 204, 205–6, 241
Manchester Art Gallery 305
Manchester Guardian 209, 285, 294, 371
Mansfield, Katherine 247
Manson, Rosamond 217, 246, 257
Manson, Ruth
  Pléneuf lodgings 257, 264, 274
  relationship with Gwen 217, 246, 256, 257, 274, 346
  wartime experiences 234, 246, 256
Maria Katerina 60–2
Maritain, Jacques 311, 313, 314
Maritain, Raïsa (Oumançoff) 311, 314
Marlborough, Duchess of 107
Martigues (Villa Sainte Anne) 204–7, 211, 291, 336
Matthiesen, Francis 356–7
Matthiesen gallery 356, 358–9
Matisse, Henri 181, 209, 231, 275
Mère Poussepin 221–2
Metsu, Gabriel 32
Meudon convent 220, 221–3, 276, 278–9
Mimi (nursemaid) 10, 11
Modersohn-Becker, Paula 117
Modigliani, Amedeo 183, 231, 236, 319
Monsell, Elinor 32, 38
Montgomery, General 364, 365
Moore, Henry 319
Moore, Thomas 108
Moorehead, Alan 373
Morgan, Evan 286
Morrell, Lady Ottoline
  affair with Henry Lamb 206
  appearance 171–2, 339
  character 171–2, 263
  Chateau Noir visit 206
  death 339
  health 321, 339

portrait by Augustus 172
relationship with Augustus 171–4, 177, 206–7, 321, 339
visiting Augustus's caravan camp 197
Morrell, Philip 172, 173, 206
Murray, Gilbert 196, 376

Nash, Paul 228–9
National Gallery 24, 243, 366
National Gallery of Wales 384
National Museum of Wales 359
National Portrait Society 228
Nettleship, Ada
  career 30, 42
  Christmas with Ida and grandchildren 125
  custody issues 163–4, 166–9, 174–5
  death 338
  death of Ida 154–5
  death of Pyramus 226
  dressmaking 30, 42, 48
  finances 42
  grandson David's Christmas visit 149
  hostility to Augustus 42, 64, 65, 167–9
  Ida's funeral 157
  letters from Augustus 163–4, 167, 168, 174, 195, 226, 284
  response to Ida's wedding 64–5
  view of Dorelia 167
  view of Ida's marriage 123, 125, 133–4
Nettleship, Edith 175, 309, 318
Nettleship, Ethel 155, 168–9, 325, 381n
Nettleship, Ida *see* John (Ida)
  appearance 40–1, 48
  Augustus's drawing of 31
  engagement to Clement Salaman 37, 41
  family background 30, 42
  finances 47
  Florence trip 41
  friendships 30, 37
  Gwen's letters 51
  Gwen's portrait of 48
  Paris life 46–8, 51–2
  Paris studies 45, 49n
  quoted 44
  relationship with Augustus 35, 41–2, 64–5

Nettleship, Ida (*cont.*)
  relationship with Gwen 30, 35, 45, 46, 50, 53, 63
  Slade studies 30, 41
  wedding 64–5
Nettleship, Jack 30, 42, 65, 75, 76, 169
Nettleship, Ursula
  death 381n
  letter from Augustus 157, 168
  letters from sister Ida 74, 137–8
  mother's death 338
  sister Ida's illness 155
Nettleship family
  background and careers 30, 42
  custody issues 168–9, 174–5, 201
  Ida's allowance 68
  response to Ida's marriage 123, 134, 169
  response to Ida's wedding 64–5
New English Art Club (NEAC)
  Augustus's submissions 81, 121
  creation 53
  deadline for submissions 88
  exhibiting Augustus's work 80, 81, 170, 196, 228, 240
  exhibiting Gwen's work 53, 162, 184, 187–8
  Gwen's submissions 188, 247
  Gwen's work not displayed 77
  letter to Gwen not forwarded 225
  picture of the year 80
  reviews of Augustus's exhibits 121–2, 138, 149, 261
  reviews of Gwen's exhibits 162, 190
The New York Times 223, 383
Newlin Price, Frederic 344, 345, 349, 350
Nicholson, William 195, 199
Nona *see* Watkins

O'Casey, Sean 329
O'Donel, Nuala 110, 151, 159, 179, 219
Orpen, Grace (Knewstub) 57, 89
Orpen, William
  Chelsea Art School 88–9, 91, 131, 138, 139
  Chenil Gallery role 301
  marriage 89
  Normandy painting holiday 57–8
  Paris Peace Conference work 261
  relationship with Augustus 40, 44, 58, 60, 88–9, 251–2
  Slade student life 34, 40
  wartime career 251–2
  works 52
Oumançoff, Véra 311–14, 315

Paris
  Académie Carmen 49, 50, 51, 52
  Montparnasse 46–8, 94, 263
  Peace Conference (1919) 261–2, 266
  Salon d'Automne 267, 270, 276, 280, 294
  Salon des Beaux Arts 294
  Salon des Tuileries 294
  siege (1918) 256–7
  Société des Artistes Français 294
  Studio Colarossi 49n, 159
Phelps, Elspeth 65
Picasso, Pablo
  Augustus's interest 175
  Augustus's meeting 165
  Gwen's meeting 295
  influence on Augustus 166, 285
  influence on Gwen 183, 265n
  'Manet and the Post Impressionists' exhibition 209
  Montmartre studio 165
  works 165, 279
Piermé, Canon 314–15
Pleiades Press 357
Pléneuf 257–8, 259, 274
  Chateau Vauclair 264–7
Plunkett Green, Olivia 337
Pol, Willem 377
Polignac, Princesse de (Winarretta Singer) 179
Pound, Ezra 190, 236, 248, 280
Powys, John Cowper 376
Powys, Theodore 329
Puvis de Chavannes, Pierre 59, 75, 158, 165, 166, 191

Quinn, Paul
  appearance 186
  Augustus's portrait of 185–6
  death 192, 298–9, 300, 302
  health 296, 298
  influence 190–1

INDEX 433

letters from Augustus 199–200, 202, 203, 208, 210, 226, 228, 230, 238
letters from Gwen 244, 247, 259, 268, 272, 273–4, 294, 295, 297
New York Armory show 213n, 228
patronage of Augustus 186–8, 193, 198, 201, 278
patronage of Gwen 185, 188–91, 193, 215, 232, 245–6, 258, 266, 274, 293–4, 300
portrait by Augustus 185–6, 198
relationship with Augustus 186–8, 278, 293
relationship with Gwen 189–92, 221, 243–4, 275, 278–9, 298–9
relationship with Jeanne 274, 293–4, 296, 299
Vauclair plans 268, 271–2
will 299

Ranks, Mr (Pleiades editor) 357, 358
Read, Herbert 366
Rembrandt 1, 25, 43, 44, 55–6, 59, 69, 121, 384
Rilke, Rainer Maria
 beliefs 117–18, 150, 184–5
 death 311
 Gwen's letters 356
 relationship with Gwen 117–18, 218, 311, 312
 Rodin's amanuensis 117
 view of Claire de Choiseul 181
 wife Clara 117, 181
Roché, Henri-Pierre 278, 296
Roche, Louise 346–7, 353
Rodin, Auguste
 affairs 107
 appearance 102, 181
 art collection 118
 death 3, 254
 drawing 118
 finances 113, 162, 179, 237–8
 Gwen modelling for 101, 102–3, 111
 Gwen's letters 111, 112, 114–17, 118–19, 142, 151, 158, 159, 161, 180, 182, 254, 356, 357, 358n
 health 244–5, 268, 296
 home in Meudon (Villa Brillantes) 109, 112, 215–16, 237, 245, 254
 letters to Gwen 112, 115, 142, 161, 180, 182, 237–8, 357
 New York exhibition 191
 open Saturdays 104, 160
 reading 112
 relationship with Camille Claudel 113
 relationship with Claire de Choiseul 178–82, 207, 223
 relationship with Gwen 2, 4, 103–4, 107–10, 111–18, 120, 141–2, 143–4, 150–1, 158, 161–2, 180–2, 223, 237–8
 relationship with Rose Beuret 107, 112, 254
 religion 218
 studios 103–4, 107, 111, 160, 181
 works
  bust of Claire 179
  bust of Gwen 148, 150
  erotic sketches 117
  Whistler memorial 107–8, 111, 161, 180, 182
Rothenstein, Albert 54, 65, 68, 84, 243
Rothenstein, Alice (Knewstub)
 cycling tour of France 61
 home in Hampstead 59, 80
 Kensington cottage clean-up 59–60
 letter from Augustus 135–6
 letters from Gwen 95, 308
 letters from Ida 74, 105, 123, 125–6, 134, 154
 painting holiday in Normandy 57
 relationship with Ida 92, 105, 125, 126, 133
 social life 80
 wedding party for Augustus and Ida 65
Rothenstein, John 358n, 366, 370, 374
Rothenstein, William (Will)
 appearance 54
 career 54, 77
 Chelsea Art School role 89
 Chenil Gallery role 301
 cycling tour of France 61
 death 380
 home in Hampstead 59, 80
 Kensington cottage 59–60

Rothenstein, William (*cont.*)
  letter from Ida 123, 158
  letters from Augustus 60, 69–70, 72, 73, 74, 75, 85, 121, 165, 175, 187, 252
  London network 80, 169
  marriage 57
  'Moderns and Old Masters' exhibition 56
  Paris network 54
  Paris visit with Augustus 58
  painting holiday in Normandy 57
  promoting Augustus's work 54, 56, 120
  relationship with Augustus 54, 55, 59–60, 91, 139, 157, 187
  relationship with Ida 105, 123, 133, 137
  Society of Twelve 122
  view of Dorelia 77
  view of Augustus's behaviour 84
  view of Augustus's later work 284
  view of Augustus's Liverpool sketches 69, 73
  view of Gwen's work 162, 305
  wedding party for Augustus and Ida 65
Rousseau, Henri 191, 298
Royal Academy 53, 120, 285–6, 294, 373, 377n
Russell, Bertrand 265, 369

Salaman, Chattie (Baldwin Wake) 304
Salaman, Clement 37, 65
Salaman, Dorothy 65
Salaman, Louise (*later* Bishop) 37, 53, 57n, 126, 343
Salaman, Michael 350
Salaman, Michel
  appearance 26, 35
  background 26
  Chelsea Art School role 89
  friendship with Augustus 26, 34, 60–2, 80
  gypsy caravan 128
  holiday in France 60–2
  letters from Augustus 69, 81, 130, 136, 338
  letters from Gwen 56–7, 58, 63, 75, 76, 304
  letters from Ida 44, 48, 85
  letters to Gwen 304, 306
  marriage 128, 139, 304
  portrait 61
  relationship with Gwen 57, 62, 63, 75, 304, 306
  Slade studies 26
  travels 76
  wedding of Augustus and Ida 65
Salmond, Gwen
  Chelsea Art School role 89
  finances 47
  friendship with Gwen 30, 46, 49, 75n
  friendship with Ida 30, 45, 46, 65, 133
  marriage 302, 375
  painting holiday in New Quay 72
  Paris life 46–8
  Paris studies 45, 49, 52
  portrait by Augustus 158
  portrait by Gwen 48
  Slade studies 30
  teaching career 76
  wedding of Augustus and Ida 65
  works 87
Salvation Army 9, 33
Sampson, John
  appearance 70
  death 338
  letters from Augustus 134, 135, 145, 156, 226, 261
  marriage and children 71
  relationship with Augustus 70–2, 73, 74, 84, 198, 284
  relationship with Roma people (gypsies) 70–1
Sampson, Meg
  letters from Augustus 145, 156, 226, 231, 338
  letters from Ida 136, 137, 143, 153
  marriage 71
Sampson, Michael 338
Sands, Ethel 171–2
Sargent, John Singer 40, 54
Satie, Eric 190
Saturday Review 208
Schepeler, Alick (Alexandra)
  appearance 140
  Augustus's plans for summer holiday 143, 145
  background 140
  career 139, 380
  death 380

INDEX

letters from Augustus 140–1, 143, 145, 147, 165, 170, 229
portrait 170
relationship with Augustus 139–41, 145–7, 149, 150, 171, 378
Sculptors' Gallery, New York 294
Second World War 354, 360, 361–2
Segonzac, André Dunoyer de 195
Shaw, George Bernard 239–40, 364
Shone, Richard 384
Sickert, Walter 54, 80, 122, 210n
Sime, Sidney 228
Slade, Charles 198
Slade School of Fine Art
  Antiquities Room 22–4, 28
  Augustus's enrolment 3, 20
  Augustus's first day 22–3
  Augustus's friendships 26, 31
  Augustus's painting studies 31–2
  building 22
  Chenil Gallery 301
  Gwen's enrolment 27
  Gwen's friendships 30–1, 57, 95
  Gwen's modelling experience 52
  Gwen's painting studies 32–3
  'John Beauty Chorus' 241–2
  Lewis's expulsion 80
  life drawing class 28, 55, 245
  Life Room 24
  Melville Nettleship Prize for Figure Composition 45
  NEAC exhibitions 53
  study of works by students and alumni 170–1
  Summer Competition 44–5
  Vivien's studies 325, 335n
  wedding of Augustus and Ida 65
  Whistler's visit 32, 49
  women students 4, 9, 21, 22–3, 27, 28–9
Smith, Augusta *see* John
Smith, Leah (aunt) 9, 11, 13
Smith, Matthew 302, 319, 375, 380
Smith, Rosina (aunt) 9, 11, 12, 13
Smith, Thomas (grandfather) 9, 12, 316
Society of Twelve 122, 228
The Spectator 56, 284n, 335, 372
Steer, Philip Wilson 25, 40, 44, 65, 68, 120
Stevenson, Frances 262n

Strachey, Lytton 153, 249–50, 260
Stulik, Rudolf 241
Suggia, Guilhermina 282–3, 284n, 378n
Sullivan, Mary 349
Symons, Arthur
  appearance and character 207, 272
  friendship with Augustus 217, 241, 272, 273
  health 273
  letters from Augustus 207, 250
  relationship with Gwen 269, 271–3, 277–8, 342
Symons, Rhoda 271–4, 277–8, 342

Tate Gallery 55n, 277, 284n, 305, 357, 384
Tenby
  Augustus awarded Freedom of 379
  Augustus's children's visits 83, 105, 274
  Augustus's return visits 34, 38–9, 42, 44–5, 72, 274, 379
  beach 7–8, 39
  childhood of Augustus and Gwen 2–3, 7–8, 12–19, 31, 102, 119
  Edwin's death 339–40
  Edwin's life 3, 12–14, 19, 46, 58, 307
  Gwen's return visits 45, 72
  Ida's visit with children 83
  move from Haverfordwest 12
  religion 218, 219, 371
  Winnie's return visits 148
Terry, Ellen 30
Thomas, Dylan 327–8, 365, 380
The Times 208, 210, 228, 248, 335, 374, 383, 384
Tonks, Henry
  appearance 23
  Augustus's wedding party 65
  Blast critique of 248
  career 23
  NEAC role 53
  portrait of Rodin 237n
  quoted 22
  Slade teaching 23–4, 25, 28–9, 49, 118, 120
  view of Augustus 59
  view of Augustus's drawing 40, 55
  view of impressionists 32
  view of Mrs Everett 33
  view of women students 28–9
  war service 239, 251

Tooths Gallery 334
Toulouse-Lautrec, Henri de 54, 57
Tree, Iris 241, 287
Tristan (son of Augustus and Mavis) *see* Cole
Tyrwhitt, Ursula
  appearance 30, 36
  Augustus's drawing 31
  illness 316
  joint exhibition suggestions 247, 302–3
  letters from Augustus 39, 61, 242, 285, 337
  letters from Gwen 77, 87, 93, 104, 107, 115, 161, 182, 184–5, 189, 191, 216, 218, 220, 223–4, 225, 231, 234–5, 238, 245, 254, 256, 257, 258, 259, 264, 271, 278, 280–1, 298, 308–10, 316, 342, 344, 350, 351, 352
  letters to Gwen 158, 189–90, 243, 245–6, 254, 264, 298
  marriage 217, 302
  meeting Rodin 160
  Moroccan travels 353
  relationship with Augustus 36, 38–9, 40, 41
  relationship with Gwen 158, 159–60, 162, 189–90, 217, 223–4, 237, 245–6, 247, 257, 278, 302–4, 308, 316, 348–9, 352, 353
  Slade studies 30
  wartime experiences 243
Tyrwhitt, Walter 217, 302, 316

Van Gogh, Vincent 206, 209, 252, 287
Van-t-Hoff, architect 230–1
Venice Biennale 331n
Véra *see* Oumançoff

Walker, Maynard 344, 350, 351, 385
Warren Gallery, London 345
Watkins, Nona 269–70, 280, 311, 356
Watteau, Antoine 25, 31, 43
Waugh, Edna *see* Clarke Hall (Edna)
Waugh, Rosa 35, 77
Westhoff, Clara 117, 181
Westminster School of Art 77–8
Westray, Grace 38n
Wheeler, Charles 381
Wheeler, Mortimer 323
Whistler, James McNeill
  appearance 26, 49
  Augustus's meeting 50
  Gwen's studies with 49–50, 67
  influence 26, 32, 48, 49, 67
  memorial 107–8, 111, 161, 180, 182
  Slade visit 32
  teaching in Paris 49–50
  winter ball 50, 51n
White, John 336
Whitman, Walt 17, 41–2, 75, 194, 293, 370
Wilde, Oscar 26, 30, 54, 58
Wildenstein Gallery, Bond Street 356
Winbourne, Lady 212
Wood, Christopher 286–7
Woolf, Virginia 2, 173n, 261, 284
Wright, Mavis *see* Cole

Yeats, W. B. 169–70, 186, 190, 328, 368

Zoe (daughter of Augustus and Chiquita) *see* Hicks